This book provides a practical road map for anyone wishing to implement a successful program for children with behavior management problems. It is designed for parents and caregivers of children with challenging behavioral difficulties, but its applications are not limited to this group alone. Anyone working with children who are struggling with behavior management difficulties should have this valuable book available to them.

—Ronald T. Brown, Ph.D., ABPP, is professor of public health, psychology, pediatrics and psychiatry and behavioral sciences and dean of the College of Health Professions at Temple University

This is a terrific book that will be a valuable resource for parents with children and adolescents. Kapalka has written a highly readable, practical book that incorporates the latest ideas about handling difficult children. It is filled with great examples that will help all parents. This book will go to the top of my suggested readings list.

—James H. Bray, Ph.D., author of *Stepfamilies: Love, Marriage, and Parenting in the First Decade*

A wonderful resource, this book is succinct, practical, and clearly written. It offers many useful suggestions and plans that can be easily carried out within the context of parenting training and behavior therapy. I wholeheartedly recommend this book to psychologists, mental health practitioners, parents, and graduate students in training. I will personally use it in my practice and on my syllabi.

—Margaret Alvarez, Psy.D., MSCP, Brain Behavior Center in Pomona, NY

There is no user's guide to being a parent, but Kapalka has provided the next best thing. This easy-to-read book provides clear and concise strategies that all parents can employ with their children. Parents, educators, and counselors alike can effective solutions to many troubling parenting dilemmas. Best of all, Kapalka has offered parents a method for creating a healthy family environment in which parents and children have the opportunity to be responsible, respected, and happy.

—Matt Englar-Carlson, Ph.D., associate professor of counseling at the California State University at Fullerton

This is a must-read for every parent concerned about their child's behavior. Kapalka offers solid, concrete recommendations that are well-grounded in the psychological literature, providing parents with wise advice and needed practical tools that allow them to deal with being overwhelmed by their child's behavior. I especially enjoyed the real-life examples and was impressed with the down-to-earth approach that Kapalka adopts in offering his suggestions. It is a well-written, engrossing text that I recommend with unqualified enthusiasm.

> —Stephen R. Wester, Ph.D., is associate professor in the
> Department of Educational Psychology at the University
> of Wisconsin, Milwaukee

This book pulls together the best practices in parenting today to address the problems of parenting the strong-willed child. Kapalka has effectively identified key areas of parenting problems, spelled out an effective approach to resolving the difficulties, and described how to move from conflict to cooperation. This easy-to-read text will be a blessing to parents in need of effective guidance, as well as to practitioners who work with them. It is highly recommended for its practical applications, reasonable guidelines, and helpful examples.

> —Arthur Horne, Ph.D., distinguished research professor emeritus
> in the Department of Counseling and Human Development
> Services of the College of Education at the University of Georgia

Kapalka has written a very readable and useful book on parenting skills. The book is well organized and cuts to the heart of the issues and potential solutions for parents and therapists alike.

> —Mark Stevens, Ph.D., director of University Counseling Services
> at the California State University, Northridge, and president
> of Division 51 of the American Psychological Association

Kapalka has written a wonderful book, giving parents an excellent addition to works from Barkley and others. His writing demonstrates that he understand difficult children and the problems parents run into when they try to help them grow up successfully in an ever changing environment. Perhaps most importantly, Kapalka clearly understands what it takes to be a competent parent. He is gentle yet firm in his convictions when advising his readers to embrace their roles as parents. This book is now required reading for my patient-parents and my post-doctoral fellows.

> —John Courtney, Psy.D., MP, is assistant clinical professor of psychiatry and neurology at Tulane University Health Science Center

This book gives parents an easy-to-read understanding of their out of control child. The practical understanding Kapalka offers helps parents better understand what is occurring in their children. Being "out of control" becomes far more predictable with the insights and strategies this book offers. I can certainly recommend it for my patients and their families.

> —Thomas M. Kozak, Ph.D., is a licensed psychologist in Texas and Michigan

Kapalka's clear yet theoretically well grounded approach lays out a roadmap for parents that stresses the positive and optimizes the chance to experience success—for both the parent and the child. This book will serve as a wonderful resource to the parents of impulsive children with limited self-control. I heartily recommend it.

> —Leslie H. MacCardell, Ph.D., is a clinical child psychologist in private practice

I highly recommend this book because it is very practical, easy to understand, and detailed in its description of steps parents can follow to manage behavior problems both in and out of the home. The book's progression and repetition of the content makes this difficult topic easy for parents to learn. It should be a very valuable treatment resource for therapists who work with parents needing help with child behavior management problems. I certainly plan on using it in my practice. It should be a very valuable contribution to the parenting literature.

> —Ed Kovach, Ph.D., psychologist in private practice in
> Clarksville, TN

A wonderful addition to the list of books I recommend to the families with whom I work. As a child psychologist who works with children who are strong-willed and hard to manage, I found this book to provide a comprehensive and well-thought out plan for child management. Kapalka took the concepts of Russell Barkley and expanded on them in an extremely thorough and user-friendly way. Kapalka provides lots of detailed examples and specifics about the sometimes-complex interventions. This book should be read by all who have children.

> —Linda Alverson-Eiland, Ph.D., child psychologist in private
> practice in Birmingham, AL, and president of the Alabama
> Psychological Association.

Parenting an out-of-control child is a lonely experience. Family, friends, and even therapists can be quick to blame and quick with advice, but useful answers have been hard to find—until now. This book provides simple, effective ways for parents to get their defiant and out-of-control child back on the right path. Combining the best of psychological science with years of clinical experience, Kapalka describes powerful solutions in nine easily implemented steps. This guide will be a godsend for parents and their out-of-control children, restoring peace, sanity, and renewed hope for the future.

> —Jonathan Rich, Ph.D., psychologist and author of *The Couple's*
> *Guide to Love and Money*

Parenting Your Out-of-Control Child

An Effective, Easy-to-Use Program for Teaching Self-Control

GEORGE M. KAPALKA, PH.D., ABPP

New Harbinger Publications, Inc.

Publisher's Note

This publication is designed to provide accurate and authoritative information in regard to the subject matter covered. It is sold with the understanding that the publisher is not engaged in rendering psychological, financial, legal, or other professional services. If expert assistance or counseling is needed, the services of a competent professional should be sought.

Distributed in Canada by Raincoast Books

Copyright © 2007 by George M. Kapalka
New Harbinger Publications, Inc.
5674 Shattuck Avenue
Oakland, CA 94609
www.newharbinger.com

Acquired by Melissa Kirk; Cover design by Amy Shoup;
Edited by Amy Scott; Text design by Tracy Carlson

Library of Congress Cataloging-in-Publication Data

Kapalka, George M.
   Parenting your out-of-control child: an effective, easy-to-use program for teaching self-control / George M. Kapalka.
      p. cm.
   Includes bibliographical references.
   ISBN-13: 978-1-57224-484-9
   ISBN-10: 1-57224-484-4
   1. Problem children--Behavior modification. 2. Parenting. 3. Parent and child. 4. Self-control in children. I. Title.
HQ773.K36 2007
649'.64--dc22
                              2006039643

09 08 07

10 9 8 7 6 5 4 3 2 1

First printing

To my wife, whose confidence and unwavering support were instrumental in my ability to complete this project, and to my parents, who helped me appreciate that patience, understanding, and consistent limits are integral components of effective parenting.

Contents

Foreword

For the past twenty-six years, I have dedicated my professional life to studying, understanding, and helping troubled children and their families in a variety of settings, including several schools, a university-affiliated psychiatric hospital, a private psychiatric hospital, a community mental health center, and several private practice organizations. Across these different environments, I have consistently worked with parents who are concerned about their children's behavior, which has been out of control. One of the most common complaints of these parents is that they have experienced great difficulty finding clinicians who know how to work effectively with disruptive and disobedient boys and girls. Many of these same parents have been disappointed by the lack of useful self-help books about how to manage hyperactive and defiant children. Likewise, teachers, counselors, psychologists, and other professionals have repeatedly reported to me that they find it difficult working with children who don't fit in with the rest of the world and, consequently, wish they had more resources to assist them in their therapeutic interactions with this population.

In light of this state of affairs, Dr. George Kapalka, associate professor of psychological counseling at Monmouth University, is an answer to a prayer. Dr. Kapalka is a respected researcher, a talented practicing psychologist, and a leader in the counseling profession. For approximately two decades, Dr. Kapalka has designed and conducted investigations exploring several clinical approaches to helping disruptive, inattentive, and defiant children. Combining the results of these investigations with related findings from the professional literature and his own observations obtained from his extensive experiences counseling children and their families, he has designed a systematic approach to managing youngsters who have trouble following rules and meeting the expectations of the adults in their lives. To our great fortune, Dr. Kapalka has shared his ideas in this outstanding book.

Parenting Your Out-of-Control Child will be helpful to many readers. Parents who have been at their wits' end about their children's behavior will find Dr. Kapalka's book to be a priceless resource. By carefully following Dr. Kapalka's recommendations, parents will gradually see their children become more attentive, less argumentative, less violent, and more enjoyable to be around. In addition, mothers and fathers who apply Dr. Kapalka's child management strategies will feel better about themselves and more confident in their parenting abilities. They will sense a difference in the climate of their home, discovering that home is a more peaceful place. They will also feel more hopeful, happy, and relieved as they witness their sons and daughters become better at responding to adult requests, making friends with other children, and completing important tasks, such as homework and chores. Mental health and educational personnel will also benefit from reading *Parenting Your Out-of-Control Child* because it provides a step-by-step guide for professionals who want to teach parents how to bring their children's behavior under control. Practitioners can use this book as a teaching tool, asking parents to read and apply each principle prescribed by Dr. Kapalka and then monitoring the parents' progress in utilizing it with their children. Professionals will also find that this book is an excellent resource for their direct interventions with children. For example, exasperated teachers, worn out from the stress associated with instructing children who are disruptive in the classroom, can use this book as a guide to classroom management and thereby create a less chaotic and more pleasant classroom environment. In summary, *Parenting Your Out-of-Control Child* is a superb and versatile resource for parents and professionals alike.

I am grateful to Dr. Kapalka for his many contributions to the professions of counseling and psychology. For years, I have learned a great deal from his many publications and conference presentations on helping children and their families. *Parenting Your Out-of-Control Child* is the latest in this string of contributions, and the information it provides will enhance my efforts to assist parents and their children. I salute Dr. Kapalka for his fine work.

—Mark S. Kiselica, Ph.D., HSPP, NCC, LPC
    Professor of Counselor Education
    The College of New Jersey
    Fellow, American Psychological Association

Acknowledgments

The author would like to acknowledge the work of Dr. Russell Barkley, whose pioneering contributions to our understanding of children with attentional and behavioral disorders continue to inspire generations of researchers and clinicians.

Does This Sound Familiar?

Stevie is a six-year-old, active child. Usually, he doesn't listen when his mom asks him to pick up his toys, turn off the TV, or wash his hands for dinner. Often, it's a battle that includes refusal to obey, crying, and screaming. Today, it's 3:30 P.M. and Mom is about to go out to run some errands, including a trip to the bank that closes at 4:00 P.M. She's in a hurry. Stevie is playing on the living room floor with his blocks. Mom is already dreading what's about to happen next. She comes into the room. "Stevie, it's time to pick up your toys. We have to go out."

"In a minute, Mom!"

Mom leaves the room to go put on her shoes. In two or three minutes, she comes back into the room. Stevie hasn't moved; he's still playing with the blocks. "Stevie, pick up now because Mommy is in a hurry."

"But I just want to finish building the tower!"

Not even waiting for his response, Mom leaves the room again. She gathers her purse, checkbook, and shopping list. From the kitchen, she yells, "Stevie, are you picking up?"

Stevie gives no response. Mom continues to gather what she needs for the errands. She goes into her bedroom and looks for the car keys. From there, she shouts, "Stevie, what did Mommy tell you to do?"

Stevie, again, gives no response. Mom is already getting very angry. She knows the pattern. Next will come his opposition, screaming, yelling, perhaps a physical confrontation. She tries again, calling from her bedroom, "Stevie!"

"I'm almost done, Mom!"

Now Mom is getting really mad. She knows that while she and Stevie are out, the blocks can't just sit in the middle of the floor because the dog may start chewing on them, and maybe even hurt himself in the process. On the other hand, if she has a battle with Stevie, she'll miss the bank. She's thinking, "Why can't he just listen to what I say? Does he enjoy driving me crazy?" She storms into the room, yelling "What's the matter with you? Didn't you hear what I said? Pick up those darned things now!"

"No, I don't have to!"

Now she is fuming. She is thinking, "My own flesh and blood telling me I can't tell him what to do? If I ever did that to my own parents, I'd have my head handed to me on a silver platter!" It's now almost 3:45, and she is getting desperate. She tries a scare tactic. "Stevie, if you don't pick them up right now, I am putting them all in the garbage! I mean it! Pick them up now!"

Stevie continues to play, and Mom continues to rush around the house, trying to get ready to leave. She is putting on her coat. Finally, she storms into the room. Stevie is still playing. She sees red and screams in anger, "What the heck is wrong with you? Didn't you hear that I will throw them away? I mean it! Pick them up now!"

"I don't care!"

Mom comes over and yanks Stevie by the hand, away from the blocks. The blocks he had in his hands go flying all over the room. He starts crying, screaming, and yelling "You can't make me" and "I hate you." She gives him a hard smack on the behind and tells him to go get dressed. He is just sitting on the floor, screaming and carrying on, throwing blocks at her. She bends down and starts to pick up the blocks herself, all along shouting at Stevie that he is driving her crazy and someday he will have children of his own and she wishes that they treat him like he treats her.

Sound familiar? This is a common interaction between parents and their out-of-control children. Perhaps you've experienced it yourself. Perhaps you've seen your sister, brother, friend, or your own children do this with their children. What happened? What went wrong in the interaction with Stevie? Why didn't Stevie listen to what his mom told him to do? Could she have done something to improve the likelihood that Stevie would listen? The answers to these questions are complex and involve a combination of many factors, such as Stevie's basic personality, the behavioral habits he has developed, and the behavior of his mother.

Judging from Stevie's behavior, we can safely assume that Stevie is one of those children who have tendencies to not listen to parents' commands and also may be one of those children who have problems transitioning from one behavior to another. Perhaps the mother's approach in the example would've worked with most ordinary children, but Stevie may be one of those more difficult children with whom the ordinary way of doing things may not work; if so, he requires a different approach.

Many parents feel that just because they are the parents, children should automatically recognize that their word is law and must be obeyed. Although some children today still respond to this philosophy and listen accordingly, many do not. This approach may have worked many years ago, but times are different now. Most children today won't listen to parents just because they say so. The above example makes this clear. When the mother asks "What's the matter with you?" or "What's wrong with you?" this is most likely a response to her outrage that her son isn't obeying her just because she said so. Most children today need a reason to listen to their parents that is more substantial than "Because I said so."

How Can This Book Help Me?

This book will help you understand the reasons why children exhibit out-of-control behaviors. While just understanding those reasons is not enough to change things, it will help you develop a more constructive set of expectations. Knowing why your child is behaving the way he is will help you understand what you can do about it and how you can implement techniques to help reduce your child's problems with acting out.

You will also learn how to control your own emotional reactions so that you remain more calm. The more you learn to control yourself and your own reactions, the more effective you will become in successfully managing your child's behaviors. Breaking the cycle of escalation will allow you to remain in control and therefore short-circuit the spiral that leads to most out-of-control behaviors.

This book will help you give your children reasons why they should listen to you, and to help them understand what will happen when they do or don't listen. You will learn how to identify and implement proper consequences for your child's positive and negative behaviors. Throughout the book, there are examples of common behavioral problems that parents experience with their out-of-control children. With each, I'll help you understand what went wrong and why the child acted out. You will develop necessary strategies to reduce acting out and increase the degree of control you have over your children's behaviors.

What Can I Expect from This Book?

Before you proceed, it's helpful for you to know what you can expect to gain from reading this book and using the strategies it describes. First, please understand that there are no quick fixes, and no strategy in the world will instantly turn an out-of-control child into a compliant one. Bringing your child under control is possible, but it will require work, effort, and a commitment of your time. This book offers you a set of tools that are proven to be effective in reducing child management problems, but these tools need time to work, and you'll need to use them consistently.

To further expand on that point, please don't approach the strategies described in this book with a wait-and-see attitude. That is, please don't say "I'll try to use these to see if they will work." This kind of approach will almost surely destine you to failure. The approach within this book is effective and proven through years of research and clinical practice, but it will only work if you have enough faith in it to truly alter the way that you address your child on a permanent basis, not temporarily just to see if it will work. Any hesitancy on your part when you implement the following procedures will be perceived by your child, and the intervention won't be as effective.

The best way to approach this book and the techniques contained herein is to conclude to yourself that you are ready to do something different, something founded on much research and clinical support, something that will help you turn things around with your child. If you are like the typical parent of an out-of-control child, you probably have already tried everything you could think of to change your child's behavior, and nothing has worked. So, what do you have to lose? Have faith. The procedures in this book do work, and results from many research studies confirm their effectiveness (Kapalka 2001a, 2001b, 2003a, 2003b, 2004, 2005, 2006). The amount of change you can expect varies from child to child, depending on such variables as your child's personality, your own personality, and the dynamics of your home. However, if you are willing to commit the effort and perseverance required to implement the following strategies, you'll see results.

You'll also need to give it a commitment of time. You can't expect to attain much change with an out-of-control child unless you decide that you need to change your approach, permanently. Learning new habits, skills, and techniques is a laborious process. While this book is divided into manageable steps, each of which most parents can easily accomplish in a typical week or two, obtaining long-term change takes time and perseverance. If you *are* willing to commit the time, effort, and resolve that it will take to bring difficult behaviors under control, this book will give you the ways to do so.

How Do I Know This Program Is Effective?

The program contained in this book was developed in the 1990s. As a clinical child psychologist for nearly two decades, I often work with out-of-control children. Parents of those children need help to break the escalation patterns that are so common in children with out-of-control behaviors. For many years, resources have existed for clinicians to help parents implement strategies that reduce conflicts and improve the manageability of their children. For example, behavioral contracting has long been known to be effective. Available resources for parents, however, rarely provide the kind of detailed instructions that assist parents in developing an effective behavior contract, and a poorly implemented contract is not likely to be very effective. Thus, I began to identify those components of behavioral contracting that appear to make it most likely to be successful.

Clinicians working with defiant children often follow a program designed by Russell Barkley (1997). I found components of this program helpful, but it was also my experience that revising the program made it more effective with out-of-control children. Gradually, I significantly expanded the program, revised certain steps, and added others. Consequently, components of the program contained in this book are loosely based on Barkley (1997), with significant additions and changes. If your child is defiant and argumentative but not often out of control, Barkley's book with Christine Benton, *Your Defiant Child: Eight Steps to Better Behavior* (1998), may be a good resource for you. However, if you feel that your child is out of control and you need something more intensive, read on.

Once this new program was complete, I performed a number of studies to research its effectiveness. Each step of the technique was researched and the results are available in professional literature (Kapalka 2001a, 2001b, 2003a, 2003b, 2004, 2005, 2006). The studies revealed that each step resulted in a 25 to 65 percent reduction in behavioral problems. When you consider the combined effect of utilizing many of the steps, the overall reduction in problems was very significant. Thus, you can be confident that the program you are reading is based on sound psychological principles and is backed by empirical, scientific evidence of its effectiveness. In addition, you can expect that the more steps you implement, the greater the benefit that you will experience.

How Do I Use This Book?

This book describes a parenting program that involves the use of nine separate (but related) procedures that collectively will help you bring your child under control. Each step is designed to address a specific problem that out-of-control children commonly exhibit. The steps must be mastered individually, and you must be comfortable with using a step on a daily basis before you proceed to the next one. Even though the steps each address a different problem, they build upon one another, and you need to truly master step 1 before you proceed to step 2, you must have mastered steps 1 and 2 before you should proceed to step 3, and so on. Consequently, it is recommended that you only attempt one step every one to two weeks. In this way, you'll give yourself and your child enough time to get used to the new way of doing things, and you'll then be ready to proceed to the next step.

The steps are designed to work in sequence. The sequence of steps is not accidental; it is designed to help you master the steps in order because each step builds on the steps you master before it. Consequently, please don't jump around and try to pick and choose the specific interventions you want to use with your child. You may get some benefit from doing so, but the program won't be nearly as effective. Instead, master all of the steps, in sequence. Once you have completed steps 1 through 6, you may then pick and choose whether any (or all) of steps 7, 8, and 9 will be helpful, and you can administer those in any order, as needed. However, before you get there, please complete steps 1 through 6 in order.

Each of the nine steps is accompanied by summary checklists. These sheets are intended to be used as reminders to keep you on track. As you proceed through each step, post the sheets in a conspicuous place where they will act as reminders to you. Seeing these checklists posted where you spontaneously see them will help you remember the details of each technique. The more you consult them, the more success you will experience with the implementation of each step.

The placement of these checklists is up to you, but I have a few suggestions. For example, if you have a five-year-old that does not yet read, you may want to place the checklists on the refrigerator in the kitchen, or a similar area in your house that acts as a general message board. If the checklists are located in a place that is frequently visited throughout the day, you will see them often and they will remind you about what it is that you are focusing on for that week. Conversely, for a ten-year-old that reads well, you may want to use a more discreet place that you visit frequently but your child does not—for example, the back of your bedroom door.

This brings up an important question: Should you tell your child that you are following a program to help bring his behaviors under control? Generally, I do not recommend that. It is not necessary for you to announce to your child that you are about to get tough. Keep it to yourself, and let your actions do the talking for you. Those steps that require preannouncements to your child are clearly identified in this book.

What if your child discovers the checklists and asks you about them? At that point, you should not lie, but it is not necessary to give your child extensive details. It will be sufficient to say that you are following a program that hopefully will help both of you get along better and minimize the conflicts that you have been experiencing. Do not make your child feel like this program is intended to "fix" him. This will make your child feel defensive and his reaction to the program may become quite negative. Instead, make this a joint effort—a program that will "fix" *both* of you—that is, a program that will "fix" the way you talk to each other and the way that rules are applied around the house.

Finally, please don't skip the following two chapters and proceed directly to the parenting steps. Although you can derive some benefit from the parenting program even if you don't read the chapters that precede it, your administration of the steps won't be as effective. As a parent, your success in bringing your child under control depends on several factors. You must gain some understanding of why your child is behaving the way he does. You must also understand why you react the way you do and what, specifically, you need to change about your own reactions to become more effective as a disciplinarian. You must also understand the philosophy and basic principles of child management that will help you bring your child's behavior under control. Only then will you be able to get the most benefit from mastering the program described in this book. The combination of all of these factors, rather than just the use of the nine steps, is what will bring about the most change in you and your child.

So, roll up your sleeves and get ready to start on an important journey. It will require time, commitment, and effort, but in the end you and your child will build a closer, more positive relationship. In the process, you will help your child develop the self-control necessary to become a well-adjusted adult.

CHAPTER 1

Why Do Children Misbehave?

So, why *are* some children so difficult to manage? In the example presented in the introduction, a number of factors contributed to Stevie's noncompliance and the subsequent escalation of the conflict with his mother. Some of these factors pertain to Stevie, and some have to do with his mother's behaviors and reactions.

Child's Personality and Characteristics

Some personality factors make it more likely that a child may become out of control. Of these, impulsivity is the most notable. The more prone a child is to quick reactions without much forethought, the more likely he is to misbehave. When confronted with a situation in which we don't get our way, we all experience a negative reaction. Those who are not particularly impulsive possess the ability to think through the situation, evaluate response choices and the consequences of each option, and select a behavior that results in the most desired consequences. Unfortunately, individuals who are impulsive spend little time thinking through the consequences of their behaviors and act too quickly. Often, those actions result in negative consequences that the individual didn't anticipate, and the result is a negative reaction, including frustration and anger.

Impulsivity is the result of many factors, most significantly the underactivity of the brain's frontal lobes. In its most notable form, this insufficiency causes psychological disorders such as attention-deficit/

hyperactivity disorder. It's important to remember, however, that impulsive children don't necessarily have a psychological disorder.

Although extreme impulsivity is a sign of a more serious problem and most likely requires appropriate treatment, many children exhibit less severe symptoms of impulsivity that, nevertheless, result in behavioral difficulties. In general, impulsive individuals exhibit limited self-control; their diminished ability to think through the consequences of their behaviors often results in their inability to adapt to situations that don't turn out as they would like. It can be said that impulsive children are known to have difficulties with thinking through their actions and often exhibit behaviors characterized by limited self-control.

What makes impulsivity particularly troubling is the way in which it interferes with the person's ability to learn from experience. When required to choose a behavior in a particular situation, those with sufficient ability to stop and think before they act are able to process the situation long enough to recall similar situations, the behavior they chose in the past, and the consequences they experienced. This allows them to learn from these situations. When faced with a similar choice, they can select a response that worked best in the past (or, at least, stop selecting the behavior that generally resulted in negative consequences).

However, impulsive individuals with limited self-control don't think through each situation sufficiently to recall prior experiences, so they are much more likely to make the same poor choices over and over again. This point is very important to remember: Impulsive children require repeated exposure to consistent consequences before they eventually begin to think before they act and start to learn from prior experience.

Parents' Attitudes and Expectations

To understand Stevie's behavior, other factors must also be considered. For example, his mother was in a hurry. In her mind, Stevie had her at a disadvantage because she had to leave regardless of what happened with Stevie, even if he didn't listen. This made her feel that she didn't have control over the situation or control over Stevie's behaviors.

Mental preparation for a difficult task is absolutely essential. We have to be in the right frame of mind when we are about to undertake something that is difficult to do. For example, we may rehearse ahead of time what may happen in order to avoid being caught off-guard. This allows us to think of possible responses to many eventualities.

Day to day, this is so commonplace that we don't give it a second thought. After all, how many people go to a job interview without preparing themselves for what will be said and how they'll respond? Or, how many people go to an examination of some sort without preparing themselves for what will be asked?

We also prepare ourselves for interactions with difficult people. For example, most people will rehearse in their mind a forthcoming conference with their boss or coworkers, especially if they know that the topic will be a difficult one and may evoke strong emotions. How about dealing with that relative who commonly pushes your buttons? Most people try to anticipate what may be said during the interaction and prepare themselves for various options to help them stay in control.

What is it, then, about thinking through a situation that helps us stay in control? The biggest factor is that when we prepare ourselves, we are less likely to get caught off-guard. Without sufficient preparation, we often experience the feeling of loss of control—for example, when someone throws us a curve and says or does something we didn't expect. Then we experience a surge of negative emotions, and we feel that we've lost control. As a result, we get stressed and angry.

So, how do you prepare for an interaction with a child who often doesn't listen? The answer lies in understanding what you want to accomplish, understanding the nature of the response of the child, and planning for all eventualities so that you're never caught off-guard by anything that he says or does.

The Goals of Parenting

During speaking engagements, I'm often asked what the goals of parenting are and the best ways to achieve them. This is obviously a complex question that has many answers, but generally I think that parents have the obligation to facilitate the child's growth and development and prepare the child for adulthood.

The first of these goals, facilitating growth and development, is attained through providing an environment in which the child's physical, emotional, and educational needs are met. The physical and educational needs are met by providing a safe environment for your child, attending to your child's health and nutrition, encouraging and monitoring school attendance and progress, and offering some cognitive challenge and stimulation to facilitate growth. The emotional needs, however, are more elusive, although no less important. These include the ability to provide your child with a home environment filled with caring, empathy, and respect. In addition, parents must allow their child to develop as his own person, with his own personality, even if that personality is different from either of the parents and even if the personality is different than that which the parents wished their child to have.

The Strong-Willed Child Grown Up

Consider the following example: Marcie is a twenty-seven-year-old woman who regularly comes to a counselor because she says that her husband treats her poorly, is very bossy, and takes advantage of her all the time. He orders her around and she has to serve him and his friends when they come over, even though they are lewd and offensive to her. She then has to clean up the mess. Marcie's boss also takes advantage of her and constantly has her working extra hours without proper overtime pay. He also asks her to perform the duties of other coworkers, even though Marcie's job has nothing to do with their duties. The counselor works with Marcie to help her recognize that she doesn't have to do what other people say just because they say so, and that she's a person who can exercise her own will and set limits on others.

Sometimes, her mother sees the counselor with Marcie. Upon hearing Marcie recount some of her stories, she remarks, "Marcie was such a strong-willed child. We used to have to spank and punish her a lot to get her to do what she was supposed to do. Why can't she be strong-willed to other people like she used to be with us?" One day, in the middle of the session, Marcie quietly says to her mother, "I guess you beat all the defiance out of me."

Now, think about this example: Joe is a thirty-two-year-old divorced man who is currently unemployed. He has been married twice, and each of his marriages ended when his wife left and told Joe that she could no longer live with him. Joe has a six-year-old son with whom he has little contact because the child's mother took Joe to court to increase the child support. Consequently, Joe is so angry at her that he doesn't want to have anything to do with her or the child.

Joe has few friends, and he frequently gets into arguments with them because he challenges people when he doesn't get his own way. On some occasions, he was beaten up and suffered broken bones and one stab wound. Joe has never held a job for more than a few months because, as he put it, "When my boss starts ordering me around, I tell him off and then I walk." Joe also admits that he has gotten fired many times.

Joe maintains no contact with his family. His brothers distanced themselves from him after some arguments, and Joe voluntarily doesn't stay in contact with his parents because "They have been trying to tell me what to do and run my life ever since I was a child. I can't stand this."

Now, a third example: Dennis is a thirty-five-year-old businessman who heads a small but successful greeting card business. Five years ago, Dennis had an idea that the large greeting card companies didn't pay enough attention to the specialty markets, and didn't produce greeting cards that catered to the specific needs of doctors, attorneys, teachers, and people in many other occupations and professions. When he first started out, he was told by his family, friends, and just about everyone in the business that he couldn't single-handedly take on the giants in the greeting card business and expect to win. However, through hard work and perseverance, Dennis did just that. He's not rich, but his business is successful, and Dennis feels a sense of pride in what he's accomplished.

Dennis is also a respected member of his community. Two years ago, Dennis discovered that his town's water supply was tainted with dangerous levels of chemicals from a pharmaceutical company in the area. Although at first no one was responsive to his complaints, Dennis continued to contact community organizations, environmental groups, and the media. The pharmaceutical company eventually improved their filtering procedures, and the town's water supply is now considerably safer.

Dennis is married and has two children. His wife remarks that she enjoys his strength and courage: "I've known him since we were kids, and he's always been that way. When he sets his mind to do something, no one can stop him. He still gets upset when things don't go his way." She says, however, that he is also warm, kind, and compassionate.

What do these three people have in common? One obvious similarity is that they were all strong-willed as children. These strong-willed tendencies, however, progressed differently as those individuals grew up and became adults. For Marcie, her defiance and strong will were eliminated. Joe's defiance persisted into adulthood and affected his ability to have a stable life. In Dennis, the strong-willed nature became an asset, and he was able to use it to accomplish personal success and respect within the community.

If, in fact, these three individuals all started out with similar tendencies as children, what then accounts for such different outcomes as adults? The answer, at least partially, lies in the manner in which their strong-willed natures transformed during development. Marcie's spirit was broken, and she learned that it isn't worth it to stand up for herself and attempt to have things in life go her way. Joe's defiant tendencies continued into adulthood to such an extent that his judgment now remains poor and he must still always get his own way, even though it is obviously to his detriment at work and in his personal life. Dennis, on the other hand, seemed able to retain strength of will and perseverance to get his own way when it really matters while having the good judgment to avoid being bossy when it isn't necessary. Thus, he is able to be tenacious but compassionate and kind.

How do we, as parents, affect the way in which our children's nature evolves into adulthood? It's probably becoming clear by now that some strength of will is an asset to a person. For it to become a strength rather than a liability, however, your child must develop the ability to judge a situation and determine when fighting for his own way is necessary and beneficial, and when getting his own way will result in cutting off his nose to spite his face. As parents, we don't want our children to lose their resolve and become like Marcie. Likewise, we hope that our children won't grow up to be like Joe. Instead, we want our children to retain strength of will and perseverance but be able to moderate it by good judgment, like Dennis. But how do we do that? It is, first and foremost, a matter of expectations.

Appropriate Expectations

Consider the following example: Michael is coming in with his eight-year-old son for treatment at a local outpatient counseling center. He says that his son, Michael Jr., doesn't listen to what he tells him. The father, in fact, gets so angry at Junior that he admits that he sometimes has been on the brink of physically abusing his son when he blatantly says things such as "No, I don't have to" and "You can't make me."

In treatment, the father disclosed that he can't stand the defiance and views it as a direct assault on his authority as a father. Junior is only eight years old, and it isn't his place to question anything that the father is saying. In other words, "Junior must obey because I said so. I would have never defied my father because I would get the crap beat out of me. I think I'm too soft on my son, or he wouldn't do this to me."

The above example is all too common. It exhibits two disturbing trends: the parents' expectation of blind obedience from their children, and the parents' perception that the children's misbehavior is an act deliberately performed to usurp their parental authority.

When given the choice of Marcie, Joe, or Dennis, most parents would choose Dennis as a model of how they'd like their children to be when they grow up. On one hand, they expect their children to blindly accept everything that they tell them to do; on the other hand, they expect the children to simultaneously develop the ability to stand up for what they believe and exert strong will as adults. However, these two expectations are contradictory. A child who blindly accepts every-thing that parents say will *not* become an adult that is independently minded and tenacious. The ability to persevere and try to get one's own way starts early in life and won't evolve if squelched. No child can magically become a strong and persistent adult without developing these tendencies gradually as a child.

Facilitating the Development of Good Judgment

We all want our children to grow up to be healthy, happy, well-adjusted, and strong adults. We want them to learn to think for themselves and make the right decisions, but we must recognize that the journey to attaining these goals starts at birth. The way we parent our children has a lot to do with the degree to which they will, in fact, grow up to be happy, well adjusted, and strong. If you scorn your child every time she expresses her own will, the eventual result will be an adult who is unhappy, feels poorly about herself, and lacks self-confidence. In other words, your child will grow up to be like Marcie. This doesn't mean that the misbehaviors should go unchecked. If your child doesn't learn to use good judgment, he may grow up to be like Joe. How, then, do we balance our approach and help our children develop to become adults like Dennis?

One way to do so is to focus on the behavior rather than the attitude. In other words, don't expect your child to do what you say blindly, without any objection. Even though your job as a parent may be easier, you're much more likely to turn your child into a passive adult. Instead, expect your child to question what you ask or command, and don't view this as a test of your authority.

Remember, your child doesn't yet know how to differentiate between settings in which exerting his own will is desirable and those in which it is not. If you want your child to grow up to be self-confident and mentally strong, this must start at home, when your child is young. Don't squelch it. Don't punish your child for the initial reluctance or refusal.

Remember, what your child does is much more important than what he says. (One exception to this is when your child becomes verbally or physically aggressive. That needs immediate action on your part and ways of handling this are addressed later in this book.) If he exhibited reluctance or protest but still made the right choice of behavior, don't punish (or scold) him for the initial reaction. If he made the wrong choice of behavior, allow the consequences to become the tool by which he eventually learns to make a better choice.

Keep in mind that you don't want to break your child's spirit. You want to encourage his attempts to exercise his will, but you also want him to learn the difference between doing so all the time and doing so when it is necessary and proper. In other words, you want your child to have a choice about whether to comply with your command or request. In this manner, your child will learn self-control. You want your child to comply with your command because he knows the consequences of complying and not complying, and because he decided which of these consequences he desires. Your goal isn't to force compliance but to teach your child the consequences of complying or not. This is a crucial distinction.

If your child doesn't listen, it doesn't mean that you weren't successful as a parent. Your job is to teach (and administer) proper consequences, and you can do this regardless of whether your child complied with your command. If your child doesn't comply, you haven't failed as a parent. You would have failed only if you didn't administer appropriate consequences.

If you can clearly establish the parameters beforehand, especially with regard to the consequences that your child will experience after either an appropriate or inappropriate behavior, you'll eventually teach your child to make the right choices, and this book will help you do so. This teaches your child to exercise reasoning and judgment. This point is so important that keeping just this point in mind, even if you don't follow anything else in this book, will make a significant difference in how you interact with your child and what you expect of him. Consequently, he'll grow up to be happier and better adjusted.

Other Factors

When children have behavioral difficulties, additional factors are often involved. Parents' attitudes and expectations, as well as family dynamics, often contribute to child management problems within the home.

He's Doing It On Purpose!

Parents of difficult children sometimes become abusive, and much research has been conducted on child abuse to try to understand its causes, dynamics, and ways to prevent it. Research has identified some characteristics that increase the likelihood that a parent will physically abuse a child. Some children are more likely to be abused than others: Boys are more likely to be abused than girls, especially boys who have behavior problems, and particularly those who are seen by their parents as strong-willed, defiant, and out of control. Obviously, however, not all of those children are abused. What differentiates those parents that become physically abusive from those who don't?

Research suggests that one important factor is the parents' belief that their child is misbehaving on purpose; that is, the child knows the right way to behave but is misbehaving to spite the parents or make them angry. It has been my experience that many parents of out-of-control children share this belief. At times, they see their child behave appropriately. Consequently, during those times when he misbehaves, they assume that he has purposefully decided to do so. This belief is further strengthened when parents experience their child's verbal challenges of authority, such as when the child says, "You can't make me" or "I hate you." However, this belief is incorrect as well as counterproductive; it only serves to exacerbate the parents' anger.

Instead, recognize that out-of-control children are usually impulsive and tend to follow the path of least resistance to get what they want. They are likely to repeat what has worked for them in the past to obtain the consequence that they want, even if the manner of doing so was inappropriate. As many noted behaviorists have pointed out over the years, it is the consequence after the behavior that determines whether that behavior will be performed again. If a behavior results in a consequence that your child considers desirable, he is more likely to perform this behavior in the future. If not, the likelihood of performing the same behavior is diminished.

The strength of the association is also important. If your child got what he wanted as a result of the same behavior for a long time, he won't stop trying just because it failed to work once or twice. When you evaluate why your child is behaving in a specific way, try to think about the consequences of that behavior in the past. Has he gotten what he wanted as a result of this behavior? When you attempted to obtain compliance, did your frustration and anger often cause you to give up? If so, chances are that your child has learned that frustrating you results in the consequence that he wants (e.g., he doesn't have to do what you said), even though it may have been preceded by a screaming match. Think back to the example of Stevie and his mother. He refused to pick up, and the mother eventually did so herself. What is the child likely to remember? What is the child likely to do again the next time this situation occurs?

Children will try different tactics to get their own way. For example, think about a child who gets punished by being grounded. The child may at first whine, cry, and argue with the parents. If none of these attempts work, the child will eventually accept the situation, although some children will carry on longer than others. However, if the child, through crying and whining, gets the parents frustrated enough to rescind the grounding (maybe to get some peace of mind and stop the protests), he'll most likely try this behavior in the future after being grounded again. Many parents in this situation will think that their child got them angry on purpose, just to get his way. This is not true. Instead, he learned how to get what he wanted; getting the parents angry, from the child's point of view, is just a by-product, rather than the direct goal, of the behavior. He'll do it again because it worked, not because he really sets out to make the parents angry. From the child's point of view, the end does justify the means.

Mental Preparation

How, then, do you stay one step ahead of your child? First, if you keep in mind that your child isn't premeditating to make you mad, and recognize that your job isn't to get compliance at any price, you'll be able to stay calm (more on that in the next chapter) and think more clearly. With clarity of thought, more options will become apparent to you.

Since your job is, first and foremost, to administer appropriate consequences (positive and negative), you'll be able to think of many consequences that you wouldn't have considered if you became angry. The manner of administering consequences is the focus of step 2. For now, just keep in mind that you can stay in control even if your child doesn't listen, and you can turn every situation into an opportunity to teach him about his choices and consequences. View each confrontation as a "teachable moment," not a battle to be won or lost.

As a parent of an out-of-control child, you can probably predict the situations where problems will occur. For example, your child may usually act out when he's asked to stop an activity that he's enjoying (e.g., to turn off the TV or stop playing video games), when he's asked to do something he doesn't want to do (e.g., clean his room or go do his homework), or during times of transition when he has to stop one activity to start another, such as in the previous example with Stevie. This predictability allows you to plan for these trouble spots.

Instead of dreading a situation that you know is usually troublesome, prepare yourself simply by allowing yourself a little more time. Be consistent and never threaten anything you aren't willing to implement. "Scaring" your child into compliance (e.g., Stevie's mother's hollow threat to throw the toys away) is seldom, if ever, effective. Instead, prepare yourself with a series of realistic consequences that you can administer if your child doesn't comply (covered later in the book). Each time you threaten without following through, you actually lose ground. Your child will have learned that you don't mean what you say and he'll be less likely to listen to *any* threat that you state in the future.

Family Dynamics

When children act out, family conflicts, relational patterns, and presence of significant stressors often contribute to these problems. Most families experience at least some domestic squabbles. Parents frequently disagree about discipline and methods of parenting. Children who are difficult to parent are especially likely to evoke disagreements between parents on how to approach and discipline them. Each parent feels that he or she has the right approach, and therefore tries to convert the other parent to that way of thinking. Some of this is normal and can be expected in most homes. It can even be productive, as long as the disagreements are approached with a constructive attitude and don't happen in front of the children. In some families, however, these squabbles lead to significant conflicts between parents that may occur within earshot of the child. This has obvious implications for the child's self-esteem. Every child feels bad when he hears one parent berate the other because of something that he did.

Lack of Parental Unity

In some homes, the disagreement may lead one parent to override the other parent's decisions and step in to take over. This makes it obvious to the child that the parents are not in agreement on how to handle the child's behavior and gives him an opportunity to play one parent against the other. In these situations, the children almost always end up getting away with more misbehaviors than they would have if the parents were more consistent. It also has a damaging effect on the children because they feel that their home lacks unity and strength. It also frequently erodes a marriage (often beyond repair), because one parent feels undermined by the other. If you are in this kind of situation, I urge you to attempt to resolve it by calmly communicating with your spouse to stop the inconsistency in front of the children. If you cannot resolve it on your own, I urge you to seek appropriate counseling.

High Stress Level

Children are also significantly affected by living in a home in which there is a high daily level of tension and stress. Although most families experience financial pressures, troubles with in-laws, disapproval of each other's friends, and so on, in some homes these topics lead to open hostilities. As discussed earlier, children are very affected by such conflicts and are likely to reflect the home's problems in their own attitudes and behaviors. Again, by way of preparation, I urge you to address these conflicts with your spouse, either by talking one on one or by seeking counseling. If your home is one in which these conflicts continue, you are not likely to make much headway with your child's behavior.

Lack of Structure

Finally, when faced with the task of parenting a difficult child, the more structure you can implement within your home, the more your child's problem behaviors will decrease. Out-of-control children tend to act out most when something is unexpected and catches them off-guard. Children lose control most often when parents, out of nowhere, tell them to do things such as get ready to go out to a bank or a store (such as in the example with Stevie), stop an activity and start another one, or get ready for bed. In general, the more consistent and predictable you can make your child's environment, the more likely you are to decrease the acting out, since this routine will give him some time to mentally prepare for what's coming. It is very desirable to set routines within your home that regulate the time to get up, eat meals, do homework, have free time, and go to bed. The rest of this book will assist you in performing many of these tasks, but, in general, remember that the more consistent, structured, predictable, and routine your child's daily life is, the less he'll act out.

Because such a major part of children's reactions is dependent on the parents' mental state and ability to control their negative emotions, before we proceed into the actual nuts and bolts of the specific interventions, I will address some ways in which parents can stay calm and handle their frustration and anger.

CHAPTER 2

Prepare Yourself

Two attorneys leave the courtroom after a trial. Mr. Smith, who represented the plaintiff, approaches Mr. Jones, who represented the defendant. Mr. Smith says, "I'm sorry I lost my temper in the courtroom. I guess the emotions just ran so high. Congratulations on winning the case. I'm a little surprised, though. I thought the facts were on our side." Mr. Jones replies, "They were, my friend. However, the side that stays calm is the side that is in control."

In the previous chapter, we learned about Michael and his son, Junior. As you recall, Michael gets very angry at his eight-year-old son for being defiant and for mouthing off to him. Although Michael appears to get angrier than most parents, just about every parent feels anger and frustration when their child misbehaves or challenges their authority. While frustration is a normal reaction, intense anger prevents parents from thinking clearly. As Mr. Jones in the above example points out, the one who stays calm is usually the one who remains in charge. In other words, as you attend to your child's behavior problems, you must be able to stay calm. But how do you do that when your child appears to be pushing your buttons, saying and doing the very things that make you the most angry? As the saying goes, "knowledge is power." Thus, to become able to control your reactions, you'll need to understand how the anger response develops in your body. This knowledge will assist you in developing tools to keep your anger under control.

The following is an example that is often used to illustrate the psychological and physiological processes that we go through when we encounter an emotion that evokes a strong reaction. While this example doesn't directly relate to parenting, the processes that it outlines are similar to those that parents often experience, especially during an encounter with a child that seems out of control. Whenever we feel threatened, whether by something or someone that can hurt us or by a child who is acting out, we experience a similar reaction.

The Emotional Reaction

A man is crossing a wide (two lanes in each direction), busy road. He looks both ways and waits for a moment when there is no traffic immediately to either side, so he can get across. He rushes through, but about halfway across, while he is in the middle of the road, he hears the loud, unmistakable sound of a truck horn warning him that it is approaching. He looks over and sees an eighteen-wheeler charging his way at a high rate of speed. He shouts "Oh, no!" and rushes across as fast as he can. After he gets to the other side, he wipes the sweat off his forehead and says, "Boy, that was close!"

What emotion was the man feeling in the above example? Most likely, fear. But what does fear have to do with anger? Well, it just so happens that the process through which we experience fear is similar to the process through which we experience anger. Therefore, I'll review what the man experienced internally in the above situation. Then, I'll apply it to situations that make us angry.

Stimulus

The fear response in the example above started when the man heard the truck horn while he was in the middle of the road. The horn can be described as the trigger for the fear response, or more scientifically, the *stimulus*. The stimulus is not something over which you have control. It just happens, and you must deal with it when it does. Now, it can be argued that the stimulus was at least partially caused by the man's carelessness in crossing the street at the wrong moment. Good point, but for now, let's just say that the first stage of the fear reaction is the stimulus.

Interpretation

The moment the man experienced the stimulus (the truck horn), he reacted to it and got out of the way, right? Well, not exactly. Several things happened between the time the man heard the horn and moved out of the way, although these things happened very quickly and almost automatically.

After hearing the truck horn, the man first had to become aware of what he was hearing. He quickly searched his memory for what this sound might be and looked over to see what was happening. When he saw the truck, before he took any action, his thought processes must have immediately interpreted the event for him. Otherwise, although he may have heard and seen the truck, he may not have interpreted it as being a danger.

For example, what if he was crossing the road on an overpass instead of being right on the road? In that situation, had the man heard the truck horn while he was in the middle of the overpass, he would've looked to see what made the noise, but he would've quickly interpreted that he was safe on the overpass and wouldn't need to move out of the way. The point is that before you take any action, you must interpret a stimulus. This happens very quickly and almost outside of your awareness, but it does happen—otherwise you wouldn't know how to respond to the stimulus. In the above example, it's clear that it happened because the man shouted "Oh, no!" Many people may be even more graphic in what they may utter at that moment. At any rate, stage 2 of the reaction is the interpretation of the stimulus.

Physiological Arousal

Through your interpretation of the situation, the stimulus is identified as one that requires action (e.g., getting out of the way of the truck), and you must mobilize your physical resources to be able to act in the most effective way. Your sympathetic nervous system is activated and, in turn, activates parts of your body to go into an immediate state of physical arousal in order to maximize your ability to perform an action. This physiological arousal includes the increase in blood pressure and heartbeat, redistribution of blood flow away from digestive organs and into muscles, sweating (to accommodate the increased metabolism in the muscles), pupil dilation, and increase in respiration to oxygenate the blood.

Everything that the body is doing at that time is designed to give greater strength and agility. In the above example, speed is very important for getting out of the truck's way. It's clear how the arousal of the above physiological systems would, in fact, allow the man greater speed to get out of the way. In the example, he wiped away sweat after he got to the other side, a sign of the physiological changes that quickly took place inside his body. Thus, stage 3 of the reaction is the physiological arousal to be ready for action. In fact, stages 2 (interpretation) and 3 (physiological arousal) are collectively known as the fight-or-flight reaction, because humans must quickly decide, and be physically ready, to fight the danger or run away from it.

Response

Now that the man in the example knows what to do, and is physically ready for it, next he performs his chosen response—the physical act of getting out of the way of the truck. Keep in mind that while he performs the response, he is committed to it, and it is an all-or-nothing situation. He has to perform the action quickly; he'll have no time to change his mind in the middle of the response. He'll simply complete the action that he chose, and he'll have to do it as quickly and efficiently as his body will allow. Thus, stage 4 of the reaction is the actual behavior, or, in scientific terms, the response. To sum it up, the four stages of the reaction are stimulus, interpretation, physiological arousal, and response.

Preparation

Actually, two more stages need to be included in the process. First, consider that the man's state of mind affected his readiness for action before he was in the situation where he experienced the stimulus. The man knew, even before he stepped into the road, that it was a busy road and that he had to be vigilant because crossing it would be dangerous. He was mentally prepared to act quickly, and his body already maintained a state of slight arousal, although not nearly as intense as the arousal he experienced in stage 3 of the reaction.

The man's reaction would have been somewhat different if he had been surprised by a charging eighteen-wheeler on a quiet country road that seldom sees any traffic, rather than on a busy four-lane road. He wouldn't have been as ready to react, and his reaction to the stimulus may have been more delayed. Thus, preparation is really the initial phase of an emotional reaction.

Consequence

Consider also the consequences of the entire episode and how they affect a person's behavior in similar situations in the future. In this example, the man's response was relief ("Boy, that was close!") and recognition that his action was effective in handling the stimulus. If he ever finds himself in a situation where he has to cross the same road again, he'll probably be even more careful next time, but he'll cross the road, knowing that he can handle it even if he gets surprised by a truck while crossing.

What if the situation had turned out slightly differently? What if the man twisted his ankle while trying to get out of the way and barely escaped with his life because the truck missed him only by a couple of inches? After such an encounter, the man may be reluctant to cross that road again, and if he had to do it, his expectation/preparation would've included much more arousal and fear even before any vehicle came his way. Thus, when we talk about an emotional reaction, we must really consider six stages: preparation, stimulus, interpretation, physiological arousal, response, and consequence.

Note that I've been referring to an *emotional* reaction rather than a *fear* reaction specifically. This is because the above sequence of events takes place with any emotional reaction, particularly one that is negative in nature (e.g., fear, frustration, or anger). It is a generic model of human emotional reaction and applies to a wide variety of human experiences.

The Emotional Reaction of a Frustrated Parent

Of course, the specific response of interest to us is the anger and frustration that a parent experiences when faced with a child who is out of control. Let's again use the example of Stevie and his mother (from the introduction) and the stages of emotional reaction I've just outlined to understand the mother's reaction and the process involved in the escalation of her anger and frustration.

Preparation

To start, the mother was already expecting to have a battle with her son, and she was dreading the interaction. She recalled the previous experiences she had had with him and remembered that many of them resulted in a conflict and confrontation. She already started the interaction with her son by thinking, "This will be trouble. Here we go again. Why do I always have to go through this with him?" Thus, in the first stage of her emotional reaction, she had already prepared herself for yet another bad incident with her son.

Also, it's likely that her own feelings of inadequacy as a parent further exacerbated her negative mind-set. She felt that she had lost control over her son, and she was angry. Most parents of out-of-control children view their children's behavioral problems as indicators of their own failure to bring the child under control. This belief only escalates their anger toward the child. Each time your child acts out may serve as yet another reminder to you that you fail to be in control. Your child may make you feel powerless and you may resent your loss of control. For Stevie's mother, the mental preparation she experienced even before she approached Stevie made it even more likely that she would have a negative response to her son, even if he really didn't act out in a major way.

Because her body language, voice intonation, and choice of words signaled to her son that she was on edge, Stevie was beginning to feel the same way and his reactions were likely exacerbated by the tense mood that was beginning to develop. Difficult children are particularly sensitive to those tense feelings and respond negatively when they encounter them (as observed, for example, by Barkley et al. 1991). The more edgy and annoyed you are when approaching your child, the more likely your child is to respond to the situation aggressively, as if to fight fire with fire. Consequently, a confrontation will probably occur.

Stimulus

Next comes the stimulus—Stevie's defiance. But if you carefully examine the sequence of events in that example, you'll notice Stevie wasn't all that defiant at first. Yes, he was reluctant to obey, but he didn't say he wasn't going to do it. Although he didn't obey when his mom gave the command, his actions weren't very challenging or defiant at first. Thus, the stimulus (from the mother's point of view) was noncompliance, not defiance.

Interpretation

In the mother's mind, Stevie was at it again, and she expected to have a problem with him, so she interpreted his response as a confirmation of her expectation. This interpretation escalated the situation further. From this point forward, anything that Stevie did further confirmed what his mother had already expected. Short of saying "Yes, Mom," almost any behavior that Stevie exhibited was going to be interpreted by her as a further sign of trouble. Her interpretation, however, may not have been entirely accurate, and it unnecessarily escalated her emotional reaction. She became increasingly angry with each thing that Stevie did or said.

Physiological Arousal

With the anger came physiological arousal. As we all have experienced during times of anger, the mother's blood pressure and heart rate likely increased, her breathing became more rapid and shallow, and she felt a rush of adrenaline that made her more ready for action. When a person is within such a state of arousal, she's physiologically and mentally ready to strike. As that state progresses, it becomes more and more difficult to respond rationally. She becomes more ready for a battle, and even minor annoyances will precipitate an explosion.

Response

Not surprisingly, the mother responded to Stevie's noncompliance with behavior that was both physically (yanking him) and verbally (yelling at him) aggressive in nature. Stevie, of course, picked up on his mother's anger and also escalated his behavior. From there, the situation went downhill. His reaction was surely exacerbated by his mother's loss of control over herself as the situation escalated and her open display of anger at Stevie. As she got angrier, the two of them reached a point of no return, and the situation became a confrontation. From there, the conflict escalated even further, and Stevie became out of control.

Consequence

Although the example ends there, you can speculate about what happened after this confrontation. Stevie got yelled at yet again by his mother, so he probably felt poorly about himself and the situation. His mother said some hurtful things to him (such as "What's wrong with you?") that surely made him wonder, after he calmed down, whether there really *was* something wrong with him.

Likewise, the mother probably experienced a negative reaction. The conflict she had expected happened again, and her feelings of frustration and inadequacy to handle Stevie escalated even further, so that she'll be even more ready for another battle in the future. She probably also felt bad, in retrospect, about some of the things she said to Stevie and blamed herself for not having enough self-control to stop saying hurtful things to him when she is angry. The entire incident just proved to her, in her own mind, that she's unable to control Stevie, that she's a bad parent, and that she has a child who won't respond positively to anything that she says or does.

The Emotional Reaction of a Parent Who Remains in Control

So, how to break this cycle? There are things that you can do in each of the six stages of emotional response to make a difference in how you react. Even if you're able to intervene at only some of these stages, this will help you to stay calm. When you're calm, you can think more clearly. If you're able to intervene at several of the stages, you'll experience an even greater difference in how you react and you'll become a more effective parent.

Preparation

To start, you must avoid preparing for a battle. As Stevie's example illustrates, if you expect a battle, you'll get one. You'll interpret each thing that happens as more proof of what you expected. Instead, prepare yourself for the possibility that the situation *may* escalate. Even if it does, you'll have the tools necessary to stay in control. Remember the example of the two attorneys from the beginning of the chapter.

To stay calm and in control, take a few deep breaths before you approach your child. It's best to take slow, deep breaths where you fill your lungs completely over about four seconds, hold all the air in your lungs for about one second, and slowly exhale to get all the air out. Repeat this procedure two or three times in one minute. While doing so, say to yourself, "I will stay calm. I will not lose control no matter what he does. It will be okay. One of us has to act like a grown-up, and it will be me." Doing so will not only help you prepare yourself mentally; you will also maintain your pulmonary and circulatory function at a slower pace, making it easier to stay calm.

It will help you to remember that it's not your job to get compliance at any price. It's your job to teach your child the consequences of his actions. Even if he doesn't comply, you haven't lost. True, it may be less convenient if you have to pick up the toys because your son refuses, but it doesn't mean that it will always be that way or that you have failed as a parent.

If you know that certain commands and situations require more time and effort on your part, don't wait until the last minute to get into the situation. Stevie's mother allowed herself to be in a hurry and felt the added pressure of meeting a deadline. If she had allowed herself more time to start getting Stevie ready to go out, the situation may not have escalated. True, she still might have picked up the blocks in the end, but she would've been better able to administer an appropriate consequence for Stevie's lack of compliance. This would have made her much more effective than she ended up being in our example. Over time and with consistency on the mother's part, it is likely that Stevie's noncompliance would start to diminish. Again, at the risk of belaboring the point, your most important job as a disciplinarian is to administer consequences, not necessarily to force compliance. As such, you'll teach your child about how the world will respond to his or her choices of behaviors.

Finally, remember that a child's tendency to have willful or defiant characteristics has little to do with what you did as a parent. Rather, the child's dispositional tendencies, which are usually genetic, determine the child's basic personality style. You didn't cause it, and you can't change it. Your job as a parent is to help the child develop the good judgment to moderate these characteristics and to be able to decide how much willfulness or defiance is okay to exhibit in any given situation.

Stimulus

This is the one stage that you can't control, because you can't stop your child from performing the stimulus—the action of saying something or doing something that is noncompliant, defiant, or otherwise inappropriate. Even here, you can make a difference, although indirectly. By following the steps outlined in this book and remaining calm and consistent, over time you can help to diminish your child's behavioral difficulties.

Interpretation

This stage is absolutely crucial to successful anger control. How you interpret your child's behavior the moment that it happens will greatly determine whether you'll get angry or remain calm and in control. The more personally you take the behavior, the more likely you'll be to get angry. The more you feel that your child is misbehaving to spite you or just to get to you, the more enraged you'll become. Instead, view your child as a goal-directed person who's merely trying to get his own way in the best way he knows.

Don't expect him to like what you tell him to do. Instead, help your child make the choice between positive and negative behaviors by helping him recognize the consequences that each choice will bring. Whatever your child's choice, as long as you administer the appropriate consequence, you did your job as a parent. Even if you have to pick up those blocks in the end, isn't a slight inconvenience worth it to be able to teach your child a valuable lesson? Wouldn't you prefer to be the one to teach your child those consequences, instead of having your child learn the hard way after he grows up? Since you care about your child, any consequences that you administer will likely be much kinder. Won't it give you a good feeling to know that you've prepared your child to be able to make better decisions as an adult?

Physiological Arousal

If you are successful in avoiding negative interpretations of your child's actions, you probably won't need to do much to control your physiological reaction. The body's arousal depends almost entirely on whether you interpret that there's a need for you to get angry or excited in the first place. In other words, if you don't personalize or exaggerate your child's misbehavior, you won't experience the physiological arousal that leads to an anger outburst, and you'll stay in control.

Still, if the situation becomes volatile and your child is really pushing your buttons, there are things that you can do. When the physiological arousal takes place, you experience a rush that is hard to ignore. It happens very quickly. You may not focus on it when it happens, but you can recognize it if you really try. With practice, you can become aware of your breathing becoming more shallow, your voice and speech changing character (people speak louder and, usually, faster), even the rush you feel as your pulse and blood pressure increase. All of these can become signals that you are angry and must calm down.

When you feel the rush, that blood-boiling feeling, it's time to get out of the sight of your child. Go into another room, go outside, even go into the bathroom and lock the door in order to regain calmness and composure. It's helpful to sit or lie down. Take deep breaths in the manner we discussed earlier in this chapter (a cycle of inhaling for four seconds, holding for one second, and exhaling for four seconds) at a frequency of about three to four deep breaths per minute, in between which you should breathe normally. This procedure takes about five minutes, but it is very effective. While you are doing it, try to imagine a peaceful place, such as a beach, the woods, or an overlook in the mountains. Although there are some times when your immediate action is necessary (e.g., when your child is about to do something dangerous), in the most common situations with your child you'll be able to delay your response until you are calm. You'll make a better choice of your actions; thus, you'll be more effective.

Stevie's mother could've done this in the example. True, she would have missed the bank, but wouldn't this have been better than having another hurtful, counterproductive confrontation with her child? Remember your own priorities as a parent: What is more important, your schedule or your child's (and your own) emotional well-being? As the saying goes, "Somebody has to be the grown-up."

If, for some reason, you weren't able to prevent the rush of anger from occurring and you weren't able to remove yourself from your child's presence when you got angry, try not to lose control, despite your anger. Keep in mind that you and your child are *both* human beings who deserve to treat each other with respect and dignity.

Response

When you respond, try to be calm but deliberate. Step 1 will give you suggestions of how to address your child. Do so directly and focus on what it is that you want your child to do. Don't personalize or comment on your child's personality. Don't bring up past conflicts. Redirect your child to think about the choice he has between positive and negative behaviors and the consequences that follow each choice. Remember, this is a teachable moment, an opportunity for your child to learn from this experience.

If you recognize that you're angry, try not to say or do things that you know you'll regret later. You can apologize for something that you said or did that was hurtful, but you can never take it back, so the damage caused by it won't really go away.

If your child begins to have a tantrum, keep in mind that you'll be more productive if you don't stoop down to his level. If your child becomes aggressive, you won't win by doing the same. Stay in control of what you say and do. If you are so angry that you need to hit, hit something else—not your child. If you need to scream, turn and do so away from your child and not directed at him. If you find that your child regularly gets you to a point of explosion and you're unable to stop yourself, get help. Counseling can be very effective in helping you develop appropriate anger management skills. You'll be doing so for yourself and for your child.

Consequence

If a confrontation has occurred, especially one in which emotions have escalated, calm down and try to think through what happened. Don't allow yourself to experience thoughts such as "Well, there he went again. I knew this would happen." Similarly, don't blame yourself or feel that you caused the confrontation.

Instead, try to analyze the sequence of events. What did your child say, and how did you react? Did he catch you off guard? If so, why? Was it a behavior that never happened before, or was it that you just didn't prepare yourself adequately for something that happens regularly? If so, make a plan for how to handle this same situation when it happens again—prepare yourself, stay calm, and think about your options before you initiate the interaction. Much of what you will learn in this book will help you address these kinds of situations.

Remember, even though whatever you did appeared to be ineffective, you can learn from it and try to avoid doing the same thing in the future. Accept that people (both you and your child) learn by making mistakes. Without mistakes, you don't have the opportunity to try out what works and what doesn't. What you did may not have worked. So, treat it as a lesson and think of what else you can do next time.

The Program

The forthcoming chapters present a set of tools that will help you address the most common behavioral problems that out-of-control children exhibit. Keep in mind that you'll need to implement each step gradually, and you may not see much difference after you've implemented just one or two steps. It doesn't mean that they aren't working. Gradually, positive changes will take place that may not become apparent until after you have implemented several of the steps.

Keep in mind that you must be calm and in control. Avoid asking, "Why is my child doing this?" Instead, ask, "What can I do about it?" If you are consistent, if you structure the child's daily routine and make the environment more predictable for him, and if you continue to administer immediate consequences for both positive and negative behaviors, in time you'll reduce behavioral problems and help your child grow up to be a better-adjusted, happier adult.

CHAPTER 3

Step 1—Give Effective Commands

After reading the preceding chapters, you should now have a greater understanding of why your child has behavioral problems that are difficult to manage. You should also have some sense of what it will take to improve these problems. In the following chapters, you will learn specific strategies to address the usual trouble spots that parents often experience with out-of-control children. As mentioned earlier, you will gain the most benefit from the following steps if you read only one chapter at a time and try to implement only one step every one to two weeks. It's best to proceed slowly. The steps are easy to implement, but you'll need time to get used to each step and to include it in your daily routine. Each step becomes most effective when you are so familiar with it that using it becomes automatic. Likewise, your child will also need time to get used to your new management style. As I pointed out previously, children respond best when their environment is routine and predictable. Consequently, they need time to adjust and to learn what to expect from you.

If you just started to read here and have skipped the previous chapters, please go back and read them. Although you can benefit from -continuing to read further, you won't derive the full benefit of the program. Your ability to administer the following steps will be diminished and you'll be more likely to give up once you experience failure. Your success is more probable if you read the previous chapters, which cover the topics that are absolutely essential to making this program work.

Getting Started

For the first week, focus only on two aspects of your interaction with your child:

1. How to give a command to your child

2. What to do when your child obeys the command

For starters, select some commands with which you usually have problems obtaining compliance from your child. These should be direct, simple commands that require a single action, such as "Pick up your toys," "Go wash your hands," or "Turn off the TV." Don't use commands that call for more complex actions, such as "Clean your room," or "Do your homework." The way to obtain compliance in these types of situations will be addressed in later steps. For now, focus on very direct, simple commands that require a single, specific action by your child.

Parents give commands to their children several times each day. If your child does not have a difficult personality, your way probably works much of the time. However, difficult children need to be addressed differently. Let's return to the example of Stevie and his mother from the introduction. Her attempts to command Stevie to pick up his toys were sandwiched between all the other activities she was doing before she left the house. Again, if Stevie was not a difficult child, this probably wouldn't pose a problem. Out-of-control children, however, need your undivided attention when you are trying to get their compliance. You can't expect to do two or three things at once and then attempt to get compliance. Instead, stop what you're doing, approach the child directly, and don't resume any other activities until your interaction with the child has ended. Obviously, this will require you to reserve more time for each instance in which you seek compliance from your child, particularly when you initially start to implement the following procedure.

The Effective Command

As outlined in checklist 1 at the end of this chapter, there are three components to an effective command:

1. Attentional cue

2. Command

3. Follow-up look

Let's look at each of these in detail.

The Attentional Cue

Not only must you give your child your undivided attention, you must also get attention from your child. In the example of Stevie and his mother, the mother was issuing commands to Stevie while doing other things, sometimes in another room, and she had no way of knowing whether Stevie even attended to some of her commands. Consequently, the first thing to do when you are about to issue a command is to get undivided attention. This is accomplished through the attentional cue.

The simplest way to cue your child to pay attention is to call his name. However, it's not sufficient to call your child from another room, around the corner, or up the stairs (while you remain downstairs). The most important aspect of the attentional cue is to get eye contact. Walk closer to your child and call his name, ask your child to come into the room where you are, or go to the room where your child is. Even if you stay in another room but get your child to look at you (for example, through an open doorway), you increase the likelihood that your child will listen. If calling your child's name is not enough, tell your child, "Look at me." If this is not sufficient, go to him and get his eye contact by turning his head, adjusting your own position so that you can catch his eye, or any other reasonable way that results in direct eye contact with him. Remember, long-distance commands with no eye contact are a sure way of decreasing compliance.

Face-to-face commands are more likely to be respected and followed. Why? There is something binding about human eye contact, as if a contract was actually set between two people and the listener understands that he must follow what was said. Although it isn't a guarantee of success, it greatly increases the likelihood of compliance, and parents of out-of-control children need to stack the deck in their favor. This by itself may not result in compliance, but when combined with the other techniques you'll utilize, it will certainly help.

Getting eye contact has an additional benefit. Some children get so involved in an activity that they tune out much of what is going on around them. Even if they briefly acknowledge that someone is talking to them and telling them something, they are likely to pay limited attention to that, and process it very little. Children with attentional difficulties, such as ADHD, are very likely to behave in this manner. When they don't comply, it may not be an overt sign of defiance; instead, it may be that the command you issued didn't fully register. Getting the eye contact momentarily breaks what they are doing long enough for them to process what was said. Afterward, they are more likely to perform the desired behavior.

What happens when you don't get eye contact was well illustrated in the example with Stevie. Many of the commands were given while the mother was in another room. It was as though obtaining compliance from her son was secondary in importance to her other tasks, such as gathering her things or looking for keys. Stevie, undoubtedly, picked up on this dynamic and knew that he had more opportunity to get his way. This "knowing" was more instinctive, rather than thought out and premeditated; nevertheless, he knew that he was more likely to get away with defiance if his mom was in a hurry and couldn't give the matter her undivided attention. To summarize, through eye contact you break the child's activity, get his full attention, and send a message to him that you expect him to attend to what you're saying. In short, eye contact communicates that you mean business.

The Command

Once you obtain eye contact, it's time to issue the command. Now, there are about as many ways of issuing a command as there are people doing so, and no one strategy works for everyone. However, there are several principles that do work, and keeping those in mind will help you increase your child's compliance.

Eye Contact

First, remember to issue the command *while* you are looking your child right in the eyes. Don't look away until you finish telling your child the command.

Be Respectful but Firm

Next, remember that you must address your child in a respectful but firm manner. Both components of this statement are equally important. The respectful part is crucial. Think about your own life and people you've known who were in positions of authority over you. You probably remember some of them more fondly than others. Those you respected and still remember kindly were respectful of you and addressed you with consideration and kindness. On the other hand, those you disliked the most were the ones that made you feel unimportant and treated you as if you were inferior. In fact, you were probably more likely to follow a command given by a "nice" boss than a "nasty" one. It is true that we respect those who respect us.

When I lecture, one of the most frequent laments I hear from parents is that their children don't respect them; yet, I see so many parents command their children with an angry voice, sometimes barking commands at them, and sometimes accompanying those commands with demeaning remarks. Parents who want respect from their children must first give it. Children are people too and deserve to be treated with dignity.

Having said that, remember that the command must also be stated firmly. Out of desperation, parents often give commands to children in a plaintive manner, almost as if they were begging their child to obey. Likewise, parents sometimes preface a command by asking their child, "Do me a favor …," and then they wonder why their child isn't listening. All parents have probably done this from time to time, and with some children this may work well. An out-of-control child, however, will interpret this statement literally and feel that compliance is optional. Obviously, you don't mean it this way.

Likewise, parents often ask a child to do something by starting, "Would you please …" Again, this isn't a good idea, because this form of a question can be answered very easily by saying no. An out-of-control child may say no anyway, but don't set up the situation in a way that makes it easier for him to do so. Instead, say what you mean in a manner that commands attention. Instead of asking, *tell* your child in a respectful but firm voice what you want him to do. Speak deliberately and clearly, with a tone that commands attention, but without yelling.

To summarize, position yourself so you can see your child, call his name or ask him to look at you, and while maintaining eye contact state an instruction to perform a concrete action (for example, "Please start picking up now").

Nonverbal Language

Your nonverbal communication must also be commanding in manner. By nonverbal communication, I mean your body posture, your hand gestures, your facial expression, the tone of your voice, and the manner in which you speak (such as how rapid your speech is, or whether your voice goes up and down or breaks while you speak). Generally, take a commanding posture (standing up may help), and keep your hands next to your body. Don't grimace; show a deliberate facial expression. Use a firm tone in your voice (it may help to raise your voice very slightly, but remember, no yelling), and produce words in a calculated, deliberate manner.

The younger your child is, the more important it is for you to communicate your commanding attitude through nonverbal language. Remember, the younger your child, the more limited is his ability to reason with words and respond to verbal communication. Think about your child at age three or four months. He probably already responded to you and your feelings and expressions, even though he had little ability to understand any of your words. The way he was able to receive your messages was through the expression on your face, the posture of your body, and your voice intonation.

In fact, a young child's ability to recognize facial expressions is universal. Many studies have been performed in which infants were presented with pictures (or videos) of faces with various emotions on them. The same person was always shown, but each time with a different facial expression of emotion. The infants correctly recognized each emotion and exhibited responses appropriate to each emotion (e.g., they laughed when it was a happy face, and cried or withdrew when the face was sad or angry). Moreover, when the images of the human face with different emotions were shown to infants from different cultures, the results were identical.

Remember that young children pay less attention to your words and respond mostly to the nonverbal messages you convey with your body, your face, and the tone of your voice. The older your child, the more he focuses on the verbal message, but he'll remain tuned-in to your nonverbal language as well. If your words say one thing (e.g., "I want compliance"), but your nonverbal communication sends another message (e.g., "I'm not sure if this is going to work"), your child will pick up on your hesitancy, and the likelihood of compliance will diminish.

And herein lies a dilemma. Your nonverbal communication can't be faked. It reflects your true feelings. If you are hesitant, your child will know, even if you try to convince yourself (and your child) that you are decisive and firm. What, then, is a parent to do? Well, since you can't fake it, don't merely *try* to convince yourself that it will work, *do* convince yourself that it will work. Have confidence that you'll make it work. As discussed in the previous chapter, if you prepare yourself by expecting realistic outcomes, understanding that your job as a parent is to stay in control and administer consequences, and remaining calm and in control, you truly will believe that what you do will work, and your nonverbal language will convey that message to your child. That's when he'll recognize that you really mean business.

While I'm on this topic, I should point out that although you must adopt a commanding posture, if possible you should avoid violating your child's space. Children, like adults, value their privacy and space and become agitated when their space is violated. In an interaction in which you are commanding your child to perform an action, the situation may become more tense, and violating your child's space can push him over the edge into an explosive reaction that otherwise could have been avoided. Of course, eye contact is even more important, so get close to your child if this is the only way that you can get eye contact and only after you've tried less invasive methods of obtaining eye contact.

Do Not Negotiate or Argue

As part of your firm approach, be prepared to fend off your child's protests and attempts at negotiations. Don't bargain with your child, and don't debate your point. Don't continue to explain why you want him to perform the action you commanded. Generally, it's okay to give your child one reason, briefly and to the point, but don't over-explain or repeat what you already said once. If your child continues to ask, it's okay to say "I already explained it to you" or "Because I said so." Remember, you're not asking your child to approve what you commanded.

Listening to parents interacting with their children, I sometimes get the impression that they want to convince their child that what they are asking is the right thing to do, in the hopes that their child will then agree to do it. This is inappropriate. First, it isn't your child's place to judge what you tell him to do. Second, it isn't your place to convince him of the appropriateness of your command or to make excuses about why you want something done. Can you imagine your boss at work doing this with you? Or a superior officer in the armed forces asking the subordinates to accept a direct command? In this way, the parent-child relationship *is* a superior-subordinate relationship.

In sum, if your child questions your command, give a brief explanation, only one time, or state "because I said so," and do not respond to all further protests or questions.

One Thing at a Time

Your command should include only one action that you want your child to perform. This is very important—only one item at a time. If you want your child to perform several actions, command him to do the first and to come and see you after he has completed it. Then command him to complete the second action and to come and see you after that one has been completed, and so on. This, again, has implications for compliance. It's much easier for your child to ignore or defy a command that calls for multiple actions (a so-called "chain command") than a command that calls for just a single action. Think about those children that have some attentional difficulties. At best, they'll focus on just the first or last command; at worst, they'll ignore all of them. And telling a very young child to do more than one thing at a time surely spells trouble, regardless of whether your child is out of control.

Ask Your Child to Repeat the Command

Finally, you might want to ask your child to repeat the command back to you. This isn't essential, but it may be very helpful if your child has some tendencies toward attentional problems or if you're unsure whether your child truly processed what you said. Those children who get too engrossed in activities and find it hard to stop them will be forced not only to attend to what you say (when you seek the eye contact) but also to repeat it back to you. This interrupts what they were doing and increases their ability to process what you commanded.

To summarize what we covered thus far:

- Position yourself so you can see your child.

- Call your child's name and/or ask him to look at you.

- State a specific command in a firm voice, such as "Please start picking up now," "Please pick up your coat now," or "Please turn off the television now."

- If your child asks you why, state a brief explanation, such as "Because it's dinnertime," or "Because we have to go out," and respond to all further questions by ignoring them, or stating "I already told you why" or "Because I said so."

- After you state your command, you may want to ask your child to repeat the command to you by asking, "Please repeat what I just told you to do." Correct any inaccuracies and state, "Yes, please do it now."

The Follow-Up Look

Once you've issued the command, you must do one more thing: absolutely ... nothing! Nothing except to stand and look at your child for an additional fifteen seconds or so. Don't move. To time yourself, count (silently) from 101 to about 115 or 120. This may seem strange at first, but think about what this will accomplish. It will put pressure on your child to process what you said. This is one of the reasons why you must obtain eye contact, state the command firmly, have appropriate body posture and tone of voice, and so on. Parents instinctively know when they need to increase pressure on their children to obtain compliance, but they usually pressure their children through yelling or becoming disrespectful and demeaning. These methods escalate conflict and lead to altercations. Standing and silently looking at the child will put pressure on your child but without escalating conflict.

Think about your own experiences: Have you ever had anyone stand and look at you after you were told to do something? Do you remember how uncomfortable you felt? If you can't relate to this point, do an experiment. Ask your spouse or a friend to ask you spontaneously to do something and then to stand and look at you until you do it. I'm sure that you'll experience the feeling of pressure. That is exactly what you want to convey to your child, and doing so through just standing and looking at him is humane and effective.

If your child asks why you're looking at him, you can respond in several ways. You can ignore the question, or tell him you're looking because he still hasn't done what you asked him to do, or say that you are doing so because you want to. Remember, though, that you don't owe your child an explanation. Most children will want to do what you asked just to get you off their back, and that's a good beginning.

While looking at your child, avoid responding to what he might say. Your child may impulsively start to protest when you first issue the command and may at first say no, but when he sees that you aren't going away and that you're not going to let up, he'll feel the pressure you are putting on him and start to comply. Here is a classic example I have witnessed many times. When asked to pick up his toys, a child at first says, "No, I'm not finished," but when the parent continues to stay and look, the child starts picking up, all the while saying "I don't want to" or "You can't make me." The parent in this situation didn't need to respond to anything that the child said because, even though he protested all the way, the child picked up the toys.

Positive Feedback

If the procedure worked and your child complied with your command, you *must* give your child positive feedback. Remember that your goal is to administer proper consequences that communicate to your child the results of his behavior. These consequences must be immediate and must follow both positive and negative behaviors. When your child makes the right choice, give immediate positive consequence, and when he doesn't, give an immediate negative consequence. Negative consequences are addressed later in this book. For now, administer positive consequences only.

Every time your child obeys you, give him a sign of your appreciation and approval. There are several ways to give positive feedback. Verbal ways to do so include sayings such as "Thank you," "Great job!" "Cool!" "Way to go," "I like it when you do what I ask," and "I really appreciate it when you listen to me." These are even more effective when supplemented by nonverbal signs of approval (a smile, a wink, or a hug). Remember, however, that although children are very sensitive to nonverbal messages, many children, particularly younger ones or those with tendencies toward attentional problems, may not make the connection that your wink or smile is in direct response to the behavior. Consequently, try to make sure that you always use both verbal and nonverbal means and you'll more effectively drive the point home. This will make your child feel good, and he'll want to feel this way again in the future. If he makes the connection that doing what you asked resulted in a consequence that made him feel good, he'll want to repeat this behavior in the future.

Bear in mind that your child may not be used to hearing positive comments from you. Out-of-control children experience frequent conflicts with their parents, usually more than once a day. They get used to the screaming and yelling, and they expect to be scolded and punished. They don't, however, expect to be rewarded, and at first they may have no idea why you are being nice to them and they may not know how to handle it. I have worked with many parents who, after starting this procedure, reported to me that their children didn't know how to handle praise and, at first, became uncomfortable. In fact, I have observed much of this firsthand. It may take some time before your child feels comfortable with hearing good things said about him and his behavior. You'll need to offer much consistent praise before your child figures out, and starts to expect, that listening to you and doing what you say will actually make him feel good in return. As you help your child learn that a compliment feels good, you won't want to minimize its effect by including any negative content. Avoid back-handed compliments, in which you acknowledge positive behavior on the one hand ("that was good") but scold on the other hand ("but next time, do it the first time I ask").

This point becomes even more important in light of the fact that there is an actual physiological difference in how positive and negative feelings are processed by the brain. Negative feelings are usually experienced more intensely, and reaction to them is more immediate. We're much more likely to remember the events that caused us to feel negatively than the ones that made us happy. Perhaps there once was survival value in this difference—the events that made humans feel scared or angry were probably those that were more dangerous, and the chance of survival increased if humans quickly learned to avoid them (and consequently remembered that experience). Whatever the cause of this phenomenon, it is real and has important implications for this program.

When you give your child positive feedback, your child registers that feedback less strongly than an interaction during which he is yelled at or punished. This means that you'll need to work extra hard to counterbalance years of conflicts and negative feelings. Keep in mind the reason for doing so—if the child can experience, perceive, and remember that complying with your command will make him feel good in the end, he'll want to experience that again. This will happen, but it'll take time, perseverance, and a lot of praise. Giving positive feedback must become second nature to you; it must settle so deeply into your own behavioral patterns that you'll automatically give your child a sign of approval every time he obeys you.

Putting It All Together

To review, the command-giving procedure is made up of three parts: the attentional cue to get eye contact, the actual command (stated in a firm but respectful manner), and the (approximately) fifteen-second follow-up look to increase pressure on your child. Since this is probably different than what you've done previously, your child will be caught off-guard. Furthermore, just by doing this procedure, you are already putting more pressure on your child to obey than you probably have in the past. This step alone may work to increase the rate of your child's compliance with your commands. If your child does comply, you *must* acknowledge that by giving him positive feedback.

Let's take another look at the example of Stevie and his mother to see what the interaction might have looked like if the mother had followed the procedure described in this chapter:

Stevie is playing with his blocks. His mother comes into the room. She approaches Stevie and says, "Stevie, please look at me."

Stevie continues to play. His mother walks closer to Stevie and says, "Stevie, I said please look at me."

Stevie looks up. The mother, while looking Stevie in the eyes, says, "Stevie, please pick up your blocks right now because we have to go out."

Stevie starts to protest and says, "But I'm not finished yet!"

The mother doesn't respond, just continues to stand there and look at Stevie. Feeling the pressure, Stevie reluctantly starts to pick up the blocks. His mother says, "Thank you for picking up. I like it when you do what I ask."

If this procedure doesn't seem immediately effective, don't stop. It is an effective technique, even though it may not work immediately for your child. It is a foundation upon which you will build further interventions, which are discussed in the upcoming chapters. For now, focus on giving effective commands and administering positive feedback whenever you get compliance. It must become second nature to you. Deal with noncompliance as you've done before. Use this command-giving procedure with your child for about one to two weeks before you proceed to the next chapter, which will help you handle situations in which this procedure, by itself, does not produce compliance.

Checklist 1

Step 1: Give Effective Commands

Realistic expectations:

- No child obeys 100 percent of the time, and difficult children have more problems with following directions and commands. They are often impulsive; consequently, they are defiant. No approach will result in eliminating all compliance problems, but specific techniques can help.

Why do children behave the way they do?

- Children don't misbehave just to get you mad or to get back at you. They misbehave because

  - they can't follow the command;

  - they don't know how to do what the parents ask;

  - they see no reason why they should obey;

  - they can get what they want by not listening.

- Remember, children's behaviors are goal directed: They use whatever means they know to get what they want.

Personality factors:

- A strong-willed child will grow up to be a tenacious adult. Strong personality is an asset in life; the goal of parenting is not to break the strong will but to help children develop appropriate judgment and self-control.

Procedure

1. **Attentional Cue**

   ■ Call your child's name.

   ■ Get eye contact; no long-distance commands.

2. **Command**

   ■ Address your child in a respectful but firm manner.

   ■ Stand with a commanding posture but try not to violate your child's space.

   ■ Speak deliberately and clearly with a commanding tone, but no yelling. Don't ask your child to do you a favor; you don't mean that. Just state, calmly but firmly, what you want your child to do.

   ■ State only one item that you want your child to do. If necessary, ask your child to come back and see you when finished.

   ■ Don't debate or overexplain (maximum of one brief explanation). Don't bargain with your child.

   ■ It may be helpful to ask your child to repeat the command.

3. **Follow-Up Look**

   ■ Stand and look at your child for about fifteen seconds.

If your child obeyed the command, make sure to give praise.

CHAPTER 4

Step 2—Give Effective Warnings

How did you do with step 1? If you're like most parents proceeding through this program, you probably found that step 1, by itself, produced some compliance from your child, but it didn't work all the time. If you haven't seen any change at all, it may mean that you haven't been following some of the recommendations from the previous chapter very closely. Perhaps you forgot to get eye contact, or you didn't speak clearly and deliberately. Did you remember to wait silently and look at your child for about fifteen seconds after you issued the command? (Remember, state just *one* command.) Or, you may have a child who is so out of control that utilizing step 1 alone won't make much difference. In that case, don't give up. Continue to address your child in the manner described in step 1. It may not seem to work now, but in combination with the upcoming steps, it will make a difference.

When step 1 doesn't work, its failure is usually due to several trouble spots that may occur along the way when a parent is issuing a command. Again, let's examine the interaction between Stevie and his mother.

Noncompliant Interaction

The interaction described in the example with Stevie is very common—so common that it is recognized as one of the most frequent trouble spots in parenting a difficult child. It has become known in the psychological literature as a *noncompliant interaction*. It doesn't result in compliance, and the interaction itself actually makes it *less* likely that the child will obey because of the specific sequence of events that takes place. As described by Dr. Russell Barkley (1997) in his book *Defiant Children*, the noncompliant interaction involves repetition loops that escalate the situation. When a child does not comply with a command, a parent usually begins to repeat the command. Each repetition does not produce compliance, and with each repetition the parent feels more and more frustrated. You know the pattern. When you tell your child, "Pick up your toys," and your child ignores you or keeps saying "In a minute," your frustration increases, your voice rises, and before you know it, you're yelling because you don't know what else to do.

When you've had enough, you start threatening, but because you are already angry, you probably threaten with consequences that are not realistic ("If you don't pick these up, they are going in the garbage!"). Because your child knows that you probably will not follow through and are only trying to scare him, this "scare tactic" is also not likely to produce compliance, which only results in escalating your frustration and anger even further. This situation usually ends when a parent threatens (or administers) corporal punishment, or backs off and acquiesces—or both. None of these is a desirable outcome.

The situation with Stevie clearly followed this pattern. As I pointed out in the previous chapter, there were problems with the manner in which the mother issued the command. When Stevie did not comply, his mother entered the first repetition loop as she repeated her command several times. Each repetition failed to produce compliance, resulting only in the increase of her anger. Each time she repeated the command, she was faced with Stevie's noncompliance. As she continued, she didn't become any more effective. Instead, she got more and more angry. It seems that the more she repeated herself, the more she recognized that she was ineffective; the more angry she became, the less likely Stevie was to comply. This continued until she felt that she had to do something else, and she entered the second repetition loop when she attempted to scare and bluff Stevie.

That's when she decided to threaten to throw Stevie's toys away, apparently in a last-minute attempt to gain compliance. However, this also proved ineffective. Why didn't it work? Any child of at least low-average intelligence, despite his young age, is able to reason and recognize simple cause-effect relationships. He may not be old enough to be familiar with the price of toys and appreciate their true value, but he surely knows that his parents spent some money buying these toys and he knows that they're not about to throw that money away. After all, by doing so, they would hurt themselves more than the child. Stevie (instinctively) knew this and was not about to be bluffed.

Furthermore, Stevie's mother surely must have used this (or a similar) threat in the past and didn't follow through with it. Why should Stevie expect her to follow through with it this time? In the end, this scare tactic was ineffective and only caused her to become even more angry. Often, parents use a scare tactic like this as a weapon of last resort when they're desperate and don't know what else to do. When this also fails, it often pushes them over the edge (as was clearly evident in the example with Stevie).

Since her attempts at scaring Stevie didn't work, his mom then turned to physical confrontation. Many parents, when faced with the ultimate loss of control over their child, become physically aggressive with them, perhaps (at best) through slapping or spanking, or (at worst) through physical abuse. This approach, of course, doesn't produce the desired results, and their child is no more likely to be compliant in the future. On the contrary, being hit by the parent has very negative effects on the child's self-esteem and strains the parent-child relationship very significantly, so that the child is even less likely to do what the parent says in the future.

On the other hand, if parents don't choose to be aggressive, they may instead acquiesce and perform the stated task themselves. Sometimes they do both. Stevie's mom, after all, not only became physical with Stevie, but she also acquiesced and picked up the blocks herself. In a choice between aggression or acquiescence, the latter is probably the better choice, because it doesn't have detrimental effects on the child's self-esteem. Ultimately, however, neither of these two options is desirable; neither produces compliance, and more importantly, neither carries immediate consequences for your child. Either way, the situation will not teach your child about the consequences of his behaviors.

How, then, can a parent improve the child's ability to obey? How can you break the chain of events and turn a noncompliant interaction into a compliant one? Some of the techniques to do so have already been presented in the previous chapter; there are ways of issuing a command so that it's more likely to be obeyed the first time around (see step 1). To be most effective, get eye contact, state one command, and continue to look at your child for about fifteen seconds after you've issued it. But what if that doesn't work? Read on.

Compliant Interaction

Researchers and clinicians, especially Dr. Barkley (1997), have developed a technique that helps eliminate the repetition loops. It *is* okay to repeat a command to your child, but there's a way to do it that maximizes the likelihood of compliance.

Step 1

When repeating a command, first make sure that you've followed *all* of the recommendations in step 1. Make sure that you don't repeat the command until after you've looked silently at your child for about fifteen seconds. This will feel like a long time, but resist the temptation and do *not* repeat the command until after that time has passed. If you allow enough time to put silent pressure on your child, you may not need to repeat the command.

Repeat Step 1

If you did allow the recommended time and your child still didn't comply, repeat the command, but remember to follow all of step 1 again. Get eye contact again, and then say, "I said …" and state the command again. Then, stand and look at your child for another fifteen seconds. In essence, you are repeating the entire step 1 procedure, but this time you'll reintroduce your command by telling your child "I said …," and you should raise your voice *slightly* (no yelling!) to convey to your child that you mean business and you won't just go away and forget about it if your child doesn't listen.

By repeating yourself only once, you are eliminating the first repetition loop. You are also eliminating the process by which you work yourself up and get angrier with each repetition of your command. Instead, because you'll remain calmer, you'll be able to think more clearly, and this will make a significant difference in what is about to follow.

If, after you've repeated yourself once (and allowed time for another extended look), your child still doesn't obey, it's time to get tough. It's time to give your child a warning, or an ultimatum.

The Warning

Yes, it is okay to threaten your child (I prefer to think of it as an announcement of a consequence), but there's a way to do it that maximizes the likelihood of effectiveness. First, think of your options. Remember, you're still calm, so you can now select a consequence for your child that will be realistic, and you'll be more likely to follow through with it. Not only will your child recognize your determination, but he'll also recognize that you are warning him of an action that isn't a hollow threat and that you're likely to administer the stated consequence. Then, he'll be more able to consider the options and make an informed choice of behavior.

Avoid, at all costs, using the threat of physical punishment. Many parents get seduced by its effectiveness with very young children. True, scaring a young child with getting hit with a belt will probably be effective in getting compliance from your child (for the time being), but have you thought about the downside of using this method? This is, in effect, parenting by fear. Do you really want your child to fear you? This will have very serious implications for your relationship with your child. He won't feel as close to you. He likely won't want to communicate with you. He will likely avoid and resent you. Children who are hit also exhibit lower self-esteem, as has been documented by many studies (such as Gershoff 2002). Do you really want a compliant child that is unhappy? In addition, compliance by fear is only temporary. What will you use in the future, when your child turns twelve, fourteen, or sixteen? The methods proposed in this book offer long-term solutions that can be started now and utilized consistently as your child gets older, when the threat of physical punishment is no longer viable or practical.

Select an appropriate consequence (I provide some suggestions in the next section) and give your child a warning. It should be given exactly in the same manner as the command-giving procedure described earlier (and in step 1): Get eye contact, then say, "If you do not ..., then ...," and, again, stand and look at your child for about fifteen seconds.

Let's review what we've covered thus far.

First, perform the sequence covered in the previous chapter:

- Position yourself so you can see your child.

- Call your child's name and/or ask him to look at you.

- State a specific command in a firm voice, such as "Please start picking up now," "Please pick up your coat now," or "Please turn off the television now."

If your child obeyed, give praise (verbal and nonverbal). If not:

- Maintain visual contact.

- Again, call your child's name and/or ask him to look at you.

- State, "I said, please start picking up now," "I said, please pick up your coat now," or "I said, please turn off the television now."

If your child obeyed, give praise (verbal and nonverbal). If not, administer a warning.

- Maintain visual contact.

- Again, call your child's name and/or ask him to look at you.

- State, "If you do not pick up now, I will pick it up for you, but I will take it away and you will not play with it anymore," "If you do not pick up your coat you will not play with your video games until you do so," or "If you do not turn off the television now, I will turn it off for you, but you will not watch it for the rest of the day."

If your child obeyed, give praise (verbal and nonverbal). If not, administer the consequence you announced (see below).

The Consequence

If your child still doesn't comply after you have given the warning, administer the consequence. Do it quickly. Remember, the more immediate the consequence, the more effective it will be. It's a teaching tool. Your child must make the connection between the behavior and the consequence. The more quickly you administer it, the more likely your child is to learn from it. Administer the consequence calmly but firmly and swiftly. Sometimes you may need to use a consequence that cannot be administered until later (such as sending your child to bed a half hour early). If this is the case, state the consequence immediately and be sure to follow through in administering it at the appropriate time.

Examples of appropriate consequences for noncompliance include:

Having toys put away for a day or a few days

No TV for the rest of the day

No video games for the rest of the day

Having to go to bed a half hour early

Missing a favorite dessert

Remember, it isn't necessary to scare your child with extreme consequences that you aren't really willing to administer. Even if you do administer a more severe consequence, you'll probably run out of punishments very quickly, after only a few episodes with your child, and then what consequences will you have left?

With a young child, it is okay to use time-out for noncompliance. The way to do this is to warn your child that he'll go into time-out if he doesn't do what you said. If he still defies, remove your child to a chair or couch or a corner of the room, and keep your child there for about two minutes. After the time is up, let your child out of the time-out spot, but immediately have him do what you told him to do before the time-out took place. If he refuses again, repeat the time-out (again, give warning), and keep doing so until you get compliance. This procedure is especially effective with a two- to five-year-old child. For children that young, this is probably the procedure of choice to get compliance (used, of course, with the other steps covered here).

For a child that is six or seven years old, this procedure can be used, but it isn't as effective as a warning of a different sort, such as losing the toys or missing a favorite activity. This procedure is even less appropriate for children who are eight to ten years old or older. Of course, time-out for children of all ages is very effective as a method of controlling temper tantrums. This is discussed more in the next chapter.

What about those children who don't seem to respond to negative consequences? When I initially help parents implement this step, many of them express that they have tried all different types of punishments with their child and none have worked. In my experience, however, children who don't respond to negative consequences are truly rare. More commonly, I encounter parents who have tried negative consequences before, and their child seemingly did not respond, but on closer scrutiny, the consequences were not administered consistently. In other words, although the parent often threatened a consequence (such as "No video games for the rest of the day") for noncompliance, the parent did not always follow through, and so the child did not experience that every warning consistently resulted in the stated consequence. Or, parents sometimes do not utilize sufficient time and opportunity for repetition for the consequences to really teach their child. They administer a consequence (such as "No TV for the rest of the day") once or twice, and on the third occasion, when this warning did not produce compliance, conclude that their child does not care about being punished and so this approach will not work. Instead, parents must keep in mind that their children have to experience the consequence many times (at least five or six, maybe more) before they make the connection that a warning really does announce that a consequence that they will not like will be administered.

Please also be aware that step 2 may not produce the desired results the first, third, or even the fifth time you administer it. That doesn't mean that it won't work. Many children, particularly those who are impulsive, are known to have difficulties learning from experience. One child may be exposed to a consequence once or twice and learn from it, while another child may need that exposure six or eight times. It doesn't mean that the consequence won't work, only that the child needs more time to learn the lesson. Often, these are the children whose parents say that the negative consequences don't work. The truth is, the parents haven't persevered long enough to give the consequence enough time to work.

Keep in mind that your goal isn't to get compliance at any price. Rather, it is to administer consequences, both positive and negative, following the child's behavior. Each interaction with your child should be a learning experience for the child about how the world will respond to his behaviors.

As much as possible, avoid administering any consequences that weren't mentioned in your warning. Don't surprise your child by adding things to make the negative consequence more severe. This won't produce the desired effect. It will only agitate the child. Adding more negative consequences won't teach your child nearly as much as sticking to those consequences that came with an explicit warning.

When Your Child Changes His Mind

If, after you've administered the consequence, your child then changes his mind and now wants to perform the desired behavior, don't let him do it. Tell him, "It's too late now. Next time, do what I ask when I ask you to do it." Continue to administer the consequence you selected, and don't change your mind.

Praise

One final but very important point: If, during this procedure (but before the negative consequence had to be administered), your child obeyed the command, remember to give him praise. Don't give any less praise if your child obeyed you after the repetition of the command (or even after the warning) than you would have had he listened the first time you said it. Helping your child to listen on the first try will come later.

As stated before, when praising your child, avoid giving back-handed compliments such as "You did that so well, but why couldn't you do it the first time I asked?" Don't even mention that it took a warning to get the compliance. The fact is, you got the compliance, so give your child praise and make him feel good about obeying you.

Putting It All Together

Let's see how Stevie's mother could have intervened by following the techniques covered in steps 1 and 2.

Stevie is playing with his blocks. His mother comes into the room. She approaches Stevie and says, "Stevie, please look at me."

Stevie looks up. His mother, while looking Stevie in the eyes, says, "Stevie, please pick up your blocks right now because we have to go out."

Stevie starts to protest and says, "But I'm not finished yet!"

His mother doesn't respond. She just continues to stand there and look at Stevie. She is counting silently from 101 to about 120. Stevie continues to play with the blocks. When she reaches 120, she says, "Stevie, look at me."

Stevie looks up. His mother says, "I said, please pick up the blocks right now."

"But Mom, I just want to finish building the tower!"

Stevie's mother does not respond to his statement. She just stands there and again continues to look at him for about fifteen seconds. When that time is up, she says, "Stevie, look at me."

Stevie looks up. His mother says, "If you don't pick up the blocks right now, I will put them away for you, but you won't play with them for the rest of the week."

Stevie starts picking up the blocks, but he protests, saying "I wasn't finished," "It's not fair," and so on. His mother ignores what he says and tells him, "Thank you for picking up the blocks. I like it when you do what I ask."

As recommended before, use this procedure for at least one to two weeks to become used to it before you proceed with the next step in the sequence.

But what do you do if your child starts acting out somewhere along the way? If the acting out is limited to verbal outbursts, ignore it. That will be addressed later in the book. If your child becomes physically aggressive, attend to it immediately in whatever way you would have handled it thus far. The next step covers how to handle temper tantrums.

Checklist 2

Step 2: Give Effective Warnings

Procedure for Compliant Interaction

1. **Preparation**

   ■ Stay calm.

   ■ Always stay one step ahead of your child.

   ■ Reduce distractions in the room.

2. **Initial Command**

   a. **Attentional Cue**

      ■ Remember the eye contact.

   b. **Command**

      ■ Firm, respectful, clear, one at a time.

   c. **Follow-Up Look**

      ■ Stand and look for about fifteen seconds.

3. **Repeat Command**

   ■ Stay calm; no yelling.

   ■ Same three components as above, but raise your voice *slightly* and say "I said ..."

   ■ Note: Repeat the command *one time only!*

- While standing and looking at your child for about fifteen seconds after the command, think of a realistic consequence.

- Keep in mind the goal of the consequence: to help your child learn.

4. Warning

- Stay calm; *no yelling.*

- Same three components as above, but now inform your child of the consequence: "If you ..., then ..." Remember to stand and look at your child for another fifteen seconds.

5. Consequence

- Stay calm.

- Administer the consequence (positive or negative).

If your child obeyed the command, make sure to give praise.

CHAPTER 5

Step 3—Learn How to Handle a Temper Tantrum

By now, you should be following the combined command-giving procedures described in steps 1 and 2. You should be able to put more pressure on your child in appropriate ways that do not escalate conflict, and you're sending your child a clear message that you mean business. Noncompliance is something you're simply not going to ignore, and if your child persists in defying you, there will be negative consequences.

Because you're getting tough, your child will likely have a reaction. She may not like your new attitude, since she's now under more pressure to do what you expect. This may lead her to become more easily agitated, and you may see an increase in temper tantrums. This "fighting-back" response is temporary. Nevertheless, you need to be ready for it and attend to all temper tantrums immediately.

What Is a Temper Tantrum?

Parents have different ideas about what constitutes a temper outburst. It is important to recognize that some temper outbursts are mild and may not require much action to control them. For example, if your child yells out "That's not fair," yet does what she was told, the mild outburst of emotions is best left alone. Similarly, if your child, when angry, goes up to her room and slams the door, that kind of emotional flare-up is also best left alone. If your child doesn't act out while angry but calls you a name or says "I hate you," this behavior should not be addressed through the procedures described in this chapter. Upcoming chapters (especially step 6) address these kinds of outbursts and how to handle them.

Let's define a temper tantrum as an encounter during which your child starts to continuously scream, yell, wail, carry on, and doesn't stop when you say "Stop it." When it includes physical aggression, it's more than just a single act of throwing to the floor a toy that your child happened to have in her hand when you told her to start picking up; it includes more serious physical violence, such as throwing something at you, throwing something across the room, breaking an object, hitting you, or beginning to thrash about in a fit of anger. Those kinds of temper tantrums respond best to the procedures described in this step.

How should you handle those types of outbursts? There are many ways of attending to your child's temper tantrums. Probably the most effective procedure is the time-out. Now, perhaps you're thinking, "I tried time-out, and it doesn't work with my child." There are about as many ways to do time-out as there are people doing so. You've tried *a* version of time-out, not *the* version of time-out. True, the particular variation you tried may not have worked. In this book, however, you'll find a version of time-out that is specifically fine-tuned to the needs and behaviors of out-of-control children. This particular version of time-out may be more likely to work for you than those you may have tried before.

Using Time-Out

Time-out is a punishment procedure that is particularly effective as a consequence for temper tantrums. It works by removing your child from the situation that caused the outburst in the first place, and placing her into a stimulation-free environment. This accomplishes two things. By changing the setting, it forces your child to stop whatever she was doing, and it removes the stimulation that caused the outburst. It also forces her to be in a place devoid of stimulation, where she can't do any of the things she'd like to do. It is, partially, punishment by boredom.

Choosing a Time-Out Spot

When you initially decide to implement time-out, you'll first need to select an appropriate time-out spot. The place that you choose must meet several criteria. It must be entirely free of stimulation. Your child needs to be isolated in the time-out spot, away from her usual activities (e.g., watching TV, playing with toys, interacting with siblings, participating in conversations with you). Many choices are available that meet these criteria: placing your child in a corner in such a way that she is facing away from stimulation; placing her in a hallway or on the stairway, sitting on one of the steps; placing her on a chair or couch in the living room or family room; placing her in the bathroom. Depending on your household and your child, any of these can work, and you can surely think of many more places where you can place her for time-out.

Remember that the place must be free of stimulation. If you selected a corner in the room, or a chair or a couch, make sure that, during time-out, your child isn't near a TV that someone else may be watching, there are no toys nearby, and no one will come near her and start a conversation. Also, keep any pets away so that your child won't play with the dog or cat while she is in time-out.

In many homes, a remote bathroom (not the master bathroom) works well. You may want to prepare the room by removing shampoo bottles, shaving accessories, hair dryers, and so forth. As long as all that remains is the soap and some towels, the room can serve very well as a time-out spot. Although there is water there, most children won't play with it while in time-out. They'll be too angry to think about play.

As a last resort, use your child's own room for the time-out spot. This is really the last resort, and it is much preferred to use a different place for time-out. Sometimes, however, particularly with an older child, there may not be any other places that are suitable. If you use your child's room, remember several points in preparing the room accordingly. First, remove all toys from her room. They will have to be kept in another location, such as a chest in the family room or in a hallway closet. Using your child's room for time-out while she has all of her belongings in that room will not be effective. It isn't really a punishment for her to go to a place where she can play with anything she wants. Likewise, there must be no TV or computer in the room, or these must be disconnected when time-out is implemented. Music is okay, as it can have a calming effect on your child (especially for older children). If you use your child's own room for time-out, the only stimulating items that should be kept in the room are a stereo and your child's books (or other academic items).

To further minimize stimulation, you shouldn't be in the time-out spot with your child. This will only prolong the confrontation. Your child will likely attempt to engage you in an interaction while she's in time-out. Obviously, you must keep an eye on your child to make sure that she's okay, but while she's in time-out, don't make much eye contact, speak to her, or answer questions that she may ask.

If your child becomes aggressive while in time-out, or if she won't remain in time-out, you'll need to stay in the time-out spot with her in order to restrain her. (The specific restraint procedure you should use is discussed later in this chapter.) Remember, however, that even if you have to stay with your child in the time-out spot to restrain her, avoid interacting with her and attend only to the restraint procedure.

Very young children will probably need to be held in the time-out spot. A two- or three-year-old child, when placed on a chair or a couch, isn't likely to stay there for an extended period of time. Expect to hold your child in the time-out spot, at least until she gets used to the procedure and recognizes that, one way or another, you'll make sure that she stays there until the time-out is over.

Preparation

Once you select the appropriate spot, there is more preparation to be done before you attempt your first time-out. Be ready to spend a lot of time with your child during your first time-out intervention. The average initial time-out confrontation lasts about forty-five minutes (Barkley 1997). When you first implement time-out, pick a quiet day—one without deadlines, guests, or unusual distractions. Take the phone off the hook, and don't answer the doorbell. Be ready to give your child your undivided attention until the encounter is over.

Keep in mind that your child's reaction to the time-out procedure will initially be much stronger than it will be after she gets used to it. She'll initially try to pull out all the stops to test whether you'll follow through on what you started. Be ready for it. Don't start the initial time-out encounter and stop it midway through, or your child will feel as though she won and that her protests were effective in breaking your attempt. Then you'll have a much more difficult time trying it the next time. So, don't do it until you have selected an appropriate time-out spot, allowed enough time, controlled any distractions, and rehearsed it in your mind so you are ready to do it all the way through, no matter what your child may try to do to stop you. Remember, the first encounter will probably be the worst. Each one after that will become easier as your child gets used to your new attitude, your follow-through, and your readiness to do whatever you need to do to take control of her behaviors.

The specific time-out procedure differs somewhat depending on whether physical aggression is part of your child's temper tantrum. The next section covers what to do if your child is screaming, yelling, and carrying on verbally, but is not physically aggressive.

Time-Out for Nonviolent Tantrums

First, get eye contact with your child, if possible, and then tell your child to stop. Try not to yell, but speak firmly and loudly enough for your child to hear. Stand and look at her for about fifteen seconds.

If she continues, warn her by saying, "If you don't stop, you'll have to go into time-out." As before, get eye contact *and* warn her. After warning her, wait about fifteen seconds; just stand and look at your child.

If she still doesn't stop, tell her that it's time for time-out. Try to get her to go into the time-out spot on her own, but get your child there forcefully if you must. Place your child in the time-out spot and say,

"You have to stay here until I say you can leave." If your child continues to act out while in the time-out spot, say, "If you don't stop, you'll have to stay here longer." If your child attempts to leave, return her to the time-out spot, forcefully if necessary, and repeat the command.

Once your child remains in the time-out spot and begins to calm down, start timing. The amount of time she'll spend in time-out depends on several factors, particularly your child's age and the seriousness of the offense that got her into the time-out. Generally speaking, one minute per year of age is the rule. Thus, a five-year-old gets a five-minute time-out, a seven-year-old gets a seven-minute one, and so forth. However, some research suggests that shorter time-outs with young children are also effective (Kapalka 2001b). I generally recommend that for children five years old or younger, a two-minute time-out is sufficient, while for older children, you may apply the one-minute-per-year-of-age rule.

Remember that your child must be relatively quiet (some crying is okay as long as it is no longer a full-blown tantrum) before you start timing. If you like, you can remind your child, midway through a particularly long acting-out episode while in time-out, that her time has not started yet and won't start until she calms down. Other than that, avoid interacting with your child and don't answer her questions.

It's important that you not tell your child the actual amount of time that she is to stay in time-out. If you set a timer, do so for yourself, not for your child. It will be most beneficial when you send her the message that you are the one who decides when she has to go into time-out and when she can leave. This may appear to be a minor point, but you want to remind your child, in obvious and subtle ways, that you are in control of the situation and that you'll decide her consequences. This reinforces your authority as a parent—an important component of parenting an out-of-control child.

The Release

Once your child has served the time-out sentence, go to the time-out spot and ask her, "Do you know why I put you here?" Be calm and talk to your child. Don't yell or lecture. Get the child to recognize on her own, at least to some extent, the reason why she was placed in time-out. Tell her, "Every time you do this, I'll put you in time-out," and release her from time-out. You want her to learn that you won't tolerate certain behaviors and that these behaviors will lead to the same consequences whenever they occur. If your child is only two or three, rather than asking her why she was placed in time-out, just tell her why you placed her in time-out and that you'll do it again if the same behavior reoccurs.

After time-out, it may be helpful to return your child to the same activity that made her act out in the first place. Why? Because you want her to be exposed to the very same situation again and have the opportunity to make a better choice (and experience a different consequence if she makes a better choice). Let's consider the following example: Five-year-old Jessica is playing with toy animals. Her mother wants her to pick up and get ready for dinner. She commands her to do so, but Jessica continues to play. The mother walks over and starts taking the toy animals away. Jessica then starts crying, screaming, and hitting her mother. Jessica is placed in time-out. After she serves the required sentence, she is released. If her mother does not return her to the toy animals, Jessica may not have learned about this specific situation. However, if she is placed back in front of the toy animals, she now has to handle the same situation. Jessica may indeed make the wrong choice again, and another time-out episode may ensue. However, the more this situation is repeated, the more likely it is that she'll eventually learn to pick up without hitting her mother. In this way, she'll begin to learn how to control herself and to control an impulse to do something that may get her in trouble in the future.

Bear in mind, however, that you must follow through on administering a consequence that you may have already announced before the time-out. For example, let's say that in a situation like that described with Jessica you warned your daughter that unless she started picking up she would not be allowed to watch TV for the rest of the day, and she ignored this warning. You proceed to pick up the animals yourself and announce the consequence to your child. If she then has a temper tantrum, time-out will be administered for the temper tantrum, not for the noncompliance. Because you already punished your child for noncompliance, don't try to get your child to pick up the toys again after the time-out is over. Just finish picking up the toys yourself and make sure that you follow through on your stated consequence (no TV).

So, to review, the time-out procedure (for nonviolent tantrums) consists of a command to stop, a warning, and the removal into the time-out spot. Once there, your child must be relatively quiet and stay there until you allow her to leave. After serving the minimum sentence, she should be reminded about why she was placed there. Then she can be released to continue with her previous activity.

1-2-3 Magic

For young children, up to about age five or so, the time-out procedure can be modified somewhat. Instead of commanding your child to stop and then warning her about the impending time-out, you can substitute a 1-2-3 procedure (Phelan 2003). When your child starts acting out, approach her, look straight into her eyes (if possible), and firmly say, "You have to stop by the time I count to three—this is one" and extend one finger on your hand. Wait about five seconds, while looking right at her. If she continues to act out, say, "This is two" and extend two fingers on your hand. Again, wait about five seconds and keep looking at your child. If she still continues after that interval is over, say, "This is three, and now it's time-out" and remove her to the time-out spot. This procedure works very well with young children, but the other procedure, with a command and a warning, also works well for some young children. You may want to try both to see which one feels more comfortable. Remember, however, to select one to use on a continual basis, and stick to it consistently.

Time-Out for Violent Tantrums

The procedure described thus far is appropriate to use for nonviolent temper tantrums, but what if your child becomes violent? Violent temper tantrums need to be handled similarly, except there should be no command to stop and no warning. In other words, any violent act (such as throwing something at you, throwing something across the room, breaking an object, hitting you, or beginning to thrash about in a fit of anger) should lead to the immediate placement of your child in time-out. In this way, the amount of violent behavior will be minimized, and you'll send a strong message to your child that no amount of violence will be tolerated. Also, for violent temper tantrums, a longer time-out sentence is appropriate. Two minutes per year of age works well with many children. However, this may need to be modified for children age five or younger. For practical reasons, it may be necessary to stay with the shorter, minimum sentence, even for violent tantrums. It may simply be too difficult to keep a five-year-old child, especially an active one, in the time-out spot for ten minutes. (Remember, your child must be relatively quiet while in the time-out spot.) Also, since young children have a limited concept of time, there may be no benefit to a longer time-out; ten minutes will feel about the same as five minutes to a typical five-year-old.

Restraint Procedure

Let's discuss the restraint procedure. By *restraint procedure*, I mean a method of maintaining your child in the time-out spot while she continues to be violent. On the other hand, if your child isn't being violent but merely tries to get out of the time-out spot before the time is up, your child shouldn't be restrained. Instead, place your child back in time-out and tell her to stay there until you say it's okay to leave. You may need to repeat this many times at first, but your child will eventually learn to accept it.

Typical situations that may require a child to be restrained in time-out include kicking the wall, throwing things that are within reach, getting up off the chair and knocking it over (or throwing it), and hitting the parent. When any of these acts occur, immediately implement a restraint procedure.

It is best to place your child in a standard chair commonly found in a kitchen or a dining room. Move her there if the time-out spot was initially in another location. Place your child on the chair and hold her by the wrists. Get behind her (while holding her wrists) and bend her arms until they are bent at the elbows, backwards, around the backrest of the chair, with wrists below the child's backside. It may be a struggle to get her arms into this position at first, but once you accomplish that, the hold will be comfortable for you and for your child.

There are several reasons why this type of restraint is preferable to the bear-hug procedure that is so popular. First, if the situation has escalated to the point where your child continues to be violent, she may try to hurt you in some way while being restrained. Your child may attempt to bite, kick, or scratch you. The bear hug, unfortunately, makes these easier for her to do. The hold from behind, on the other hand, allows you to stay away from your child's reach, so that she can't kick you or bite you. Once you become skilled at holding your child's wrists firmly with your thumb and index finger of both hands (placed around your child's wrists), you'll see that your child's fingers are too short to reach and scratch you.

Second, the stronger the child, the more strength it takes on the part of the parent to keep holding the child in a bear hug. The wrist restraint, on the other hand, will allow you to have significant physical leverage over your child. It takes very little strength to continue to restrain a child in this way, and the hold is very effective in restricting her actions.

Finally, a bear hug has a tendency to be very invasive. After all, a large portion of your body comes in contact with a large portion of your child's body. Consequently, a bear hug significantly violates her space, which may agitate her even further. The wrist hold, on the other hand, results in only a small part of your child being held, and since you are behind her, the violation of space is minimal.

While you are restraining your child, it is important that you calmly say, "If you stop, I'll let go of your hands." Say this in a repetitive manner, in a low, almost chanting, tone of voice. When you feel your child stop squirming, let go of her hands but instruct her to stay in the chair. Be on the alert. Your child may become violent again, and you'll have to quickly reapply the wrist restraint. During the first confrontation, you'll likely have to repeat this several times. Don't be discouraged. Your child will eventually learn that you won't give in and that you won't tolerate violent behavior. Then, future time-out episodes will become shorter and less violent. When your child calms down, start timing the appropriate sentence.

Putting It All Together

The procedure described in this chapter will take some time and effort, but gradually you will see a decline in acting out. When appropriate, give your child a warning before utilizing time-out. Over time, the warning will be enough and your child will learn that the warning is a signal for her to make a choice about what to do, and what consequence she will experience if she makes the wrong choice. However, do not use the warning for violent behaviors. Your child must learn that once she has "crossed the line" and acted out violently, she has already made the wrong choice and now must experience the consequence.

As with the preceding steps, give yourself at least a week or two of practicing the time-out procedure. Don't continue with step 4 until you feel comfortable using steps 1–3 and until your child gets used to the procedure so that each time-out episode is relatively short and calm. This may take some time, so be prepared to pause for a while before continuing with further parts of this program.

Checklist 3A

Step 3: Learn How to Handle a Temper Tantrum

For violent acts, skip steps 1 and 2 below and take your child straight to the time-out spot.

Procedure

1. **Command**

   ■ Tell your child to stop what she is doing.

   ■ Try not to yell, but speak loudly enough for her to hear and attend to you.

   ■ Maintain eye contact when possible.

   ■ Wait about fifteen seconds.

2. **Warning**

   ■ Announce that if she doesn't stop, she will go to time-out.

   ■ As above, use a commanding tone, and try to get eye contact.

   ■ Wait about fifteen seconds.

3. **Take Your Child to the Time-Out Spot**

   ■ Try to get your child to go on her own.

   ■ If necessary, get her into the time-out spot forcefully.

   ■ Say, "Stay here until I say you can leave. You must be quiet."

- Restrain your child if necessary.

- If your child doesn't stay, return her to the time-out spot and repeat as above. Repeat this as many times as necessary.

- Once she is relatively quiet, start timing but *don't tell her how long you want her to stay there.* If you set a timer, do so for yourself, not your child. Minimum sentence: two minutes (up to age five), or one minute per year of age thereafter.

4. **Release**

- Go into the time-out spot and ask, "Do you know why I put you here?"

- Don't challenge your child into a confrontation; don't yell or lecture. Just get her to recognize the reason why you placed her in time-out.

- If your child is very young, just state the reason why she was placed in the time-out spot.

- Say, "Every time you do this, I will put you in time-out."

- Return her to the previous activity (very important).

Checklist 3B

Creating a Time-Out Spot

The time-out spot must be free of stimulation. It's best to use a place where your child can be isolated—no TV, computer, toys, or activities. Stay with her if the restraint procedure is needed (see below) but avoid interacting with her.

Possible choices

- Stand in a corner of a room (dining room, living room, hallway, etc.).

- Sit on a stairway.

- Stay in a bathroom.

- Sit on a chair or couch in the living room or family room.

- As a last resort, use your child's own room for time-out, but only if no computer, TV, or toys are kept there.

- For young children, use a chair or a couch. Stay out of your child's view, but keep an eye on her to make sure she remains in the time-out spot.

- Some children may need to be kept physically in the time-out spot (see below); a chair works very well.

Restraint Procedure

- Place your child in the time-out spot.

- Say, "Stay here until I say you can leave. You must be quiet."

- If she acts out, place your child in a standard chair and hold her from behind by the wrists.

- When restraining your child, make sure to stay out of her reach to prevent her from hitting, kicking, and biting.

- Repeat to your child: "If you stop, I'll let go of your hands, but you have to sit here."

- When your child stops, let go of her hands but instruct her to stay in the chair. Be alert; she may start acting out again. If she does, quickly return to the wrist restraint.

- Don't be discouraged if you have to repeat this many times during initial implementation. Your child will need time to learn the rules of this procedure.

CHAPTER 6

Step 4—Implement a Behavioral Contract

Now that you are using techniques that improve the way you issue commands and handle temper tantrums, it's time to move on.

Children's refusal to do their chores and homework are among the most frequent complaints I hear from parents. These problems cause parents and children to argue on a regular basis. In fact, in some households, in order to avoid arguing, parents don't expect their children to perform any household duties. In essence, these parents give up and conclude that they simply can't get their children to do any chores. In other homes, parents constantly argue with their children and frequently dole out punishments such as grounding or taking away TV privileges. These punishments are often ineffective; consequently, parents continue to argue with their children and gradually begin to feel that their children won't respond to anything they try. There must be a better way.

Well, there is, but you'll need to do some things differently. Essentially, you'll need to implement a structure at home where your child earns every privilege that she wants by performing her responsibilities. This method is called a *behavioral contract*.

You may have tried some version of this procedure before and may have been unsuccessful. Don't despair. As with the time-out, there are many different ways of designing behavioral contracts. The way that is described in this book is effective with difficult children, so read on and have faith—you *can* make it work.

The behavioral contract is absolutely crucial for you to administer. It's one of the most effective ways to decrease management problems with your child. In fact, my experience has been that the behavioral contract is so important that without it, parents won't attain much improvement in the problems they encounter with their children. In addition, implementing a successful behavioral contract will greatly assist you with the remaining steps in this program. Give yourself time to get this part of the program off the ground, and don't proceed further until you have it running smoothly. This step will probably take you at least two weeks. Don't rush it; take your time. The better the contract, the easier it'll be to implement the remaining steps covered in this book.

What Is a Behavioral Contract?

A behavioral contract works on the principle of dispensing appropriate consequences following your child's behaviors—positive consequences after positive behaviors and negative consequences (or, at the least, lack of positive consequences) after negative behaviors. In short, you'll reward the behaviors that are appropriate and punish those that are not. The moment I mention the term *reward*, many parents object and tell me that I'm asking them to bribe their children. Well, not exactly.

Rewards, Not Bribes

A philosophical distinction must be made between bribes and rewards. A bribe is something that is given to a person to entice them to perform a behavior that is improper. For example, politicians get bribed to support a specific position on an issue, company executives are bribed to perform special favors for individuals, and so on. As you can clearly see, these actions are wrong, and the recipients are paid, in effect, for selling out their principles and doing what they shouldn't do.

A reward, on the other hand, is a positive consequence one receives after performing a task that is proper and necessary but requires some time and effort. For example, capable students are rewarded with good grades, commendations, and certificates. A reward is a show of appreciation. A reward makes a person feel good and allows a person to feel a sense of accomplishment.

For some people, just the feeling of accomplishment is enough of a reward. However, it isn't realistic to expect this of your child. First of all, the ability to feel good just by conquering a difficult task mostly applies to adults, and very few children are able to exhibit this kind of mature behavior. Second, out-of-control children rarely want to perform a behavior that requires effort and time and that isn't fun. To expect them to do so only to get a sense of accomplishment (or because it's the right thing to do) is simply unrealistic.

Even adults expect rewards on a daily basis. Would people go to work every day if they didn't expect to be rewarded with a paycheck? Of course not. Just because you get paid for performing your job, does that mean that you are being bribed to do so? Again, it's obvious that the answer is no. In fact, if you carefully examine most of our day-to-day activities, you'll discover that most of what we do is because we expect to get some type of reward.

Most Rewards Are Free

Usually, when I first present to parents the idea of rewarding their child, the parents think that I'm asking them to start buying things for their child. This is a major misconception. Although a limited type of monetary reward (e.g., a small toy or an allowance) can be included in a behavioral contract (more on this later), the basic contract is established with no monetary outlay of any kind. In other words, you wouldn't be buying things for your child as rewards—you'd use the rewards that are free and available to you every day. The idea is to implement an exchange at home through which your child will earn privileges by performing certain behaviors.

Preparation

To start, get a box of poker chips at your local five-and-dime or toy store. The chips are not expensive—just a few dollars for a box. Instead of poker chips, you can use other types of chips, including chips from some board games, even bingo markers, but poker chips really work well. They're large, so they're tangible and feel significant to a child. It's also easy to keep track of how many you have, and they don't get lost easily.

With very young children, chips may not mean much because the child may have not yet sufficiently developed the concept of quantity. In addition, a child of three or four years of age may not be able to see any value in the chip, since he may not yet fully understand the idea of exchanging the chips for something more tangible. Instead, you may want to get a set of stickers (it helps to have your child go with you to the store and select a set that he really likes) and start a sticker book where you will place stickers on a page as he earns them. Devote one page per day so that you can keep track of how many stickers your child earns each day.

List of Responsibilities

Next, you need to make a list of duties that you want your child to perform. Start by writing down, for yourself only, the tasks that you want to have him do every day. It's important to start with only the things that you want done on a daily basis, not the responsibilities that occur once every few days, or once a week. Those will be addressed later.

What daily duties should you include? Well, that's entirely up to you. However, here are some suggestions. Start small, a maximum of about five or six items, and include only things that are part of your child's daily routine, such as getting out of bed in the morning after no more than two prompts, dressing himself, remaining in his room until dressed, coming down for breakfast by a specific time, getting out of the house to catch the school bus by a specific time, brushing teeth or washing hands without having to be repeatedly asked to do so (e.g., before and after meals and in the morning or at bedtime), and so forth. Each task on the list must call for a single, specific behavior.

Don't include anything about school performance or homework—that'll be addressed in the next step. Don't put on the list the things that you want your child *not* to do, such as "Don't argue with your brother," or "Don't hit your sister." These concerns will be addressed later. Don't put things on the list such as "Clean your room." Keep in mind that your definition of "clean" is probably very different than your child's. Don't put anything on the list that is vague and open to different interpretations by you and your child. If you want to include items that have to do with keeping your child's room clean, break the job down into specific components, such as "bed made," "nothing on the floor," "all clothing in the closet," "all laundry in the laundry basket," and "all books on the shelves or on the dresser." Remember, each item on the list must be a single, specific behavior. Define each behavior very precisely, so that there'll be no question in your child's mind as to exactly what it is that you want. To start, the responsibilities must be simple and easy to be checked and monitored by you. This will significantly cut down on arguments with your child.

Be sure to make your list appropriate for your child's age. A preschool child doesn't read yet, so you'll need to read each item on the list to him every day. In addition, make the list very short, and make sure that your child can perform the tasks.

Once you've made your list, it's time to assign point (chip or sticker) values to each of the items. Start by assigning the value of one chip to the easiest item on the list, one that takes the least time and effort. Then compare the other items on the list to that one item and assign the other items the number of chips that are comparable with the time and effort that each task requires. In addition, assign higher chip values to items that your child is most reluctant to perform. Keep in mind what tasks and chores have caused the most conflict between the two of you, and assign point values to these accordingly.

Take some time to talk with your child and explain that, starting tomorrow, you'll be implementing a new system at home. Inform your child that there are some responsibilities that you want him to perform every day and that you'll show your appreciation by giving him some rewards. Your child will undoubtedly say, "What rewards?" At this point, it's best to ask your child to make a list of rewards that he'd like to earn, and write them down. Do *not* criticize your child for putting inappropriate rewards on the list. After all, just because your child places it on the list, it doesn't mean that you have to honor it. However, you need to make your child feel that he has input into this new program and that you'll at least consider what he wants.

List of Privileges/Rewards

Next, select from your child's list of rewards those items that you accept as appropriate and add additional rewards that you jointly discuss with him. Primarily include privileges as rewards. Examples include viewing TV, playing video games, using the computer, riding a bicycle, having a friend over, extending bedtime, renting a videotape, or going to a video arcade in the mall. These privileges shouldn't be given out for the entire day at once, but rather in shorter chunks of time, up to a limit you set beforehand. For example, the TV should be earned in thirty-minute intervals, computer and video games should be earned in fifteen-minute intervals, the bicycle (and time outside) can be earned in one-hour intervals, bedtime can be extended in fifteen-minute intervals, and so on.

Your child will undoubtedly list some items that require a monetary outlay. There are a few ways to handle this. One way is to include, as one of the rewards on the list, an item from a grab bag. The best way to do this is to take your child to a toy store or a five-and-dime store and ask him to select ten or fifteen items that cost no more than about $2 each. Then put them in a bag and periodically allow your child the ability to earn a trip to that grab bag to select a toy from it. It's a good idea to allow only one grab-bag reward per day, and perhaps only three or four per week.

As a way to include some of the more expensive items that your child wrote on his list, ask your child to accumulate chips over a longer period of time to earn a more substantial item, such as a video game cartridge. Make each chip worth a small amount of money (e.g., a quarter), and tell your child that he can accumulate enough chips (as per the exchange rate) to be able to, in time, earn a game cartridge. Remember, you control the exchanges, so don't allow your child to talk you into buying things that you don't want him to have or that you can't afford. It's important to start the program with items (and their respective worth) that will be agreeable to you from the start. Avoid recalculating exchange rates after you've implemented the contract. You don't want your child to lose confidence in the entire program and feel that you don't hold up your end of the agreement. Also, decide what rewards you're comfortable with and allow your child to earn only those items that you'll be able and willing to give him.

When you figure out the exchange rate (i.e., the amount of chips your child earns in one day and the amount of chips he can spend), allow for some surplus. In other words, allow your child to earn about 15 to 25 percent more chips in one day (providing that he does everything on the list) than he would typically spend buying the daily privileges (including the amount of time you usually allow him to watch TV, play with video games, use the computer, and so on). This allows him to start accumulating chips for some of the bigger items.

A sample behavioral contract could look like this:

Responsibilities:

Getting out of bed after no more than two prompts	2 chips
Getting dressed by yourself	1 chip
Staying in your room until you are dressed	1 chip
Coming down for breakfast by 7:15 A.M.	1 chip
Getting out of the house by 7:40 A.M. to meet the school bus	2 chips
Making your bed	2 chips
Washing your hands before each meal without being asked	1 chip each
Brushing teeth in the morning and at nighttime	2 chips each

Rewards:

TV (per thirty minutes)	1 chip
Video games (per fifteen minutes)	1 chip
Going outside to play (per hour)	1 chip
Extend bedtime by fifteen minutes	1 chip
Trip to the grab bag	6 chips
Renting a videotape	10 chips
Earning a $20 video game cartridge	50 chips

Getting the Contract Started

Pick a day when you want to start the program, and put it into effect that morning. It's best to start on a Monday. The weekend is a good time to make lists of responsibilities and rewards and get grab-bag items. It also gives your child a sense of a fresh start at the beginning of a new week. Because this is a new experience for your child, select a week that is relatively quiet and doesn't involve extended visits from family members or other interruptions in your family's daily routine.

Have your child keep his own chips. Each time he performs an item on the Responsibilities list, immediately give him the necessary chips. Likewise, each time he wants to do something that is on the Rewards list, he must give you the necessary chips to earn that activity.

Once you start the program, follow through on every item on both lists. Each time your child performs the desired action, you *must* be watchful and give your child the amount of chips that were earned. Don't forget to do this; your child will lose confidence if you don't keep your end of the agreement. Also, don't tell your child, "I'll give you the chip later." Do it immediately. Remember, as a parent you are most effective when you administer immediate consequences. A chip is a consequence, a positive one for a positive behavior. It will teach your child the most if it is given immediately.

If you've set up a list of chores that need to be done in the child's room (e.g., nothing on the floor, bed made, all dirty clothes in the laundry basket), make sure that you set a time to inspect the child's room and give the chips for each of the components that are completed. Make sure that your child knows what time that will be, and make sure that you use the same time every day. It's best to set a consistent daily inspection time and stick to it as much as possible. Remember, the more predictable your child's day is, the fewer management problems your child will have.

Likewise, be consistent in requiring the chips from your child to cash in on the items on the Rewards list. Be ready to restrict your child's ability to do what's on that list, unless it is bought back with the chips. If your child protests and begins a temper tantrum, attend to the tantrum (as discussed in the previous chapter), but continue to follow through with the program.

Don't advance your child any chips that allow him to do something that he hasn't yet earned. When your child wants a privilege from the list but hasn't earned the chips, this presents a terrific opportunity for you to help your child learn that positive consequences—privileges—must be earned by positive behaviors. If the child wants to go outside, for example, but hasn't earned enough chips because he hasn't performed some of his chores, this would be the perfect time for you to remind your child that if the chores get done, he'll earn the chips to go outside. Don't deviate from this procedure even if your child previously earned the chips but can't find them right now. By sticking to this, you'll send a clear message to your child that you are serious about following through with this program. You'll also encourage your child to improve his ability to keep track of his things and know where they are when he needs them.

Sometimes your child may have spent all the chips and may not have an opportunity to earn any more chips for the remainder of the day. In the aforementioned list, most of the chips are earned in the morning. If the child had a bad morning and didn't earn any chips, he can now earn only a limited amount of chips for brushing his teeth and washing his hands.

In that case, you can do one of two things: You can stand firmly by the contract and restrict your child from doing anything on the Rewards list until the next morning, or you can give your child a job for which he will earn some chips. If you do the latter, however, do so sparingly. Remember, you don't want your child to get the idea that you will accommodate him with other tasks so that he can earn the chips he needs to do what he wants. He needs to learn that he has to perform what's on the list or be restricted from what he wants to do. You must send that message to your child very clearly.

Sometimes I hear parents lament that their child doesn't seem to care if he is restricted from an activity. These parents feel that their child doesn't care about any consequence (positive or negative) they try to administer. This, however, is very deceiving. When a child says, "I don't care" to parents after he is punished or restricted, parents often take that too literally. Children do *not* like to be restricted. They *do* miss being able to do the things they want to do. However, they don't want the parents to know that these things matter. Children sometimes get into power struggles with their parents. They want to communicate to the parents that they control their own lives and make their own decisions. They *want* the parents to feel that they have lost control.

Think about it: If your child lets you know that your restriction really got to him, he'd be admitting openly to you that you're in control. Instead, from his point of view, it's in his best interest not to admit to you that the consequence was, in fact, effective. By saying, "I don't care," children are trying to tell their parents, "You can't get to me," even though the consequence probably just did. So, don't listen to these statements. Remain consistent. After a day or two (or three) of being restricted, even the most out-of-control child will realize that it's not fun living this way, and he'll start to play by your rules. However, if you really have a child who doesn't mind staying in his room without TV, computer, telephone, or toys for weeks, he may be depressed and I urge you to get help as soon as possible.

Who's in Charge?

Some final comments about implementing the contract: It is very important that parents are the only individuals who monitor the chores, give the chips, and accept them back when their child earns a privilege. Older siblings should not do this. Throughout this entire program, the recommended interventions not only structure your child's day, but also establish you as the one who controls your child's consequences. Don't pass this control onto anyone else, especially your child's siblings.

When using babysitters or extended family members to watch your child, it's best not to involve them in what you are doing. Some of this may change as the contract expands later on, but for now, you should be the only one who monitors your child, gives the rewards, and allows him to buy back privileges. If you are going out and the babysitter will be watching your child, have him buy back the specific privileges from you before you go; then leave appropriate instructions with the babysitter about what your child is allowed to do and for how long.

What About an Allowance?

For a child that is old enough (in your judgment as a parent) to have an allowance, it's effective to tie it into this program. Make each chip worth, say, twenty-five or fifty cents and allow your child to exchange the chips for an allowance, up to an established limit. It's best to tell your child that the allowance is given on the same day each week, and only exchange chips for allowance on that day. This will also help your child learn to plan his spending habits for the week and will help him learn money management and organization skills.

What About Siblings?

If you have more than one child at home, it may be beneficial to start the program with all of your children. Remember to make the list of chores age-appropriate for each child. This may help you structure the day for the whole family, so you may feel some relief because it'll help you organize who does what at home. Use a different color of chips for each child; otherwise, you'll have to attend to constant complaints about your children trading chips or accusing each other of stealing them.

Also, an important note about including chores in the contract: First, remember that the chores you'll start with are simple, daily ones. In addition, make sure that the chores you assign each child don't interlock with the chores of another child. Say, for instance, that you expect one child to clear the table, another to wash the dishes, and yet another to dry them. What if something goes wrong along the sequence? What if the child that clears the table refuses to do so? Then, the other children will either have to do it for him or forgo the ability to get their own chips. In a situation like that, it is best to assign the whole dish chore to one person at a time, on a rotating basis. This will be covered further in step 6, when the contract is expanded.

Modifications for Young Children and Adolescents

Although the behavioral contract procedure is effective for children of all ages, some modifications may help make it more effective for very young children and for adolescents. As pointed out earlier, instead of chips, young children may respond better to stickers. For a specific number of stickers, allow your child a special privilege, such as watching a special TV show or renting a special video. Conversely, for an adolescent, use age-appropriate rewards, such as the privilege to use the telephone, television, or video equipment (DVD player, VCR), having friends over, and getting rides from you (to go to the mall or visit a friend). Make sure each has a consistent value that you will expect every time, as per the list. Also, for older adolescents, it may not be necessary to use chips. Rather, you can use a one-to-one exchange for a privilege if a chore is completed; for example, a teenager will be able to use the phone only after all the room chores on the list are finished.

Putting It All Together

Get the chips (or stickers), make the lists, and implement the contract. Be consistent and firm. Remember to give the chips each time a target behavior is performed, and collect the chips each time your child gets a privilege or a reward. Immediate presentation (or collection) of the chips is one of the prerequisites for the contract's success.

If your child misbehaves but still performs the chore from the list, give the reward anyway. Don't punish him by withdrawing the reward that he earned by performing the chores. In other words, don't take away any chips during this step. Remember, you want to make your child's environment consistent and predictable so that he knows what to expect. For now, find another consequence for the transgression. For example, you may restrict your child from watching television for a day but allow him to use the chips to earn another privilege that is on the list.

And finally—please always remember to *praise* your child for performing each item on the list of responsibilities. Giving the reward isn't enough. Your child must hear that you like what he did and that you appreciate his sense of responsibility. Please refer to the examples of praise listed earlier in this chapter.

Give yourself at least two weeks before you proceed to the next chapter.

Checklist 4A

Step 4: Implement a Behavioral Contract

Procedure

1. Preparation

- Get poker chips (or, for a young child, stickers). If administering the contract with more than one child, make sure each child's chips are a different color.

- Start by making a list of responsibilities that you want your child to perform every day. Initially, don't include weekly or sporadic tasks. Start small. The things that work best at first are things that involve a daily routine or schedule, such as:

  - Getting out of bed in the morning after no more than two prompts

  - Staying in own room until dressed

  - Getting out of the house by specific time each day

  - Brushing teeth or washing hands (before/after meals, etc.)

  - Making own bed

- Don't include behaviors that you want your child to stop doing (e.g., fighting with siblings). To start, the responsibilities must be simple, clear, and easily checked and enforced.

- Ask your child to make his own list of rewards. Don't criticize him for putting inappropriate things on the list. After all, you don't have to agree to what he wrote.

- Use privileges as rewards. Examples:

  - Thirty minutes of TV

  - Fifteen minutes of video games or computer time

  - One hour of riding bicycle

  - Bedtime extended by fifteen minutes

  - Renting a videotape

- Include a grab bag of inexpensive items that your child can redeem, one at a time, with chips. It helps to go to a store with him and have him select the items.

- When figuring out the exchange rate, make sure that he can earn a little more in one day than he can spend in one day.

2. Getting the Contract Started

- Your child will keep his own chips (e.g., in a jar in his room).

- Your child will earn chips for performing certain duties and then use these chips to earn privileges (and small prizes) at home.

- Only you, the parents, have the authority to give the chips and authorize the exchange of chips for a privilege/reward.

- If he misbehaves but still performs the chore, give the chip anyway. Find another consequence for the transgression. Don't take away a chip that he has just earned.

During this step, do not punish by taking away chips. Use rewards only.

Checklist 4B

List of Responsibilities

Name: _____

RESPONSIBILITY	AMOUNT

Checklist 4C

List of Privileges/Rewards

Name: _____

PRIVILEGE/REWARD	AMOUNT

CHAPTER 7

Step 5—Address
Homework-Related Problems

Note: You can skip this chapter if your child isn't in school yet, or if she is on vacation from school. Please come back to it, however, when your child starts school or returns to school after the vacation is over.

As you may have recognized by now, one of the biggest reasons for implementing the behavioral contract is to help your child learn that performing positive behaviors earns positive consequences and that the amount of effort is proportionally rewarded by the magnitude of the consequence. With a properly administered contract, your child frequently experiences those lessons and the behavioral problems diminish. Sometimes, your child may still refuse to do certain things, but at least now you can administer proper consequences consistently, so that over time your child can reassess whether that choice is worth the consequence. Now, it's time to start expanding the contract to other problematic areas. For the remainder of the book, we will use the contract as a main tool and adapt it to address various types of problems. This chapter focuses on school-related issues, especially problems with homework.

Homework problems occur in many forms. Some children refuse to sit down and do homework. Others have problems staying on task and take several hours to complete assignments. Some children constantly ask for help and show little independence in doing their work. Others constantly forget their books, notebooks, and whatever else may be needed to complete the homework. Some children lie about whether work was assigned and constantly tell their parents that no homework was assigned by teachers when, in fact, homework *was* assigned and needs to be completed. Many children have a combination of these problems. In this chapter, I'll discuss methods of addressing all of them, and how the behavioral contract plays an important role in improving homework-related problems.

Choose a Homework Setting

It's important to set up a home environment that is most conducive to effective homework completion. To start, select a place in the home for your child to do homework. The place should be free from distractions and close enough so that you can monitor what your child is doing while there. The place should be quiet, but not isolated. Examples of places that work well include the kitchen table (if you're not preparing food at the time), the dining room table, or a desk in the child's room (as long as the child doesn't have a substantial amount of distractions in the room, such as a TV or video games).

Speaking of TV, the homework setting needs to be outside of the view (and sound) of the TV that other family members may be watching at the time. You may just elect to turn the TV off. However, some children have more difficulties working in an environment that is too sterile and devoid of any stimulation. They may do better with a limited amount of activity around them. Sometimes it's a good idea to either allow the child to see the TV screen but turn the sound off, or turn off the TV and turn on the radio in the homework spot. You may want to experiment to learn what works best. In addition, the homework spot should be away from the telephone and any place where siblings are playing.

Establish a Homework Time

When is the best time to have your child do homework? This is very individual and depends on your child's personality, your schedule in the home, your preferences, and extracurricular activities that may determine when she will actually be at home to do homework. Activities, sports, and clubs all occur at different times; your child's homework time may need to accommodate these schedules. However, as much as possible, your child should have the same homework time each day. The times that usually work best are about a half hour after the child gets home from school, about one hour before dinner, or immediately after dinner.

Doing homework immediately after school generally doesn't work well for many children. They may feel overloaded after doing a lot of work in school and need a little break before they do homework. Also, for many children, especially in early grades, the time right after school may be the only time when they can see their friends, so homework time should be set in such a way as to allow them to participate in at least some social activities. Whatever time of day you choose for homework time, it's important that you try to keep it consistent from day to day. One of your goals is to structure your child's day and make it more predictable for her. A routine that repeats every day will eventually become internalized, and your child will learn to expect it.

Some specific times don't work well. For example, it isn't a good idea to have your child do homework right before she goes to bed. In the evening, the mind is not as sharp as earlier in the day, and it is much harder to concentrate. Likewise, in the morning before she goes to school is not advisable. Most households are rushed in the mornings and hurrying to get homework done while trying to leave the house on time prevents the student from being able to devote the kind of effort and energy required to learn from the assignments. Left on their own, however, children often choose these times to do their homework. As a parent, you should intervene and set a consistent time that is more appropriate.

Also, if you have several school-age children in the home, it may be to your benefit to set the same homework time for all of them. It will be easier for you and your children to remember that everyone has homework time at the same time, and you'll have an easier time monitoring your children and minimizing distractions. If you establish a common homework time, make sure to separate each child into a different homework spot.

Begin a Homework Checklist or Journal

Further preparation is needed for implementing a procedure that successfully addresses a wide variety of homework problems. More specifically, you'll need to solicit the participation of your child's teacher so that you have daily communications from school. In this way, you'll be able to monitor the amount of homework that your child gets each day. The best way to accomplish this is to implement some type of daily written record of your child's assignments that will be checked by the teacher for accuracy at the end of each class or school day.

Nowadays, most schools have adopted their own system of assisting their students in keeping track of homework. Some schools use homework journals or planners that are completed each day by the teacher or by the student. These usually resemble a notebook in which the work assignments are written. Sometimes, instead of a journal, teachers give each student a sheet at the beginning of the week that has spaces for homework in each subject to be recorded every day. This provides a convenient weekly record of all assignments in one place that can quickly be checked at a glance.

If your child's school doesn't have any of these systems in place, you can develop and implement one yourself. Get a blank, small notebook for your child in which the teacher (or your child) will write the assignments each day. This procedure is particularly effective for younger children. For a child in fourth grade or higher, you can make up a variety of homework sheets that she can fill out (an example is provided at the end of this chapter). The sheets can be used either daily, in which case your child gets a blank sheet from you every day to fill out, or weekly, in which case she gets a sheet each Monday and uses it for the entire week. Either can work, and each has its benefits and drawbacks.

The weekly sheet is more convenient, but some children may lose it in the course of the week. For many children, the daily sheet, although somewhat more cumbersome for you (because you have to make sure that plenty of blanks are available and you have to remember to give it to your child each morning), works better, particularly if your child tends to be disorganized.

Obviously, you must enlist the teacher's assistance. At first glance, this may seem difficult, but my experience has been that most teachers are happy to help implement this procedure. After all, if your child has homework problems, the teacher probably already has, unsuccessfully, attempted many different ways to address this problem. Most teachers are very happy to get assistance from the parents of children with homework problems.

Depending on your teacher's preference, either she may fill out the journal (or homework sheet) herself, or ask your child to do so. If she prefers the latter, make sure that she signs or initials the journal or sheet at the end of each day; otherwise the entire procedure won't work. If your child has more than one teacher, each teacher should check and sign the portion of the journal or homework sheet that pertains to her subject. The teacher should sign the form as your child is being dismissed from class. If there are no assignments given to your child that day, the entry must say "no homework" (or something similar), and it must be endorsed by the teacher. This is very important—otherwise, you won't know whether your child is correct about having no homework, or whether she simply didn't write it down. One more thing: All entries in the journal or homework sheet must be made in nonerasable pen only.

Establish Homework Rules

Once you have the setting and time established at home, and the use of a homework journal or checklist has been arranged with the teacher, it's time to set the homework procedure. Your child must bring the journal or homework sheet home each day, together with all the work that is to be completed, including all handouts, books, and notebooks. Then, at the start of the homework time, your child must show you the homework sheet completed for that particular day (signed or initialed by the teachers) and all the materials necessary to complete all of the work.

What do you do if the homework journal or checklist isn't signed, or if your child forgot a book or other item needed to complete the work? Any of these instances constitutes an incomplete homework preparation by the child, and the consequence will be that your child doesn't earn a pass that day to buy back certain privileges established in the behavioral contract (this is discussed in more detail later in this chapter).

Doing the Homework

First, help your child organize the work by locating and categorizing, by subject, all work that has to be done. Then, instruct her to start working on one assignment only. When that assignment is done, have her come to you and show you the completed work. Check it. The assignment is considered done when all of it is completed, most of it is correct, and it is legible. Don't get particularly picky about neatness. As long as it's legible enough for the teacher to accept it, it's considered done. If it's really sloppy and/or if most of it is obviously incorrect, send your child back to redo it. If she asks for help, handle it in the way discussed later in this chapter.

When the assignment is finished, instruct your child to start working on another one and to show it to you when it's done. If she is having particular problems with remaining on task during homework, it may help to reward her for each completed assignment by giving her one chip. However, if you do so, give the chip only if the assignment is finished correctly the first time, not if it has to be redone.

Earning a Privilege

To teach your child that successful homework completion is rewarded by positive consequences, restrict certain privileges until after homework time. Although in the previous step you developed a contract that specifies how your child earns certain privileges, you still control *when* your child can exercise the option to "buy" them during any given day. For example, don't allow your child to cash in the chips to watch TV or play video games until after homework is done. In this way she is restricted from buying certain privileges, even if she has the necessary chips, until after homework time is over. This allows you to increase her motivation to complete homework. Furthermore, if your child forgot something on the homework checklist or if the list is not signed, don't allow her to buy back the privilege that was restricted. This means, for example, that your child won't watch TV that day or play with video games. She can only buy the restricted privileges if the signed checklist (or journal) and all work was brought home and all of the work was completed. As you can see, this also serves as an added motivator for children who tend to procrastinate or take a very long time to do homework. After all, they'll be restricted from doing what they want until they are done with homework.

Providing Assistance

What if your child asks you for assistance, or says, "I can't do this assignment"? First, monitor whether this happens on a regular basis. If it does, address this problem with the teacher. It's possible that, for some reason, your child may not be learning an academic skill at an appropriate pace. The teacher may need to know this to consider modifying the curriculum or assessing your child for possible learning problems.

When your child asks for assistance, give it, but don't complete the assignment for your child. Just do a starter item or two with her and then have her complete the rest under your monitoring. If she refuses to try, tell her that she'll sit there until she decides to attempt the assignment. And remember, send her back to do it again if it is done haphazardly.

Putting It All Together

This procedure, although seemingly complicated at first, is actually easy to administer. You will structure your child's homework routine and help her develop productive work habits. Gradually, she will internalize those rules. To help motivate her, she will be restricted from a privilege until after she completes the assignments. If she forgets assignments or neglects to have the journal or sheet signed by teachers, she will not earn that privilege for that day, and so she'll work harder to keep track of homework assignments. This approach is effective in improving your child's homework performance, but don't be discouraged if it takes a week or more to get this procedure off the ground. Don't give up. Stick to your guns, even if it means that your child won't watch TV for a week until she begins to bring home all that is required. Remember, you're administering proper consequences and sending a message to your child that homework is very important. As before, give yourself at least one to two weeks before proceeding on to the next chapter.

Checklist 5A

Step 5: Address Homework-Related Problems

Procedure

1. **Choose a Homework Setting**

   - Prepare a setting for your child that is free from distractions but isn't too quiet or isolated. Examples of homework spots that work best: dining room table, desk in the child's room, kitchen table.

   - The place needs to be quiet and outside of the view of the family TV, beyond earshot of the telephone, and away from other children playing.

   - It is sometimes helpful for the homework spot to have a minor stimulus present: either a radio quietly set to a popular music station, or a TV on but with the sound off.

2. **Establish a Homework Time**

   - Your child needs to have a set homework time that will be the same every day. The times that work best are about a half hour after the child comes in from school, about one hour before dinner, or immediately after dinner.

   - Don't set the homework time immediately before bedtime or in the morning before your child goes to school.

   - If you have several children in the home, it's helpful for all your children to have the same homework time.

3. Begin a Homework Checklist or Journal

- Establish a homework journal or checklist with your child's teachers.

- The child or teacher fills in the daily homework assignments, and the teacher must initial each entry.

4. Establish Homework Rules

- If your child forgot the homework checklist, or if it isn't filled out properly, she won't earn the after-homework privileges for that day.

- If she brought home the checklist but is missing any of the assignments and/or the books necessary to do all of the work, she won't earn the after-homework privileges for that day.

5. Doing the Homework

- At the start of homework time, your child must show you the homework checklist filled out for that day.

- Help your child get organized at the start of the homework time; help her locate all the assignments listed on the checklist, and the books necessary to complete them.

- Have her do one assignment at a time and bring it to you to check when done. Then, have her start on the second assignment, and so on.

6. Earning a Privilege

- Your child is restricted from buying back certain privileges established in the behavioral contract, even if she has the chips, until after homework time. Examples: TV, video games, going out, having friends over, phone time. It's usually best to pick just one or two of these.

■ After the homework is done and you've checked it, your child can buy after-homework privileges with the chips she's earned through the behavioral contract.

7. Providing Assistance

■ Give assistance only when your child asks or says that she doesn't know how to complete an assignment.

■ Don't do the work for your child. If assistance is needed, do a starter item or two with her and then monitor as she works on the remainder on her own.

■ Check each completed assignment. If one was obviously done haphazardly (i.e., all or most of the items are clearly wrong), or if it is unusually sloppy so that it is barely legible, have her do it over before she proceeds to the next assignment.

Checklist 5B

Daily Homework Checklist

Name: _____ Date: _____

SUBJECT	ASSIGNMENT	TEACHER'S INIT.

CHAPTER 8

Step 6—Expand the Behavioral Contract

After completing steps 4 and 5, you now have a solid behavioral contract implemented with your child. By now, your child should be having fewer problems, and homework performance should be improving. Now it's time to further expand the behavioral contract to include more problem areas of out-of-control children.

The suggestions in this chapter are not meant to be implemented all at once. This chapter is designed to help you continue with the contract and expand it to include more and more of the problems that you may encounter with your child. Extend the contract slowly, and always give your child about a week or two to get used to each new change.

Reviewing the List of Responsibilities

If you haven't done so already, you may want to add more items that have to do with personal hygiene, keeping the child's room clean, and so forth. This is also the time to add sporadic chores to the list. Thus far, you've only asked your child to perform tasks that are expected every day. Now, you can add those responsibilities that don't occur every day but need to be done once or twice a week, such as taking out the trash and helping to clean the house.

Remember, don't interlock or overlap the chores between the siblings. Instead, rotate the larger jobs between all children, or have each child assist you in one part of the job and reward each child separately and independently of the others. Make sure that each child knows exactly what the reward will be for each job.

Per-Need Responsibilities

You may also add "per-need" jobs that you want your child to perform only when you need the job done. These are the jobs that come up infrequently, such as cleaning the basement or attic, cleaning your car, cleaning the yard, bagging the leaves in the fall, or helping you with a project. Usually, these items are not placed on the list (the contract), but are announced to your child when the need to do these tasks arises. Always make sure your child knows beforehand how much he'll earn by doing the job.

Chunking Responsibilities

Now may also be a good time to start "chunking" the responsibilities. Instead of rewarding your child for each component of a routine, now you can give the reward only if the entire sequence is completed. Until now, you gave your child a separate chip for making the bed, making sure nothing is on the floor, putting dirty clothes in the laundry basket, and so on. Now you can start chunking these tasks into a single responsibility, such as "room is clean at inspection time," and you may give a chip reward only when the whole "chunk" of tasks is complete. In this way, the routine becomes an all-or-none task, in which the reward is only earned after the entire routine is completed.

This greatly improves your child's ability to internalize the sequencing of common daily routines. Make sure, however, that even after you start chunking, all the components of that chunk are still clearly listed on the Responsibilities list so that your child understands exactly what it is that you expect. As always, remember to praise your child each time he did what you asked, whether he receives a chip reward or not.

First-Try Compliance

Adding "on the first try" commands is a good way to teach your child to become more compliant. This procedure, popularized by Barkley (1997), involves giving your child an extra chip if, when you ask him to do something, he does it immediately, without your need to repeat the command. At first, announce to your child each time you will implement this procedure. For example, "I'm going to ask you to do something now, and if you do it immediately, I'll give you a chip." Then, ask him to perform some kind of a task. As before, these tasks should be simple, direct, single-action items, such as picking up toys, helping set the table, and turning off the TV because it's dinnertime or bedtime. After you use this method several times with a warning, you can then inform your child that you won't remind him anymore about rewarding his compliance on the first try but that you *will* continue to reward him every time he immediately complies with your command. Be careful, however: Once you say this, you'll have to remember to reward the desired behavior when it happens, or the procedure will lose its effect.

Over time, you can start to fade the continuous reinforcement and switch over to a more intermittent schedule. For example, tell your child that he'll earn five extra chips for each day during which he complied on the first try with at least ten commands. In this manner, you'll gradually teach your child to be compliant without expecting a chip each time. Be careful, and don't progress to this last suggestion too quickly; your child may lose motivation to continue to try if your expectations are set too high. Praise your child each time he complies on the first try. Over time, you want him to become more compliant because he likes to hear your praise, not just because he'll earn extra chips.

Reviewing Rewards and Privileges

By now, your child may have started to accumulate some chips. Don't be concerned. This only means that the program is working as planned. Sometimes, when a child has saved many chips, he may stop earning more and start to again refuse to perform the duties on the list. Do *not* discontinue the contract. This is temporary. Continue to require your child to buy back privileges, and encourage him to spend the chips. As he spends more chips, the motivation to earn them will return.

Add More Rewards

Just as you expanded the list of responsibilities, it is important to expand the list of rewards. Include some items that your child may buy back with a larger amount of chips, such as toys, books, videotapes or DVDs, and CDs. Chances are, you may buy some of these things for your child anyway, so make your child earn them. Likewise, go out of your way to entice your child to spend chips on extra activities that may come up. For example, offer to take your child to an amusement park where he can spend a lot of chips on rides, or take him to a video arcade and allow him to spend chips playing games.

In addition, expand the regular privileges that your child can earn by encouraging privileges such as a sleepover party or staying over at a friend's house. Make the value of these activities more significant but still within realistic reach so that your child can feel that these are reasonably possible to earn.

Hoarding

If your child seems to be hoarding the chips and isn't buying back the privileges on the list (and refusing to perform many of the tasks on your Responsibilities list), your list of rewards/privileges may be too limited and your child may still have enough "free" activities that he likes to do that aren't included in your program. Make sure that your list is broad enough to include the common activities that your child likes. For example, with regard to playing outside, require the child to buy back time outside *and* the ability to ride his bicycle.

With a child who hoards chips and doesn't want to spend them, another technique may be useful. You can designate a "chip clean-out" weekend, during which he has to spend all of the chips that he has collected thus far. At the end of the weekend, the value of all of the remaining chips expires and the program begins from scratch. Performing this once in a while may be effective. Don't implement this too frequently, however, or your child will learn that saving chips is pointless and this will diminish his motivation to earn the chips at all.

Fluctuations in Motivation

Understand that your child will go through periods of greater and lesser motivation. There will be days when he'll earn and exchange many chips and days when he'll refuse to do anything, regardless of the consequences. Don't be concerned—you're not doing anything wrong. As the saying goes, "Children are people, too," and like adults, they have moods. On some days they'll be more cooperative; on other days, more difficult. Just be consistent and stick to the program.

Occasionally, an out-of-control child refuses to participate in the program and doesn't earn any chips to exchange them for privileges. This situation may require the parents to gather all of the child's toys and place them somewhere in the house in a locked chest. The child then has to earn, with chips, the ability to play with each toy for a specific period of time; for example, one chip per toy per half hour. In that case, two toys per half hour would require two chips. Most children don't require this drastic approach, but if your child isn't responding well to your efforts thus far, don't be afraid to get tough.

Costs

Another procedure to implement as you expand the contract is to include chip costs. In other words, you'll now start to punish your child by taking chips away for certain behaviors that you want to eliminate. To start this procedure, you'll need to make another list and label it "Costs" (not "Punishments"). A sample form is provided at the end of this chapter. Start by listing only one behavior that you want to punish. Common behaviors for which this works well include cursing and using bad language, aggression, failure to remain in their room after a predetermined cutoff time at bedtime, or taking something without permission. Some examples are discussed below.

Be *very* specific, clear, and precise in defining what the behavior is and how much it will cost your child each time it happens. Make sure that it is a behavior that you will observe yourself. Don't rely on the reports of others (e.g., siblings or a babysitter) to tell you that the behavior occurred. If you didn't see it or hear it, don't take the chips away.

Verbal Outbursts

Verbal outbursts that aren't severe enough for time-out are good candidates for initial chip costs. For example, if your child, when disciplined or restricted, blurts out an obscenity, it can cost the child five chips per episode. If your child says several obscenities during a single episode that are punishable by chip costs, give only one punishment. However, if a minute or two later your child does it again, give him another chip punishment. If you use this suggestion, make sure to specify every phrase and word that you want to target. Don't be vague and just say "all curse words." This will only generate future squabbles about what is and isn't an obscenity. Instead, state exactly what you don't want to hear. Remember, the more predictable your child's environment, the fewer management problems you'll experience.

Physical Aggression

Another candidate for chip costs is physical aggression. Even though, as discussed in step 3, this will immediately result in time-out, it may be beneficial to back it up with a chip punishment as well, particularly if your child has a problem with aggression that results in spending much time in time-out every day. Again, as in the previous example, define very precisely what action you'll punish and how many chips it will cost your child. For physical aggression, the punishment should be greater than for inappropriate language, but remember to give only one punishment per episode, even though your child may have committed several aggressive acts in that one episode. When you set the chip costs, don't set them so high that one or two episodes will result in your child losing all of his chips. If that happens, what will you use when your child does that behavior again? After all, you have to be consistent. You can't advance chips to him that weren't yet earned, and you can't put a child into a "minus" account and take chips away later after they are earned.

Limits on Chip Costs

One final point about chip costs. At any given time, do not work with more than one or two behaviors for which you'll be taking chips away. Any more than that will result in confusion, and your child may begin to lose the chips too quickly, which may limit his motivation to continue with the program. After one problem has been eliminated (e.g., when your child stops using inappropriate language) you can move on to another problem that you want to address. Just make sure you wait for at least one to two weeks before you make the change so that you don't encourage the child to return to his old habits.

Putting It All Together

As explained at the start of this chapter, the suggestions contained herein are much too extensive to implement all at once. Instead, expand the contract gradually. For example, at first, include some more chores, chunk one of the routines, expand the Rewards list, and start working on one behavior with chip costs. Let this work for a week or two before you expand the contract again. Always give yourself and your child enough time to become used to the changes implemented before you proceed further. Some further techniques for expanding the contract are provided in steps 7, 8, and 9. It isn't mandatory to complete these in sequence, and you only need to implement those that you feel are needed. When you are ready to proceed, continue on and read the chapters that outline these steps.

Checklist 6A

Step 6: Expand the Behavioral Contract

Procedure

Reviewing the List of Responsibilities

- Extend the list of responsibilities.

- Add sporadic chores to the list. Make sure the exchange is clearly stated.

- Add "per-need" chores that you'll ask for spontaneously. Always make it clear how much your child will earn by doing the task.

- Start "chunking" the chores that go together, but only if your child already had at least two-thirds compliance with these chores separately over the past week.

First-Try Compliance

- Add "on the first try" commands. When you first implement this, warn your child each time one of these will be utilized.

Reviewing Rewards and Privileges

- Extend the list of daily privileges.

- Extend the list of more sporadic privileges, such as staying over at a friend's house or having a sleepover at the house.

- Allow your child to earn a lot of chips over a period of time for a larger reward, such as a game cartridge, DVD, or CD.

- Don't be concerned if your child is hoarding the chips and exchanging them sporadically. If necessary, restrict his ability to play with toys unless earned. Consider a sporadic "chip clean-out" weekend.

- Make sure that your child has no other way to earn a privilege except through exchanging the specified number of chips. Be firm.

Costs

- Introduce chip costs for specific transgressions. Start with one behavior that will be punished. Be very clear, and define precisely what the behavior is and how much it will cost each time it happens. Make sure it's a behavior you can observe yourself rather than getting reports from others, such as siblings or babysitters.

- At any given time, work with no more than two behaviors that will be punished by taking away chips.

Checklist 6B

List of Costs

Name: _____

COSTS	AMOUNT

CHAPTER 9

Step 7—Manage
Out-of-Home Situations

Pause for a moment and review your progress. By now, you have implemented several important behavioral techniques, and your child should be exhibiting notable improvement. Behavioral problems should be diminishing, although it's normal to expect some day-to-day fluctuations. Like most of us, children also have good days and bad days; on some days your child will seem more cooperative, and on other days she'll seem more difficult. Consider that the level of behavioral problems you experience during any given day is related to your child's ability to exercise self-control that day.

Like any other skill, self-control will not be the same day to day. Think about yourself and your own self-control. Do you have days when your self-control isn't as good as it is on other days? Do you have days when it's harder to resist the urge to eat junk food or buy an impulse item? Do you have times when it's so easy to skip dessert, and other times when you get second helpings, even though in the back of your mind you know you shouldn't? Do you have days when you see an item you like in the store window and pass it by because you know you really don't need it and shouldn't spend the money, and other days when you go in and buy it anyway? It's important to remember that children, like grown-ups, also have days when their self-control diminishes, and the reasons for this aren't that different from your own at times when it's harder to resist dessert or buy that impulse item.

Self-control is related to so many factors. It depends on how we feel on any given day, and when we feel stressed, angry, troubled, or sad, we're less able to resist the impulsive urge to perform an action. Remember that children experience the same feelings and reactions; similarly, their ability to exercise self-control is affected by these factors. In addition, children's self-control is also related to the amount of excitement they feel during any given moment, and the more stimulated they feel, the more difficult it is for them to exercise self-control.

Before proceeding to additional steps and techniques, take stock and review how consistent you have been in using the previous steps. Do you remember to obtain eye contact *before* you issue a command to your child? If this is difficult for you to remember and use consistently, please go back and review step 1. Do you continue to argue with your child after the command has been issued? If so, please go back and review step 2. Does your child still throw frequent temper tantrums? Perhaps reviewing step 3 will help. Any remaining problems with homework? Do you continue to implement the techniques suggested in step 5?

And, most important, how is the behavioral contract working? By now, you and your child should be on cruise control for much of the day-to-day tasks and chores. Some daily variation is expected, but your child should be generally more cooperative with morning routine, bedtime, basic chores, and so on. If you're still experiencing problems in these areas, perhaps you should pause to review steps 4 and 6 before proceeding further. Are you consistent with giving your child chips or stickers each time he earns them? Are you consistent with charging for privileges and rewards? Is the contract designed with sufficient opportunity for success? Are you careful not to overuse the costs and punishments? A smooth-functioning behavioral contract is an important prerequisite for the success of the additional techniques of steps 7, 8, and 9, so please take any extra time you need to improve the contract's implementation before you proceed to the additional steps.

A well-implemented behavioral contract is a powerful tool. It allows you the flexibility to add additional tasks and situations that still need to be addressed, while providing opportunity for your child to receive immediate, tangible, and verbal feedback after a behavior—a positive consequence for appropriate behavior and lack of a positive consequence (or a negative consequence) for inappropriate behavior. When used consistently over time, it allows your child to learn that appropriate behaviors result in positive consequences and improves her ability to think before she acts and to make the right choice when deciding how to act in a given situation. For the remaining steps of the program, we will use the contract you already established in steps 4 and 6 to help you reduce three additional common problems that difficult children often exhibit.

It was important for you to complete steps 1 through 6 in order because each step built upon the previous one and the success of each step made it more likely that the next step in the sequence would also be effective. For the remaining steps, however, proceeding in order is no longer important. Each of the following three steps addresses difficulties in specific settings by extending the basic use of the behavioral contract. This chapter focuses on reducing problems in out-of-home situations (e.g., places of worship, stores, or restaurants). Step 8 focuses on problems with interruptions, and step 9 addresses problems with transitions. Please feel free to complete these three chapters in any order you wish, based on your needs and the needs of your child.

Why Are Problems in Out-of-Home Situations So Common?

Out-of-home situations often present a particular challenge. Outside of their home environment, children often exhibit more problems with self-control. The reasons for this are complex, but some factors are important to keep in mind.

First, a different setting doesn't feel like home, where your child is used to certain patterns of behaviors and consequences, so your child may be less likely to know what to expect. In addition, many out-of-home settings inherently have less structure. In a supermarket or a department store, there is less supervision and the expectations about what constitutes good behavior are much less clear, at least from a child's viewpoint. Your child may wonder about several things: How far can I wander away from Mom before she starts yelling? How fast do I have to run before I get in trouble? Is a trot still okay when a full run isn't? What items on the shelves am I allowed to touch before I get into trouble? How much noise can I make before Mom starts yelling?

Another important contributor is the increased stimulation that children experience in many out-of-home settings. In a supermarket or a department store, there are many people walking all around, bumping into each other, talking to each other. There are lights and colors that grab your child's attention, moment to moment, and therefore minimize the likelihood that your child will continue to think about self-control and good behavior. There are noises (and, in a restaurant, smells) that divert her attention and make her curious about what's going on. Put this all together, and she is likely to become overstimulated. When this occurs, her ability to utilize self-control is greatly diminished.

For example, when visiting family, children often come in contact with cousins (whom they may not see that frequently) and become excited about the opportunity to play with them. This play may involve a lot of physical activity. All in all, children may become so stimulated by the setting and the activities that utilizing good self-control may be very difficult.

Out-of-home settings may also be characterized by rules and expectations that are more difficult than those children are accustomed to in their own homes. For example, when visiting family members who don't have children residing with them, your child may find that certain behaviors that you allow at home aren't permitted at someone else's house. This difference in rules and expectations is most apparent in places of worship, where the expectation to be quiet and sit still may be very difficult for most young children to meet. All in all, out-of-home situations often present a special challenge that requires specific attention and a specialized approach.

Consider the following situation:

Five-year-old Bobbi is about to go into the supermarket with her mom. Before going in, Mom says, "Now, Bobbi, if you behave while we're in the store, I'll buy you a piece of candy when we leave."

Bobbi says, "Okay."

Bobbi and Mom proceed into the store. Immediately, Bobbi starts to wander off. Mom is busy attending to her shopping list and doesn't immediately notice that Bobbi has wandered away. After a few moments, she calls out to Bobbi, who has now wandered to the next shopping aisle. "Bobbi, where are you?" She doesn't answer. Mom goes over to the next aisle and notices Bobbi looking at a box of cookies on the shelf.

"Can we get these, Mom?" Bobbi takes the box off the shelf.

"No, we can't!" Mom responds, while taking the box out of her hands and placing it back on the shelves.

Bobbi protests, "But why?"

Mom doesn't answer and says, "What did I tell you about behaving? If you keep this up, you won't get your candy!" Mom grabs Bobbi by the hand and drags her back over to the aisle where she was previously shopping.

Bobbi starts to whine and complain. Her voice is becoming louder. "But why not? I want cookies!"

Mom ignores her and goes back to her shopping. She lets go of Bobbi's hand. Bobbi runs away, and goes right back to the cookies and picks up the box again. Mom chases her, grabs her hand while yanking away the cookie box, and says, "Why aren't you behaving? I swear, you'll get no candy when we leave."

Bobbi starts to cry and falls on the floor. Mom has to drag Bobbi away while she is screaming and carrying on. Mom comments about getting a few more gray hairs every time she goes shopping with Bobbi.

Mom again returns to shopping, this time trying to hold on to Bobbi's hand. Bobbi continues to cry and carry on and grabs various items on the shelves, putting some of them in the shopping basket. Whenever Mom notices, she takes these out and places them back on the shelves. She again reminds Bobbi that behaving like this won't get her the candy she promised. Sometimes, Bobbi breaks free and Mom has to chase her, grab her by the hand, and drag her back in order to keep her close. Bobbi continues to scream and cry.

As they approach the checkout counter, Mom sees candy and gum hanging on the racks next to each cashier line. She points to these and says, "Bobbi, if you behave while I am paying, you'll get the candy I promised." She lets go of Bobbi's hand and begins to place the items from the shopping cart onto the cashier's conveyer belt.

Bobbi grabs one of the candy packages and puts it in the basket. Mom notices, takes it out, and says, "Bobbi, that's it. I've had it. No candy!" Bobbi starts to cry and tries to run away from Mom. She grabs Bobbi by the hand and drags her back while Bobbi is kicking and screaming. Shoppers in other lines are beginning to notice, and Mom becomes embarrassed. She says to Bobbi, "Just wait until we get home! Now, you'll really get it. Wait until I tell your father what you did!"

She struggles to pay the bill and proceeds out of the store, dragging along Bobbi, who continues to scream and cry. In the parking lot, Bobbi again tries to run away from Mom. She grabs Bobbi and shoves her in the car, screaming at her that she's driving her crazy and she doesn't know what to do with her anymore.

What went wrong? Is there a way to address these problems and improve Bobbi's behavior in a store? Although the answer is yes, many parents often give up and, after a few tries, choose not to take their children to a store; instead, they ask an older sibling, spouse, another family member, or a babysitter to watch their child at home while they go shopping. This is not a practical solution. Hiring a babysitter each time you need a few items from a store may be too much of a financial burden for many parents, and family members may get tired of babysitting too frequently. What's most important, however, is that removing a child from this situation deprives her of an opportunity to learn and practice additional self-control skills. Consequently, it is crucial to continue to take your child into these settings. However, there are many aspects of the above example that need improvement. The following suggestions are originally based on ideas of Barkley (1997), significantly expanded and elaborated, and their effectiveness in the current format is confirmed by my own research (Kapalka 2003a).

Set Realistic Expectations

Taking your child to a store, restaurant, someone's home, or a place of worship requires preparation. First, it's important to consider what behaviors your child is likely to exhibit that will be most problematic. Before a trip to the store, think about which problems your child has previously exhibited that were most annoying or difficult. This will help you focus on specific problems, an important component of success in improving her behavior in these settings.

In addition, it will help you think realistically. Are you expecting that your five-year-old will sit quietly through a religious sermon? That may not be possible. Perhaps you need to plan built-in breaks every fifteen minutes or so to go outside and give your child a breather. Always keep in mind what's realistic to expect of your child, given her age and personality.

The Plan

To address behavioral problems in out-of-home situations, you'll need to utilize the principles and strategies previously covered in several steps of this program, which will now focus on the particulars of the out-of-home settings.

As outlined in checklist 7 at the end of this chapter, here are the components of a plan of action that will help minimize problems and improve your child's self-control:

- Set the rules.

- Set the reward for following the rules.

- Set the consequences for not following the rules.

- Go into the target setting.

- Administer the appropriate consequence.

Let's cover each of these components in detail.

Set the Rules

Before going into the target setting, make sure that your child clearly knows what you expect. Prepare yourself, and focus on what it is that you want your child to accomplish. This is best done in the car, right before you go into the target setting. Use the procedure described in step 1 and obtain eye contact with your child.

Once you have her attention, set a few specific rules. The younger your child, the less you should expect. For example, a four-year-old can only follow one rule at a time, whereas a typical nine-year-old should be able to follow two or three rules. Explain to your child the rules that you want her to follow. The rules need to be stated in a manner that is clear and sufficiently detailed so that you are leaving little to your child's interpretation. In other words, define exactly what it is that you expect. Don't say general things such as "Be good" or "Don't misbehave," which assumes that your child knows what you mean and what you expect, and this usually isn't true. Instead, be very specific: "Don't run away from me," "Don't take things off the shelves without my permission," and so on.

Tell your child that you'll give her only one warning or reminder of the rule while you are in the target setting. Have your child repeat these rules to you to make sure that she understands what you expect, including the fact that you'll give her only one warning. This will help your child recognize that the warning is a signal. Because the warning won't be repeated, it will be more meaningful. When a child hears a warning over and over, it becomes an empty threat and the child learns that it isn't likely to be administered. Instead, teach your child that you give only one warning.

Set the Reward for Following the Rules

Tell your child clearly and specifically what she will earn for following your rules. Again, be clear and detailed. A good example of a reward is earning five chips or stickers (as per the contract you've already established). This underscores the need to have a well-functioning behavioral contract before attempting this step. If your child is used to the idea that good behaviors allow her to earn points (in the form of stickers or chips) that can be exchanged for privileges and rewards, she'll easily recognize the value of trying hard to earn additional points.

Sometimes, it may be preferable to set a direct, primary reinforcer (i.e., using a consequence that in itself has a rewarding value) rather than a secondary reinforcer (one that only becomes valuable when exchanged for something else). Especially with a child that is five years old or younger, it may be better to reward your child immediately after the completion of the task. Stickers work well with some children. You can also use a treat (such as a piece of candy) or a similar, tangible reward. However, it's important to do so only after a clear, detailed, and realistic rule was initially set. The reward is given only after your child was successful in following the stated expectation. If you use food as a reward, try to do so infrequently and continue to search for other reinforcers that your child will like. It is not advisable to teach a child that food is a frequent reward because she may grow up to reward herself too freely with food treats, and such behaviors contribute to weight management problems. Still, with some out-of-control children for whom nothing else seems to work, using food to teach better behavior is probably better than continuing a cycle of intense conflict and not using anything at all.

Make sure you set a reward that is commensurate with the level of difficulty of the target setting. For example, your child should earn a greater reward for following the rules in a difficult setting (for example, in a place of worship) than for a short trip to the store. When setting rewards for a car trip, it's helpful to break the trip into segments and have your child earn rewards during each segment of the trip. If you are visiting friends or family, let them know what your rules are so that your child knows that everyone in that setting has the same expectations of him. Sometimes, when visiting others, you may need to adjust your own expectations for your child's behavior in order to accommodate the rules of your host, even if those rules are different from the rules you set at home. It's important to send your child a consistent message about what is acceptable and expected within a given setting.

Set the Consequences for Not Following the Rules

If your child doesn't follow the rules, she won't get the reward. In many situations, this may be sufficient and is a natural consequence for not following the rules—if your child doesn't earn something, she won't get it. Sometimes, however, it may be helpful to set a negative consequence for breaking the rules, especially if breaking the rules may result in significant consequences (e.g., when the child may place herself in danger by running away from you). The most appropriate negative consequences are commensurate with the reward the child would've earned if the rules had been followed. If your child earns five chips for following the rules, she loses five chips for not following the rules. In some situations (for example, places where following a rule may be especially difficult, such as a place of worship), this additional motivator may improve the likelihood of success and help your child try harder. Have your child repeat the stated consequences to you—what she'll earn by following the rules, and what she'll lose by not following them.

Go into the Target Setting

After the rules and consequences are clearly set, you are ready to go into the target setting. Monitor your child's behavior to make sure that the rules are being obeyed. At first break of the rules, or when your child is about to break them, warn her of the rules and the consequences. It's important that you give your child *only one* warning. If your child is able to follow the rules through the duration of the trip, praise her, point out how much you appreciate her ability to exercise good self-control, and administer the positive consequence as soon as it's practical. Help your child feel a sense of accomplishment about her achievement.

Administer the Appropriate Consequence

If, after you issued the warning, your child breaks the rules again, inform her of the loss of reward or negative consequence and administer it as soon as it is practical. Try not to make it sound vengeful. You do not want your child to feel any worse than she already does. Instead, point out to her that she will have another opportunity in the future to try to succeed.

When Time-Out Is Necessary

Out-of-control children, upon learning that they have lost a reward or will receive some negative consequence, often become upset. It is important to attend to this situation immediately. If you see that your child is becoming angry and is beginning to get worked up, intervene right away. Pull her aside and attempt to calm her down. Try not to do this in front of others. Your child will likely become more upset if she gets embarrassed in front of other family members, friends, or strangers who witness the event. Instead, find a quiet, private spot, and speak softly and calmly, even if your child doesn't do so. Remain composed and in control, and don't yell at your child; that will only upset her further. Ask your child whether she needs a minute or two to calm down. If you see that your child is too agitated to return, take a little more time.

If your child truly loses control and begins to have a tantrum, administer time-out (see step 3) as soon as possible. Find an isolated spot where you can place your child to calm down. When visiting family or friends, you can use a bathroom, bedroom, or den where no one else is at the time. In a restaurant or a store, you may use a stall in a public restroom. When no practical place seems available, you may place them in the car.

Time-Out in the Car

To administer time-out in your car, remove your child to your car and place her inside, preferably in the backseat. Give your child instructions that are consistent with step 3. Communicate to her that she'll be in the car until she's able to calm down. Close the doors, but don't get in. Instead, stand next to the car and make sure that your child remains inside. Try not to make direct eye contact, because it will only incite her to engage you further in the tantrum. It may be helpful to turn away, but keep an eye on the car and your child. If your child is truly out of control and begins to behave dangerously while in the car, get in next to her and hold her on the backseat.

Be sensible about when to use your car as a time-out setting. Don't do so in extreme weather (e.g., in the height of summer or winter) or when the car is parked in a busy spot where your child may become endangered if she opens the door. Be mindful of what items you have in your car, and make sure that nothing in your child's immediate vicinity can be harmful or dangerous. Beyond these simple, common-sense precautions, the modern automobile is actually quite safe as a time-out spot. Without a key in the ignition, most cars can't be started or shifted into gear, so the car can't become mobile.

After your child has calmed down sufficiently, return to the setting but don't give any further opportunities to earn rewards. If your child acts out again, repeat the time-out.

Putting It All Together

Consider how the example of Bobbi and her mom would look when the techniques described in this chapter are implemented:

While Mom and Bobbi are still in the car, before they enter the store, Mom says to Bobbi, "Bobbi, please look at me." When she does, Mom says to her, "We're going to go into the store, and I have two rules for you to follow. First, you have to stay next to me and not wander away. Second, don't place anything in the basket that I don't say is okay. Please repeat these two rules to me."

"Okay, Mom. I have to stay by you and I can't put things in the cart unless you say it's okay."

"Very good. Now, let me tell you what will happen if you are able to follow these rules. First, I'll buy you a piece of candy when we are on the way out of the store. Second, when we get home, I'll give you five chips to place in your jar. Now, please repeat to me what will happen if you follow these rules."

"I'll get a piece of candy—and you'll give me five chips."

"Very good. Now, let me tell you what will happen if you don't follow these rules. I won't buy you any candy, and when we get home, I'll take five chips out of your jar. Do you understand? Please repeat to me what will happen."

"Okay, Mom. You won't buy candy, and you'll take five chips away."

"Very good. Remember, I'll only give you one warning before you lose these things. Do you understand?"

"Yes, Mom."

"Very good. Let's go in. Try hard. I'm sure you'll do really well with these rules."

Mom and Bobbi go in the store. The first time Bobbi wanders away, Mom gets her and says, "Bobbi, while we were in the car, what were the two rules I asked you to follow?"

Bobbi explains these to Mom, and Mom helps Bobbi along in case she forgot. Then Mom says, "Okay, Bobbi, now what did I say will happen if you do and do not follow these rules?"

Again, Bobbi explains these to Mom and Mom helps her along, if needed. Then Mom says, "What just happened? Why did I have to go get you?" Mom helps Bobbi recognize that she just wandered away. Then Mom says, "Okay, Bobbi, as I said in the car, this is your one warning. If you break either of the rules again, you know what will happen."

Mom and Bobbi continue shopping. If Bobbi completes the trip while successfully following the rules, Mom praises her, buys the candy on the way out, and puts five chips in her jar right after they get home.

On the other hand, if Bobbi breaks the rules again, Mom repeats the above interaction and helps Bobbi remember what the rules and consequences were and what action she just performed that broke these rules. She calmly reminds Bobbi of the consequences and attempts to complete the shopping trip. If Bobbi becomes upset, Mom goes into a corner of the store and tries to calm Bobbi down, giving her a moment to compose herself. If Bobbi works herself up into a tantrum, Mom leaves the shopping cart, asks one of the clerks to watch it for her, and takes Bobbi out to the car to implement time-out. When Bobbi calms down sufficiently, Mom and Bobbi return and complete the shopping trip.

A Worthwhile Investment of Time and Effort

This interaction, especially if Bobbi breaks the rules and doesn't earn the reward, takes more planning, time, and effort on the mother's part. However, the extra time and effort is a worthwhile investment, considering that Bobbi is likely to learn something from this interaction. Doing this only once won't guarantee that Bobbi won't have problems again on the next trip to the store, but consistency in using this procedure will likely result in diminishing problems over time. On the other hand, the interaction described earlier in the chapter didn't result in any appreciable learning, and Bobbi was still likely to exhibit problems in the store during subsequent shopping trips.

As with all other techniques, consistency and repetition greatly improve the likelihood of success. Use this technique with your child two to three times a week, perhaps every other day. Depending on the level of difficulties that you experience (and your child's age), you may need to start with just one rule and relatively short trips. As your child begins to exhibit success, you can then gradually expand the time and add additional rules to be followed. As before, work on this technique for at least two weeks before proceeding on to address other problems.

Checklist 7

Step 7: Manage Out-of-Home Situations

Procedure

1. Set the Rules

- Before going into the target setting, get eye contact and explain to your child the rules that you want her to follow.

- Set no more than two or three rules.

- Be clear and specific. The rules should not be "Don't misbehave," but should be very precise, such as: "Don't run away from me," or "Don't take things off the shelves while in the store."

2. Set the Reward for Following the Rules

- Tell your child clearly and specifically what she'll earn for following your rules.

- Examples of rewards: five chips, earning a snack you will buy while in the store, earning a small prize, choice of dessert, getting a "freebie" privilege, choosing a videotape for the whole family to watch.

- Make sure you set a reward that is commensurate with the level of difficulty of the target setting. For example, your child should earn a greater reward for following your rules in a difficult setting (e.g., in church) than for a short trip to the store.

- If setting rewards for a car trip, break it up into segments and have your child earn rewards during each segment of the trip.

- When visiting friends or family, let them know your rules, so your child will know that everyone has the same expectations of her.

3. Set the Consequences for Not Following the Rules

- Your child doesn't get the reward.

- Have your child repeat the rules, rewards, and consequences to you before you go in.

4. Go into the Target Setting

- At first break of the rules, or when your child is about to break them, warn her of the consequences. *Only give her ONE warning!*

5. Administer the Appropriate Consequence

- If she breaks the rules again, inform her of the loss of reward. Don't let her earn any more rewards this trip.

- If she becomes uncontrollable, give her a time-out in a spot such as a bathroom, an empty corner, or a chair in the waiting room.

- If no other appropriate place is available, use the car for time-out:

    - Interrupt whatever you are doing and take your child out to the car.

    - Place her inside the car and close the doors (don't get in).

    - Give instructions, as during the in-home time-out procedure.

- Stay outside of the car and make sure your child is inside. It may help to turn away from the windows so she won't engage you in conflict.

- After appropriate time has elapsed, inform her that you will now return to the previous setting but no reward will be given. If there is further acting out, repeat time-out.

If your child followed the rules, make sure to give praise and reward.

CHAPTER 10

Step 8—Teach Your Child to Stop Interrupting

If you've just completed the implementation of the technique described in the previous chapter—congratulations! You're well on your way through the program. By now you should be seeing significant overall improvement in your child's behavior problems. In the last step, you learned a method of expanding the use of the behavioral contract to address additional problems, those you may encounter in out-of-home situations. If you skipped the previous chapter, I encourage you to go back and read the first few paragraphs of that chapter before you proceed with the step described in this chapter. It's important to make sure that the behavioral contract you have implemented is working well and running smoothly.

A well-implemented behavioral contract is a powerful and flexible tool. Not only does it allow you to address day-to-day problems that your child has been having, but it can be used to address more sporadic problems and difficulties in specific settings and situations. It is effective because, through the use of consistent consequences, it gradually teaches the child to think before he makes a choice of behavior. Over time, this stop-and-think approach becomes more automatic, and overall improvement is noted across the board. Along the way, you can tailor the contract to address specific problems.

One of these problems is interrupting adults, a behavior that is typical of very young children (maybe age two or three) but that generally improves with age. Still, some children old enough to know better continue to interrupt adults and seem unaware that there is a right time and a wrong time to approach a parent.

Consider the following example: Seven-year-old Jimmy is watching television in the living room. Nearby, in the kitchen, his mother is preparing dinner. The phone rings and the mother answers. About a minute into the conversation, while she is on the telephone, Jimmy walks into the kitchen and begins to talk to his mom.

"Mom, Mom," he tugs on her sleeve while she's trying to continue to focus on her telephone conversation. "Mom, Mom," he continues to repeat.

Mom pauses the telephone conversation and says, "What do you want? Can't you see I'm on the phone? You'll have to wait until I'm done."

Jimmy pauses for a moment, but then starts again: "Mom, Mom," he repeats while the mother again tries to ignore him. After a few moments, Mom again pauses the conversation.

"I told you, I'm on the phone! What is it?"

"My teacher said that you have to call her to change the date of your meeting."

"Okay, tell me later—I'm on the phone."

Mom again returns to the conversation. Jimmy pauses, starts to leave the kitchen, and then stops and turns around and approaches Mom again. "Mom, Mom, Mom ..."

Mom again tries to ignore him, but after a minute or so of his repeated interruptions, she again pauses the conversation. "What is it this time? I told you I'm on the phone!"

"Mom, Mom, Mom ..."

"Go to your room. I'm on the phone!"

"But Mom, I just need to tell you that you have to sign my permission slip to go on the class trip to the museum next month."

"Can't you see I'm on the phone? What's wrong with you?"

Jimmy starts whining and gets louder. "But you have to sign the permission slip ..."

Mom is now losing patience. With the telephone in her hand, she tries to drag Jimmy out of the kitchen while he is now crying and trying to stop her. He continues to protest loudly, "But I have to tell you something and it's important! Moooooom!"

By now, his mother is furious. She shoves him out of the room, yelling that now he has done it and he is grounded to his room through the weekend. He is screaming and crying and says, "You're a horrible mom and I hate you!"

Mom tries to return to the telephone conversation, apologizing to the other party on the phone. She complains that she doesn't understand why Jimmy acts this way and that she thought that he'd grow out of this by now and start to act his age. Jimmy continues to scream, "You're a horrible mom and I hate you!"

This is a good example of a common situation that occurs regularly in many homes, where a problem behavior that is initially annoying escalates into a major conflict that upsets you and your child. You may wonder: Why is it that my child often interrupts adults on the telephone and during in-person conversations with other adults? What can I do to stop this? There are many factors that contribute to this problem, and understanding these may be helpful to the parents of children who have problems with interrupting.

The above example holds many clues. As the mom points out toward the end, Jimmy has engaged in this behavior since he was little. Apparently, Mom found it easier to tolerate his interrupting when he was four years old, but she feels that by now he should have learned better manners. It's true that most young children tend to interrupt adults. This is an impulsive act. Young children possess little self-control, and most thoughts or urges that come into their minds are converted into action. A young child will approach his parents with a thought or a question whenever he thinks of it, regardless of what the parents may be doing at the time.

Why Do Children Interrupt?

Why do some children outgrow this tendency while others seem to continue to interrupt well into their middle childhood? The answer lies in the children's overall ability to use self-control. Those children who tend to have continuing problems with impulse control in later childhood are likely to exhibit this tendency in many ways: poor judgment, frequent lying (usually in impulsive attempts to cover up acts for which they think they'll get into trouble), blurting things out, not being careful around traffic, and so on.

One of the ways that children exhibit impulsivity is through interrupting adults. Here, the mother in the above example is right—Jimmy continues to exhibit a problem that most children outgrow by his age. Most likely, Jimmy is an impulsive child with poor self-control that causes many behavioral problems, one of which is interrupting adults. In other words, Jimmy is the kind of child whose parents need help to address behaviors that are difficult to control, and you're likely reading this book because you are the parent of a similarly impulsive child. Hopefully, what you are reading in this book is helpful to you in your quest to diminish those problems.

"He's Interrupting on Purpose!"

Sometimes, you may feel that your child purposefully waits until you get on the telephone, or until company comes over, to start talking to you. It's as though he is purposefully waiting to interrupt and annoy. Be careful not to make this assumption, as it tends to vilify your child. Parents who believe that their children misbehave specifically to make them mad generally get very angry at their children and overreact to their transgressions.

Instead, recognize that children exhibit this behavior in many situations. Only sometimes do parents feel that it is a problem; at other times, this behavior may seem tolerable, even acceptable. Interruptions illustrate this point. In all likelihood, your child frequently approaches you, spontaneously and out of the blue, to say something that just came into his mind. When you are performing a common household task, you may not notice that he just interrupted you. Similarly, when you watch television or chat with your spouse (or another household member), you also may not notice that your child is impulsively approaching you (or someone else) to talk about something he just thought of. However, when this occurs at an inconvenient and annoying time, such as during a telephone conversation, you may not recall that this happens at other times as well and you may feel that he is awaiting the most inopportune moment to interrupt.

Additional Contributing Factors

Additional components of the above situation contributed to such an escalation of the conflict. The mother wasn't consistent in her instructions, and rather than giving specific commands, she usually expressed her expectations in the form of a question. In addition, she was not consistent. There was no reason for Jimmy to stop interrupting, other than to avoid Mom's annoyance (which, by itself, is usually not a sufficient reason for a child to change a habit or a behavioral pattern). In addition, Mom was becoming more and more annoyed and agitated as the incident continued, and her own agitation contributed to Jimmy's escalation. Eventually, he lost control, no doubt further exacerbated by the fact that he overheard his mom embarrassing him on the telephone to the person with whom she was conversing.

Preparation

Before I get to specific instructions about addressing interruptions, I want to restate a few general principles. Never put your instructions in the form of a question. Always make them clear and specific (see step 1). It's best to state your instructions before a situation occurs, and remember the importance of eye contact (again, see step 1). When that's not possible, interrupt what you are doing (e.g., ask the person on the telephone to wait for a moment) and, using the procedure in step 1, state your command. Control your own level of anger and frustration, and don't insult or embarrass the child—that will only lead to significant escalation of conflict and a tempter tantrum.

The Plan

Now that you understand why children interrupt, how do you address this problem? We will follow a technique briefly discussed by Barkley (2000), significantly expanded and elaborated upon through my research (Kapalka 2003b) and practice. The principles and steps are similar to those that you used to address out-of-home situations in step 7:

- Set the rules.

- Set the reward for following the rules.

- Set the consequences for not following the rules.

- Practice the situation.

- Repeat the process.

Now we'll address each of these components in detail as it pertains to preventing interruptions.

Set the Rules

It's best to establish the structure necessary to address this problem before you become involved in a telephone conversation. Select a day when you are ready to begin working on this problem. At the start of the day, using the techniques outlined in step 1, set the rules for what you expect of your child when you are on the telephone. Be clear and specific, and focus on that which is most important. For example, say, "When I am on the telephone, don't interrupt. Wait until I am through to tell me whatever you want to tell me." You may want to ask your child to repeat to you what you just said.

Set the Reward for Following the Rules

Next, set the reward for following the rules. Tell your child clearly and specifically what he will earn for following your rules. Again, be clear and detailed. Because you now have a functional behavioral contract in which you give chips or stickers as rewards for good behavior, it will feel natural to you to offer a chip reward ("When you follow these rules and don't interrupt me while I am on the telephone, I'll give you two chips"). Your child has gotten used to the idea that good behaviors allow him to earn these rewards, so he'll easily recognize the value of trying hard to earn them. With very small children, it may be better to reward the child immediately after the completion of the task with a piece of candy or a similar tangible reward. However, it's important to do so only after a clear, detailed, and realistic rule was initially set. The reward should be given only after the child was successful in following the stated rule.

Set the Consequences for Not Following the Rules

Next, set the consequences for not following the rules you just elucidated. First, your child won't get the reward that you previously indicated. In many situations, this may be sufficient and is a natural consequence for not following the rules. If he doesn't earn something, he won't get it. Sometimes, however, it may be helpful to set a negative consequence for breaking the rules. The most appropriate negative consequences are those that are commensurate with the reward your child was going to earn if the rules were followed. For example, if your child was promised that he would earn two chips for not interrupting, he will lose two chips if he interrupts the conversation. Have your child repeat the stated consequences to you: what he'll earn by following the rules, and what he'll lose by not following the rules.

Practice the Situation

Once the rules and consequences are clearly set, practice the target situation. Here, you'll have to implement some things differently than you did in the previous steps. Sure, you can wait for a phone call. However, there are too many variables that cannot be controlled in this manner. You don't know when you will receive a call, and this will make it difficult for your child to continue to remember the rules you just set. Moreover, the duration of the conversation will be unpredictable, and as the conversation becomes longer, it'll be more difficult for your child to continue to exhibit sufficient self-control to suppress the impulse to interrupt you.

Instead, this step will be most effective, and you'll experience the greatest improvement, if you create frequent opportunities for your child to practice this task. Let a friend or relative (use more than one person if you can) know that you'll be calling them several times a day over the next one to two weeks to allow your child to practice not interrupting you on the phone. "Dummy" calls also work. At the start of the day when you're ready to begin to work on this problem, tell your child that you have to make several phone calls today and each time you're on the phone, you have some rules for him to follow. Set the positive and negative consequences. Have your child repeat these rules and consequences back to you. Then, after a few minutes, place a practice call: Call someone (or just pretend that you're calling) and stay on the telephone for just a few minutes. Determine the length of these "conversations" by your child's age. The younger your child, the shorter they should be (initially). For a four- or five-year-old, a two- to three-minute call is sufficient to start. For a child who is seven or eight, a conversation of five minutes or so would be fine.

Before you place the "call," it's helpful to tell your child, "I'm about to place a call. Remember what we said before about the rules and the consequences." Then, make the call. Watch the time to make sure that you don't exceed your initial target length. If your child comes into the room while you are calling, you may want to remind him of the rules you discussed with a hand gesture—for example, raise your hand in a "stop" motion—but don't give any warnings. If your child interrupts, pause the call you are making. Calmly escort your child out of the room, remind him of the rules you previously set, and go back to finish the conversation. After you get off the telephone, approach your child, calmly review what happened, and state that he'll have another chance to try again later.

Repeat the Process

It's very important to make these practice runs repeatedly. The first day you implement the procedure, plan at least five practice runs. The more opportunities you give your child to practice a situation, the more learning will take place. Don't be discouraged if your child interrupts the first few times you run through the "call." It may take a few tries before he is able to exercise enough self-control to suppress that urge. Obtain a baseline of at least four or five consecutive successes before you extend the time of your conversations. After a baseline is obtained, increase the time of the call by approximately two minutes, and practice again until you obtain another baseline of success. Gradually extend the time until you reach the length of a typical telephone conversation.

Some readers may ask, "Okay, but what do I do when I receive a call and my child interrupts?" You can easily incorporate this into the procedure. While the phone is ringing, remind your child about the rules that were previously set, and proceed as above. The more practice opportunities you give your child to master this skill, the more that skill will transfer to other similar situations, and you'll begin to see a decrease in your child's interruptions.

Using This Technique in Other Situations

The technique described herein is flexible and may be used to master other settings and problems with interruptions in other situations. For example, if you want your child to stop interrupting your face-to-face conversations with others, you can similarly create practice opportunities. As with the "dummy" calls, you can instead create practice runs of short conversations during which you'll allow your child to gradually become able to suppress the impulse to interrupt. After you obtain a sufficient baseline, gradually start increasing the length of the conversations.

Putting It All Together

Children interrupt because it is hard for them to resist the impulse to say something whenever the thought comes into their minds. By implementing the technique outlined in this chapter, you are creating opportunities for your child to practice resisting this impulse. Placing phone calls is a convenient way to do so. Before the call, make sure to set the rule, the consequence for following the rule, and the consequence for not following the rule. Make sure your child understands. Place the calls and administer the consequences after each call. Repeat this often. Remember, "practice makes perfect," so the more practice opportunities you give your child, the more success you'll experience. When your child is successful in resisting the impulse to interrupt a phone call, expand this procedure to address other situations your child commonly interrupts (for example, in-person conversations).

As before, work on this technique for at least two weeks before you proceed on to other problems.

Checklist 8

Step 8: Teach Your Child to Stop Interrupting

Most commonly, children interrupt parents on the telephone. Pick a quiet day when you can spend thirty to sixty minutes initially on the procedure outlined below. You'll need to do it daily for at least one to two weeks, so be sure to allow sufficient time in your schedule.

Procedure

1. Set the Rules

- On the day you begin the procedure, before making the first call, explain the rules to your child: He should stay quiet and not interrupt you for the duration of the call.

- Be clear and specific. The rule should not be "Don't misbehave," but "Don't interrupt me when I'm on the phone."

2. Set the Reward for Following the Rules

- Tell your child clearly and specifically what he will earn for following your rules. One or two chips per call works best.

3. Set the Consequences for Not Following the Rules

- Your child doesn't get the reward.

- You may also use a comparable chip cost for not following the rules.

- Have your child repeat the rules, rewards, and consequences to you before you begin.

4. Practice the Situation

- Prepare a friend or a relative to whom you'll make several calls per day for the next one to two weeks in order to get your child used to allowing you interruption-free phone calls. Use more than one person if you can. "Dummy" calls can also work.

- Set the duration of the initial call. It should be about two minutes for children under age five, and about five minutes for older children.

- Tell your child you're going to make a call. Remind him of the rules and consequences you discussed earlier.

- If your child breaks the rules, pause your phone call to inform him of the loss of reward. Continue with your call for the duration you set beforehand.

- If your child becomes uncontrollable, use time-out.

- *If your child followed the rules, make sure to give praise and the promised reward.*

5. Repeat the Process

- If your child wasn't successful, repeat the process about fifteen minutes apart.

- If successful, repeat the process until you get four to five consecutive successful calls.

- Then, increase the time by two minutes or so and try again until you get four or five consecutive successful calls at the new time interval, then increase again and repeat.

Incoming Calls

After about two weeks of mostly successful outgoing calls, start to use the above procedure for incoming calls.

- When the phone is ringing, quickly remind your child about the rules and consequences (positive and negative).

- Take the call, and limit the duration, as in the above procedure.

- As with outgoing calls, repeat the procedure, and, when repeatedly successful, increase the duration of calls.

CHAPTER 11

Step 9—Help Your Child with Transitions

You have come to the final technique described in this program. You now have a sizeable toolbox of techniques that you can use to address a variety of problems. Overall, you should now be noticing a significant improvement in your child's behavior problems. In the previous two chapters, you learned methods of expanding the use of the behavioral contract to address additional problems with acting out in out-of-home situations and interruptions. If you skipped the previous two chapters, I encourage you to go back and read the first few paragraphs of chapter 9 before proceeding with the step described in this chapter. It's important to make sure that the behavioral contract you have implemented is working well and running smoothly.

A well-implemented behavioral contract allows you to successfully address day-to-day problems, and it also works well in addressing more sporadic problems and difficulties in specific settings and situations. Through the use of consistent consequences, it gradually teaches the child to think before he makes a choice of behavior. Over time, this becomes more automatic, and improvement is noted across the board.

The contract can be used to address a variety of problems. For instance, some children act out while transitioning from one activity (such as playing with toys or watching TV) to another (such as getting ready to go out or to bed). Consider the following example: Nancy is five years old. She can be a handful, and turning off the TV, washing her hands for dinner, and cleaning up her toys is often a problem. She is argumentative, and when prevented from having her way she has tantrums and loses control.

Nancy is watching cartoons on TV in the living room. It is time for dinner, but Dad is expecting that, as usual, Nancy will not want to leave the TV and will refuse to come for dinner. Dad comes into the living room. "Nancy, you have to turn off the TV, it's time for dinner."

Nancy proclaims, "No!"

Dad leaves the living room and begins to set the table. In a few minutes, Dad calls from the kitchen, "Nancy, turn off the TV now because we have to eat dinner."

"No, the cartoon is not finished yet!"

Dad begins to serve the food. From the kitchen, he yells, "Nancy, you have to come now!"

Nancy gives no response. Dad continues to bring out the food. From the dining room, he yells, "Nancy, I told you to turn off the TV now!"

Nancy, again, gives no response. Dad is getting very angry. He knows that this is when Nancy starts screaming, yelling, and kicking. Dad tries again, "Nancy!"

"I don't want to eat. I'm not hungry."

Dad is getting really mad. He knows that letting Nancy skip dinner will result in Nancy becoming very hungry an hour later and demanding dinner, and he'll have to reheat dinner for her, an additional task that he would rather avoid. He's thinking, "Here we go again." He storms into the living room, yelling, "I said turn off that TV now! What's the matter with you? Didn't you hear what I said?!"

"No!"

Dad doesn't know what to do. The dinner is already served, and extending this interaction much longer will make the meal cold. He goes over, grabs Nancy by the arms, and drags her off the couch. The TV is still on. Nancy starts screaming, yelling, crying, and kicking. She is squirming and tries to pull herself away from Dad. She succeeds and falls to the floor, flailing about in an out-of-control fit of anger. Dad thinks, "I knew this was going to happen!"

Dad again grabs Nancy by the hand and drags her into the dining room. He sits her on the chair at the table. Nancy continues to thrash about. Accidentally, she hits the place setting and silverware goes flying all around.

Dad pulls Nancy's chair back from the table, and starts shouting, "What the heck is wrong with you?! Knock this off or you are going to go to bed now!" Nancy just keeps crying. Dad lets Nancy just sit there for a while, crying and screaming, and after a few minutes he pushes her chair back toward the table, and places some food on Nancy's plate to eat. Nancy is still carrying on and pushes the plate away. Dad is thinking, "No wonder I feel so stressed. When will we even be able to get through a meal with her in peace?"

Why Are Transitions Difficult for Some Children?

Why do some children tend to have such difficulties stopping a current activity and transitioning into a different one? What can be done to address this? As with all behavior problems, there are many contributing factors. Understanding them may be helpful to parents of children who commonly have these difficulties.

Look at some details from the above example. Nancy's dad experiences this problem on a regular basis. When Nancy is involved in one activity, she's resistant to transition away from it. One reason is obvious—Nancy is enjoying what she's doing and she doesn't want to stop. Consider a situation where you, a normally functioning adult, are asked to interrupt an activity that you are enjoying. Let's say you are watching an interesting television show and someone approaches you and tells you that you have to stop. What is your reaction? You probably think to yourself, "No, I don't want to. I'm not finished." However, before you put these thoughts into words, you probably reason through the situation. You may think to yourself, "I don't want to, but it's dinnertime, so I guess I have to do it." Thus, before you select a response and decide what you will do, you reason through the situation and then select an appropriate response.

Many children, however, don't have such well-developed abilities to reason through a situation, and so your child's initial response is likely to be, "No, I don't want to. I'm having too much fun." What your child does next depends on her self-control. Children with good self-control may pause, think, and recognize that Mom said it's dinnertime, so even if I don't want to, I have to come. However, a child who has poor self-control will have difficulties suppressing that initial impulse and will react negatively, opposing your attempt to transition her away. Nancy is that kind of child and her parents need help in addressing the many problems that stem from her impulsivity and poor self-control. The techniques described in this book target many of these problems.

Preparation

The above example is also notable for the father's expectations. Because he has experienced similar problems many times, he expects the worst. With every one of Nancy's refusals, Dad becomes angrier and more agitated. As Dad escalates, so does Nancy. Eventually they both reach a point of no return in their self-control and anger, and the interaction turns into a physical confrontation. Instead, it would have been more productive for Nancy's father to remain in control and not let his anger and frustration dominate his response. If he remained calm, in all likelihood Nancy wouldn't have escalated nearly as much and the interaction wouldn't have resulted in such an unpleasant confrontation.

There are additional components that contributed to the problem. The father obviously did not follow good practices of issuing a command, as stated in steps 1 and 2. Consequently, his commands weren't nearly as effective as they could have been, and they resulted in his needing to repeat himself several times. With each repetition, the situation escalated. The father also did not prepare himself sufficiently. When addressing a situation that has, in the past, resulted in difficulties and conflicts, it's crucial to make an extra effort to stay calm.

The Plan

So, how should you address problems with transitions? Again, we will expand on a technique briefly mentioned by Barkley (2000). Follow the principles that were previously used in steps 7 and 8, modified slightly to address the particular needs of this problem:

- Set the rules.

- Set the reward for following the rules.

- Set the consequences for not following the rules.

- Give sufficient warnings.

- Implement the transition.

- Practice.

We'll review each of these components as it pertains to addressing problems with transitions.

Set the Rules

As with steps 7 and 8, it is necessary to establish appropriate structure before the situation takes place. In advance of the actual time when you have to transition your child from one activity to another, follow the techniques outlined in step 1 and set the rules for what needs to occur during a transition. Be clear and specific. For example, "In a few minutes, we'll have to come to dinner, so when I tell you to turn off the TV, you'll have to do so."

You are preparing your child ahead of time so that when the transition comes, she is not caught off guard. Children with poor self-control become more upset when a change in activities or a change in expectations comes out of the blue. Without sufficient warning, their brain does not have a chance to prepare, and so the oppositional reaction is likely to be much stronger. Instead, you must help your child's brain prepare for what is going to happen.

Set the Reward for Following the Rules

Tell your child clearly and specifically what she will earn for following your rules. Since you now have a functional behavioral contract where you give chips or stickers as a reward for good behavior, it will feel natural for you to offer a chip reward, such as, "When you turn off the TV when I tell you, I'll give you two chips." Because your child has gotten used to the idea that good behaviors allow her to earn these rewards, she'll easily recognize the value of trying hard to do so. With very small children, it may be better to reward the child immediately after the completion of the task with a piece of candy or a similar tangible reward. However, it's important to do so only after a clear, detailed, and realistic rule was initially set. The reward is given only after your child was successful in following the stated rule.

Set the Consequences for Not Following the Rules

Next, set the consequences for not transitioning. First, your child won't get the reward that you previously indicated. In many situations, this may be sufficient and is a natural consequence for not following the rules. If she doesn't earn something, she won't receive it. Sometimes, however, it may be helpful to set a negative consequence for breaking the rules. The most appropriate negative consequences are those commensurate with the reward she was going to earn if the rules were followed. If she was promised that she'd earn two chips for turning off the TV when needed, she will lose two chips if she doesn't comply. Have her repeat the stated consequences to you: what she'll earn by transitioning appropriately, and what she'll lose by not doing so.

Give Sufficient Warnings

It's important to give your child these instructions ahead of the actual time of transition. This gives your child some time to prepare herself mentally that a transition will take place. When a transition is expected, it makes it easier for your child to exercise self-control, even if the transition is not desirable (e.g., when your child has to terminate an activity that she enjoys in order to come to dinner).

Sufficient warning must be provided. Sometimes, you may want to follow a "three bells" approach. This is similar to what is used in theaters and at concerts during intermissions: One bell means that the audience must prepare to return to the theater, two bells mean that the show will begin soon, and three bells mean that the show is starting now. This works well when applied at home. The first "bell" occurs when the parent sets the transition rule with the child. The second "bell" should be a warning that reminds the child that the transition is about to take place. It should occur a minute or two before the actual transition. The third "bell" signals the start of the actual transition.

Try to make the time frame of the transition's occurrence meaningful to your child. With a child who comfortably tells time, it's okay to have her look at the clock and state that the transition will take place in, say, five minutes. Then, the second "bell" can come about two or three minutes later. With a younger child who doesn't yet have a sufficient concept of time lapse, giving a number of minutes is usually not meaningful, because she can't relate to how long a time frame is actually involved. Instead, it is better to find a time frame that's meaningful to the child. For example, if the child is watching a TV show, a parent can say, "When the next commercial comes on you'll have to turn off the TV." Another suggestion is to use timers. Set a timer for five minutes and place it within your child's view. Then about midway through the period, come in and give her a reminder (the second "bell"). The third "bell" occurs when the timer goes off and the transition must begin.

Implement the Transition

Once these rules and consequences are clearly set, implement the transition. Be firm but calm. Don't issue any more warnings, and transition your child immediately, regardless of her response. If your child transitions successfully, administer the positive consequence and praise her for doing such a good job following your rules. If she doesn't transition as you asked, don't allow her to continue with the activity. Turn off the TV or video game player or pick up the toys. Don't yell or begin a conflict. Just inform your child of the appropriate negative consequence (as per the rules you set previously).

What if she begins to have a tantrum? You may have to administer time-out, as described in step 3. This underscores the need for you to be prepared for whatever responses you may get from your child. Again, allow enough time and don't place yourself in a situation where you feel rushed and cannot do what you know is necessary to sufficiently address a situation. If a time-out is not feasible (for example, when you have to get ready to leave the house), help your child along with the transition, even if she is crying and carrying on. Most important, follow through with what you said would happen and administer the negative consequence you previously set as soon as it is practical.

Practice

As with the other techniques described in this book, it is necessary to practice this step as often as possible. The more opportunities you give your child to get used to this new way in which you'll implement transitions, the more she'll become used to this technique and begin to comply. When you first begin this technique, practice several transitions per day (involving various situations). As your child becomes accustomed to this technique, she will begin to exhibit more self-control at transition times, and you'll note an improvement. Be consistent and give it time. The longer you use this technique, the more likely you are to see positive changes.

Putting It All Together

During transitions, children act out primarily because they find it hard to resist the impulse to continue with the present activity. By utilizing a warning, you are preparing your child's brain to process the change that is forthcoming. Remember to use a time frame that is meaningful to your child. Set positive and negative consequences, and implement the transition. Afterward, administer the appropriate consequence.

Checklist 9

Step 9: Help Your Child with Transitions

Transitions from one activity to another are often difficult. Your child may try to continue with the ongoing activity or may become agitated and start acting out.

Procedure

1. **Set the Rules**

   ■ About five minutes before you need the transition to take place, warn your child that at a specific point you'll need her to perform a specific action.

2. **Set the Reward for Following the Rules**

   ■ Inform her of a special reward she'll earn for transitioning when stated.

3. **Set the Consequences for Not Following the Rules**

   ■ You may also set a negative consequence for not transitioning when needed.

4. **Give Sufficient Warnings**

   ■ About two minutes before the transition, issue a "second bell" warning.

5. **Implement the Transition**

   ■ Use an attentional cue (such as "Look at me").

   ■ Give the transition command. Remind your child of the reward for doing it immediately.

- Look at her for fifteen to twenty seconds after the transition command.

- If your child is compliant on the first try, dispense reward and praise. If noncompliant, administer the consequences and proceed with the transition.

6. Practice

As with the procedure for interrupting, practice this technique as often as possible.

CHAPTER 12

Putting It All Together

Congratulations on completing the program! Getting here means that you have exhibited dedication, patience, and perseverance. In completing this program, you learned to use behavioral techniques that allowed you to address many of your child's behavioral problems. I hope that using these techniques has helped you attain improvement in your child's behavior and overall manageability. By now, your child should no longer appear "out of control."

Long-Term Management

Like most parents, you have probably also learned that consistent use of the techniques described in this book requires ongoing effort. Maintaining a behavioral contract is a task that takes time. Many parents ask, "How long do I have to keep using these procedures?" The answer is, "It depends."

Steps 1 and 2

Some techniques should be utilized on an ongoing basis, without stopping. Steps 1 and 2 fall into this category. Using this method of issuing commands should become a new way of life for you. I strongly recommend that you use the checklists that accompany these steps and review them frequently. Children who have impulsive tendencies and self-control problems tend to return to old patterns of behavior quickly if parents discontinue some techniques. Accept that from this point forward you will always have to seek eye contact before issuing a command, reduce distractions when you do so, have your child repeat the command to you, and so on. If you find yourself forgetting the procedure, reread those steps and review the checklists. Even when your child becomes a teenager, continuing to use these steps will help you communicate your desires and expectations to him in a clear, consistent manner.

With teenagers, you may need to modify the follow-up look technique (step 1) to some extent. Teenagers exert themselves by challenging authority. It is an attempt on their part to figure out how much control they have over their own life and destiny. Being stared at may cause them to stare back in an attempt to win this contest of wills. Instead, obtain eye contact (or, at least, make sure you have your teenager's attention) and issue one clear, specific command. Then, instead of continuing to look right at your teenager, stay in the vicinity to communicate to him that he isn't off the hook and that you intend to stick around until you obtain compliance. You'll still be effective, and your teenager will get the message. When it comes to step 2, however, don't change the manner in which it is done. Avoiding repetition when giving commands is important for children of all ages. This step will likely continue to be effective throughout the teenage years.

Step 3

How long will you need to continue to use step 3 (time-out)? That depends. Most parents find that as they continue to use all of the techniques described in this book, their children behave more calmly and temper outbursts diminish. There are good reasons for that: You are now expressing clear and consistent expectations, the consequences are more obvious, and your child is learning more self-control. Over time, your need to use time-out may diminish. Still, you should maintain some rudimentary structure to attend to a tempter tantrum, just in case one occurs.

Remember, you're most effective as a parent when you're not caught off-guard. Preparation is a major prerequisite to successful behavior management. When you have little need for time-out, begin to encourage your child to use his own room as much as possible to work out those times when he may feel angry or upset. Encourage removal to his room as a means of getting himself under control. Help him along to get there, if necessary. If he hasn't yet acted out sufficiently to require you to administer a negative consequence, encourage him (and assist, if necessary) to go to his room to calm down, and don't make it sound like a punishment. Be clear in communicating to your child that he isn't in trouble. He can come out and join you whenever he feels ready. In this manner, your child won't view this intervention so negatively and will be much more likely to cooperate with it. This technique works well all through the teenage years.

Steps 4, 5, and 6

What about the contract? How long will you need to use the point system? In my experience, this component of the program is one that parents are most likely to discontinue when the child's problems begin to significantly diminish. I understand why this is the case. Ongoing maintenance of the contract requires time and effort. As your child begins to perform what's expected of him regularly, continuing to keep track of the list becomes a task that you may feel is no longer necessary. Similarly, as the overall problems diminish, you may feel that you no longer need to restrict your child's privileges and continue to charge for each one.

Whether it is a good idea to discontinue the contract depends on your child. More often than not, when the contract is discontinued, the child begins to gradually exhibit more problems. At first it may be sporadic, but over time, the problems may return to prior levels. With young children, and those children who are very impulsive and exhibit significant problems with self-control, it's best to continue to use the contract indefinitely, although it can be streamlined significantly. Consider the suggestions made in step 6, especially chunking.

You may also find that your child may get to a point where maintaining a comprehensive contract is no longer necessary, but there may be one or two aspects that require continuing attention (e.g., homework).

In this situation, you may use a one-to-one exchange by which completion of homework earns your child a specific privilege (e.g., the ability to get on the computer that day). This approach works especially well for a teenager, who can earn a given privilege (e.g., the use of a cell phone) by compliance with a specific rule (e.g., coming in before curfew the night before).

School performance and behavior are areas where children frequently continue to benefit from a behavioral contract. Children who have difficulties with self-control often also exhibit these difficulties in school. Younger children may struggle with out-of-seat behaviors, call out, and have difficulties with sharing; older children may be argumentative with teachers and have problems following directions. Difficulties such as these lend themselves well to a behavioral contract.

A behavioral contract that tracks the child's daily progress with regard to a finite and limited number of specific problems can be developed with help from a teacher. You may ask the teacher to rate your child's daily progress in remaining on task, not speaking out of turn (without being called upon), and remaining quiet during class (not talking). For each, you may ask the teacher to rate the day on a scale of 1 (poor) to 3 (excellent). For young children (ages four to five), you may instead use a face system by which the teacher draws a happy face for excellent, a straight face for okay, and a sad face for poor.

Restrict your child from watching TV (or another privilege) until he shows you the daily progress report from school. Then, depending on the amount of points that are indicated on the report, your child will earn a proportional amount of the privilege that day. If your child lost the report, you'll have to assume that all indices were in the poor category and restrict privilege accordingly. This approach is highly flexible and can be customized to meet your child's needs. At the same time, it provides a valuable backup that reinforces your child's need to use appropriate self-control in school. A system of this type can successfully be used with your child well into the teenage years. As your teenager gets older, you can use a ride to see friends, use of a cell phone, or even the use of the family car (for teens who drive) as privileges that can be earned through the contract.

Steps 7, 8, and 9

Steps 7 and 8 are meant to be used on an as-needed basis, and few parents administer these interventions long-term. These steps help your child gradually develop sufficient self-control to suppress the initial impulse to misbehave. If you use these procedures to help your child learn self-management skills while young, he'll continue to use these skills as he gets older.

Step 9 can be used indefinitely. Continuing to follow this procedure during transitions is likely to help your child develop a method of preparing himself for stopping an activity that he is enjoying when it is necessary to do so. This can be useful even when your child becomes a teenager. For example, if you find that your fifteen-year-old creates a scene each time you go to pick him up when it is time to come home, using step 9 and selecting positive and negative consequences meaningful to his age will likely minimize these problems. Along the way, your child is learning frustration tolerance, an important personal skill that will help him become a better-functioning adult.

Working with Extended Family and Babysitters

Another aspect to consider is the use of these techniques with extended family members. Your child's aunts, uncles, and (especially) grandparents may have an ambivalent attitude toward your behavior management program. In particular, it's not unusual for older individuals to be skeptical of some of the behavioral interventions that we have been discussing. Generational issues are important to consider. Parenting a child thirty or forty years ago was different than it is today. Many factors contribute to this difference, including social expectations, media influence, community standards, and a host of other issues that are generally beyond our individual control. Older individuals often have difficulties accepting these changes.

If you need to rely on extended family members on a regular basis to assist you with child care, consider streamlining the contract. In a manner similar to that discussed earlier with regard to school behavior, you may select a behavior or two that you want your child to work on while being watched by the family member (or babysitter). When you return, obtain a brief report from that person about your child's behavior specifically as it pertained to the rules you set beforehand. Then, in accordance with the consequences you established, administer a positive consequence for following those rules or a negative consequence for not doing so. In this manner, regardless of whether the extended family member or babysitter believes in the approach, you can still help your child learn self-control in that setting by dispensing the appropriate consequence afterward.

Conclusion

As I pointed out at the beginning of this book, the techniques described herein are not quick fixes and require ongoing effort, perseverance, and time. I hope that you've seen firsthand how using these techniques has helped your child become more manageable.

More important, by using these techniques you have helped your child develop better self-control. Managing one's impulsive tendencies and developing the ability to stop and think before you act is a major developmental task. When mastered, it helps individuals become more successful adults. The strategies described in this book were designed to help you teach your child through the consistent use of positive and negative consequences. Attaining predictability is an important aspect of this process. Over time, your child will learn to accurately anticipate that positive behaviors will meet with positive consequences, and negative behaviors will meet with negative consequences. This book was designed to help your child learn this important lesson and to help him become more manageable (and nicer to live with) in the process. I hope that you feel a sense of accomplishment and pride. You are helping your child develop a skill that will help him become a better adult.

References

Barkley, Russell. 1997. *Defiant Children: A Clinician's Manual for Assessment and Parent Training.* 2nd ed. New York: Guilford Press.

———. 2000. *Taking Charge of ADHD: The Complete, Authoritative Guide for Parents.* Rev. ed. New York: Guilford Press.

Barkley, Russell, and Christine Benton. 1998. *Your Defiant Child: Eight Steps to Better Behavior.* New York: Guilford Press.

Barkley, Russell, Mariellen Fischer, Craig Edelbrock, and Lori Smallish. 1991. The adolescent outcome of hyperactive children diagnosed by research criteria: III. Mother-child interactions, family conflicts, and maternal psychopathology. *Journal of Child Psychology and Psychiatry* 26:705–715.

Gershoff, Elizabeth. 2002. Corporal punishment by parents and associated child behaviors and experiences: A meta-analytic and theoretical review. *Psychological Bulletin* 128:539–579.

Kapalka, George. 2001a. Avoiding repetitions improves ADHD children's compliance with parents' commands. Paper presented at the annual meeting of the American Psychological Society, Toronto.

———. 2001b. Two-to-four-minute time-out is sufficient with young children. Paper presented at the annual meeting of the American Academy of Child and Adolescent Psychiatry, Honolulu.

———. 2003a. Reducing ADHD children's management problems in out-of-home settings. *Resources in Education*, ERIC # ED474462. http://www.eric.ed.gov.

———. 2003b. Reducing ADHD children's problems with interrupting at home. Paper presented at the annual meeting of the American Psychological Association, Toronto.

———. 2004. Longer eye contact improves ADHD children's compliance with parents' commands. *Journal of Attention Disorders* 8:17–23.

———. 2005. Reducing ADHD children's problems with transitions. Paper presented at the annual meeting of the American Psychological Association, Washington, DC.

———. 2006. Efficacy of behavioral contracting with ADHD children. Paper presented at the annual meeting of the American Psychological Society, New York.

Phelan, Thomas. 2003. *1-2-3 Magic: Effective Discipline for Children 2–12*. 3rd ed. Glen Ellyn, IL: ParentMagic.

Photograph by Thomas VanDyke

George M. Kapalka, Ph.D., ABPP, is director of the Center for Behavior Modification in Brick, NJ, and associate professor of psychological counseling at Monmouth University in West Long Branch, NJ. He earned a doctorate in clinical psychology from Fairleigh Dickinson University and holds board certifications in several areas of practice, including clinical psychology, psychopharmacology, child mental health services, and learning disabilities. He has authored nearly 100 research studies, publications, and professional presentations, and currently he is editor of the New Jersey Journal of Professional Counseling. He is school-certified in New Jersey, heads a state-approved independent child study team, and is a member of medical staff at Meridian Health Systems' Brick Hospital.

Foreword writer **Mark S. Kiselica, Ph.D.,** is a licensed psychologist, a nationally certified counselor, a licensed professional counselor, and a professor of counselor education at the College of New Jersey. He is author of more than 100 professional publications, including *Multicultural Counseling with Teenage Fathers,* the *Handbook of Counseling Boys and Adolescent Males, and Counseling Troubled Boys.* Kiselica served as a consulting scholar to the Federal Fatherhood Initiative during the Clinton Administration, and he is a fellow and former president of the Society for the Psychological Study of Men and Masculinity.

more titles for **children with special needs** from new**harbinger**publications

The Best American
Sports Writing
2006

GUEST EDITORS OF
THE BEST AMERICAN SPORTS WRITING

The Best
AMERICAN
SPORTS
WRITING™
2006

Edited and with an Introduction
by Michael Lewis

Glenn Stout, *Series Editor*

HOUGHTON MIFFLIN COMPANY

BOSTON • NEW YORK   2006

ISSN 1056-8034
ISBN-10: 0-618-47021-2   ISBN-13: 978-0-618-47021-1
ISBN-10: 0-618-47022-0 (pbk.)   ISBN-13: 978-0-618-47022-8 (pbk.)

Printed in the United States of America

MP 10 9 8 7 6 5 4 3 2 1

Contents

Contents

Foreword

NOW THAT THIS PROCESS is over for the year, of all the stories and columns that I read this past season I find myself thinking of only one. Oddly enough, it was not the "best" story I read this year. It didn't even make the book. In fact, I didn't even forward it to guest editor Michael Lewis. Nevertheless, I think that story may have informed this process more than anything else I read this year.

There is a tendency in putting together a collection like this to look for stories that are "perfect," without seams or rough edges, stories that tie up all loose ends and leave few questions unanswered. These are both rare and worthy finds that make the labor of this book worthwhile for the reader, for me, and, I suspect, for the authors themselves. All writers hope to find that perfect story in which every word the subject speaks is full of wisdom and insight, every scene carries us deeper into its own noise, and the words somehow align to deliver the tale in perfect synchronization with the moment; such transcendent stories can carry deep personal resonance and meaning.

Of course, that doesn't happen very often. Too often the actual facts of the potential perfect story result in rough edges, questions, banalities, and cliché. So what does the writer do when the story veers off course?

There is, of course, only one real answer, one so obvious that it feels a little preachy even to bring it up: report the truth and follow that wherever it goes. I guess it is somehow a measure of our age that it is necessary to bring this up, for the veracity of our language and the words we use has never been more at risk.

Simply put, too many who call themselves writers have chosen to lie, ranging from the big lies of such pariahs as Jayson Blair and James Frey to the smaller lies of any number of plagiarists that are uncovered almost weekly, to the fully compromised writer who looks in the mirror and knows he or she owes more to a corporate sponsor than to any internal and eternal ethic. Each new such revelation, ranging from fibs, falsehoods, and pure propaganda to outright lies, chips away at the bond of trust between the reader and the writer. Too many readers, accustomed to such invention, either become incredulous before genuine efforts, believing that *every* story contains some form of embellishment, or, even worse, expect every story to reach the visceral and counterfeit perfection of some discredited "masterpiece," a thoroughly false standard that very few real stories actually reach.

That is why I find myself thinking of the story that didn't make the book, because at first I thought it would. Its main subjects were two people who were similar yet different, each of them uniquely compelling. Owing to no fault of their own, they experienced a very similar tragedy and were thrown together. As their dual stories unfolded, the story seemed to be falling perfectly into place. You could see it coming — the two subjects would overcome their outward differences and initial distrust, bond through their tragedy, and reach a certain level of insight through a friendship that would spur each one to transcend the situation, enabling the reader to experience a catharsis. From the opening paragraph I saw where this story was headed and knew, absolutely *knew*, that it would go to the very top of that very small pile I accumulate each year.

Except it didn't. The two protagonists didn't overcome their differences. They didn't bond or find transcendence through the other — hell, they didn't even become good friends. The impulses and accidents that brought them together did not last, and in the end they were not just estranged but virtual strangers who independently reached a kind of uneasy and uncomfortable peace with their predicament. The story went from "feel good" to "feel nothing" — interesting but empty.

I was deeply disappointed. How could a story that was going so right end up so wrong? What did I miss? What did the writer miss? I read the story again and then again to see if there was some small revelation hidden anywhere that would explain what happened, bring the story back together, and deliver the neatly wrapped package I'd expected.

It wasn't there. No matter how badly I wanted to read it, it simply wasn't there. I was miffed, even a little angry. I felt cheated. How could this very talented writer have missed such a fat pitch? Why did the writer dampen the rising crescendo and settle for a quiet *pfft*, the deflation of expectation?

Then it hit me. The writer had followed the story, not steered it, reported it instead of creating it. The writer had written the truth, not massaged it. The writer hadn't pounded the story into a template that didn't fit the facts, or — even worse — written a false story that cynically served some other agenda.

Nope. Where the reporting encountered loose ends that couldn't neatly be tied off, well, those loose ends had been left loose because they were loose. Questions asked that were not answered lingered in the air, still unanswered, because the lack of an answer was even more authentic than either leaving the question unasked or speculating about an answer never given. The closer I looked the more I could see, clearly, where the author had probed for more and pushed the borders of the story looking for a way out, so the failure to find the big finish wasn't a question of effort or skill. The facts simply left nothing to discover and offered no place else to go. This writer knew well enough where to quit and, even better, why. The story ended in a whisper because that was where the truth ended, because the truth is always the end of the story and never the beginning, and the only good reason to write in the first place. The truth may be black or white, but find enough of it in one place and it sometimes comes out gray. Ambiguity, after all, is a fact too. The only failure in the story came from my anticipation of a different end and a certain measure of embarrassment because I had expected the facts to conform to my own narrow perspective, rather than follow what they were teaching me.

Although few stories I read each year make this point so clearly, I have read many, many similar stories; in the past I might have dismissed them too easily, viewing them as "failures" rather than as the significant moments of success they represent. They may not be perfect masterpieces, they do not appear in this book, and they do not win awards. There is nothing wrong with that. More importantly, though, is that they do not compromise the truth in an attempt to win awards. Without the veracity of these authors and their dedication to the truth, how would the "best" stand out? If *everybody* faked it, how would we recognize the truth?

This question is particularly important in an era when the independence of journalism is so often and so easily and so correctly called into question, when teams, leagues, networks, governments, and other not always independent entities produce something they call "content." In an attempt to control the news and circumvent writing and reporting that is beholden to no other standard but the truth, they deliver coercive hosannas masquerading as reportage, then have the audacity to refer to this garbage as somehow more pure because it is "unfiltered" by the media.

This odd convergence and blurring of the line between content and commentary, often absent any reporting at all, results in something made of words, but not anything I recognize as writing. The mere fact that in the present day words can appear almost instantaneously, almost anywhere, anytime, is no excuse. Just because the field has evolved to include new, electronic-based media does not mean that the essential standards have changed. The lust to entertain does not justify using reality as if it were plastic, or treating the truth as if it were flexible. There is no defense for viewing sources and basic independent reporting as disposable relics and then acting as if making stuff up made one some kind of postmodern literary insurgent. Pardon me while I throw things across the room — but just when did the truth become an anachronism?

In such a politically charged climate, I feel the need to make the claim that every story that has appeared in this series is, as far as I know, "true." As editor of this series since its inception, I proceed on the assumption that the readers, the author, and myself have joined together into a covenant in which we trust the facts of a story to be real and that together we inform and teach and learn from one another by following the story wherever it goes, shedding any preconceived notions along the way. Yet I must say that each time another writer admits to making it up my level of distrust rises and I worry that I might someday be hoodwinked. Once upon a time I believed everything I read until given a reason not to. Now I question everything I read and look for reasons to believe. As I look over the seventy-five stories or so I forwarded to Michael Lewis this year, it strikes me that if they are united by any one criterion, it is that they were the stories that gave me those reasons, that tasted authentic, that didn't feel contrived or created or calculating. Whatever the color of the truth uncovered by each author, it was celebrated for the shade that it was.

Every season I read every issue of hundreds of general interest and sports magazines in search of writing that might merit inclusion in *The Best American Sports Writing*. I also survey the Internet and contact the sports editors of some three hundred newspapers and hundreds of magazine editors and request their submissions.

Everyone reading this is encouraged to send me stories they've written or read in the past year that they would like to see reprinted in this volume. Writers, readers, and all other interested parties should feel free to alert me to either your own work or that of someone else for consideration in *The Best American Sports Writing 2007* according to the following criteria:

Each story:

- Must be column-length or longer.
- Must have been published in 2006.
- Must not be a reprint or book excerpt.
- Must have been published in the United States or Canada.
- Must be received by February 1, 2007.

All submissions must include the name of the author, the date of publication, and the publication name and address. Photocopies, tear sheets, or clean copies are fine. Readable reductions to 8½-by-11 are preferred. Submissions from online publications must be made in hard copy, and those who submit stories from newspapers should submit the story in hard copy as published. Since newsprint generally suffers in transit, newspaper stories are best copied and then mounted on 8½-by-11 paper and, if the story also appeared online, with the appropriate URL attached. There is no limit to the number of submissions either an individual or a publication may make, but please use common sense. Owing to the volume of material I receive, no submission can be returned or acknowledged. I also believe it is inappropriate for me to comment on or critique any individual submission. Publications that want to be absolutely certain their contributions are considered are advised to provide a complimentary subscription to the address listed below. Those that already do so should make sure to extend the subscription.

No electronic submissions will be accepted, although stories that only appeared online are eligible. Please send all submissions by U.S. mail — midwinter weather conditions often prevent me from receiving UPS or FedEx deliveries — and please try to hit the deadline. This past year I received dozens of stories too late to be considered. In the event that a story is selected for publication, your publication will be contacted concerning rights and permissions.

Please submit either an original or clear paper copy of each story, with the publication name, author, and date of the story's publication, to:

Glenn Stout
P.O. Box 549
Alburg, VT 05440

Those with questions or comments may contact me at baswed@sover.net. Copies of previous editions of this book can be ordered through most bookstores or online book dealers. An index of stories that have appeared in this series can be found at glennstout.net.

Thanks again go out to Houghton Mifflin for allowing me to continue to work on such a gratifying project, particularly my editor Susan Canavan, Will Vincent, and Beth Burleigh Fuller. Thanks also to Michael Lewis for his meticulous commitment, the Web site sportsjournalists.com for posting submission guidelines, and Siobhan and Saorla for our ongoing experiment in living with words. And thanks again to all the writers whose hard work and honesty bring value to this project.

GLENN STOUT
Alburg, Vermont

Introduction

ONE OF THE STRANGE things about people who write for a living is their tendency to dismiss the subjects most important to people who don't write for a living. Even as sports has taken up a position at the center of American life it remains peripheral to American literary life. The literary world treats books and articles about political events with utmost seriousness — even as a fantastically large number of Americans, to judge from their talent for avoiding the polls on election day, don't have the faintest idea what all the fuss is about. Books and articles about sports, and the ideas underpinning sports, remain on the bottom shelf, alongside the self-help books and celebrity memoirs. And yet sports is the one thing Americans can be relied upon to feel passionately about. There may be Americans glued to C-Span, but their numbers are overwhelmed by ESPN's addicts. There may be political leaders who inspire loyalty, but there aren't any — so far as I know — who cause grown men and women to paint their faces and tattoo their chests and howl like werewolves. For every little boy or girl who wants to grow up to be a member of Congress there are, oh, about one million who intend to become major league baseball players or professional basketball players or ice skaters or gymnasts. Americans' deadly seriousness about the games they play is probably not a good sign for their democracy, but it is unquestionably a sign. You can't govern what people care about. And what people care about is the writer's path to their inner lives.

The chance to help to rectify this imbalance between what people care about and what good writers write about has been one of the pleasures of being asked to make the final selections for this year's edition of *Best American Sports Writing*. Here we dignify the work of writers who happen to have tackled material that is, in one way or another, related to sports. They won't be winning any literary prizes, but their work is important. They aren't merely writing about sports. They're describing who we are.

I should confess up front that this is a collection of stories with no very good theory to unify it. I've just picked out the twenty-seven magazine and newspaper and Internet articles that I found the most interesting, of the seventy-five or so thrust upon me by the man who actually edited this volume, the shockingly diligent Glenn Stout. (Glenn apparently has read every article about sports ever written in America.) Several writers are represented here more than once: they are not blood relations of mine. So far as I know, I've never met any of the writers whose work I've selected. Literarily, the pieces don't have much in common with each other. Some are among the most finely written things on any topic; others are distinguished less by the quality of their prose than by the beauty of the story they tell. They range from elaborate narratives to simple opinion pieces, and they illustrate, among other things, how many different species of writing can be herded into literature's null set: "nonfiction." Their subject matter is also all over the place: basketball, baseball, football, arena football, golf, boxing, pool, scuba diving, poker, cheerleading, cycling, poaching, softball, rodeo, track, wrestling.

Still, taken as a whole, I think these stories add up to a bit more than the sum of their parts. For a start, they suggest certain trends in American sporting life. The most striking of these is the rapid eliding of the distinction between sports and competition. In a free market economy, premised on competition, that distinction is always under siege. The American businessman has drawn for decades on sports metaphors to enliven his work and make him feel more interesting — and less sedentary — than he is. Now it seems that anyone with a hobby that involves mostly a lot of farting around seeks to infuse his activity with the dynamism of an actual athletic event in which people sweat and suffer. Poker on ESPN should have been treated as an early warning signal. Poker players used to be guys avoiding their wives. Now, apparently, they are professional athletes.

As a nation, we seem to be replacing actual movement with the idea of movement. We treat our most fattening activities as intense calorie-burning exercise. Among the side effects of this trend is to make it possible for the aged, the infirm, and the obese to experience, as competitors, the thrill of victory and the agony of defeat. We may be a nation of fat people, but we're still all players! (We aren't alone in this desire; anyone who has watched Englishmen "compete" at darts knows that there is no limit to what might be considered an athletic event if the audience is willing to go along with the ruse.) In a nod to the trend, this collection includes pieces about not only poker but also fishing, scuba diving, and cheerleading. I remain unsold on the idea that poker belongs in the same category as, say, heavyweight boxing. My unthinking prejudice against cheerleading, however, was changed by Pamela Colloff's delightful piece on the subject. Like a lot of the writers in this book, Colloff takes on a far bigger subject than she pretends. Her ostensible target is a Texas cheerleading camp and the response of serious cheerleaders everywhere to attempts by the Texas legislature to ban sexually suggestive sideline dance routines. But her lovely piece is also about people striving and setting higher standards than their audiences for themselves. If, as Colloff tells us, more than half of the deaths and disabling injuries that have occurred in American high school sports in the past twenty-two years have been suffered by cheerleaders, cheerleading is either a sport or an act of insanity.

As a rule in American sports writing, the less physical exertion the activity under inspection requires, the more likely the writer is to make fun of it. No one here pokes fun at boxing; every boxing piece I've ever read treats the sport with the seriousness of a heart attack. Poaching bass from golf courses, on the other hand . . . well, there may have been a funnier and less reverent sports story written in America last year than Charlie Schroeder's account of the quest for big bass in the water hazards of America, but I haven't read it. As I write this I can hear the serious sports reader muttering to himself, *Poaching fish from golf courses is not a sport, it's a crime, and no responsible editor of a collection of* America's Best Sports Writing *would treat it as such.* I couldn't agree more! But I also feel that, when the criminals exhibit the competitive fanaticism of Michael Jordan, exceptions must be made. And unlike, say, playing poker, poaching bass from golf courses has the same internal logic of a real sport: the bigger the fish, the harder it is to steal. As a golf course poacher explains to Schroeder, "If you find a pond with big bass in it, it's usually one that has NO TRESPASSING signs around it and requires a nighttime mission. The more protected the ponds are, the bigger the fish are."

Another trend, touched on by this collection, is the intellectualization of sports. It's all getting a lot more complicated out there, on the court and the field. Or rather, just off the court and just off the field. There has been for some time now, in many American sports, a kind of informal R&D movement seeking to uncover their hidden secrets. Interestingly, the movement is manned almost entirely by outsiders. Statistical analysis is finding a new home in American sports and leading people with a gift for it to question, far more deeply than it has ever been questioned, the wisdom of insiders. Baseball, with its counterculture of geeks and nerds who analyze baseball statistics and search for new baseball knowledge, has led the way, but the other major sports aren't far behind. In the past couple of decades the outsiders have acquired new tools: more accurate salary and performance data than ever before, a computer to analyze them with, and an Internet to argue with others about the analysis. The guy who makes his living as the general manager of a professional sports franchise now faces a small army of shockingly well-informed fans, many of whom suspect they could do his job better and regard him as guilty until proven innocent. Neal Pollack's piece "The Cult of the General Manager" gets at this phenomenon. Michael Sokolove's defenestration of the American basketball player does too, in another way: by establishing that the journalist, if he has the nerve to try, can plausibly condescend to people three feet taller than himself.

The American sportswriter, like the American fan, is no longer content to shout his abuse from his bleacher seat. Of course there are still plenty of sportswriters who conceive of themselves mainly as shouters: their job, as they see it, is to tell the reader who to love and who to hate (though they're usually much better at whipping up hatred than love). Open the sports pages in any major American city and you will find a columnist — he's always a columnist, never a reporter — who hasn't bothered to learn anything new in decades, hurling vitriol at others. This character has built his entire career on the theory that there's never been anything new to learn in sports — and thus exempted himself from the responsibility of ever having to learn anything. But there is something new to learn. The ever-greater body of knowledge about sports — how to build teams, how to value players, how to evaluate strategies — puts the writer who bothers to educate himself in a position to undermine entire sports franchises. He can speak directly to the owner about the incompetence of the general manager — and the owner will listen! For the poor people who actually make their living by building the teams and valuing the players, life has become a lot less cozy than it used to be. Just as the general managers around the NBA are settling in for their second cup of coffee, they pick up the *New York Times* magazine, flip to Sokolove's piece, and discover that this guy is actually dangerous. *This scribbler . . . who probably never even played the game . . . is making me look like a fool!*

Finally, the reader of this collection will notice the tendency of writers to use sports as a filter for America's great social debates. This isn't so much a trend in sports writing as its permanent condition. Whatever happens to be going on in American politics and society — a war in Iraq, a civil rights movement — inevitably plays out on American courts and ball fields. This collection includes stories about a cyclist with Parkinson's disease, a sprinter without a foot, and a wrestler without arms. None of these athletes is having quite such a tough time competing as the lady basketball coach in rural Texas suspected by the locals of being a lesbian. In sports, sexual inclination seems to be taking the place once occupied by race: Jackie Robinson is now gay. This collection includes two stories about homosexual coaches and players, another about a boxer who killed an opponent in the ring after the opponent called him "queer," and a fourth about a pitcher for the Cincinnati Reds whose chief distinction, apart from his ninety-four-mile-per-hour fastball, is that he was raised by lesbians. All achieve a poignancy that they might not have achieved if they were set in an arena outside of sports; all, in a way, rise above the cultural debate on homosexuality. We Americans still expect our games to be fair; we expect that the best man or woman will be given a chance to win; we are now conditioned to be upset by discrimination on the playing field. We might be disturbed when a woman is demoted by her Wall Street employer after her coworkers discover she is a lesbian. But when that woman is a hotshot basketball coach who has inspired her girls to play their way into the Texas state championship game, we're ready to march in the streets.

Sports, as literary material, offers up this wonderful opportunity: to change the terms of any debate. Walk into any intractable debate and throw a basketball into the middle of it and it becomes, for a brief moment, less intractable. Months before *Brokeback Mountain* introduced the notion to mainstream America that male homosexuals could be (a) manly and (b) in love in a way that was recognizable even to a straight person, Ben Paynter was dreaming up one of my favorite openings in this collection:

> Just because this is gay rodeo doesn't mean Shorty likes to see men acting like women. While finishing a cigarette a few moments ago, he heard two men catcalling effeminately to each other.
> "Shit," he said quietly. "Those are the ones who give us names."

That's the other thing about sports writing that I, for one, find appealing. It enables the writer to cram on to the page an awful lot of life that otherwise might be left off. Sports is the literary category that tolerates the most outrageous liberties: the writer doesn't need to be relevant. He needs only to be interesting. Once he has established that this character he's decided to describe plays or coaches some sport, he is allowed to take readers pretty much anywhere he can talk them into going. A lot of the pieces in this collection are, in this sense, literary. They pretend to be about one thing when they are in fact about another. Steve Friedman uses golf to write about his relationship with his father. L. Jon Wertheim, in a truly spectacular performance, uses arena football and Jermaine Ewell to etch a portrait of stoicism. You finish Wertheim's story, which he wrote for *Sports Illustrated*, and you know that people are still capable of seizing control of their own experiences. No matter how they might have suffered, no matter how they might have been victimized, they can refuse to be defined by their suffering or to be cast forever as victims. If he never plays another down, Jermaine Ewell has escaped the cliché that the world would like to make of him, and the writer has too.

A lot can be done with sports by a gifted writer, and a lot of that is done right here. I'd like to point the reader especially to one piece: J. R. Moehringer's story about the ancient homeless softball genius, "The Unnatural Natural" — the hobo Roy Hobbes.

"Here he comes!" someone shouted.

At last, walking slowly toward us from the parking lot, was a man built very differently from the men gathered around me. He had none of their midwestern roundness, none of their low-slung solidity. He was tall, lean, somewhat frail, and instead of clomping along on big feet, as the others tended to do, he picked his way forward delicately, as if someone had told him to watch out for broken glass.

What Moehringer achieves writing about sports would be the envy of any writer writing on any subject.

When I finished reading through this collection, I found myself feeling a little bit better about the world around me. At any given time, it seems, there are a surprising number of writers of serious literary ability who are out there beating the bushes and scaring up moving and delightful stories — even when high literary culture has no particular interest in them. They are doing the important work of explaining us to ourselves. What's reassuring about great sports writing is what's reassuring about great sports performances: facing opposition, and often against the odds, someone, at last, did something right.

MICHAEL LEWIS

The Best American
Sports Writing
2006

PAUL SOLOTAROFF

There Is Nothing Special
About Kyle Maynard . . .

FROM MEN'S JOURNAL

HOW SAD, CLIFF RAMOS SAID TO HIMSELF. Someone had to take
that child's mother in hand and explain to her it was hopeless. In
his thirty-odd years as a wrestling coach, Ramos had heard of tough
cases before, including a high school kid who fought on one leg,
compensating for the loss of limb with strength and feral cunning.
But the son of the woman on the phone that morning was way past
the pale of bad luck. He was so far out there on the hardship graph
that Ramos could do nothing for him. All he could think to do, by
way of help, was to let his mom down easy.

"She called me to enroll Kyle in juniors and then started to describe him," says Ramos. A taciturn man in his early fifties with salt-
and-pepper hair and the build of a lifelong athlete, he is the coach
and architect of a championship squad at Collins Hill High School
in Suwanee, Georgia. "I cut her off quick, saying that whatever his
challenge, our youth coaches could more than handle it." But
Anita Maynard came back at him, insisting he had to hear this, and
finished what she had to say. Ramos put the phone down trying to
make sense of it, and thought, *What, he means to wrestle with no arms?*

Well, no, as Ramos saw for himself later that day, Kyle meant to
wrestle with no arms *or* legs. He'd been born with a preposterously
cruel congenital insult: the spontaneous (and still barely understood) amputation of each of his four limbs in utero. But here he
was, all sixty-five pounds, a gorgeous, tow-haired twelve-year-old
boy with a certain aura. Ramos knelt to say something nice to Kyle

and was mesmerized by the seriousness of his gaze. He decided, then and there, to take him on personally, though he knew the idea was risible; no one in the several thousand years of the sport had won without upper limbs. Legs you could work around, but hands? Come on now. That's why they call it grappling.

As for Kyle, he had no notion of what he was getting himself into, and it wouldn't have much mattered if he had. From birth he'd been a kid you couldn't say no to, insisting on doing everything the other kids did, and making life miserable until you let him. A few nights later he got down on the mat with Ramos, who tucked his own arms into the top of his track suit to simulate Maynard's impairment. So grateful was Kyle for the chance to compete that he made two silent vows to Ramos. The first was that he would never embarrass him by getting pinned in a match. The second was that he'd work like a young man possessed to get his coach a win.

Although he weighed next to nothing, Kyle was strong through the trunk and could clamp down hard with his stumps, which ended between the elbow and shoulder. Ramos and Kyle's father, a former wrestler named Scott, improvised a series of holds for Kyle and taught him some basic rolls. But whatever they managed to contrive in practice went to hell in his middle school matches. He got beat, and beat badly, that whole first year by a string of novice wrestlers, kids who smacked him around the circle, then danced off to catch their breath. On the car rides home, Kyle would convulse in sobs, convinced he was shaming his family and coach. He wanted so much to emulate his father that it killed Kyle to let him down. On his worst days he'd moan about wanting to quit, but Scott, a hard case, wouldn't hear it. "No one named Maynard walks away a failure, and besides," he'd lie, "I lost every bout my first year as a wrestler too. If you can just get through it and take your lumps, you'll dominate next fall."

But the next fall came and the losing went on, lancing fresh holes in Kyle's spirit. He raged at his father, who rode him but good, making him watch videos of his errors in matches, then fix them ad nauseam in the basement. On the playback, Kyle saw the camera rattle and dip because his father was screaming so loud. "You fight only well enough to lose," Scott said. "I'll keep on you till you get that out of your system and learn what it takes to be a winner."

That spring the county championships were held nearby, bringing much of the town of Suwanee out to watch. Kyle, who competed in a low weight class, got a bye when his semifinal opponent fell sick, and passed into the seventy-five-pound finals. There, he met a polished kid who would go on to wrestle varsity in high school for one of the elite teams in the region. But as skilled as he was, he wasn't ready for Kyle, who tore after him from the opening bell. Nose to nose in the center ring, Kyle seized the boy in a barrel roll and flipped him on his back. Too shocked to flee, the boy grabbed him head-on, and again Kyle tossed him to the mat. The large crowd jumped to its feet, ignoring the other match, screaming for the limbless hometown kid who'd won its heart while losing all season. The first period ended and his opponent regrouped, but in the second period Kyle came on even harder, rolling the kid over a total of eight times to win by mercy rule. The ref waved his arms and raised Kyle's stump; the place went bedlam.

"I looked in the stands and saw my folks going crazy and my sisters and grandparents hugging, and this feeling I'd never felt before hit me," he says. Now nineteen years old and engine block–thick through the chest and shoulders, he sits in his dorm room at the University of Georgia, where he's a freshman and the star attraction of the wrestling team. "I knew then I wasn't just put here to wrestle or be an example to other [handicapped] kids. No, I was here for one thing, and that was to *win*, and I was going to go to any lengths to make that happen."

In conjuring the life of an amputee wrestler, you can land pretty quickly on the shores of folklore, describing a kid who could have been invented by Gabriel García Márquez. It's a question less of fact than of size and scale. Most of us proceed in steps so small that we can't remember the route that brought us here, to this place and this time and this self. But Kyle Maynard's path moves in leaps, not steps, and it would be easy to lose him in the myth, to treat him like a shorter Paul Bunyan. To do so would be to miss the point of him, though, which is that courage isn't an option but a duty.

Begin, then, with the miracle that led things off: the fact that Kyle lived at all. Sometime before birth, likely the first trimester, he was stricken with a condition called amniotic band syndrome (ABS). In layman's terms, the inner lining of the womb rips, and loose strands of membrane encircle the fetus, choking off blood to its limbs. Nobody knows why this happens; heredity has been ruled out, but no unified theory has emerged. ABS is rare — one in 3,846 babies is born missing all or part of an appendage — and severe cases like Kyle's are overwhelmingly likely to miscarry or end in stillbirth. (Quadruple amputees are so rare that statistics don't even exist on how many there are.) To compound the mystery, Kyle's parents were healthy, and when they went in for a sonogram, it showed no damage.

"Scott was in the army at the time, finishing his tour at Fort Myer, and we went to the VA hospital to have it done," recalls Anita, a tall, trim blond with a year-round tan and the pep of a former majorette. "The technician thought he saw something, so he called in the doctor, who looked things over and announced that Kyle was fine. And then six months later came this beautiful white-haired baby who, by the way, had no arms or legs. The news just crushed us — I mean, really plowed us over — but we were first-time parents who had to go raise our child."

In lieu of dialing lawyers or taking to bed in depression, the Maynards searched for other cases and managed to come across two. The first was a three-year-old boy in Maryland who fed himself and raced about on his stumps. The second was a man in Fort Wayne, Indiana, where the Maynards settled to be near Anita's family. He was a fully functional adult who earned a living as a graphic artist and drove a modified van. Heartened to learn that life was navigable without limbs, the Maynards laid down an iron rule: Kyle was to be treated as a typical child, with no breaks or allowances thrown his way. As early as six months, he was put on the floor and strongly encouraged to crawl. At eighteen months, they strapped a spoon to his arm and told him to use it or starve. "We didn't mean it literally," says Anita, laughing, while glancing over at Scott. "Well, *I* didn't anyway, but I'm the softy. He's the hard one, or thinks he is."

In the basement rec room of their brick colonial in this sprawling Atlanta suburb they moved to in 1997, the Maynards are gathered on a nippy Sunday, the sounds of a televised ball game in the background. On the couch with his mother are Kyle's three sisters, one blonder and more beautiful than the next. Much like their brother, they are soft-spoken kids with a streak of midwestern shyness, and seem a little in awe of the attention Kyle's gotten in the past ten months or so. There was a segment on HBO's *Real Sports with Bryant Gumbel* last year, an hourlong appearance on *Larry King Live*, and a front-page story in *USA Today*, plus a book deal, speaking engagements, and an Abercrombie & Fitch shoot. The spotlight baffles the girls, as it does their parents: no one here has the least idea why people find Kyle — or his family — special. They have managed so seamlessly to mainstream him that they've forgotten why it was necessary to do so.

"People think we pushed him toward sports and all, but that was Kyle's doing," says Scott. "From the age of five he's been a rabid fan, and all he ever talked about was playing football. So when we moved here, I thought, *Shoot, let's do it; let's get him into peewees and see what happens.* And he did really well at it, playing nose tackle on defense, and if you ran it up the gut there, he'd bring you down."

But kids stomped on his bandaged feet, which point backward and can't be shod. (Kyle's legs end where the thighbone begins, and the left one is longer than the right.) Anita feared that without an after-school activity, he'd sit at home and mope, so she acceded to his desire to wrestle, hoping he wouldn't get hurt. "In the good-cop/bad-cop deal we had going, Scott was the drill sergeant who cracked the whip, whereas my job was to surround Kyle with other kids, make sure he was social at all times," she says. "Our mantra with him was, 'Normal, normal, normal,' because we never knew any better."

Nor, as it developed, did Kyle. A rambunctious kid who was constantly underfoot, driving his mother crazy — "At thirteen months he would crawl in the broom closet and yank my vacuum wands down" — he excelled in school and was early with milestones, learning to read and write by preschool. Bringing his arms together, he could hold a brush or pencil in the crook. (Implausibly, his handwriting is stellar, and he cleanly types fifty words a minute.) He had a yardful of friends who made room for him at play, installing him in goal during their street hockey games and at lineman for rough touch football. The only time he ever felt odd or excluded was when doctors, in their ignorance, stooped to meddle. During a bad year while he was in kindergarten, he tried out prostheses after a specialist told his family they'd change his life. Ugly and painful, they did just that, leaving him stuck in his noisy wheelchair and dependent on an aide. When he threw off the extensions before school one day, Kyle's pals let out a roar. "They love him the way he is," reported his teacher that afternoon when Anita came to pick him up. "With arms and legs — or whatever you call those things — he doesn't seem to be like Kyle."

Still, to judge Kyle Maynard by his competence is to sell him short. Let others applaud him for fitting in, cobbling together an honorable life from such unwieldy parts. He could care less about breaking even; his goal, his fixed mission, is to go where no one, limbed or otherwise, has gone before.

On a bitter morning in the middle of January, the tail of a storm dropping the wind chill to freezing, Maynard meets me at the student field house, having steered his motorized chair a long way through the gusts. (On a campus so large it takes up much of the town and requires students to drive or catch buses between classes, Maynard, who is carless, must plan his day around the big blocks of time he needs to get places.) He is dressed, as usual, in a T-shirt and shorts, laughing off the unseasonable cold that has fellow students bundled as if for ice fishing. We head for the weight room, which, like everyplace else here, is full to bursting with tanned blonds. When Kyle wheels in, every eye in the room trails him to the stretch mat. Two floor attendants help him set up, tying plates to the chains he uses to bench.

As today is a light one (he has a rematch tomorrow against a kid who outwrestled him last fall), Maynard begins with low-end weight, doing flat-bench flys with 250. At 120 pounds, he can bench-press three times his weight, and in early March he traveled to the Arnold Classic in Ohio to shatter the modified bench-pressing world record for a teen by lifting 360 pounds. I watch, dumbfounded, as he glides through sets, easily firing up fifteen reps, then popping off the bench for dips. When he's done he clambers down and scuttles to the pec-dec station. Here he sets the pin at 230 and grunts through short-stroke sets, snapping the stack with perfect form, then guiding it down slow to rest. When you stand to one side, your view partly obscured, it's possible to forget that Maynard has no arms, to find the big-shouldered kid with quartz features the benchmark of male development. What's harder to lose sight of is his age; he's impossibly strong for nineteen.

"That's what comes from losing," he says, catching a breath between chest work and triceps. "I got so mad at being manhandled that I said, 'Quit, or stop whining and do something.' There are two words I live by — 'no excuses' — and so I started with two-pound plates and slowly worked my way up." It took him a while to find his form, because nothing in the gym is set up for him. But between his father and Coach Ramos, they figured out how to simulate bench press by hitching chains to his stumps. (The thick chains are rigged to padded cuffs, which in turn slip over Kyle's arms.) "And by the time summer passed I was definitely stronger, or at least strong enough to get my own shots in."

Though it was several months, still, till that first win at county, he'd become a bantam wrestler no one wanted to fight, bashing opponents with his cudgel stumps and battering them with his head. He worked out maniacally after school, and often had the weight room at the top of Collins Hill High to himself. One day Ramos poked his head in late and saw Kyle bent over, pouring sweat. "He was probably a ninth-grader then and far down the roster, but I thought to myself, *There's a winner.* Anyone who works that hard with no one watching is going to be unstoppable one day."

From way back in boyhood, Kyle's fantasy of fantasies was to become a varsity wrestler. He idolized the starters on Collins Hill's powerhouse squad, thrilling to see them at the mall or pictured in the local daily. Under the direction of Cliff Ramos, Collins Hill High has become the premier program in the state of Georgia, finishing in the top three each of the past six years and cracking the nation's top fifty last fall. There are about sixty-five kids on its active roster, and a number of them go on to scholarships at Division I or Division II colleges. Kyle spent three years waiting his turn, competing on the very good junior varsity team and handling himself ably at ninety-five pounds. Finally, as a senior, he wrestled his way on to the varsity team, certifying his status as a god on campus and catching the eye of national media. Not all the attention was celebratory, though. "I got letters and e-mails from around the country saying, 'C'mon, people let him win,'" says Ramos. "It never occurred to them that a kid with no arms could overpower guys his size. But they don't know Kyle, or anyone like him, because there is no one like Kyle."

If you think a limbless teen can't outpoint his foes, you've never

seen Maynard scamper side to side, darting for a hold. Wrestlers
may start matches on their feet, but bouts are won and lost on all
fours, and Maynard is already down there, waiting. Moreover, his
foes' weight takes up full-length frames, but Maynard's is concen-
trated in his trunk, giving him advantages in strength and balance.
These are offset, of course, by a long list of deficits, prime among
them the lack of hands to grasp and control opponents and legs
with which to take them down. "I do what I can with the moves
I've got, but a good wrestler can usually negate them," he admits.
"Where I'll have three or four counters, say, a guy with arms and
legs will have a dozen. And the real trouble comes when he sees me
on film and can prep for the limited things I do."

What no one can properly train for is Maynard's motor, his tire-
less, pit bull drive to dominate. Few, if any, two-minute stints of
peak exertion are more taxing than a round of wrestling, and a
high school match has three of them, with no rest periods. Giving
away length and skill in bouts, Maynard made up for it by being re-
lentless and went 35–16 as a 103-pound senior. (He also kept his
vow to Coach Ramos by never getting pinned.) Along the way, he
beat champions from other states, then suffered narrow losses in
the state tournament. Still, he managed to land a spot at nationals.
There, he was mobbed by thousands of fans who'd seen him on
HBO, swarming his mat while he stretched for matches and begging him to sign their programs.

"He was almost like a rock star — we had to have our own guards
just to get through the arena," marvels Ramos. "It stunned some of
his teammates, who came up to me later and said, 'Kyle's good but
he's not *that* good.' Can you imagine a higher compliment? They'd
completely lost sight of the fact that he was wrestling with no arms
or legs."

If he sets aside red-state, blue-state issues, one of the first things a
northerner notices down South is how comparatively gracious its
teenagers are, treating guests not with reflexive irony but a sunny
brand of formal respect. On campus, jocks and frat boys hold
doors for you, and sorority girls stop when asked directions, smiling as you repeat them back. Though his family didn't move to
Georgia till he was almost twelve, Maynard is an exemplar of southern manners, meeting your gaze warmly and giving smart answers

to questions he's had put to him many times. Even around his parents — the ultimate stress test for kids — he's unfailingly courteous and even-tempered, letting slide their mild attempts to run his life. He's on the road two weekends of every month, earning big money on the lecture circuit, and is waiting to take delivery on the ultimate SUV, a chromed-out International MXT with specially modified pedals (price: six figures; approximate wheelbase: one and a half Hummer-lengths). Additionally, he signed a lucrative deal to write his autobiography. I learned most of those details from his family, however; Maynard views such proffers of fact as a crime akin to bragging.

But on the day of his four-school round-robin tournament, a different Maynard shows up. He is surly, fire-eyed, monosyllabic; no one, not even his teammates, goes near him. While they banter and stretch, checking the smallish crowd (the men's basketball team is hosting Kentucky, siphoning off much of the student body), he wanders over to the edge of the mat, doing freakishly hard drawbridge lifts. (Lie flat on your gut, pull your legs up off the ground, and raise your chest off the mat. Now repeat that thirty times, then call an ambulance.) As he blasts out reps, foes from Clemson, Mercer, and Newberry gape at his show of strength. Even those who have seen Maynard wrestle before nudge the guys next to them and whisper. In a combat sport that hinges on bravery and the willingness to give and take pain, the sight of a limbless kid without fear is enough to scare off competitors. One time in high school, his opponent tapped out, resigning before the match even really started. That hasn't happened in college, but there are lots of ways to duck him; one is to flunk the morning weigh-in and come in over 125.

That, or something like it, is what happens today. Maynard's foe, the kid from Newberry College who narrowly edged him last fall, has shown up five pounds overweight and will compete in the next bracket up. The wrestler who fills in for him is a wiry teen whose thighs are about the size of Kyle's arm-stumps. From the start, it's abundantly clear that he wants no part of Maynard, shuffling out of reach or fending him off with stiff-arms to the head. Over and over, Maynard charges after him and finally grabs his leg, using it to shove him from the circle. This earns him a lead and changes the kid's tactics; in the second round, he gets on the mat and grapples. But even born with four limbs, he can't lock up Maynard, who takes him down with a shoulder to the jaw. Maynard is safely ahead now but keeps on grinding, whacking away at his foe's ribs. By the end of the bout, the boy can hardly stand. If this were anyone but Maynard, you'd call it a walkover.

I catch up to him in the hall outside, where he has wheeled off to decompress. He seems strangely down after a lopsided win, and shrugs when I point it out. "I'm bummed that the first kid came in heavy. He's the best in my weight class, and I trained hard for him."

"Well, a W's a W, right?"

He shoots me what, for him, is a filthy look. "It's not about padding my won-lost record; it's about competing at the highest level. Otherwise, why practice three hours a night? I can win whenever I want to at video games."

Kyle confides that he's thought about transferring to a top-tier, Division I school. Because of Title IX, college wrestling at Georgia and its Southeastern Conference rivals has been downgraded to a club-level sport, meaning the athletes themselves pay to play it. Maynard and his teammates must fund everything from plane tickets to school tuition. (It isn't, of course, the only sport thus affected; on campuses around the country, baseball, tennis, and soccer have been lopped off budgets entirely.) Maynard is among the lucky ones on his team, earning a half-scholarship in academics because of his A-minus record in high school. Still, he hungers to take it to the next level, defying all odds and the advice of friends who tell him, politely, to stay put. Cautions Ramos, his old coach at Collins Hill, "There's only so many ways you can get around the problem of having no arms and legs. I've had better wrestlers — with all their extremities — try Division I and fail."

We head back into the wrestling theater, where the crowd has grown. While we were out, Maynard's team fell behind to a very good Newberry squad. Crestfallen, he slides out of his chair and scoots to the edge of the mat. He is down on all fours, screaming encouragement; the veins in his forehead bulge. I return to my seat in the pullout bleachers, beside an elderly man with two grandkids. Clad in red sweatshirts and UG Bulldog hats, the young boys are emphatic fans, hopping up and down at each fall. While one of them explains the point system to me, the other nervously chews his sleeve, groaning at Georgia's mistakes. "C'mon," he mutters, "circle, circle! There's your shot now, take it!" But things get worse, not better, for his 'Dawgs, who drop match after match for an hour. Then, near the end, Georgia makes its run, winning at the higher weight classes. For the nail-biting finish between superheavies, the crowd gets up on its feet. "Suck it up!" yells the young boy. "You're not tired now — be like Kyle!"

On my last night in town, I meet the Maynards for dinner at a mall near their home. In Suwanee, Outback Steakhouse is considered glitzy, and on a weekend evening the line for a table rivals that at Spago or Nobu. As we pace out the wait, something notable happens over and over. Strangers approach and, with the deference of monks, ask if they can speak to Kyle. "You changed my life," says a blue-haired lady visiting from Maine. "I watched you on *Larry King*, and you so inspired me. I'm coping with a lot of health issues myself." Following behind her are two hockey players from Canada's University of Guelph, who are in town for a semipro game. "Dude, you fuckin' rock," says the shorter of the two yobs. "I said, if that guy can get up and train each day, there's no excuse not to go a hundred miles an hour and skate through fuckin' brick walls."

Maynard's parents, devout Christians, wince through smiles. "We hear that a lot, though usually with less cursing," his father says once we're seated. "Maybe they were delirious from hunger."

I ask Kyle how he copes with the attention, which, as near as I can tell, is constant. His website is clogged, his cell phone keeps ringing, and wherever he goes, he's buttonholed by people who stop to tell him their stories. As a young man famous for surmounting hardship, he's become a kind of lodestone for the disadvantaged, or in some cases, the merely unhappy. That kind of onus can oppress a kid who's six months past his prom, and who, in his first year of college, is juggling a full course load with a varsity athlete's schedule.

"Well, no, it's great that people get hope from my story, and if it helps even a couple of 'em, that's amazing. But —" he pauses a moment, and I lie in wait for his first harsh utterance all week, "the truth of the matter is, it feels hollow sometimes. I don't really deserve all this."

The chatter around the table stops dead. "What do you mean?" asks Anita.

Kyle fusses with his shirttail, picking the words carefully; it's clear he's been brooding on this a while. "Look, there's hundreds of thousands of wrestlers in the country right now, and out of all of them, I'm maybe above average. And for this kind of spotlight — going to parties at Hef's mansion and winning an ESPY and all that — I feel like I should be great. Hands or no hands."

"Isn't that a little unfair?" says his father. "You've done a lot of things in a real short time that nobody in their right mind thought were possible."

"But that's exactly my point," he counters. "Just because I've done 'em means that anyone else could've, if they were in this chair. And as far as being a hero, I don't think so. That's the guys in Falluja, fighting and dying."

This launches a discussion of sensible goals, the mere mention of which makes Kyle bristle. He has already game-planned the next ten years, culminating in a career in on-air journalism as a news anchor or sports-talk host. That much, his parents stand behind; it's the step before it that scares them stiff. After graduating, it is Kyle's avid intention to become a steel cage fighter, competing on the Ultimate Fighting circuit à la his idol and mentor, Randy Couture. (Kyle met the reigning light-heavyweight champion at one of his matches in Las Vegas. They get together when possible, usually at Couture's bouts.)

That no one has entered this savage sport without limbs to kick or punch with doesn't faze Kyle. Any wall can be scaled or jumped over, he says, if you put in work and embrace pain. "Whenever I get tired or my lungs start burning, that's when I kick up the jams," he says. "Because pain, to me, is just another word for weakness leaving the body."

Well, certainly that's one view. Another is that pain is vital information, like a YIELD sign at an on-ramp. You can blow right past it to get places faster, but you can also get crushed by an eighteen-wheeler doing seventy in the slow lane. In his haste to silence the mean-spirited and stupid — the folks who called up HBO and said, "Bullshit, he can't do that" — Kyle has put himself in harm's way, letting indignation call the shots. As a high school senior, he broke his nose four times, but refused to get it set or go see a doctor who might rule him out of regionals. He's torn a pectoral muscle benching 410, has chronic spine problems that he ignores in order to wrestle, and rarely gets back from practice before midnight, with three hours of homework ahead of him. There's also the little matter of his autobiography, which the publisher expects from him early this summer at some eighty thousand words.

Still, there's more than just masochism at work here, or the supernormal drive of the disadvantaged. When you stand next to Kyle Maynard or see him on television, something very potent comes across the wire, and it's more complex than courage or hope. The word that springs to mind is a quaint one: *nobility*. And even that term isn't equal to the task. He makes you want to be better — not a better person, but a better, truer version of who you are; stronger, braver, and ready to meet the world on its terms. It's easy to see why he drew a crowd of fifteen thousand for a speech at the Junior Olympics, or why corporate executives fly him in to talk at their sales conventions. He isn't merely the sum of his mastered shortcomings; he's a winner with the humility of a fighter who lost a lot once and learned some hard lessons along the way. Anyone can talk when he's on top of the world, but it's the guy who got there from a long way down that can really teach you things you need to know.

In the past couple of decades we've developed ways to calibrate life's unfairness. We no longer speak, say, of the paralyzed as crippled or the brain-damaged as retarded, instead using such blocky constructions as "-challenged" or "other-enabled." Clumsy though the words are, they represent progress, an earnest attempt to view the impaired as full-blooded fellow creatures. What we haven't yet done is to coin new language for those who are clearly superior, those men and women whose dynamism advances our entire species. Call it genius or merit or inborn goodness, what they have in spades is the power to go forward, to test the bounds of what's known. We are lucky to have them, and luckier still to know them, and the least we owe them is a name. Until someone has a better idea, I humbly submit the term "Maynards."

The next day, on my way out of town, I stop at Collins Hill High to see Coach Ramos. It would be hard to overstate his fondness for Kyle, or the part he's played in the boy's life. In the fall of 2003 he mass-mailed tapes of him to local and national media; a copy made its way to HBO, and soon the land-rush started. I find Ramos alone in the wrestling room, laying down mats for varsity practice with a craftsman's slow precision. He walks me over to the Wall of Fame, where the stars of the past decade are pictured. Here are his state champions and finalists, kids who lettered for two and three years and went on to wrestle in college. But the boy most prominently featured is Kyle, photos of whom are clustered in a small shrine.

"I'm a pretty tough fellow — just ask some of my guys here — but there were times during practice I'd have to turn away because I was all choked up," says Ramos. "What he did defied physics, let alone wrestling — you can't just take someone and throw him on his back if you don't have arms to do it — but every day he did the impossible. He put us on the map, brought all this attention to a small-town school in Georgia, and made every kid work harder by example. I've been at this twenty-nine years, and there are days I come in here and don't really have much energy. Then I look at that wall and see his picture up there and think, *What would Kyle do?*"

JEFF DUNCAN

Desire Without End

FROM THE NEW ORLEANS TIMES—PICAYUNE

IT'S A TYPICAL SIGHT on an October night in Louisiana: a group of coaches leading a high school football team into battle.

But nothing is even remotely typical about this night, or these coaches, or their players, or the school they represent.

They are a New Orleans school, but they are driving to the game from their new campus at Camp Timpoochee in Niceville, Florida, five hours away.

To prepare for the game, they have had just one week of class and one full practice in pads, on a potholed, unlined field that is better suited for sack races than football.

En route to the game, the team caravan has to stop at a sporting goods store to buy helmets for some of the players, and maroon T-shirts for the coaches.

Before heading to Porter Field at St. Martin's Episcopal School in Metairie to face the Crescent City Christian School Pioneers in their first game of the season, the team makes one more stop: Desire Street Academy, a fledgling New Orleans school for seventh-through twelfth-grade boys.

It is their school, an offshoot of the Desire Street Ministry, in the heart of the Ninth Ward and founded by Mo Leverett in 1990 to serve the impoverished, crime-ridden Desire-Florida neighborhood. Now it is in ruins.

On this night, on the way to their first game, the members of the Desire Street Academy Lions are seeing their decimated building, and their devastated neighborhood, for the first time since August 29.

After the tour, they board the bus quietly and head to their game across town.

"They had to see it," said assistant coach Mickey Joseph, a former standout athlete at Archbishop Shaw High School. "I think it helped them start to appreciate this place a little more, knowing they're not going back anytime soon.

"They know they're not going back now."

When Leverett planned the construction of Desire Street Ministry's new school building five years ago, he did so with its rough Ninth Ward neighborhood in mind.

He knew only too well that windows were an invitation for trouble in the crime-ridden Desire-Florida area; a few years back, a bullet crashed through the glass door of his back patio and rattled around the floor just feet from his wife and daughters.

Flying bullets and thrown rocks wouldn't threaten the students inside Desire Street Academy. Leverett fortified the walls in the new building with stone and concrete and included only a few windows in the 36,000-square-foot fortress.

Figuratively and structurally, Desire Street Academy was built to withstand any hell that impoverished urban life could deliver.

Any hell, that is, except high water.

On the morning of August 29, Hurricane Katrina's storm surge tore a fifty-foot-wide breach in the floodwall that stretches from Lake Pontchartrain to the Mississippi River and protects the Ninth Ward. The force of the current lifted train boxcars and eighteen-wheeler trailers at the France Street rail yard and deposited them a football field away.

The Desire Street Academy's plush $3 million complex, two blocks northwest of the breach on the west side of the Industrial Canal, was directly in the path of the onrushing floodwaters.

Water burst through the gym windows, poured over the basketball court, and eventually rose past the first seven rows of bleachers.

When Leverett returned to the building to survey the damage a month after the storm, he found a dead crab in the parking lot and half a telephone pole resting on the stage in the gym.

The contents of his office had been tossed on the floor like toys in a kid's playroom. In the next room, a wooden bookcase had punched through a wall in the office of Danny Wuerffel, the former Heisman Trophy winner and New Orleans Saints quarterback who now serves as the school's development director.

In half a day, Katrina destroyed what Leverett and his staff worked fifteen years to build.

Katrina scattered Desire's faculty and students across the country.

Leverett, most of the staff, and several students evacuated to a Presbyterian church camp in Jackson, Mississippi. Wuerffel, wife Jessica, and twenty-two-month-old son Jonah, whose Lakeview home was destroyed by the Seventeenth Street Canal breach, worked their way to his parents' house in Destin, Florida. School principal Al Jones stayed with family in Baton Rouge.

Most of the students, however, did not have the means to evacuate, and they fought for their lives in the swamped city. Some wound up stranded on rooftops. Some huddled with the masses in the Louisiana Superdome and the Ernest N. Morial Convention Center, or waited for buses on Interstate 10.

Gathered with staff at the camp in Jackson, Leverett anguished each time his cell phone rang.

"I was getting calls from these kids in the Superdome and Convention Center saying, 'Coach, get me out of here,'" Leverett said. "Everybody was fending for themselves and doing as they saw fit. [One student] was scared. He was literally losing his mind and begged me to do something."

Leverett called Wuerffel and board members to plan a rescue mission. They told him the city was off-limits. The National Guard would not let them in.

"Some of the kids were highly dependent on our ministry," Leverett said. "Our school had become more than just a place to go to before these kids went home to be with their families. We had become their families."

Leverett and Wuerffel made a commitment to keep the ministry afloat.

The next morning, Wuerffel woke before sunrise, went to the neighborhood church in Destin, sat at a piano, and quietly played an old hymn:

> In every high and stormy gale,
> My anchor holds within the veil.
> His oath, his covenant, his blood
> Supports me in the whelming flood.
> On Christ the solid rock I stand;
> All other ground is sinking sand.

"I must have played that song for an hour straight," Wuerffel said, "singing and crying."

One of the kids Leverett and Wuerffel worried about was Deangelo Peterson.

Peterson stayed behind with family to ride out the storm at their apartment on Bullard Avenue in eastern New Orleans.

A wiry six-foot-three, Peterson is built like an NFL wide receiver, with sinewy arms, long legs, and massive hands that belie his sixteen years.

Peterson's preternatural frame was vital on the Tuesday after Katrina, when high water surrounded his second-floor unit in the Wind Run apartment complex.

"The water was rising," Peterson said. "And it kept rising."

Using every inch of his frame, Peterson propped his nieces, ages seven months and three years, above his head and waded through the chest-high water to the safety of a nearby hotel. He returned to rescue his mother, his sister, and an aunt.

"I was a little bit scared, but I knew I could walk through the water," Peterson said.

The group survived at the hotel for three days, with minimal food and water, before military troops rescued them by boat and took them to the Convention Center.

Three days later, officials took Peterson and his group to Louis Armstrong International Airport, where they slept on the ground for a night before being evacuated to a shelter in San Antonio.

Desire Street officials found Peterson by sending a local pastor to the shelter with a bullhorn to call out his name.

Heath Davillier, a bright-eyed eighth-grader with an infectious smile, waded through chest-high water from his home on Bienville Street and headed toward the Superdome. He couldn't make it.

"The water was nasty, and it was up to my neck," the pint-sized fourteen-year-old said. "I had to carry my bag over my head to keep it dry."

Deeper water blocked their path to the Superdome, so the group of eight found their way to an Interstate 10 ramp and tried to make their way across the Crescent City Connection. Halfway across, an RTA bus picked them up and dropped them at Worley Junior High

School in Westwego. They stayed there for three days, sleeping on the gym floor and subsisting on a diet of granola bars, fruit cups, and water.

Three days later, a relative picked them up and took them to Baton Rouge, where Heath reconnected with Desire officials.

"I couldn't wait to get back here," said Davillier, a point guard on the Desire basketball team. "This is where all my friends are, and I knew I would get a good education here. They try to help you as much as they can here. This is like my family."

Day by day, other students began to surface. The school opened an administrative office in Atlanta. Officials established a "people locator" database on its Web site and sent staffers into shelters with Desire Street Ministries T-shirts to locate evacuees. In other spots, they asked church volunteers to post fliers with the ministry's phone number and Internet address. Wuerffel used his media connections to make appearances on TV and radio.

"We needed to resuscitate our school," Leverett said.

One by one, the lost were found. Some were as far away as Kansas City, Missouri. Most were in Texas. On a three-day reconnaissance run through east and south Texas, a group of coaches rescued forty-seven boys, picking them up in passenger vans borrowed from local churches.

Students in more isolated locations were flown in on private jets whose cost was donated by supporters. Some used frequent-flier miles of board members to fly commercial.

In the end, the staff located almost 75 percent of the school's 192 students. The whereabouts of about 30 are still unknown to the school.

"The way those kids were calling, we knew we had to go get them," said head football coach Byron Addison, who, along with his coaching staff, helped organize the bus run. "It was all on them. They wanted this."

On October 3, the academy reopened its doors as a boarding school on a donated patch of peaceful countryside in the Florida Panhandle.

Camp Timpoochee sits at the end of a narrow dirt road on the outskirts of Niceville, hidden among a thicket of oak and pine trees along a bluff overlooking Choctawhatchee Bay. Once a playground of the Euchee tribe of American Indians, the area known as Stake Point is a favorite of artifact collectors, who still find remnants of pottery along its sloping, sandy beach.

First and foremost, Timpoochee is a 4-H camp. Deer roam the woodlands, dolphins play in the bay's warm, shallow waters, and box turtles creep along the forest paths.

"This is not normal for any of us," said Jones, a native New Orleanian. "But we're still Desire."

To function as a school, though, Timpoochee needed work. During a few frantic weeks in late September and early October, a transformation took place.

Desire Street staffers worked with contractors to enclose an outdoor pavilion and create a set of classrooms. They converted log cabins into dorms. They cleaned and reorganized a cafeteria, a recreation hall, and a handful of wood-paneled administrative offices.

"I like it so far," Peterson said. "It's fun. You get to hang out and sleep with your friends. It's like college."

And like college, hijinks are common. Eighth-grader Eric Green said he and his friends are fond of late-night canoe excursions in the bay. On a recent Sunday night, Jones happened upon a midnight pillow battle being waged between cabins. He discovered the sortie when he noticed "a big white blob" moving across the darkened courtyard.

"We're still learning as we go," Jones said. "This is new to all of us."

Still, as idyllic as Timpoochee is, it's not home. Other than the presence of an outdoor basketball court, it has little in common with the students' former homes. For all the problems the Desire-Florida neighborhood has, for most of the students, it's all they've ever known. And many are desperate to go back.

"I want to go home too," Jones said. "We all want to be in New Orleans. We're just going to have to tough it out. If we can get through the transition stage, we have the perfect opportunity to train the total kid here."

Desire demands a lot from its students. The school day runs from 8:00 A.M. to 4:00 P.M. The college preparatory curriculum remains unchanged at Timpoochee. Students are tutored in English, math, science, arts, music, physical education, and Bible study. There are also elective courses in construction and culinary arts. Study halls are conducted nightly. Cornrows and braids are prohibited. Students must stay to the right at all times when walking down hallways. Cursing is strictly forbidden. Lights-out is at 10:30 P.M.

The discipline and structure are vital at Desire, where more than two-thirds of the students are raised by single parents or extended family members.

Deep-pocketed donors provide partial sponsorships for the majority of students because few can afford the $6,000 annual tuition. Sponsorships are determined by need (income and family size) and merit (academics, citizenship, athletics, and parental participation). Each student's family is required to pay or work for $500 toward the tuition amount.

Before the storm, Desire's enrollment was a healthy 192, a nearly 300 percent increase from its original 70 in 2002. The goal was to increase to 240 in 2006.

Katrina derailed those plans. It decimated enrollment and plunged the academy into debt.

The ministry's board of directors has tapped its national pool of supporters. Assistance has poured in from across the nation.

The University of Florida, where Wuerffel starred in the mid-1990s, donated $50,000 from pay-per-view proceeds after the Gators' game against Louisiana Tech.

Larry Arrington, dean for extension at Florida's Institute of Food and Agricultural Sciences, offered the use of Camp Timpoochee.

An Atlanta-area church recently donated $66,000 to buy a new bus.

On one October night, a local family dropped off a television set that wasn't being used at home. A couple of hours later, a truckload of desks arrived.

Three rooms at the facility are overflowing with school supplies, backpacks, clothing, and linens.

And yet, it's not enough.

The demands of operating a boarding school have stretched the ministry's resources and fifty-person staff thin. Staff members' work schedules had to be restructured to comply with U.S. wage and labor laws. Counselors were hired to assist the staff and help them cope with the stress. More "dorm dads" were added to supervise the boys overnight and give the beleaguered staff a break.

The school's expenses have increased fourfold, Leverett said. The demands have forced Leverett and Wuerffel to spend the majority of their time on the road in fund-raising efforts.

"We've had to raise a truckload of more money," Leverett said. "We've got a lot of challenges to survive as an organization."

Despite the hurdles, school officials felt it was imperative to revive the District 10-1A football program.

Football is an integral part of the school's mission, as indicated by its well-pedigreed staff. Leverett was a kicker at Tennessee-Chattanooga and an assistant coach at Carver High School. Wuerffel was the 1996 Heisman Trophy winner while at the University of Florida and a fourth-round draft pick of the Saints in 1997; he played six seasons for the Saints, Chicago Bears, Green Bay Packers, and Washington Redskins. Principal Jones was a standout defensive end at St. Augustine High School and Tulane University, and coached at Walker High School. Joseph, the offensive coordinator, was a star quarterback at Shaw High School and University of Nebraska standout. Head coach Addison prepped at Carver and played collegiately at Grambling State University.

"After all that they've been through, we owed it to them to play," Joseph said. "These kids have worked so hard to get to this point. This is what they wanted."

The Lions arranged to play an abbreviated schedule of games back in Louisiana starting October 10, only days after their new equipment arrived.

They made their official LHSAA debut against the Crescent City Pioneers in uniforms that were rescued from high shelves in Addison's flooded-out home two days earlier. Their nifty helmet decals with the block "DSA" and Lions logo had not arrived yet, so the players played in plain black helmets.

At the opening kickoff, one assistant was still peeling the "XL" sticker off his just-purchased "coach's shirt." Water coolers and marker boards would not arrive on the sideline until midway through the first quarter.

On the Lions' first play from scrimmage, they lost a fumble and one of their best players when running back Byron Weber injured his knee.

On the next play, Crescent City rambled twenty-five yards for a touchdown. Fourteen seconds into their season, the Lions trailed 7–0.

From there, it only grew worse. Two more quick touchdowns gave the Pioneers a shocking 20–0 first-quarter lead. The margin grew to 35–6 at halftime.

Bankrupt of confidence, the Lions' play and attitudes devolved in the second half. They played two snaps with ten players. They jumped offsides and were penalized for delay of game repeatedly. They fumbled twice, threw three interceptions, and nearly snapped the ball over the punter's head and between his legs on consecutive attempts. Players argued with each other and talked back to coaches. One player threw his helmet into the fence behind the team's bench. Another tried to pull off his shoulder pads and quit on the spot. Another broke down in tears.

It was a startling contrast to the promising start of the Lions' season. Four days before Katrina, the Lions had defeated Abramson High School in their jamboree. Back in the spring, they had tied St. Bernard (12–12) and Douglass (6–6).

By the time it was over, Crescent City had drubbed the Lions 50–14. In the hectic rush to schedule the game, school officials forgot to arrange for postgame shower facilities. So the players and coaches boarded the bus for the five-hour ride to Niceville dirty and defeated.

They arrived back at Timpoochee at 5:30 A.M.

The season got worse before it got better. Off the field, some students left the program and came back; others left for good. Enrollment, which started at about eighty, had decreased to less than seventy by the time the first academic quarter ended in late November, prompting the administration to begin accepting students from its waiting list, which numbered into the hundreds before the storm. The school opened its doors to about a dozen new students for the second quarter.

On the field, Desire lost to St. Charles Catholic 47–12 and then to Fisher 45–6. In their first three games, they were outscored 142–32 and produced more penalties and turnovers than points.

"There was considerable digression in the four weeks after the storm," Leverett said. "[The players] have had to deal with so much. The bottom line is emotionally there was a very thin layer of capacity to deal with disappointment. They spun out of control when they had to deal with adversity. It was a more difficult experience than I realized."

Essentially, the Lions had become sacrificial lambs. Each game required a ten-hour round-trip bus ride. The home crowds grossly outnumbered their smattering of staff and students in the visiting stands.

But the team played on, and in the manner of the best Hollywood movies, its perseverance was rewarded. In its final game of the season, Desire Street defeated Ridgewood 36–8.

"It was one of the best sporting events that I've been a part of," said Wuerffel, who guided Florida to college football's Division National Championship in 1996 with a 52–20 win against archrival Florida State in the Sugar Bowl at the Superdome. "It meant so much more than just winning a football game to these kids."

Leverett hopes to make Desire's mission more manageable next year. He's in the process of purchasing a church facility on twenty-four acres in Baton Rouge, where he plans to run the school next season while the Ninth Ward is being rebuilt. Officials hope the Louisiana location will help them attract many of the displaced students who couldn't make it to Florida.

"Our school is a very important school in our city and in our state," Leverett said. "I think it's highly important that we preserve Desire Street Academy. It's addressing what was at the heart of the problem in New Orleans in many ways. It's the only one of its kind. It's desperately needed."

Environmental contractors have cleaned the old facility in the Ninth Ward. The building is structurally sound and salvageable, Leverett said. The Desire-Florida neighborhood, however, faces a more uncertain future. Leverett said he wants to become a catalyst in the area's redevelopment.

Time is not on Desire's side. The ministry's lease at Camp Timpoochee expires May 20.

"I'm not entirely sure how it's all going to shake out," Leverett said. "But I remain committed to the goals of our ministry. Hopefully, we can be a launching point for the rest of the neighborhood.

"I miss New Orleans like crazy. I'm in a nice place on the Emerald Coast. I can ride my bike around the neighborhood and not get shot at, but it still don't feel like home. The Ninth Ward of New Orleans, that's where my heart is. I can't shake that."

No one knows for sure when the Ninth Ward will be ready for Desire's return. Like so much else in New Orleans, its future is clouded by uncertainty.

Only one thing is certain: the experience of being away has changed the people at the school.

"It's been difficult," Leverett said, "but in the end we'll look back on it and say it was worth it. We kept something going that is extremely important during one of the worst tragedies the city has ever seen. In the absence of families and resources, we made a difference."

KURT STREETER

The Girl

FROM THE LOS ANGELES TIMES*

A Surprise in the Ring

Do girls box? she asked, turning to her father one evening. *Is it okay for girls to box?*

Well, yeah, mija, *they do,* he answered. *Sure, it's okay for girls to box.*

They were sitting on the bed in his cramped apartment, faces lit by a flickering TV, eating pizza, watching a pro boxing match. Seniesa loved to watch fights with him, loved the way boxers settled their differences, using fists to express what was inside. She was just a kid, a girl enthralled with a man's sport, but she wanted to express herself like that.

Dad? Can I box? Can I learn how to box?

Joe Estrada was shocked, he would remember afterward, but he didn't want to let his daughter down, not with what they had been through. *Yeah,* he said, eyes still on the TV. *Sure,* mija, *you can do that, if you really want to. I'll take you to a gym in a couple of days. I promise.*

He didn't mean it. Boxing wasn't for girls. Not for his girl, a pretty one with thin bones, a delicate nose, and rosy lips. He had lived by his fists, both on the streets and in prison. All he wanted was to protect her. For weeks, he did nothing to make his promise real.

* Quotations in this story are designated in two ways: Those heard by the writer are enclosed in double quotation marks. Those recalled by others in interviews are in italics.

But she grew adamant. She read a book about Muhammad Ali, got a poster of him and tacked it to her wall. She admired his confidence, the way he would not back down, just like her father, she would proudly say, and the way Ali had grown up, just as she had — an outsider looking in. She wanted to become a champion boxer, bold and strong, just like Ali.

Besides, if her father trained her, he would be with her, no matter what. Both needed that, desperately. They needed it to save each other.

The more he put off boxing, the more she pressed.

Finally, guilt got him. One Monday afternoon, he drove her to a gym on a busy street in East L.A. When he parked, she sprinted from the van to the entrance. They walked inside, unsure what was next.

Do you train kids here? Joe asked.

The manager looked down at Seniesa, leaning against her father's side. *How old is she?* he asked.

Eight, Joe said. *Almost nine.*

She's too small, the manager said. *We'll train her, when she's thirteen.*

She walked from the gym with her head down. Joe tried to console her, but actually he couldn't have been happier. Good, he thought, that's the end of this boxing thing. Then, inside his van, he looked at her and saw her staring out the window.

What's wrong, mama? he asked.

She couldn't speak. Tears filled her eyes.

It hit him then how much this meant, how badly she just wanted the chance to step inside a ring and put gloves on and let go.

A few days later, deciding to try once more, he took her to a gym near her home where a group of boy boxers trained.

One of their coaches had grown up with Joe. Two decades before, they were in the same gang. Then Joe Estrada and Paul Gonzales took different paths. Joe scuffled along the gutter. Now forty-two, he had climbed out, but he could easily tumble back, leave Seniesa, even go back to prison. Gonzales, for his part, had risen from the gang and the projects and become a famous boxer.

Joe and Seniesa approached him, near the ring.

Puppet? Is that you? Gonzales asked, calling Joe by his gang name. He had long figured Joe was in jail — or dead. When he remembered Puppet, he thought of a young man with hair below the shoulders, roving eyes, and a tattoo reading "Maryann" burned into his right forearm.

Before him now stood another man: just plain Joe, hair closely cropped, eyes firm, the "Maryann" X-ed out and his gang tattoo covered by a flower, heart, and cross. And then there was the surprise, peeking from behind him, a small girl with smooth, light brown skin and hopeful eyes.

Paul, this is about my daughter, Joe said. *She wants to box. She practically dragged me down here.*

Seniesa was too shy to look him in the eye.

Gonzales was stunned. He would never forget it. *She wants to be a boxer?* he asked. *She's a beautiful little girl. Why on earth would you want her to box?* In his heart, though, Gonzales knew he could not say no. Figuring he owed Joe, he swallowed his doubts.

Sure, he said, *there's a place for your girl here.*

The trainers found Seniesa (pronounced Seh-NEE-sa) an old pair of gloves, showed her a few simple defensive moves and a basic punch. It was but a few days later when she stepped into the ring to box for the first time. Joe felt relief; he was certain she would be hit and then give up. After all, her opponent was a boy.

To Seniesa, it was riveting. She saw the boy, about her size, standing in the corner across from her. She saw men hanging on the ropes, watching, wondering what would happen. They made her nervous. She heard one of them yell: *Attack him, attack him, go forward, see what it's like!*

So she hit the boy.

He smacked her back.

She backed off, uncertain, leaving an opening. He released a hook that plowed into her stomach.

Air sucked from her lungs. She couldn't breathe. She bent over.

Joe gripped hard on the ropes, struggling to keep from leaping in and calling it off, struggling to keep himself from lecturing the boy: Hey, kid, what the hell are you doing, hitting my little girl like that?

Seniesa heard one of the men shout: *Breathe from your stomach, girl! From your stomach!* She breathed in once, she breathed in twice. She stood up straight, like a dreamer rising from a nightmare.

She zeroed in on the boy, her small fists a blur: *whapwhop-whapwhop-whapwhop.*

He tried to shield himself, but now Seniesa was angry, and her blows kept coming. *Whapwhop-whapwhop.* Her fists moved faster than his arms. *Whapwhop.* She saw his legs go shaky.

Stop! a trainer yelled, applauding with the others. Nobody wanted to see the little boy get hurt.

What Seniesa felt was more than good: it was unforgettable. She walked over to her father and hugged him.

He caught himself beaming. My little girl, he thought, she can fight.

Mija, *aren't you afraid?* he asked as he drove her home to her mother's apartment. *You're the only girl out there. Boxing is hard, mama.*

No, Dad, she said. *I'm not afraid.*

The little boy Seniesa pummeled never showed up to box again.

The Only Girl in the Place

She was a surprise. I had set out to write the story of a boy, near manhood, full of promise, one step from making it big as a boxer.

I searched the weary Latino neighborhoods of East Los Angeles, scattered with boxing gyms. One was fashioned from an abandoned jail, another from an old building that rose from the street like barracks, another from a rundown church where the pews had been replaced with a large canvas ring, and still another from an old body shop with walls splintered by bullets.

They were filled with young men. Some fought because the boxer, proud, tough, and loyal to the craft, was so revered in these parts. Some fought because they had been pushed to turn their machismo into something useful, even if it meant taking blows, countless blows, again and again. Some were tender and some were hard. Some were high school kids with stubble chins, tough nicknames, and new tattoos, and some were children as young as six.

The gyms of East L.A. have produced a long line of great fighters. Paul Gonzales was one. Richie Lemos, world featherweight champion in 1941, was another. The most recent and most famous was Oscar De La Hoya, a world titleholder in six weight classes. But for every fighter who has made himself into a name, scores upon scores have tried and failed. When I stopped by the Hollenbeck Youth Center, I heard about every young man who was training there. I was impressed. Each showed confidence and hustle and hard punches. In a loud, bustling arena that smelled like old socks, I watched for hours, searching for the next De La Hoya.

Then, one day, in late August of 2002, my attention drifted past the boys and past the ring. Over there was a girl, the only girl in the place.

Her fists sliced through the air, and her feet skipped lightly as she punched a heavy bag filled with sand, dangling from a rafter by a chain. Next to her, eyeing every move, stood a thin man wearing a T-shirt with the sleeves torn off. Seniesa and Joe. I hadn't imagined this. She was not a teenager, not even a he. I knew that female boxers fought professionally. There were movies about them. But I did not know that girls still in grade school boxed, their eyes fixed on future fame, just like the boys.

Intrigued, I walked over and sat on a wooden box. Joe smiled but didn't say a word. Seniesa worked on a single punch, a round right hook. She peered over her red gloves at the bag. When she was ready, she bent her knees, corked her body, first to the right, then to the left, and let her thin arm release. *WHUMP!*

Her punches were solid, smooth, well-coordinated, bringing to mind the form of good male boxers. I decided to come back. Soon, I became a regular. As time passed, Seniesa and her father began to confide in me. I learned that this small girl not only wanted to be in the ring, she *needed* to be there — not just for herself, but for her father as well.

She had challenges far bigger than her next fight. Her neighborhood, for one, where kids got shot for as little as standing on the sidewalk. Her mother, for another, who didn't really want her to box. Her brothers, who always seemed to be on the edge of trouble. And her uncle, a turbulent man who lived close to trouble himself. Her life was filled with unpredictability, sneak attacks, ambushes, and obstacles lurking to surprise her.

Even her own father could be a problem. He was an ex-street gangster, ex-doper, ex-convict. He was a father who, for all his goodness with her, was only one more angry confrontation away from going back to prison. Then she would lose him, maybe forever. Still, he towered above everything else in her life. If not for him, she would not be here at this sweaty gym.

But a girl?

I thought she'd quit. What girl could want the loneliness she would find in the shadows of a sport so very male?

Then I listened to the sound: *WHUMP!*

The girl.

It was her fist, plunging into the bag, swinging it in all directions. Seniesa possessed a remarkable punch. She reared back and hit the bag again. *WHUMP!* This girl — oh, but this girl had power. *WHUMP!* I shuddered. The sound of her blows, so solid, persuaded me to forget about boy boxers.

I stopped my search for a new De La Hoya. He paled beside this little girl, her dreams and her courage, fighting to redeem her father. She knew that he needed her to help him stay straight, as much as she needed him to train her to box.

Life in "the Zone"

Growing up, Seniesa Estrada had found there was a lot to learn about her father.

He came from Tijuana, where he and his mother lived in a dirt-floor shack with no bathroom and no running water, where a chicken from the backyard was a feast. In Los Angeles, they settled in Aliso Village, a crime-ridden housing project near downtown.

By eleven, he had joined Primera Flats, a gang that "jumped him in" by testing how much of a licking he could take. In what became a trait for life, he fought back — not just to survive, but to dominate. He called it going into "the zone," an anger that built and built until finally he snapped, feeling nothing but rage and raw energy. It turned him into one of the toughest fighters in the neighborhood.

At fifteen, he was an enforcer and a drug dealer. When he wasn't fighting, he was selling: weed, acid, PCP, uppers, downers, crystal meth. He snatched purses, robbed grocery stores, and stuck up jewelers. He was arrested, jailed, then got out and started selling, fighting, and robbing again.

Once, he would recall, an enemy gang tied his ankles to the bumper of an Impala and dragged him through a park. Pavement ripped at his flesh until, somehow, the rope snapped and he got away. Paul Gonzales saw him afterward and would remember, "He had his shirt all tore off, and his back was just thrashed." Joe would recall two other close calls: When a rival held a pistol to his head and pulled the trigger. *Click-click*; it jammed, and he escaped. Then, when he was shotgunned by a tough from the Third Street Gang, ricochets crashing around his head. He held his best friend, who was hit and struggling to sip air. The friend died in his arms.

Those days stayed with him like scars. Dangerous as they were, they suited him. What he liked most was to square off with bare fists at Pecan Park, two street gangsters on the grass, the violence contained only because everyone in the circle around them was armed. Nothing, not even being with a woman, made him feel better than standing firm, sinewy, olive-skinned, with piercing eyes, just him against the other guy, hitting, being hit, the joy of landing a stiff punch behind an ear.

It was a small step from there into "the zone." Once, in a brawl over one of his girlfriends, a challenger crashed a crowbar over Joe's brow. Anger engulfed him. It built until he lost track of who he was, where he was, and what he was doing. He wrested the crowbar away, rose, and chased his assailant. He tackled him. He lifted the crowbar high and brought it down on the other man's head.

That was Joe the *terrorista*. Then there was Joe the Robin Hood, as he would come to call himself: charming, smooth, cool, doting on his mother, bighearted like her, doling out money from his drug sales to anyone who needed it, buying toy trucks and Barbie dolls for neighborhood kids.

Like his mother, he was meticulous: he wore spit-and-polish Stacy Adams shoes, crisp Pendleton shirts, and pants with a crease he ironed himself, perfectly down the middle, just so.

Long before Seniesa was born, drugs took her father hostage for the first time, and the drugs tortured and defeated him as no back-alley thug ever could.

His undoing was heroin. He could not say no to the way it made him feel. When he was twenty-two, heroin turned his hair stringy and wild, his face pasty, his body bone-thin. The stone-cold gangster, the sharply dressed street tough, became a strung-out junkie.

Most mornings, he found himself on the outskirts of Aliso Village, by a liquor store at the corner of First Street and Utah, under shot-out street lights and shards of glass, shaky, desperate, willing to do anything for another fix.

Sometimes a teenager ran by in a gray sweatsuit and a black cap.

It was Paul Gonzales. He too was in Primera Flats, but with help from a street cop who coached him, he also was an up-and-coming boxer, training with an eye on the Olympics, rising before dawn to jog from the projects to downtown and back.

Puppet, you all right, man? Gonzales asked one morning, slowing to a walk. He would remember feeling bad, because he had always looked up to Joe.

Doin' okay, Joe replied. *Hangin' in there.*

Joe, you gotta get clean, man. You gotta get off that stuff. It's killing you.

He knew Paul was right. He watched him run off, across the First Street Bridge, toward the downtown skyscrapers peering through the morning fog. Good Lord, he thought, I could have been like Paul. If I didn't love the gangs and the streets and the drugs so much . . . I could have been a boxer.

Not long afterward, Seniesa's father went to the penitentiary.

The reason is burned into his memory and was laid plain at his preliminary hearing. In late 1979, a woman in Aliso Village bolted from her bed. Someone was breaking into her house. As she reached to call the police, a Primera Flats gangster known as Pee Wee pushed a .38-caliber pistol into her face.

Put the phone down, he said. *I'll shoot.*

She looked up at Pee Wee, then saw Joe. She knew his mother and had known Joe since grade school. *I don't know why you are doing this,* she said.

Pee Wee demanded her stereo, her TV, her money. *Bitch,* he said. *I will shoot you.*

That was more than Joe could take. *Hey, Pee Wee,* he said. *Don't shoot her, I know her family.*

From there, Joe's recollection and the woman's differ. Joe said he up and left. But she swore otherwise: Joe and Pee Wee looted her apartment.

To avoid trial, Joe pleaded guilty to robbery. He was already on probation for another stickup. "He cannot function in the community without resorting to criminal behavior," a probation officer told the judge, who sentenced Joe to three years in California State Prison at Susanville.

Prison was tough. He raged and fought to stay alive. But it was good for one thing: it got him off heroin and helped him gain a semblance of self-control.

Back on the streets in time for the 1984 Summer Olympics, Joe stood among the spectators at the Los Angeles Memorial Sports Arena to watch Paul Gonzales in the ring, fighting the way Joe wanted to fight. Gonzales won a gold medal.

Twisting Out of Control

Even before Seniesa was born, her father had a feeling.

He had married Maryann Chavez, a girlfriend from Primera Flats, who stuck by him through all the drugs and prison, and they had two sons. But now, when Maryann got pregnant again, Joe felt deep in his soul that this was a girl.

In anticipation of her birth, he gave her two names: Seniesa, after the daughter of a friend in his gang, and Carmen, after his mother. He crawled on his hands and knees, dousing the bathroom floor with Pine Sol and using a toothbrush to clean the corners of the nursery where his little angel would sleep.

She was born June 26, 1992, at White Memorial Medical Center in Boyle Heights. For all his eagerness, Joe missed the moment. Maryann had begged him to go call her father, to say the baby was coming. He ran down a hallway to a phone booth, and Seniesa slipped suddenly into the world. When Joe walked back in, he saw a nurse with a baby in her arms, wrapped in a soft blanket.

Yes, he said, holding her. *A girl. My little girl.*

She weighed six pounds, eleven ounces. Her face was round and pudgy, her scalp matted with brown peach fuzz. She wailed like a banshee.

He looked into her amber eyes. Nothing had ever come close to this. He felt warmth. Certainty. Pure love. With Seniesa, he would carve out a new and special role, a role he would cling to like hope itself. He would be her guardian, the protector of his little girl.

She would need one. Home was in El Sereno, an enclave in eastern L.A. divided street after street by a handful of gangs. He would see to it that nothing would hurt her. He rose in the dead of night when she cried, three, four, five times, to feed her, hold her, and place her at his side, rocking her back and forth, back and forth.

In the morning, he dressed her in a blue bonnet and lay her on a pillow in the living room. *You are going to be special, little mama,* he whispered. *Special.* In the evening, he put her on his chest and sat back in his La-Z-Boy and watched boxing, describing the action, blow by blow, long before she could understand.

One afternoon when they were alone, she struggled to her feet. She gave him an unforgettable look. Her legs shook. She clung to the top of the coffee table. Slowly she began to tumble. He wrapped his hands softly around her.

Try again, mija, he whispered. Her face tightened with determination as she worked to regain her balance. She took a right step, a left.

That's it, little girl. Come on, mija, *come on, keep going.*

She took a few steps more. Only then did she hesitate. Again she began to pitch backward. He caught her. Her father would not let her fall.

Not long after that came her first word. He was there to hear it, in the kitchen one morning as he made a bacon-and-cheese omelet.

Daddy.

How it felt, seeing those first steps, hearing that first word: Daddy. As if he were a good man, a decent and even honorable human being.

For his new family, Joe worked hard with his brother Rick at the family shop, building signs and installing them at strip malls all over the city. After the kids were born, Maryann stayed home, and it took all Joe could do to make enough money. Sometimes he left work at midnight, then rose before dawn to drive to another job.

To fight fatigue, a coworker offered cocaine.

Joe said no. He knew where drugs could lead.

But then, when Seniesa was just a few months old, he gave in. One line led to another, then another. After a few weeks, he was hooked again, sucking thick ridges of coke up his nose seven times a day.

Even then, he tried to be a daddy. He kept phoning home from work. *How's she doing, is she okay?* he asked. *Is my baby okay?*

In front of the TV, she would sit with him, lying in his lap, curling under his chin, cooing, even when he was high. For the backyard, he got her a swimming pool. Its sky-blue metal sidings rose four feet above the ground. Everyone wanted to splash around with Seniesa, teach her to swim. But there was only one person who could coax her into the water without a struggle: her father.

Inevitably, he grew erratic. Maryann began to fear him. Their quarrels grew ugly. When he came home, she huddled with Seniesa and the boys in a bedroom, cordoning him off in the living room, demanding he stay there and sleep on the couch.

The night before Seniesa's first birthday, he went out smoking, drinking, and snorting. He arrived late for her party. Head throbbing and in a cold sweat, he slunk through the celebration, a knot in his stomach. Everyone could see he was back to his old ways. And they knew he was failing as a father. It was Maryann who tied the piñata to an oak tree, grilled the hot dogs, poured the sodas, and fussed over their daughter. He stayed on the periphery — at a party for his little angel.

One night, when he came home from a long work trip, Maryann had left him. She took the kids. The house was bare. Everything of any importance was gone. Worst of all, Seniesa was gone.

He stopped working. He twisted out of control. Soon enough, he was back on heroin.

Seniesa didn't see him for months. Then, when she was about three, she began asking for her father.

Her mother, thinking it would be okay, let her visit him.

Seniesa saw a bare floor, a mattress in a corner of the living room, covered with a few blankets. She met pushers, junkies, and street gangsters. Some had enemies, and they were turning her old home into a death trap. Once, when she was not there, an addict was killed on the front steps.

Joe tried to protect her. When she came to visit, he told his housemates to put away their drugs and guns. He gave them a few bucks, told them to leave, go buy some pizza. Nobody, he said, was to let anything happen to his little girl.

But he couldn't bring himself to change, even for her.

One day, when Seniesa was not around, he asked himself: Why on earth go on? He couldn't find an answer.

He slumped into a chair, determined to stop the pain.

He put a chalky chunk of heroin into a spoon with a dab of water and heated it with a match until it bubbled. He plunged a needle into the crook of his arm, pushed on the syringe, and let the concoction smooth through his body.

He would forever feel the shame. As the heroin enveloped him in its warmth, he saw an image of his little girl, in a floppy white hat with a rose on top, just like the one she wore in his favorite photograph. He felt heartbreak. But he wasn't done. He stumbled into the bathroom and shot up again, knowing well that a second dose might be enough to kill him.

Two junkie roommates found him. They filled the bathtub with water and ice. They dumped him into it, pulled him out, slapped him, propped him up, and walked him in circles on the living room floor.

He slept, then woke, sore, spent, and thankful to be alive. He had to leave, flee, straighten out. He needed his family back. Needed his little angel.

For months, he lived like a stray dog, with anyone who would take him in. He slept on couches, in cars. He holed up in a studio apartment on a run-down street near the clanking East L.A. train yards.

His brother, Seniesa's Uncle Rick, took him to church. Even before the sermons, Joe was in the bathroom, snorting coke.

Finally, one night, he sat on his bed in his dim room, all alone. He knew that if he did not stop drugging, he would lose his kids, lose his life, lose Seniesa forever.

He opened his black leather-bound Bible to John 3:16: "For God so loved the world that he gave his only begotten son . . ."

God did this for me, sacrificed his child, Joe told himself, in wonderment. For me, a crook and an addict. Even with all the unspeakable pain I've caused. Even I can be forgiven.

He felt hair rising on his arms and on the back of his neck. He stood up from the bed, feet planted firmly in the gray carpet. He clutched the Bible to his chest with both hands.

Please, Jesus, help me, he prayed. *I know you are there, just show me.* He fell to his knees, tears rolling from his eyes. His words and what was happening became etched in his mind. *I just want my family back. I just want forgiveness for the things I have done. I just want to prove that I am a good man.*

All the while, things were not well with Seniesa. She had grown aggressive. She was snake-hip skinny, and her light brown locks flipped off her shoulder and into the air as she plowed through life, attacking it, a one-girl storm. Again and again she crashed her bike, once flipping herself over the handlebars. Again and again she ran into her mother's sliding glass door. She slammed her forehead against it in full sprint, as if on purpose.

To Maryann and Joe, she seemed angry, frustrated perhaps with his struggle. How could he protect her if he couldn't save himself? Maybe she was afraid. He was hardly around; maybe she feared that someday he might never be.

A Magnet for Fighting

Somehow, slowly, Seniesa's father found the strength.

Maybe it was his newfound faith. Maybe it was the damage he saw in his family, the pain to Seniesa. Maybe it was all of this, in an overwhelming way. Somehow, he no longer wanted to go out at night and find trouble. It took time, but Joe finally began to confront his past.

Seniesa was about six when he started to turn around. He kicked drugs and went back to work at the sign shop. There was too much hurt between her parents for reconciliation, but not between Joe and the kids. He saved money, bought a van, and took them to movies, to Disneyland, and to Dodger games. He helped coach the boys' baseball teams.

But he lived alone and was lonely. Sometimes, when he called Maryann's apartment on weekends to see if the kids wanted to come over, the boys preferred to stay home.

Not Seniesa. She always begged her dad to pick her up.

When he didn't call her, she called him. *Daddy, Daddy, when are you coming to see me?*

With him, she was sweet and playful. Shy, even. And Joe noticed that when he was around more, she stopped inflicting her aggression on herself.

Instead she turned it outward. She began attracting fights like a magnet. At home, at school, at parties, she wrestled, scratched, clawed, and tried to lay a good whipping on any kid she thought had slighted her.

Once, she bloodied a little girl's face so badly that Maryann swore she would never take her to another birthday party.

Then there was the day Maryann and Seniesa waited in line at the Social Security office near their home. Maryann couldn't believe her eyes. Seniesa motioned to a little girl, waving at her to come closer.

What's going on? her mother asked. *Stop acting so embarrassing.*

She's staring at me. I don't want no one staring at me, Seniesa said.

She scowled at the little girl, who stood near her own mother and stuck out her tongue.

Seniesa was ready to brawl. *Want some of this? Come get it. I'll kick your butt. You don't want to mess with me.*

None of this surprised Joe. Sure, he thought, she needed to calm down, but there was something about her courage that made him happy. "Her way of reacting to frustration, to fear, is like my own," Joe would say, looking back. Her way of reacting was to fight.

So it was that at his apartment one day in late 2000, while they sat on his bed, as they often did, eating pepperoni pizza, napping, and watching professional fighters on TV, she asked if she could box. Would he teach her?

At eight, she was old enough to know what might happen to her father if he ever went back to fighting on the streets.

It was too much, perhaps, to expect either of them to have wondered if she was asking to fight in his place. No, she seemed to want this for herself, to become a champion. But did she realize that this could be a way to show the world that her coach — her father — was in fact a good man, despite his past? That she could redeem him?

Whether she realized any of this, it was true that she would be making something good out of the aggression she felt inside.

Her father wondered if it would be too much. Shouldn't she be hanging out with her girlfriends, playing hopscotch and double Dutch?

Seniesa wanted no part of that.

She wanted to be a boxer.

"Dang, She's Good. Dang, She Is Tough."

She looked formidable, even against a boy named Frankie.

Seniesa was ten, long-limbed and lithe. She strode across the ring, tentative at first, then gaining confidence with each step, shoulders back, chin tucked, gloved fists wagging.

Frankie Gomez was her age. But he'd been boxing for four years, more than thirty bouts, almost all victories. He was stronger and more experienced, so he sparred as her foil. He worked on his defense while she worked on her offense. He punched only to hold her off.

"Come on, baby, come on," chanted Joe Estrada, forty-four, her father. "Hit him. Hit him."

With each combination, she forced Frankie to step backward. For every step he retreated, she took a step forward, coiled quickly, and let the gloves fly again.

Whap-whap-whap: the sound of a BB gun. Her ponytail whirled around her head. *Whap-whap-whap*. She pressed against him.

He fought back, throwing a right-left combination, his fist mashing her nose, followed by a punch that glanced against her shoulder and knocked her to the left. Sweat flew from her thin arms and glistened on the silver-painted canvas.

Frankie weaved and ducked and turned, creating little openings that she tried to seize. Some of her punches hit his gloves. Some hit his chin.

He grimaced, feeling the sting.

"Come on, Seniesa." It was Joe, again. "Hit him. Attack."

Whap-whap. Whap-whap. Step by step, she forced him across the ring, twenty-five feet square.

Then her father told her to finish him off. "Last ones, baby. Power punches, baby."

I stood against the ropes, a foot away. Joe's sweaty green T-shirt smelled like sour buttermilk. I saw a gleam in Seniesa's eyes.

She stepped forward, right fist leading.

From outside the ropes, a cross-section of the neighborhood — gang thugs, muscled men, scrawny boys, teenage girls, and middle-aged mothers — clapped loudly, especially the women. "Go, girl, go!" they shouted. "Dang, she's good. Dang, she is tough."

"Come on, *mija*," Joe said. "Come on. Come forward. Are you tired?"

"No," she huffed, around her plastic mouthpiece. She homed in on Frankie, who leaned against the ropes. *Whap-whap-whap*.

And it was over. Frankie reached out to touch her gloves, appreciative of her work.

Joe kissed Seniesa on the forehead, where her hair parted in the middle. "Good, *mija*, good. That's the way. You're gonna be a champ."

Being a champ. It was what she wanted. It was what Joe wanted for her. She was four-feet-eight and just under seventy pounds when I first saw them. He was an ex-gangster, had done hard time, and was not long off heroin. She had a dream: to win an Olympic gold medal, then to become a champion boxer, like her hero, Muhammad Ali. Her dream was Joe's dream.

If she made it come true, I realized, she would have to do it against long odds. The Olympics still didn't have events for female fighters. She could not get many matches; few girls wanted to box. She would have to do it despite her mother; Maryann Chavez worried about injuries and wanted her to become a cheerleader. She might even have to do it despite her father; Joe was her coach, but he was an ex-junkie with a blistering temper and a street instinct for revenge. One slip could send him back to prison.

Divorced from Maryann in 1996, Joe brawled with her boyfriend about a year and a half afterward. It was one of the upheavals in Seniesa's family that had a way of ambushing her. All it took was Seniesa's complaint that the boyfriend had twisted her arm.

Joe's anger flared. A few evenings later, he lay in wait outside Maryann's apartment. As the boyfriend left, Joe appeared.

Don't be f—— with my kids! he said, and he launched a fierce barrage of blows. With pride, he would recall that he had dropped the boyfriend in his tracks.

Joe stood over him. *Seniesa, that's my baby,* he said. *Don't you ever touch her again.*

Seniesa didn't see the fight. But she did see the boyfriend barge back into her mother's apartment, blood pouring from his face. He had a swollen eye and a fat lip. Seniesa's grandfather was there. He had known Joe for years. *Don't go against him,* she heard her grandfather say. *That fool is crazy. He will kill you.*

Maryann thought Joe was jealous of her boyfriend. But to Seniesa and her father, the brawl was about defending Seniesa. She was proud, grateful even, that he would go to such lengths, but she knew what might happen if he ever killed someone. He'd already served time for robbery. This could take him away from her for life.

Boxing was still new to Seniesa: the tournaments, held in sweaty, tinderbox gyms in the middle of tough neighborhoods; the spectators, breathing down on the ring, hoping for a knockout; the air, heavy with cigarette smoke and the smell of stale beer. Boxing was hard, ugly. But even when she lost, she loved every bit of it.

By the fall of 2002, she had started winning, and not just in spar-ring matches with boys like Frankie. Her reputation grew. Police Athletic League champ. Silver Gloves champ. The best little girl fighter in East Los Angeles. Sometimes it scared opponents away. They would find out they were fighting Seniesa Estrada, and they wouldn't show up.

She could always count on Joe. Always.

"I see her becoming an Olympic gold medal winner," he said. "And after that, a pro, champion of the world." We were standing outside the ring at the Hollenbeck Youth Center, a noisy athletic emporium on First Street, watching her train. His voice sharpened, mimicking Ali: "Cham-PEEN of the world. Float like a butterfly, sting like a bee."

He reminded me that several women boxed professionally, and that women's boxing was at least being considered for the Olym-pics. "I guess I'm living my life through her," he said. "I always wanted the chance to be Olympic gold medal champion. Just like Paul Gonzales. I see her becoming something that I could have been . . . if I would have not been around the environment that I was."

Like her father, Seniesa was enamored of the violence she could wreak with her fists. "I love how it feels," she told me. She noticed my brows rise. She looked me in the eye, something she didn't of-ten do. "I like to hit people." In the ring, she said, she lost track of time and her surroundings. All she felt was a flash of energy, and all she saw were her own boxing gloves, lashing out, striking a nose, a cheek, a stomach. It was something similar to what her father felt in a street fight. It was what he called entering "the zone."

But she did not want him to go back to the streets. She sighed and shuddered when she thought about it. She knew she was doing this for him as much as for herself. "It helps him," she told me. "Helps give him something that's, like, good to do." She knew she must keep doing as he told her. "My dad keeps motivating me to keep boxing. He keeps telling me to practice and train.

"He says, 'We have to do this.'"

"Not Afraid of Nothing"

"Three-three-three!" Joe yelled.

A three was a left hook. A two was a straight right.

It was October 2, 2002, four days until the Desert Showdown, in Thermal, near Palm Springs. I watched her drill and spar and run miles through a park, then climb back into the ring and slam her fists into her father's big gloves as he shouted numbers that signaled the punches he wanted her to throw.

She pounded his mitts, rapid-fire. *Whop-whop-whop.*

Each blow came with an *"oomph"* — first from her pursed lips when she threw them, then from Joe when he took them. As she waded toward him, fists up, he began jabbing softly at her head, to keep her honest.

When they finished, he wrapped his arms around her narrow shoulders. "Nobody can beat you, baby. *No-bah-dee!*" They leaned against the ropes. "She's fierce, Kurt. She's not afraid of nothing. *Nah-thing.*"

At school that day, a girl had slapped Seniesa. "They were playing," Joe said, "and the little girl started getting rough and hit my girl. Seniesa, what did you do?"

"Smacked her back. Smacked her in the jaw."

He patted her shoulder.

"That was the end of it," she added.

I reminded Joe that he frequently spoke of his Christianity. At school, wouldn't Jesus counsel Seniesa to turn the other cheek?

"Kurt, there's a time and a place for that," he said. "Sometimes you have to hit back. That's in the Bible too."

He turned to Seniesa. "Honey," he said, "you're ready for this weekend."

They left the afternoon before the tournament, everyone in Joe's maroon van: Seniesa and boy boxers from her gym, who trained with her every day and were becoming her surrogate brothers.

They were boisterous and cocky. She was guarded, trying to figure out her place, still too unsure to look them in the eye. They were thick and powerful, with meaty hands, callused skin, and ropes of muscle that snaked around their shoulders. She was soft-skinned and bony. What muscles she had were still not visible.

The boys looked tough, with shaved heads or stubby crew cuts. She looked pretty, hair done up in a trademark ponytail, bunched together and tied with a colored band. They wore rumpled black shorts and smelly shirts. She wore blue shorts and pressed T-shirts, white and pink, adorned with cartoon kittens, smiley faces, and sweet sayings: FBI — Forever Beautiful and Innocent. They had fight names, such as *El Terror*, embroidered on their shorts. She had no fight name, just the nicknames her family had given her: NeeNee and Pookie. At ringside, onlookers sometimes called her, simply, the girl.

The van pulled up at La Familia High School. Two beige canvas rings had been set up in a baseball field. Joe and Seniesa checked in with tournament officials. Dozens of boxers, their families and trainers milled around. They came from as far away as Utah. Most were Latino, but only a few were girls.

An official told Joe that his daughter would fight someone named Kelly, from Arizona. Walking in the grass not far from the ring, Seniesa spotted a girl her size, wearing boxing shorts. *Are you Kelly from Arizona?* she asked.

The girl nodded.

Seniesa sized her up.

Later, at the hotel where she, her father, and the boys were staying, she told me: "I'm gonna beat that girl, Kelly from Arizona. Beat her up."

She looked in her bag. "Gloves, headgear, pads. Good," she said, quietly. She sat down. Then she got back up and went through the bag again. "Gloves, headgear, pads. Got it."

"Nervous?" I asked.

"No," she said. Her voice rose. "I trained so hard for this." She swore she had no butterflies, but her face betrayed her. It was gray.

Noon came and sent the temperature to one hundred degrees. At the school, mariachi music blared, and the air filled with the aroma of grilled pork, beef, and corn. Two teenage boys fought. The crowd moaned with each stiff punch, every quick hook. Men hollered, jumped, and high-fived. "He got 'em good!" "That boy got skills." "That boy got straight *cojones!*"

Near the ring, Seniesa sat in a chair as a trainer wrapped her hands tightly with gauze and white tape. Then she rose and walked among the boxers and officials.

"Did you see Kelly from Arizona?" she asked.

To another, she said, "I'm fighting Kelly from Arizona. Have you seen her?"

She spotted Joe. "Dad, do you see her? Do you see Kelly from Arizona?"

She shadow-boxed. Her taped fists hammered the air. "I've been waiting for this one," she said. She turned away. I could see her talking to herself as she punched. "I'm not nervous. I'm not nervous."

Joe walked toward us, head down. "Bad news, baby."

Seniesa stopped. She looked up.

"She's not here," Joe said. "Kelly from Arizona is not here. They don't know what happened. She left."

"What does that mean? Kelly from Arizona isn't here?"

"Well, it looks like she went home. You don't have a fight. There's no one for you to fight."

Silence.

"Oh," she mumbled, voice sagging. She looked away, toward a thicket of nearby palm trees, mouth open slightly, as if she wanted to say something. "Oh."

Slowly, gingerly, she took her puffy boxing gloves and stuffed them into her bag.

They walked back to the van, his arm around her, the only sound coming from the crunch of their feet on parking lot gravel. Both stared at the ground. She began to unwrap the tape from her fists.

"I can't believe this," Joe said, angrily. They were leaving without a fight. He wanted to swear, but he tried not to around his angel. "Just a bunch of garbage," he said. "Just a real bunch of bull."

On the freeway back to Los Angeles, he told her not to worry. She would get more fights. She just had to hang in there. But his words could not make the devastation go away. He glanced at her.

She was crying, using the tape to dab away the tears.

A Mother's Misgivings

If it wasn't an opponent fleeing, or her father brawling, then it was her mother. Maryann could ambush Seniesa's dreams just as surely as any other challenge outside the ring. Seniesa didn't get home from the tournament until nearly midnight. It was a school night, and her mother was waiting up. She was upset.

Maryann wasn't keen on boxing. If Seniesa wanted to box, she'd let her, but she worried that her little girl was going to suffer a brain clot, worried that she would break her nose and lose her prettiness. She wanted her daughter to become a cheerleader and hoped that she would soon discover boys. Then, maybe, she wouldn't care so much about boxing.

Barely in the door, Seniesa looked into her black bag and realized that she had left her math book at her father's house. Maryann's unhappiness doubled. Maybe the forgotten book was a sign, she said: *It's not good to spend so much time boxing.*

With that, Seniesa picked up the phone. She would recall choking back tears. *Dad*, she blurted. *Help.*

Maryann took the phone away and told Joe to meet her downtown, at a midpoint between El Sereno and where he lived. *Bring the math book.*

Joe couldn't have cared less about the math book. He feared that Maryann would make Seniesa quit fighting.

You bitch, he would recall shouting into his cell phone. *Don't tell her she can't box.*

Bitch? Don't you call me a bitch!

They raged at each other. Maryann had a new boyfriend. He took the phone, hoping to make peace.

Joe told him not to butt in.

The boyfriend said he had every right to butt in.

I'm coming over right now! Joe said. *You wait.*

Seniesa looked up. Her mother's boyfriend paced near the door. Seniesa was shocked at how fast a forgotten book had turned into chaos. She braced herself. *Oh, man*, she would remember thinking, *I bet it's gonna end up in a fight. I bet.*

Her father had been ready for bed, in his long white boxer shorts with his white tube socks pulled snugly to his knees. He started to put on his jeans, but then he began having doubts: *Don't be stupid, man. You don't need to be going over there. You're gonna get there, and Maryann is gonna call the cops, and it's gonna be nothing but bad. And if you do fight, what's your little girl gonna think? This will scare her. This won't be good for her to see.*

He took off the jeans and slipped them back into a drawer. The math book was forgotten.

Seniesa was glad nothing happened. Cops could mean prison, and prison could take him away from her for a long time. Besides, she was fond of her mother's new boyfriend, who had a past like her father's. She did not want them to fight.

But one evening soon afterward, when her father drove her home, her mother and the boyfriend pulled up at the same time. Seniesa walked to the porch and turned to see the two men get out of their cars and walk toward each other.

What's up, dog? her father said. *You were talking a lot of s* ——. *You still want to get down, or what?*

Seniesa watched her mother's boyfriend take off his shirt. The two men began throwing punches. Her mother's boyfriend rushed at her father, bending, clutching, not letting go. Her father hit him in the head, got him in a headlock, and twisted him to the ground. They cursed, swore, and jabbed.

Finally, the boyfriend got loose and stalked off, yelling.

Seniesa claimed later that she had felt no fear. She had seen street fights before, she said, and even had fallen to the floor one time at the sound of gunshots outside her mother's apartment. This wasn't about to faze her. "My dad had control," she told me, describing his dominance of the fight. We were eating lunch. She sat next to her father and chomped away on a French fry, not a care in the world. "It wasn't even like a real fight."

To Joe and Maryann, the fight was very real. Maryann got a restraining order, on the grounds that Seniesa's father was a menace.

Joe felt awful. Here he was, supposedly turning his life around, supposedly a God-fearing man, and his street instincts were still getting the better of him. He was still fighting, still letting his anger loose, right in front of the kids and the neighbors and Maryann.

"Hopefully, one day," he told me, "I will learn not to get involved in stuff like that. Hopefully, one day, I will see it isn't worth it."

It took weeks before Maryann let him pick up Seniesa at her apartment again. When he did, he was forced to stay half a block away. He parked his van down the street and called on his cell phone to say she should come out.

In the next few months, Seniesa entered four tournaments. Each time, she couldn't get a match. She got trophies and belts by default. They meant nothing. She didn't earn them by hitting anyone.

Maybe her mother was right. Maybe boxing shouldn't be such a big deal. Maybe boxing wasn't for her. Maybe boxing was just not for girls.

She knew her dreams were her father's dreams, and she knew that if she quit, he would be without his redeeming angel.

But his brawling and the restraining order were keeping them apart.

They were in Joe's van, leaving the gym one afternoon, when Seniesa began to tell him what she was thinking. She was tired of training so much and not getting any fights, tired of seeing boy boxers get plenty of them, while she got so few.

Dad, she said, *I think I should quit.*

Life Throws Some Unexpected Punches

Her words hung in the air. *I should quit.* She looked away from her father.

He was stunned. He didn't know what to say, but he knew he had to say something — and fast. To him, "quit" was a four-letter word. So long as she was his daughter, Seniesa Carmen Estrada was not going to quit. She had put too much into boxing.

They both had. Boxing was as important to Joe Estrada, forty-four, as it was to Seniesa, who was ten. Her dream was his dream: that one day she would win a world championship. Besides, coaching her was helping him stay away from his gang, free of drugs, and out of prison.

In his van, musty with sweaty shirts, worn-out gloves, and moldy hand wraps, they rode through East L.A., past Lincoln Park, one of his hangouts during his gang days. He reminded her of that. Then past Central Juvenile Hall, where he had spent so many weeks he couldn't count them. He reminded her of that too.

Dad, she said, *it's too hard.*

She trained at least two hours a day, five days a week. But not many girls boxed, so it was difficult to get fights. She faced other obstacles too. Her mother, divorced from her father, didn't think much of girls boxing. Seniesa lived with her, so it was not easy. Even her father could be a problem. If he didn't control his street instincts, stay off drugs, and quit brawling, the cops would take him away. She would lose him.

Boxing was for their future, as much as to redeem his past.

They drove into her neighborhood. He wrapped his hands tightly around the steering wheel. He worked to keep his cool, fearing she would tune him out if his voice rose. She slumped in the front seat, frowning. It was a long ride. Both would remember it well and the words they spoke. *You have to keep fighting,* he told her. *You have to, even if I have to drag you to the gym. You are going to be special, little mama.*

They pulled up in front of her mother's apartment. She stayed in the van. He kept talking. *Of all of us in this family, you are going to make something of yourself. And I am going to keep you around me and keep you in this and show you the way. Show you not to make the mistakes I did. And that is going to make me feel like I have done something good. I did a lot of bad in my life, but that's okay, because with you, I have helped make something good.*

He would not let her end up like her two brothers. One was a high school dropout, too familiar with the streets. Joe feared the other was not far behind. Both had been good at sports. Both had quit.

Seniesa, you can't quit.

He leaned over to hug her.

Already, she was feeling better. Yes, it was hard. Yes, her father was a problem, and he would become more of one in ways she couldn't imagine. But she needed him to tell her that boxing was okay, that everything would turn out fine, that girls could fight.

He kissed her forehead.

Tell me what you want to do, he said. *Do we stay with boxing?*

Yeah, Dad. Yeah. We do.

Soon afterward, she wrote him a poem, misspelled here and there, to say thanks for being there. He tacked it to a wall in his bedroom, near his pillow. Each morning, it was one of the first things he saw.

> Maybe it's the way you make me luagh
> Maybe it's the way you push me in boxing when I feel like qiting
> Maybe it's the way you buy me things
> Maybe it's the way you hug and kiss me
> Maybe it's the way you tell me right from wrong
> Maybe it's the way you make me get good grades
> Maybe it's the way you make me go to school
> Maybe it's the way you support me
> Maybe it's the way you tell me what I am doing wrong in boxing

"What If She Gets Hurt?"

Too nervous to eat, Seniesa toyed with her omelet.

"Gabriel hits like a girl!" said Ronny Rivota, a gruff coach who trained the boys at her gym. "Hits like a woman. He's a puss. Can't hit. Can't take no pain."

The boy boxers, including Gabriel, were sitting with Seniesa around a table in a restaurant. The boys hooted and high-fived.

Seniesa stared toward the street. She was used to this. She tried to ignore them. They know I don't hit like a girl, she would recall thinking. They know I'm tough. They know I fight as good as they do.

They know.

It was May 18, 2003, and we were in South El Monte, where she would box in a Junior Olympics tournament for girls and women. Finally, she was guaranteed a fight. Winning would be a big step toward the biggest tournament of the year, the Region VIII Silver Gloves Championships, a face-off among the best young fighters from California, Arizona, Utah, Nevada, New Mexico, and Colorado.

The boys had come to cheer her on. Confident as she was, her face was pale, and her right leg shook, trembling lightly against her father's.

I asked for a prediction.

She looked away. "Dunno," she shrugged, nervous about her prospects. "Don't want to talk about it. . . . Gimme a piece of paper."

I tore a page from my notebook.

She took my pen. MAKE HER HURT, she scratched out quickly. MAKE HER CRY. MAKE HER NOT WANT TO FIGHT ME AGAIN.

Inside, the gym smelled soapy. It had been cleaned because the fights would be on local cable TV. Gauze and white tape encased Seniesa's fists like little casts, and she wore shorts that drooped down her thin hips to her knees.

Her father paced, his gaze far off. He leaned toward her. "You okay, little mama?"

She nodded.

He kept close to her ear, whispering instructions: *Counterpunch, box with skill instead of just slugging, be patient with this other girl.*

Seniesa listened, but something was wrong. She was tense. She balled her fists and began to move her arms, flexing them out from her tight shoulders, slowly at first. Then she built momentum, loosening, skipping lightly on her toes. Finally, her fists whooshed through the air, and she threw a blur of jabs, hooks, and rights in rhythm with her feet.

But when she stopped, her legs trembled, and she rubbed her eyes. I sensed that she was not feeling right.

"Okay, okay," she agreed, "I'm nervous. My mom . . . She usually doesn't come."

Joe thought it might be something more. Was she upset about the conversation at breakfast? "All that talk about Gabriel and the boys this morning, don't let it bother you."

She cocked her head, surprised that he misunderstood.

"All you gotta do is keep winning," he said. "Vegas and turning pro, that can happen to you, little mama. Why not you? You can be like that. This is the school of hard knocks, though, baby. Just keep going and don't worry. You can do it."

She nodded, mouth closed, tossing punches, then swaying gently, side to side, shaking tension out of her arms. Finally, in the packed bleachers, she spied her mother. Seniesa walked toward her. They hugged.

If Seniesa was nervous, Maryann was more so. She had come to the tournament to applaud her daughter, but she sat stiffly, wringing her hands. She didn't say much. When she did, her words rushed out frantically, so fast they were hard to understand. Maryann's worry was one of the obstacles to Seniesa's dreams. It could ambush anyone's confidence. "You feeling okay, Seniesa? Everything's fine, right? Sure you're okay?"

Seniesa nodded. She was fine. She walked away, straight toward the ring.

Maryann turned to me. "It's what she wants, but I don't feel too good about this," she said. "What if she gets hurt? What if she gets a blood clot in her head? That can happen."

In the ring, Seniesa could barely peer over the top rope. The crowd, about 150 people, applauded, but only politely. Earlier fights had featured teenagers close to becoming women. These were two little girls.

They greeted each other by touching gloves. I noticed that Seniesa's opponent, Rosa Medel, had muscles. Her calves were thick. I saw biceps. She could bully Seniesa.

Seniesa waited in her corner and listened to Joe. Headgear covered much of her face, but I could see wary eyes. She looked worried, numb.

At the opening bell, Rosa took the fight to Seniesa, forcing herself upon her with left-right combinations.

Seniesa evaded, stood her ground. Then she countered, parrying like a bullfighter, thrusting back with jabs and hooks to Rosa's head and gut.

In the second round, Seniesa's replies began to sting. She steeled herself. Once, near my side of the ring, Rosa smacked her squarely in the face. Seniesa did not flinch.

On a stool behind her corner, Joe did.

Seniesa answered with rights and hooks, forcing Rosa backward. When Seniesa threw a right-handed punch, Joe threw one, shadowboxing. When she threw a left, he threw a left.

Maryann sat in the crowd, biting her nails, looking down, putting a hand over her face.

By the third and final round, Seniesa was dictating the fight.

They might have been little girls, but now the crowd hungered for more, and cheers echoed through the gym.

Rosa dropped her hands as her energy drained.

Seizing the moment, Seniesa darted in, then out, like an angry bumblebee, slashing uppercuts and straight jabs to Rosa's unguarded chin, eyes, and nose.

The bell clanged. The girls hugged. Twice. Seniesa spoke into her opponent's ear: *Good fight, good fight.*

Judges tallied their points and declared Seniesa the winner. In the middle of the ring, she jumped into the air and raised her fist. Then she recovered, replacing a smile with a stone face: of course she won, what did people expect?

She received a tall trophy. It stood almost as high as her waist. She lugged it with her as she walked to the bleachers, her father behind her. She held the trophy out for her mother to see.

Maryann gave it a quick once-over. Then came her questions: "Does your head hurt? Can you see me good? Did you get hit hard, baby?"

"I'm fine," Seniesa said, looking at the trophy, then at her mother, then away.

If she had little patience for such questions, Joe had even less. He muttered, to no one in particular, that his little girl was never going to be hurt. "She's too fast. Too skilled."

As always, Seniesa was not satisfied until she had judged the fight for herself. One of the boys had taped it. She took his video camera and hurried away from both of her parents. Toward the back of the gym, she sat alone, on a metal chair, clutching the camera in her right hand. She examined her every move, every feint, every punch, looking for flaws.

Did she see any?

She shut off the camera and turned to me. "There was, like, a whole bunch of things I could've done better." She paused, searching for the right words. "But it was good."

Then she remembered what she had written on the page from my notebook.

"I don't think she is gonna want to fight me again."

Another Son and Brother

Without warning, Seniesa's problems grew beyond her mother's fears. This time it was her father's past, and it ambushed her truly and severely, in a way she could not have guessed. One evening before her victory, I walked into the Hollenbeck gym, and her head was down.

Joe took me aside.

"I have a surprise for you," he said. He paused. "This is my son. This is Frank."

I knew two sons. One was Joey, the other was Johnny. But Frank?

He was older, short and pudgy, with a wispy mustache. He wore baggy shorts and an old gray T-shirt. Joe had told me about two daughters, out there somewhere from his early days in Primera Flats, when the gang was more important than family. But he had never spoken of another son. There had been rumors that after Joe went to prison, one of his girlfriends delivered a baby boy. Joe never tried to find out.

Then, just the other day, he said, the truth had walked up.

Like Joe, his newly discovered son had been a junkie. Hoping to stay off the streets and away from drugs, he had tracked Joe down. He wanted his father to help him heal.

So it was that Seniesa discovered she had another brother.

In the gym, she ran laps around the basketball court, in a pack with the boy boxers. But she ran slowly, her head bowed, her feet taking small, shuffling steps. When she passed her father, she stole a glance up at him.

He was standing next to Frank, near the ring.

"I am going to be there for you, *mijo*," Joe was saying. "You are going to be my son."

Days passed. Seniesa was tense. One day, the boy boxers were sparring a few feet away. She ignored them. She positioned herself straight ahead, to make it appear that she was staring toward a fierce game unfolding on the basketball court.

But I could tell she was not watching basketball. Her eyes darted toward Joe. She could not hear what he was saying, but the more she stared, the more tense she grew. Her mouth puckered slightly. Her face tightened, as if she were trying to solve a difficult puzzle, trying to figure out what this was going to be like.

Frank was determined to know Joe. The best way, he thought, was to become what Seniesa was: a boxer.

Soon, Seniesa got less of her father's attention. She watched as he cradled Frank's hands and wrapped them gently in gauze and tape. From outside the ropes, she watched as her father stepped inside with Frank. She watched as her father taught Frank how to wear his headgear, how to glide across the ring. She watched as her father put on the heavy mitts and held them out as Frank plodded toward them, trying out jabs and hooks for the first time.

Frank eased next to Seniesa whenever he could. He called her his sister, although the boy boxers had to remind him how to pronounce her name.

He asked her for boxing tips.

Although he was getting in the way, she obliged, teaching him what she knew.

But something was amiss.

One evening, Frank joined Seniesa, their father, and the other boxers to watch TV at a friend's house. The boys teased Frank because he had shaved his head to stay cool in the ring. They saw an Oscar De La Hoya fight. Joe sat on a beige couch, and Frank took Seniesa's usual spot next to him. His left leg nudged against her father. When Joe spoke, Frank gazed at him, mesmerized.

Seniesa stayed on the floor.

"Look at Oscar, how smart he is, mama. How he measures his guy," Joe said to Seniesa. "This is how to do it, mama. He hasn't even been hit yet."

Seniesa barely nodded.

I'd never seen her respond to her father this way.

Frank and Joe hollered encouragement at the TV, but she slunk into the kitchen and stayed there, slouching, cradling her face in the palm of her hand, eating sausage pizza and slurping a Coke. Often, I saw her glance into the den at Joe and Frank.

In time, however, Joe's relationship with Frank began to fray. Busy for several weeks with new work at the sign shop, Joe had little time for boxing.

One afternoon, I ended up driving Frank home from the gym. He sulked, complaining that Joe was avoiding him. Frank had a girlfriend and a baby and no job. He wanted financial help. If he didn't get it from Joe, he said, he would go back to selling drugs.

A few days later, I found Seniesa at the gym, just outside the ring. "What's up?" she said, nodding at me. She extended a hand. We slapped palms and knocked knuckles, a standard East L.A. greeting.

She bounced on her toes, more cheerful than she'd been in weeks.

"Seen Frank lately?" I asked.

"Nope," she said, with a hint of satisfaction.

That evening, near midnight, Frank called my cell phone, voice cracking, speaking through tears. He was convinced that Joe was avoiding him, and now was when he needed his father the most.

"I wish I never met him," he said. "He's distancing himself from me. I can feel it. I opened up to him, found him, found out he was real. And look what happened. My dad talks a good game. He tells me if I need money to call him and he will help. I need money now, and he is not there." I could hear him sobbing. "He is too busy for me. He is with Seniesa, probably . . . He has his little girl, she makes him proud."

I went to bed thinking of Seniesa, her father, and the rest of her family. I wondered about Joe, laboring to put the past behind him, working to prove his goodness. He lived like a monk, in a room at his mother's house. It was a simple life meant to decrease distraction. Distraction could cause him to lose balance, loss of balance could lead to old habits, and old habits could lead to prison. Joe had his job, a TV, and Seniesa's poem. He had Seniesa and her boxing.

It was Frank or Seniesa. Room did not exist for both.

A Respite from Boxing

Seniesa liked to go to her classroom when it was empty and sit down with her teacher and talk. Occasionally it was about the obstacles to her dreams. Now she was less worried about Frank than she was about the rest of her family.

Her other brothers, for instance. Joey was nineteen, thin and tough. He helped Joe at the shop, but at night he hung out on the streets. Johnny was fifteen, rangy and shy. He also was spending time on the streets, failing school because he hardly went. Maryann worried so much she couldn't sleep, imagining the worst, her heart pounding as she closed her eyes and saw them both being killed.

When darkness fell on the streets of El Sereno, which echoed often with gunfire, Seniesa would demand that she and her mother drive through the neighborhood, looking for the boys. She wanted to pick them up and bring them home to safety. "I told you, Mom, he's not going to class," she said one evening, as Maryann spoke of Johnny's grades. "He's getting straight Ds. He's being so stupid. Mom, what are you going to do?"

For Seniesa, the talks with her teacher at El Sereno Elementary School offered a respite from her family, even from boxing. When I visited her classroom, I saw a charming teacher's pet, carefree, eager to please, the most popular girl in her class, the best actress in the school play, a top student who did what she was told.

Her teacher was impressed with how Seniesa went out of her way to befriend a kid the others picked on and was captivated by how she drove herself. She thought Seniesa would be the first in her family to graduate from college. "I will be shocked if she does not make something special out of her life," she said.

Seniesa surrounded herself with other girls. They walked to the playground, joking about who was taller, smaller, who had the cutest jeans and the coolest shoes. They were careful not to talk about boys. "We're B-F-F," Seniesa said, one arm around Victoria, lanky with long brown hair. She pointed to her own notebook. I saw BFF scrawled in large blue letters on the cover and a list of girls' names below it. "B-F-F. Don't you know what that means? Best Friends Forever." Her eyes sparkled as she laughed. "That's us. B-F-F."

One day, Maryann sat with me in her living room and talked

about her children and their prospects, her eyes darting, as they always did when she was stressed.

"I can't worry about Seniesa right now," she said. "It's sort of like Joe and Seniesa are one side of it. And then there's me and the two boys. I don't let anyone talk bad about my boys. And Seniesa, if I say anything bad about Joe, she is all, 'Don't you say anything bad about my dad.' Those two, you can't tear them apart for nothing."

Seniesa walked in and sat next to her mother.

"NeeNee," Maryann said, "why don't you stay home today? Stay home, and let's go to Starbucks. What do you think?"

"I'm supposed to be with my dad," Seniesa replied, unimpressed with the offer, even if Starbucks was one of her favorite places. She heard a horn. She looked through the shutters. She saw Joe, pulling his van into the driveway. Without a word, she rose from the couch and bolted out the door, smiling as she skipped down the sloping driveway in her white high-tops. Joe leaned through the driver's window and kissed his daughter on the forehead. She reached up to him, grinning, clasping his shoulders with her small hands.

Maryann peered through the blinds at them. "He spoils her," she said, shaking her head. "All she ever wants is to be around her father. Maybe she does think she is saving him. Look at that."

Pushed to the Edge

It was a rest day, and Seniesa was at home when it happened. Her neighborhood could mount sneak attacks too. Joe was at the gym with the boy boxers. We stood together, laughing, catching up. He bragged about Seniesa.

Suddenly, a commotion flared on the basketball court.

"What you gonna do now, mother ——?" It was a street tough named Johnny, shouting at Marlon, a strapping boy in his late teens who had dropped out of training but still hung around the ring. Johnny wore baggy jeans and a muscle T-shirt. He bore down on Marlon with a stiff-legged strut.

Marlon backpedaled, unsure what to do.

Johnny pushed him.

Joe's eyes narrowed and grew dark.

I looked at Johnny's baggy jeans. Did he have a gun in his pocket? Was there a place to dive for cover?

Johnny pushed Marlon again and yelled at him about a girl.

Joe boiled. "Marlon, don't take nothing from him!" he shouted. "Don't let him punk you like that."

Marlon backed away, showing weakness. Joe knew that showing weakness was a way to end up dead. "Hit him back!" he yelled. "Hit him back!"

The gym fell silent.

Johnny kept pushing.

Marlon kept walking backward.

Joe shook his head. He handed me his cell phone. "This is wrong," he muttered. A metal railing stood between us and the action. He gripped it hard, as if he were about to jump over.

But something held him back.

"Straight right, Marlon! Don't take nothing from him!" he shouted. "You know what to do, boy. Don't take that s ——."

Marlon stopped retreating. He cocked a fist and released a perfect right. It landed flush on Johnny's jaw, sending him to the floor like a dropped rock.

"Yeah, that's the way, baby!" Joe yelled. "Don't take s —— from nobody! *No-bah-dee!*"

But Johnny rose. He looked at Joe and me. He banged a fist to his chest and pointed at Joe. "F —— you, mother ——!" he yelled, walking toward us.

My legs tensed. If he pulled a gun, I was ready to run.

Joe would not back away. "Shut the f —— up," he shouted, "and leave the kid alone!"

Johnny kept walking, straight toward us.

"You don't want to mess with me, homes," Joe said.

Johnny kept walking. He picked up a metal chair.

"I ain't taking your s ——," Joe said. "I'm ready to rumble, dog."

Johnny flung the chair. It twisted toward us. I ducked, and it crashed down against Joe's back, ripping his shirt, tearing his skin.

"Bitch!" Joe shouted.

Johnny grabbed a broom and broke it in half over his leg. Long splinters of wood protruded from one end.

Joe picked up a dustpan with a wooden handle. He slammed it hard against the railing and snapped off the pan. Now he had a sharp stick of his own.

He and Johnny squared off, circling each other.

Joe hunched slightly, bent his legs, and wielded his stick. I saw up close that he was about to lose control, about to swing and slash until only one of them stood. Joe was almost in "the zone."

But he stopped. He was thinking of Seniesa, he told me afterward. What if he hurt this kid, got arrested and convicted? One more felony and he could get twenty-five years. He would lose Seniesa and their dream.

Joe threw his stick to the ground.

Johnny lunged at him, raking him with the broom handle.

They grappled, chest to chest, legs trembling.

Joe grimaced, working to hold Johnny's right hand, which gripped the stick.

Johnny broke free and slammed Joe over the head, so hard that a large chunk of the stick broke off.

Joe clutched him again, this time in a headlock.

They turned and twirled. Sweat ran down Joe's chest. I could hear him gasp. Johnny freed his stick hand and stabbed. Blood flowed from Joe's arms. I saw more on his chin. "Is that all you got?" Joe growled. "Mother ——, is that all you got, punk?"

It took several large men to break it up. They yelled: "Cops coming!" Johnny broke free and fled, swinging his stick and stabbing another man. Blood streamed from the man's forehead.

"Kurt, we gotta go," Joe said, walking fast to his van. Both of us knew Johnny might bring back a gang and try anything, maybe spray the place with bullets.

The boy boxers piled in. "Go, Joe, let's go. Come on, let's go."

Joe started the engine.

"I gotta get the kids outta here," he told me. "And you'd better get outta here. You okay? We'll talk about this later."

That night, we spoke on the phone.

He was contrite: "I shouldn't have fought that kid. I really shouldn't have."

He was reflective: "My worst quality is my anger. Always has been. You saw it. I couldn't keep away from that, seeing Marlon get punked. I couldn't let it go . . . I had to keep control of him and myself, as mad as I was. I was about this close to going into one of those where I used to go into, where I blanked out and just went off."

Then he turned defiant: "That guy doesn't know who he is mess-ing with. I don't gangbang anymore, but I'm from Flats gang. I got pull. All I gotta do is make one call, and we will go after that guy. I can put him in his place with one call."

He was thankful that his little girl had not been there. "Oh, man, I'm just so glad she had the day off. She would've been scared. And you know, I don't want her to see me like that anymore."

Joe did not tell Seniesa about the brawl.

She found out about it the next day from a boy boxer. She told me it didn't scare her. She betrayed no emotion at all. If anything, she felt pride. "That was kind of cool, how my dad backed up Marlon."

Seniesa seemed unburdened by the idea that anything bad could ever happen to her father. Maybe it was the dream they shared and her role in his redemption. Still, she was aware of the risks, what her father's anger could lead to.

One day, not long afterward, I asked if she knew her father could go back to prison if he ever got in trouble again — and for a long time.

She looked at me. "I know," she said. "But it's not going to happen."

"I'm Gonna Win. But You Never Know."

"Down, then up, baby," her father said as he stood behind the ropes and watched. "*Rapido, rapido.* Set him up, set him up. Then come with the Duran."

Seniesa bounced on her toes, holding her gloves in front of her face and weaving toward the other boxer, a boy one year older and ten pounds heavier. He retreated against the ropes. She jabbed. She hooked. She backed off.

His body melted deeper into the ropes. He threw a few meager punches, then drew away.

"Duran," her father said.

She evaded a blow by bending slightly to her right. In perfect position, she coiled tightly, right arm bent, right fist suddenly down, near her waist. When she released, her fist took off, making a small U, curving at first, and then straightening into the air before landing — *whap* — in the kid's gut.

Seniesa Estrada, eleven, had changed gyms, to Solid Rock Boxing, an old storefront with a single ring, where a onetime street hustler named Gil Valdez was helping Joe Estrada, forty-four, her father, train her. She had learned an array of punches. One she called "the Duran," a powerful roundhouse like the one perfected by the legendary champion Roberto Duran.

But it would take the Duran and more to make Seniesa a champion. Outside the ring, the world had a way of ambushing her. If it wasn't her mother, who smothered her with worry that she could be hurt, then it was her brothers, who hung out on the streets where they could be killed, or her father, an ex-addict who exploded with such anger that it could get him back into trouble with the police. Seniesa herself was conflicted. Part of her wanted to be the warrior of her dreams, but another part wanted to stay a little girl. Before long, she would face her toughest opponent, a girl just like her in so many ways. And the girl was tough.

Tougher than this kid in the ring, whose name was Richard. He trudged to his corner. Blood formed around a nostril. His trainer lit into him. "Come on, you've got to hit her first, or you're gonna get hurt out there. Stop fighting like you are scared of her. What's wrong with you?"

Richard spit out his mouthpiece. "She's so quick," he gasped. "So quick."

His trainer sent him out for another beating. For a minute, he and Seniesa traded a series of close blows, until she backed him against the ropes again.

"Duran." *Whap.* "Duran." *Whap.* "Duran."

Richard covered himself with his arms and gloves. He wanted it to end. Finally, the last bell sounded. In his corner, he held himself against the ring, resting his forehead on the top rope. A tear rolled down his cheek, and he rubbed his side, where so many of her punches had landed. "It hurts," he muttered, touching his stomach. "It . . . hurts."

Seniesa sat down next to him at a large table ringside. She jammed her gloves into her black bag. She avoided my questions, as if it would ruin her magic to acknowledge that she could now hold her own against almost any boy her size in East L.A. When she zipped up her bag, she walked off to her father.

Richard watched her, smiled, and shook his head. "She hits too hard," he said. He laughed at this, the fact that a girl could be so good. All he could do was laugh. "Seniesa hits too hard."

Seniesa the warrior was as cold and hard as her punches. At night, she dreamed of fighting in a ring surrounded by cameras, flashing lights, and people. She woke throwing jabs and uppercuts.

In the daytime she imagined being a famous fighter, having money, enough to buy a house. A house not in a place "all stuck up, like Beverly Hills," she said, but not in El Sereno. A house with a pool and a slide. Her father would live with her. The future was far off, but she was working hard to make it real.

She didn't care that, on one occasion, she had overmatched another girl by so much the referee stopped the fight in thirty seconds, to prevent a knockout. "Once you step in the ring, nobody makes you go there," Seniesa told me, watching video of the short-lived fight. "If she wasn't ready, it's not my fault. If you are not up to it, too bad for you."

Seniesa the little girl, however, could be warm and fun-loving. After tournaments away from Los Angeles, she always insisted on swimming in the hotel pool. She giggled and shrieked with delight as she jumped again and again and again into the warm water.

"This is so much fun!" she said, climbing out and looking at her father. "Dad, can we stay over, and then stay and, like, swim here all day tomorrow? Dad, someday, let's, like, let's get a big pool like this one. Dad, can we?

"Dad, when I am professional?"

Her dreams, ever present.

"I See Her Changing"

She was becoming more confident, but also more wary. She was growing up.

Now, when the boy boxers teased her for being short or skinny, she barked back with a gleam in her eye. She taunted one for his paunch, another for his girlfriends, still another because he struggled with English.

Around adults, though, it was different. Once, she had bubbled with questions and quick answers. "What is your wife like?" she would ask me. "Where do you live? What is the name of your cat?

Pablo? Dang, that's no cat name. My cat is Sunny. That's a cat name."

Now, though, her questions stopped. She meted out her answers. She trusted less. Even with her father, the bright, shiny exuberance dimmed. "I see her changing," he said one day. "She don't say much. Part of it is where she is growing up, the things she sees and experiences. It can be kind of crazy around where she lives. After a while you sort of stop being a kid. You have to if you want to survive."

On September 2, 2003, Seniesa went from fifth grade, at the top of elementary school, into sixth grade, at the bottom of middle school. She stood just a shade under five feet tall. She was stronger and looked more like an inverted pyramid: widening shoulders tapering steadily to her skinny ankles. Her face looked different too. Narrower, the flesh around her eyes tightening, maybe from the punches. It made her cheekbones more prominent.

She tried not to attract attention. In fifth grade, she had gladly let me come to her classroom. By the sixth grade, it was embarrassing, and it took months for her to decide that I could visit. The first time I did, she played sick and stayed home.

In fifth grade, everyone knew she boxed. In sixth grade, she worried about people finding out. A kid who once looked for trouble, now she was trying to avoid it. "If people know I'm a boxer," she explained, "they are going to be trying to talk a lot of stuff. I'm going to have to show them they can't mess with me."

She didn't even tell her teachers.

In an early piece of homework, she let slip that she loved fighting. Lupe Arellano, the teacher who assigned it, thought she meant causing trouble in class and fighting on the playground.

I'm not going to have any problems with you, am I? Arellano asked. Seniesa said no, but it took her weeks to open up to Arellano about boxing, her neighborhood, and life at home. "She has a lot of stuff on her plate," her teacher told me one day, flipping through Seniesa's homework. "From what I gather, there are things in her life that she just has to be strong and suck it up and deal with. Seniesa keeps her feelings bottled deep down."

But the ambushes would not stop.

Early one morning, her father's cell phone rang. Her Uncle Rick, who had taken him to church and helped him give up gangs and drugs, was in jail. Despondent over a troubled marriage, he had cornered his wife and shot her twice. She barely survived.

When Joe picked up Seniesa the next day to go to the gym, he told her about it, and tried to reassure her about himself. He said he was okay, when clearly he wasn't.

Her body went numb. She wanted to box, but part of her wanted to take care of her father. She saw the hurt in him. There were bags under his eyes, his voice was faint, and he rubbed the back of his neck as he wondered and worried.

Had he missed the signs that something was wrong with his brother? He knew that Rick would have to pay a price, but he was not sure Rick could survive it. He feared that his brother might kill himself to avoid prison.

Then there was a more practical matter: the shop. Rick was his partner. Joe built and installed the signs. Rick paid the bills, managed the inventory, and lined up new customers. Could Joe shoulder the whole burden? He didn't know.

Seniesa's uncle had been a rock. He always brightened when she came to the sign shop. She could close her eyes and hear him: *Hey, champ, how's it goin', champ? What ya doin' today, champ?*

But now her uncle's fate was weighing her father down. Joe was desperate to talk about it to the person who understood him best: Seniesa. He wanted to tell her how he felt. But was it the right thing to do? How many problems could a little girl take? He hesitated.

Of course, she knew what was eating at him. As weeks went by, she could tell by the way his shoulders slumped and how he seemed tired and testy. "There's nothing I can do," she told me one evening, shaking her head in disbelief and frustration, standing outside the gym, watching cars go by.

Her eyes fell. "I'm a kid."

But there was something she could do. Instinctively, she knew it. Together, they had boxing.

A Showcase Event

Seniesa and her father stepped up training for the Region VIII Silver Gloves Championships. They had been on her mind for a year. Now it was December 2003, and the tournament was coming up in the second week of January. It was one of the biggest regional events in amateur boxing, a chance to show the world that Seniesa was the best girl fighter around.

Days before, she decided to challenge me to a boxing video game on the TV at her house. She picked Roberto Duran. For me, she chose a little-known fighter named Zab Judah. From the start, her Duran forced my helpless Judah against the ropes. "It's gonna be just like this at the regionals. I'm gonna break out the Duran."

"Really?" I asked, scowling, trying to get my poor fighter off the ropes, determined not to let an eleven-year-old girl whip me. "Feeling pretty confident?"

She decked Judah. He lay on the canvas, knocked senseless.

"Don't you feel pressure?" I asked. "All those people watching? The stuff with your uncle? It's a pretty big deal for you and your dad."

"I feel pressure," she said. "Some people, they've been saying I should win in one round, because they say I am good. But what if I don't?" She paused, looking at the floor. She fidgeted and crossed her arms.

"I think I'm going to win," she added. "No, I know I'm going to win. But if I don't do good, if I lose but I try hard and do what my dad says, I don't think he will be mad. I hope he won't be mad. I'm not gonna lose. I mean, the only way I lose is, sometimes, I just don't throw enough punches. I hesitate to throw punches. I get sort of anxious. Not nervous. Anxious. I'm gonna win. But you never know."

In fact, she might not even make weight.

She had started the week knowing she would have to drop three pounds — down to seventy-five — or be disqualified from her weight class. She could move up to the next weight division, but there weren't any girls in that division for her to fight.

All week long, she starved herself. To lose weight, she drove herself ruthlessly. She ran wind sprints in an alley, dodging cars and being careful to keep her sneakers out of the mud. She put on her heavy blue sweat suit and her boxing gloves, and she ran around the block, four, five, six times, spitting on the sidewalk to get rid of fluid. She sparred. She worked at the big red bag, her eyes intent, fierce.

Never had I seen her so determined.

"Pump that jab, sweetie. Double it up, double it up," her father said, standing by a floor-to-ceiling mirror near the heavy bag. "Whoever you are fighting is going to be feeling your pain this weekend, mama. We're gonna take this thing, sweetheart, I can feel it."

With each blitz of punches, she breathed out — *whoosh! whoosh!* Sweat flew from her pink shirt. The sound of her fists drowned out everything else. *Whap-whap-whap-whap-whap-whap.* Steady, like a metronome. She stopped, hunched over, gloves on her knees, sucking air. "Need water," she said. "Need water."

"Baby, that was more than one punch a second," Joe said, offering her a drink. "That's the way." He patted her slumped shoulders, slick with sweat.

She shadow-boxed in front of the mirror, mesmerized, lost in her reflection, in the way she bent, the way she turned and flexed her knees, how she shot her arms out like springs, how she evaded an imaginary opponent with a steady weave.

She came out of her trance, bent over again, and held her stomach.

"I don't have the idea that I could lose," she said. But as she spoke she slumped to the carpeted floor and lay there exhausted. "I'm tired now, but I'm planning on winning."

Making Weight

Two evenings later, Seniesa and her father drove to Norwalk to register and watch the draw naming her opponent. It was in a large conference room at a recreation center. As happened so often, she was virtually alone in a sea of men and boys. A referee told her there was just one girl in her division, and she was from Arizona.

"I bet it's Kelly," Seniesa said. "Kelly from Arizona." Kelly had mysteriously disappeared from a match with Seniesa in Thermal fifteen months earlier. Seniesa clenched her fists, then relaxed them, clenched, relaxed. Beating Kelly would be sweet.

In the crowd, she spotted a girl in shorts, roughly her size. She tapped her shoulder. "Are you Kelly?"

No, the girl said. She was just there to watch her brother.

Dejected, Seniesa retreated to the back of the room. Joe stood there, arms folded, leaning against a wall, alongside the boy boxers, who had fights of their own. The room filled with people, two hundred at least.

Seniesa kept clenching her fists. She was still a pound or two overweight. Tomorrow she would have to step on the official scale. If she was too heavy, she couldn't fight.

"Go, go, get moving," said Gil, the coach from her gym. "Run until I tell you not to."

She jogged down a dark hallway, then back. Down, then back. She looked grim, eyes cast toward the floor as she plodded. She stopped only to bend into a water fountain and spit. I've gotta fight, she would remember thinking. I've been waiting so long for this one tournament. I've gotta fight.

For half an hour she ran, finishing just in time to hear someone announce: "In the female junior division, seventy-five pounds . . ." She rushed to the table up front. "Seniesa Estrada, Los Angeles, against Daveena Villalva, Phoenix."

Her opponent wasn't Kelly after all. Who was this new girl? Who was Daveena?

A referee pointed her out. Daveena was wiry and pretty, dressed in a black warm-up suit.

From across the room, Seniesa eyed her, trying not to stare. Daveena appeared calm and casual, talking to a man, maybe her father.

Seniesa sidled next to her, shoulder to shoulder, taking advantage of the fact that Daveena did not know who she was. Seniesa pretended to look toward the officials, but her eyes kept glancing at her opponent. She seemed to be trying to imagine what Daveena would become in the ring.

She walked back to Joe, worried. "Dad, you think I might weigh too much?"

"No, *mija*," he said, trying to ease her fears, even though he wasn't really sure she would make it. "Don't worry. You're gonna be fine. This should be a lesson. You gotta stay away from McDonald's."

Weigh-in wasn't until the next morning, but she wanted to check herself now, on the official scale. It stood in the middle of another conference room, this one at a nearby hotel. The boy boxers went with her. She demanded to weigh first. She needed to strip to her underwear, so the boys stood guard in front of the doors.

Get in there, they said. Good luck.

After two minutes, she bolted out, grinning. "I'm right at seventy-five," she announced. "I'll make it. I'll qualify. If I don't eat nothing tonight."

The boys extended their right fists. She tapped their knuckles with hers.

As the boys weighed themselves, Seniesa joined Laila, Gil's girlfriend, nineteen and willowy. Seniesa cast her eyes at Laila's shiny red pumps. She asked to try them on. They were much too big. She walked unsteadily past her father and announced that when she got older she planned to wear red pumps, pretty clothes, and makeup, just like Laila.

She and Laila held hands and walked through the hotel lobby, peering into a gift shop window. They spotted a beige stuffed puppy with large ears and droopy eyes, a name tag, and a pink bow tied around its neck. "Oh, so cute, it's so cute!" Seniesa said, bouncing up and down, tapping the window, pointing at Sad Sam, the stuffed beagle.

"Dad, could I get him?"

"Not now," Joe said, his mind on boxing.

The boy boxers rolled their eyes. Rarely had they seen Seniesa like this.

Laila turned to me, chin held high. "She does girl stuff with me," she said. "With all this boxing, it's good for her."

Seniesa ate nothing that night. Realizing her dreams was not easy. She slept without Sad Sam. Growing up wasn't easy either.

She awoke tired, out of sorts, weak. Her arms felt heavy, she would recall. Her stomach ached. Her face was ashen. She was hardly able to speak. At the weigh-in, she and the few other girls in the tournament used a small bathroom for women. She walked inside. A female referee joined her to record the proceedings. Near the toilets was the scale.

She stripped to her underwear and stepped as gingerly as she could onto the footpads of the scale. She held her breath, she told me afterward, and focused on its digital numbers. She tried to keep from trembling.

The numbers climbed: sixty-eight, sixty-nine, seventy-four, seventy-six, seventy-seven . . .

Then settled down, to seventy-five.

Oh, yes, she whispered.

Back out in the hallway, she saw her father, standing next to the boys.

"Make it?" Joe asked. "Well, tell us. Did you?"

She reached out to slap his palm.

He swallowed her in hugs and high-fives.

"Made it, yeah," she said. "Made it. Made it."

Although she had gone hungry the night before, she could barely eat. At a Jack in the Box, she nibbled on potatoes and eggs. She and the boy boxers went to the arena early. Seniesa sat on a concrete bench, next to Laila and me.

"Did you see her yesterday?" Laila asked her. "The girl you are fighting?"

"Yeah, I seen her. She was over there last night. She don't look tough."

"So, are you going to kick her ass or what?"

Seniesa paused. "Well, I'm not gonna let her kick my ass." She tightened her lips and stared at the gravel. Then she gave in. She couldn't be a warrior every minute. "Oh, remember that stuffed dog last night? Oh, I want one. I thought about it all night. I wish I could have one. I wish."

Two Small Girls

Two hours to the opening bell.

Seniesa sat at the top of the bleachers, in baggy shorts and a droopy blue top with SOLID ROCK BOXING on the back in large letters. She was alone, face pale, skin clammy. She didn't talk. She stared at the front doors of the gym.

Daveena walked in.

"Whoa," Seniesa said, reflexively.

Parents beside her, Daveena moved toward the ring.

Seniesa stared at her like a lioness eyeing a mouse. Her gaze never left Daveena. Unaware that anyone was watching, she breathed out, then breathed in deeply, rubbing her thin legs with her hands. "There she is," she muttered softly. "There she is."

Seniesa's father arrived to help wrap her fists. She tried hard, she would remember, to push a feeling from her mind: somehow, something was not right. She felt sluggish, weak from losing those extra pounds so fast.

Maryann arrived with her boyfriend and Seniesa's godmother. Maryann was fidgety. She wanted Seniesa to win, but she was worried, as always. "I'm hoping that [boxing] is just a stage she is going through," she had told me a few weeks before, at a McDonald's near the Home Depot where she worked all day before going to Dodger Stadium at night to sell hot dogs and popcorn. "I just worry. You know, brain clots. I don't want her getting one. What if she breaks her nose? My baby is pretty. . . I still want her to be a cheerleader."

Seniesa didn't want to lose this fight, not in front of her mother or any of them. Then there was her father. She could tell how much this meant to him. All she had to do was watch him pace.

Fifteen minutes to the bell.

Joe rubbed Seniesa's shoulders, sensing her nervousness. He took a small black swatch of Velcro and bundled her braided hair. Seniesa bit her lower lip. She stared at the ring. Two boys were slugging it out, and the crowd roared.

Three minutes to the bell.

Near the ring, Daveena shadow-boxed. She wore black trunks. Her face was taut and serious.

Seniesa wrapped her arms around herself. She shivered, as if she had a cold.

"What's wrong, *mija?*" Joe asked. "What's wrong?"

"I'm fine. I'm ready."

She walked a few steps away, whispering: "I'm ready, I'm ready."

One minute to the bell.

The announcer called Seniesa's name. She put her head down and marched to the ring, followed by Joe and Gil. She climbed through the ropes. Joe stood in her corner, chomping hard on gum.

The crowd, nearly five hundred people by now, hushed at the sight of two small girls. Then people began to clap and cheer.

"Come on, NeeNee!" Seniesa's family yelled. "You can do it, NeeNee!"

"Let's go, Chickee!" countered Daveena's family. "You're the one, Chickee!"

Now it was up to them.

Delivering Real Pain

The referee, a tall man wearing a crisp white uniform, brought the girls to the center of the ring for instructions, then sent them back to their corners.

Daveena bounced on her toes, ready to spring across the ring and attack.

Seniesa swiveled her hips. She looked grim. She stared at her opponent. This was her moment. She could not let herself lose.

The bell clanged. The girls moved toward each other. Daveena held her gloves high, in front of her face. Seniesa held hers just above her waist.

Daveena threw the first punch, a quick right that grazed Seniesa's shoulder. Daveena began winding back her right hand. Seniesa saw a target and punched a left into her opponent's stomach. Daveena wasn't fazed. She stepped forward and threw a left that smacked against Seniesa's head.

A pattern developed: Daveena became the aggressor, throwing more punches, but fewer hard ones; Seniesa became the counterpuncher, often on her heels, punching fewer times, but with clearer results.

An exchange near the end of the first round was typical. Seniesa bobbed and shuffled, to make herself harder to hit. Daveena hopped forward — literally hopped — and punched Seniesa in the face. Seniesa stepped back and planted a Duran in Daveena's gut. *Whap.*

Daveena kept coming. She hit Seniesa with a hard right to the left cheek. Seniesa backed off, shielding her face with her shoulder. Then she stopped, turned her hips, cocked her right arm, and let loose. Her glove slammed hard into Daveena's liver.

The ring shook. Daveena grunted.

BIG punches, I scrawled in my notebook.

At the bell, Seniesa walked back to her corner and sagged, listening to Joe's instructions as she gulped down water. Then she rose slowly from her stool and waited. She looked drained, feet flat, shoulders slouched, limp arms dangling at her sides. It looked to me as if she didn't want to fight.

But she had to.

The second round replayed the first. Daveena came after Seniesa with blind aggression — inefficient, but impressive to the ringside judges. She threw the first six punches. Only one hit its target, a hard left jab that landed flush against Seniesa's nose.

Seniesa conjured up a response, summoning energy from somewhere deep and stopping Daveena's next advance with a jab to the face. Daveena's head jolted backward. But she charged again.

Seniesa's knuckles crashed once more into her face. Again, her head jolted back. How much more could she take?

The bell clanged.

So far, the fight seemed too close to call. The crowd could feel it. Both corners knew that whoever won the third and final round would go home happy.

When it began, Daveena's punches pushed Seniesa and spun her.

But then Seniesa strung together her reply, a series of hard lefts that jolted Daveena's head to one side, then the other. "Oooh!" the crowd roared with each punch. "Oooh!"

Daveena frowned, grimaced, but hardly slowed. Her aggression seemed instinctive, as if she were fighting for her life.

The girls clutched and backed off, then launched into a violent exchange of jabs and uppercuts. I caught myself wondering about the sanity of it all. These young girls were delivering pain. Real pain. They took hard shots to the head, to the liver and kidneys. I looked at Seniesa, breathing hard, sweat flowing, face blotched with red, mustering herself for one last push. Maryann's fears, at that moment, seemed well placed.

Finally, the bell split the air.

Seniesa walked to her corner and put both hands on the ropes to keep herself from falling. Her head drooped. Sweaty hair clung to her neck.

Then she walked to the middle of the ring, acknowledging the crowd the way pro fighters do, with a stomp of the feet and a bow in each direction. Usually, she did this crisply. This time, she shuffled through it with little enthusiasm.

Daveena and the referee joined her. Seconds passed. Anticipation filled the gym. Finally, the announcer's voice crackled over the loudspeakers.

"How about a nice hand for both of these young ladies. Both of them are warriors."

Daveena closed her eyes.

"And the winner, in the girls' seventy-five-pound division . . ."

Seniesa looked up at the klieg lights.

"By decision, in the red corner . . . Da-vee-na Vill-al-va!"

Seniesa slammed a foot to the canvas. She turned toward her corner and tried to walk away. Only the referee's grip on her hand kept her from bolting to her father and out of the ring in anger.

Daveena leaped into the air and thrust her arms skyward.

She turned to Seniesa. Amateur boxing is emotion-filled and gritty-tough, but after each fight, tradition calls for opponents to shake hands. Daveena wanted to.

Seniesa refused. She couldn't even look at Daveena.

Tears welling, she went to her father. "Come here, *mija*," he said. She couldn't look at him either. He drew her into his arms. "It's okay. You did real good. I thought you won. That was robbery. I mean, come on, what do you have to do to win the fight?" His words, usually enough to make her feel whole, were no solace.

In the locker room, she ripped the gauze and white tape off her hands and began to change her clothes. She looked up. There stood Daveena. She wanted to change too.

Seniesa gathered her gear and walked out in a huff.

There was one ray of hope: Joe. He stood, ramrod straight, waiting by a big metal door that led out of the gym. The muscles around his eyes were tight.

Before she ran to her mother's car, she turned to her father. This time, her eyes met his with a sad look, a look that begged forgiveness.

The Fight of Her Life

There was nothing for this pain.

Although she had lost, her father bought her a tall trophy with a fighter on top, inscribed "Seniesa Estrada, Regional Junior Champion." He surprised her with it. She took it to her bedroom and placed it near her pillow. It didn't help.

Sucking a lollipop, she watched a videotape of her fight. "Maybe I did win," she said. "I didn't do as badly as I thought." It didn't help.

She stayed away from the gym. When she finally went back to training, she was stale. She talked about other sports and practiced with a basketball team, against her father's wishes. It didn't help. Even her teachers noticed that something was amiss. Seniesa goofed off, and her grades fell. She interrupted class with chatter and gossip.

She was nearly twelve now, and losing her first big match had taught her something. It showed her, said Lupe Arellano, one of her teachers, that she was not invincible, and it forced her to realize that there was more to life than boxing. "She is testing out what it is to be an ordinary girl," Arellano said. "Maybe it's good for her. She's just a kid. Now is the time to test and figure out where she belongs."

It was a time, also, to test herself against family obstacles. Her father, Joe Estrada, forty-five, who shared the dream of her becoming an Olympic champion and then a world champion, was in a tailspin of his own. His brother, Seniesa's Uncle Rick, was facing trial for attempted murder and could get twenty-five years to life. Joe feared that Rick would kill himself, maybe provoke someone in prison to kill him.

Joe hardly slept. He spent long days running the family sign-making business without his brother's help. It distracted him from training his daughter as a boxer. In his shop one day, as he arranged metal and vinyl letters, his scarred and battered hands faltered, then stopped. He looked up. A few years earlier, he said, he would have cracked under this pressure. He would have been going out again, maybe drugging, maybe heading straight for the gutter, maybe heading back to prison — or a coffin.

Luckily, he had his little girl now and the dream they shared. Seniesa's boxing had long meant his own redemption. It was keeping him straight. "I gotta be there for her," he said. "I don't want this affecting her, because she hurts when I hurt. We're tied together. She's my glue, holding me together."

Still, Uncle Rick was a problem he had to talk about. She was just a little girl, but she understood her father best. At lunch one day, eating hamburgers and drinking Cokes, he would recall, he told her how tired he was, how worried and distracted and stressed.

What do you think, mija? he asked. What could he do for his brother? What should he do about the business? Should he close the sign shop? *What should I do?*

I know it's hard, she said, stepping up to the challenge. She would never forget looking at him, tears in her eyes. *Dad, you can do it,* she said. *You've been through so much. This is nothing compared to what you've been through.*

She didn't need to say more. Her presence, her concern, and her boxing were enough. If only she didn't let her loss in the ring, so unexpected, so painful, cause her to quit.

A New View of Boys

It might help if she beat some boys.

The thought came naturally. It had helped before. But now it was cloaked in complexity. Although she needed to beat them in the ring, she was discovering that boys could be attractive.

She was the leader of a tight-knit group of sixth-grade girls, giggly, rambunctious, brimming with nonstop talk about shopping, food, and music. But boys?

Truth was, her teacher told me, she had spotted Seniesa holding hands with a boy.

I asked Seniesa about it. She stared at me as if I were a ghost. Then she smiled and blushed. "Miss Arellano," she said, "should mind her own business."

Her friends squirmed. One asked: was it true that she actually got into a boxing ring and fought boys? If that was true, she must be pretty good.

"What do you mean, pretty good?" Seniesa said. Her voice grew sharp and stern. "You know I fight boys. And sometimes, I hit them so hard they get all bloodied up. What do you mean, pretty good? I'm more than pretty good. I make boys bleed."

Her father encouraged the idea. Maybe it would get her confidence back.

An opportunity came one day when Seniesa was sick with a cold. It was February 23, 2004. She sat alone in her gym in East L.A., watching boy boxers work out. A team from Hawaiian Gardens was on its way over to spar. Only bragging rights were at stake, but at least it was something.

When the team arrived, Seniesa was playing paper-rock-scissors with a neighborhood girl, looking sad, cast-off.

An eleven-year-old boy from Hawaiian Gardens, named Ulises, climbed into the ring against one of the boys from East L.A. Ulises fought with strength and skill, and he pummeled the kid from Seniesa's gym. Ulises' coaches claimed he was new to boxing.

Joe suspected that wasn't true. Could Ulises fight a girl?

"Sure," his trainer said.

"Tell your kid not to hold back," Joe replied. He turned to Seniesa. "You don't feel too sick, right?"

Her eyes grew. She nodded: right.

"Get ready," her father said. "You're gonna fight."

She sprang to her feet and stretched her arms toward him. He slipped her boxing gloves onto her fists. "He has a big right," her father said. "Just slip the right. Don't stay back. Don't draw away. Slip it and hit him in the jaw with your overhand left. They are getting cocky, mama. We don't like that. Let's take this guy."

At the bell, Seniesa smacked Ulises with a series of hooks, jabs, and uppercuts. She forced him to the ropes, punching fast, down to the body, up to the head. The gym filled with her crackle-and-pop.

Ulises was shocked. Then he began to fight back, smacking her in the body and the face. She winced. Her head jolted, but she stayed close, steering clear of his right as she hammered him back. With each of her body blows, I could see and hear the results.

Ulises' mouth formed an O. "Ugh," he groaned. "Uhh. Uhh."

"*Vamos, Ulises, vamos!*" his coaches yelled. "*A la derecha! A la derecha!*" To the right. To the right.

Sweat poured. Fists rose and fell and arced through the hot, humid air. Joe and the rival trainers roared. So did onlookers from the neighborhood, who had filed into the gym.

"Duran, Seniesa, Duran!" It was the punch she had named after the champion Roberto Duran.

"Come on, Ulises, come on!"

"Show your stuff, girl, show your stuff!"

One woman yelled louder than the rest. "*Vamos, mama! Vamos, mama!* Show 'em you're a true Mexican! Show 'em you're a girl! Show 'em the power of a girl!"

Seniesa gained the upper hand. She circled, wheeled, ponytail flying, boxing as if she were chasing a demon.

At the end, the crowd applauded in awe. Seniesa and Ulises embraced in mid-ring.

Suddenly, she seemed calm, happy. She stood tall, something I hadn't seen in weeks.

"She was good," Ulises said as he walked to the back of the gym to get a drink of water. His white shirt was soaked, his gait stiff. "She just kept coming. Coming and hitting me."

Joe slipped an arm around his daughter, and they walked out into the darkness of early evening. Seniesa had a smile.

"Nobody can touch her," he said, shaking his fist. "*No-bah-dee.* My little girl is back."

Believing Again

To regain momentum, Joe seized almost any opportunity for her to box. One was the Junior Olympics. Despite her mother's worry that she looked too pale to be in the ring, Seniesa won by a second-round technical knockout. Twice she went to Arizona. Both times she beat a girl ten pounds heavier.

In the last of those bouts, when it was announced that Seniesa had won, the hometown crowd booed, hissed, and shook their fists. Joe tried to hurry Seniesa away, but she raised her right arm in defiance and pointed a middle finger skyward.

"Don't do that, mama, don't!" Joe yelled over the din.

As they drove back to their hotel, he shook his head. He couldn't believe his daughter had flipped off the crowd.

"What?" she asked, with a sly smile. "I was just saying, 'I'm number one! I'm number one!'"

Her father shook his head again, but he let it go. Inside, he felt contentment. She believed in their dream again.

Even Lupe Arellano, her teacher, could see that Seniesa was feeling better about herself. She had sharpened her focus and pulled up her grades.

In her school journal, Seniesa wrote: "I'm a Mexican. A girl who lives in El Sereno. Not a lot of money. An American citizen. I have the attitude. Proud of my achievements."

She was the only one in her sixth-grade class who had clear-cut goals, Arellano said. "Most of the kids, they are at that stage where all that matters is immediate gratification. But for her, it is long-term dedication. She is saying, 'I want to go to the Olympics one day. Nobody will stop me. If you don't like it, too bad for you.'"

What would finally restore Seniesa's full confidence, her father knew, would be to win a rematch with Daveena Villalva, who had defeated her at the Region VIII Silver Gloves Championships that January.

It was Seniesa's first big defeat — and it started her slump. Now that the gloom was lifting, she wanted revenge. Daveena lived in Arizona, and Seniesa had seen her at both of her Phoenix matches. But Joe could not talk Daveena's father into another bout.

With each refusal, Seniesa's lust for vengeance grew. "She don't want to fight," Seniesa told me. "Ooh, I hate her."

In truth, Daveena wanted very much to fight. They were a lot alike, these two girls.

At her flat, one-story prefab house in a largely poor and largely Latino neighborhood south of downtown Phoenix, where I visited one afternoon, Daveena was running laps near a boxing ring that her father, who coached her, had built on their dirt lot.

Like Joe, David Villalva had been a street tough. Now he was a welder and tree trimmer who bred pit bulls in eighteen wooden kennels next to the ring to make extra money. Just as it had been with Seniesa, boxing was Daveena's idea. David didn't want his daughter anywhere near it. But then she sparred for the first time — like Seniesa, against a boy. And, like Seniesa, she beat him so badly that her father changed his mind.

The Villalvas were a warm, close family. As Daveena jogged past the dog kennels in 108-degree heat, she saw me and trotted over. She introduced herself and extended her hand. She had soft skin, dark round eyes, round cheeks, and straight black hair that fell below her shoulders.

I was struck by her poise. Like Seniesa, she was a charmer, but she was more at ease, more open. She looked steadily at me as she answered my questions.

Like Seniesa, she was angry. She hated the way Seniesa had treated her, how Seniesa refused to shake hands after Daveena won, how Seniesa stomped out of the ring, then stormed out of the locker room when Daveena walked in.

David worried about Daveena's anger. Too much of it could drive her to be overly aggressive, he feared. That could blind her to danger. And that, in turn, could make her vulnerable. She needed to simmer down, he said, before she boxed Seniesa again.

I watched her hammer punches into a big red training bag and then spar against a boy.

Daveena was aggressive. She was powerful. She was just as aggressive and powerful as Seniesa.

Oh, there would be a rematch, Daveena assured me. "The last fight, I thought I did very good. We'll fight. Soon, I hope."

Spring was turning to summer when a tournament in Tucson known as the Turquoise Gloves offered an opportunity.

Joe tried again.

This time, David agreed.

Seniesa saw her father's excitement.

And she saw his relief; his brother Rick's trial was finally over. A jury had acquitted Seniesa's uncle of attempted murder and convicted him instead of lesser charges: assaulting his wife with a deadly weapon, using a firearm to cause great bodily injury, and inflicting great bodily injury. The judge sentenced him to ten years in prison. It was less than Joe had feared, and he thought his brother could endure it.

She saw another change too. Slowly, her father was becoming a peacemaker. In an argument pitting him, along with another coach, against a rival trainer, Joe's anger flashed. He wanted to end it with his fists. Seniesa could see it by the veins in his neck. But her father stepped back from the fury that was part of his nature, what he called "the zone."

Let's cool off, he said. *Fighting ain't worth it, fighting won't do nothing to solve this. They think we're cholos from the streets. We ain't gonna give them the satisfaction.*

Seniesa came to realize that her father could walk away from a fight. Maybe the dream they shared was changing him.

Even so, as the rematch against Daveena drew near, the world ambushed her again. It was after dark when she rode with her mother, Maryann, past a neighborhood liquor store called Mickey's. They saw a crowd. Then they saw yellow tape, and then legs in black pants sticking out from under a blanket.

Was it one of Seniesa's brothers?

Johnny?

Maybe Joey?

Maryann stopped the car, rushed toward the body, and asked frantically: *Who is that, dead on the ground?*

It was no one in the family. But Seniesa woke that night to crying in the living room, as her mother and Joey talked about the victim, a woman the family had known, and the apparent killer, whom they knew as well.

Seniesa told me it froze her with fear.

But she knew she should not dwell on it. Where she lived, it

seemed, sometimes murder just happened. Her father said she had
to be ready mentally, or she would lose to Daveena. She had to forget the killing.

You gotta let go of that, Joe would remember telling her. *This is your
test. It's time to focus, time to go to Arizona and take care of business.*

Dreaming of Daveena

Finally, there was only one thing on Seniesa's mind: Daveena. At
night, Seniesa dreamed about her, of battling her for three straight
days, all day long, each day its own round.

In her dreams, she beat Daveena badly, every day.

"In the beginning, when they call our names, I'm gonna shake
her hand fast, because I don't even want to look at her," she said to
me, her voice cold. "I just want to beat her up, and that is it."

I replied that Daveena was a kid much like herself, a good kid
who wanted to win just as much as she did. If they lived in the same
neighborhood and went to the same school, I said, I could imagine
their being good friends.

"No way," she shot back. "I don't like her."

Anger was powerful fuel, and I could see that some of her tough
talk had become part of psyching herself up.

The fight would be on June 26, her twelfth birthday. Her father
promised her $400 as a birthday gift, but to get it, she had to win.
His tactic surprised me. It was clear that Seniesa needed no extra
motivation.

The fight had become something special to Joe, however, a kind
of survival test.

"God bless her and her family," he said, speaking of Daveena. "I
wish them no harm. No, nothing really personal. It is just that this
is a brutal sport. A very brutal sport. And once you get in that ring,
I am sorry, but my girl is going to beat your girl. My girl is going to
hurt your girl. After we step out of that ring, then they can go and
play dolls and whatever they want to do, talk about Barbie and Ken.
But when they are in that ring, I am sorry: it is about hurting you
before you hurt me. That is just the way it is."

We left for Tucson the day before the fight, taking along a team
of boy boxers from Seniesa's gym. The next morning, no one
spoke of her birthday. In her hotel room, she sat apart, fidgeting,

toying with her braids, checking her bag to be certain she had all of her gear.

Every so often, she rose to work tension out of her thighs. The boys were playing a video game. She ignored them. She twisted and pulled a foot up behind her, balancing. She looked like a thin brown heron, standing on one leg.

A boxing ring squatted at the center of the El Casino Ballroom, in a Tucson barrio. Above it hung a disco ball. The hall was filled with hot, June-in-Arizona air. It smelled of dust. Bright lights blazed onto the canvas. There were enough folding chairs for at least five hundred people, and the place was filling up fast.

Seniesa had no trouble making weight. When she and Daveena stepped onto the scales, they weighed the same: seventy-seven pounds.

The two girls hardly acknowledged each other. Both tried to look unbothered, unfazed, but I saw them peek at each other when they thought no one was looking.

On their way to lunch, Seniesa and her father walked past the Villalvas. Daveena was eating Doritos. She held out the bag.

"Want some?" she asked.

Seniesa seemed shocked that Daveena had even spoken. She pulled back, ducking the Doritos like a punch. "Nah," she replied and walked away. "I'm fine."

After lunch, an eight-year-old boy approached. "Can't do it," he gasped, weeping. "Can't." It was his turn to fight, and Joe had helped teach him to box. Joe took a moment and massaged his tiny shoulders. "Just try it. If I see you don't like it, I'll stop the fight. I won't let nothing bad happen to you."

They watched the boy's bout, and when he won, Seniesa hugged him and her father. Then she slung her bag over a shoulder and walked away from the ring, her lips pursed. Her own moment of reckoning was coming.

An hour from the bell, Seniesa had dressed in her shiny blue shorts, crisp blue tank top, and black Adidas boxing shoes, spotless, carefully wrapped at the ankles with thin strips of white tape. Like Daveena, she stared into the middle distance. I watched them both. They rubbed their eyes. They stretched their arms.

"You ready?" I asked Seniesa.

"No, I'm not ready," she said, her voice dripping with sarcasm.

She cracked a smile. She no longer had trouble looking me straight in the eye. "Yeah, I'm ready. Of course. I was born ready."

The Big Moment

Twenty minutes to the bell.

Over each of her taped fists, Joe slipped puffy blue boxing gloves.

"Don't like these gloves," Seniesa said.

Joe stopped her cold. "No, no, no. No excuses today, mama. No excuses."

She and Daveena moved near now, just a few feet from the ring. Referees examined their headgear and their gloves. Each girl's face was solemn, expressionless.

Daveena bounced on her toes, then stood firm and still. Her fists rested on her hips. She stared at the ring.

Seniesa tossed hooks into the air, lips tight.

David and Joe patted each other on the back. "Good luck," each said to the other.

Seniesa and her father walked up to the ropes. Ronny Rivota, a coach for the boy boxers, followed, leaning in and reminding her of the game plan: stand firm, counter Daveena's forward motion with heavy artillery, with all of your power. "If she hits you," he cautioned, "control your anger."

She peered over his shoulders, her eyes round, large, and focused.

"You ready, girlfriend?" her father asked.

"Yeah."

"Okay, right hand, left hand, right hand. Remember, she don't throw straight punches. Come up, then over."

Seniesa didn't acknowledge him. She was lost in a world of her own, stretching, swaying, bouncing on her toes.

For weeks, Joe had prepared for this moment, staying up late, night after night, as he watched a tape of the first Seniesa-Daveena fight, counting blows, convincing himself that his daughter had been robbed. He told me he would know just what to say to Seniesa as she entered the ring to fight Daveena again.

Bending down, he blurted stream-of-consciousness into her ear.

"Pound on her," he told her. "The referees are stopping fights today. Let the referees stop it. Come on, baby, she don't hit harder than Richard [one of the boy boxers]. Remember that. You've got to show it to 'em now. They think they beat you, but they did not have the skills to beat you. She don't have half the skills you have. C'mon, mama, you are ten times, a hundred times better than she is. Skill-wise and every way, baby. You can do this, mama. God is with us. It's you and the Lord in there, mama. Ask the Lord to give you strength. I can't go in there with you, but God is with you all the time, baby. Let's do this. We've waited a long time for this, mama. I'll tell you right now, they think they won the first fight, but I know there is doubt in their mind. Let's do this, baby doll."

Seniesa nodded — yes, yes, yes.

But in truth, there was little anyone, even Joe, could say to interrupt her focus and get inside her head. This was the biggest moment in the life she shared with her father, a rehearsal for the many tough fights they hoped to have in the future. She wanted to win this fight more than she had ever wanted anything. She was already in the state of trance she had inherited from her father.

She stepped through the ropes and into the ring. A few seconds passed. *Clang!* The opening bell echoed through the ballroom.

Ready for More

Seniesa and Daveena rushed at each other, releasing six months of anxiety since their last duel.

Seniesa led with a left that grazed Daveena's gloves.

It gave Daveena a moment's hesitation. Then she charged.

Seniesa backed away. But in this fight, unlike the last one, she stopped, braced her back leg, pushed off, and fired a nifty combination — jab, cross, jab, cross. The punches, more powerful than anything she had thrown before, slammed into Daveena. They stung.

But this was not a girl Seniesa could intimidate. This was Daveena, the wind-up boxer. She fixed on her target, and she kept coming, always kept coming, just as she had in their first bout. She stalked forward, throwing curved punches, refusing to let up.

Seniesa worked against the forward motion like a crafty old master. Full of energy, ready to strike, she swayed inside Daveena's blows, slipping most of them. She threw fast, heavy replies with her right, then her left.

Daveena's head jolted backward. *Whap.* Her head slapped from side to side, left to right. *Whap-whop.*

At the bell, Seniesa brimmed with confidence and speed.

"Relax, mama!" her father said.

He was happy, so happy that he offered no instructions. Just keep doing what you are doing, he said, because what you are doing is winning.

She nodded, ready for more.

In the second round, she opened with an uppercut, then a stiff left hook.

Men and women in the chairs, who hadn't expected to see girls box, spat their astonishment into my ears: "Goddamn!" A Duran to the gut. Then another. "Damn!"

"Keep going!" her father yelled, so loudly that the referee stopped the fight for a moment, turned to Joe, and told him to calm down. He did, but he still twitched with every punch his daughter threw and flinched with every blow she took. It was like voodoo; he felt everything.

Daveena, facing a new kind of onslaught, evaded many of the blows. She kept charging, driving toward Seniesa with her punches. Some landed solidly against Seniesa's sides. They turned her and twisted her.

"Let's go, Chickee! Fight, Chickee!" Daveena's family and friends screamed, on their feet near the ring.

Then, just before the bell, Seniesa landed a hard shot that nearly forced Daveena off her feet. Several of Daveena's fans fell into their seats with worry.

But they didn't give up. They rose when the third and last round got under way, cheering loudly as Daveena found new strength. She whaled away with haymakers. *Whap!* Several found their mark, *whap-whap,* rocking Seniesa to her heels.

Soon, though, Daveena lost strength.

Seniesa had weathered the aggression, and now she pounced. Right hand. Duran. Right hand. Duran. Backpedal. Stop. Jab.

Just like practice, just like her father had told her, just like she had dreamed.

Then she tired too.

The girls took each other's measure near the middle of the ring, looking for an unguarded spot, hoping for a second wind. There was no time. *Clang!* The final bell. It was over. Six months of waiting and wanting, just like that.

Joe clutched Seniesa. She looked excited and nervous, spent but pleased.

David hugged Daveena, her face fixed with calm, as if she were preparing to accept gracefully whatever the judges decided.

The judges gathered their scorecards, the outcome was tabulated, and a referee in white held a warrior's arm in each hand.

There, in the middle of the ring, they stood, for five, ten, fifteen seconds. Each girl's face was filled with hope — and dread.

"Ladies and gentlemen," the announcer said into his microphone, his voice warbling as it ran through the speakers. "Ladies and gentlemen, please give a hand for our fighters."

The crowd cheered and stomped.

"We have a winner . . ."

Seniesa's legs shook.

"And the winner, by decision, is . . ."

Daveena looked toward heaven, prayerfully. One second passed, then another.

"Se-nie-sa Es-tra-da!"

I should not have been shocked when all she showed was simple satisfaction: a quick jump into the air, a clenched fist raised for a moment. Anything more would have signaled doubt. Seniesa's stance, upright but nonchalant, said enough: Do not be surprised by what I do. Seniesa Carmen Estrada can take care of herself.

She shook Daveena's hand firmly, even helped her through the ropes and out of the ring. The officials gave Seniesa the championship belt, and she walked to her father with it slung over her shoulder. She slapped his palms.

"Is that clear enough for you?" he asked, alluding to the moments when she did have her doubts. "Is that clear enough?"

She smiled but said nothing, letting him vent to someone in the crowd — "Last time, we got robbed. We got robbed on that last one" — letting him bask in what she had created.

Soon, we stood under the sun, in the dirt parking lot. I asked Seniesa how she had felt in the ring.

Stronger than ever, she said. She knew she was hitting hard, because she could feel, against her knuckles, the softness of Daveena's flesh. She said she was glad it was over, because now she no longer needed revenge. The grudge was gone. Then she looked down near her feet and spotted an anthill.

Joe spoke excitedly, words tumbling. "Oh, man, I am sky-high. This makes it all worth it. Everything was just like I said it would be. Her aggressiveness. I told her to step in and land combinations. I told her to hit hard and not hold anything back."

He kissed her forehead.

She smiled, and then she bent down toward the anthill.

"You did as good as I thought you were going to do, mama," her father said.

She dabbed her finger in the dirt, announcing that she had never seen such large black ants. Gone was the warrior who had fought so fiercely in the ballroom, making strangers holler and cry. Suddenly, Seniesa was just like any other kid.

Her father didn't notice. "There's something more important than that fight that my daughter learned today," he said. "There's no giving up or giving in. It's like my life. You don't give up, no matter what happens. If you lose a fight, or if something worse happens, like what happened in my life, no matter what, you keep coming back, keep coming back, keep coming back."

He touched her neck with his fingers. He seemed to be talking to himself as much as to her, reminding himself of where he had been and how far he had come. Tijuana. Primera Flats. Prison. Addiction. Aggression. The loss of his family, the loss of his little girl. And then, the long road back.

"That's what I have to teach. Don't give up, don't give up, don't give up."

Now his past was far away. Seniesa's fight helped make this clear. Still, though, she was only a little girl, twelve years old on that very day. This was too young to put her life and his life and how they fit together into complete perspective. Nor did she really need to.

She crouched down on her thin knees, hovering over the ants.

"Dad?" she asked, tugging his shirt. "Dad?" she asked again, looking up. "Can we go?"

He nodded.

She bounded off, brushing past him.

"It's just that, I love you, *mija*," he said.

"I know," she said. "I love you too, Dad."

Flipping Out

FROM TEXAS MONTHLY

THEY HAD NAMES LIKE KAYLEE AND HAILEY and Ashley and Brittany, and they all had long legs and glossy hair and tan summer skin. More than a thousand of them — 1,345 cheerleaders from across Texas — had come to Southern Methodist University, in Dallas, on a sticky afternoon in June for the first day of cheer camp, and a clutch of mothers and squirming little sisters was taking in the view. On the lawn outside Dallas Hall, girls in starched cheerleading uniforms the bright colors of Life Savers built pyramids and performed midair toe-touch jumps and a dizzying number of standing back handsprings; the nimblest ones were lifted ten feet off the ground, where they each wobbled on one leg, grinning, before dropping into the outstretched arms below. Clipboards in hand, an army of clean-cut instructors from the National Cheerleaders Association stood watch, taking notes and appraising them, as the girls offered encouragement to one another ("Awesome job, Bailey!"). At the end of the day, they dusted themselves off and walked arm in arm to their dorm rooms, smiling and clapping and, of course, cheering. As they made their way across campus — *We've got spirit. Yes, we do!* — a thousand ponytails swayed back and forth.

I had come to SMU in hope of understanding what it was about cheerleading, exactly, that had sparked such hostility just a few weeks earlier at the Texas Legislature. While pressing issues like balancing the budget and financing public education had been put on hold, the House had found the time to consider HB1476, or "the booty bill": legislation that prohibited cheerleading squads, marching bands, and dance and drill teams from performing at public schools "in a manner that is overtly sexually suggestive." The bill, which inspired an intense, two-hour floor debate that included the spectacle of legislators shaking pom-poms and blasting KC and the Sunshine Band's "Shake Your Booty," had been ridiculed in newspapers ("Bunch of Sis, Boom, Baloney!") and on cable news and late-night talk shows. "You wouldn't have the Texas Rangers out there busting the cheerleaders and putting them in cuffs, would you?" Bill O'Reilly asked the author of the legislation, Houston Democrat and lay preacher Al Edwards, on *The O'Reilly Factor.* *The Daily Show* piled on with a segment called "No Child's Sweet Behind," which featured correspondent Bob Wiltfong bumping and grinding during an interview with Edwards. "Is it any wonder Texas has become a national punch line?" marveled *Austin American-Statesman* columnist John Kelso, who suggested that the Legislature create a watchdog group to monitor cheerleading and call it the Bipartisan Observational Organization on Booty, or BOOB.

But a majority of lawmakers, who voted to pass the bill, failed to see the humor in it. During the floor debate in the House, Republican Carl Isett, of Lubbock, called for a return to "old-fashioned morality," citing sexually suggestive cheerleading — along with out-of-wedlock births and throwaway marriages — as evidence of the moral decay of our time. "If I take my twelve-year-old son to a high school football game, I don't want to have to cover his eyes when the cheerleaders are on the field," he said. Linda Harper-Brown, a Republican from Irving, praised the bill as "a shot across the bow" for school districts, which would have lost funding under its provisions if they did not ensure that their cheerleaders' routines were sufficiently wholesome. Representative Edwards went so far as to suggest a link between "overly sexy performances" on the sidelines and a host of social ills. "We see, as a result, more of our young girls getting pregnant in middle and high school, dropping out of school, having babies, contracting AIDS, herpes, and cutting off their youthful life at an early age," he said. "And members, it's part of our responsibility to do something about it." While legislators who opposed the measure criticized it for being everything from a sexist bill (no one was regulating football players' behavior) to a publicity stunt, the rhetoric from supporters — which included the local chapter of Phyllis Schlafly's Eagle Forum — seemed to suggest that cheerleaders posed a threat to the moral fiber of the children of Texas every time they walked onto a football field.

That cheerleading, of all things, found itself in the crosshairs of a culture war was unlikely enough; that it happened in Texas, which introduced the world to the Dallas Cowboys Cheerleaders thirty-three years ago, was stranger still. In the end, the booty bill failed to reach the governor's desk; the Senate refused to consider HB1476, and it died before the end of the regular legislative session. The House succeeded only in passing a resolution that called on the Texas Education Agency to monitor school performances for sexual content. No videotapes of raunchy cheerleading routines ever surfaced, and even Edwards was hard-pressed to name a school whose squad had crossed the line. But the stigma has lingered. Just before the start of the school year, Texas Education Agency commissioner Shirley J. Neeley sent a memo to every superintendent in the state, directing them to monitor their districts' cheerleading squads, marching bands, and dance and drill teams for any "overly sexually suggestive" routines and cautioning that "inappropriate performances are unacceptable and should not be tolerated." It was a strange imperative, given what I had seen that summer day at SMU, when girls had whiled away an afternoon reciting upbeat cheers. Then again, it has been a long journey from pleated skirts and saddle shoes to accusations of indecency. Why, when cheerleading is more popular than ever, have our feelings about it grown so complicated?

If there was a moment in history when sex became forever associated with the sidelines, it happened on the hot, humid afternoon of September 17, 1972, when the brand-new Dallas Cowboys Cheerleaders — seven professional dancers who Cowboys general manager Tex Schramm had promised would add a "touch of class" — paraded onto the field at Texas Stadium in front of 55,850 spectators, wearing only hot pants, go-go boots, fringed vests, and satin blouses tied snugly above the midriff. Part Vegas showgirl, part girl next door, the women wore royal-blue-and-white uniforms that allowed for plenty of jiggle and signaled the start of a new way of seeing the cheerleader in the public imagination. (Until that fall, the Cowboys' game day entertainment had featured the CowBelles and Beaux, a group of local high school students who had worn matching varsity sweaters and performed pom-pom routines.) Just as Schramm had intended, his new squad soon had Dallas talking; breathless news reports speculated, contrary to fact, that the cheerleaders were not wearing bras under their trademark blouses. "We were an overnight phenomenon," remembers Dixie Luque, a member of the original squad who is now a real estate agent in Plano. "When we came off the field, there were fans waiting at the end of the ramp wanting our autographs and gentlemen throwing roses from the stands, asking if they could take us to dinner. And you've never seen so much mail! None of us imagined — we were just a bunch of girls who loved the Cowboys and loved to dance. I mean, who would have *thunk?*"

Of course, the cheerleader had always been an object of desire; she was the unattainable girl at the top of the high school caste system, the prettiest one in the class. The Dallas Cowboys Cheerleaders were not technically cheerleaders — they didn't cheer — but their name evoked those old associations and only magnified them. Coming at the height of the women's movement, their uncomplicated brand of femininity held monstrous appeal, though it wasn't until January 1976, when the Cowboys played the Pittsburgh Steelers in Super Bowl X, that they secured their reputations as national sex symbols. TV cameras rarely focused on the sidelines then, since professional cheerleading squads were still a novelty; the Steelers had no one other than their fans to cheer them on. But during a break in the game, a cameraman let his gaze wander to the edge of the field. Gwenda Swearingen, the former Miss Corsicana contestant–turned–Dallas Cowboys Cheerleader who had caught his eye, looked back — and winked. Seventy-five million viewers across America were watching. And so, as the story goes, the first pinups of the gridiron were born. Soon there were swimsuit calendars, made-for-TV movies, *Love Boat* cameos, shampoo commercials, and public appearances with thousands of screaming fans. The Cheerleaders were so popular that in 1977 their cheesecake posters outsold Farrah Fawcett's.

The Cowboys franchise traded on the squad's all-American, mass-market eroticism, at the same time careful to keep its image squeaky-clean. Cheerleaders were not allowed to fraternize with players, perform where alcohol was served, smoke cigarettes while in uniform, or even chew gum on the field. They were, after all,

"America's Sweethearts." To drive the point home, their director, Suzanne Mitchell, reeled off a list to a *Dallas Morning News* reporter of all the dignified jobs her girls were busy holding down when they weren't high-kicking at Texas Stadium. "They're teachers and secretaries, PE instructors and stewardesses," she told the paper in 1977, adding, "We don't pick these girls up at go-go joints." The success of the squad required its image to remain above reproach; after the release the following year of the X-rated film *Debbie Does Dallas* — which featured a group of cheerleaders trying to finagle a trip to Big D so they could audition for a squad whose blue-and-white uniforms looked awfully familiar — the franchise sued for a trademark violation and won. When Jerry Jones announced in 1989 that he wanted to outfit the squad in halter tops and spandex and relax the rules that kept cheerleaders from socializing with players, more than a third of them quit, complaining that the team's boorish new owner was trying to undermine their "traditional virtues" and "high moral standards." ("I feel like we are a sacred, sacred organization," one cheerleader said.) Jones eventually backed down.

These days, the thirty-seven women who are the Dallas Cowboys Cheerleaders spend much of their time at the team's headquarters, in Irving, in a chilly dance studio with blond-wood floors and mirrors that extend from floor to ceiling. On the wall is a list of aphorisms that urge them to be better: "Wear a cheerful countenance at all times." "Look at the sunny side of everything." "Give so much time to the improvement of yourself that you have no time to criticize others." On the opposite wall stands a scale. Outside, the foyer is lined with blown-up swimsuit calendar photos in which cheerleaders are pictured in tiny bikinis crawling on all fours across expanses of sand or running their hands through their sea-soaked hair or arching their backs at the water's edge. The women who are picked to be Dallas Cowboys Cheerleaders — more than a thousand audition each year for the honor — must still adhere to the same strict code of conduct and be able to dance for upwards of four hours in sweltering heat (longer, if the game goes into overtime) without ever letting their smiles falter. Each cheerleader must attend rehearsals at least four nights a week and stay at her audition weight or risk getting cut from the squad, a rule enforced with occasional weigh-ins; she must also reaudition for her job at the end of the football season. Although the pay has risen from $15 per game to just $50, no one is complaining. "It pays for gas and panty hose!" one cheerleader told me. "Pretty much every girl who's come through these doors saw the Dallas Cowboys Cheerleaders on TV when she was a little girl and knew that's what she wanted to be when she grew up," explained former cheerleader Courtney Sparks, who recently retired from the squad. "This is a childhood dream."

I had visited the dance studio that July afternoon to ask the Dallas Cowboys Cheerleaders what they thought about the debate over cheerleading. Carefully sidestepping any questions about politics, Laura Beke and Elizabeth Davis sat and talked with me, emphasizing that they and their fellow squad members were always mindful to be "ladies" and "role models" and were proud to be part of "a classy organization." "We wear more clothes than most people do on the beach," offered Beke. Several other cheerleaders — women in their early twenties with perfectly sculpted bodies and manes of blond hair — were busy teaching DCC Camp, the cheer and dance instruction that the squad gives to local girls each summer. Over the thumping beat of RuPaul's "Looking Good, Feeling Gorgeous," the cheerleaders stood in front of the bank of mirrors, counting to the music ("Step five, six, seven, eight!") while they effortlessly walked through a dance routine. Behind them, a motley crew of junior high school students — girls with mouths full of braces, pudgy girls with acne, flat-chested girls who hadn't hit puberty yet, girls with frizzy hair and glasses — watched in rapt amazement. Studying themselves in the mirror with fierce concentration, they tried to follow along. They thrust their chests forward and swiveled their narrow hips back and forth, awkwardly aping the cheerleaders who were dancing in front of them, trying for all the world to look like someone's idea of sexy.

Seventeen miles northeast of Dallas is the suburb of Rockwall, a mostly white, middle-class enclave of big-box stores, chain restaurants, and subdivisions that, as one resident observed during my visit, might more aptly have been named Wonderbreadland. Although its 5A football team, the Yellowjackets, has for years maintained a near-perfect losing streak, its varsity cheerleading squad has given Rockwall something to brag about. In January the girls won second place at the National Cheerleaders Association's annual competition, where they came in just three one-hundredths of a point behind the Kentucky high school that cinched the title in their division. Rockwall's success was not unexpected; most of the girls on the squad have taken cheer and gymnastics lessons since they were in kindergarten and can perform the most demanding stunts with such grace and ease that even when they are spinning in midair ten feet above the ground, they seem to be doing nothing more demanding than breathing. The eighteen-member squad includes two sisters, Hannah and Caroline Wilson, whose great-grandmother, Chug Linn, cheered for Rockwall during the 1930–31 school year. Before she died this summer, Linn was able to recollect little of her life through the fog of Alzheimer's, but she never forgot the Rockwall High School fight song ("For the boys, we'll yell and yell and yell!"), which she would recite faithfully, from start to finish, whenever she was given the opportunity.

Rockwall's first game of the season, against the North Garland Raiders, featured none of the provocative sideline moves that had caused so much hand-wringing in Austin. As the Yellowjackets tried to move the ball that August evening, their cheerleaders did back handsprings down the length of the field and stood on the sidelines urging the team on, shouting in unison: "Go orange! Go white! Go 'Jackets! Fight, fight, fight!" Their uniforms were not what one would wear to church on Sunday, but they were hardly offensive either; a fitted top covered the midriff, and a flouncy skirt, which grazed the top of the leg, was worn over black spandex shorts that revealed nothing more than a pair of well-toned thighs. Climbing onto one another's palms, the cheerleaders ran through their repertoire — soaring above the field in arabesques and scorpions, bottle rockets and basket tosses — while the boys battled it out on the field below. (Overcome by the heat, the Yellowjackets' mascot periodically dashed off the field to remove her enormous plush-covered head and gulp down water, wiping the sweat from her face with her furry orange arms.) When one of Rockwall's players suffered an injury and lay grimacing on the forty-yard line, each cheerleader knelt at the edge of the field and looked appropriately solemn. And during the third quarter, when the team needed a little extra encouragement, they leaped into the air again and again

with broad smiles, yelling, "Let's go, Rockwall!" In spite of their efforts, the Yellowjackets still lost, 20–17.

Sitting on the yellow school bus that ferried them to and from
the game that evening, the girls talked about their frustration over
the way cheerleading had been maligned this spring. "We're not
trying to offend anyone," Hannah Wilson said. "I mean, the worst
thing you can say about us is that we all like to be the center of attention." Perhaps mindful of the image that they wanted to project,
the girls talked at length about the church missions they had partic-
ipated in, the most recent of which had taken several members of
the squad as far as Ghana. "We are truly, truly blessed," one girl told
me. Their sponsor, an upbeat English teacher and former cheerleader named Holli Loveless, drove the point home. "Cheerleading has always tapped into issues like sex and power, but these girls
are morally strong," she said. "They are well rounded in their family lives and spiritual lives." The squad was particularly exasperated
by the way that one of its members, Kristin Turner-Wurm, had
been portrayed this spring in the *Dallas Morning News*'s free spin-
off, *Quick*; a front-page article on HB1476, which ran under the
headline "The Dirrty Rule," was accompanied by a photo of her
performing a stunt in a sports bra. The image had been taken out
of context, she explained; she had been photographed practicing
at Cheer Athletics, a Garland gym that is famous not only for turning out winning squads but also for toughening up its cheerleaders
by making them practice without air-conditioning. "I don't wear a
sports bra when I perform. I wear a uniform," she said. "They
made what we do look bad."

As the school bus made its way back to Rockwall, the cheerleaders passed around bubble gum and sent text messages to one another in the dark. One girl hunched over a binder, doing her
homework by the light of her cell phone. The sound of pop culture
filtered through the conversation now and then, as when one girl
started singing the Black Eyed Peas' hit "My Hump." But when the
bus swung into the Rockwall High School parking lot, the girls all
chimed in:

> Hail, dear old Rockwall!
> How we love you
> > Ever you'll find us
> > Loyal and true.

When they had finished, head cheerleader Bronwyn Hill stood up and yelled, "Make sure to tell the guys they had a great game!"

In a simpler time, before anyone had heard of the booty bill, a Texan named Lawrence Herkimer got the idea to fasten dyed crepe-paper streamers to the end of a wooden stick. He called his invention a pom-pom. (Later, when he discovered that the term meant something rather crude in Hawaiian, he changed it to "pom *pon*," but the original name stuck.) In 1956 he and his wife began making pom-pom kits out of their garage in Dallas, and girls across the Southeast soon started clamoring for them. After Herkimer applied for a patent, the uniform business he owned, Cheerleader Supply Company, started producing pom-poms wholesale. And so the cheer industry was born.

"Mr. Cheerleader," or just "Herkie," as the seventy-nine-year-old Herkimer is called, is credited with creating everything from cheer camp to the spirit stick and for turning Texas into the cheerleading capital of the world. He conceived of his most imitated invention — the herkie — during World War II, when he was a cheerleader himself at North Dallas High School. (The herkie, which involves thrusting one leg forward in midair while crooking the other back at the knee, is still a sideline perennial.) While an undergraduate at SMU, Herkie conducted the first-ever cheer clinic, teaching fifty-two girls at Sam Houston State University, in Huntsville, the art of public speaking, gymnastics, and rhyme; it was so popular that he made it a fixture at SMU and then at colleges around the nation. When he founded the National Cheerleaders Association in Dallas more than half a century ago, he launched the city's reputation as the epicenter of all things cheerleader. Herkie has since retired to Miami Beach, where he isn't quite as limber as the day he performed thirty-eight back flips for a Cheer detergent commercial. (Doing a herkie now, he joked over the phone, would require "a crane and some piano wires.") On the subject of the Legislature and HB1476, which I asked him to weigh in on, Herkie was philosophical. "There have always been humorless people," he said. "They made the same complaints fifty years ago: 'These girls need to cover up — they're half-naked,' or, 'It's disgusting how they are throwing their legs apart.' You can read something ugly into anything, you know."

Cheerleading has changed since the days when Herkie taught

girls to do pom-pom routines to the tune of "Lollipop." The technical skill and athleticism that are required by squads like Rockwall's have made cheerleading more than just a popularity contest. At many 4A and 5A high schools, the baseline at tryouts is no longer poise or a pretty face; it is a rounded-off standing back handspring, a technique that only students who have had years of practice in gymnastics can execute. (Splits and cartwheels went out of fashion around the same time as Keds, feathered hair, and "How Funky Is Your Chicken?") Routines have become so dazzling now that one annual competition is broadcast on ESPN. The acrobatics have come at a price; in the past twenty-two years, cheerleading has accounted for more than 50 percent of catastrophic sports injuries — that is, injuries involving hospitalization or death — among girls in high school and college. At cheer camp, where instructors stress the importance of safety, it is not uncommon to see girls in splints, hobbling around on crutches, or occasionally pushing the least fortunate member of their squad around in a wheelchair (bedecked in the squad's school colors, of course). Early last year, a cheerleader at Prairie View A&M University was paralyzed from the neck down when her squad failed to catch her after throwing her in the air.

Because modern cheerleading is so physically demanding, many of its boosters think it should qualify to be a sport in its own right. But just as calling the Miss America pageant a "scholarship competition" elicits eye rolls and snickers, so too does the CHEERLEADING IS A SPORT slogan that is emblazoned across so many girls' T-shirts. School districts have been slow to recognize cheerleading as an activity that is on par with other girls' sports. If anything, cheerleading suffers from a double standard; while some administrators are "grounding" squads — forbidding their members to perform stunts as a way of heading off accidents — no school districts have benched their football teams as a safety precaution. And so cheerleaders find themselves in a Catch-22; the more they ask to be taken seriously, the more dismissive their critics become.

Their detractors have included feminist theorists and academics, who have weighed in with essays like "Postmodern Paradox? Cheerleaders at Women's Sporting Events" and "Hands on Hips, Smiles on Lips! Cheerleading, Emotional Labor, and the Gendered Performance of 'Spirit.'" Why, they ask, should girls participate in an activity that still requires them to wear hair ribbons, lipstick, short skirts, and happy faces when Title IX long ago opened up other opportunities? Waving pom-poms at football games was one thing in the fifties, when chanting "Two bits, four bits, six bits, a dollar," provided the only chance for girls to participate in school sports, but another thing entirely, they point out, when their role models are Venus Williams and Mia Hamm.

The argument against cheerleading was most forcefully articulated by *Sports Illustrated*'s Rick Reilly, who devoted a column of his — "Sis! Boom! Bah! Humbug!" — to the subject in 1999. "I guess this is like coming out against fudge and kittens and Abe Lincoln, but it needs to be said," he warned his readers. "I don't hate cheerleading just because it's about as safe as porcupine juggling. I also hate it because it's dumb. The Velcroed-on smiles. The bizarre arm movements stolen from the Navy signalmen's handbook. The same cheers done by every troupe in every state. What's even dumber is that cheerleaders have no more impact on the game than the night janitorial staff. They don't even face the game. They face the crowd." But such criticism has not had much resonance in Texas, where cheerleading is bigger than ever. All-star cheerleading — in which squads compete against one another and exist independent of school teams — is currently one of the fastest-growing athletic activities for girls in the nation, with Texas being home to one out of every four all-star squads. More than four hundred cheer gyms have opened from Beaumont to El Paso, each with a more exuberant name than the last: Atomic Cheer, Spirit Explosion, Cheer Factory, Cheer USA, Lonestar Cheer, Planet Cheer, Tumble Town, Wild About Cheer. The industry that Herkie helped to establish more than half a century ago now generates hundreds of millions of dollars a year. So popular has cheerleading become that the Dallas suburb of Garland has forty-eight squads, twelve of which are for kindergarteners alone.

A half-hour's drive north of Garland, at Pro Spirit, in McKinney, I watched a peewee squad practice one afternoon. Pro Spirit is housed in a cavernous metal building on the western edge of town, where the subdivisions start to give way to grassland and the effect is that of entering a place set apart from the rest of the world. The walls are covered with shadow boxes filled with ribbons and medals and photos of girls triumphantly hoisting colossal trophies above their heads. On the day I visited in July, several dozen mothers sat in a darkened room that looked out onto the blue mats where their children were learning how to tumble; above them hung a sign that read POSITIVE PARENTS. POSITIVE COACHES. POSITIVE KIDS. POSITIVE RESULTS. The glass partition they sat behind was lit in such a way that they could observe their children but their children could not see them. In sparkly outfits that glimmered under the fluorescent lights, the four- and five-year-olds executed near-flawless routines in miniature; one girl was held up in the air (with the assistance of her coach) by four equally tiny bases. Their mothers gave unseen thumbs-up signs and applauded; the girls gazed back at the opaque glass, flashing their practiced hundred-watt smiles. They had a certain girly glamour to them despite the occasional runny nose. Each girl was honing the skills she would need ten years from now, one mother told me, to win a spot on her high school cheerleading squad.

Although Representative Edwards could not name a specific high school cheerleading squad or incident that spurred him to action, he didn't pull the issue out of thin air either. The National Cheerleaders Association issued a warning in 1995 that is still given to every squad that attends its annual competition. "Deductions will be given for vulgar or suggestive choreography, which includes but is not limited to movements such as hip thrusting and inappropriate touching, gestures, hand/arm movements and signals, slapping, positioning of body parts and positioning to one another," it reads. All facets of a performance, it continues, "should be suitable for family viewing and listening." (Although the wording is broad, it is far more precise than the definition that Edwards gave his colleagues for overly sexually suggestive cheerleading: "Any adult that's been involved with sex in their lives will know it when they see it.") The National Cheerleaders Association issued the warning after its judges began noticing a change in tone at competition. Hemlines had crept to the top of the thigh, and uniforms were showing more and more midriff. Of most concern to judges was the music that a few squads had selected to perform to. (Last year a college squad was cautioned that it would be penalized if it presented the routine it had prepared to 50 Cent's bawdy "Disco Inferno.") "We are the gatekeepers," explained the National

Cheerleaders Association's vice president of marketing, Karen Hal-terman, when I visited the NCA headquarters, in Garland, this summer. "Our entire culture has been desensitized to explicit sex-ual content. We don't want to impose or even define morality, but we must have parameters."

Whether cheerleaders are singing Big & Rich's "Save a Horse (Ride a Cowboy)" in the locker room or taking up practice time mimicking the dance moves in Ludacris's "P-Poppin'" video — and what *P* stands for can't be printed in this magazine — popular cul-ture has put its imprint on what was once considered just good, clean fun. "If I tell my girls to come up with their own routine and I come back to polish it, my jaw drops when I see what they've done," said coach Billy Smith, of Dallas's Spirit Celebration. "When I tell them that we're going to have to change the routine, they'll say, 'But this is what Beyoncé is doing!'" And yet contrary to what was argued on the House floor, raunchy performances — at least at the high school level — usually stay off the playing field; coaches know that their squads will be penalized at competition if their routines are off-color, and cheerleading sponsors are not eager to showcase their girls shaking it at games that will be attended by parents and members of the school board. So where are these risqué routines that so inflamed the passions of the Legislature? Over and over again, I heard the same answer from parents and coaches, all of whom were white and asked not to be quoted by name: "It's a prob-lem at the *black* high schools." They read particular significance into the fact that the bill's author, Representative Edwards, is Afri-can American. "Go to an inner-city football game, and you'll see what I mean," one coach advised me.

So I went to the first football game of the season at South Oak Cliff High School, in a gritty pocket of Dallas that could not have looked more dissimilar from Wonderbreadland. But at its heart, South Oak Cliff was no different from Rockwall; despite the finger-pointing from the suburbs, there was no bumping and grinding that Friday night, no booty shaking or "dropping it low." The most offensive move of the evening was one very PG-rated shimmy. The squad had on the most demure cheerleading uniforms I had seen: loose-fitting athletic shorts and matching black tank tops with let-ters that spelled out BEARS. Wearing dabs of glittery eye shadow and ponytails secured with white, star-spangled ribbon, the girls beamed up at the crowd as they did herkies along the sidelines. Perhaps there was a cheerleading squad somewhere in Texas that night whose routines would have made our legislators blush, but it was not to be found in South Oak Cliff. Then again, as long as there are cheerleaders, there will always be those who pass judgment on them; they are athletes in short skirts, stranded between the same impossible expectations that all women find themselves caught between. They must be attractive but not too sexy. Fit but not too athletic. Confident but not too outspoken. If the cheerleader is the symbol of perfect womanhood, she will never measure up until we figure out exactly what it is that we want women to be.

None of that mattered on that warm August evening, when the South Oak Cliff cheerleaders called out in unison to the players on the field, "You make the touchdown! We'll make the noise!" The fans roared back their approval. Little girls studied the cheerleaders, waving miniature pom-poms in the air; lanky boys leaned over the railing, trying to catch their attention. The cheerleaders were beautiful under the stadium lights — young and radiant, with an aura of celebrity to them — and even when their team fumbled and fell behind, they kept on cheering.

JAMES BROWN

Dirty Moves

FROM THE LOS ANGELES TIMES MAGAZINE

AT 4:30 ON SUNDAY MORNING I roust my boys out of bed and tell
them to use the bathroom. When they're done, each takes his
turn stepping onto the scale beside the tub. They're groggy, of
course. They're slow to react, but they don't protest. My older son
understands the importance of a single ounce in wrestling, and the
younger is quickly learning. The slightest difference in weight can
mean having to compete in the next division, potentially giving
away nearly five precious pounds to your opponent. That might not
sound like much, but it is when you're already little more than muscle and bone. Stripped to his boxers, Logan tops the scale at 111.
He's a pound and one ounce over the weight for the division in
which he prefers to wrestle, where he's strongest, between 105 and
109. Logan curses, the most popular four-letter expletive in the
book.

"Don't cuss," I say, though his father is hardly a model of civil
speech.

Logan steps off the scale.

"I knew I shouldn't have eaten that banana last night," he says.

"You might still make it."

"How?"

"By the time we get there," I say, "you'll probably have to use the
bathroom again. That's another three, maybe four ounces. And
you can always run around the gym a couple times."

At twelve, Logan has been wrestling competitively for five years,
and he does not like even the slightest disadvantage. Little Nate, on
the other hand, is only six and weighs in at thirty-four and a half

pounds, close to the limit for his class. I pat him on the head as he steps off the scale.

"Good going," I say.

"What?"

"You're on weight."

"Oh," he says. "Is that good?"

"It's very good."

This is his first year in competition, and he's excited, wanting to follow in his brother's footsteps and win his own shelf full of medals and trophies. I'm confident that he will. The youngest in the brood is often the toughest, having on a daily basis to fight off the tortures and teasing of his older brothers.

By five we're in the car, headed for El Monte High School in the San Gabriel Valley. It's a good seventy miles or better, and we need to be there between six and seven for weigh-ins. Miss those and you don't wrestle. Nate is snuggled in the back with a blanket and a pillow. Logan sits shotgun but with the seat reclined, huddled under his Levi's jacket, so that he too can sleep while I drive. I sip coffee and try to keep my eyes open. It's still dark, and fortunately there aren't many people on the road. We make good time. Shortly after sunrise, we pull off the freeway, drive a few more miles, and then turn into the parking lot of the high school. Already it's beginning to fill up.

The registration tables are situated outside the main entrance to the gym. I get in line with the other parents and wait my turn with Nate. Logan, meanwhile, takes this opportunity to run around the gym, hoping to shed those last ounces. A few minutes later I step up to the table and show the woman in charge my kids' USA Wrestling cards.

"What team are they on?"

"We're independent."

"Excuse me?"

"We don't have a team," I say. "It's just me and my two sons."

"I'm sorry, sir," she says. "They have to be on a registered USA team or they can't wrestle."

We used to have a team but it disbanded a couple of years back when the coach's three boys graduated from USA Wrestling's youth programs to high school wrestling. Now, from time to time, especially when the people working the registration tables are new to their job, I have problems. But I'm prepared. I know the bylaws by heart, down to the page stating that independents are allowed to compete as long as they're accompanied by a registered Copper Coach with a current Copper Coach card. And that person would be me. I'm about to rattle all this off to the woman when the man working the table beside her, a man who's registered us several times in the past, speaks up.

"No, we take independents. We don't get many, but we take them. I know this guy," he says. "You're from the mountains, right?"

"Lake Arrowhead."

He whistles.

"Long drive," he says.

Once I've signed them in and paid the entry fees, I search out Logan, catching him as he rounds the corner of the gym at an even jog. He's worked up a sweat, though he's not breathing heavily, the sign of an athlete in shape.

"Did you use the bathroom?" I ask.

"Yeah, but I barely had to go."

I look at my watch.

"Better quit running," I say. "There's only twenty minutes left for weigh-ins."

"I don't think I'll make it."

"So you wrestle up a division. It's no big deal," I say. "You're tough."

"Yeah," he says. "Except that kid from Norwalk goes one-tens."

He's referring to the boy who beat him for first place at an earlier tournament. It was a close match, Logan leading by two points going into the last round when he took a chance, made an error, and the other kid capitalized on it.

I try to be upbeat. I try to turn his self-doubt around on him.

"That's good," I tell him.

"Why?"

"Because you need the competition. You learn more from your losses, not your wins. Besides, you'll get him this time."

Gang graffiti mars the walls of the boys' locker room, and the lockers themselves are mostly busted and broken. This is where weigh-ins take place, and it's packed with kids from the competing teams. The Outkasts. The Terminators. Fontana Boyz and the Scorpions. All have team warm-up suits while my sons are simply dressed in jeans and T-shirts. Clearly we stand out, and not solely for lack of uniforms. We are one of the few white families in an overwhelmingly Mexican-American community. I don't know if it's my imagination or not, if I invite it somehow, or if it's just part and parcel of the nature of this sport, but we occasionally get that dirty, lingering look that suggests we're not welcome here.

In the last ten years or so, wrestling also has become more popular with girls, which is terrific, but because of their presence in the locker room — and there are only a few here this morning — it's mandatory that the boys weigh in wearing their wrestling singlets. For Logan, that means forsaking another couple of ounces, and sure enough, when he strips down to his singlet and steps on the scale, he's over the mark.

The man working the scale jots down Logan's weight on a clipboard. Then he writes "110½" on my son's arm with a black felt-tip pen. Next in line is Nate, and he's been watching his brother. He knows to wait until the man signals him to step forward, and I admire this about him, that at six he's already well-mannered and mindful of his surroundings. He weighs in at thirty-four pounds, meaning he'll wrestle thirties. The divisions are separated by five-pound increments.

As my boys are putting their clothes back on, I notice Logan staring at something, his eyes narrowed. I look in the same direction. The kid from Norwalk is staring back at him, just as meanly, from the other end of the locker room. I put my hand on Logan's shoulder, which seems to break the spell.

"What're you doing?"

"He's trying to psyche me out."

"Don't go there with him," I say. "Don't let him rattle you."

"I'll kick his ass."

"You're here to wrestle," I tell him, "not fight. That's exactly what he wants you to do — lose your temper and screw up."

But I can see he's not listening. I know my son well. We're very much alike in temperament, quick to anger, and when he gets like this it's impossible to reach him. For better or worse, and I suspect it's for the worse, this ugly thing will just have to run its course.

The younger children, between the ages of five and eleven, wrestle in the morning. The older ones, twelve to fifteen, compete in the afternoon. In Nate's first match he goes up against a tough lit-

tle kid from nearby Fontana, birthplace of that fun-loving fraternity known as the Hells Angels. Because I am a card-carrying Copper Coach who has paid all the necessary fees and dues and attended all the mandatory seminars, I'm allowed in my son's corner
on the mat. The other fathers and mothers have to stand on the
sidelines, which are cordoned off with yellow caution tape, and
watch the team coach instruct their sons and daughters. I hand the
bout sheet to the scorekeepers and then take Nate aside. He's nervous, shifting his weight from one foot to the other. I kneel down so
we're looking eye to eye.

"What's the game plan?"

"Go for points," he says. "Don't worry about the pin."

Those are my exact words.

"What else?"

"Just relax," he says, "and do my best."

"Good."

The teenage referee, likely a volunteer from the high school's
wrestling team, calls Nate out to the mat. I give him a pat on the
back, a gentle nudge to get him moving. The other kid is waiting
for him. He's crouched over, his knees slightly bent, hands out to
his sides. It's the proper stance. Nate assumes the same position.
They shake hands and then the ref blows the whistle.

It's hard to imagine brutality among six-year-olds. It's hard to
imagine how a coach, or a father, could in good conscience teach a
child to inflict pain on another child in a fair and clean sport. But
in the first round the Fontana boy tries to bend Nate's arm, and
when he can't do it, because Nate is holding strong, he strikes him
in the crook of the elbow. Once. Twice. Three times. The ref is slow
to respond, and when he finally does, when he stops it, it's not even
with a penalty. Then, in the second round, the kid grabs Nate from
behind, locking his arms around Nate's waist. Leaning back, lifting
him into the air, he slams my boy face down into the mat.

I see him squint in pain.

I see him fight back the tears and I want it stopped. Right now.
This is not what wrestling is about. This is not how I've taught my
kids. Slamming also merits a penalty for unnecessary roughness,
but the ref again fails to note it. I'm a second away from calling the
match when I see it, this glint in Nate's eye, his face suddenly hard-
ened with resolve. The boy is on top of him, and Nate locks the

kid's arm under his own and rolls him, perfectly, onto his back for a one-point reversal and three-point near-fall. The round ends a moment later, and Nate returns to his corner.

I drop to one knee, so he can hear me better.

"You're doing great. That kid's a dirty wrestler but you're smarter, you're faster. This is the last round," I say, "and you're behind by two points. I want you to go for the takedowns. Don't worry about anything else. He's leading too far with the left leg and that's what you want. That left leg. After you take him down, let him back up, okay?"

"Let him back up?"

"Right."

"What for?"

"Because you're going to take him down again. Only the second time, I want you to hang on, just ride him out till it's over. Escapes are only worth one point and takedowns are worth two, and you're going to win this match by one point."

And that's what he does.

When the match is over, Nate walks off the mat victorious, smiling proudly.

Unfortunately his next couple of bouts are even tougher, though by no means as violent as the first. He loses two by narrow margins but wins his last by a pin and earns himself a fifth-place ribbon out of the twelve in his division. Not bad for his first tournament. Logan wrestles later that afternoon, winning three in a row and qualifying for the final bout for first or second place in the 110 weight class. His opponent, of course, is the boy from Norwalk, who also has won three in a row, all pins.

In Logan's corner, as I'm rubbing his arms, loosening him up, I tell him pretty much what I told his brother.

"Go for the takedowns. Go for rolls and reversals. If the pin presents itself, great. But this kid is strong. Don't butt heads with him."

"I'm stronger."

"You probably are," I say, though I'm not so sure. "I want to see some good smart wrestling out there, not some brawl."

Unlike street fighting, there are rules here. The intent is not to injure, and moves like chokeholds and certain types of arm-bars are illegal. Wrestling is about controlling your opponent, not destroying him, and I try to instill in my sons a sense of respect and principle for the sport. For Logan, fixated on avenging his narrow loss, it's a tough sale today, and I'm worried when the ref calls him out to the mat. I'm worried that this could turn into a real free-for-all.

The ref hands him a strip of red Velcro, which Logan wraps around his ankle, identifying him for the scorekeepers. The kid from Norwalk hustles out, waving his arms, doing a kind of goose step. He's cocky. He's arrogant, and I want it even more now, for Logan to beat him, to knock that ego down a few notches. If nothing else, it would serve the kid well later in life.

They shake hands.

The ref blows the whistle and Logan shoots in, not wasting a second, catching the boy off guard and taking him down for two quick points. I'm on the sidelines, excited now.

"All right," I shout. "Now turn him. Get him on his back."

In the heat of battle, and given the headgear that wrestlers wear to protect against cauliflower ears, it's hard for Logan to hear my instructions. So I have to really shout, as does the opposing coach, a stout, potbellied man with a goatee. His wrestler escapes and gets to his feet, but not before Logan rocks him onto his back, scoring a near-fall for another three points. The first round ends with my boy leading five to one. Logan returns to his corner breathing hard.

I hug him.

"Good work," I say. "Another takedown and that'll put you ahead seven to one. Lock him up. Ride him through the second round. Got that?"

Logan nods.

"Keep that lead going into the third," I say, "and it's over."

The rest period ends. Logan returns to the mat, and about halfway through the second round he scores yet another takedown. I suck in a deep breath. I let it out slowly. Assuming he doesn't get pinned, there's no way that the other kid can catch up. He's done it. He's won, and I'm proud of him. That he didn't lose his cool. That he wrestled smart.

Then something happens. Something bad.

The kid works himself free. The kid scrambles to his feet, and I don't believe that what happens next is an accident. I don't believe that his hand catching in my son's headgear is an innocent mistake, any more than I do his pulling the straps down across Logan's

eyes, blinding him. Why the ref doesn't call it for what it is — a bla-
tant foul — is beyond me. Logan takes it for granted, as any good
wrestler might, that the ref will shout for a time-out, and it costs
him, this assumption, this belief that sport is fair. It's a disappoint-
ing but necessary lesson, and I blame myself that Logan has to
learn it this way, for not having taught him earlier that in sport, as
in life, you must often assume the worst in another.

Dazed, confused, he stands up straight, and the other kid rushes
him, like a lineman taking out a quarterback. He rams him in the
stomach. As his back strikes the mat I actually hear the swell of air
forced from his lungs, and inside of five seconds the referee blows
the whistle. Logan has been pinned. He gets to his feet and rips off
the red Velcro strip from around his ankle and throws it in the ref's
face. That's when I snap, when the other coach, the guy with the
goatee, starts screaming at my son.

"You apologize," he says.

"Go to hell," Logan says.

He steps toward my son, but I'm there now, between them.

"You discipline your kid," I say, "I'll discipline mine."

"Your boy's a sore loser."

"Your boy's a cheater."

For a few seconds we just stare each other down. I know I've
crossed a line I should never cross, especially in front of my children, but how much can you reasonably take before you lose it? He
turns away, and it's good that one of us does it.

On the ride home that afternoon I ask my sons what they would
like for dinner. "Anything," I say. "You name it." This is tradition.
This is my offer after every tournament, win or lose, as a reward for
a day well spent together. Typically, from Logan anyway, it invites a
single word — steak, say, or shrimp. He loves both. And I love to
cook either for them. Today, however, when I pop the question, I
receive no answer. I look at Nate in the rearview mirror. Already a
welt is forming above his left eye — the result, I imagine, of a well-
placed elbow or knee to the face, a blow I hadn't noticed. His arm,
where the first kid struck him, is also bruised and sore. I watch him
rub it. I watch him bend it up and down, slowly, like it must hurt.

"How about you, Nate?" I say. "Want anything special for dinner?"

All I get is a shrug.

For a while I let it go. For a while we drive in silence. Logan is pretty beat up too, with bruised ribs where that kid speared him and, from another bout, scratches on his neck and down one side of his face. I wonder if it's worth it, if maybe it's time to hang it up. I don't want to ask the question, because it's always been my favorite sport, because I live through my kids, as parents often do, but it seems the right thing now.

"Maybe we should try something else," I say. "Like soccer. Or baseball."

"What are you talking about?" Logan says.

"We don't have to wrestle, you know. There are other sports."

"No way," he says. "I'm nailing that stupid Mexican next time."

Half my childhood was spent in Los Angeles, the other half in East San Jose. My stepmother is Mexican. My stepbrother and stepsister are Mexican, and two of my lifelong best friends are Mexican, one so close to the family the boys call him uncle. Uncle Orlando. I've experienced hate, and I've experienced the sort of acceptance and love that transcends it. My son, I think, ought to know better. I raise my voice.

"What'd you just say?"

He bows his head.

"Nothing," he says.

"I don't want to hear you talk like that again. You understand me? No more cussing either. I've had it." He's quiet. I shake my head. I look at him again, hard. "You're mad because he cheated. That's it. That's all. Don't get it mixed up. Mexican has nothing to do with it."

I would like to believe my own words, and I do. I would like to believe that I can offer my sons a better world where there is no racism, no cheaters, no parents who teach their children to hate and hurt others. But I can offer them no such thing. At best I can only instruct so that they might suffer less, and so that in surviving they know when to suspend the rules, for their own protection. As we drive home that evening, both boys staring silently out the window, bruised and shaken, I make them a promise.

We will have steak tonight.

We will have shrimp too. The works. And afterward, when calm has prevailed, I will lead them to the middle of the living room floor and lovingly show them the moves I eventually had to learn, those dirty ones, the kind designed to hurt.

STEVE FRIEDMAN

Driving Lessons

FROM TRAVEL AND LEISURE GOLF

Okay

MY FATHER TELLS ME to grip the seven-iron "like you're holding a bird in your hands and you don't want to crush it," and I say, "Okay," which is what I always say to my father when I think he is criticizing me, or when I have absolutely no idea what he's talking about, or when I'm filled with a vague and guilty rage toward him, or when all three are happening at once. I say okay when he talks about investment strategies and tax shelters and the enduring value of discipline and why I should buckle down and write a bestseller and when he tells me the story of the ant and the grasshopper, which he started telling me when I was two years old. I'm forty-nine now, and I've been saying okay for forty-seven years.

"You want to sit, not bend," he says after I slice one.

"Okay," I say.

"Both hands working together now," he says. "Belly-button focus."

I hook one.

"Uh-huh. Okay."

"Keep your lower body still."

I swing with savage intent, and miss.

"Okay."

"But not completely still."

Another whiff.

"Oh, I see now. Okay. Yeah. Okay."

We face each other, holding clubs, alone together on a weekday afternoon at a driving range. It is a brilliant, sunny spring day in St. Louis, home of my father, and of my father's father, and — after he'd immigrated from Hungary — my father's father's father. I have come here from New York City, where I moved to twelve years ago, because my father has agreed to teach me to play golf.

I asked because I wanted to understand his life better, because I wanted to find out what he was doing all those Wednesday afternoons and Saturday mornings and Sunday summer evenings, whether golf was a cause or a symptom of his failed marriage to my mother. I asked because I wanted to learn what my father found in the fairways and on the greens that he didn't find at home, or at work, and whether he was still looking for it.

After he'd agreed, I put off the trip for five years. Because I was busy. Because I wasn't sure I wanted to know the answers to my questions. Because neither my father nor I had ever discovered much joy in our teacher-pupil sessions, whether they involved cutting grass or changing oil or polishing shoes. And then my father had emergency bypass surgery and a subsequent bout of mild depression, and shortly after that his parents got ill and died. I helped write the eulogies that my father delivered. And so, filled with a sense of loss and impending mortality — his and mine — I called to finalize the details of the golf lessons.

There would be three days of lessons, he said, at least a few hours a day and maybe more, culminating in a nine-hole match for which we would be joined by my older brother, who was flying in for business. Okay, I said.

He told me to read *Harvey Penick's Little Red Book*. He told me to buy or borrow a couple of irons and go to the driving range and work on my swing. He told me to practice, especially the short game, "because if you really want to play golf, if you're serious about this, that's what you do, you practice the short game."

What I heard was, "You don't really want to play golf. You're not serious. You're not serious about the short game, not serious about making money, not serious about getting married and having children and not serious about making a success of yourself."

"Okay," I'd said, half a country away. "Okay, okay, okay."

And now, hour four of day one, I'm hooking and slicing and whiffing and topping in St. Louis. If I'd read a solitary page of Penick's book, would I be wiser? If I'd made a single trip to a driv-

ing range in New York, would I be better? If I'd done my homework, would either of us be happier? Does my father sense how I
have already failed him?

"We're going to work on the fundamentals this week," my father
says. "Stance, grip, putting, the short game, and the basic swing."

"Okay," I hiss, and when I look up, he is frowning, in pain, as if
he knows what my okays really mean. I think he does know. I hate
when he worries about me. I like it too. I think he has been worrying about me for a long time.

"But most important," he says, "is that we're going to teach you
to have fun. That's the most important thing."

He tries so hard. He worries so much. I want to reassure him. I
want to make him proud. I want to promise that I will practice the
short game and hold my club like an endangered bird, that we will
stride down lush fairways together for many years to come.

But I don't, of course. I can't.

"Okay," I say.

Big Boy

My father and I are walking in a parking lot, and from time to time
I reach out to feel his thigh. I'm nine years old. This is my earliest
memory that involves golf. My father tells me that next month he is
going on a weekend trip with some of his friends to Illinois to play
golf, and he says I'm a big boy now and I can keep a secret and not
to tell Mommy, he's going to surprise her. Okay, I say, and I touch
his thigh again, which is knotty with muscles. It's a big parking lot.
I'm a worried child and I blow saliva bubbles to pass the time and
to calm myself, and I am fiercely concentrating on blowing a big
one as we walk and I reach out again to touch my father's thigh and
then I hear a strange voice and something is wrong and I look up
and it's a strange man and then I'm sobbing and here comes my father, laughing, rubbing my head, picking me up in his arms. Somehow I have wandered off, lost in my head, but never out of sight of
my father, who has watched his dreamy boy with what? Amusement? Bafflement? Fear for the future? I bury my face in his neck
and his hand covers my entire head.

When we get home, I run into the kitchen. "Mommy," I sing,

"Daddy's going to Illinois to play golf with his friends." Betrayal as casual and effortless as sneaking a cookie before dinner. I don't know why I did it.

Really Serious

Our second day at the range, I hit one straight and true.

"That's great!" my father says. "That's really, really great."

It's as if I've announced plans to marry, get a business degree, and move back to the Midwest, all at once.

"Now try it again. Just do the same thing again."

A capital idea, except that I, of course, have no idea what I just did. Consequently, I slice one, then hook two, then whiff, then slice four in a row.

"You're getting it," my father says, with transparent dishonesty. "Let your hands move from eleven o'clock to one o'clock." I've never understood the clock designations for direction. "And swing from the inside out." He might as well be speaking Uzbek.

"Yep, okay," I say.

I'm a good athlete, but I've never been a quick study at sports that require balance. What I possess is a dumb, mulish capacity to absorb pain and humiliation until I master a physical movement. And once I master it, my appetite and skill grow exponentially. I remember the moment on my snowboard when I felt balanced, when a mountain of certain doom morphed into my own snowy playground; the instant that the eighteen discrete mechanical parts of a jump shot merged into one fluid motion; the chilly afternoon when I realized I could rock from one foot to another on my Rollerblades without falling. With golf, though, my straight shot seems to have nothing to do with any choices I have made. It precedes only hours of anguish.

The afternoon drags on, with me screwing up nine of every ten shots and my father offering encouragement that I'm sure is criticism. He mentions every few minutes that people "who are serious" about learning to play golf work on their short games. He says that people who "really want to play golf" practice a lot. If you're "serious" and "really want to play golf," you visualize great shots; you believe in yourself; you learn to play as a kid. He actually says this.

"The great players, the ones who are really serious, who really want to become the best, they learn to play as kids."

What does that make me?

"Okay," I mutter through clenched teeth, slicing and hooking and whiffing. "Okay, okay, okay."

Then I hit another one straight and true. I can't believe it.

"You're a natural, Steve!" my father exclaims. "You're really getting this."

Ten Minutes

On the way home from the range, my father suggests we stop for coffee. I think he senses how miserable I am. "How about Starbocks?" he says, which makes me grind my teeth. Does he mispronounce words intentionally? Where did he ever come up with "bocks"? Why am I such a bad son?

We roll onto one of the superhighways that roam the hills and floodplains of suburban St. Louis, the endless swaths of pavement that stretch to the horizon every way you look. I have always possessed a terrible sense of direction, and in the past decade St. Louis has become more confusing than ever to me. I ask how far we will be going.

"Ten minutes," he says, which makes me clench and unclench my fists. Ever since I was a child, prone to car sickness and embarrassing vomiting episodes, I would ask my father how long before we arrived at our destination. I wanted facts, exact times. I longed for the reassurance of certitude. But he offered me the same demonstrably dishonest pabulum. Two blocks, fifty miles, three state lines, it mattered not: "We'll be there in ten minutes."

He had been so looking forward to my visit. His wife — he was recently remarried — is off seeing her children and grandchildren in California. She is a kind woman, acutely aware of how my father yearns to connect with his grown children, and I suspect she arranged the trip for that reason. "So it'll be just you and me," he told me on the phone one evening (after suggesting reading lists and practice regimens). "We'll golf and see some movies and go out to dinner. We'll catch up. We'll have a good time."

And here I am, rocking myself in the passenger seat of his car, grinding my teeth and clenching my fists, a carsick seven-year-old in a forty-nine-year-old body. A body that isn't serious. A body that doesn't really want to learn his father's game.

Advice

Here are some reasons I never took up golf:

I'm twenty-one, a college senior, and there is a fat brown envelope in the mailbox of the house where I live in California. I share the place with five others, and we cook together and drink beer and listen to the Grateful Dead and play Frisbee and talk about how empty our parents' lives are. I had recently announced to my parents my plan to become a newspaper reporter. In the envelope is an article about the glut of journalists immediately post–Woodward and Bernstein. It is the midseventies, and I'm part of the glut. The article talks about saturation in the field, declining salaries, and shrinking profits at newspapers. At the top, in my father's scrawl, is a short note.

Maybe you should consider business. At least take some accounting courses.

I'm almost thirty, have been fired from a newspaper job for my dissolute habits, and am now writing speeches for Southwestern Bell Telephone Company. I wear a suit and tie every day and take naps every Saturday afternoon. I suffer from insomnia and chronic stomachaches. When I receive an offer to work on a magazine, I can't recall ever being so happy. I call my father to share my joy.

"You're taking a 30 percent pay cut?" he asks.

"Uh-huh," I say.

"And there's no 401(k) at the magazine?"

"Right," I say.

"And no dental?"

"Yes, but . . ."

"I don't understand," he says. "I don't understand why you're doing this."

I'm forty-five and my father and I are sitting in a café in Colorado. For the past five years, I've been scraping together a life as a freelance writer. A tongue-in-cheek advice book, a collaboration with a professional athlete, some newspaper articles, a fairly steady string of magazine assignments. I recently finished a dark first-person account of a long winter in the mountains and a near emotional breakdown. It's the most personal thing I've ever written; my favorite story, and I just found out that a small literary magazine will publish it.

"You have a lot of talent," my father says.

"Thanks, Dad," I say. "That means a lot to me."

"No, really, I mean it. You should write a *real* book with all your talent."

"Thanks, Dad," I repeat. One thing we agree on is that my first two efforts weren't *real* books. "Thank you."

"No, really," he repeats. "You should really write a book. A real book. Have you thought about a book? It just seems a waste, with all your talent, not to write a book."

He is trying so hard. Was any father ever more encouraging to a son?

"Well, you know that piece I just sold to the literary magazine, about the winter and all that?"

He nods. I know he read it.

"Well, I'm thinking about expanding that into a book."

He looks at me, confused.

"Who would want to read that?" he says.

The Launcher

At our first practice session, I spotted the bulbous oblong poking out of my father's golf bag and asked about it. That is one of his drivers, he said, the Cleveland Launcher, but it would be awhile before it came out of the bag, because people who were serious about golf worked on their short games.

I have always been something of a magpie, attracted to shiny things and quick fixes.

"Okay," I said, then added that I thought I understood the short game. I told him that I had a strong feeling that I could really hit it straight with the Launcher.

"I know a guy who changes clubs like I change underwear," my father told me. "It doesn't help his game any."

Well, sure, I said. Okay. Nevertheless, I told him I thought the graphite technology might suit my stroke. I have no idea what graphite technology is, but I would have said anything to get my hands on the Launcher.

"It's not the driver," he said. "It's the guy hitting it."

Yeah, I understood. Okay. But what about all *his* gadgets, I said. What about the time we were watching television together and an ad came on for Callaway's first Big Bertha and he called the 800 number and bought one?

"It's not the arrow," my father told me. "It's the Indian."

I have been whining for three days.

"Today," my father tells me on our third day of practice, as we stand at the driving range of Meadowbrook Country Club, "we are going to work on putting and chipping, we'll review your swing and" — dramatic pause — "maybe we'll let you use the Launcher a few times."

I nearly yelp with joy. Because of the Launcher. And because the instruction is almost over. This is the last day of practice before our match tomorrow, and my older brother has flown in from Oregon to join us. Don is two years older, a lawyer and businessman with a wife and child, college funds that have been gaining interest since before his wife was pregnant, and an aggressive-but-not-too-risky retirement strategy. He is as calculating and shrewd in his approach to golf as he is to life. Don, it should probably go without saying, has an excellent short game.

Don takes a wedge and two irons and starts hitting.

Before I can swing the Launcher, my father wants to try something new with me today. He wants to introduce me to his Inside Out machine. It is another of the gadgets he buys, in direct violation of his arrow/Indian philosophy. Then again, he has always been a man of contradictions. He tells me to keep my feet still, to do the bird grip, to focus on my navel, then he adds, "But when you get up to hit the ball, trust your body. Don't think of anything." He stresses the supremacy of man over tools but later says, "If you're really serious about golf, you'll get fitted clubs." He stresses that lessons help any golfer, even the professional, that any golfer who "really wants to play" should be open to learning. Does he take lessons? "No, because it always screws up my game for weeks afterward."

So I shouldn't be surprised when Mr. It's Not the Arrow now

places a thing that looks like a cross between an automatic sprin-
kler and a mechanical shoe-shine machine in front of me, sticks a
ball underneath it, and tells me to swing.

"Inside out," he says.

Would it do either of us any good if I asked what in the world he
was talking about?

I slice the ball.

"Try again," he says.

And I do. And I slice again. I try seven times and slice seven
times.

"The ad says that on the seventh swing you'll be going straight
and long," my father says. "Here, let me try."

While he works with the Inside Out, I slip the Launcher from the
bag and smack one. I adore the heft, the soft little ping, the distance. I smack another. Meanwhile, Don experiments with irons
and wedges, asks for exact distances to various flags, makes inquir-
ies about how fast the greens are. And there we stand, a man and
his two grown boys. My father mutters and curses at the Inside Out
until, like magic, on the seventh try, he hits a towering drive 260
yards, and then another and another. Don squints, adjusts his grip,
chips, drives, toys with his swing, chips some more, asks people
driving by in golf carts about the greens. I whale away with the
Launcher, spraying balls everywhere, with lots of energy and very
little direction.

Keeping Score

Day four: on the first tee the Launcher fails me, and I whiff. Maybe
I fail myself. It's different here on the course. There are trees to
worry about, and middle-aged women waiting to play behind us,
and a scorecard, and my shirt keeps coming out of my shorts,
which, my father tells me, is a violation of Meadowbrook Country
Club policy. I try again and dribble one about ten feet and he tells
me to remember about my grip, and to swing from the inside out,
and to relax, to have fun, to let my body take over. I whiff again.
Finally, I ground one about eighty feet.

"That's all right," my father says. "You're on the fairway. You're
in good position."

"No matter how bad you are," my pragmatic older brother tells me, "if you're fast, no one will refuse to play with you."

I sprint after my ball.

It goes this way for three holes, my father and brother playing slightly above par, me hacking and whiffing and slicing and sprinting.

On the fourth hole, I find myself three feet from a water hazard, then dribble three balls into the water. My father reaches into his bag for his folding, snap-jawed mechanical ball retriever to snatch the balls from the pond. "Best investment I ever made," he says.

Once, Don, eyeing the green, asks whether it's 135 or 140 yards away. I tell him that even good players are a pain in the ass when they're so sluggish, and does he have to be so calculating about everything, can't he just hurry up and smack the ball? He tells me to shut up.

Once, I seven putt. Once, I lose a ball in the woods. My father offers advice for awhile but eventually sees how it's adding to my misery.

On the seventh hole, he pulls me aside.

"You know, the score doesn't matter," he says. "This is just your first time. The thing that would make me happy is if you get to like this enough that when you go back to New York you decide to go out and play by yourself."

A Golf Story

In the last years of my paternal grandparents' lives, they told me a story about my father. It's a golf story. It doesn't start out that way, but trust me.

My father is four years old and his baby brother, a two-year-old whom everyone calls Sonny, is sleeping in his stroller one morning when he stops breathing. That afternoon, his mother makes my father noodles and milk — his favorite — and she cries, but she doesn't say anything about why Sonny is gone, or where he is, or if he'll ever come back.

She cries for the next two years, and she doesn't mention Sonny for almost seventy years after that. But my father doesn't cry.

He is sixteen years old, a high school student, a letterman, a star in football and basketball and track. He works hard. He practices. He wants to be a doctor. He is serious and really wants to do well.

He is eighteen years old, a college freshman at the University of Michigan, and it is winter break and his parents are driving him to Union Station in St. Louis, where he will board a train to return for his second semester, but he has a stomachache, he feels sick. "Let's take him home, Herman," his mother, my grandmother, says, and they do, so he can sleep and get over his stomach flu.

The next day they drive him back to the train station. But he feels sick again, so they return home. On the third day, in the car on the way to Union Station, my father feels sick once more, and his mother tells him he doesn't have to go to Michigan, he can stay home and go to school at Washington University. So he does. He goes to school in St. Louis, and he gets married to his high school sweetheart and has two sons and thinks he's too old to go to medical school. He needs to support his family, so he works as a manager in the same drugstore chain as his father.

He is twenty-six, and he needs more money to support his family. He tells the president of the company that if he doesn't get a raise, he will have to look for work elsewhere. The president wishes him well.

He answers a blind ad in the newspaper, an ad that calls for "smart, hardworking young men." He has a wife and two boys — the youngest of whom tends to get lost and blow bubbles when he's daydreaming and throws up in the car — and a mortgage, and now he is a life insurance salesman. He makes cold calls. Sometimes he doesn't come home until nine or ten o'clock at night. At breakfast, he pores over thick booklets so he can take the test that will allow him to become a Chartered Life Underwriter. He has pens and calendars made with his name on them.

He is thirty-five years old, and now there's a third child — a little girl — and sometimes he clenches his jaw when he's getting ready to go to work in the morning, and one night when his sons can't sleep they hear him in the kitchen cussing to their mother about the people in the head office. Sunday nights he takes his children to Steak 'n' Shake for hamburgers, "to give your mom a break," and on the evenings when it's the second son's turn to ride in the front seat there is a serious speech about enjoying oneself, how it's important to relax, that there's no need to hurry into marriage, that "you have the rest of your life to be responsible." The boy is eleven years old.

At night, the boy's father goes to sleep before anyone else in the house, because he's so tired. On Saturday mornings, though, he wakes whistling, beaming. On Saturday mornings he plays golf. He comes home in the early evening smelling of grass and grinning. He has his Saturdays, and sometimes Wednesday afternoons, and the occasional summer Sunday evening, and his annual trip to Illinois with his friends.

He returns from those trips expansive, talking about "honor" and how in golf "there's no referees, you have to trust yourself and the people you're playing with," and how "I've never met a man who cheats on the golf course who I like in life," and how "if a man plays square, you can trust him with anything." A few times he brings home a first-place trophy. "Bigger than the one in the U.S. Open," he says, laughing.

He is sixty-one, divorced and remarried for ten years. He is more relaxed now, less worried, less tired. He plays golf a lot, sometimes with his new wife. His children have never seen him so happy. When she is diagnosed with inoperable brain cancer, she insists that he keep playing golf, and he does, until her last two months, when he stays at home with her, feeding her and taking care of her in the bedroom, which she doesn't leave. When she dies, he grieves, of course, and he has some fainting spells. And then he thinks of Sonny — he hasn't thought of Sonny in decades — and for the first time he cries for his little brother and he can't stop.

Ten years pass, and he has chest pains and emergency bypass surgery and a bout with depression and a few girlfriends who don't work out. And then he meets someone who doesn't golf but says that if it's important to him, she'll learn.

And now he is seventy-four, married for the third time. He tells his children he loves them often, spoils his thirteen grandchildren and step-grandchildren with bicycles and computer games and toy trucks and trips to the zoo and sleepovers and ice cream sundaes in the middle of the day. Not one of them knows what a step-grandchild is. The word would mystify them. He is a lifetime member of the Million Dollar Round Table, which, in the life insurance business, is as good as it gets. He is one of the most successful salesmen in the country, an innovator who sold the first group tax-sheltered annuity in the world.

(I know what a group tax-sheltered annuity is now. I know that it has earned his company many billions of dollars.

"Your company should name a building after you," I say one afternoon, between a slice and a hook.

"They don't even know my name," he replies.)

He paid for his three children's college education, offered them choices and career opportunities he might have dreamed about but could never pursue. He skis, owns property in a resort town, winters in Palm Springs, works when he wants, travels when he wants. All of that came to him because he was serious, because he really wanted it. Hard work and thrift and seriousness of purpose have formed the bulwark for him against pain and loss, but they haven't been enough. Still, what else is there?

Isn't it obvious?

There are Saturdays and Wednesdays and summer Sunday evenings and a place where he can breathe fresh air and stretch and play, where honor means something and where people don't cheat.

I want to tell him how proud I am of him, how I wish I could live up to the example he set, how I envy him his discipline and success and self-sacrifice and generosity. I want to tell him how much he means to me. But I can't. So I vow to do the next best thing. I will hit a good shot in our match. If I need to be serious, I will be serious. If I need to really want it, I will really want it. Whatever it takes, I will do it.

Anything, to hit a good shot.

You Never Know

I don't, of course. I don't hit a good shot. If it were that easy, if striking the ball cleanly and with strength and purpose and something approaching artistry were as simple as just distilling all the resentment and misunderstanding and rage and wounded feelings and guilt and gratitude and love a son holds toward his father into a smooth and honest and powerful swing, there would be legions of scratch golfers launching millions of elegant drives all over the world. There would be so many multitudes of white dimpled balls arcing across empty skies that no one would be able to see the sun.

But it's not that easy. So I whiff and hack and sprint and goad my brother, who plays with grim cunning. I kid my father about the ball retriever and ask him to tell me stories of the trips to Illinois, and I beg for tales from his early days in the insurance business and of his best shots and his favorite afternoons on the golf course.

I give up, and I relax, and I cheer on my father, and if you're a golfer, or a father, or a son, of course you know what happens next.

I can still see it leaving the Launcher, flying away, a blur of white against the deep green of the trees, the baby blue of the midwestern afternoon. A white smudge, low to the ground, a vector bending toward the distant green.

A mystery.

"Great shot!" my father yells. He applauds. "That's a great shot!" he yells again, and applauds some more.

"I don't know how I did it," I say as he comes over to pat me on the back.

It doesn't matter, he tells me. What's important is that I did it, and that I'm having fun. I may not play golf when I return to New York City. I'm not sure if I'll go to the driving range with friends. I don't know if I'll ever pick up a club again.

It doesn't matter. It truly doesn't matter.

We walk together, up the fairway, my father and I, playing golf. He will shoot a 42 for the nine holes. I will finish at 86.

We are blessed.

"That's the great thing about this game," he tells me, his arm around my shoulder. It is a mild, sunny day, and the grass is soft and springy and the Emerald City of the final hole beckons. This is the lush fairway I imagined. "Even if you have a bunch of bad shots," my father says, "you never know when you're going to hit a good one. And that good one can save you."

PAT JORDAN

Card Stud

FROM THE NEW YORK TIMES MAGAZINE

DANIEL NEGREANU IS A VEGETARIAN, without much interest in food. "I ate two days ago" is the kind of thing he says. His disdain for food is a reaction to his mother, who is obsessed with food. Mommy, as he calls her, likes to serve people food, then sit down and smile at them as they eat. When Negreanu was growing up in Toronto, Mommy sent him to school with his lunch packed in a brown bag. When he went to McDonald's with friends, she gave him a brown-bag lunch. When he got his first job as a telemarketer ("I lasted a day," he says), Mommy packed him a brown-bag lunch. When he got his next job at Subway ("I was a good sandwich maker"), Mommy packed him a brown-bag lunch. These days, when Negreanu goes to work at night at the Bellagio casino in Las Vegas, Mommy packs him a brown-bag lunch.

Daniel Negreanu (pronounced neh-GRAH-noo) is a small, slightly built man of thirty. His job in Las Vegas, where he has bought a house for Mommy, is playing poker for eight hours a night or more, for pots as high as a million dollars, with older men named Eskimo Clark, Jesus Ferguson, and Texas Dolly Brunson. Negreanu looks small, boyish, defenseless, with his bottle of water and Mommy's brown-bag lunch at his feet. Often during his poker games, Mommy calls from home. If he's winning, she says: "Good. That's enough. Come here, I made some cabbage rolls." If he's losing, she says: "Today is not your day. Come home, I'll make you some mamaliga." If he's breaking even, she says: "Nothing is happening. Come home, I made some fresh vinete."

Poker is no longer the sole preserve of unshaved, cigar-smoking older men in cheap motel rooms. It has become a game of the young, most of whom have made their poker bones playing online poker. Negreanu says they learn as much about poker in a year as he did in seven years playing cash games. "I see Internet kids with a $250,000 bankroll," he told me. "I had to hustle up games to get a bankroll, which is why I consider myself a bridge between the old-timers and the kids. I have a hustler's skills, but I'm up on what's happening now too. Some old-timers don't keep up with the kids and get passed by. They don't respect their intellect."

Many of these young players, like Negreanu, David Williams, Phil Ivey, and John Juanda, have become instant celebrities because of their TV exposure at the World Series of Poker and on the World Poker Tour. "We're the new rock stars," says Negreanu, who had a first-episode cameo in the ESPN poker series *Tilt.* Hollywood stars like Tobey Maguire, Ben Affleck, and James Woods treat such players as if they are the real celebrities. "Poker is hot because it's everyone's sport," Negreanu says. "Most guys can't play football or hockey. They're fat and out of shape, but they can play poker at home. Poker is the purest form of reality TV. Nothing's scripted. There's drama. Real people with real money on the line."

Last year *Card Player* magazine named Negreanu the poker Player of the Year. Jeff Shulman, a publisher of the magazine, says, "Daniel Negreanu wins so much he's a freak of nature." Texas Dolly Brunson, who is seventy-one and has won nine lesser World Series of Poker competitions and two grand-prize WSOP championships, says: "He may be one of the all-time greats. Maybe the greatest ever."

This week, someone will win a grand prize of more than $5 million in No Limit Texas Hold 'Em, the main event at the World Series of Poker, which begins on June 2 at the Rio All-Suite Hotel and Casino in Las Vegas. It's a prize Daniel Negreanu has never won, even if he is already one of the best poker players ever. "He's on an amazing roll," Brunson says. "The only thing that can bring him down is if he forgets who he is."

Since Negreanu moved to Las Vegas in 2000, he has won more tournaments, thirty-plus, and more tournament money, about $6 million, than any other player. He has also won millions of dollars in private cash games at the Bellagio. "If I had to play $100 games,

I'd shoot myself," he says. "I like million-dollar cash games." Cash games are dangerous. A player gambles with his own money. Often Negreanu brings hundreds of thousands of dollars to those games. If he loses, he has to go deeper into his own pocket. He once lost $156,000 on a single pot in a cash game.

Tournaments are less dangerous. Each player puts up an entry fee of, say, $10,000; that is the most he can lose. But if he survives late into a tournament he can win hundreds of thousands, even millions, on his $10,000 investment. Last year at the WSOP, an attorney from Connecticut, Greg "Fossilman" Raymer, won $5 million, and David Williams, a twenty-three-year-old college student, finished second, winning $3.5 million. Negreanu himself won $1.8 million at a Bellagio tournament last year and another $1.1 million at a tournament in Atlantic City. When Negreanu first started playing tournaments in the late '90s, a sponsor occasionally covered his entry fee, and he had to split his winnings fifty-fifty with the backer. But since 2000, Negreanu has used his own money for cash games and tournaments.

Negreanu claims not to have much interest in money, except as a means of keeping score. After he won that $1.8 million at the Bellagio, he bought six videos and put the rest of the money in poker chips in a lockbox at the casino as if it were a bus station locker. The chips are still there. The $1.1 million Negreanu won in Atlantic City was converted into $300,000 in cash and an $800,000 check. Back home in Las Vegas, he discovered that he left the check in his hotel room; the maid threw it out, and Negreanu had to fly back for another check. "I don't believe much in banks," he says. "Although I do have one bank account with not much in it, just a couple hundred thousand." He also doesn't believe in credit cards, or buying anything he can't afford to pay cash for, which is why he always travels with a wad of $100 bills held together with an elastic band.

Negreanu has two basic rules for playing poker. First, maximize your best hand and minimize a mediocre hand. Too many novices play too many mediocre hands when not bluffing, which increases their chances of losing. Great players only play hands when they have "the nuts," or unbeatable cards; otherwise they fold hand after hand. Second, play hours, not results. Negreanu sets a time limit for his play and sticks to it, whether he's winning or losing. If he goes beyond his time limit, he risks playing "tired hands" when he is not sharp. (Before a tournament, Negreanu gives up alcohol and caffeine. "I do nothing to numb my brain," he says, "except watch poker film — just like an NFL team before the Super Bowl.")

Negreanu says that most great players are geniuses, then lists the kinds of genius they must have: (1) a thorough knowledge of poker; (2) a mathematical understanding of the probabilities of a card being dealt, given the cards visible; (3) a psychological understanding of an opponent; (4) an understanding of an opponent's betting patterns — that is, how he bets with the nuts and how he bets when bluffing; and (5) the ability to read "tells," or a player's physical reactions to the cards he is dealt. Negreanu is a master at reading tells, although he claims it is an overrated gift, since only mediocre players have obvious tells. The best players, of course, have poker faces.

Negreanu says he can break down opponents' hands into a range of twenty possibilities after two cards are dealt. After the next three cards are dealt, he says, he can narrow the possible hands to five, and after the last two cards are dealt, to two. "It's not an exact science," he admits, "but I can reduce the possibilities based on the cards showing, his betting pattern, tells, his personality, and my pure instinct."

Shulman, *Card Player*'s copublisher, connects Negreanu's success to his personality: "Daniel controls a table by getting everyone to talk and forget they're playing for millions," he told me. "He makes every game seem like a home game — you know, guys drinking beer and eating chips. They forget what's happening. Plus, Daniel is the best at reading an opponent's hands, as if their cards were transparent. He gets guys to play against him when he has a winning hand and gets them to fold when he has nothing. He's the King of Bluffing. You know some guys can beat bad players and not good players, and some vice versa. Daniel does both."

Beyond Negreanu's knowledge and considerable intelligence, what makes him truly great is his aggressiveness in a game — his ruthlessness, some might say. He once bluffed his own girlfriend, also a professional poker player, out of a large pot at a tournament. "I bet with nothing," he says, "and she folded. To rub it in, I showed her my hand. She was furious. She stormed into the bathroom, and we could hear her kicking the door, screaming, smashing stuff.

When she came out she kicked me in the shin and said, 'Take your own cab home.'" She is no longer his girlfriend.

Negreanu began preparing for his poker career when he was a five-year-old with "grandiose dreams" in Toronto. He was a change-of-life baby (his mother had nine previous miscarriages) raised in an Old World Romanian household. Before they moved to Toronto in 1967, his mother, Annie, and his father, Constantin, were so poor in their native country that, according to their son, they seldom had enough to eat. As a boy, Negreanu says: "I was big on numbers and reading people. Mommy would take me to a mall, and I'd see a couple, the woman rolling her eyes, and I knew she was sick of him but he loved her." As a young teenager, Negreanu was short, so, he says, he never got the number-one girl — "Only maybe number three" — but he was personable and adaptable enough to fit in with all the school cliques, the "blacks, nerds, cool kids."

By sixteen, Negreanu was skipping school to play pool. He showed up only for tests, usually "acing them," he says, especially his math tests. "My math teacher was a moron," he told me. "I'd go up to the blackboard and show him a better way to do it." It was at the pool hall that Negreanu learned poker, becoming a regular at the house games there. He then taught his classmates to play and ran a daily game in the cafeteria. One day a kid wrote him a $300 check to cover his losses, and the next day Negreanu was in the principal's office. "The principal told me the kid stole the money from his mother. I said, 'What's that got to do with me?' He expelled me. I said: 'Why me? He stole!'"

By the time he was seventeen, Negreanu was playing for as much as $1,500 a night: "I played noon to 8:00 P.M. every day and won $45 an hour." At twenty-one, he made enough money to finance a trip to Las Vegas. But he lost the money quickly and returned home humbled, beginning a vicious cycle that lasted more than a year. Negreanu would hustle up a bankroll in Toronto, go to Las Vegas and lose it, return to Toronto for another stake, and so on. Eventually he had an epiphany: he had to stop being so aggressive. "I realized I can't always be the bull," he says. "I gotta rein it in and play some defense."

A few months later in Las Vegas Negreanu had his first big success. At twenty-three, he became the youngest player to win one of the smaller World Series of Poker competitions. Shortly after that, he began to win regularly in Las Vegas in both cash games and tournaments, and soon he had settled there. Negreanu was on a roll that lasted until he was twenty-six, when he fell in love with a woman he refers to as Delilah.

"I got careless," he says. "I thought I had plugged all my leaks at nineteen." Leaks can be alcohol, drugs, gambling, women. In Negreanu's case, he was winning so much money so quickly that he couldn't spend it fast enough. He began to splurge on expensive dinners, order bottles of Champagne, then try to play high-stakes poker. "I began to lose $30,000 a night," he says. And Delilah was distracting him from poker; she never understood that it was his job and not a game. She called him during his games, pleading with him to come home because she was lonely. Negreanu was getting calls from two women while he played poker, his girlfriend and Mommy. Even worse, they were jealous of each other. "If Mommy made me breakfast, Delilah's feelings would be hurt," Negreanu says. "So she'd make me breakfast. Same with lunch and dinner. Jeez, I was eating two breakfasts, two lunches, two dinners every day." Shortly after he broke up with Delilah, Negreanu went on a winning streak and formulated another poker rule: "Avoid the poker table when there's a crisis in your life."

Today Negreanu has no crises in his life. He is rich, famous in his field, and happily in love with a woman named Lori Weber. He says she's easygoing, self-assured, and jealous of neither Negreanu's poker nor his mother. (His father died when Negreanu was twenty-two.) "I laugh at how much his mother adores him," Weber says. "Let her do it. It makes her happy."

One afternoon in early January, Negreanu and a lifelong friend from Toronto, Jason Morofke, were navigating their way through a crowd of poker players and fans in the lobby of the Atlantis Paradise Island resort in the Bahamas. They were there for the PokerStars Caribbean Adventure tournament. The Atlantis is a sunny adult theme park. Rock waterfall pools. An underwater re-creation of Atlantis. A comedy club. A disco. All forms of gambling. The Atlantis is where people who don't know how to entertain themselves go. Negreanu, wearing a baseball cap pulled low over his eyes and a jacket with its collar pulled up around his neck, could walk only a few feet before being recognized and asked to pose for photographs. Morofke said, "He's a celebrity now, but he's still the same guy he was at seventeen."

Negreanu plays his celebrity role graciously, which is why Steve Wynn, the Vegas casino impresario, hired him to be the poker ambassador at his new casino, Wynn Las Vegas, which opened in April. But in private, Negreanu is skeptical about poker players being viewed as celebrities. "I hate idolatry," he told me. "They're just nerds trying to be great men."

Negreanu entered a conference room crowded with men and a few women seated at the thirty or so poker tables. He circulated among them, glad-handing the players; he seemed to know everybody. Whenever he enters such a crowded poker room, he told me, he can look around and see all the players he has lent money to. "In any given room," he says, "I can see a million dollars of my money out there. Some guys I back in games, some I give personal loans, one guy I put in drug rehab. I guess you could say this is my leak. I was really soft in my twenties. I used to go to L.A. with $30,000, win $20,000, and leave with $20,000." He shrugged.

Shulman told me that Negreanu is loved like no other poker player. "College kids love him because they think he's one of them," he says. "Mothers love him. He does things no pro athlete does. He answers all his e-mails. He has no ego. I haven't seen this in any other sport."

Texas Dolly Brunson told me: "I didn't like Daniel at first. He was too brash, loud, always partying . . . But he turned his train around. Now he's one of my favorite people. You know, poker transcends age. There's just this bond when you put your feet under the table and your hand in the pot."

Negreanu found his table, number 14, and sat down beside Morofke. He acknowledged the eight other players around him. Only one was a seasoned pro, Yosh Nakano, from Los Angeles. The others were ordinary-looking young men who would like to become Daniel Negreanu someday. They tried not to stare at him, but every so often they sneaked a glance. Even the dealer couldn't help smiling at Negreanu. Before the game began, a woman stopped by to say hello to Negreanu. She was Evelyn Ng, the former girlfriend Negreanu bluffed out of a pot. I asked if the story was really true.

"Yes, it's true," she said, then faked a kick at his shins. She told me the problem with their relationship was that both of them were poker players with big egos. "I had trouble taking his advice," she said. "He wanted me to play like him, aggressive, but I was more conservative, so we broke up." They later tried dating again but decided they were better as friends. "Daniel's a great friend," Ng said.

Over the next four hours, Negreanu played poker. He was nervous at first, but as the games assumed a rhythm of their own, he relaxed. There was not much talk between games, since the players didn't know each other. There were a few grins, however, when Nakano nodded off during a hand. "He's been playing for four days straight in L.A., without sleep," Negreanu whispered to me.

The game continued in silence, players folding hand after hand before the final cards were dealt. It was boring. Poker is no sprint; it's an endurance race. But then Negreanu became hot and won six out of seven pots. He put $10,000 into the eighth pot and smiled at one of his opponents, a beefy man. "I'm trying to get you all in," he said, "'cause I got you beat." But the man wouldn't bite. He flicked his cards toward the dealer. Negreanu said, "I had two aces," but he didn't show his cards. He showed his cards a few hands later after he bluffed a player out of a pot with a pair of threes. He hugged his chips and said, "My bluff of the day, gentlemen."

A few hands later, Negreanu bet $3,000 — "'cause I got the best hand." He tossed a head fake at Morofke. "You only got ace-king." Morofke folded. By the time the first session was halted for a dinner break at 8:00 P.M., Negreanu had built his $10,000 entry fee into $42,000. (He would end up with $11,000, finishing seventy-fifth.) Negreanu went up to his hotel suite with Morofke to relax for an hour before the second session at 9:00 P.M. He took off his sneakers and lay down on the sofa.

"The guys at the table weren't very good," Negreanu said. Then, glancing at Morofke, who is a landscaper and plays poker only occasionally, he added: "I don't mean you. You played okay, but you played too many hands. A good player wants to avoid confrontation unless he has the nuts. A few times I wanted them to think I was bluffing by taking a long time to place a bet, but even then I had the nuts. I'm walking through these guys 'cause they're letting me be aggressive. They're laying down like lambs at the slaughter." He grinned. "My job — taking money from chumps."

GREG GARBER

A Tormented Soul

MIKE WEBSTER NEVER MADE IT to his son's tenth birthday party in Lodi, Wisconsin. Lying in a dark room at the Budgetel Inn, some twenty minutes away in Madison, he was bed-bound in a haze of pain and narcotics, a bucket of vomit by his side.

Webster was often laced with a varying, numbing cocktail of medications: Ritalin or Dexedrine to keep him calm. Paxil to ease anxiety. Prozac to ward off depression. Klonopin to prevent seizures. Vicodin or Ultram or Darvocet or Lorcet, in various combinations, to subdue the general ache. And Eldepryl, commonly prescribed to patients who suffer from Parkinson's disease.

After seventeen seasons in the National Football League, Webster had lost any semblance of control over his once-invincible body. His brain showed signs of dementia. His head throbbed constantly. He suffered from significant hearing loss. Three lumbar vertebrae and two cervical vertebrae ached from frayed and herniated discs. A chronically damaged right heel caused him to limp. His right shoulder was sore from a torn rotator cuff. His right elbow grew stiff from once being dislocated. His knees, the cartilage in them all but gone, creaked from years of bone grinding against bone. His knuckles were scarred and swollen. His fingers bent gruesomely wayward.

"He was too sick to come to my birthday party. He didn't even call me and I was mad," Garrett Webster remembered recently. "Now I understand that there was something wrong."

Ten years later, there is only a faint strain of resentment in his voice. His father, the celebrated Hall of Fame center for the Pittsburgh Steelers, is gone now. Still, the mental snapshots, those harrowing memories, persist of the stoic man they called Iron Mike:

- Desperate for a few moments of peace from the acute pain, repeatedly stunning himself, sometimes a dozen times, into unconsciousness with a black Taser gun. "The only way he could get to sleep," said Garrett.
- Glassy-eyed like a punch-drunk boxer, huddled alone, staring into space night after night at the Amtrak station in downtown Pittsburgh. "Living on potato chips and dry cereal," said Joe Gordon, a Steelers employee.
- A formidable man, at six-foot-two and 250 pounds, who sometimes forgot to eat for days — sleeping in his battered, black Chevy S-10 pickup truck, a garbage bag duct-taped over the missing window. "Sometimes he didn't seem to care," said Sunny Jani, the primary caregiver the last six years of his life.
- Writing wandering journals in a cramped, earnest hand so convoluted in their spare eloquence that, upon reading them in his lucid moments, he would be moved to weep. "You had absolutely no idea what was going through his mind," said Colin, his oldest son.
- The powerfully proud former athlete, anguished and curled up in a fetal position for three or four days, puzzling over his life, contemplating suicide, and, in later years, placing those sad, rambling calls, almost daily in the later years, to friends and family when he couldn't find his way home. "All I see is trees," he'd say apologetically, almost in a whisper.

When Webster died in Pittsburgh on September 24, 2002, at the age of fifty, the official cause was heart failure. That was absurd, of course. Few players showed more heart than Webster in his marvelous seventeen-year NFL career. In the end, his body and brain left him a defeated man.

Webster's Steelers won four Super Bowls in six seasons from 1974 to 1979 and rank as one of the league's greatest teams. There has been a football renaissance in Pittsburgh, where this year's Steelers finished the regular season with only one loss and reached the AFC Championship game. They won't be going to Jacksonville, but with quarterback Ben Roethlisberger no longer a rookie, running back Jerome "The Bus" Bettis contemplating another season, and the core of a savage defense back, square-jawed Bill Cowher may be coaching his team in Detroit this time next year.

Nine players from the Steelers' 1970s dynasty are enshrined in the Pro Football Hall of Fame. Eight of them — Terry Bradshaw, Franco Harris, Jack Lambert, Joe Greene, Jack Ham, Mel Blount, Lynn Swann, and John Stallworth — reveled in the franchise's return to glory. Their missing comrade is a footnote worth considering. Amid the fervor and fanaticism that enveloped the Steel City this season is Webster's reminder of the daunting price the game can sometimes extract.

Sometime later this year a collision is likely to occur in a Baltimore courtroom. Civil action number WDQ-04-cv-1606, *The Estate of Michael L. Webster v. The Bert Bell/Pete Rozelle NFL Player Retirement Plan and The NFL Player Supplemental Disability Plan*, is working its way through Maryland's U.S. District Court.

The NFL already has paid Webster and his estate more than $600,000 — $100,020 annually for the last three years of his life, plus a $309,230 retroactive payment made in December to cover his disability from 1996 to 1999. Webster's surviving family — ex-wife Pamela, fifty-three, and four children, Brooke, twenty-seven; Colin, twenty-five; Garrett, twenty; and Hillary, sixteen — wants more. A lawsuit directed by Jani, the administrator of Webster's estate, seeks an additional $1.142 million in disability payments, plus legal fees and expenses, going back to his retirement after the 1990 season. The suit argues that Webster was mentally disabled when he left the game and that by denying Webster "active football" disability the NFL's pension board committed an "abuse of discretion."

"This isn't a knee that became inflamed after an old injury — this is about Mike Webster's brain," said Cyril Smith, co-counsel for the plaintiffs. "He was hit in the head thousands of times and suffered many concussions at a time when the dangers weren't widely recognized. The evidence is clear that he was completely disabled by March of 1991."

As evidence of Webster's diminished cognitive command from 1991 to 1996, the family cites the loss of assets over a period of several years that once amounted to an estimated $2 million to $3 million or more.

"Are you telling me that seventeen seasons in the NFL didn't factor into his bad business decisions?" Garrett Webster said. "World-famous athletes, at the end of their careers, people say you're stupid and lazy. But that's what football does to you."

The NFL contends there is no empirical evidence that Webster was disabled before 1996, noting that no doctor who assessed Webster in the original case saw him until after 1996. Regarding his competence, the NFL points to the same business dealings referred to by the estate.

"It's a very sad case," said Doug Ell, the lead attorney for the NFL retirement plan. "He was a great, great player. He tried to run all these businesses, all these companies, and, ultimately, it's not clear that any of them succeeded. The board can't say a guy is permanently disabled just because his businesses failed."

This much is certain: Webster's life and career were, in so many ways, a worst-case scenario for physical and emotional well-being. With a family history of mental illness and heart disease, Webster played a compromising position in an exceedingly violent game for an extended period of time. He competed in an era when the rules governing contact were far more liberal than they are today and the development of safer equipment, particularly helmets, was embryonic. Webster's toughness, a quality that compelled him to play in 177 consecutive games, exacerbated his injuries, just as experimentation with anabolic steroids might have led to later liver, kidney, and heart ailments. His immense pride worked powerfully against him; in a city noted for the exquisite steel bridges that span its three rivers, Webster resisted when friends and former teammates reached out to help.

Some people will see the suit as a referendum on the NFL and its treatment of former players who are irreparably injured in their service to the league. Others view the case as a transparent, after-the-fact money grab.

"The kids deserve it," Jani said, "because of what their dad went through. They basically sacrificed their father to this game. If somebody told them, 'We'll take care of your dad [but] we gave him a spaghetti brain and we'll give you a million dollars,' they would say, 'No, thanks. I'd rather have my dad.'"

This is one of the few things all four children agree on.

"Mike's story needs to be told," Pam Webster said from her home in Lodi, where she lives with three of her four children. "I don't want this man to die in vain.

"They're gladiators. When the game is over, these guys have to go home. And when it's over, a lot of them don't have a home to go to."

Blood and Guts

Merv Corning, the southern California portrait artist, has been commissioned by the NFL to paint more than three hundred portraits since 1967. None is more haunting, particularly in retrospect, than his vision of Mike Webster.

Flanked by four gleaming Super Bowl trophies, Webster sits on the bench, his gnarled hands holding a towel. His thin blond hair, white at the temples, matted with sweat. Deep-set brown eyes, too small for his large, round, and nobly scarred face, engage with jarring intensity. His black and gold jersey, grass-stained and bloody, a splattering on the bridge of his misshapen Roman nose for effect.

"He hated it," said Webster's oldest son, Colin, who lives just north of Pittsburgh. "He said, 'Every time they paint me, they put blood all over me. Why do they have to do that?'"

Somehow, blood and the implied guts seemed appropriate. It was the way he played the game.

Webster was born on March 18, 1952, in Tomahawk, Wisconsin, a swashbuckling address of origin fit for a man who cut a swath as wide as his hero, John Wayne. He was an All-Big Ten center at the University of Wisconsin, but at six-foot-two, 225 pounds, there were questions about his relatively spare frame in the NFL. He was drafted in the fifth round of the 1974 draft by the Pittsburgh Steelers — Lynn Swann, Jack Lambert, and John Stallworth were taken ahead of him, giving the Steelers four future Hall of Famers among their first five picks — and his manic work ethic amazed his coaching staff and teammates alike.

It was a discipline born of insecurity. Webster did not consider himself a great athlete, but believed he had to work harder than most players. His self-esteem was sadly but not inexplicably lacking, for he came from an alarmingly dysfunctional family. His father was an overbearing disciplinarian, and one doctor noted that Webster grew up with "episodes of marked physical abuse." His parents, both described by Webster as alcoholics, divorced when he was ten, and the family house burned down a year later. His younger brother, Joseph, spent more than a dozen years in prison for a sex-related offense.

So Webster hit the weights hard and in a few years he had packed another thirty-five pounds of muscle. Webster also began to display the effects of anabolic steroids — which had yet to be banned by the NFL — including the acne, the radical mood swings, the thinning hair. Later, he would matter-of-factly tell a physician, Charles Cobb, that he had experimented with steroids in his twenties. He and teammates Jon Kolb, Steve Courson, and Steve Furness were the core of a group that slammed the iron with abandon in the basement of the Red Bull Inn in nearby McMurray. Although Webster publicly denied it, steroid references can be found several times in his voluminous medical records.

"And if I did," he would tell friends, "it was legal back then."

In the days before today's form of free agency, even future Hall of Famers had to put in their time on the bench. Webster played behind Ray Mansfield for two seasons before becoming a regular in 1976. He started fourteen games, six at guard and eight at center, and went on to start at center for each game of the next nine seasons. Going back to his rookie season, Webster played in a remarkable 177 consecutive games despite a variety of injuries that would have taken less committed players out of the lineup. Only a dislocated elbow ended the streak in 1986. He was ruthlessly diligent; how many NFL players had a blocking sled in their front yard?

The position of center requires, above all, intelligence; remembering the snap count is the least of the position's worries. The center assesses the defense and calls out the blocking assignments. Steelers quarterback Terry Bradshaw admitted at Webster's 1997 enshrinement at the Pro Football Hall of Fame that his center called as many plays at the line of scrimmage as he did. Webster, a devoted student of film before it was fashionable, sometimes based his calls on the subtle positioning of defenders' feet or shoulders. Line play is a function of leverage, and Webster, as head coach Chuck Noll said on many occasions, was almost technically perfect. He played with precision that belied his monstrous biceps — set off by trademark short sleeves — and a barely controlled fury.

"I can see him now, sprinting out of the huddle to the line of scrimmage before everyone else," said Harry Carson, the former New York Giants linebacker, sitting in his home in leafy Bergen

County, New Jersey. "To me, that's what it was all about. He'd come out so pumped up, you'd get pumped up right along with him. I looked at Mike as being the leader of that group — everything revolved around him."

Webster, the veritable epicenter of one of history's great teams, played in Pittsburgh for fifteen seasons and appeared in 220 games, still franchise records. Including two seasons in Kansas City, 1989 and 1990, Webster played in 245 career games, the most ever by a center at the time of his retirement. Offensive linemen generate few statistics, but consider this: Webster was voted to nine Pro Bowls. When he entered the Hall of Fame, it was the highest total ever for an offensive lineman and second only to Bob Lilly's league-record eleven. In 1994, Webster was named to the NFL's seventy-fifth-anniversary team, a group more elite than those with brass busts in Canton. The Steelers, meanwhile, won four Super Bowls in a span of six seasons. Webster was a captain of three of those championship teams.

Those honors, however, came with a caveat, as Webster came to realize in his later seasons. There would be a necessary physical price to pay for his longevity; mental toughness would congeal into physical frailty. Because of his place in history, Webster was particularly vulnerable. The savage head-slap, as practiced by Deacon Jones and others, officially had been outlawed by then, but that didn't stop defensive linemen from using the maneuver in the '70s and '80s. Helmets, thin plastic shells by today's enlightened standards, did little to absorb the shock. And, because his hands were occupied when snapping the ball, Webster sometimes had a difficult time warding off those initial hits.

When he was finished, Webster had broken most of his fingers, suffered permanent damage to five vertebrae, and effectively ruined his knees, right shoulder, and right heel. More troubling were the constant headaches that began to dog him in his last few seasons with the Steelers. The record books dutifully note his 245 regular-season games, but there were nearly 100 more, taking his 19 playoff games and more than 75 preseason games into account. Factor in the grueling training camps in Latrobe, Pennsylvania, and practices throughout the season, and it's probable that Webster endured more than 25,000 violent collisions.

Webster's oldest son, Colin, tells the story of the doctor who, upon examining an MRI of Webster's, asked if he had been in a car accident.

"Yeah," the old center said, "about 350,000 car accidents."

Despite this, Webster was never treated by team doctors for a concussion, according to medical records submitted in the case. The Steelers' trainers, too, note he never complained of concussion symptoms. Still, it is probable, based on discussions with doctors and former players, that Webster suffered a significant number of head injuries during his career that today would be classified as concussions.

Webster's other son, Garrett, references Oliver Stone's NFL opus *Any Given Sunday*. Al Pacino, in the role of coach Tony D'Amato, is lecturing James Woods, who plays Dr. Harvey Mandrake.

"Pacino tells Woods to stop worrying so much about injuries," Garrett said. "He tells him, 'You cannot take away an athlete's confidence in his body. When you take that away, you steal his heart.'

"There was an unwritten rule in the NFL — if you can play, under any circumstances, you play."

Webster played through the pain and, almost certainly, through the debilitating effects of postconcussion syndrome, the same condition that hastened the retirement of Carson in 1988, New York Jets wide receiver Al Toon in 1992, and former Steelers running back Merril Hoge in 1994. Today, NFL doctors will tell you, there still is much they do not understand about the effects of brain trauma. In the '80s, they knew next to nothing.

The Steelers and Giants met thirteen times in preseason and regular-season games when Webster and Carson played. Carson, a middle linebacker, locked up with Webster many times.

"I was one of the hardest hitters in the league," Carson said. "I was willing to stick it up in there and deliver a massive shot to the head with my forearm. I can't tell you how many times I did that to Mike. When he passed away, I was saddened. I thought perhaps what I did might have contributed to the neurological problems that he had. But Mike would not blame me. That's just the way it was.

"I got postconcussion syndrome too," Carson said. "I got mine. It's an occupational hazard that's part of the game."

Pam Webster, contemplating the hindsight of an eighteen-year marriage that began on a blind date in college and ended six months before Webster's death, said there were signs that something was wrong in the mid-1980s, a good five seasons before the end of his career.

"Small things," she said. "Anger at inappropriate times, a sense of disorganization, personality changes with no warning, getting lost, getting easily distracted. He poured his heart and his soul into the game of football, but . . ."

But he was slowly, literally, losing his mind.

Man on the Moon

When Neil Armstrong walked on the moon thirty-five years ago, he became the first man to set foot in another world. That giant leap for mankind was a high-water mark for humanity and, by implication, nothing in the celebrated astronaut's life would ever approach the magnitude of that moment.

So it often is with players in the National Football League, for those who live in that world, even briefly, sometimes struggle when they are forced to leave it.

Very few — former Bills quarterback Jack Kemp (U.S. Congress), former Vikings defensive tackle Alan Page (Minnesota state supreme court justice), and former Raiders offensive lineman Gene Upshaw (director of the NFL players' union) are exceptions — manage to turn their NFL experience into a stepping-stone to a higher calling. To be a physical specimen of the head-turning order, to make vastly more money than ordinary people do and to live an appropriately outsized lifestyle, to play in arenas filled with sixty thousand adoring fanatics, to exist in an environment where people want to name their children after you — well, that can skew even a healthy sense of perspective.

"When you're an elite athlete and you reach a certain level of success, you have a different set of rules," said Garrett Webster, the youngest son of Mike Webster, the center of the Pittsburgh Steelers' dynasty of the 1970s. "He had people to handle all of those things that need to be handled. Then, when you retire from the NFL, you're done. Just like that.

"For seventeen years, you have somewhere to be, every minute of every day. The coach tells you what to do and all the details are taken care of. All of a sudden, you're on your own."

In February 1988, when the Steelers left Webster unprotected under the NFL's Plan B system, the league's first stab at free agency, Webster retired. He was the last active member of that select group of Steelers to play in all four Super Bowl victories. Five days later, the Kansas City Chiefs announced he had been hired as an assistant offensive line coach. Some years earlier, Webster had left the Steelers for two days to join Forrest Gregg's coaching staff with the Cincinnati Bengals. His coaching career with the Chiefs didn't last much longer. With the blessing of the team's hierarchy, he played center in Kansas City for two more years before retiring for good after the 1990 season.

"It's been seventeen wonderful years," Webster said at the time. "But one thing you learn in this game is reality. It's time."

Reality, at least initially, was a pleasant prospect. Two months shy of his thirty-ninth birthday, Webster contemplated his off-field options with typical enthusiasm. Family and friends say he considered coaching, broadcasting, a career as a chiropractor and a stockbroker, as well as various business opportunities. He didn't make the seven-figure salaries that today's players enjoy, but football afforded him a comfortable living. His first signing bonus, in 1974, was only $8,000 — his ex-wife Pam said he spent it all in three months on three cars — but he made $400,000 in his last season with the Chiefs, apparently invested wisely and conservatively, and had in excess of $2 million in assets, including three annuities that provided a steady, if unspectacular, income through the early 1990s.

Kansas City offered Webster another assistant coaching job in July 1991, but he left the position a few weeks later when NBC offered him a broadcasting trial. He was assigned as an analyst for two preseason games, but when NBC followed up with a modest contract offer for a limited schedule, Webster passed on his first regular-season assignment, saying it conflicted with his family's move from the Kansas City area to Wisconsin.

Feeling adrift, Pam had convinced Mike to relocate the family to the place where she grew up, Lodi, Wisconsin. They moved into a large Victorian house, where the four children had plenty of space. But by then the symptoms that Pam first noticed in Pittsburgh began to manifest themselves on a more regular basis. Mail, bags and bags of it, piled up. Bills weren't paid. According to records, Webster stopped filing tax returns in 1992 and didn't for the last eleven years of his life. This, from the man who knew the tax laws in every state when he was a player. The electricity was turned off. Sometimes spare change was scrounged together to buy macaroni and cheese or toilet paper. Eighteen months after the Websters moved in, the bank foreclosed on the house.

"It was like living in a tornado," Pam said. "A counselor told us that we were living in so much stress we didn't know what stress was. Mike would leave for days at a time and I didn't understand that he was sick. I just figured he was mad at me.

"One thing I found out later was that after football, 60 percent of marriages fail. There was no structure, nobody handling the details. It was horrible."

The couple separated in 1992, and Pam would initiate unsuccessful attempts to divorce Mike in 1994 and again in 1996. Finally, six months before he died, Pam officially divorced her husband of twenty-seven years.

So, where did all the money go?

"I still don't know," Pam said. "We were set for life. We had $90,000 in college funds (invested in tax-sheltered zero coupon bonds) for each of the kids. But then the money would disappear, and we tried to follow it. People took advantage of him. He always blamed the attorneys.

"When your mind isn't working straight you aren't going to make good decisions."

Joe Gordon worked for the Steelers for twenty-nine years, most notably as the team's director of communications. He had dealt with Webster often in his later years with the Steelers and worried about his post-NFL life.

"It was obvious to me that he was naive in business," Gordon said from his Pittsburgh home. "He was too inexperienced to recognize that too much of this was pie-in-the-sky. In football, if you were tough enough you could overcome adversity. Unfortunately, that didn't transfer to his life after football."

After Webster began petitioning the NFL for disability benefits in 1999, the league commissioned a thorough background check of him for throughout the 1990s. Of particular interest were his business dealings. The report, completed in January 2001, details a tangled web of bad judgment and failed ventures:

- In 1990, Webster was the CEO and treasurer of a Pennsylvania business known as Pro Snappers Inc., which no longer exists.
- He listed himself as an employee of Distinctively Lazer, a graphic printing company in Pennsylvania, in a 1992 loan application with PNC Bank.
- In 1992, he was an investor in Terra Firma Development Trust, a Pittsburgh real estate company.
- Webster Asset Management Trust was formed by Webster in 1993, with a capital contribution of $230,000, but soon passed into nonexistence.
- That year, Webster listed Olympia Steele Sports Management of Pittsburgh as his employer on a hospital admission form.
- Later in 1993, Webster was among several names on an application for a business known as "Tins, Totes and Tees." During this time, he carried a business card with the title of director of operations for the Lestini Group.
- He was listed as a director of the National Steroid Research Center in 1994 and later that year formed Webster Business Enterprises, Ltd., which also failed.
- The Chiefs, partly in sympathy, offered Webster a job as a strength and conditioning coach in 1994, but like so many things it never worked out.

In the wake of these business failures were several lawsuits and, as a result, Webster's annuities, sacrificed as collateral for hundreds of thousands of dollars in bank loans, were seized. After 1994, his only income was a modest compensation for signing autographs at card shows and speaking engagements. In 1996, the Internal Revenue Service filed a tax lien for $251,015.

"It is without question that Mr. Webster attempted to work at any number of businesses after his career as a player ended, mostly in the capacity as investor," investigator Thomas A. Keating wrote in his report to the NFL. "I was unable to find any evidence that any of them succeeded."

The separation with Pam in 1992 was another damaging blow to Webster's sense of family and his sense of self. It was instrumental in establishing a vagabond existence for the former center. For the next five years, from 1993 to 1997, he would not have a permanent address. "Homeless" was now a word that described Iron Mike Webster. He spent time in Kansas City, Pittsburgh, Philadelphia, and rural parts of West Virginia and Wisconsin. Sometimes he stayed with friends, but more often he stayed in cheap hotels — he was a regular at the Red Roof in Robinson, Pennsylvania. When he didn't have the cash, he slept in his car, a gas-guzzling late 1970s Cadillac and, later, a Chevy S-10 pickup truck. He'd fall asleep wherever it was warm and people didn't disturb him — the airport, the bus station, the train depot.

With his brain deteriorating from the hits suffered during a seventeen-year NFL career, Webster suffered from dementia and was often disoriented. The multiple medications he took for pain — since he had no health insurance after he retired, he paid for these out of pocket — certainly had a muddling effect. On numerous occasions, he would call his family from somewhere between Pittsburgh and Wisconsin, a daunting nine-hundred-mile, seventeen-hour ride, to say he wasn't going to make it.

"That was the standing family joke," Pam said. "Where's Dad this time, Ohio? The police in [nearby] Columbus [Wisconsin] would recognize him at the train station and call to tell us he was okay."

But, clearly, he wasn't.

In September 1996, Webster was examined by Dr. Jerry Carter of Allegheny General Hospital, who produced a comprehensive psychological profile. Webster, Carter said, constantly dwelled on his crumbling financial situation and an inability to help his family.

"He has periods of despair during which he feels hopeless," Carter wrote. "He states he thinks about suicide every day, although he doesn't think he would ever act on it. He states this is because God would not want him to do that and he can't help his family if he is dead. During some of his periods of despair, he states he curls up into a fetal position and may remain in this position off and on for three to four days.

"Often during these times, his mind races, trying to find solutions for the problems he has, although he is unable to find any solutions."

A few weeks before this analysis, Webster was discovered in this catatonic state in the Amtrak station in downtown Pittsburgh. The manager recognized Webster and immediately called the Steelers. Gordon took the call.

"He told me Mike had spent the entire night in the station," Gordon said. "Since it was only a mile from Three Rivers Stadium, I told him I'd be right over."

Gordon spoke briefly with Steelers owner Dan Rooney, grabbed $200 out of petty cash, and raced to the station. He found Webster sitting in the waiting room, surrounded by an array of papers, brochures, and photographs of sports stars like Muhammad Ali, Arnold Palmer, and Mickey Mantle. He excitedly told Gordon he had obtained a distributorship for promotional pieces for a sports memorabilia company.

"I asked him where he was staying," Gordon remembered. "He said he had a place, the Red Roof Inn, but I said, 'Why don't we put you up in the Hilton for the weekend?' That was the hotel we used, and we made a reservation for him and I gave him the money and dropped him off."

Webster stayed there for three months.

Eventually, in November, Gordon persuaded him to check out. Sometimes the daily phone and room service charges were more than the cost of the room itself. The Steelers quietly paid the "significant" bill, according to Gordon, and Iron Mike Webster, with the weather turning colder, walked back onto the street.

Wandering Through the Fog

Through a leaden curtain of fog, you can just make out the gleaming towers of Pittsburgh industry rising to the south of McKees Rocks. It's only a five-minute drive into downtown, but this grimy section of the city feels like another country altogether.

Go past the flat, faded warehouses, past the decaying homes built snug against the dung-colored brick streets, turn onto Broadway, and follow it through a working-class neighborhood to the Blue Eagle Market. The blue "A" in Eagle is missing on the dingy white façade, but inside it is warm and ordered. The snacks and sodas and sundries are stacked neatly in rows. Judging by the haggard appearance of some of the customers, necessities are purchased here, not items of convenience. This is where you'll usually find Sunny Jani, a small Hindu man with a pleasant, round face. Jani, thirty-four and a terminal Steelers fan, runs the store for his parents.

For the last six years of Mike Webster's life, from 1997 to 2002,

Jani was his most consistent, most constant companion. Walk into the back office and you will see Webster's number 52 jersey, autographed, hanging in the corner. They met in 1994, when Jani asked him to sign autographs at a card show he was promoting at the Holiday Inn in Greentree. Webster was only scheduled — for a fee of $1,500 — to stay for two hours, but he insisted on taking care of everyone. Three and one-half hours later, after his last labored signature, Webster, wearing long blond hair, a cowboy hat, and boots, got up, and Jani drove him back to the Red Roof Inn in Robinson.

"Mike Webster, at Red Roof? You've got to be kidding me," Jani said, leaning back in his leather office chair. "I had heard on the radio that he was sleeping in his car, but I didn't believe it. This is Mike Webster, Mr. Steeler. Three months later, he walks into the market and we talked about a business relationship. I started booking him all over the place."

Webster often slept in his black pickup truck in the parking lot behind the Blue Eagle Market. He spent hundreds of hours in the back office, sometimes sleeping overnight on the green couch against the back wall. Eventually, Jani became his caregiver, the one who managed his meager money from a joint checking account. Sometimes, when referring to Webster, he uses the word "us." Of all the people in the world, why did Iron Mike allow Jani to help him?

"Because he *wasn't* Terry Bradshaw or Mel Blount," said Webster's youngest son, Garrett, who considers Jani a father figure. "If you were destitute ten years from now, would you want your friends to see you? Sunny was devoted to him and my dad knew that."

It was Sunny, more than anyone, who had to clean up after the elephants. But to him, it wasn't a chore at all. For when he looked at Webster, he didn't see the derelict so many others did; the rabid Steelers fan saw his personal hero of two decades before. It was Sunny who usually drove Webster to the doctor and card signings. Sunny was the one he called when, inevitably, he found himself in trouble. One time, it was 2:00 A.M.

"Mike says, 'I'm pulled over by the side of the road and I don't have any money and I don't know where I am,'" Sunny remembered. "So I told my wife, 'I've got to go get Mike, rescue him.' I got in my car and drove nine hours to get him. It was, like, nine hours. He was almost to Milwaukee.

"Later, I got smarter. I'd stash $50 bills and $20 bills in the back of his truck. I'd say, 'Mike, go to the back of your truck and inside the cap I duct-taped some money.' I loved him, sure, but I didn't want to get up at two in the morning."

Jani laughs to punctuate the thought, but Webster's dependence on him proved costly. He and his wife, Marcia, used to argue about it all the time; Marcia insisted that he spend more time with his children, Alexis, ten, and Devin, eight. It was, Jani conceded, a factor in their recent divorce.

When former teammates offered help, Webster usually refused it. He was too proud to accept handouts. Former linemates Tunch Ilkin and Craig Wolfley, now Steelers' radio analysts, rented him a $300 apartment in nearby Bridgeville, but Webster never stayed there. He did stay with former teammate Steve Courson for three months, and he allowed Ilkin and Wolfley to fly him home to Wisconsin for the holidays in 1997.

Webster constantly worried about money, but rarely for himself. When he made a $1,500 check from a card show, he would typically send more than $1,000 via Western Union to Pam in Wisconsin to help take care of the two youngest children, Garrett and Hillary, and maybe $200 to his oldest daughter, Brooke, who was living in Canada at the time. Since the payments were irregular, at best, Jani had to convince him to keep a few hundred dollars for himself. Eventually, Pam was forced to sell her house and car and take a job as a cleaning woman. Scrubbing other people's toilets, she would reflect on how quickly things fell apart.

In 1997, Webster's condition continued to worsen. The daily headaches, he told Dr. Patrick Sturm of Tri State Pulmonary Medicine, were "blowing the top of his head off." His days were filled with pain from his numerous football injuries. He often slept only a few hours each night, usually sitting up in a chair because the ache was too great to lie down. By that time, he was taking Vicodin regularly and, at different times, Darvocet, Ultram, and Lorcet. He also had a regular prescription for Ritalin and used Paxil and Prozac to dull his demons. Sometimes, the only thing that brought him relief was a black Taser gun. He would ask Sunny or his son Garrett to stun him into unconsciousness, usually in the thigh but sometimes in the back and neck. When no one was there, which was often, he would try to do it himself.

Webster no longer had a real sense of time or commitment. Often, when Sunny came to pick him up for card shows, he couldn't summon the effort to shower, shave, and dress. Food held little interest for him; his weight dropped to 225 pounds, down from 260. His sense of taste was indifferent at best. The things he liked best were Coca-Cola and Copenhagen, a steady dose of caffeine and nicotine. Jani and his sons constantly had to remind him to eat. When he had money, he'd indulge himself with Pringles, Little Debbie pecan rolls, and waffles at Denny's. When he didn't, he simply didn't eat — sometimes for days at a time. For a while, Jani took to leaving milk and snacks at the door of his motel room; Webster wouldn't always accept the food if it was given to him face-to-face.

One of his favorite places was the Kinko's in Moon Township, where he could hang out twenty-four hours a day. He'd make copies and organize his request for NFL disability. He'd read there — biographies of JFK and Churchill mostly — and sometimes sleep. If Jani was looking for him, even at midnight, that was often where he was. They would go shopping at Kmart and Wal-Mart, where he'd stock up on $6 shirts, duct tape, and Super Glue. One day, in a typical haze, he tried to glue a couple of his rotting teeth back into his jaw.

It was odd: in one moment, autographing fans' artifacts, he would astonishingly recall a first and last name from a dozen years in the past. In another, he would head out into the frigid snow without a jacket. Webster, who fluctuated between anger and hopelessness, was aware it was happening too; he would write for hours in his journal and, later, in a more lucid moment, burst into tears when he couldn't follow the meandering train of thought.

While Webster's twelve years of life after football were filled largely with pain and confusion, there was a seven-month respite in 1997, from late January to late July, when he approached happiness. He was elected to the Pro Football Hall of Fame, the highest professional honor for a football player, and the concept warmed him like the sun on a spring day. At the banquet before the enshrinement speech, in a cavernous hall, Webster caught Jani's eye as they were introducing him with the usual long-winded hyperbole.

"They're talking about me," he whispered, tapping his finger to his chest as if they were talking about someone else.

In a sense, they were. Word of his struggles had leaked into the public domain, and there were worries that he would embarrass himself during his enshrinement speech. But fortified by eighty milligrams of Ritalin and supported by former teammates and the proximity of family and friends, he somehow managed. They cleaned him up and got him a sharp-looking tuxedo. Terry Bradshaw, his old quarterback and presenter, stepped under center one more time, and the fans in Canton, Ohio, roared with delight and gave him the longest and loudest ovations of the day. Webster rambled a bit and digressed often; his speech consumed twenty minutes — double his allotted time — but he got through it. With football as the metaphor, he seemed to be talking about his current life.

"You only fail if you don't finish the game," Webster said, adding that, contrary to reports, he still had his four Super Bowl rings. "Sometimes you can be down and struggling, but as long as you keep working at it, you win. The important thing is that I'm here and moving forward."

Webster left the ceremony with bitter feelings that typified his growing anger and paranoia in the final years. After the announcement of each incoming class, the Hall of Fame flies the enshrinee and the guest of his choice to Hawaii for a weeklong celebration at the Pro Bowl. Webster brought his four kids and was furious when the Hall of Fame refused, in accordance with its guidelines, to pick up the extra tab. When they deducted the expense from the money he earned signing Hall of Fame memorabilia, Webster threatened to resign from the Hall of Fame — something he seriously considered until his death.

The day before the ceremony, Stan Savran, a Pittsburgh television and radio personality, asked Webster if he'd be interested in working as an analyst for a television show on Fox Sports Net. Webster agreed. Every Monday after the Steelers games, Webster would show up at Three Rivers Stadium at 1:00 P.M. to tape a five-minute segment. Savran didn't find out until later that Webster was commuting the seventeen hours from Wisconsin for his fee of $300.

"One time the Steelers' receptionist told me he was an hour away and that he might be little late," Savran said. "I had no idea he was living in his car outside his ex-wife's house and driving all that way. He missed only three or four of the shows, which was amazing considering the condition he was in. His mental state, at that point, was fractious. He wasn't the guy I had known."

In February 1999, Webster made headlines again. Police arrested him for forging nineteen prescriptions for Ritalin after he walked into a drugstore in Rochester, twenty-five miles west of Pittsburgh. They took Webster away in handcuffs. Jani used his four Super Bowl rings as collateral for a loan from a lawyer friend to pay the $2,000 bail. They're still in the lawyer's possession today, diamonds set in gold, sitting in a safe deposit box in nearby Altoona, according to Jani. Webster's doctor had left him with a pad of signed, blank prescriptions. Since Webster moved around a lot and would often lose his pill vials, he would sometimes stop for Ritalin at the local Eckerd, CVS, and Rite Aid — all in the same week. The public embarrassment, certainly, was worse than the probation he received after pleading no contest.

A press conference was organized to put a positive spin on Webster's situation, and the call went out to former teammates.

"It was basically damage control," Hall of Fame cornerback Mel Blount said. "I just remember me and [linebacker] Robin Cole being there. It was interesting that players he went through the wars with didn't step up. But in their defense, Mike was so proud. He didn't let anyone help him."

Sometimes, when people were persistent — or discreet — Webster did accept help. Franco Harris, the Hall of Fame running back and successful owner of Super Bakery Inc. in Pittsburgh, handed him an envelope after they crossed paths in 1999. Webster was stunned when he later discovered it was a check for $5,000 — he promptly sent most of it to Pam and the kids.

Webster first considered asking the NFL for disability in 1995, but never followed through. He told friends the one-page application was too complicated. But after a 1998 medical appraisal suggested brain damage, Robert Fitzsimmons, a friend and Wheeling, West Virginia, attorney, initiated a claim in April 1999. Fred J. Krieg, a clinical psychologist at Marshall University, was one of those who examined Webster in preparation for the claim.

"He would have reminded you of a street person," Krieg said from his office. "It didn't take long to see that Mike Webster had difficulty with higher order executive functioning, frontal lobe stuff. When you talked to him, there were so many symptoms it was pretty obvious what was going on. That's how it is with traumatic brain injuries."

Dr. Jonathan Himmelhoch, a professor of psychiatry at the University of Pittsburgh, examined Webster six different times. His conclusion: Webster was "totally and permanently disabled" and had a "traumatic or punch-drunk encephalopathy, caused by multiple head blows received while playing center in the NFL."

The Bert Bell/Pete Rozelle NFL Player Retirement Plan and the NFL Player Supplemental Disability Plan, following a protocol established in the league's 1993 collective bargaining agreement, authorized a "football degenerative disability pension" that paid Webster $100,020 annually, beginning in November 1999. Dan Rooney, the Steelers' owner, had privately lobbied the pension board on Webster's behalf.

This temporarily eased Webster's financial situation. Although he still sent most of each month's check to Pam and the kids, Jani was able to secure a lease at Waterford Apartments in Moon Township. The ground-level unit, at the back of building number 3, is a study in beige elegance. Jani, who wanted Webster to live in comfort after so many years of scuffling without a bed of his own, paid the $1,500 monthly rent out of their joint account. But after fifteen months, Jani said, the IRS seized the NFL disability check and, after missing three rent payments, Webster and his son Garrett — who, at six-foot-nine, 345 pounds, was playing high school football and living with his father — were thrown out.

They moved into an $800-per-month apartment, also in Moon, where they lived in something approaching squalor. They didn't have any furniture and slept on the floor. When Jani visited he would find fast-food wrappers and other trash strewn about. It was Garrett, at the age of seventeen, who played the role of father. He placed a flag in the front window, so his dad would know which apartment was his. Still, sometimes late at night, Webster would find himself knocking on the wrong door when the key wouldn't fit.

The Mel Blount Youth Home, about twenty miles south of Pittsburgh in Washington, Pennsylvania, is a refuge for disadvantaged and delinquent kids. Work ethic and self-sufficiency, the trademark values of those old Steelers teams, are stressed. Blount and Webster were teammates for ten seasons, which is why Blount remembers, all too vividly, a card-signing show in New Jersey.

"It was 2001, the year before he died," Blount said. "For those of us who were able to walk away from the game, well, we feel fortunate. The human body wasn't designed to take those kinds of blows. It's a shame something you love so much — in Mike's case, something you do for a living — can take such a drastic toll on your life.

"I spent some time at the show talking to Mike. It took me a while to realize he didn't even know who I was."

Sifting Through the Ashes

There was a time, around the turn of the twentieth century, when Pittsburgh was known as "The Forge of America." But by the early 1980s, just a few years after the Steelers won their fourth Super Bowl, Andrew Carnegie's dynamic creation had foundered. More than 100,000 steel-related jobs left the city, and now information technology is the leading industry.

Andrew Mellon, a contemporary of Carnegie's, was a spectacularly successful financier. Today, Mellon Financial Corporation is a financial services company with $2.8 trillion in assets. One of Mellon's subsidiaries, Mellon Global Securities, provides custodial services for the National Football League's player benefit plans totaling about $1 billion.

The ex-wife and four children of late Steelers star Mike Webster are looking for about $1 million of that money sitting in downtown Pittsburgh. They are suing the NFL retirement plans in Maryland's U.S. District Court — the plans are based in Baltimore — claiming that Webster was completely disabled when he retired after the 1990 season.

"I think we have a good chance," said Colin Webster, the oldest of Webster's two sons, who lives outside Pittsburgh. "Basically, his whole life was ruined as a direct result of what these people did."

In the fall of 2002, a day after he had watched his son Garrett play a game for Moon Area High School, Webster was rushed to Sewickley Valley Hospital. His lips were a dangerous shade of green and he was nauseous; he had been sniffing ammonia because he was convinced that if he fell asleep he might not wake up. Two days later, early on the morning of September 24, surrounded by his family, Webster died at Allegheny General Hospital. If the coroner was a Steelers fan, he might have noted that the time of death, 12:52, linked quarterback Terry Bradshaw (number 12) and his favorite center (number 52) one last time. A heart attack was blamed — an earlier angioplasty failed to correct the damage — but there was also extensive liver and kidney damage.

Later that morning Webster's caretaker, Sunny Jani, called the Steelers with the news. Joe Gordon of the Steelers met him an hour later at the Joseph M. Somma Funeral Home in Robinson. They picked out a simple casket, the Westridge model. The entire bill was $6,861.50, but Steelers owner Dan Rooney covered most of it with a check for $5,000.

Two years after the grim fact, Jani sighed and a smile played on his face.

"If Mike found out Mr. Rooney paid for the funeral," Jani said, "he would have been really upset."

The day of the funeral was mild and drizzly, but not surprisingly, so many who were there say it was chillingly cold. More than two hundred mourners gathered at the hilltop funeral home to pay their final respects. Bradshaw, Franco Harris, Lynn Swann, Dan Rooney, and Chuck Noll were among those who attended the eighty-minute service, along with former Giants player Harry Carson and ex-Packers linebacker Dave Robinson.

"We should never allow the passing of a loved one to be the drawing card to keep our family together," Bradshaw said.

"I had great respect for Mike," Carson said. "He was the best at what he did and I considered myself the best at what I did. I felt I had to be there."

The Rev. Hollis Haff remembered Webster's joy in quoting lines from John Wayne's character Rooster Cogburn in *True Grit*. For Webster was, in so many ways, football's version of the cantankerous, one-eyed marshal. He played for seventeen seasons in the NFL, and also taking his playoff and preseason games into account, his career total was nearly 350 games. Webster used to joke that he had played the equivalent of seven football players' careers.

When Webster died, former Steelers running back Merril Hoge felt a deep twinge of sadness — and fear. Hoge played with the Steelers from 1987 to 1993, overlapping two seasons with Webster. His career ended in 1994 with the Chicago Bears after he suffered his second concussion of the season.

The trauma had a serious effect on his brain. Early on, Hoge carried his own telephone number in his wallet. Sometimes he got lost walking around his neighborhood. It took him three or four years to learn how to read again. He now functions well as an NFL analyst for ESPN, but still struggles with bright lights and when he helps his children, Kori, eleven, and Beau, eight, with their homework.

"When Mike passed away, you couldn't help but think about it," Hoge said. "There's always a sense of the unknown with these injuries. Will it expedite Alzheimer's? Will it lead to mental illness? At the same time, it helped me realize I made the right decision to retire. I could have challenged it, but ultimately I was jeopardizing my life. When you see it in that perspective, it was a good decision."

Pamela Webster, who divorced Webster six months before he died, pleaded for some peace and quiet during a phone conversation last month. It's not easy to find private space with three kids — Brooke, twenty-seven; Garrett, twenty; and Hillary, sixteen — in a one-bedroom house. The two younger children will continue to receive $1,300 a month for college from the NFL until they turn twenty-three, and Pam has a job at a small medical clinic in a nearby town, but despite a children's fund that netted donations of more than $80,000 in the wake of Webster's death, Pam said it's not enough.

"There is nothing to take care of the kids," Pam said. "The NFL needs to take care of its own. Veterans don't have insurance and they're lost after the game. They need to step up to the plate and give these guys their just deserts."

In 1999, the NFL awarded Webster an annual disability of $100,020, which he received the last three years of his life. Last month, the Webster estate received a payment of $309,230 for another three years of disability, going back to September 1996. The NFL pension board, made up of three former players, two team owners, and Miami Dolphins president Eddie Jones, voted unanimously in January 2003 — four months after his death — to grant Webster's estate the dispensation.

"Everybody on the board," said Doug Ell, an attorney for the NFL, "wanted to know what happened to this poor guy."

Nevertheless, Ell said, the Webster estate's request for additional disability fails to meet the retirement plan's eligibility requirements.

Retroactive benefits, according to the plan, may cover up to a forty-two-month span from the date the first claim was filed. In October 1999, the plan's retirement board awarded Webster benefits dating back to September 1996.

The estate, meanwhile, argues that the board committed an "abuse of discretion" in not compensating Webster for being completely disabled for the additional period from the time of his retirement, March 1991, to September 1996. The case is likely to be decided sometime later this year.

"Both sides have filed motions asking the court for summary judgment," said Cyril Smith, co-counsel for the Webster estate. "In a claim of this nature, it's unlikely to go to a jury. Ultimately, it's up to the judge."

With the arrival of the most recent check from the NFL, the estate is now said to be somewhat solvent. The IRS is, apparently, in the process of being satisfied. A lawsuit by one of Webster's former partners recently was settled for $65,000. There still are some minor housecleaning items such as defaulted loans and an outstanding insurance claim, but Jani said there will be some money for the family regardless of the lawsuit's outcome. He plans to use some of the money to retrieve the Super Bowl rings; Brooke, the oldest, will get the first one from the 1974 season, Colin the second (1975), Garrett the third (1978), and Hillary, the youngest, the fourth (1979).

With the surprising success of this year's Steelers team, the old players from those great Super Bowl teams are in great demand these days. The autograph signing business has never been better.

"We could have made some money," Jani said. "But I don't know if he'd be happy for the team. Toward the end, he was so hateful with football. In the end, he said football got the best of him — and it did."

Colin Webster, more than any other family member, has been an outspoken critic of the Steelers and the NFL. Surrounded by rabid fans, he said he can't bring himself to watch a Steelers game.

"They have this huge pension fund and they aren't helping these people," Colin said. "I think, when it's all over, justice will be done."

In the rare moments when Pam Webster isn't consumed with trying to support her children, guilt filters into her consciousness.

"Mike Webster was not a quitter, but I feel I quit on Mike," Pam said. "I should have given it more time, more effort. It's my biggest regret."

She said she hopes the lawsuit shines a harsh light on the NFL's treatment of former players.

"Someday," she said, "I hope there's a Webster Rule, where they're not allowed to play so long."

"They say it's a business — that's completely fine," Garrett said. "But if you're going to make it a business, then when you f —— up, you have to pay for it. Enron, well, they made a mistake and they had to pay. The NFL needs to solve this problem. Create a retirement exit plan, give ten-year players health care.

"Something bad happened and mistakes were made. How can we correct it in the future?"

After the funeral, they cremated Webster. Jani, Pam, and each of the children have some of his ashes. Jani keeps his in an urn on the mantle over the fake fireplace in his home.

"I went through the benefits board of the NFL and I was denied — twice," Carson said. "They look at things quite differently than the way things are. Let me be as honest with you as I can. The average person will question why Mike did certain things, or didn't do certain things. When you're trained to be a leader and push your way through pain and injuries . . ."

Carson, one of the hardest-hitting linebackers in NFL history, stopped for a moment.

"I can very much identify with the struggle he went through," he continued. "For a player to die at fifty — which is too young for an athlete, a person, period — it's painful. For a person who never did anything as great as winning a championship and struggled to such great heights, you just won't understand.

"Some of us find a safety net when we fall through a crack. We are somehow able to grab hold. Others fall right through — and nobody even notices."

DAVID GRANN

Stealing Time

FROM THE NEW YORKER

ONE SUMMER NIGHT NOT LONG AGO, Rickey Henderson, the greatest base stealer and leadoff hitter in baseball history, stood in a dugout, pinching the front of his jersey and plucking it several inches from his chest — "peacocking," as some players call it. He went through the same pregame rituals that he has performed since he was a rookie outfielder with the Oakland A's, in 1979. He sorted through a bunch of bats, asking, "Which one of you bad motherfuckers has got a hit in you?" Picking one up with resin on the handle, he cocked it back, waiting for an imaginary pitch, and talked to himself in the third person, the words running together so fast that they were nearly unintelligible: "Let's-burn-Rickey-come-on-let's-burn."

Henderson is accustomed not only to beating his opponents but also to lording his abilities over them. As a ten-time All Star for the A's, the New York Yankees, and seven other teams, he stole more than fourteen hundred bases — a record that is considered untouchable, like Joe DiMaggio's fifty-six-game hitting streak. He scored more runs than Ty Cobb, Babe Ruth, or Hank Aaron. Bill James, the oracle of baseball statistics, wrote, "Without exaggerating one inch, you could find fifty Hall of Famers who, all taken together, don't own as many records." Or, as Henderson puts it, "I'm a walking record."

As Henderson stepped onto the field, he stopped abruptly. A foul odor was seeping from under the dugout. "Where's it coming from?" one of his teammates asked. Several players bent down, trying to find the source of the smell; previously, the manager had found a dead rat in the stadium.

"I think it's coming from over here," one player said. "See that hole?"

Henderson tried to ignore the commotion and resume his routine. He walked toward the batter's box, moving casually, as if he were out for an evening stroll. An opposing player once noted that it took him longer to get to the batter's box than to drive to the stadium. Henderson has said that his slow approach is a way to get into a pitcher's head; opponents have said that it is simply another means for Henderson to let the world take stock of him. As he reached the batter's box, informing the world what Rickey was going to do to the ball, he again seemed disconcerted, and looked up at the crowd: there were only six hundred or so fans in the stadium, and many of the women had dressed up, as part of a promotional Eighties Night, in sequins and lace stockings, like Madonna in her "Like a Virgin" phase.

Earlier, Henderson had confessed to me, "Last night, I dropped down on my knees and I asked God, 'Why are you doing this to Rickey? Why did you put me here?'"

An announcer called his name on the scratchy PA system: "Now batting leadoff for the San Diego Surf Dawgs . . . RICKEY HENDERSON."

The man who once proclaimed, "I am the greatest of all time!" was, at the age of forty-six, playing in the Golden Baseball League. It wasn't the majors. It wasn't even part of the minor league farm system. It was an independent league, which consisted largely of players who had never made it to the minors, or had washed out of them. Created by two Stanford business school graduates, the league — which began operating this spring, with eight teams in Arizona and California — is widely considered to be the bottom of the bottom. Yet it is here that Henderson suited up for $3,000 a month, less than he could bring in selling a piece of memorabilia from his days in the majors.

"Come on, hot *dawwwg*, let's see what you can do!" a fan yelled.

Henderson tapped the dirt out of his cleats and got into his crouch, staring at the pitcher, a twenty-four-year-old right-hander for the Mesa Miners. Several nights earlier, Henderson had singled and stolen second base, sliding head first in a cloud of dust, to the delight of fans, but this time he hit a weak liner to the second baseman for an easy out. As he made his way to the dugout, one of the hecklers in the crowd yelled, "Hey, Rickey, where's your fucking wheelchair?"

Other baseball greats have insisted on playing past their prime: at forty, Babe Ruth, in his last major league season, batted .181 for the Boston Braves. But Henderson's decision to go so far as to join the Surf Dawgs — which, the team's former publicist admitted, was frequently assumed to be a girls' softball team — has been a source of astonishment. His last stint in the majors was in 2003, when he played part of the season for the Los Angeles Dodgers. He hit a mere .208, with three stolen bases. (His last productive season was in 1999.) The Dodgers management, concluding that time had finally defeated "the man of steal," as he was often called, unceremoniously released him. He had played 3,081 games, putting him fourth on the all-time list. He was forty-four years old, and most fans reasonably assumed that he would retire and wait for his induction into the Hall of Fame. Instead, he played the 2004 season with the Newark Bears, in the independent Atlantic League, before switching to the Golden Baseball League. Manny Ramirez, the Boston Red Sox slugger, who played alongside Henderson in 2002, has said that Henderson must be "crazy," and a sportswriter declared that it would take "a team of psychiatrists" to figure him out. Even one of his three daughters, Alexis, asked, "Dad, why are you doing this?"

A few hours before the game against the Miners, I found Henderson sitting on a metal chair in the Surf Dawgs' locker room, with his shirt off. He insisted that he was no different from anyone else in the league: he simply wanted to make it to the majors. But he also seemed shocked by his own predicament, by the riddle of age. As he put it, "There are pieces of this puzzle that Rickey is still working out."

He stood to put on his uniform. He is five feet ten, and, like a Rockette, most of his height seems to come from his legs, which he calls "the essence of my game"; they dwarf his torso, which always appears to be pressing forward, as if he were bursting out of a starting gate. His eyes betray frequent shifts in mood — they squint with displeasure, then widen with delight — and, during games, he often hides them behind wraparound sunglasses. He put on his jersey, which was white, with powder-blue sleeves, and pulled his pants above his hips; when he slipped on his cap, only the creases on his forehead and around his mouth confirmed that he was as old as many of his teammates' fathers. Extending his arms, he said, "Look at me. I ain't got no injuries. I got no problem with my eyes. My knees are good. The only problem I have is a little pain in my hip, and it ain't nothin' a little ice can't cure."

Henderson knew that he had only a few months to prove to a scout that he was able to play at the highest level — the major league season ended in October. He told me that not long after he began playing for the Newark Bears he called Billy Beane, the general manager of the Oakland A's. Most of Henderson's greatest achievements in baseball, including his first World Series ring, in 1989, stemmed from his time on the A's, and he told Beane that he wanted to return to the team more than to any other. "Then I could go out the way I came in," he said. Beane responded that the A's, which are currently vying for a spot in the playoffs, had no room for him. Nevertheless, Henderson said, "I ain't giving up hope. I know if people would just come out to see me play they would realize that Rickey is still Rickey."

He arrived hours before a game, and would slash at balls as they shot out of a pitching machine at eighty-five miles an hour, while the Surf Dawgs' adopted theme song blared over the loudspeakers: "Who let the dogs out? Woof! Woof! Woof! Woof!" On some mornings, he could be seen running up and down the bleachers. Jose Canseco, who played with Henderson on the A's, and who helped to fuel the explosion of performance-enhancing drugs in the major leagues, has said of Henderson, "That's one of the guys who's not on steroids!"

"They kept that shit a secret from me," Henderson said. "I wish they *had* told me. My God, could you imagine Rickey on 'roids? Oh, baby, look out!" He laughed in an easygoing way. "Maybe if they weren't juicing there'd still be a spot on a ball club for me. People always ask me why I still want to play, but I want to know why no one will give me an opportunity. It's like they put a stamp on me: 'Hall of Fame. You're done. That's it.' It's a goddam shame."

As Henderson was talking to me, one of his teammates, who had tousled hair and looked to be about eighteen, walked over. He was holding a baseball and a pen in his hand. He said to Henderson, "I feel funny asking, but could you sign this?"

Henderson smiled and signed the ball.

"Thank you, Rickey," the young man said, holding the ball along the seams, so as not to smudge the ink.

Henderson turned back to me, and said, "I'll tell you the truth. I'd give everything up — every record, the Hall of Fame, all of it — for just one more chance."

Base stealers are often considered their own breed: reckless, ego-centric, sometimes even a touch mad. Ron LeFlore, who stole ninety-seven bases with the Montreal Expos, was a convicted armed robber; Ty Cobb, who was called "psychotic" by his authorized biog-rapher, used to slide with his spikes in the air, in an effort to take out the second baseman; even Lou Brock, who was more gentle-manly, believed that one of his greatest assets was unbridled arro-gance. Henderson, by all accounts, was a natural-born thief. Lloyd Moseby, a childhood friend of his who played for the Toronto Blue Jays, told *Sports Illustrated*, "Rickey hasn't changed since he was a lit-tle kid. He could strut before he could walk, and he always lived for the lights."

Henderson grew up with little outside the game: when he was two, his father disappeared, abandoning the family, and after his mother moved to California to find work, he and his four brothers remained in Pine Bluff, Arkansas, for several years, in the care of a grandmother. In 1976, when Henderson was seventeen, the Oak-land A's drafted him in the fourth round and assigned him to one of their minor league teams, in Boise, Idaho. From the beginning, he was intense, moody, and flamboyant. If he hit what looked like an easy groundout, he sometimes refused to run it out, to the con-sternation of the manager. But when he thought the opportunity was ripe, his speed was unparalleled. One night in Fresno, Califor-nia, in 1977, he stole seven bases, tying a record for a single game. Two years later, in the middle of the season, the Oakland A's called him up to the majors.

With his new money, Henderson hired a group of detectives to find his father. "I didn't care if he was a bad guy or a good guy," Henderson told me. "I just wanted to know him." The private eyes reported back to his mother, who informed him, "Your father is dead. He died a few years ago in a car accident." In 1980, however, Henderson found an unlikely father figure in Billy Martin, the

A's new manager. Martin was a pugnacious drinker who, on at least one occasion, slugged one of his own players. But he and Henderson shared an in-your-face approach to the game — Martin hung on his office wall a poster that said, "There can be no rainbow without a cloud and a storm" — and together they developed a manic style of play, known as Billy Ball, that was as terrifying as it was exhilarating. As Henderson has put it, "Billy was the publisher of Billy Ball, and I was the author."

Because the A's didn't have a lot of power, they couldn't rely on three-run homers and big innings; they had to manufacture runs, to create them out of the slightest opportunities. As the leadoff hitter, Henderson was the catalyst, or, as he likes to say, "the creator of chaos." He had remarkable strength (twice, he finished the season with a higher slugging percentage than Mark McGwire), but his principal role was to be a nuisance, a pest — to "get on base, any damn way I can," and begin wreaking havoc on the defense.

As part of his strategy, he had developed one of the most distinctive and infuriating batting stances ever seen. Each hitter has a strike zone that extends roughly from his chest to his knees. Henderson, by collapsing his shoulders to his knees — by practically doubling over — made his strike zone seem uncommonly small; one sportswriter quipped that it was "the size of Hitler's heart." With so little room for the pitcher to throw a strike, Henderson would frequently eke out a walk. (In 2001, he broke Babe Ruth's record for total walks, and is now second, behind Barry Bonds.) Or he would crush the ball — he is one of only twenty-five players in history with more than three thousand hits. Once he was on base, the chaos began: he would often steal second, then steal third; he stole home four times. In his first full year, he broke Ty Cobb's American League record of 96 stolen bases in a season, which had stood since 1915; two seasons later, he blew past Lou Brock's major league mark of 118. Thomas Boswell, of the *Washington Post*, wrote, "Not since Babe Ruth hit fifty-four home runs in 1920 — thirty more than anyone else had hit in a season — has one of baseball's fundamental areas of offensive production been in such danger of major redefinition. . . Now, perhaps for the first time, a player's skill is challenging the basic dimensions of the diamond."

His mere presence on the base paths was a force of psychic disruption. Distracted infielders made errors, and pitchers, finding themselves unable to concentrate, gave up easy hits to subsequent batters. As the former Yankee captain Don Mattingly has said, "Basically, he terrorizes a team." Henderson would score in ways that made his heroics nearly invisible: he would often get a walk, then steal second, then advance to third on a ground ball, and, finally, come home on a routine fly ball to the outfield. In other words, he regularly scored when neither he nor his teammates registered a single hit.

But there was also something out of control about Henderson. A base stealer takes his team's fortunes into his own hands; if he decides to run and gets thrown out, he can devastate a team's chances for a big inning. In 1982, Henderson didn't merely set a season record for steals; he also set one for being caught (forty-two times). The very traits that won him praise — bravado, guile, defiance — also made him despised. During a 1982 game against the Detroit Tigers, when he needed only one more base to tie Brock's record, he singled but had no chance to steal, because there was a slow base runner on second. Violating every norm of the game, Billy Martin ordered the man on second to take such a big lead that he would get picked off. Henderson's path was now clear, and he took off, sure that he was safe at second, but the umpire called him out, allegedly muttering, "You got to earn it."

Baseball has an unspoken etiquette about lopsided games, and Henderson's habit of stealing when his team was already trouncing an opponent was widely seen as unsportsmanlike. In 2001, while Henderson was playing with the San Diego Padres in a game against the Milwaukee Brewers, he took off in the seventh inning, when his team was leading by seven runs. The Brewers' manager, Davey Lopes, who had been one of the most aggressive base stealers of his day, was so incensed that he stormed onto the field, yelling that the next time Henderson came up to bat the pitcher was going to "drill" him. The threat was clearly in earnest, and Henderson was removed from the game. "We're old school," Lopes said later.

And it wasn't just the way Henderson ran the bases that irked traditionalists. In 1985, after being traded to the Yankees, he was asked what it would be like to play on the same field that once knew Joe DiMaggio and Mickey Mantle, and he replied, "I don't care about them . . . It's Rickey time." When he hit a home run, he would stop and watch it go over the fence, then arc ostentatiously around first base, one elbow outstretched like a bird's wing. Instead of simply catching a ball, he would make a show of snatching it out of the air. "I don't appreciate that hot-dog garbage in my ballpark," the former Orioles catcher Rick Dempsey, who once had to be restrained by an umpire from attacking Henderson, said.

Henderson earned a reputation for creating tumult off the field as well. He held general managers hostage with his contractual demands. "I've got to have my money guaranteed," he'd say. Or, in one of his more Yogi Berra–like phrases, "All I'm asking for is what I want." Once, when he couldn't find his limousine upon leaving a ballpark, he was heard saying, "Rickey don't like it when Rickey can't find Rickey's limo." In 1989, the A's signed him to a four-year contract worth $12 million, which made him the highest-paid player in the game; but less than two years later, after several players surpassed that sum, he demanded a new contract. The pitcher Goose Gossage, who played with Henderson on the A's, once said, "Henderson set a new standard for selfishness. He made Jose Canseco look like a social worker." By the end of his career in the majors, Henderson was recognized as one of the best players of all time, but in the view of many players and sportswriters, he was also "greedy," "egomaniacal," "Tropical Storm Rickey," "the classic baseball mercenary," and "the King of I." In other words, he was the last player anyone thought would join the Golden Baseball League.

"I can't be late," Henderson said.

He was at the Los Angeles airport, waiting for a morning flight to Yuma, Arizona, where, for a July game against the Scorpions, the Golden Baseball League was hosting Rickey Henderson Night. (The first thousand fans to arrive at the game would receive Rickey Henderson bobble-head dolls.) The league, realizing that Henderson helped give it legitimacy, had offered him various perks to sign on, and unlike the rest of the players, he didn't have to endure long bus rides to away games — he flew by commercial airplane. And so, while the team was spending five hours on a bus to Yuma, Henderson picked up his bags and boarded the plane. He was wearing an elegant tan shirt and matching pants, and a gold Rolex studded with diamonds. During his career, he has earned more

than $40 million in salary alone. He owns dozens of rental proper-
ties, as well as a 150-acre ranch, near Yosemite National Park, where
he spent time in the offseason with his wife and their daughters. He
also has a Porsche, a Rolls-Royce, a Bentley, a BMW, a Mercedes, a
Cadillac, a GM truck, a T-bird, and a Ferrari. "I've told major
league clubs, 'Don't worry about your bank account — I'll play for
free,'" Henderson said. "This ain't about my portfolio."

As he waited for the plane to taxi to the runway, he checked his
cell phone to see if his agent had called with any word from the majors. "Nothing," he said. After holding power over general managers for so long, Henderson seemed uncertain what to do now that
they held power over him. He had even considered crashing a Colorado Rockies tryout for high school and college players. He knew
that his reputation had probably hurt his chances of being brought
onto a team as an elder statesman and bench player. "There's always that concern: will Rickey be willing to come off the bench?"
Henderson said. "I would. If you let me retire in a major league
uniform, you won't hear a peep out of me." Henderson regularly
scoured the news reports for injuries and roster changes in the majors, to see if there might be an opening.

"Who's that new guy they got playing center field for the Yankees?" Henderson asked me.

"Tony Womack," I said.

"Womack, huh?" he said, then added in frustration, "My God,
you mean to tell me I ain't better than him?"

He placed a call on his cell phone, and began talking over the
roar of the engine. The stewardess, who seemed unusually tense,
asked him sharply to turn the phone off. He said that he would, but
requested that she ask him nicely. Within moments, security of-
ficers had boarded the plane to remove him.

"What the hell's going on?" he asked.

"Is that Rickey Henderson?" a passenger asked.

"Look how cut he is," another said. "I hear he never lifts weights
— he only does push-ups and sit-ups."

"You'll have to come with us," an officer told Henderson.

I stood up to get off with Henderson, and the officer asked who
I was.

"That's my biographer and lawyer," Henderson said.

The passengers began to shout, "You can't take Rickey!" But the stewardess wouldn't relent, although Henderson said that if he had done something to offend her he was happy to apologize. The plane took off without us.

"See, man?" Henderson said to me. "I cause controversy even when I don't do nothin'. That's the way it's always been."

The airline, seemingly embarrassed by his removal, tried to find us another flight, but the next one to Yuma didn't leave until the evening. "I gotta make my game," Henderson said. "It's Rickey Henderson Night."

Eventually, the airline found us a flight to Imperial, California, which was about an hour's drive from Yuma; from there, the airline said, it would provide a car to take us to the stadium. When we arrived at the Imperial airport, a middle-aged man standing in the baggage claim area said, "Rickey, what brings you to Imperial?"

"Got a game tonight in Yuma."

"In *Yuma*?"

"Playing in a new independent league over there."

"You trying to make it back to the show?"

"That's the plan."

"Well, I sure wish they'd give you a shot. They never treat us old guys well."

We drove in a van across the desert to Yuma, which is known primarily for a prison that once housed outlaws from the Wild West. When we reached Desert Sun Stadium, Henderson seemed taken aback — it was little more than a field with bleachers and a water tank looming over it. "It ain't Yankee Stadium, is it?" Henderson said.

The temperature was 109 degrees, and it was hard to breathe. Henderson signed autographs and posed for photographs with fans — "I'm, like, the Babe Ruth of the independent leagues," he said — and then went into the clubhouse to suit up. The bus for the rest of the team had already arrived, and the players were lounging in their underwear; a few were chewing sunflower seeds and discussing a rumor that a scout from a major league organization had appeared at a recent game.

By now, Henderson knew most of his teammates' stories. There was Nick Guerra, a former college star who worked a construction job in the mornings to support his family. There was Scott Goodman, a slightly pear-shaped power hitter, who once hit eighteen home runs for a minor league team affiliated with the Florida Marlins but was released anyway. And there was Adam Johnson, perhaps the most promising player on the team, a twenty-six-year-old starting pitcher who had lost only one game all season. The manager, Terry Kennedy, who had played fourteen years in the major leagues as a catcher, and whose father had played in the majors as well, told me, "I sometimes call this the Discovery League. Everybody here is trying to discover something about themselves — whether they should continue pursuing their dream or whether it's time to finally let it go."

Henderson and Goodman went out to the batting cage together. Goodman, who was among the league leaders in home runs and RBIs, had been struggling with his swing in recent games.

"How you feeling?" Henderson asked him.

"Last night, I wasn't getting my bat out right."

"I don't mean last night. I'm not worried about last night. How do you feel now?"

"I don't know," Goodman said. "It's like I'm not getting my weight behind anything." He went into the cage and swung at several pitches.

"See your foot?" Henderson said. "You're stepping too far in, instead of toward the pitcher."

Goodman inspected the divot in the dirt where his front foot had landed. "You're right," he said. "I never noticed."

Kennedy told me that he had initially worried how Henderson would fit in with the team, especially considering his perks. "I was never into guys who chirp," he said. But, to his surprise, Henderson had gone out of his way to mentor other players. "I don't want to go too deep into his head," Kennedy said. "But something's clearly going on in there. I think maybe he's trying to show clubs that he's willing to be a different player."

After a while, Goodman and Henderson returned to the clubhouse. They put on their road uniforms, which were gray and navy blue, and walked onto the field, their cleats leaving marks in the sticky grass. Despite the heat, more than four thousand people had come out for Rickey Henderson Night — the biggest crowd in Yuma since the opening night of the season. As Henderson took his position in center field, a yellow Volkswagen Beetle, with a pair of rodent-like ears attached to its roof and a curly tail sticking out of its trunk, circled the grass. "It's time to exterminate the competi-tion," the stadium announcer said. "Truly Nolen Pest Control — We get the bugs out for you." After the first inning, Henderson sat on the bench, his uniform already soaked with sweat, while cheer-leaders danced on the dugout roof over his head. The announcer said, "See if you can answer tonight's trivia question! The question is: what year was Rickey Henderson originally drafted by the Oak-land A's?"

"Nineteen seventy-six," one of Henderson's teammates said.

"I wasn't even born then," another said.

At one point, with Henderson playing center field, a shot was hit over his head and he began to run, unleashing at least a memory of his speed. He looked back over his shoulder, trying to bring the ball into focus, and made a nice catch. "Thataway, Rickey!" his teammates yelled when he came back to the dugout.

Even though Henderson played well, with two singles and a walk, the Surf Dawgs lost, 5–0. His wife, who had come to see him play that weekend with two of their daughters, told the team's general manager, "Why won't he just quit and come home?" As he left the field, fireworks began to explode in the sky above him, the finale of Rickey Henderson Night.

One afternoon before a home game, Kennedy approached Hen-derson at the ballpark and asked if he would teach the other play-ers the art of stealing. Kennedy knew that, in recent years, base stealing had been all but forgotten in the major leagues. Team owners, convinced that home runs brought people to the stadium, had built smaller and smaller ballparks; at the same time, players made their muscles bigger and bigger with steroids. Since 1982, when Henderson broke the single-season record for steals, home run totals had risen by 61 percent, while the number of stolen bases had fallen nearly 20 percent. But Kennedy knew how devas-tating stealing could be: he had been with the San Francisco Giants in the 1989 World Series, when Henderson and the A's swept the Giants in four games and Henderson set a postseason record, with eleven stolen bases.

Henderson agreed to give a demonstration, and there was a buzz as Goodman, Johnson, and the other players gathered around first base. Henderson stepped off the bag, spread his legs, and bent forward, wiggling his fingers. "The most important thing to being a good base stealer is you got to be fearless," he said. "You know they're all coming for you; everyone in the stadium knows they're coming for you. And you got to say to yourself, 'I don't give a dang. I'm gone.'" He said that every pitcher has the equivalent of a poker player's "tell," something that tips the runner off when he's going to throw home. Before a runner gets on base, he needs to identify that tell, so he can take advantage of it. "Sometimes a pitcher lifts a heel, or wiggles a shoulder, or cocks an elbow, or lifts his cap," Henderson said, indicating each giveaway with a crisp gesture.

Once you were on base, Henderson said, the next step was taking a lead. Most players, he explained, mistakenly assume that you need a big lead. "That's one of Rickey's theories: Rickey takes only three steps from the bag," he said. "If you're taking a big lead, you're going to be all tense out there. Then everyone knows you're going. Just like you read the pitcher, the pitcher and catcher have read you."

He spread his legs again and pretended to stare at the pitcher. "Okay, you've taken your lead; now you're ready to find that one part of the pitcher's body that you already know tells you he's throwing home. The second you see the sign, then, *boom*, you're gone." He lifted his knees and dashed toward second base. After he stopped, he said, "I'll tell you another of Rickey's theories." Nearly all base stealers, he explained, begin their run by crossing their left foot in front of their right, as they turn their bodies toward second. That was also a mistake. "If you cross over, it forces you to stand straight up to get into your stride," he said. "That's the worst thing you can do as a runner. You want to start out low and explode."

As Henderson was conducting his demonstration, members of the opposing team arrived and began to look on. He said that the final touch was the slide. Before Henderson, the great base stealers typically went feet first. Henderson decided that it would be faster — not to mention more daring and stylish — to go in head first, the way Pete Rose, who was never a major base stealer, occasionally did. Yet each time Henderson tried the head-first slide he would bounce violently, brutally pounding his body. Then, one day, while he was flying to a game, he noticed that the pilot landed the plane in turbulence without a single bump. Henderson recalled, "I asked the pilot, I said, 'How the hell did you do that?' He said the key is coming in low to the ground, rather than dropping suddenly. I was, like, 'Dang. That's it!'" After that, Henderson said, he lowered his body gradually to the ground, like an airplane.

Henderson concluded by saying that if the base runner studied the pitcher, made a good jump, and slid well, he should beat the throw nearly every time. And if for some reason he was caught, the moment he got back on base he should try to steal again. As Henderson put it to me, "To steal a base, you need to think you're invincible."

"Look at your head," the Surf Dawgs' hitting instructor said to Henderson one July afternoon. "You're dropping it down."

"I know it," Henderson said, stepping back in the batting cage. He took several more swings, but nothing seemed to be going right. "Come on, Rickey, you're better than this!" he yelled.

In July, his batting average had plunged from .311 to .247 — one of the lowest on the team. (Recently, it climbed to .270.) In May, he hit only one home run; he had none in June. "He still sees the ball well," Kennedy, who was leaning against the cage, said of Henderson. "But he doesn't have the bat speed to get around."

After a dismal series against the Samurai Bears, an all-Japanese squad that had the worst record in the league, Henderson began staring at the ground in the outfield. Kennedy turned to his coaches and said, "I think we've lost him."

Kennedy, believing that Henderson was ready to quit, later called him into his office. "I understand if you're through," Kennedy said.

"No, man, it's not that. It's just my damn hitting. I can't get it straight."

As the weeks wore on, it became clearer that the defiant mindset that had made him a great base stealer had, in many ways, trapped him in the Golden Baseball League. He was forever convinced that he could do the impossible. "When I went to play with the Newark Bears, I was sure I would be there for only a few weeks — that a major league team would call me," he said. "But one week became two weeks, and now it's two years and I'm still waiting for that call."

Trying to improve his average, he started to experiment with his trademark crouch; he stood straighter at the plate, until he was an almost unrecognizable figure. "I remember at the end of my career I began to doubt my ability," Kennedy said. "I knew what I wanted to do, but my body wouldn't let me do it. And I called my father and said, 'Dad, did you ever start to think you weren't good enough to play this game?' And he said, 'I did, and once you do you can never get it back.'"

During the game against the Scorpions in late July, after Henderson had singled and was on first, he got into his three-step lead. I had been traveling with the team periodically throughout the season, waiting to see him steal. The crowd implored him to run, and several times the pitcher threw to first to keep him close. "Here he goes!" a fan yelled. "Watch out!" But when the pitcher went into his motion, Henderson didn't move. He stood there, frozen. "What's wrong, Rickey?" another fan yelled. "Can't you steal anymore?" On the next pitch, Henderson took his lead again and wiggled his fingers. The pitcher seemed to dip his shoulder when he was about to throw home — his tell — but Henderson didn't break. After several more pitches, the batter hit a ground ball to short and Henderson was easily thrown out at second. As Henderson returned to the dugout, he shouted, "Goddam cocksucking sun was in my eyes. I couldn't see a goddam motherfucking bullshit thing." He sat in the dugout with his head bowed, and for the first time since I had seen him play he didn't say a word.

Two weeks later, in the middle of August, as the Surf Dawgs' season was nearing its end, word spread in the clubhouse that the Oakland A's had just phoned about a player. Kennedy came out and told the team the good news: a Surf Dawg was being called up to Oakland's AAA farm team. It was Adam Johnson, the pitcher. Afterward, Henderson told me, "I'm happy to see one of the guys get out of the league, to get a chance to move on." He seemed genuinely glad for him and refused to mention his own circumstances. On another night on the field, however, he pointed to the Surf Dawg logo on his jersey and said, "I never thought I might end my career in this uniform." I asked if he would retire at the end of the season. "I don't know if I can keep going," he said. "I'm tired, you know." As he picked up his glove, he stared at the field for a moment. Then he said, "I just don't know if Rickey can stop."

DAN KOEPPEL

Standing Still

FROM BICYCLING

IT IS A DAMP TUSCAN AFTERNOON, and we've got a wind behind us. The breeze pushes the bikes along, even upward into the hills, but even so the rest of the cycling group has long since left Davis Phinney behind again.

He and I are alone, chatting, laughing. The man beside me was the first American to win a road stage of the Tour de France; he was the first American with enough muscle and nerve to snatch forty-mile-per-hour sprints from European hardguys, and in the mid-'80s led the fabled 7-Eleven team that pioneered this country's way into the Grand Tours and Classics; he once starred in a Super Bowl television commercial and, in an endorsement deal, his face appeared on two million Slurpee cups — all before Greg LeMond won his first Tour, before Lance Armstrong got his driver's license.

We dawdle up a tiny climb. The face is the same. The legs are still muscular. At the top, we lean our bikes against a sandstone wall and step into an empty café. Phinney orders a coffee. He's lived in Italy for nearly three years, and his espresso habit has gone native; he takes it black and sugared thick. He extends his right hand to grip the tiny cup, awkwardly, because Phinney is left-handed. For a second, my eyes sweep downward. Phinney's dominant hand is pressed into his hip. He's trying to keep it still. But the effect of Parkinson's disease is obvious.

He's trembling.

Thousands of miles have been pedaled since a sixteen-year-old boy — with scientists for parents and an older sister who did far better in school — stood in a Boulder, Colorado, park and discovered what he'd been put on earth for. It was 1975, the height of America's first post-automobile-age bicycle boom, and in the mountains northwest of Denver, the two-wheeled vogue found its most thrill-rich manifestation: European-style road racing. Davis Phinney was witnessing the premiere Red Zinger Classic. (Later the Coors Classic, this was the first attempt to bring multi-day, Tour de France–style events to the United States.) Phinney saw the riders, the speed, and, especially, the power of the sprinters as they exploded toward the finish, and knew what he wanted to be.

"I was going to race bikes," he says.

Within weeks, he'd found an oversized Peugeot to ride. Within months, though his bike didn't fit and he wore his father's rock-climbing helmet and a woolen thermal undershirt as a jersey, Phinney was in breakneck competition with Boulder's young cycling stars. There was Ron Kiefel, who would end up becoming one of Phinney's closest friends and, on 7-Eleven, his leadout man in European sprints. There was Alexi Grewal, who would become Phinney's Olympic nemesis.

Back then, I was as obsessed with being on two wheels as Phinney was. But I spent most of my time pedaling the back roads around New York City with a set of panniers strapped to my Schwinn. There was a velodrome not far from my grandmother's house in Queens, but the world of bike racing seemed terribly distant. One day a racing fanatic at a snobby Manhattan bike shop told me that the athletes to watch were a young Nevadan named Greg LeMond and a five-foot-nine Rocky Mountain powerhouse named Phinney. Stuck in the urban East, with little skill for racing and my only idea of what it might be like coming from the 1979 movie *Breaking Away,* I noted the names, but it was hard to visualize Phinney's brand of cycling.

In his hometown of Boulder, he was as adored as Reggie Jackson, the slugger who helped the Yankees win a pair of late-decade World Series, was in mine. Michael Aisner, who promoted the Red Zinger/Coors Classic race, says the Boulder stages were pandemonium: "You'd never believe it. When those riders came through North Boulder Park, there would be sixty thousand people, all screaming for Davis."

I wouldn't have believed it. But soon, the whole country would.

A year before the 1984 Los Angeles Olympics, Phinney married Connie Carpenter. A stunning athlete — nearly six feet tall, with flowing red hair and two years Phinney's senior — she'd competed in the 1972 Winter Olympic Games as a fourteen-year-old speed-skating phenom. In the early '80s, she and Phinney started a passionate romance. (Ron Kiefel says his training partner spent four days off the road when he hooked up with his future wife. "They were locked in a room together," he recalls.)

Phinney had upgraded his undershirt-and-climbing-helmet style to a consciously well-groomed, media-friendly persona and begun racing in Europe for 7-Eleven. ABC Sports fell in love with the medal-contending couple, and began promoting them.

"There were no two athletes with more attention — or expectation," Aisner says.

Phinney told me his Olympic story one day last fall as we drove across Tuscany to one of the Carpenter/Phinney bike camps. In the months leading up to the Games, he says, he became more and more certain that both he and Carpenter could win the gold medals everyone expected. He'd especially convinced Carpenter of her own potential. Three years earlier, she'd finished third by just millimeters at the world championships in Prague. In analyzing her loss, Phinney pointed out that his wife had been the strongest rider but lacked an essential sprinter's skill: the ability to throw the bike forward, at the last instant, pushing it ahead of the body to burst across the finish line and get the edge in a dead heat. It was an art Phinney demonstrated, and Carpenter practiced, day after day, as the Games approached.

Carpenter raced first. I remember watching the women's road race at my friend's house. Like many fans, I didn't know much about the women, though the television hype had made me aware that Carpenter and Phinney were, as a broadcaster put it, "a matched pair." Carpenter and her chief rival (and teammate), Rebecca Twigg, spent the sunny afternoon dicing with each other. After nearly fifty miles of pedaling a circuit around Mission Viejo, neither had put any distance on the other; Twigg approached the finish with a slight lead.

"Maybe a half wheel," Carpenter remembers.

She threw the bike.

I'd never before seen a race with world-class competitors; although what Carpenter did seemed like stuff I'd attempted on my Sting-Ray as a kid, I understood how different and amazing it was, this gigantic redhead with perfect timing and perfect grace accomplishing something that seemed not to surprise her.

"It was," Carpenter says, "a gift from Davis."

A few days later, Phinney wheeled onto the same course (though the length was doubled to one hundred miles). "I felt so strong that morning," he remembers. But late in the race, Alexi Grewal took the lead, and on the final climb, Phinney couldn't keep up. Steve Bauer, a Canadian who also rode for 7-Eleven, joined the chase and eventually finished second. Phinney finished fifth.

"I couldn't close the gap," Phinney says. "My legs weren't there."

We'd reached the Mediterranean coast; we were passing Pisa, and I could see the famous crooked tower from the highway. "It was a bitter, bitter blow," Phinney says. "For years, I'd done nothing but win. I'd anticipated nothing but victory."

There was a brief silence. The hardest thing, he said, was learning to take less seriously the pity people heaped on him. They'd recognize him as the half of that famous couple that didn't fulfill destiny, usually with a sad shake of the head and a downcast glance. But Phinney had a ready antidote: racing — and winning. In 1986, he became the first American to win a road stage in the Tour de France (LeMond had won a time trial), and he prevailed again in a hotly contested sprint into Bordeaux the following year. In 1988, in the Liège-Bastogne-Liège Classic, a team car stopped short in front of Phinney; he went through the back windshield, fracturing a vertebra and opening a wound in his face that took 130 stitches to close. He returned to the United States and, five months later, entered the Coors Classic, finally standing atop the podium in the race that had inspired him, completing an amazing comeback before hometown fans.

Such determination in the face of hardship is, of course, the hallmark of a winning athlete. It brought Lance Armstrong back after cancer, and Greg LeMond back after a gunshot wound forced him to sit out the 1987 season. But this final hardship of Phinney's is different. It's striking after his peak. There are no more races for him to win. Even if there were, his disease wouldn't allow it. Cancer is a killer, but the lucky and determined can get better.

Those with Parkinson's have no such opportunity.

"The other fathers think I'm drunk," Phinney cracks one day at his son Taylor's soccer game. The boy is a star, fluent in Italian

and deadly accurate with a corner kick; his teammates (and teammates' sisters) love him. On the sidelines, Phinney shuffles, slurs
his speech, and shakes.

His joke actually reflects a common first impression of those with
the young-onset version of Parkinson's. (About one in a hundred
people over age sixty have the disease; under age fifty, the ratio is
less than one in a thousand.) The symptoms are caused by the de-
struction of brain cells that produce dopamine, a chemical that
helps regulate the body's movement and pleasure functions. (Sex,
chocolate, and heroin all feel good because they stimulate dopamine receptors.)

Phinney began to notice what he now realizes were early symptoms toward the end of his racing career. After winning the national pro road championship in Philadelphia in 1991, Phinney
started to get intense leg cramps, usually during long car or plane
rides. By '93, when he retired, he was experiencing fatigue, mysteri-
ous aches, and tingles. He and Carpenter had begun their bike-
touring business, and Phinney says he was too busy to worry about
such vague symptoms. Taylor had been born in '90, daughter Kel-
sey in '94, and Phinney was also an in-demand personality for
broadcast television; cycling was finding a place on cable networks
and would become increasingly popular as the era of Lance Armstrong dawned. But the aches and pains continued, and the couple
found themselves shuttling to doctors and chiropractors and MRI
facilities.

One of the problems was that youthful Parkinson's is so rare
that it doesn't usually occur to a diagnosing physician; Phinney's
fitness might have masked more severe symptoms. The likely cul-
prit, the couple believed, was probably related to the 1988 windshield crash.

"It wasn't blissful denial," Phinney says. "The thing about Parkinson's is that it comes at you like some kind of poison vine, advancing up a wall by just an inch a year. It takes over your system so
slowly, and with such subtlety, that you don't notice it until it has a
grip around your throat."

There's no single marker for Parkinson's. The presence of the
disease is confirmed by its symptoms, along with some basic tests
that measure response to dopamine-altering medication. Phinney's
diagnosis finally came after his hand began shaking so much that

he couldn't hold a microphone on a broadcasting job. On a cold Denver evening in 2000, he and Carpenter sat in a neurologist's office as the doctor explained the disease and what the future might hold.

"It was a strange relief," Phinney says. "But it was also a sobering bucket of cold water, right in the face." They drove silently back toward Boulder. Halfway there, they stopped at a Mexican restaurant. As Carpenter watched, her husband downed shot after shot of tequila. "I just needed to check out," Phinney says.

The 1984 Olympic gold medalist drove her stricken husband home. Neither of them knew what they'd do. "But I knew," Carpenter says, "that we weren't going to do nothing."

I attended my first Carpenter/Phinney camp in 2003. I wanted to spend a week cycling beside one of my heroes. I knew that Phinney had Parkinson's, but as we rolled through the Dolomites, stopping at cafés, his symptoms seemed mild. I didn't notice that he often kept his left hand in his pocket, or that he'd grip something to keep his tremors from becoming apparent.

"I was hiding," Phinney says. "I got good at thinking about everything I'd do, not getting caught off-guard. There were tactics I'd adopt to keep myself from looking overtly disabled."

Carpenter and Phinney moved to Italy in 2002 so he could get away from the pressure, from the fast-paced lifestyle, from things that would cause him stress and aggravate his disease. But their bike camps aren't the typically lazy, catered vacations offered by many companies. In handouts Carpenter gives to her guests, she instructs them to both *vai tranquillo* — take it easy — and go hard.

"Give," she says. "Give your all."

Before those Olympics, back in '84, Carpenter told everyone she'd win, then quit the sport immediately. She kept her word. More than twenty-five years after her last race, she still possesses a steely intensity that I've seen in only one other athlete I've met up close: Lance Armstrong. You never get the sense that Carpenter became an athlete for the glory. It feels more like she simply held herself to a deeply personal and ferociously high set of internal standards. Her perfectionism makes her an ideal host in Italy. She will get you up that hill. She will make sure you learn how to make impeccable tiramisu. She will ensure that you have no choice but to adore your bike, adore your wine, adore your life — that you live and relax with passion.

Carpenter, says Max Testa, a close family friend who was Phinney's doctor for much of his career, "is taking almost as big a hit as Davis. But she's the one who has to keep everything under control."

Last autumn, I rode with Carpenter and Phinney again.

During a dinner at a Tuscany hotel, Phinney dispensed with the silverware and ate with his fingers — it's easier that way — while joking to his companions to "watch out for flying food." He told me he's practicing making eye contact with people who notice his shaking. "It's time," he said, "to bring this bad self out into the open."

I'm too much of a fan to be able to get very deep inside that bad self. I know that my filter of admiration keeps me from understanding how Phinney and his family, and his oldest friends, can cope. I won't pretend that I can portray how they manage to believe in the future as they watch a man who once epitomized the gorgeous physicality and aggression of professional bike racing struggle with a disease that is degenerative, disabling, and slithering in its malice. I don't imagine that I can climb inside Phinney's head as his thoughts drift from the person he calls Shaky Davis to his old self. I don't know if his heart is overwhelmed by sorrow and admiration, one twisted against the other, as mine is when our tours into the hills of Tuscany end and he quietly returns to his quarters to sleep, his exhaustion hidden behind closed doors, while Carpenter shoos guests away.

Seeing the disease in plain sight — the same thing that, at first, made me heartsick — inspires hope. Neither Phinney nor Carpenter sugarcoats. "I know the normal course of the disease," Carpenter told me one night. Phinney says, "I know things down the line look pretty grim for me."

But over and over you see the two of them throw themselves, with a perfectly timed instinct, past the dark moments. At the Tuscany camp, Phinney was trying to adjust his seat post, dropped the hex wrench, and couldn't pick it up. He began laughing and said, "I hope everybody's amused."

One evening in Bassano del Grappa, the walled medieval city just east of their Italian home, I shared a pizza with Carpenter. "It *is* hard to wake up every day, and know that the person you live with is getting beaten up," she told me. "But what I also see is Davis trying to live the best way he can. There are so many of us who don't have the specter of disease haunting us who can't manage doing that."

I don't think either Phinney or Carpenter is hiding from the truth, or denying the future. They're returning to the United States, partially because soon Phinney will need more-aggressive treatment, possibly brain surgery. They've started a foundation to help fund Parkinson's research; last year an inaugural charity bike ride raised more than $170,000, enough to help launch several projects in Cincinnati. (The Davis Phinney Foundation is affiliated with the Neuroscience Institute at the University of Cincinnati and University Hospital.)

I think they're simply people who don't know how to lose. It is the key to Phinney's bravery, to Carpenter's strength, and to whatever the future holds. It is an idea that is utterly alien to most of us — those of us who are mortally ungifted, who come apart merely from witnessing the suffering of our heroes. But it is the idea that keeps them going, that makes every day feel like a triumph.

STEVE ONEY

Fallen Angel

FROM LOS ANGELES

ON A FRIDAY MORNING in November 2001, several hundred mourners filed into the spacious sanctuary of Trinity Life Center, a Pentecostal church just east of the Las Vegas Strip, to pay final respects to one of the congregation's most unlikely members, Robert "Bo" Belinsky, who had died of a heart attack a week earlier at the age of sixty-four.

Gathered on Trinity Life's pews were people who had known Belinsky in many of his incarnations. Up front were the former ballplayers who on May 5, 1962, had watched the left-handed pitcher for the Los Angeles Angels take the mound at Chavez Ravine and throw California's first major league no-hitter. In one row were Dean Chance, the Angels' 1964 Cy Young Award winner and Bo's closest friend on the team, and Albie Pearson, the Angels' center fielder at the time. Nearby were Dick Williams, most famous for managing the Oakland Athletics to consecutive world championships during the 1970s but on the night of Belinsky's masterpiece left fielder for the opposing Baltimore Orioles (in three at-bats Williams struck out twice and fouled out), and Steve Barber, the Orioles' starting — and losing — pitcher that evening. These men had been best acquainted with the old Bo, the one who in the wake of his singular triumph used his good looks, charm, and knack for getting his name in the newspapers to woo Hollywood starlets, among them Ann-Margret, Tina Louise, Juliet Prowse, Connie Stevens, Mamie Van Doren, and *Playboy* Playmate Jo Collins. Their Belinsky was the rebellious, sporting-world Casanova who pointed the way for the athletes as sex symbols who followed. Before Joe Namath, there was Bo.

Elsewhere at Trinity Life were those who'd seen a different Belinsky, whose largely unpublicized post-baseball descent into alcoholism and cocaine addiction took him to such depths of degradation that for nearly a decade he seemed past redemption. Some, like Mark Greenberg, former vice president of business development at the Betty Ford Center in Rancho Mirage and current executive director of Michael's House, a treatment facility for men in Palm Springs, were involved in Belinsky's rehabilitation. Others, in the manner of Alcoholics Anonymous members everywhere, were known to Bo merely by first names and last initials. These mourners possessed a keen awareness of his travails. As Belinsky once put it at an AA meeting, "It's a terrible feeling when you're in pain and you know you're going to remain in pain. You tell yourself, it's gotta get better, but no, the game is just starting. There's no limit to going down the tubes."

Belinsky's service also attracted a few Las Vegas notables — chief among them boxing promoter Bob Arum — but most of the others in attendance were either members of Trinity Life or friends Bo had made during his twelve years of residency in the city. People like Rich Abajian, general manager of Findlay Toyota, Irving Marcus, director of guest relations at Arizona Charlie's Casino, Lou Rodophele, a retired plumbing supplies distributor from Boston, and Don Richardson, sales manager of Saturn of West Sahara. These people knew Belinsky as a genial soul who despite perilous finances always overtipped waiters and frequently quoted from the Bible. To them, Bo's religious conversion was both brave and undeniable. "I had a spiritual awakening," he liked to say. "It was a beautiful thing. There's a power greater than any other power on this earth, and it came into my life and left me with a feeling that no matter what happens, everything is going to be all right."

It was an impressive funeral, but as the Reverend Randy Greet stepped to the pulpit, it became obvious that the body of the man who was being remembered was not on the premises. The reasons, like so much with Belinsky, were complicated. Married and divorced three times and estranged from his three children and only sibling, Bo had left no instructions regarding the disposition of his remains. Until the legalities could be sorted through, his body would stay at the undertaker's. Later Don Richardson would comment, "Nothing was ever easy with Bo." Yet the absence of Belinsky's corpse also spoke to a deeper enigma, one rooted in Bo's sense of alienation. "Nobody could ever figure me out," he once remarked. "I wouldn't show what was really inside me, inside Bo Belinsky I was just a façade I'd carried along all my life." On another occasion he said, "I was born apart. My mother was Jewish, my father Polish Catholic. To Jews I was a Polack. To Poles I was a kike. I was removed — removed from people in my family, people in my school. Even in my youth, I didn't know where to park myself."

Two days before his death, Bo Belinsky was at work in the showroom of Findlay Toyota on Auto Show Drive in the Las Vegas suburb of Henderson. The former pitcher suffered from an array of illnesses, most seriously bladder cancer and diabetes. The diseases, along with a recent hip replacement operation, the years of substance abuse, and one unconquered vice — he chain-smoked unfiltered English Oval cigarettes — had taken a toll on Bo's appearance. Skin pallid, eyes dark circled, and hair sickly gray, he was not well. Yet as he gazed out the dealership's windows onto the lot, where the sun burst off Camrys and 4Runners, he seemed happy. "Bo was proud of what the last ten or eleven years had been like," says Rich Abajian, his boss, who spent time with him that November morning. "He was proud that he could conform to a business structure. He and I had the longest employer-employee relationship in his life."

Findlay Toyota was perfect for Belinsky. The dealership's owner, former University of Nevada Las Vegas basketball standout Cliff Findlay, believes in hiring retired athletes (among others who have worked for him are onetime National League batting champion Bill Madlock), while Abajian, a boyish, fifty-one-year-old charismatic Christian, enjoys helping people in trouble. "I work with people who've had problems," he says as he indicates the spot where Belinsky's desk sat. "I give people second chances, third chances, and usually I don't get much back. But once in a while with people like Bo, things work out. This place became his world. And that's rewarding."

Belinsky's job at Findlay was that of a public relations emissary. He represented the dealership at celebrity golf tournaments and gave Toyota-touting talks to civic groups, but according to Abajian, while Belinsky's position provided him with a high profile, he never behaved like a big shot. "By the time Bo got to us, he'd learned humility. He'd go wash a car. He'd walk new salesmen around the lot. He'd keep our morale up. In the car business, if by two in the afternoon nothing is happening, it can get depressing. But Bo would walk around the dealership saying, 'It's gonna be okay,' which meant a lot to me."

Once a week Belinsky ate breakfast with Irving Marcus at Arizona Charlie's, a rambling casino on the north side of Las Vegas that attracts mainly locals. He liked talking to the eighty-five-year-old guest relations director about boxing and gambling. Occasionally, Bo ducked into a sports bar called Instant Replay for lunch. Every Sunday there were services at Trinity Life. But otherwise, Bo stayed to himself in the tiny apartment he rented at the Duck Creek Condominiums not far from work. There, night after night, he ate supper, watched old movies on television, read the Bible, and took obsessive care of a tabby cat named Choo-choo.

At the end Belinsky's existence was subdued. In fact, it may have been the life he was best suited for all along, not that those who knew him at the height of his glory or the nadir of his madness would have predicted that it would turn out like this. Indeed, when he was in the midst of it all, Bo — who over the years had put his thoughts regarding these matters on tape — could never have imagined such a finale. Speaking of his seasons with the Angels, he said, "In those days it was all sex and champagne, champagne and sex. The two were a lot like each other. When it was good, it was good, and when it was bad, it was still pretty good." As for the dark times, he was appalled: "I was an alcoholic of the worst kind, not only dangerous to myself but to my loved ones and friends — and they fled from me."

Even before Bo Belinsky arrived at the Angels' 1962 spring training camp in Palm Springs, he was famous. He had done what in those days was unthinkable for a rookie — held out for more money. He was insulted by the Angels' $6,000 offer. Anything under $8,500, he said, and he'd stay home in Trenton, New Jersey, hustling pool. After the club agreed to renegotiate his deal at midseason, he accepted the $6,000, but his labor action had made big news. When he reached the team's Desert Inn headquarters, he was whisked to the swimming pool, where reporters had gathered for a press conference. Turned out in dark sunglasses, cashmere sports jacket, yellow sports shirt, tight pants, and suede shoes, Bo dazzled this hardened bunch. Boasting of the "compromise" he'd exacted from the Angels, the self-professed "crazy left-hander" scoffed at the "yes sir, no sir . . . zis-boombah" attitude of conventional athletes. "He gave them what they wanted," team publicist Irv Kaze subsequently reflected.

Unlike most big leaguers, the twenty-five-year-old Belinsky had never played an inning of high school baseball, spending his after-class hours on the streets of Trenton, where his family had moved when he was a baby and his father eventually opened a TV repair shop. By ten Bo had smoked his first cigarette, by twelve he had lost his virginity, and by fourteen — thanks to evenings spent at Joe Russo's Pool Hall — he was an accomplished pool shark. Under the tutelage of an old hand known as "the Goose," Belinsky learned not only how to sink complicated combinations but how to seek out marks. At sixteen, in a neighboring small town, he made his first big score, taking $1,200 off a seasoned hustler named "the Masked Marvel." For the remainder of his teens, Bo, apprenticing himself to the likes of "Cincinnati Phil" and "the Farmer," worked the Eastern Seaboard, preying on the gullibility of grown men. Along the way he acquired the cunning that would carry him through the first years of adult life. As he would later proclaim: "You gotta remember the laws of hustling. You never hustle anybody. They hustle themselves. You never try to snow a snowman."

From an early age Belinsky possessed a live left arm, and summer days often found him on Trenton sandlots blowing fastballs by hitters. On May 15, 1956, after a scout saw him strike out fifteen opponents, Belinsky signed a contract with the Pittsburgh Pirates' Brunswick, Georgia, farm club for $185 a month. When he arrived at the team hotel, he didn't even own a baseball glove. Instead he carried a pool cue. From the start — he went AWOL from Brunswick to hustle pool — his minor league career was dodgy. In Pensacola, where his 13–6 record marked him as a comer, he had to be smuggled out of town under a blanket to avoid a statutory rape charge. In Miami he and a roommate were accused of drilling holes in their hotel bedroom wall to spy on the Miss Universe contestant staying next door. Finally, after six years of spectral lights and long bus rides while playing for Knoxville, Aberdeen, Stockton, and Little Rock, he was drafted by the newly minted Los Angeles Angels. During winter ball in Venezuela in 1961 he had developed a screwball. The difficult-to-control pitch can be a devastating asset, as it allows left-handers to throw a ball that breaks away from right-handed batters, making it hard to hit. In Belinsky's case, as sportswriters duly noted at the time, the screwball was also something of a metaphor.

The Los Angeles Angels and Bo Belinsky were made for each other. The club was entering only its second year of existence. So much did owners Gene Autry, the singing cowboy, and Bob Reynolds, a former Stanford All-American football player, resent being overshadowed by the better-established Dodgers that although they played their home games at Dodger Stadium, they refused to refer to the park by its given name. Their home field, they maintained, was Chavez Ravine. Autry and Reynolds were looking for someone who could make them both a contender and a rival for the city's affections. They were not only willing to tolerate the eccentricities of a pool shark turned pitcher, they were prepared to celebrate them.

Belinsky won his first three decisions of the 1962 season. Still, only 15,886 were in attendance at Chavez Ravine on May 5 to see him face the Baltimore Orioles. The game that these fans took in, declared Bud Furillo of the *Los Angeles Herald-Examiner,* "made history." Over nine innings Belinsky dominated the opposition. Wrote Braven Dyer of the *Los Angeles Times*: "I can report that the Birds didn't even come close to getting a hit." Though Belinsky walked four men, he struck out nine and faced only one serious threat — a bases-loaded jam in the fourth. When the Orioles' last batter popped out in the ninth, giving the Angels a 2–0 victory, the city had witnessed its first big league no-hitter. Bo Belinsky, not Dodger great Sandy Koufax, would forever hold the record. After the game, as his teammates celebrated, Belinsky posed for pictures, including one with former vice president Richard Nixon, California's Republican gubernatorial candidate that year.

Among the handful who saw Belinsky pitch that night was sixty-five-year-old gossip columnist Walter Winchell. For three decades Winchell — with his punchy items, access to places high and low, and, on his radio and television broadcasts, trademark salutation ("Good evening, Mr. and Mrs. North and South America and all the ships at sea") — had been an unavoidable presence in American journalism. Of late, however, he had been slipping. Frequently descending into red-baiting and Kennedy bashing, his work seemed increasingly dated. Still, because his column appeared in the *New York Daily Mirror*, the nation's second-largest-circulation daily, and the *Los Angeles Herald-Examiner*, he possessed a huge readership. Moreover, he narrated the popular television drama *The Untouchables*.

Winchell recognized Belinsky as a great source of copy who could restore relevancy to his work. (The pitcher reminded the columnist of his younger self — a city kid, a Jew, and a handsome rogue with an eye for a well-turned ankle.) A few days after the no-hitter, Winchell published his initial item on Bo: "New York–born no-hitter rookie Bo Belinsky of the Angels should be in *The Untouchables*. His fastball is that unbelievable." Several days later, there was this: "Bo Belinsky, pitching curves and catching headlines. The most exciting player to hit the major leagues since Mantle's debut." A few days later still, Winchell convinced Belinsky to join him onstage at the Ambassador Hotel's Cocoanut Grove in a comedy sketch to cheer up headliner Eddie Fisher, who was lovesick over losing Elizabeth Taylor to Richard Burton. By early June, Winchell and Belinsky were inseparable. Cruising Los Angeles in the pitcher's new candy apple red Cadillac convertible, which a local dealer had provided in return for promotional considerations, the two took in premieres, attended parties, and made after-hours clubs. Each was hustling the other, and both were getting what they wanted.

Thanks to Winchell, Belinsky suddenly seemed bigger than baseball. When he started a game at Chavez Ravine the night of June 1 against the powerhouse New York Yankees, a then-record crowd of 51,584 (among them Marilyn Monroe, Bob Hope, and Ann-Margret, who the *Herald-Examiner* reported "came to plead for Bo") filled the stadium. While the Yankees beat Belinsky that night, it nonetheless seemed that he could do no wrong. Even at the time, however, Bo knew it wouldn't last. "I needed that no-hitter like GM needs more engines," he said years later. "I wasn't ready to handle it. All the pretty blonds, the actresses, the notoriety." The task of keeping up appearances — a task that had consumed Bo since he worked his first pool room — had become infinitely more demanding.

At 5:00 A.M. on June 13, as Belinsky, accompanied by Dean Chance and two young women, steered his Cadillac through Beverly Hills, he made his first misstep. While stopped at the intersection of Wilshire Boulevard and Roxbury Drive, the foursome, on their way home from the Cocoanut Grove, got into an altercation. Ultimately, thirty-three-year-old Gloria Eves jumped from the car, blood pouring from a jagged wound over her left eye. "He's beating me up," she screamed. It was at this point that Officer B. E. Gruenzel arrived on the scene. While the policeman concluded that Eves, who refused to press charges, had sustained her injury accidentally, the incident took some of the shine off of Belinsky's image. Blared the headline in the next day's *Times*: "Belinsky, Chance Fined After 5 A.M. Ruckus."

The fallout continued for several weeks, and it hit Belinsky — who went out of his way to absolve the married Chance of wrongdoing — the hardest. "Someone should talk to Bo and give him some advice," Eddie Fisher told the *Times*'s Hedda Hopper, who also reported that Gene Autry had admonished the pitcher, informing him, "Hollywood will wine you and dine you as long as you win, but you . . . start losing a few games and they'll forget you're alive."

In the wake of this highly visible lapse — which cemented the improbable friendship between the streetwise Belinsky and Chance, a slow-talking farm boy from Wooster, Ohio — Bo did go on a losing streak. After Belinsky started the season 7–2, his record fell to 10–11, and he narrowly averted being traded by the Angels' old-school general manager, Fred Haney, who disapproved of the pitcher's antics. Nonetheless, 1962 had been an astonishing year for the Angels, who finished in third place, and for Bo.

By season's end, Belinsky had moved into a bachelor's pad atop La Presa Drive in the Hollywood Hills's Outpost Estates. The one-room apartment, which featured a lavender Formica bar, a black sunken tub, and a king-size bed, looked out on the Los Angeles skyline through enormous windows. This would be the heart of Bo's romantic universe, the lair to which he'd invite not only starlets but such exotic diversions as Queen Saroya of Iran, the ex-wife of the shah. "Bo's idea was that every day should be thrilling," says a sportswriter who knew him. "By that he meant the most gorgeous women, the biggest tits, the best sex — and then he could talk about it to fifteen people the next day. 'Live fast, die young, and leave a beautiful corpse' — Bo lived by that line. I didn't think he'd make it to forty."

Belinsky even had dates with such elegant older women as actress Paulette Goddard and tobacco heiress Doris Duke, but he took none seriously. All that changed one night in late 1962 when Winchell, who was sitting with Bo at Hollywood's Peppermint West disco, picked up the phone and invited Mamie Van Doren, the star of *Sex Kittens Go to College*, to join their party. Though the actress for whom Universal Studios created the "bullet bra" rejected this first invitation, she accepted when it was tendered again the next evening and spent several hours on the club's dance floor with Belinsky. "He could do the mashed potato better than James Brown," she says. "He was a sexy dancer." Bo and Mamie went their own ways that evening, but by the time the Angels' 1963 spring training camp was under way, they were together. On April 1, the two were engaged.

For Belinsky, the 1963 season was a wash. He pitched poorly, but he and Mamie were happy. "Bo was just full of sex," she says. "We'd be up all night making love, and the next day he'd wonder why he didn't have a fastball. We spent a lot of time in his apartment. He'd walk around naked. He was always splashing on Aqua Velva cologne. I'd done that commercial, 'There's something about an Aqua Velva man.'"

On May 26, with his record a dismal 1–7, Belinsky was sent down to the Angels' AAA farm team in Hawaii. Though Fred Haney hoped Bo would feel chastened, the pitcher was overjoyed. He loved the islands, where he learned to surf and, with Van Doren far away, resumed chasing women. Minor league baseball seemed a purer form of the sport: no front-office politics, no contract fights, just bats and balls and fans. Part of him wanted to stay there forever. But after recording some impressive victories, he was recalled to the big leagues; on his better days he knew he belonged there. Bo adored his teammates, particularly Chance. The two spent time gambling, playing practical jokes, and making scenes — the wildest of which, courtesy of Winchell, saw them hanging out with FBI director J. Edgar Hoover. "J. Edgar! Man, he's a swinger," Bo told the press afterward. "He let me shoot tommy guns at FBI headquarters. He said, 'Bo, there'll always be a place for you on the force.'"

Belinsky had fashioned a persona as both bon vivant and rapscallion. He possessed the brio of a Dean Martin, yet he also bore the antiestablishmentarian markings of a Jack Kerouac. In him, the lounge lizard and the free spirit commingled. Little wonder that he was soon guest-starring on that most emblematic of early '60s television series: *77 Sunset Strip.*

If Belinsky was ever going to fulfill the promise of his 1962 no-hitter as an Angel, he would do so in 1964. To begin with, his engagement to Mamie Van Doren was over. "He didn't trust me at all," Van Doren says. "He thought because he was doing it, I was doing it." With Mamie out of the matrimonial picture but not out of his life ("We were very sexually compatible," she says. "We couldn't stay away from each other"), Bo worked hard during spring training, and he began the season pitching well. But the Angels failed to give him much offensive support, and by midsummer his record stood at 9–8. "Bo was brilliant that season," says Bob Case, the team's then visiting clubhouse boy and a close friend. "If he'd had any help, he'd have been 15–2." No matter: Belinsky's year — and his Angels career — came to an abrupt conclusion at 3:00 A.M. on August 14 in Washington, D.C.'s Shoreham Hotel. Three days earlier Bo had lost a tough game at Chavez Ravine to the Cleveland Indians. In the locker room afterward, he told the Associated Press that he was going to quit baseball. By the time the Angels arrived in the East for a three-game series with the Senators, the wire service story was all anyone was talking about. This was evidently why Braven Dyer of the *Times* came to Belinsky's door. According to Bo, Dyer barged into his room demanding to know why he wasn't given the scoop. According to Dyer, it was Belinsky who initiated the conversation. The pitcher, he maintained, had reconsidered his retirement decision and wanted to get the word out. What happened next, however, is not in dispute. Following several nasty comments by both men, Belinsky flattened the sixty-four-year-old Dyer with a left to the head, causing blood to spurt from one ear. The twenty-seven-year-old southpaw had knocked out a sportswriter twice his age. Fred Haney suspended Belinsky. For years the pitcher would argue that Dyer had been at fault, but in time he would accept responsibility for what happened, admitting, "I screwed myself out of a job with the Angels." After just two and a half years, Bo's Los Angeles playing days were done.

Although Belinsky was finished with the Angels, he was hardly out of baseball. After spending the offseason in Hawaii, he reported with considerable fanfare to the Philadelphia Phillies. On March 1, 1965, *Sports Illustrated* featured Bo and Phillies ace Jim Bunning on a cover captioned "The Phillies — Old and New — Try Again." In Belinsky the team believed it had found an answer to its pitching problems. "I went to a great deal of trouble to get Bo," says Gene Mauch, the Phillies' manager at the time. "People said, 'You're crazy.' But I was pretty cocky and thought I could take on anybody." Convinced that Belinsky's fastball was his most effective pitch, the manager did his best to persuade him to abandon the showier but less consistent screwball. "Early on, I told him I was going to show him what he could do without the screwball." At first Mauch appeared to make headway. "Bo went to Houston and pitched a three-hitter relying on the fastball," he recalls. Then in an aggrieved tone suggesting that even after forty years what happened next still galls him, he says, "Four days later, we get to Los Angeles, Bo gets two strikes on a hitter in the first inning, and here comes the goddamned screwball. I go to the mound and say, 'One more of those and you go to the bench.'" At that moment Mauch realized that Belinsky was a lost cause. "The fastball wasn't flashy enough for Bo. Flash meant a lot to him, more than baseball did, which he saw as sort of an hors d'oeuvre to get things started — girls, parties."

Mauch, who would conclude his career as the manager of the Angels, liked Bo. "How could you not like him? He had such a great personality." But in the wake of the pitcher's insubordination, he sent him to the bullpen. There Belinsky, who had spent most of his career as a starter, stewed. Worse, he began a habit whose terrible consequences he would only see in retrospect. "I'd occasionally used greenies, amphetamines, as a starter, but in Philadelphia they had red juice [liquid amphetamines]," he later said, "and when I got into the bullpen, I started getting loaded every day, because as a reliever, you never know when you might have to play. This chemical started coming into my life. I thought I could handle it, because I was strong and still had that phony smile. But something was happening to my system."

The remainder of Belinsky's major league career was an exercise in futility. He began 1966 still in Philadelphia, but having compiled a 4–9 record the previous year, he was soon sent to the club's AAA farm team. In 1967, Belinsky popped back up in the big leagues with the Houston Astros, where he pitched indifferently but made headlines by adopting a dog and getting the club to agree to give it a locker in the Astrodome. When the season ended, he repaired to the place that increasingly enthralled him — Hawaii. There he met his first wife.

Looking across crowded Michael's Restaurant in Honolulu in January 1968, Bo spotted Jo Collins, the 1965 *Playboy* Playmate of the Year. Wearing a white backless minidress, she sat amid a gaggle of advertising men and Ford executives who'd gathered in Hawaii to kick off a promotional campaign for Lincoln-Mercury. "Bo came over and introduced himself, and everyone made a fuss over him," Collins says, "but I wasn't a baseball fan and didn't know who he was. I'd been dating Donny Anderson, a running back on the Green Bay Packers."

The next morning Collins received a bouquet of roses from Belinsky in her room at the Royal Hawaiian Hotel. Several nights later she accepted his invitation to dinner. "We went out that first night," she says, "and were inseparable afterward. I never went back to the mainland. Everybody was wondering where I was. I was with Bo."

Though Belinsky reported to the Astros' spring training camp in February, he failed to make the team and spent the bulk of the 1968 season on the Hawaii AAA club, which delighted him. "Hawaii was just his playground," Collins recalls. "He was the star of Hawaii." In June, Belinsky and Collins married. For the next two years — save for a brief return to the big leagues with the Pittsburgh Pirates late in the fall of 1968 and an abortive flirtation with the St. Louis Cardinals the next spring — Belinsky remained with the Hawaii club. On June 19, 1969, Jo gave birth to a daughter they named Stevhanie Lehua to honor their attachment to the islands.

Belinsky got his last shot at the major leagues in 1970 when he reported to spring training with the Cincinnati Reds. He made the team but only got into a few games, and in late May manager Sparky Anderson cut him. That night, when Bo returned home to the suburban town house he and Jo had rented for the season, he began to drink. By 4:00 A.M. the two were fighting, at which point Bo pulled out a .38 pistol. "He threatened me with the gun," Jo says. "I called the police, but when they came and saw it was Bo Belinsky, they let him go. So I took Stevhanie and spent the night with Pete and Karolyn Rose." Later Bo and Jo patched things up, but the career that had begun so promisingly with the no-hitter at Chavez Ravine was over. In five and a half years in the big leagues, Belinsky had won only twenty-eight games. To reporters he boasted, "I got more out of twenty-eight victories than any major leaguer in history. Anybody can be a star if he wins three hundred games. Let him try being a star winning only twenty-eight games." In truth, Belinsky was crushed. Since 1956, baseball had been all he'd known. "I never liked baseball that much, at first anyway," he later said. But by the end he'd experienced a change of heart. "That's funny, isn't it, babe?" he asked writer Pat Jordan. "Me, the guy everybody said didn't love the game enough. Ha! Man, I loved the game. I just didn't take it seriously. I don't take myself seriously, so how could I take a game seriously?"

On a November evening in 1970, Bo and Jo, now living in Malibu, were speeding down the Pacific Coast Highway in yet another Cadillac. They had just finished a dinner where they both drank too much, and they were quarreling. As the two argued, Bo lost control of the car, smashing it head-on into a steel utility pole. Jo's right arm was so badly crushed that emergency room doctors initially considered amputating it. "That was the beginning of the end of our relationship," she says. It was also the start of Bo's headlong descent into the bottle.

"When I got out of baseball," Belinsky would say, "I sat down and had a drink, and that drink never stopped." The causes of Belinsky's binge were many. "He didn't know what he was going to do, and panic set in," Jo says. Ultimately, however, the explanation went deeper. Bo's terrors had been with him in one way or another since childhood. "I didn't have a chemical problem as a kid," he said, "but I had the personality and the fear of an alcoholic, and I was ready to have the chemical catch up with the personality." Even as a sixteen-year-old pool shark, Bo had often been consumed by dread. He had developed his hustle as a tactic to, in his words, "down those people" who might hurt him. The same approach had worked, albeit to a lesser extent, in the big leagues, where the screwball replaced the pool cue and Walter Winchell stood in for the Goose and Cincinnati Phil. Once the games were done, Bo could no longer count on such props or hide behind such glib maxims as "never snow a snowman." Suddenly naked, he surrendered to the addictive disposition that had emerged when he began using speed in Philadelphia. "The disease ran over me," he said. "It caught up that quick. That's how it is. It knocks you over. Boom! A year and a half later nobody knew what to do with me."

After recovering from the injuries sustained in the car wreck, Jo accepted a job as Bunny Mother at a new Playboy Club in Denver, taking Stevhanie with her. Soon Playboy promoted her to a public relations position in Chicago. Periodically, Bo visited in an attempt to reconcile, but it was not to be. "We needed to pull our lives together," Jo says. "I was capable of that. Bo wasn't." Living with a prostitute in Malibu, Belinsky became, as he put it, "a flat-under-the-table drunk. There wasn't a sober day for quite a while. I stayed drunk for two years, blew out my pancreas, almost died. It was total insanity."

In 1972, through the intercession of his old Angels teammate Dean Chance, Belinsky was admitted to St. Thomas Hospital in Akron, Ohio, near Chance's home. "It wasn't too nice," Bo recalled. "It was a lockup type of an institution. There was a guarded gate. They'd throw you down and get you to sign." Every weekend during Belinsky's stay, a group from Alcoholics Anonymous visited. The smiles, slogans, and omnipresent Styrofoam coffee cups offended Bo's sense of cool. "I couldn't figure them out. They'd treat each other like they hadn't seen each other in years, shaking hands and spilling coffee on their shoes." Following twenty-eight days of treatment, Belinsky was released. "I had two or three dollars, and the first thing I did was I bought a bottle of wine and stuck it in a brown bag, and I went crazy. I didn't even know where I was. I wound up under this bridge in Akron. It was about eighteen degrees and slushy, and I said, 'One and a half years ago, I'm in the major leagues in Cincinnati, and now I'm under a bridge in Akron,' and I thought, 'Boy, it can't get any worse.' *Wrong!*"

Back in Malibu, Belinsky began traveling with a criminal crowd. "The pimps and gangsters in Los Angeles were the only ones who'd accept me," he recalled. "As a matter of fact, they gave me a couple of draws and were going to put me in the business, but I was too drunk. They introduced me to cocaine. I had to stop drinking, because it was bad for me, so I did cocaine."

Hair now flowing over his collar in greasy strands, boyish smile masked by a dirty mustache, Belinsky spent much of the early '70s roaring up and down the PCH on a Harley-Davidson, stoned out of his mind. "It was unreal," he said. "I never killed anybody, and I'm fortunate. The things that happened to me, the physical damage that happened to me — I just didn't care. I wanted to die. I didn't want to die. I had no idea. All I knew is that I was in pain."

Not that there weren't ways out. In 1973, Dial Press published *Bo: Pitching and Wooing* by veteran *New York Post* sportswriter Maury Allen. The author, as the jacket copy boasted, received "the uncensored cooperation of Bo Belinsky." Allen and Belinsky were equal partners, and as the release date approached, their editor became convinced that they had a bestseller. It was the age of the athlete as antihero, and the work's subject was the prototype. When *The Today Show* booked Belinsky to plug *Pitching and Wooing*, the hype began. All Bo had to do was catch a red-eye flight to JFK, where a limousine would whisk him to NBC's Rockefeller Center studio. "Much as I liked Bo," says Allen, "I was wary, for I knew there was a chance he'd miss the *Today Show* date. Not only did I talk to him two hours before the flight, but I insisted that the Dial publicists walk him to the gate in Los Angeles, and they did. The problem was, they left before the flight boarded. There was a beautiful girl on line. She and Bo started talking, and they went off and spent the night. The next morning on *The Today Show* there was no Bo. That was a killer for us. That was to have been the big break. I was so angry. I told myself I'd never talk to that cocksucker again." Allen pauses for a second before adding, "But I couldn't stay mad at Bo. He called and apologized, and I said, 'All right.'"

In 1974, Belinsky made another effort to overcome his addictions, relocating to the state that had always been charmed for him — Hawaii. There he embarked on a program that prescribed Valium and other drugs to dispel his desire for alcohol. He stayed sober several months. While walking on the beach, he met Jane Weyerhaeuser, heiress to the timber and paper fortune of the same name. Like so many others, she was at first smitten, and in 1975 they married. "She's a lovely gal," Belinsky would recall, but that was only part of the attraction. "Now I was back in the ball game. Now I could buy all the cocaine I wanted."

For a year Bo and Jane Belinsky used cocaine — he heavily, she less so. In 1976, when Jane was seven and a half months pregnant, she gave birth prematurely. "The day I brought her in for a checkup," recalled Bo, "the doctor said, 'Your wife is giving birth today.' On top of that he says, 'You're gonna have twins.' I couldn't handle the pressure. She went into the hospital, and I got loaded. I brought all my friends over, and with all the dope and everything, I couldn't even make it to the hospital. I think I was drinking. I may have had a nip. I don't know. All I know is that I was coming apart at the seams. I was dying inside. I was so dead that when I finally came to the hospital and saw those two little girls, I had no feeling for them whatsoever, and I had no feeling for Jane. All I could think about was me."

Because the twins were born prematurely, they stayed in the hospital when Jane returned home, where Bo immediately got high. It was then that he snapped, retrieving his .38. "I started shooting all over the place. Next thing I knew, I was gonna play twenty questions with my lover. I go back to the bedroom and am waving the gun around at her. I'm ready to pass out. I don't know what I'm doing. I thought I would fire it in the closet. But somewhere along the line I knew I was going to shoot her. And I did. The bullet went through her hip. Maybe a quarter of an inch up and she's dead. Simple as that. After I gave her the whack with the .38, I had seen what had happened. I walked off. I was going to put the gun right to my head and fire it. Cocked it too. Then I heard her say, 'Bo.' I was going to pull the trigger real fast. And she said, 'What are you doing? What are you doing?' And I didn't do it."

Jane's wound was not serious. "I was very lucky," she says. "The bullet didn't hit any bone. I should have called the police, but I didn't. I loved him." After a physician stitched her up, Belinsky fled to Los Angeles, where he went on a bender. 'All I wanted to do was get into the bottle, back into alcohol, so I could totally blot out this incident." But Bo could not blot it out, and following several trips back and forth between the mainland and Hawaii, he checked into another rehab clinic.

During Belinsky's first two weeks at St. John's Hospital in Santa Monica, he made little progress. "I wasn't responding to the treatment. The counselors kept saying, 'Let's get him down the street. He ain't doing it.' But the program director, Dave Thomas, kept saying, 'Let's give this guy one more day.' There's always someone in a program who won't give up on you, and that's what happened to me."

While Belinsky always had a religious bent — in times of trouble he would recite the Twenty-third Psalm — he'd rejected faith as being unhip. But shortly after Thomas interceded, this Jewish boy from Trenton opened himself to Jesus. "After all those years of not God losing me but me losing Him," Bo said, "I found Him. I had to beat myself down so low and get it down so deep and so far to be receptive. But there it was. I stopped shaking and started to swell up inside."

Belinsky then did something that a couple of years earlier would have been inconceivable — he agreed to attend an Alcoholics Anonymous meeting. "It's AA or amen for you, Bo," Thomas informed him. Bo's first meeting was in Manhattan Beach. The room was plastered with posters bearing all the familiar slogans. As Bo looked around, he told himself, "It's so corny." Yet as he heard one alcoholic after another relate their stories, he couldn't help being moved. "I thought I was a sensitive, giving person, but I started taking a cold, hard look at how egotistical and self-centered I was and how much fear and resentment ruled my life, and I started to open my eyes. I knew I would always be insane, but I saw I didn't have to drink behind it. I didn't have to be dangerous. I was given a gift. Something was happening. This was where I belonged."

Once Belinsky emerged from St. John's Hospital, he performed the suggested follow-up work of attending ninety AA meetings in ninety consecutive days. He soon began to venture out into the world, always traveling with a list of names to call should the temptation to drink arise. Astonishingly, Jane Weyerhaeuser and Bo remained together, moving to Doheny Estates, where Bo drove a Maserati and played golf at the Riviera Country Club. "He was the father of my daughters," she says. The relationship, however, did not last. According to legal filings, Belinsky beat his wife. "He grabbed me by the throat and pushed me in front of our children," she alleged. In 1981, the couple divorced, with Bo relinquishing custody of the twins. Through the years he visited them infrequently, then once they turned ten, not at all. "They always thought he'd ride out of the hills on a white horse and rescue them," says Jane. "But he never did."

As often happens with recovering alcoholics, Belinsky preached the gospel of sobriety. For much of the early '80s, he teamed with Dr. Joseph Pursch, a Laguna Beach–based psychiatrist who specializes in treating patients suffering from substance abuse. "It was the

Bo and Joe show," says Pursch. "We were contracted by business organizations, the Betty Ford Center, and several major league baseball teams to discuss the problem of alcoholism. Bo would tell his story as one who'd been to hell and back, then he'd introduce me, and I'd give the scientific facts to hang on the bones of Bo's firsthand account." At such sessions, Belinsky held little back. "It hurts me when I tell you of shooting my wife," he would typically say. "But I tell you because I love you, and if you ever forget where you were, I'll tell you again." The point was clear: if Bo could rise from the depths, so could his audiences. There was, of course, another point as well. In providing hope for the hopeless, Bo was gaining a sense of accomplishment and making the sort of personal connections of which he'd previously believed himself incapable. "You're my family," he'd tell AA groups. "You saved my life."

Not all of Belinsky's work was public. In 1980, when he heard that his former Angels teammate Eli Grba was in an alcoholic tailspin, he drove to the Yorba Linda home where Grba had crashed. "Bo and I had never been that close," says Grba. "He was too Hollywood. But he came and got me and took me to an AA meeting. I was nervous, but Bo said, 'Don't worry, Eli, they're all drunks just like you and me.'" Grba has been sober for twenty-four years.

By the mid-1980s, Belinsky was back in Hawaii and remarried, this time to a waitress named Bobbi. Living on the North Shore of Oahu, he spent his days windsurfing. In 1989, the two split. Subsequently, Bo would attempt to make light of the breakup. During an appearance at the Betty Ford Center with Pursch, he remarked, "You know, I'm not too successful with wives. So I asked Joe, 'Every time I go to Hawaii, I get married. What can you advise me about my relationships?' He said, 'Simple, stay away from Hawaii.'" Despite such stabs at humor, the divorce from Bobbi was another indication that Bo, his decade of sobriety notwithstanding, still didn't know what to do with his life.

That Belinsky would find his ultimate path on a golf course was, considering all that was to come, fitting. "I met Bo at a scrambles tournament in 1989," recalls Don Richardson, sales manager at Saturn of West Sahara in Las Vegas. "He was living on a small pension from baseball, but he loved cars, so we put him to work in sales at Saturn. We soon found out he didn't have what it took to do sales, but Rich Abajian, who was then my boss, said, 'Bo, relax. I'm gonna pay you $1,500 a month to do PR.' For the rest of his life, he essentially played golf and schmoozed."

Judging by appearances, Belinsky adjusted easily to life in Las Vegas. "Bo had a magnet that drew everybody to him," says Richardson. "He had an ability to be in a group, and everybody liked him." Building goodwill for a business came naturally to Belinsky. When Abajian moved to Findlay Toyota, he took Bo with him.

For the first time in decades, Belinsky's fortunes seemed on the uptick. In 1994, thanks to Alana Case, a successful European model and the wife of his old friend Bob Case, Bo was featured in a major fashion layout in Italy's *L'uomo Vogue*. No longer young but not yet old, he photographed well, projecting a hard-earned wisdom. In 1997, he was invited to play in an Angels old-timers game. This honor not only recognized his place in the team's history but amounted to a homecoming after the extended exile that followed the ugly 1964 incident with the *Times*'s Braven Dyer. On the field that evening in Anaheim, Bo exchanged warm greetings with Gene Autry and cavorted with his former love, Mamie Van Doren. At a news conference, he received more attention than did three-hundred-game winner Nolan Ryan, thus confirming his view that he'd gone a long way on his twenty-eight wins.

Still in all, Belinsky's Las Vegas friends often sensed that beneath his upbeat public persona lurked a profound sadness. "He kept a lot hidden from us," says Lou Rodophele. "Don, Irving Marcus, and I knew Bo very well, but none of us knew where he lived." Belinsky not only kept his address a secret but resisted the efforts of his newfound pals to make him an intimate. "On holidays I always included Bo in my family," says Rodophele, "but he'd only stay an hour or so. He couldn't stay longer because he couldn't tolerate it emotionally to see a happy family life, which he didn't have."

Out of touch with his children, Belinsky was alone. Even dalliances with beautiful women — whom he'd once hustled as avidly as he'd hustled pool — were no longer satisfying. "The fucking you get isn't worth the *fucking* you get," he'd crack to Abajian. Bo would then laugh, but he was putting up a brave front.

The gap between the face Belinsky presented to the world and his tortured private self opened on New Year's Eve, 1997. After falling off the wagon, Bo attempted suicide at the high-rise apartment where he'd long been living. First he drank half a bottle of vodka.

Then he slashed his wrists. Next he plunged a dull hunting knife into his stomach just below the rib cage and slashed downward. Bleeding heavily, he dragged himself to his unit's balcony. "He later told me he was going to throw himself off," says Rodophele, "but he was hurt so bad he didn't have the strength." Eventually, Bo crawled to a phone, and soon help was summoned.

For several days Belinsky was in intensive care at the University Medical Center Hospital. "The emergency medical technicians told me they were surprised he lived," recalls a friend. Once Bo was strong enough, Rodophele bundled him into the backseat of his Lincoln Town Car and drove him to Palm Springs, where he would again battle alcoholism. "When Bo had his relapse," says Mark Greenberg, who had gotten to know the former Angel during the years when he spoke publicly on substance abuse, "I assisted him in getting help." The help began with a stay at Michael's House, Greenberg's new employer. There Greenberg perceived that for all the progress Belinsky had made, he had yet to deal with some of the underlying reasons for his despair. "I told him to clear things up with his daughters and clean house," he said. "But that's one step I don't think he really took. He didn't make amends."

Still, Belinsky fought his way once more to sobriety. On February 28, 1998, at a clinic called Life's Journey, he signed a "No Suicide Contract" in which he agreed not to take his life and to phone Greenberg should he ever find himself entertaining suicidal thoughts. Then he returned home.

Back in Las Vegas, the members of Belinsky's circle now possessed a sharper awareness of how fragile Bo was. Rodophele, who was charged with cleaning up Bo's apartment, was shocked by what he found. "I broke down crying," he says. "It was squalid. Not only was there blood from where he'd knifed himself, but trash was piled up everywhere. You couldn't even see the kitchen table. It was covered with empty cans, unopened bills, dirty clothes. This is what depression looks like."

For the first few months Belinsky lived with a succession of friends, among them Rich Abajian and his wife, Jo Ann. As he'd done during his initial recovery, Bo kept himself clean by helping others do the same. Jo Ann had a drug problem. "Bo helped her stay sober, and she helped him," says Abajian. Adds Jo Ann, "We'd sit on the balcony and talk about our lives. It wasn't all 'Woe is me.' There was a lot of laughter. He was an inspiring gentleman." At the Abajians' urging, Bo joined their church — Trinity Life.

"I met Bo right after the suicide attempt," says the Reverend Randy Greer. "He told me that he'd had a vision of Christ that night he tried to take his life." According to Greer, Bo realized that "his life was empty. He wanted to fill that void that Billy Graham calls 'a God-shaped vacuum.'"

Trinity Life became the pivot around which Belinsky's existence revolved. Not that he acted pious. "Bo was always going to be rough around the edges," says Greer, citing as example his habit of sitting in the back of the sanctuary during services so that he could duck out for cigarettes. Equally telling, Bo continued to indulge in language better suited to a dugout than a house of worship. "He'd come up to me after church and say, 'That was a helluva sermon, Pastor Randy.'" Belinsky also resisted what for a Pentecostal is the acid test — speaking in tongues. Nevertheless, Greer believes that his new congregant found true salvation. "Bo would tell me, 'I need Jesus. Without Him, I'm lost.' He gave his life to Jesus. He wanted to be part of everything here."

On the morning of December 7, 2001, Bo Belinsky was finally laid to rest in the Garden of Peace at Paradise Memorial Gardens, a perpetual-care facility just across a busy four-lane road from McCarran International Airport. After the initial confusion as to the legalities, Lou Rodophele was appointed administrator of Bo's estate. The spot that he, Don Richardson, and Dean Chance chose for their friend is five plots away from where the remains of another tortured 1960s sports icon — former heavyweight boxing champion Sonny Liston — are interred.

As the Reverend Greer pronounced words over Belinsky's body, questions regarding Bo's troubled sixty-four years still eluded easy answers. On one level, he was a man who had it all — looks, athletic talent, stardom, and charisma. Yet he couldn't face life's realities. "God knows, Bo was of this world," his friend Dr. Joseph Pursch would later say, "but he was not for this world. He was like a child. All his life, by acting out socially and sexually, he tried to defend himself. Then he lost baseball, and he had nothing left. That's when alcohol and drugs got him." But whatever the sources of Belinsky's pain, by the end he had achieved some degree of self-knowledge. "Bo was becoming more normal, thinking about the continuity of life," says Pursch. Adds Chance, "For the first time, Bo got around quality people, and that made him feel much better about himself."

For Belinsky's brass grave marker, two of those people — Lou Rodophele and Don Richardson — selected a motif that honors his greatest achievements. Beneath an image of a baseball appear the words NO HITTER and the date 5/5/62. Next to the legend is another image — a cross. At long last, Bo had found a home.

The Sprinter

FROM SPORTS ILLUSTRATED

You know the story. There was an accident, maybe something in the genes, maybe a drunken driver crossing the divide. An arm was lost or the bones didn't form or the eyesight faded away. The upshot: something vital is missing. It's an adversity most of us cannot imagine, so we call it a tragedy. But now the victim has "overcome" it, now he is wearing USA across his chest and wheeling himself fast down a basketball court or drawing back a bowstring to launch a golden arrow. The moment provides an inspiring finale — *It's a triumph of the human spirit, Bob* — but the central fact remains; the story always bends itself around what's gone. The arm, the leg, the eyesight.

Cue the soft music, zoom in on the stony face with the thousand-yard stare. *When he was five years old,* the narrator intones, *Marlon Shirley lost his foot. . . .*

Here he comes, cutting around the curve. The midmorning light catches the metallic blur of his left leg as it swings down and pounds the rubbery track. Here he comes, the fastest man on one foot, a two-time Paralympic gold medalist, the only leg amputee to have broken eleven seconds in the 100-meter dash. On this March day the other athletes working out at the Olympic Training Center in Chula Vista, California, have no disability worse than flat feet, yet they say that Shirley's explosion out of the blocks, his graceful transition into the sprinter's lean, is something to envy. But who's kidding whom? Technique isn't what makes him remarkable.

No, it's the foot he lost in a lawn-mower accident, and though he takes pains to make sure no one ever sees the scars, Shirley isn't exactly shy. He plops onto a chair trackside, gasping, and pulls his stockinged stump out of its racing prosthesis with all the ceremony — and the audible *pop* — of a waiter uncorking a cheap bottle of wine. It's hard, at such a moment, for a first-time viewer to take in all that Shirley treats so casually: the socket custom-made in a lab in Oklahoma City, the band of lightweight carbon fiber bowed like a cheetah's hind leg, the sawed-off front half of an athletic shoe. He sits for a while in the sun, stump thrown over that $15,000 biomechanical marvel, until it's time to run again. The socket hisses as he slides the stump back in. The effect is a mass of contradiction — weakness and strength, the human and the high-tech, Captain Ahab meets Blade Runner — but Shirley has grown used to stares.

The other athletes, though, don't look twice. Shirley likes that better. He is the only Paralympian training full time at the center these days, but nobody treats him as if he's different or tries to help him too much. He jaws it up this morning with hurdler Micah Harris about a woman they met, and only if you pay close attention do you notice that Shirley's rhythm is off; he doesn't quite nail the macho banter of jocks at rest.

Now he's standing at the line with his hands on his hips, watching U.S. discus champ Jarred Rome drag a weight sled. Shirley tries again. "You know anybody from Utah State?" he asks. He mentions a name, an event the guy ran, but Rome shows no sign of recognition. "I think he became a coach," Shirley says. He pauses a beat before blurting, "He's a Vegas pimp now!"

He spits out a short, hard laugh. Rome looks puzzled and the conversation dies, but to anyone who knows Shirley's past, the words hang out there, curdling. He puts his head down and runs. It's impossible not to focus on the foot as he churns past, even though he has made it clear that his isn't that kind of story. Yes, he lost something vital once. But the lawn mower was not what crippled him, was not what threw up obstacles he may never overcome. That was something else, and it made the instant his foot slid into the blade seem like a blessing.

"One of the best things that happened to me," he says.

From the start, he was groping in the dark. The boy lay on his bed, and the lights in the orphanage would go out, and this vicious hum would begin in his head, growing louder and louder until he would scream to drown it out. The adults would come and restrain him. He fought a bit, but he didn't cry. Marlon Shirley knows that about himself, if little else: he almost never cried. He was five years old when he was sent to the orphanage. He doesn't know if, in the years before that, he ever saw his mother servicing strange men. He remembers her being gone a lot. He remembers her being passed out. But she was his mother. He doesn't remember not wanting to be with her. Then one day he wasn't.

He didn't learn why until he was twenty-two. His mom, Lindy Lebolo, was like him in one sense: she needed to run fast. She'd been moving since she was twelve, really, one of those Catholic girls bucking off Daddy's strict ways — in and out of schools, reformatories, detention centers. She wasn't that bright, but she was blond and tall and loose, attracting bad boys the way sugar draws ants. Her parents lost her; her hometown, Richmond, couldn't hold her; at eighteen she was gone. Her dad, Herman Joseph Lebolo, a pilot for American Airlines, was old-school Italian and racist too. So at nineteen Lindy hit the rebel-girl jackpot. According to her sister, Peggy, their mom found Lindy in a big empty house in Tampa, pregnant, barefoot, and with only one dress to wear, too far along to have an abortion and too scared to leave. Her boyfriend, a black pimp, kept her close and made her turn tricks. Lindy wasn't the first.

After Marlon was born — April 21, 1978 — Lindy took off for California, Minnesota, Hawaii, latching on to one screwup guy after another. The pimp's other girls would call the Lebolos in Richmond, trying to find out where Lindy was. "She wanted to get away from him and give Marlon a life," says Peggy, "but this guy was like an octopus." The way the family heard it, he caught up with Lindy in Las Vegas. She was in a phone booth. He stepped inside and broke both her hands.

Lindy had a small inheritance, but the money couldn't keep her off the street or off heroin. She set herself and Marlon up at the Blue Angel Motel, in the Vegas tenderloin, off Fremont Street. By the time he was four, Marlon says, he came and went as he pleased, holed up with a pack of street kids in a storage room at the Angel, slept under the freeway sometimes, cadged leftovers from a manager at Carl's Jr. "One night she was passed out on our bed,"

Marlon says, "and I couldn't wake her, so I cut the back pocket off her pants so I could get some money for food. I cut the pocket off with a pair of scissors." It's all fuzzy, though, his memory full of what he calls "my black holes." No matter: it was no way for a boy to live, so, Peggy says, her father told the police where to find his daughter and grandson. Marlon was five when he got picked up, wearing only a bathing suit, walking the street.

The social services people who picked him up bought him a Happy Meal. Marlon remembers the toy inside; he remembers, too, being told by his grandmother years later that his grandfather had refused to let him come live with the family in Richmond because he was half black. "My father just had a bad problem with that," Peggy says. So Marlon began the pinball life of an institutional orphan, first at Child Haven in Vegas, then at the Children's Home in Boulder City, Nevada. Within months of his arrival there in 1984, he and another boy went chasing the caretaker as he rode his rotary mower; Marlon slipped, and his foot got pulped.

"It was disgusting," he says. "They stitched most of it up, but that night nobody was there to tell me I didn't really have a foot, and I jumped out of the bed and reruptured it. That's when they amputated it."

His mother visited him once in the hospital. She didn't talk, just set down a Snoopy doll as he slept. Marlon awoke as she left. His final sight of his mother was of her back going out the door. Not long after, he was taken to get his prosthesis. "My mom must've died," he said to a caseworker at the Children's Home. "Because, why hasn't she come to see me?"

He bounced among foster homes. When he was seven, Marlon got his first good shot at adoption with a military couple. They dubbed him Michael and gave him the family name, but Marlon - couldn't settle down, couldn't stay out of trouble. The father picked him up by his legs once and banged his face against a headboard. After getting caught sneaking into his Halloween candy, Marlon was ordered to eat it all; when he vomited, the parents gave him a spoon and told him to eat that too. After eighteen months eight-year-old Marlon came home from school one day to find his bags packed and his bed standing against a wall. Shipped back to the Children's Home, he didn't complain. It wasn't his way.

"In our business everyone's a victim," says John Sprouse, then the social work supervisor at the Children's Home. "You hope that down the road the kids will go from victim to survivor. What distinguished Marlon? Not once did I see him use his foot to get something, to get pity. He just got on with life."

After all, Marlon figured he was alone. He didn't know there was someone else in the dark, searching too. In the late '80s Marlene Shirley, a Mormon living in the tiny farming community of Thatcher, Utah, with her husband, Kerry, and three children, wanted a fourth. Difficulties in her previous pregnancies didn't deter her: Marlene saw a TV news segment about orphans and took home a box full of files and pictures from Child and Family Services. Marlon's photo struck her instantly. At first it made little sense to adopt him — nine years old, needing thousands of dollars of prosthetic work — and even less when she learned about his brutal past, his mixed-race background. How would that go over in white-bread Utah? Her parents expressed reservations, files were not sent on time, red tape built up. Marlene bulled ahead. As the Shirleys' application progressed, Lindy broke four years of silence and asked to meet with Marlon. Sprouse told her to call back in a week; she never did. "Marlon was *supposed* to be part of our family," Marlene says.

But there's a reason it gets difficult to place orphans as they age: each year the baggage is heavier, harder to handle. "We tell every adoptive family of an older child: when that kid comes into your home, there will be a crisis," Sprouse says. "Your home will be turned upside down." Marlon arrived at the Shirleys' the day after Christmas 1987, and the crises began. He had no idea how to be part of a family; he got along well enough with his new siblings — Keri Beth, Tim, and Mary — but things kept disappearing, odd items like peanut butter and small tools. Marlon got caught stealing money from a teacher's purse. Marlene escorted him to juvenile court more than once. Kerry's long shifts at the fire department didn't help, but Marlon had been Marlene's idea. He lashed out at the only mother at hand.

Marlene prayed, but nothing changed. In her journal she admitted, *I sometimes dream of having back the simple days before Marlon came.* He had always been fast, and he tried playing tailback and running track at Bear River High despite his walking prosthesis. He dropped both to take a job changing tires and repairing brakes at an auto mechanic's, playing softball and basketball in the church league. When he was a junior, Marlene heard hints from Marlon about suicide — Marlon insists she was overreacting — and the Shirleys drove him to a Salt Lake City treatment center for a month of observation. That drive was the only time in his life he remembers crying.

Midway through his senior year, close to flunking out and humiliated, Marlon let Marlene have it. For two hours he detailed what a terrible mother she'd been. His girlfriend, his buddies, everyone in school knew he'd been put in a place with padded walls. "I'm going to leave home," he said, "and never come back." She admitted mistakes. He didn't care. The tirade broke her. Marlene went to her room and whispered, *Heavenly Father, I'm not sure why you wanted me to adopt him, but I've done all I know how to do. I'm at the end of my rope. I'm basically turning him back over to you because I don't know what to do.*

The end of high school loomed. Life's great crossroads, and a young man was about to hit it with no diploma, half a leg, and a headful of ghosts. "And I was heartbroken inside," Marlene says.

When Marlon Shirley walks — away from the track, wearing his street prosthesis and pants and a jaunty cap — you would never know one of his legs ends in a knob about two inches above where the ankle should be. He races to take the point in any group, and the slight dip in his stride is more a matter of style, a hint of that cocky ambulation used to warn off trouble in high school halls. It's something he works on; the comfort of limping is a constant temptation, but succumbing to it isn't an option. No, he's about action: golf, four-wheeling, in-line skating; he flies planes for fun. A bartender throws her arm over his shoulder or he meets a woman at a party? He's not telling her about the foot. "I want it to be a shock to them," he says.

"Put it like this," he goes on. "My leg is my greatest strength and my greatest weakness. I make a point of dressing well. I'm told no one takes more showers than I do. I got rid of my earrings, necklaces, anything that's a distraction, because I want people to think that I can be, you know, sexy. I want people to see strength."

On the track, of course, Shirley is defined by his disability, and he has been able to make a good living precisely because of our fascination with the weakness. But it doesn't take much for the able-bodied world to seem ghoulish, and his antennae are always up. One woman he dated seemed fine when he told her about the foot; then she went home and Googled Marlon and called him in tears: "Oh, that's so *special.*" He never went out with her again.

But let's face it, we want to see that stump and that racing foot because they are what they are — visually startling, a living nightmare. For able-bodied spectators, the Paralympics offer a chance to rubberneck a highway wreck but also feel good about it. It's revealing that Shirley was able, by 2003, to sign with companies like Visa, McDonald's, and Home Depot, but he couldn't secure a shoe sponsorship until last month, when he signed a four-year deal with Reebok worth close to $500,000. That reverses the norm; able-bodied athletes don't make the crossover to nonsports endorsements until their personas and résumés fill out. But Shirley had unprecedented assets: he had a disability that made visual impact, but he wasn't so disabled that he could make a product memorable for the wrong reason. Most important, his backstory suggested the absolutely necessary happy ending. The underlying message of disabled sports is always triumph, because who would be nervy enough to market "the agony of defeat" on top of anguish beyond measure? So everyone is a winner. Everyone is just happy to take part.

Never mind that such rhetoric appalls Shirley and his peers, who train — and live — to win. "They compete just as hard as we do," says former decathlete Dan O'Brien, the Olympic gold medalist in 1996. "Marlon reminds me of myself when I was young: he wants it bad. He thinks like a champion. He's willing to work anywhere, with anybody, to become a champion." Want to see Paralympians get mad? Confuse their endeavor with the Special Olympics. "People are happy that I just made it down the track," Shirley says. "They pat me on my head and say, 'Good for you: you won the race before you even got in the blocks.' Bulls ——! Not everybody in my sport gets a medal, and they're sure as hell not passing out gold medals before you get into the blocks."

Yet even on his terms, Shirley's turning point was irresistibly feel-good. In February 1997, just weeks after his fight with Marlene, he told her he was driving up to Pocatello, Idaho, to compete in the Simplot Games — the largest open high school indoor track meet west of the Mississippi. He hoped to get offered a college scholarship. It was nonsensical: Marlon's track experience was almost nil, and he was hobbling on crutches because he'd fractured a bone in his stump while dunking a basketball. "I have to do this," Marlon said. Marlene swallowed hard and asked if he needed money.

He entered the high jump, his discipline during his brief foray on the Bear River track team. Bryan Hoddle, who coached sprinter Tony Volpentest at the Atlanta Paralympics in '96, was sitting in the stands and saw Shirley hop over on his good leg and dive headfirst over the bar. It was ridiculous — the scissor kick and backflop are far more efficient techniques — except that Shirley cleared six feet six inches. Hoddle sought him out, asked if he'd heard of the Paralympics. No, Marlon said. "Well," Hoddle said, "you just cleared the Paralympic world record."

A month later Shirley joined Hoddle in Chula Vista for a Disabled Sports USA track meet offering prize money. When his turn came, he hopped to the bar not noticing that officials were measuring the previous jump for a world record. Too late to stop, Shirley took off, cleared two officials and their measuring tape, then the bar. By the end of the weekend he was $13,000 richer and planning to head north to train with Hoddle in Olympia, Washington. There the coach tested the six-foot-one, 190-pound Shirley for strength, "and his power levels were off the charts," Hoddle says. "They were way higher than any normal high school track athlete's."

Now, instead of being a handicap, his lost foot gave the nineteen-year-old focus, confidence, a chance to be somebody. Here, for the kid in the dark, the one with every excuse to be in jail or high, was a sudden stab of light.

He needed it. Marlon had never spoken much about Las Vegas with the Shirleys, but he had hardly left Fremont Street behind. After he went to train with Hoddle, Marlene went to clean his room, pulled out the bed — and stared. There it all was: the jars of peanut butter, lost bags of Cheetos, a case of soda, missing silverware, pliers and wrenches, supplies hoarded over the years just in case. "He had learned these survival skills of a little boy," Marlene says. "If it was under his bed he would know, *At least I won't starve to death.*"

Leaving home loosened Marlon's defenses. Memories had always flashed through his head: faces, place names, a car accident, feelings that left him physically ill. Now Marlon began to run straight at the questions: Who am I? Where do I belong? It would take him years to understand that losing his foot had been a kind of gift, but he began sensing that the Shirleys had been his salvation. A few months after he'd moved to Washington, Marlon was on the phone with Marlene, and at the end of the conversation she told him she loved him. He said good-bye and hung up. Two minutes later he called back, and for the first time he told Marlene he loved her too.

Still, she wasn't Lindy. Where had Lindy gone? In 2000 the twenty-two-year-old Marlon was glancing at some old legal papers when he noticed the scrawled name "Minnie Lebolo" and a phone number. Two months before the Paralympic Games in Sydney he finally dialed it. When his grandmother came to the phone, he said, across 2,400 miles and seventeen years, "This is Marlon." Minnie broke into sobs. "I'm sorry to tell you," she said, "but your mother is dead."

She told him the essentials: That his mother had been a prostitute. That his father had been her pimp. Why his grandfather would never take Marlon in. "Your mother loved you very much," she said, "but she never left anything for you."

The conversation left him with more questions than ever. He went to Sydney, shocked favorite Brian Frasure to win the 100 meters and broke the Paralympic record by .24 of a second with a time of 11.09, took silver in the high jump by clearing 6'2⅖", became his sport's new superstar. But what Marlon remembers most is how hollow it felt without the Shirleys there. He sent newspaper clips and a video to his grandmother, and she sent him a card with three photographs. After that he heard nothing from her. In the spring of 2002 he dialed Minnie for the second time. She told him that his grandfather was ill. He never spoke to her again.

So imagine this: you're a twenty-six-year-old man, and a reporter is filling you in on the details of your own life. That phone call with your grandmother? Your grandfather died later that day. Your grandmother? She died a year and a half ago. The reporter has spoken with your Aunt Peggy, and she has told him things no one ever told you: That your mother died of kidney failure while living in Bullhead City, Arizona, in September 1992. That she was buried on her thirty-fifth birthday in Richmond. That your grandfather was the one responsible for having you taken away from her. Peggy also told the reporter some other family history, reminders of how blood can travel: That your grandfather, like you, was a pilot. That your great-grandfather, like you, liked gadgets and driving his car out in the wild and, as a firefighter, lost a leg in an accident.

Peggy told plenty, but not what Marlon wanted to know most. "Did she tell you why they didn't talk to me?" he asks, his voice rising. "Did she tell you that?"

Here's one thing he doesn't know and may never: whether his father is alive. Here's one thing he doesn't know and will someday: whether, after retiring from sports, he can handle the shards of his broken life without drawing blood. In the spring of 2001 Shirley drove into Las Vegas for the first time as a man and promptly got lost. Pulling over to get his bearings, he looked up to find himself staring at the familiar old motel sign, the one with that twenty-foot blond blue angel rotating on top. He doesn't know whether to be bitter about his past or numb or sad. Sometimes he's all these at once. Maybe what matters is that Shirley is aware. He knows the flamboyant mess he could make of his life. His struggle to keep things clean could almost be called heroic.

"I know there's demons I'm fighting every day," he says one night at a restaurant in Chula Vista. "I've had some of the best relationships a guy could have, given my circumstances — not the sharpest-looking guy in the world, got a prosthetic leg — and, my gosh, have I had some of the best girlfriends ever. But when it comes down to it, something about me just . . ." He snaps a finger. "As much as I want a family, something makes it hard for me to do that. And it scares the hell out of me.

"I haven't gone off the deep end, but there are some emotional problems there that aren't fixed," he says. "Track and field is a big distraction. I don't have to sit and think about these other things. So . . . we'll see." A few minutes pass; then he says, "Remind me to show you my pictures."

He drives back to the training center, fast as always. In his room he picks up a blocky chrome frame holding the three small photos Minnie sent. Two are unfocused, unposed shots of Marlon and Lindy taken in Hawaii, but the third is nice: he's about three years old and sitting on her lap, naked. Both of them are smiling. "I know she wanted to be with me," Shirley says. "She must've cared for me, or she wouldn't have kept me as long as she did."

In the picture he appears full-bodied. There's the left foot, dangling: his proof. Before the picture arrived, Marlon had only memories of what the boy and the blue angel looked like then. "And I'm beginning to forget those times," he says. Gently he puts down the frame, his one way back to the way he used to be.

Last September 25, in Athens, Marlon Shirley won the Paralympic 100-meter gold medal for the second straight time. For his sponsors and his wallet and a U.S. Paralympics organization desperate for growth, this was a great relief. The branding of Shirley as "the world's fastest amputee" and "the golden boy of the Paralympic Games" could continue apace for another four years. He left Athens as essentially the same hot property, no matter that he had become a far different athlete.

Indeed, Shirley had been more than the most prominent Paralympian when the Games began. What with his aim of winning five golds — in the 100 and 200 meters, the 4×100 and 4×400 relays, and the long jump — and his oft-stated ambition to compete in the nationals against able-bodied athletes, he had the mainstream crossover potential that no one had considered when Paralympics began as a rehab program for injured veterans in post–World War II London. But by the end of the 100 final, Shirley's five-gold hopes were gutted. His right hamstring had popped, his winning time of 11.08 matched his world record, and Oscar — already people had dropped his last name — had come within .08 of a second of beating him.

"I'm running world-record speed," Shirley says, replaying video of the race on his computer, "and I can hear his legs just coming at me." He stares at the screen. "That's the most ridiculous velocity I've ever seen."

Shirley has started working with a new coaching staff. He should hit the peak of his sprinting powers just in time for Beijing, and he'll need to because South African sprinter Oscar Pistorius, despite being only seventeen and missing both legs, hit the Athens Paralympics with all the shock and force of a blizzard in July. Pistorius crushed a 200-meter field featuring Shirley and the then world-record holder, Frasure. In the semifinals Pistorius got stuck coming out of the starting blocks and still ran down the field to win. In the final Shirley ran 22.67 — a world record for a one-legged amputee — and Oscar still beat him by 11 meters, in 21.97.

"From here on out," Shirley told Frasure, "I guess I'm going to be a 100-meter specialist." Oscar had humbled him.

Such detail would only clutter the usual triumph-of-the-human-spirit story, but then Shirley's has never been that kind of story. Nothing about his tale is simple, not even the best parts. When asked whether Marlon's rise had had an impact on the Lebolo family, Peggy said, "It was just a good thing that we knew a good feeling, that he was taken care of and he was doing well and he made something out of himself. That would make Lindy proud, and he should be proud of himself too. I'm sorry he had to live with those Mormon people, but it seems he has a good head on his shoulders, if he just stays away from white girls." She didn't ask for Marlon's phone number.

Marlon isn't sure he wants to call her either. This is no inspirational video. It's his life. And despite its horrific details, it is, like any other life, a search for love and home, two steps forward and one back, no matter whether the feet are flesh or carbon fiber. Most lives don't end on the victory stand. Most victories take years, not seconds, and the only reward might be knowing when they happen. Shirley knew in Athens. His triumph came after he lost.

This was four days before the 100, just after he had watched Oscar fly so easily by him to win the 200 final. Marlon had no time for self-pity, no chance to feel empty. Up in the stands Marlene, Kerry, and Mary Shirley sat clutching a big U.S. flag; they couldn't have afforded the trip, so he had paid for them. As their plane had descended into Athens, Marlene had marveled at how far they'd come. *Is this real?* she thought. *What if I had given up?*

Now it was nearing 6:30 P.M. on September 21, and he was walking to the edge of the track. He motioned up to his family. "I'd got my ass beat hard, but it didn't matter," Marlon recalls. "The only thing that mattered was what I hate people to say about me: that I had made it there. But it wasn't that I had made it to the Games or that I had made it down the track. It was that I made it and my parents were able to be there and share it with me. They were able to see what they had helped blossom. It wasn't just a race. It showed why we were put here."

Mary took him the flag, and Marlon waved to Marlene to come down. He wanted her there. He had been chasing Lindy all his life; part of him always will. But Marlon was a cripple once, and the crutch had found him. Now Marlene was coming down the steps, smiling. Marlon unfurled the flag and pulled her close and wrapped the cloth around the both of them. He held up his head and yelled, "This is my *mom!*"

The crowd cheered. Marlene's heart filled. And for one moment Marlon's life became that kind of story after all.

L. JON WERTHEIM

Saved by Sports

FROM SPORTS ILLUSTRATED

THEY ALL HAVE A STORY. Everyone in Arena Football2 can recite a saga that purports to explain why he's playing in this quirky indoor league that's at least a Hail Mary from the NFL, earning $200 a game, and living in a motel room by the interstate. Just scan the field at the Albany (New York) Conquest's training camp, and you'll see what we mean. The guy throwing those quick out passes? He's the starting quarterback, D. Bryant. He played for Duke but transferred to Iowa Wesleyan and never found traction there. The guy rushing the passer? That's linebacker Jameel Dumas, who was a star at Syracuse before blowing out his left knee. The kicker sitting on his helmet in the end zone? Vinny Cirrincione, a local kid. By the time he realized he had a knack for booting an oblong ball through the uprights, he had skipped college to work at his parents' pizzeria.

"Everyone is here for a reason — a bad decision, an injury, a personal problem, something that derailed his career," says Albany's coach, Richard Davis, a disarmingly straight-talking Texan who himself will last only six games before being fired by the Conquest. "People see this league as a pipeline. These guys are happy for this chance, but they aren't necessarily satisfied being here. They're aspiring to the NFL. At least I hope they are!"

But this spring there was one player who was content simply to be running around the turf in Albany's Pepsi Arena. Jermaine Ewell couldn't stop smiling as he worked through the tip drills and the thug drills, absorbing and dispensing hits. Making it to the NFL had once been his obsession. But that was a long time ago. His dreadlocks poking out from a helmet that obscured the zippers of surgical scars on his head, the six-foot-one, 230-pound Ewell was simply experiencing football again: the sounds, the rhythms, the lulls followed by spasms of violence. That was plenty.

Ewell wouldn't survive the Conquest's final cuts, but that almost didn't matter. He was back on the field. At thirty-one he was nearly a decade older than some of his teammates, but he didn't look it. He hadn't played more than a few weeks of football since 1990, but he concealed that pretty well too. On the day he handed in his playbook, he picked up his bag and thanked the coaches for the audition. He was gone before most of the other players got wind of *his* how-I-ended-up-here story — the most arresting tale of them all.

They called him the Streak. Playing linebacker and fullback for the Lawrence (New York) High Golden Tornadoes, Jermaine Ewell was a brutal tackler with a rippling upper body and a sixth sense for where a play was headed. But his biggest asset was his speed. Timed in the 40-yard dash at 4.4 seconds, he was the fastest kid on the field, a DSL modem in a dial-up league. "You'd think there was no way Jermaine could make the play," says Richard Mollo, his coach then, "but he was so quick, it was like — *bam!* — and the other guy would be on the ground with Jermaine on top of him."

In the fall of 1990, Jermaine's junior season, he led the team in solo tackles. Before he was named to various all-conference and all-county teams, scouts and coaches from college programs on the order of Virginia Tech sat in the Lawrence bleachers to get a look at him. A solid senior season and Jermaine would be a lock to get a full ride in Division I-A. "He got better with every game," says Pat Palleschi, a co-captain that season who later played at Hofstra. "There was no doubt he was going to play at the next level."

Jermaine was a minor celebrity throughout the Five Towns — a string of communities on the South Shore of Long Island that includes Lawrence — but it was as much for his winning personality as for what he did on the football field. He may have been an African-American kid in a predominantly white and Jewish enclave, the son of a domestic in one of the most affluent zip codes in the United States, but he moved easily in all social circles. Despite a learning disability that kept his grades in the B and C range, Jermaine was beloved by his teachers. The odd jobs he did (mowing yards, painting houses, restoring deck chairs) put him in touch with the community's adult movers and shakers. "He was the coolest kid you could imagine," says Mollo, a father figure to Jermaine, whose dad had died a few years before. "Guys, girls, older, younger, black, white, jock, not a jock — everyone wanted to be his friend."

Syd Mandelbaum, a former Lawrence school board member who runs a hunger relief organization, offers perhaps the highest praise in the Five Towns' lexicon: he says Jermaine was "a real mensch." So it was no surprise that when trouble found Jermaine, a crowd rushed to his defense.

On June 1, 1991, the last Saturday night of his junior year, Jermaine, then seventeen, went to a "key party" — at which underage drinkers could suckle on a keg provided they surrendered their car keys to the host — and met up with a girl named Nikki Diamond. This didn't go over well with one of Nikki's old flames, Shannon Siegel. A husky former baseball star at Lawrence who was the starting third baseman at Adelphi College, Siegel was at the party with his pickup basketball buddy James "Jimbo" Peralta and three of Jimbo's pals from the Bayside section of Queens: Ian Pearl, David Donahue, and Gregory Kussoff. Nikki would later claim that, out of Jermaine's earshot, Siegel asked her what she was doing with "nigger money." (Jermaine had given Nikki $5 to pay the party's admission and beer charge.) Siegel vigorously denies having used the N-word but concedes that he and his pals had been drinking and were giving Nikki a hard time.

Regardless, when Nikki told Jermaine what Siegel had said, Jermaine was offended. But more than that, he was confused. They had mutual friends, and they'd never had a problem. Two months earlier they had been part of a small group that had driven to Manhattan to visit a club. Now, as Jermaine confronted Siegel, an army of classmates backed him up. No one raised a fist — certainly not Jermaine, who didn't even curse, much less fight. But it was made clear that Siegel and his four friends were no longer welcome at the party. "It wasn't like some sort of big feud," Jermaine recalls. "They were drinking. They said things they shouldn't have said. They left. I thought it was cool."

It wasn't cool. Siegel was reeling not only from a forty-ounce Olde English malt liquor but also from a potent cocktail of rage, immaturity, and humiliation. A few years earlier Siegel could have staked a claim to being the Man at Lawrence High. Now, clearly, there was a new Man — who liked a girl he had once liked. Worse,

Siegel had just been chased from a party by a group of kids, most of whom had been *freshmen* when he was a senior, in front of his pal Jimbo and Jimbo's running buddies. "I should have walked away," Siegel says. "Jermaine and I would have seen each other the next day and probably hugged."

Instead, Siegel and his companions peeled off in two cars, met up at a gas station, and hatched a plan. They would go to Siegel's home, arm themselves with stickball bats, return to the party, and kick some Lawrence High ass.

At the party, meanwhile, the kegs had been drained and most of the crowd had retreated to the nearby Atlantic Beach boardwalk, which runs between the Atlantic Ocean and a bay. Around midnight Jermaine was leaning on a railing and talking to Nikki when Siegel, Peralta, Pearl, Donahue, and Kussoff showed up. According to several witnesses, Siegel, the college baseball player, took the first cut. Jermaine never saw the blow coming. The wood collided violently with the right side of his head. He was likely unconscious before his head slammed against the boardwalk. For the next twenty to thirty seconds, witnesses say, the gang of five beat and kicked Jermaine's head as if it were a piñata.

Stephen Lieberman and Tony Franzese, two Lawrence kids, were hanging out on the boardwalk and heard Nikki screaming. They jumped on top of Jermaine to protect him. For their heroism they got the business end of the bats and suffered minor injuries.

By the time the beating had ended and the five marauders had scattered, Jermaine's body was convulsing. In the emergency room of Peninsula General Hospital, in Far Rockaway, he lost his pulse and his heartbeat. "Medically," the ER physician would later say, "he died in front of me." Jermaine was revived but remained in a coma. His head had swelled to twice its normal size. When Coach Mollo arrived at the hospital, doctors asked if he'd thought of what to tell his players in case Jermaine died. When Jermaine's mother, Earnestine, arrived, the doctors had a question for her too.

"Is your son an organ donor?"

Jermaine Ewell didn't die that night. Neurosurgeon Chris Overby, figuring there was nothing to lose, performed an emergency craniotomy, drilling through Jermaine's skull to remove a blood clot and repair lacerations in his brain. As Jermaine lay comatose, hundreds of Lawrence classmates and people from the community gathered in the hospital parking lot.

When Jermaine emerged from the coma five days later, he told a friend, "Shannon Siegel snuffed me." He had slurred speech, searing headaches, and no vision in one eye. He was hooked up to tubes and held down by restraints. The kid who'd had 4.4 speed a week earlier was unable to move his legs. Even the trauma specialist used the word *grotesque* to describe Jermaine's state. "If he hadn't been in such superb physical condition and with such strong organs, he probably wouldn't have survived that night," says Overby. "Statistically, he should be dead or in a persistent vegetative state."

Anyone who'd seen Jermaine put up plates of iron in the Lawrence High weight room was aware of his physical strength. But his internal fortitude surprised even those closest to him. When he was allowed to receive visitors, he cracked self-deprecating jokes and thanked folks for coming by. "From the very beginning he was so at peace with what happened to him, it was almost eerie," says Tamara Steckler, Jermaine's godmother. "He was not sure if he'd walk again, and he was the one cheering up everyone in the room."

He approached rehab the same way he'd approached football: by setting goals, training like hell, and seeing where it got him. When the pain from the headaches kicked in, he took Motrin and shook it off. When the blurred vision made him sleepy, he forced himself to stay awake and pushed on. He hadn't reached those 250 pounds on the bench press overnight, so now, too, he would work to gradually build his body back up. He went from a wheelchair to using a walker to walking with a cane.

Instead of working out twice a day in preparation for a monster senior season, as he had planned, Jermaine spent his summer in the hospital. From there he went to Gaylord Hospital, a rehabilitation center in Wallingford, Connecticut, where nurses grew accustomed to hearing him groan in the middle of the night as he rose early to start his exercises. Once he disobeyed the doctors and tried to walk down the hall without his cane. His legs gave out, he fell, and his plastic urine bag exploded. When the nurses found him lying on the floor, soaked in his own urine, he was giggling. "Guess I fumbled," he told them.

The case of Jermaine Ewell had all the markings of a cause célèbre. It was a perfect storm of topics the mass media find irresistible:

kids, sports, violence, and, not least, race. Plus it came at a time when race relations in the New York City area were at a low point. Two years earlier a black teenager named Yusuf Hawkins had been fatally shot in broad daylight for having had the audacity to walk around the predominantly white Bensonhurst section of Brooklyn. Not long after Jermaine was beaten, in the summer of 1991, Yankel Rosenbaum, a rabbinical student from Australia, would be stabbed to death by a young man in a crowd of African Americans in the Brooklyn neighborhood of Crown Heights. Without much effort the assault on Jermaine could have been made part of the same ugly tapestry: a black football star gets bludgeoned into a coma by a gang of white kids over an interracial relationship.

Except that Jermaine and his family wouldn't let that happen. Scan the newspaper accounts from 1991, and you won't find Jermaine making a single disparaging remark about his attackers. "Honestly, I was just concentrating on my recovery," he says now. "I didn't have to suppress anger or revenge or anything like that, because I couldn't spend energy on that. I had to put everything I had into getting better."

While Jermaine was still in the hospital, the Reverend Al Sharpton organized a racially charged protest on the boardwalk where the beating had occurred. Jermaine's relatives sent word that they had no interest in being involved. "He was trying to make it something it wasn't," Jermaine says of Sharpton. "This was about five guys, and four of them weren't even from here. To try and paint the entire community [as racist] was unfair." Sharpton's rally went on as planned, but without the subject of it lending his support, it fizzled.

If Jermaine treated his recovery as a competitive sport, the community was his team. When word got out that he lacked health insurance, donations rolled in. Classmates sent dollar bills, sometimes even coins. Doctors, lawyers, and bankers sent hundreds and sometimes thousands of dollars. Strangers offered to run errands for Jermaine's mom. Once he left the hospital, Jermaine couldn't go to a deli or diner without someone offering to pick up the tab.

"The way the people here supported me — and I don't just mean the money — was unbelievable," he says. "I felt that people were cheering for me, the same as when I was playing football."

Beyond a full recovery, Jermaine's overarching goal was to graduate with his class at Lawrence High. He needed a full-time tutor. He needed to take tests without time limits. But on June 30, 1992, he walked gingerly down the aisle and picked up his diploma as applause and tears cascaded about him.

Meanwhile, the five attackers had been arrested and charged with a variety of crimes, including attempted murder. Predictably their ties, tenuous to begin with, frayed quickly, and each man pointed a finger at someone else. Donahue agreed to plead guilty to second-degree riot, partially in exchange for testifying against Siegel, and was sentenced only to probation. Siegel defiantly went to trial and, contradicting many witnesses, asserted that not only had he never struck Jermaine but he had also tried to talk the other four defendants out of the attack. Siegel was convicted of first-degree assault as well as conspiracy, riot, and criminal possession of a weapon. Imposing a sentence of seven to twenty years, Nassau County Court Judge Donald Belfi gave Siegel a withering stare and said, "To jump someone from behind and to beat him as he lay unconscious is the epitome of cowardice."

After that Kussoff, Pearl, and Peralta quickly pleaded out. None of the three would spend more than three years in prison.

There were no bars or walls or spools of razor wire around Jermaine, but he too had to live with limits on his freedom and potential. He enrolled at Howard University in Washington, D.C., but dropped out when his short-term memory loss and persistent headaches made it almost impossible to keep up with schoolwork. He turned inward and seldom left his house. While he was grateful for the sympathy from so many quarters — his favorite football team, the New York Jets, named him honorary captain for a game and invited him to watch from a luxury suite — the attention began to embarrass him. "Just picking up the pieces and trying to get things back to normal," he says with a sigh, "was harder than I'd ever imagined."

He spent most of his twenties in a fog that seemed impenetrable at times. He has no doubt about what enabled him to disperse it. "Being an athlete is what saved me," he says. "It saved me that night, and it saved me throughout this whole process. *Put a goal in front of me, I'm gonna reach it and then go for the next one.* That's pretty much the essence of what an athlete does."

In time he was walking without his cane and putting on muscle.

His stamina and equilibrium improved. "Who knows," he confided to a friend one day, "I may even play football again."

If there's anything worse than going to prison, it might be going to prison as a suburban white kid convicted of an assault with racial overtones. Shannon Siegel was braced for the worst. But after spending the last thirteen years at Clinton Correctional Facility in Dannemora, New York, he says he hasn't had so much as a heated argument with another inmate. The guards back him up on this.

See, being an athlete has saved Siegel too. Smallish, somewhat pasty, and prone to stammering when he gets nervous, inmate 93A1482 may not cut an imposing figure, but when other prisoners saw him throw a perfect spiral or go deep in the hole to field a ground ball or pull up on the fast break to pop a jumper, he gained a measure of status. Siegel figures he plays sports twenty hours a week, mostly during yard time, prison's version of recess. It falls to him to fashion balls out of tape and other items. It also falls to Siegel, a former New York Mets spring training batboy, to arbitrate discussions about the best teams.

"I know you always hear it, but sports really do break down barriers," Siegel says. "You might not think that growing up on Long Island is the best preparation for maximum-security prison, but sports, you know, make differences go away."

He also uses the sports calendar to keep connected to the outside world. He has never surfed the Web or used a cell phone or downloaded tunes onto an iPod. His slang is stuck in the early '90s, and he makes references to television shows that have been off the air for years. But as long as he can read Knicks box scores or turn his transistor radio at the right angle to pick up Mets games late at night — "Go ahead and quiz me about any New York team," he pleads — life isn't completely whizzing by him.

Like Ewell, Siegel has made the best of his circumstances. He earned a college degree by correspondence and became the first inmate in Clinton's history to receive an advanced degree — an MBA from City University in Bellevue, Washington. His prison job is to help other inmates earn their GEDs. More than one hundred men have done so under his tutelage.

Still, Siegel has had oceans of time to try to make sense of June 1, 1991. What could account for his lapse in humanity? How could a college baseball player with no police record, a new Corvette, and a newer girlfriend beat another man's brains out? "I was drunk, I was young, I was stupid," Siegel says in a tone that suggests he's frustrated that there's no more satisfying answer. "I was making bad decisions, hanging out with [people] I shouldn't have. This eats at my soul every day."

Siegel also spends time wondering why the parole board regularly turns him down. He is supposed to be released next St. Patrick's Day, by which time he'll have served fourteen years. Some rapists and even killers have served less time. How could that be, especially when Jermaine Ewell's four other attackers *combined* didn't spend fourteen years in the joint? Is the board, Siegel asks, "trying to show that middle-class kids don't get special treatment?"

He's not alone in thinking he's no longer in arrears to society. Franzese and Lieberman, the other two victims, have sent letters to the parole board seeking clemency for Siegel. In 1998 Clinton superintendent Daniel Senkowski wrote to the state's Executive Clemency Bureau on Siegel's behalf. "Shannon Siegel's demeanor while incarcerated has been exemplary," Senkowski asserted. "It seems unlikely that [he] could derive any further benefit from continued incarceration. However, society is currently being deprived of the positive contributions he could be making."

In a sharp departure from his trial testimony, Siegel finally owns up to his actions that night. "For a long time," he says, "I was afraid to take responsibility. [But] the fact is, I have no one to blame but myself. Maybe I was swept up in this wave of politics and hype. But after a lot of reflection, I came to the proverbial moment of clarity: none of that mattered. The only thing that mattered was that Jermaine was injured, and lives were changed forever."

He still seethes when the topic of race surfaces. He points out that he always had black friends growing up, he's always listened to rap music, and even today he watches BET on the black-and-white TV in his cell. He claims he was "real tight" with the late rapper Tupac Shakur, who spent much of 1995 in Clinton on a conviction for sexual abuse.

Can't one embrace black friends and black culture and still be poisoned by racism? "Maybe," Siegel says, "but that's not me. Race was never a part of this."

For years Siegel felt a burning need to apologize to Ewell face to face. For years Ewell, too, wanted to confront Siegel, look him in the eye, and distill everything to a single question: *why did you do this to me?*

On a brisk Saturday in the spring of 2001, Shannon's mother, Joyce, made the six-hour drive from Long Island to the Clinton prison with Ewell riding shotgun in her car. Asked if he didn't feel funny taking a road trip with the mother of the kid who'd beaten him nearly to death, Ewell shrugs. "Maybe it was a little awkward, but she didn't do anything to me," he says. "She was a real nice woman."

As Ewell passed through the security entrance and heard the gate slam behind him, he felt a rush of panic. *What am I doing?* When he and Siegel finally met near the prison commissary, they were both flooded by years' worth of thoughts and emotions. Siegel was the one to break the silence. "Yo," he said softly. "My bad."

Yo, my bad?

"You know when you've been thinking about saying something perfectly for years, and the words just fail you?" Siegel says now. "That's what happened."

For the next three hours, the entire visiting period, they talked easily, the conversation meandering from music to mutual friends to, of course, sports. Eventually they found their way back to the assault, and Ewell got at least some of the answers he'd been seeking. Siegel apologized and reiterated his claim that race had not been a factor. Even if fate had not yoked them together, even if they had not spent their twenties in two different kinds of prison, they had plenty in common. To Ewell, this only underscored the senselessness of the beating. "You ruin two lives, you involve families, you shake up a community," he says, "and for what?"

When he returned to Long Island, Ewell didn't often mention having seen Siegel. But friends and relatives of both men say the visit accelerated their healing. "It was absolutely cathartic," says Steckler, Ewell's godmother. "Emotionally, I think his recovery started that day." Two weeks after the visit the parole board received this letter from Ewell: *On Friday April 13th, I went to visit Shannon at Clinton Correctional Facility. We had a chance to talk and out of this visit, a full reconciliation was achieved . . . I believe that Shannon has grown from this experience and has learned from his mistakes. He deserves a chance at parole and to restart his life. I am in full support of his efforts to become a positive member of society.*

By that time, lung cancer was winning the war it had been waging against Joyce Siegel. Before she died, neighbors were curious about the kid with long hair and a slight limp who paid her periodic visits. By then she was too weak to explain that it was Jermaine Ewell, checking in on her. "The way he treated my mother," Shannon says, his voice catching, "is something I'll never forget."

By last year Ewell's headaches had stopped, his vision had cleared, his equilibrium had fully returned. But when he told friends and family members that he was thinking about returning to football, they all gave the same response: you need to get your head examined. He took it literally, seeking out Overby for medical clearance. Grudgingly the neurosurgeon gave it. "He's an adult who can make choices, and physically he can play," says Overby. "I explained that when you have a serious head injury, you don't want to put yourself at risk for another. Do I want him playing a contact sport? No."

Ewell says he knows the risks, but he adds, "I have to do this for me. This isn't about making it to the pros. It's about getting back something that was taken from me."

Ken Leistner played football at Lawrence High in the '60s with Lyle Alzado and later became a chiropractor and a strength trainer for elite athletes. Like just about everyone around the Five Towns, he'd followed Ewell's recovery. "When I heard he was thinking about making a comeback," he says, "I thought, *I can help him get stronger.*"

Apart from Ewell's daily visits to a swank gym where, until recently, he was a personal trainer, he has three sessions a week with the man he calls Dr. Ken. Leistner has transformed his clapboard house on a quiet tree-lined block in Valley Stream into a spartan gym frequented by NFL players, track stars, and wheelchair athletes. Nautilus machines are scattered through the basement; the driveway is strewn with boulders and tires and a foundry's worth of iron slabs. Neighbors are inured to watching large men vomit on the curbside tulips. "Dr. Ken doesn't pretend," says Chip Morton, the Cincinnati Bengals' strength coach. "The guy is just brutal, but one of the best at extracting effort from his athletes."

Training with NFL types such as former Detroit Lions Pro Bowl linebacker Stephen Boyd and former New York Giants defensive end Frank Ferrara, Ewell held his own and developed his Body by Zeus: cables of veins up his arms, bulging pecs, fire-hydrant thighs. Leistner worked his contacts this spring, and Ewell was invited to try out for Arena Football2 teams. "The question," Leistner says, "was, how will this guy respond to taking a lick?"

The answer came during Ewell's first practice with the Bakersfield Blitz in California. During a blocking play, he collided with a 245-pound linebacker. "It was like being hit by a car," Ewell says. He took inventory of his body, determined that everything was okay, and returned to the line of scrimmage.

He didn't make the Bakersfield team, but at both its camp and the Albany Conquest's he made a good impression. "There was some rust there, which was to be expected, but I told him he was welcome back next year," says Paul Press, the Blitz director of football operations. "He was all class."

Last month Ewell was offered a job as the Conquest's strength and conditioning coach. But for now his flame for playing still burns. "I know my body can handle the contact," he says. "I haven't gotten playing football out of my system." He talks about trying to hook up with a Canadian Football League team or trying out for NFL Europe. His immediate goal is to stay in shape and continue adding mass.

So it was that on a balmy Friday morning in May, Ewell was in Leistner's driveway working out with three other football players, "taking it to the limit and then going further," Leistner says. Standing there exhausted, with sweat staining three layers of clothing, Ewell lifted an amount of weight unfathomable to most of us and tried to propel it over his head ten times. Midway through the reps, with the weight resting on his shoulders, his legs buckled and his back started to curve. He unleashed a scream that pierced the suburban calm.

"Come on, Jermaine, be strong!" yelled Ferrara. "Speed kills, but strength punishes!"

Ewell screamed again. His grip tightened, and damn if he didn't finish off the set.

The Unnatural Natural

FROM THE LOS ANGELES TIMES MAGAZINE

I CHECKED MY WATCH and peered into the distance. I was starting to think he'd never show. I was starting to think he didn't exist.

In a way I was right.

It was a warm summer night, two months ago, a slow dusk coming on. I was sitting beside a well-groomed baseball field in St. Louis, surrounded by a dozen well-groomed men in their sixties, members of a softball team called U.S. Pallet, which competes in an intensely serious league for senior citizens. The first game of a double-header against archrival Bud Light was set to begin, but there was no sign of U.S. Pallet's best player, one of the best players in the league — the man I'd come to see. His name was John Meeden, but most just called him Homeless John.

While waiting for Meeden, we talked about him, or tried to, though each attempt at a definitive statement went trailing off, because nobody knew anything. His teammates had told me the stories, the legends, "the myths," as one called them. Meeden had been homeless, they said, but no one knew why. Vietnam? Drugs? Alcohol? Every teammate had a theory, but no theory felt more plausible than the rest.

Meeden was a rare and gifted ballplayer, they all agreed, but how he got to be so good, no one could say. A few teammates believed Meeden had played organized ball as a young man. One said Meeden had signed with a major league club when he was just a kid and the pressure of going pro caused some kind of breakdown. What evidence was there for this? None. Just as there was no evidence that Meeden would ever show up tonight.

Again I checked my watch.

"Here he comes!" someone shouted.

At last, walking slowly toward us from the parking lot, was a man built very differently from the men gathered around me. He had none of their midwestern roundness, none of their low-slung solidity. He was tall, lean, somewhat frail, and instead of clomping along on big feet, as the others tended to do, he picked his way forward delicately, as if someone had told him to watch out for broken glass.

He was dressed differently too. Rather than the dapper uniform worn by his teammates, Meeden wore baggy street clothes — he preferred to play in his everyday duds, his teammates insisted — and he carried a sad little Kansas City Chiefs tote bag. Also, while every other man looked as if he'd been to the same Supercuts that morning, Meeden wore his white hair rakishly, almost foppishly, long. The wispy strands fell well below his shoulders.

Like all but two of his teeth, Meeden's youth was long gone. His sixty-four-year-old face showed the lines and leathering effects of age and hunger and hard times. Still, his eyes retained a gleam, just a glimmer, of boyishness. This became even truer as his teammates hollered their hellos. Meeden smiled and waved, and for a second he could've been that straggly kid who always shows up last for Little League.

I'd been warned that Meeden was shy. He won't talk to you, everyone said. But now he sat down next to me in the stands, so close that our knees nearly touched. I didn't know if he was being friendly or if he simply didn't see me. He began tugging an elastic brace onto his leg, fastening it around his thigh. Someone asked how the hamstring was feeling. Meeden had strained it during a recent game. He mumbled an inaudible answer while rubbing the hamstring and staring at some indistinct point in space.

I introduced myself and Meeden stopped fussing with his leg long enough to look at me. I told him I was hoping for a chance to speak with him later, privately, that I wanted to write a story about him.

His eyes widened.

Then he just giggled and trotted onto the field.

The hobo Roy Hobbs. The Unnatural Natural.

A homeless guy who clouts homers in a softball league somewhere in the heartland.

It sounded too good to be true, at first, but baseball is full of things that are too good to be true — baseball itself is too good to be true — and that's one of the things we love about it. Like no other sport, baseball caters to our need for mythology. For pretend.

Only now, looking back, do I recognize the internal pretending that propelled me to St. Louis in the first place. I told myself I wanted a good story, but in truth I wanted a simple story, one that was laid out before me, neatly arranged between two clean white lines. No trapdoors, no surprises. As I usually do when the world seems unusually crazy, I wanted to focus on something easy, just for a few hours. And I figured: What's easier than baseball? What could be more therapeutic for a flagging spirit than a nice, one-dimensional hero with a bat in his hand?

Simple.

My plan was simple too. Rather than bother with major league baseball and all the egos and press credentials that would involve, I decided to write about baseball in its blue-collar form — softball. Better yet, "senior softball," a fast-growing, slow-pitch sport in which nearly two million baby boomers now take part. The largest nationwide league is Senior Softball USA, based in Sacramento. I phoned league officials to ask if there might be one standout team or player on whom I could hang a story, and Terry Hennessy, the league CEO, told me about a St. Louis squad whose best slugger had been homeless when they "drafted" him.

I made a few more calls, and soon I was talking to Len Suess, manager of U.S. Pallet — an outfit that, like countless American softball teams, bears the ungainly name of its corporate sponsor. Suess swore it was true. Meeden, a.k.a. Homeless John, had been living in a broken-down van and roaming St. Louis in rags when he began playing for U.S. Pallet twelve years ago.

Suess, a sixty-four-year-old financial adviser, was fuzzy on some details, but he recalled that U.S. Pallet was short a man at the start of that season, and several players suggested Meeden, who had been spotted subbing now and then for another team on a nearby field. No one knew why Meeden was homeless, or why he bothered to play softball when his life was on the skids. And Suess didn't care. He approached Meeden about playing full-time for U.S. Pallet, and Meeden agreed, and thus was launched an improbably superb softball career.

I asked Suess if Meeden was as good as all that.

"Buddy," Suess said, "he can play."

Despite his frail frame, notwithstanding his training diet of leftovers scrounged from dumpsters, Meeden hit for power, showed wild speed on the bases, and played a gorgeous shortstop, Suess promised. People were still talking, he said, about the tournament three years ago when, over the course of several days, opponents simply could not get Meeden out at the plate — and in the field Meeden was even better, catching every ball in sight. He also caught the eye of another team. Chicago Classics manager Joe Yacono "recruited" Meeden on the spot, inviting him to divide his playing time between the Classics and U.S. Pallet. (This meant, essentially, that Meeden would travel with the Classics to bigger national tournaments in which U.S. Pallet didn't participate.) Soon, Meeden led the Classics to their first-ever title at the Senior Softball World Series in Iowa. Later the same year he helped them win the Senior Softball World Championship in Mobile, Alabama.

"He's one of the most fantastic softball players in the nation," said Pat Herod, U.S. Pallet's sixty-one-year-old right fielder. "Anybody who has seen him play, they know about him. Some guys have it, some guys don't. He has it."

Suess and the other players with whom I spoke didn't know where Meeden learned to play ball. It wasn't that they lacked curiosity — like good midwesterners, they merely didn't want to pry. So Meeden's skills were as inexplicable as they were remarkable. But the real story, Suess said, was what Meeden had done off the field.

While making both his teams better, Meeden had also quietly bettered himself. Through softball he'd managed to restore his health, reclaim his dignity, and make a fresh start. He'd found an apartment. He'd begun eating right. He might even have filed for assistance — though some teammates believe he's been collecting some form of government assistance for longer than he's been playing softball. Again, no one was quite sure. Only one thing was clear: "All of a sudden John started getting his act together," Suess said.

"Softball has given him a different feeling about himself," said Jim Welch, a retired sixty-four-year-old salesman who plays second base for U.S. Pallet. "He's got a sparkle in his eyes. And that smile!

He seems to be more at ease in the community and when we travel."

Just recently Meeden received an old jalopy as a gift from a teammate, but for years he had no transportation, so Welch would drive him to games. Welch didn't mind. It was a little out of his way, he said, but he was happy to do what he could for Meeden, as were most men on U.S. Pallet and the Classics.

Whenever Meeden goes on the road, for instance, his teammates gladly shell out for his airfare, lodging, food, and tournament entrance fees. In fact, Yacono found a Chicago company willing to sponsor just Meeden. In addition, Meeden's teammates give him advice about nutrition, buy him shoes and warm clothes in the winter, and sometimes help him with the complex government forms he must fill out. They help because Meeden's their teammate, and they like him, but also, it seems, Meeden's air of mystery has lent an aura to their games.

I had no reason to doubt Suess or Yacono or any of Meeden's teammates. They all sounded like sober, upstanding, straight-shooters. But I didn't really begin to fall under the spell of the legend, I didn't believe in Homeless John, until I was there, watching Meeden smack a vicious double his first time up, knocking in two runs. He stood on second base, blasé, as if waiting for a bus. He looked neither happy nor proud as his teammates clapped and cheered him.

Suess's wife, Judy, was keeping score, as she's done at nearly every one of her husband's softball games for the past forty years. White-haired, green-eyed, quick to smile, she sat on a folding chair, I sat at her feet, and we watched in the bottom of the first as Meeden darted left, gloved a hard grounder up the middle, then buggy-whipped the ball across the diamond, nailing his man by a step. Judy shook her head. "He covers more ground than any shortstop I've ever seen," she said, penciling a 6–3 on her scorecard.

Expressionless, Meeden trotted off the field. Again he sat next to me. "Nice play," I said. He giggled.

I mentioned to Meeden that I couldn't help noticing his unorthodox batting style. A lefty, he cringed as the rainbow pitch wafted toward the plate, then lifted his right knee high, uncoiled his body, and lashed at the ball. Meeden said he'd developed this style back when he first started playing with U.S. Pallet. He was so hungry and weak that he needed to wind his body as tightly as he could, like a top, to get maximum recoil on the swing.

I asked Meeden if he'd played organized baseball as a young man. He answered by telling me about the awful paper route he'd had as a kid. "It was slavery," he said. "But I didn't know you could quit. I didn't know you could say no."

A short while later I tried a follow-up. Meeden's response was to reach into his tote bag and produce a can of shaving cream, then squirt a softball-sized dollop of foam onto his palm. Seeing my perplexed look, he explained that he always rubs shaving cream into his mitt during games. "Lanolin," he said, rubbing, rubbing. "Keeps the leather soft."

His voice, I thought, was lanolin soft, which made it hard to hear. I started to say something else, but he ran away, onto the field, leaving in his wake a lovely fragrance of soap and limes.

When Meeden first joined U.S. Pallet, Judy Suess told me, he was painfully shy. He would sit in the backseat of the car and say nothing during four-hour rides to tournaments. The men coaxed him out of his shell, Judy said, by always treating him with respect, but also kidding him now and then, ever so gently, about how little he spoke.

A few innings later, Meeden gunned down a runner at the plate, and Judy remarked how healthy he appeared. A far cry from those first days, she said, when he was virtually starving. "He was rail thin," she recalled. "He looked ill. And now . . ." She gestured to the field where Meeden was crouched, awaiting the next pitch, looking indeed quite spry.

Occasionally the men of U.S. Pallet had trouble persuading Meeden to accept their help. "One time," said Herod, the right fielder, "we stopped at some little restaurant and he didn't have any money. I said, 'What do you want to eat?' He said, 'I'm not hungry.' And I knew he was hungry. So I bought him dinner. Then I offered him a big piece of pie. Pie was extra. He said, 'No.' Then he walked across the street and bought a Snickers bar at a gas station."

After a few innings, U.S. Pallet had built a comfortable nine-run lead. But in the final frame, Bud Light rallied and pushed across ten runs, winning 19–18. U.S. Pallet stomped off the field, heads down, fuming. Meeden, meanwhile, looked as calm as a Buddhist monk.

In the nightcap, Bud Light took the early lead, and it was U.S. Pallet's turn to play catch-up. Meeden smacked a triple, clearing the bases and pulling U.S. Pallet to within two runs. The hit was one of the most impressive of the night. It soared over the right fielder's head and clanged off the chain-link fence, missing a homer by a foot or two.

U.S. Pallet won. Again Meeden looked unfazed.

I looked up. He was standing over me, smiling, toweling the sweat from his arms and neck. By now he radiated the scent of shaving cream like an old barber shop. I asked if he'd like to have lunch together the next day. Sure, he said.

He lived in Alton, Illinois. His hometown. He suggested a particular McDonald's. "It's just over the bridge on your way into town," he said. "You can't miss it."

About twenty-five miles north of St. Louis, at the confluence of three big rivers — the Mississippi, the Missouri, and the Illinois — Alton lays grim claim to being one of the most paranormal places in America, rife with ghosts and haunted houses, a reputation that makes its downtown seem that much gloomier as you cross the bridge.

Looking somewhat ghostly himself, his white hair translucent in the light of day, Meeden was waiting for me at a table for two. I reminded him that lunch was my treat. He looked glad but embarrassed. He ordered a cheeseburger, small fries, and a small Coke. I asked if he didn't want more than that, but he shook his head.

Over lunch I questioned him about his life, and he answered slowly, albeit eagerly, between small bites. He wasn't good with logical signposts like chronology and cause and effect, but he became disarmingly linear, almost lucid, as he described the nervous breakdown he'd suffered in his twenties. He blamed it on a strict religious upbringing. His father and uncles were fire-and-brimstone preachers, he said, and he grew up afraid he was "letting them down." Letting God down. Eventually he fell apart. He couldn't get out of bed. Soon he was receiving painful and frightening electroshock treatments in a hospital. "It's a shame," he said, "because I was a pretty nice kid, I think."

After the hospital released him, Meeden said, he had only the shakiest sense of his place in the world. He worked odd jobs —

foundry work mostly — and married a woman who "had her own
problems." They took off for Vegas in a beat-up Ford, which gave
out halfway there. They returned to Alton and had a son and a
daughter before divorcing. Both children, now grown, lived in
other states. It wasn't clear what had become of his ex-wife. "I don't
understand myself," Meeden said. "I'd like somebody that don't
know me to tell me what I'm like, because —" He didn't complete
the thought.

I tried repeatedly to bring the conversation back to softball. He
responded to nearly every softball question with a vague non-
answer, or else a story about something wholly unrelated. Sometimes he would answer by eating a French fry.

After lunch we drove up the hill to a block of passable old Victo-
rians and bunker-like apartment buildings. Meeden's apartment,
for which he said he paid $190 a month, sat at the end of the street.
He unlocked the door and led me inside. The front room was
dark and cluttered with laundry baskets or boxes, it was hard to
tell, each stuffed with clothes or random household items Meeden
had salvaged from dumpsters. An enormous air mattress slouched
against the far wall, and a table in the near corner held an old stereo. A kitchenette overflowed with economy-sized soda bottles and
canned foods, and just down a short hall was Meeden's bedroom,
with barely enough space for a bed and a hand-held TV.

Proudly, he showed me his new stereo. He'd found it recently, he
said, along with stacks of vinyl records. Many were wet or warped,
but some were in mint condition. He set one on the turntable.
Booming crackles and pops filled the apartment, followed by the
silken baritone of Tony Bennett.

Take my haaand, I'm a stranger in par-a-diiise!

"I like that song," Meeden said.

I suggested we talk outside, on the narrow square of cement that
served as Meeden's porch. We sat on chairs facing the street, watching an off-and-on breeze fluff the trees. Again I tried to steer the
conversation around to softball. I pitched him softball questions —
literally. I all but pleaded with Meeden to say he loved the game, to
say the game had saved him, to wax rhapsodic. Instead he complained about the injuries, the mosquitoes, the way his teammates
scolded him when he made an error. I asked again if he'd played
ball in his youth. I couldn't understand his answer. I asked about

the upcoming tournament in Iowa, where the Classics would vie for their second World Series championship. Meeden said he didn't much care for that long drive to and from Des Moines.

We sat in silence, listening to Bennett.

I ventured a comment about a fine play that Meeden had made the night before. Meeden frowned. It was that frown that did the trick. Finally it hit me. I looked up — a plane was sailing through the clouds — and felt like a fool. I capped my pen, closed my notebook, and turned to Meeden. "John," I said, "you don't like softball, do you?"

He whipped his head toward me, shocked.

"In fact," I said, "you hate softball, don't you? If you had your way, you'd never play softball again. It's like that paper route, isn't it? You don't know how to quit. You don't know how to say no. You're playing because the guys have been good to you, and because you know they need you to win, but if you never played softball again, that'd be fine by you — isn't that true?"

He giggled. "I guess so," he said. "But I'm not sure I'd want everyone to know that."

At least, I think that's what he said. He had dropped his lanolin soft voice even lower, as if Tony Bennett were eavesdropping on us. But I could see in his face, and in his sly smile, that I'd guessed it, that I'd been the first to guess it, and so I started to laugh. Then I laughed harder. I laughed and laughed, and now Meeden was laughing along with me. I was laughing at the exquisite irony of the situation, the perfect silliness of an indentured senior softball player, but I didn't know what Meeden was laughing at. Did he see the irony? Did he understand that he was caught up in a softball version of "Gift of the Magi," the famous story in which a wife sells her hair to buy a fob for her husband's watch at the same time the husband sells his watch to buy a set of combs for her hair? The men of U.S. Pallet thought they were saving Meeden by letting him play, and Meeden thought he was saving them by playing, and nobody was right.

Then again, nobody was wrong. When I stopped laughing and took a long look at Meeden, I realized he *was* helping them win, and they *were* helping him live. They were giving him fresh air, exercise, good food, warm clothes, fellowship, and social contact — and he was better off, whether he liked it or not.

But maybe I was wrong. Maybe I'd merely guessed what Meeden's mood was in that one gossamer moment. If I were to ask Meeden again tomorrow, I thought, he might tell me how much he loved softball. As if reading my mind, he whispered to himself, or to me, or to the breeze: "I say stuff that I don't even understand."

The only thing certain about Meeden was that nothing could be said for certain, not even by Meeden. Except that he was a very good ballplayer. As for how good, even that couldn't be described with anything like objective truth, because people saw what they wanted to see whenever Meeden took the field. Baseball — even when it's just senior softball — almost begs us to pretend.

I stood and thanked Meeden. He peered at me, not sure why I was thanking him. I wasn't sure either. Partly I was thanking him for the laugh. But also I'd come to St. Louis for a simple story, and I'd gotten a bracing and necessary reminder that there is no such thing.

When I returned home I meant to phone all kinds of people. Meeden's kids. His teammates. The courthouse in Alton. In the end, however, I decided that I knew enough, even though I knew less than when I started.

Still, I couldn't help myself from making one last phone call.

Yacono, the manager of the Classics, told me Meeden had himself a solid World Series in Iowa, batting nearly .600. I gripped the phone tighter, waiting for Yacono to say it, shout it, exclaim that his Classics had won the whole thing.

"We took third place," he said solemnly, sounding almost as disappointed as I.

Almost.

NEAL POLLACK

The Cult of the
General Manager

FROM SLATE.COM

A FULL-PAGE AD for Monster.com in this week's *Sports Illustrated* shows a clean-cut, white, college-graduate type in an empty base-ball stadium. He's staring beatifically into the distance, maybe watching batting practice or studying the crevices in the outfield walls. "Whether you're a five-tool player or a five-tool accountant," the ad says, you're in charge of your career path. Hovering above our white-bread college grad are these words: "You are the General Manager of you."

The Monster ad left me wondering what, exactly, an accountant's five tools might be. But more significantly, it represents a breakthrough in sports metaphor. Sports commercials used to encourage people to drink beer to "bring out your best" on the amateur football field, or implied that the right deodorant would get you laid as often as Joe Namath. But the interface between consumer and sports has changed. When sports-loving kids stare wistfully into the distance now, they're not daydreaming about being like Mike or coming to the plate in the bottom of the ninth with the bases loaded. No, they're dreaming about pulling off a deadline trade or finding a "sleeper" in the low rounds of the draft.

We're in a sports age in which Executive of the Year is an award on par with the MVP, where there's always a seat for an ex-GM on *Baseball Tonight*, where Knicks fans hate Isiah Thomas not because he's dismantling them on the court, but because he's doing so from the front office. Michael Jordan is remembered as a failed executive. A general manager, Billy Beane, is the most controversial figure in baseball. His intellectual disciples Theo Epstein and Paul DePodesta are almost like folk heroes.

It's hard to say whether the growing popularity of general managers has made everyone want to play fantasy sports or if the nation's fantasy sports obsession has made everyone think they're a GM. Either way, people have lost sight of the fact that general managers, however great or however incompetent, are just guys in suits who can spot talent, endure talking to agents, and memorize a bunch of rules. One popular site, RealGM, gives armchair executives the privilege of sifting through the same arcane salary-cap labyrinths as their favorite number-crunchers. When I clicked on "GM Resources," I was asked this question: "Need to know if your team can get rid of that contract from their books early or when a player's Base Year Compensation ends so it is easier to trade a contract?" Well, I think, I would *if I were a general manager.*

If you don't care about buying, selling, and trading, the sports world has much less to offer you these days. Around baseball's trading deadlines we're flooded with absurd trade rumors while the action on the field goes relatively unnoticed. There's also little distinction made between fantasy sports news and real sports news. When I went to ESPN.com the other day, a full-page fantasy football ad popped up before I could get to the home page. I clicked through, and a ticker said I had less than a minute to make my first draft selection. If I wanted to be the general manager of me, I'd better hurry.

Meanwhile, on *SportsCenter,* I found Dan Patrick discussing "six running backs you don't want on your fantasy football team." I'm not sure who Michael Bennett plays for these days, but I do know that he is, at best, a "late-round draft risk." Even considering ESPN's lousy summer, with that idea-bankrupt "50 States in 50 Days" feature and the endless reports on Barry Bonds's knee fluid, this was disheartening. Patrick is ESPN's top talent. It was as though CNN called Christiane Amanpour back from Iraq to cover a Risk tournament. Excuse me for wanting *baseball highlights.*

I'm as susceptible to the charms of fantasy sports as any healthy American nerd-male. It's basically Dungeons & Dragons with the added attraction of getting drunk on draft day if you're in the right league. But I play fantasy baseball because I love sports, not because I love business. I wanted Carlos Delgado on my team (the Washington Balls of Anaheim) so I could see what numbers he could put up under my watch. I'm not salivating at the chance to flip him for a couple of prospects in a waiver deal.

My modest GM fantasies begin and end with baseball, where numbers rule and where such obsessions were born. Every other sport has to stay relatively pure in my mind; I've struggled for years to ignore the NBA's arcane salary cap rules, and I'm not about to change now. Regular consumers of this space know that I live and die by the Phoenix Suns, but reading about general manager Bryan Colangelo's "difficult front-office summer" appeals to me less than reading about his colonoscopy. I want to see the final product, not hear about how it was made in Santa's workshop.

As deathly dull as a general manager's machinations may be, there's obviously an audience for it. I think that's warped. Yes, athletes are overpaid, pampered assholes, but their jobs are still inherently fun and interesting. Heroes don't analyze spreadsheets. Really, who would you rather be, Tom Brady or the guy who signed Tom Brady to a long-term deal? This may be the age of the general manager. But the quarterback still has more fun.

JONATHAN MILES

What Goes Ninety-five Miles per Hour for Seventeen Days Straight Through Mud, Sand, High-Speed Smash-ups, and Marauding Bandits?

FROM MEN'S JOURNAL

WHAT I AM ABOUT TO DO HAS been denounced by the Vatican as "a vulgar display of power and wealth," drawn the ire and fire of Islamic terrorists, stranded European royalty and thrill-seeking riffraff in the Sahara, cost hundreds of millions in damages, and claimed the lives of more than thirty people. Likened to "blood sport from a science fiction novel," it's been judged the world's most dangerous legally sanctioned sporting event. Seventeen years ago *Sports Illustrated* decreed that with "any luck, or common sense," it would never happen again; yet it did, and has every year since.

Most commonly it is called the Paris–Dakar Rally, though Paris has been just a flickering presence in recent years. More accurately, it's called the Dakar Rally, and it's a bone-crushing, will-killing off-road race from Europe to the African city of Dakar, in which cars, motorcycles, and trucks slog 5,500-plus miles through the deepest orange undulations of the Sahara, with its biblical sandstorms and locust swarms and arid empty vastness, to the beautiful blue sea-spray of the Senegalese coast. Half my fellow competitors, revving their engines in the starting lineup, won't see that blue beauty — for every one that finishes, another will fall prey to injury or exhaustion or mechanical failure, and the race will leave them behind. More darkly, the odds say that at least one of us will not return alive; on average, in the Dakar Rally's twenty-seven-year history more than one competitor has died at each running.

This time, however, when it's all finished, at least five people will lie dead, including a legendary Italian racer, a five-year-old Senegalese girl, and a jovial Spanish motorcyclist who shared my team's support truck. A suspected al Qaeda operative will be arrested and charged with "plotting to kill as many participants as possible." Spain's Green Party will demand that the Spanish government extract itself from the rally, while a French lawmaker will plead with his prime minister to ban the race altogether. The rally's major motorcycle sponsor, KTM, will publicly admit misgivings about the race, wondering, as many have before, if death in the desert outweighs the bright glory of a Dakar victory.

At this moment, however, as my partner and I watch the line official count down the start of our first stage with his fingers, five, then four, three . . . the truth is, at this moment, I have no fucking clue what I'm about to do.

One day earlier, in an auto shop on the outskirts of Barcelona, I stepped back from the race car after affixing a sticker bearing my name to the left front fender. The sight, for me, was a peculiar one: I'd never raced before — I'm notorious back home, in fact, for my slow, meandering driving style. Just a couple months prior I'd been asked to take the co-driver slot in a *Men's Journal*-sponsored car. Immediately I said yes, because for anyone with a thirst for adrenaline, the Dakar Rally is the ultimate cocktail, the ne plus ultra of reckless abandon. And for another reason: like the summit of Everest, or the finishing tape of an ultra-marathon, the Dakar is something to measure oneself against, a yardstick of endurance and nerve steel. I wanted to know if I could hack it. As race rules required, I affixed another sticker to the car, just beside my name. On that sticker was my blood type.

I'm thrown back in my seat as the car vaults off the line. As co-driver, or navigator, my job is to tell my partner where to drive via the aid of a road-book (half in French), a trip computer (basically, a digital odometer), and a GPS unit bolted to the dash. Right now, though, as we begin a quick 3.7-mile qualifying run on a Barcelona beach, I'm just trying to hold on to my road-book. Being a co-driver, at this point, feels like being a toddler driven around by an angry and potentially suicidal parent: I'm strapped into a bucket seat via a five-point harness, and I really feel like screaming.

We fly too fast over a five-foot-high jump, the car's front end smacking hard and a wash of sand spraying across the windshield. "*Fuhhhhhck!*" my driver, Darren Skilton, screams. "Last thing I want to do is bust an axle in Europe." A pause. "By the way, mate," he says, "don't put your hands up when we're landing hard. You could lose them if we roll. Second-last thing I want to do is send you home with no hands."

A broodingly intense thirty-seven-year-old with short-cropped, khaki-colored hair and round, wide eyes that seem to expand when he's driving, Darren is a second-generation racer with a fierce pas-sion for speed and the desert. His father, Clive Skilton, was a drag racer in England, where Darren was born, before relocating to southern California in 1976 to compete on the American drag cir-cuit. Off-road racing came next and Darren was there for the ride. The son entered his first race at the age of twenty-three, and since then he's captured four SCORE Desert Series championships, in-cluding three victories in the Baja 1000 and a win in the Baja 2000, the longest off-road race ever staged in North America. This will be his third Dakar rally, after a sixth-in-class finish in 2000, followed by a second attempt, in 2001, that ended with a blown engine in Mali.

Our car is a five-year-old, fire engine–red Kia Sportage. The frame is stock, as is the six-cylinder, 3.5-liter engine, but the rest is all race-issue. The front end is fiberglass, to save weight, while the rear of the car is mostly engulfed by a ninety-gallon fuel tank and three spare tires. The interior is almost comically spartan, a hodge-podge of unmarked switches, dirt-encrusted gauges, an oversize tachometer, loose wires, tubular foam padding, and bare metal. Nothing about it is even remotely comfortable; after my first ride — a short spin around Barcelona — I proclaimed it an "ergonomic enema," which made our two mechanics laugh but not Darren.

The mechanics — Barrie Thompson, a Jeep racer from the high desert country of Apple Valley, California, and Todd Mason, a moonlighting pro snowboarder from Australia — will trail us in an eight-ton, four-by-four Mercedes truck, sometimes via the rally course, sometimes on an alternate route. The truck is stocked with enough parts, wheels, tires, and body panels to all but rebuild the race car from the bottom up, which, to my unschooled eye, might already be necessary. And I'm not alone: in the shop near Barcelona, where five or six cars and trucks were being readied for the race, a French driver examined the Kia for a while before asking, "Thees car — Dakar Ralleee?" I nodded. He stared at the car a little longer. "Thees year?" I nodded again. "Holy *sheeet*," he said, with a caustic Gallic laugh.

The echoes of that laugh would bang about my skull for weeks. On the way to "scrutineering," the pre-race vehicle inspection, the car's headlights kept shorting out, forcing us to drive through Barcelona either in total darkness or by the blinding white aurora of our off-road lights. Darren was restive, frowny, knotted with mechanical worries. The gear shifter stuck constantly. The alternator seemed troubled. Exhaust fumes were seeping into the car, choking us. The windshield wipers didn't function. "The trip computer isn't working," I noted, futilely pushing buttons as we zoomed along an unlit Barcelona highway en route back to the shop. "*Nothing* is working, mate," Darren said. "It's going to be a total fucking thrash all the way to Africa."

A total thrash, however, would be in very precise keeping with the original spirit of the Dakar. In 1977 a French motorcyclist named Thierry Sabine got lost in the Libyan desert while racing in the now-defunct Abidjan–Nice Rally. By all accounts it was a harrowing, hallucinatory ordeal, but Sabine apparently enjoyed it, in much the way the French enjoy Mickey Rourke movies and the works of Jacques Derrida, and decided to repeat it the next year with as many racers as would join him. "A challenge for those who go," went Sabine's slogan, "a dream for those who stay behind." One hundred and seventy competitors raced in the inaugural Dakar Rally, blasting 6,200 miles through Algeria, Niger, Mali, Upper Volta (now Burkina Faso), and Senegal. One of them, of course, died, as did Sabine himself a few years later, during the 1986 Dakar. But the thrash lived on.

"This is the *ultimate* adventure," an American named Ronn Bailey is saying to me. We're standing beside our cars at the port of

Algeciras, Spain, three days into the race, waiting to load them onto a ferry to Tangier — and thus to Africa, where the real shit begins. A fifty-five-year-old data-security magnate from Las Vegas, with a preternatural suntan and printer paper–white teeth, Bailey is here on an expensive whim. "Nine months and two days ago," he tells me, he decided to (a) race in the Dakar Rally, which meant he had to (b) custom-order a race car, and (c) quickly learn to drive it. For years he'd been hearing about the Dakar from fellow travelers he'd encountered on his solo motorcycle trips to Central America and the Arctic Circle, and, well, with about a million bucks burning a hole in his pockets, why not? "Tell me another race in which you can be a total amateur and get to compete against the best in the world," he says. And it's true: the Dakar nurtures its amateur element, opening the rally to anyone with a vehicle, the cash (fifteen grand to enter, plus anywhere from twenty grand to a million more to cover costs), and the little experience needed to qualify for a racing license. Roughly 20 percent of the car drivers, and a whopping 40 percent of the truck drivers, will be competing for the first time this year.

Though little known in the United States, the Dakar is a sports juggernaut in Europe, where France's state broadcasting company runs more than twenty-five hours of coverage and the leading drivers and riders are accorded the same status we give to Super Bowl quarterbacks. The American presence in the race has always been small — nonexistent on occasion — and something of a novelty. This year's race, however, is different: a record number of five Americans, including me, are here, most notable among us Robby Gordon, a top-tier NASCAR driver who's claimed six off-road championships and a near-win at the 1999 Indianapolis 500. Already, Gordon has made history. His victory on the rally's first day, in Barcelona, marked the first time an American has ever won a Dakar stage. Gordon, like Bailey, is a Dakar virgin. Of the Americans, only my partner Darren has raced the Dakar before.

At this point, thirteen days of racing lie ahead for this year's 162 cars, 230 motorcycles, and 69 trucks, our southward passage divided into noncompetitive "liaison" stages and white-knuckled "special" stages that get longer and more grueling as the race goes on, particularly when they hit the raw depths of the Sahara. Our second day in Africa delivers a first small taste of what those specials will entail — what the French might call an *amuse-bouche*. We're rol-licking along on a seventy-six-mile special in Morocco, south of Rabat, through green meadows where shepherds gather on rock mounds to watch us pass, and across flat nasty fields of craggy brown rocks. Our trip computer still isn't working — some sort of battery problem — so I'm forced to navigate by the landmarks noted in the road-book.

With the trip computer, navigating is not, in theory, terribly dif-ficult. At kilometer 243.5, say, the road-book will direct you to veer right off the visible trail when you come to some longer *collines avec rochers*, and even if, like me, you don't know a colline from a crois-sant, there's a rudimentary sketch indicating that these collines are round, like rocks, or maybe holes. Without the trip computer, how-ever, all I can do is guess at the mileage, and try to formulate some instructions for Darren. *Leave the trail to the right before you hit some, uh, round things.* All this at eighty miles per hour.

"Horn!" Darren is shouting. "Hit the horn! *Horn!*" I sound the horn twice — that's my job, along with operating the wipers, since Darren's hands need to stay glued to the wheel — to signal to a Mitsubishi in front of us that we want to pass. As Darren swerves left and right, searching for an opening, I return to the road-book, des-perate to know where the hell we are. A few moments later I glance up and see two things: the Mitsubishi directly beside us, three feet to our left, and a four-foot-high cairn with stones the size of medi-cine balls right in front of us. *"Holyshitlookout!"* I yell, and Darren, who's been focused on the Mitsubishi, makes a split-second choice. We slam into the side of the other car. Fiberglass shreds spew across the windshield. Our left front fender is ripped off.

"Thanks, mate," Darren says calmly. "Good eye." Thirty seconds later we pass the Mitsubishi with its mangled rear fender. Weirdly, its inhabitants do not flip us off.

We end that day's racing with an alternator failure, forced to drive 262 dark liaison miles through Morocco using only our low-voltage off-road lights to conserve the battery. Even powering my map light is too risky; I navigate by the flickering glow of my ciga-rette lighter.

Years ago, prior to the running of a Dakar, Thierry Sabine was asked at a press conference who he thought would win. "The desert," he replied. It was an honest, accurate answer. Except for a very few elite pro racers up front, the Dakar Rally is not, at heart, a contest among the competitors; the battle, instead, is between mankind — more precisely, Western mankind, with all its fire-breathing machinery and inexorable arrogance — and Africa, which has been proving itself untamable for centuries now. Yet it isn't about "beating" Africa — that, as even the first-place winners will attest, is a ridiculous notion. It's about Africa not beating you. For most of the competitors, winning the Dakar has little to do with the standings on the final day, and everything to do with *making* it to the final day.

We set out on the fifth day's course, a 149-mile liaison followed by a 237-mile special through Morocco, with a fresh new alternator and trip computer installed. And for 80 miles we're rolling well: passing cars, hitting the correct turns, eluding all the traps — the holes, the ditches, the subtle tricks the course-makers plant in our GPS codes to steer us off the route. But then, as we're running fast along a bumpy, rock-strewn trail, the front right wheel falls off — falls right off the race car — and sends us into a deadening thunk of a stop.

"*Fuhhhhhhhck!*" Darren screams, ripping off his helmet. Already that aggrieved curse is becoming a refrain. After wrenching all night on the car with the mechanics, he'd neglected to manually tighten the lug nuts. To boot, I'd neglected a major item on my daily pre-race to-do list: check the lug nuts. Bump by bump, they had worked themselves off.

Still, I think, this shouldn't be a major problem. I fetch the runaway wheel from a ditch on the opposite side of the trail, skittering across the sand to avoid a Russian racing truck careening by. The wheel is trashed, sure, but we've got two spares in the back.

It *is* a major problem, though — the lugs are stripped. In fact, they look melted. We try to steal a lug off each of the other wheels, figuring we can secure a new wheel with just three wheel studs, but they're not all uniform, and won't fit. By this time we've fallen so far behind that the support trucks — the big racing-shops-on-wheels that trail behind the factory-sponsored cars — are starting to chug by. We flag one down. The spare lugs they've got on board don't fit either. We're stranded, and out of decent options.

"All we can do," Darren finally concludes, with a wrecked sigh, "is file."

File: meaning, file new threads onto the melted lugs. One at a time, by hand. We take seats on opposite sides of the trashed wheel and tire, back to back, and hunch over the lugs, scraping at the silvery globs that once had been screw threads, eyeing them, scraping some more, trying to twist a nut onto them, cursing, scraping, trying, cursing, scraping. Small funnels of reddish sand come whipping at us, stinging our eyes. We don sand goggles and keep at it. An hour passes, then two, the sandy-edged wind increasing as the sun drips westward, the Moroccan desert eerily silent after the last-place stragglers have all passed us by.

"What's the maximum time allowed on this special?" Darren asks.

"Eleven hours, I think." The prospect of not finishing within the time limit hasn't occurred to me until now. "What happens if we don't make it?"

"We take a penalty," he says. "It's not a huge thing. The key is making it to the start of each stage. If you miss a start, you're out of the race. It's over."

"So we've got all night, technically," I say, not particularly comforted by the idea.

At twilight, with the desert washed in purple, its hills like the folds of a king's velvet robes, I'm finally able to screw a lug nut onto a third stud. We replace the wheel, load into the race car, strap on our helmets, fasten our harnesses, and pull back onto the course.

"That pretty much sucked," I say.

"It's not over yet," says Darren.

Just thirty miles later the left front hub assembly explodes — another wheel falls apart — and once again we're trailside. Darren rests his head against the steering wheel for a minute or more; he's beyond cursing, driven to something like prayer or seething or both. Then he slowly and silently gets out of the car, pulls out the tools, and goes to work.

"We may not make it, mate," he says after a while, lying beside the wheel and a jagged metal mess of parts and wrenches, trying to jury-rig a precarious fix while I aim a flashlight at the wheel and shiver in the unexpected chill of the Moroccan night. "Once you get to Africa" — turning a wrench, muttering — "the first thing the organizers do is try to break your car. (Hand me the five-eighth wrench.) That gets the weaker cars out of the race. (No, sorry, the eleven-sixteenth. Thanks.) Next, they try to break you, to get the weaker drivers out of it. If we can get this car through Morocco, I think we'll be okay."

We load back into the car sometime after midnight. "It's peg-legged," Darren says, before slipping on his helmet, "but it might make it."

Which it does, but not without another crisis.

The fumes seeping into the car since Barcelona have worsened, and are loading the interior with pungent exhaust; we slide open the postcard-size window vents in an attempt to clear out the exhaust, but all we get is colder. The fumes are affecting Darren worse than me — whether because the leak might be on the driver's side or because eighteen years of smoking Camels has inured my lungs to all other pollutants, I can't say. But sometime past 2:00 A.M., as we're cruising at ninety miles per hour on the flat moonscape of a dry lake bed, Darren starts slowing down.

"What is it?" I ask. By now we're at school-zone speeds. "Problem?"

Full stop, an engine stall, then silence.

"Darren?"

He's wearing a full-face helmet, so I can't see his eyes, but his head is immobile and tilted toward his chest. I repeat his name four or five more times before punching him, which rouses him only slightly; he makes drunk bear noises. He's blacked out from the carbon monoxide, his body weakened that much further from lack of sleep. We trade places.

Driving a race car isn't too far a cry from driving any other sports car, but driving one through Africa in the middle of the night offers a wide scree of new sensations. As I drive I keep seeing trees that aren't there — low, thick-trunked ones, like live oaks — and have to wag my head to expel the images. I always thought of mirages as heat-induced, daytime phenomena. Perhaps it's the sheer nothingness of the desert here. The brain can't accept the emptiness the eyes are seeing — it wants plants, boulders, animals, anything.

According to the road-book, balanced against the wheel, I'm currently driving through a military zone. Here in southern Morocco, where a dispute over the Western Sahara has been simmering for decades, that often means land mines, so I tightly follow the visible tire tracks, overmindful of something Darren jokingly told me in Spain: "The trick with land mines," he'd said, "is to go fast enough over them so that they blow up behind you." "Helluva trick to practice," I'd said. I step on the gas hard, envisioning what it must be like to outdrive a land mine — like dancing a jig when someone's shooting at your feet. "Slow it down, mate," Darren moans every now and then, drifting in and out of consciousness.

By the time I reach the checkered flag at the end of the course, at 4:00 A.M., the finish-line post is deserted. A few miles away, at the rally bivouac in Smara, I'm barely halfway into my tent before crumpling to the ground. I wake the next morning with my legs hanging out the tent flap.

Whether Darren ever made it out of the car to sleep that dark morning — or even made it out of his helmet — I cannot say. Shortly after daybreak, when I pull myself up after two and a half hours of sleep, he's already under the car, wrenching its guts out.

On each of the thirteen days that the Dakar Rally runs through Africa, a new, halogen-lit city rises from the sands, and then, twenty-four hours later, disappears altogether. In this phantom city you can get a bottle of wine and a plate of duck confit; an examination by a doctor; a shower, occasionally, but at least a bucket of clean water; and as many cans of Red Bull as you can carry. Its citizenry includes hundreds of administrators, cooks, physicians, and journalists, and then, as the motorcycles and cars and trucks trickle in from the course, hundreds more racers and support-crew mechanics. This is the Dakar bivouac, a military-issue compound that's assembled and disassembled daily, then flown on to the next location, in pieces, via jumbo jets and a slew of big-muscled trucks. All through the night it hums and rattles with the sounds of vehicles being torn apart, rebuilt, repaired, revved. Motors squeal, generators rumble, mechanics shout for tools in twenty languages. No one is still save the sleepers, tucked into one-man tents or crowded tight as puzzle pieces on the ground beneath canopies, earplugs insulating them from the mechanized din.

Today, however, is different. It's the morning of Friday, January 7, in Tichit, Mauritania, a desolate stone village that's changed little since the twelfth century, except to crumble. The bivouac is like a ghost town, just a cluster of tents on a sand-whipped plain with a few people milling about. Partly this is owing to the fact that support trucks are banned from the bivouac for the current "marathon" stages. But more important, it's because most of the competitors are still out in the desert, stranded, or struggling yet to finish.

We pulled in at 5:00 A.M. The special — a grueling 410-mile slog through sand dunes first, and then more than 100 miles of camel grass (clumps of dry grass rooted in hard sand mounds as tall as three feet) — was so murderous that race officials have canceled the next stage, ostensibly because of a sandstorm that's grounded the helicopters, but also because it would mean abandoning perhaps 75 percent of the competitors in the Sahara. Though we'd started 142nd among the cars, and took sixteen hours and forty-nine minutes to finish, we were the 37th car in.

Distress signals have been pouring in all night from the racers we spied out there in the dark: motorcyclists huddled together under silver emergency blankets, drivers standing beside their dead cars holding makeshift signs reading OIL GAS PLEASE or NEED PETROL. All the talk at the bivouac is about the missing or defeated: two-time Dakar winner Jean-Louis Schlesser is out of the race, his self-designed buggy broken in the sand. Four-time winner Ari Vatanen is out of gas somewhere. Robby Gordon, who rolled his car the day before, limped in with less than a liter of fuel. Ronn Bailey is nowhere to be seen.

Our car is alive, but only barely. Early in the stage we busted the transfer case, which meant we lost our four-wheel drive — an odious development in an off-road race. To cross sand dunes in two-wheel drive, you have only one tactic available: barrel up them as fast as you can, so that your momentum will carry you over the impossibly soft sand at the crest. The only problem with that, of course, is that you have no clue what's on the other side of that crest — sometimes a sheer drop, sometimes a car stuck at the bottom, sometimes both.

Near the end of the course we took a wrong turn and, instead of the mountain pass marked in the road-book, found ourselves at the edge of an eighty-foot, eighty-or-so-degree sand cliff above the plains of the Tagant desert. We got out and walked to the edge, our headlamps doing little to illuminate the ground far below. Sans four-wheel drive, there seemed no turning around. It smelled like doom.

"Why don't I run up and flag a truck?" I said. "Maybe someone will pull us out."

"They couldn't get close enough without getting stuck down here themselves," Darren said. He was staring down the cliff.

"Maybe we could swing it back up that way. It's just a short climb before it levels out some."

Darren glanced up, then shook his head. "The car can't go anywhere but forward," he said.

"Forward isn't really an option."

He got into the race car and started the engine. "Let me try something," he said.

Figuring he'd reconsidered my proposed tack, I backed away, crossing my fingers that he'd be able to turn the car back around and, with luck, get it back toward the course.

Instead, he revved the engine twice, threw it into gear, and went over the cliff.

In the Dakar, the dangers are obvious and everywhere. You're riding or driving as fast as you can through unfamiliar terrain, much of it roadless desert, often with little or no sleep and little or no food. Take a dune too fast and you can end up planted in the sand like onions. Miss one of the hazards marked in the road-book — all the holes, ditches, bumps, and dry washes cratering the desert — and you can flip, roll, or just plain crash. Animals are a constant danger: camels, monkeys, and livestock roam the trails. (One story that made the bivouac rounds concerned a donkey that walked in front of a Mexican motorcyclist. The rider jumped off the bike, but the bike kept going, hitting the donkey, and, rumor has it, cutting it in half.) And man-made hazards loom just as large, or larger. In 1996, near the Mauritania-Morocco border, a Mercedes truck hit a land mine, incinerating one of the passengers. That same year a sniper fired at a Mitsubishi support truck, narrowly missing its driver. In 2002 the threat of terrorist attacks convinced organizers to reroute the rally at the last minute.

The cliff, for us, was just the start of it. While I ran-slash-tumbled down the cliffside after the car, fully expecting to watch it roll below me and smash headlong into a rock face at the bottom, Darren crab-walked it down the sand — a twisted feat of technical driving. He was waiting for me, calmly, at the bottom. "You're fucking insane," I said.

"Welcome to the Dakar, mate," came his dry reply. "Get in."

In northern Mauritania we got another welcome. As Darren and

I were slowly climbing a boulder-strewn path, about fifteen tribes-men appeared out of nowhere and descended upon the car, open-ing the doors, yanking everything out that they could. They rifled through my backpack, even tore out the Kia's hood pins. When Darren slammed the car into reverse, then forward again, rocking through the boulders to unsettle the men's grip on our stuff, a grapefruit-size rock hit the Plexiglas driver's side window with a loud *thwack*. The window remained bowed for the rest of the race.

In Mali we hit a low-hanging tree limb, which shattered the front windshield; for days afterward we raced al fresco, gathering leaves, twigs, and a thick coat of desert dust inside the car. In Senegal we hit a hole too fast and the car went airborne, flying nose-down over the trailside foliage.

Our mechanics, driving slower and steadier, fared even worse. In the dunes of Mauritania the truck flipped onto its side. Barrie cracked his head hard enough to lose some blood, and the duo had to spend the night in the Sahara until they could wrangle help to get the bruised truck back upright.

Even the few calm, collected moments of racing were shadowed by threats: in Mauritania a rumor spread through the bivouac that the U.S. embassy had contacted the race organization, having in-tercepted a terrorist plot to ambush an American team.

When I lay down to sleep that night, I couldn't help but wonder what the hell I was doing here. Risking life and limb for pleasure is at least defensible. But risking it all for misery is another matter al-together — a demented subset of masochism. The adrenaline that had been sustaining me for more than a week was going rancid, like milk left in the hot sun. I wanted to quit. It wasn't simply that I was bloodshot-eyed, sand-encrusted, physically spent, that my hips were bruised from the violent up-and-down smashing of the camel grass crossings, that I had barely slept in two weeks and was surviv-ing half the time on hot Red Bull and baguettes. Nor was it just the machine gun–fast disasters: the three hours spent digging the car out of sand as fine as talcum powder, the midnight roadside re-pairs, the bad GPS heading we followed that took us through a nightmarish series of virgin dunes and more and more camel grass. It was all of this, yes, but also something more: I'd lost my will. At some point, when you've been hanging by your fingers from a cliff, letting go begins to feel like the better choice.

I learned of the rally's first fatality the next morning: Jose Manuel Perez, an amateur Spanish motorcyclist who'd been sharing storage space on our support truck, had died following a crash. I watched one of his teammates, a woman, get the news: she fell to the sand wailing. The next day Fabrizio Meoni, a forty-seven-year-old motorcyclist who was in second place in his thirteenth Dakar, crashed his bike a hundred or so miles out of Atar, Mauritania. He died in the desert.

"This is not a true rally," a Spanish racer told me several days later in Bamako, Mali. It was 3:00 A.M., and we were standing at a table in the bivouac, washing down our dinner with warm French beer from a can. "This is a contest to see who is tougher than who. How many dead already? Two? Every year I vow never to do it again. But then every year I do — for nineteen years. Why? Because maybe I am crazy. That must be it. I am crazy."

Insanity — while seemingly accurate, in the doldrums of poststage exhaustion — is too reductive and facile an explanation for why otherwise rational people shell out minor fortunes to suffer like mad and take the fierce chance of losing their lives. Something else is at work here, something I'm just beginning to comprehend. Today is January 15, a golden-hued day, and we're rolling fast on a 140-mile special between Tambacounda and Dakar in Senegal — the last true leg of the rally. The car, it seems, is going to finish, despite its endless traumas, and we are too, despite our traumas. "Double-down hole in three hundred meters," I tell Darren, eyes darting from the road-book to the road and back again. "Then it's shitty and bumpy in the vegetation for 1.5 kilometers."

"Does it actually say 'shitty' in the road-book?" he asks with a smile.

"My loose translation of the French," I reply.

A ticklish new sensation is washing through me, vastly different from the low psychic valleys I mined just days ago — not enjoyment, necessarily, or contentment, but more like understanding. I'm recalling something Darren told me, months ago, when I first met him in California to plan our long voyage. "Will this thing ever be *fun?*" I asked him. "No," he said, "not fun. Not at all, really. But a few weeks later, or maybe a few months, you'll think back on it and wonder if maybe it wasn't actually fun, because you'll have this great feeling of *satisfaction* about it." Satisfaction: it's a weak word, the bland stuff of consumer survey cards, yet it's precisely what I'm starting to feel, a kind of past-tense high. You do not race the Dakar to experience it, I'm beginning to see, but rather to *have* experienced it. What I've been through has plainly been awful, an acid bath for the body and soul. Yet that I'm going to survive seems glorious.

Senegal whizzes by in a greenish-brown blur, the desert having given way to dense jungle, mud huts, windy shaded trails, the promise of water and life. "Keep to the right when you see a well, about four hundred meters," I tell Darren. "Double-down descent following, it'll be stony. Then you've got a village, check speed." Villagers line the course on both sides, cheering, dancing, egging us on. What a vast difference from Mauritania, where the women cowered behind burqas and young boys pelted us with stones. Our every slow pass through a village feels like a parade. With the mud huts in our mirrors, and open earth before us, Darren guns it. The car rockets forward, its metallic scars gleaming in the African sunlight — a bright red symbol, like all the vehicles about to pour into Dakar, of speed and survival. "Nice fast trail for 4.5 kilometers," I say. "Open it wide."

We finish sixty-fourth among the cars. Of the 162 cars that started in Barcelona, 75 survived to Dakar. Of the motorcycles, 104 of 230 made it; of the trucks, 37 of 69. On the last stage, a nineteen-mile special on the beach at Lac Rose, in Dakar, we come in twenty-ninth place, one slot ahead of Robby Gordon, who finished twelfth overall. "Toughest thing I've ever done," Gordon says to me later, at the postrace party held at Dakar's Club Med. We're still drinking Red Bull, only now it's spiked with vodka. Several German racers are in the pool, singing beer-hall songs, and the dance floor is jammed, a sweaty jumble of inebriation and exhaustion and relief.

"But I'm coming back," Gordon tells me. "I've seen it, I've experienced it, and I know I can put together a team that can win it." Later at the party I'm startled to encounter Ronn Bailey, whom we hadn't seen since he fell behind on the gruesome stage to Tichit. "We drove to Dakar anyway," he says. "It was amazing — like a grand tour of Africa. Did you know there are crocodiles in the Sahara? I saw them. What a wild ride." He too vows to return. The

Dakar is a hard mistress, but still she seduces. The glory she promises, coyly, seems difficult to resist.

Whether that glory is worth the Dakar's hulking costs is ripe for argument. Auto racing, no matter where and how the races are held, will always kill and maim; NASCAR's predictable oval tracks and continuing safety innovations have not kept it from sending drivers to their graves, and likely never will. Over the years the Dakar's organizers have made serious efforts to improve safety — linking the horns of race vehicles to receivers in others, tracking each racer via GPS, an additional medical helicopter, strict speed limits through villages. Yet still the deaths pile up: just outside Dakar, a five-year-old girl was killed when she ran in front of a support truck. Earlier the same day, in Dakar, a pair of Belgian motorcyclists, unofficially following the race, were killed in a crash. With the deaths of Jose Manuel Perez and Fabrizio Meoni, that brought the race's fatal toll this year to five. It seems, darkly, that no degree of safety measures can protect the Dakar from itself. For as long as it continues, it will always be a high-speed off-road race through the wildest and wooliest corners of Africa, a competition founded on danger and colonial exoticism, designed to thwart and batter those who enter it.

Early the next morning, following the party, as the city of Dakar is stretching itself awake to the rhythmic sounds of the waves, I make a last visit to the car before it's to be loaded onto a freighter and shipped back home. Its windshield is a piece of makeshift Plexiglas. The turn-indicator lights are missing. The rooftop air intake is shredded. The right side mirror is gone, along with the left rear fender and the entire rear bumper. The front fenders are patched and held together with red duct tape. I pat its hood almost fondly, not for what it did — I will always hate it for that — but for what we went through together. "Dakar Ralleee?" I say, imitating the cynical Frenchman from the shop near Barcelona. "Holy *sheeeet.*"

GARY SMITH

The Shadow Boxer

FROM SPORTS ILLUSTRATED

IT WAS SILENT in the backseat of the car. The old boxer had just left the gay bar outside of which a gang of men had beaten him to the edge of death on a summer night thirteen years ago. He couldn't remember how or why it happened. He had given up trying.

The traffic light on Eighth Avenue turned red. His head turned toward the passenger window.

"Look!" he cried. "There I am!"

There he was, five-time world champion Emile Griffith, twelve inches from his nose, on a poster plastered across the side of a bus that had just stopped beside his window.

He stared at himself. It was him, wrapped in anguish and shadows, on a spring night forty-three years ago when he beat a man who had called him a *maricón* — a faggot — to the edge of death . . . then beyond it.

"I don't have any clothes on!" he cried.

"No, Champ, you've got your black boxing shorts on," assured his adopted son.

"But you can't see any shorts!"

"That's because you're in shadows."

"No! I'm naked!"

"But you used to be naked in the locker room."

"But . . . but I should have clothes on!"

The bus belched exhaust and pulled away. The old boxer kept staring out the window, but there was only smoke.

*

Get used to the smoke. Let it fill your lungs and sting your eyes. There's no getting rid of it, not in a story about Emile Griffith, not in the one American arena where the smoke just doesn't seem to dissipate. A policeman or a judge or a lawyer can openly be something other than heterosexual. A doctor or teacher or carpenter can be, along with, of course, an actor or a musician or a writer. Even executives on Wall Street now can. But a male athlete in a major sport?

Not one has ever emerged, not while he was still playing. Odd — isn't it? — because what sports does best is break down barriers and bring people of all colors and creeds together. Odd that no bat or ball or fist or foot could smash through *this* wall.

On April 20 a striking documentary about Emile Griffith — *Ring of Fire*, directed and produced by Dan Klores with Ron Berger and being promoted on buses all over New York City — will premiere on USA Network at 9:00 P.M. ET. Later in the year a biography of Griffith by Ron Ross, also addressing the issue of the fighter's sexuality, is expected to appear, and the rights to produce a feature film on the big screen have been sold. You'd think, under all those klieg lights and reading lamps, that the smoke's about to clear. But this is Emile Griffith. This is sports. And this is us. So the smoke may only grow thicker.

But I should have clothes on! Sorry, Champ. You're naked again, except for underwear and socks. You're approaching a weigh-in scale in front of a couple of dozen people, mostly writers and photographers. It'll be fifteen years before you retire with more championship rounds under your belt than anyone in boxing history: fifty-one more than Sugar Ray Robinson, sixty-nine more than Muhammad Ali. It's 1962, when a handful of writers — Allen Ginsberg, James Baldwin, and Gore Vidal — are virtually the only people known to be gay in all of America; even Liberace files a lawsuit against those implying he's a homosexual, for fear of what he'll lose.

"Easy, Emile," whispers his trainer, Gil Clancy.

But how can Emile be easy? The last time he and Benny "Kid" Paret — his opponent tonight at Madison Square Garden — met at the weigh-in scales, before their fight six months earlier, Benny did the unthinkable. Swished his limp wrist and hissed that word, *maricón.* Thank God the reporters pretended it didn't happen. Thank God it was 1961.

Then Paret nailed the insult to the wall of Griffith's heart, winning a controversial decision that night and taking back the world welterweight crown that Emile had snatched from him nearly a half-year before. Now it's their third fight, the clincher. The fear of what Benny might do at the weigh-in climbs up Emile's throat. "If he says anything to me before the fight, I'll knock him out," he mutters to Clancy.

Emile steps on the scales. "Watch out," hisses Clancy. Too late: Benny's already slipped behind him, wriggling his body, thrusting his pelvis, grabbing Emile's ass. "Hey, *maricón,*" Paret coos, "I'm going to get you *and* your husband."

Emile blinks, in his underwear, at a room full of boxing aficionados, reporters, and photographers. If he doesn't respond, that means he's afraid, means he's weak . . . means he may be just what Paret says he is.

Clancy steps between them. "Save it for tonight," he begs Emile.

It's tonight. The twelfth round. The whole country's watching. It's fight night on TV. The smoke of 7,600 men in sport coats and ties, sucking in and exhaling their Chesterfields and Camels and Lucky Strikes and White Owls, descends over the ring at the old Madison Square Garden. That blue nicotine fog, as Pete Hamill, a writer puffing for the *New York Post* at the time, calls it.

In the center of the smoke crouch two black immigrants from the islands. They've played basketball together in the neighborhood they share in the shadows of the Polo Grounds in upper Manhattan. Paret, twenty-five, the sugar-cane cutter from Cuba who carries his two-year-old son, Benny Jr., everywhere on his shoulders, fighting in what he has decided will be his last prizefight . . . never dreaming how right he'll be. Griffith, twenty-four, a Virgin Islander who never wished to be a fighter, who just happened to ask if he could take off his shirt on a sweaty summer day as a teenager working in a hat factory on West Thirty-ninth Street owned by a former amateur boxer named Howie Albert. Albert had never seen anything like it: a twenty-six-inch waist fanning out to forty-four-inch shoulders, all rippling with muscle. "Shoulders," says boxing writer Bert Sugar, "that you could serve dinner for six on."

The young man didn't have the lust for hurting people —

would've been happy hauling boxes of bonnets to Macy's and Gimbel's all his life — but his body was a destiny that had to be fulfilled. Albert took him to Clancy, a trainer with a growing reputation at a gym on Twenty-eighth Street. Two months after he laced up the eleventh-grade dropout, the kid was a finalist in the New York Golden Gloves. A year later he was the national Gloves champ.

Boxing solved things. It gave Emile a release for something that just didn't fit with the ear-to-ear smile he always showed the world: a monstrous rage that he felt whenever his family was insulted or his manhood was challenged. Boxing gave him — in his co-managers, Clancy and Albert — two of what he'd never really had one of: father figures. It gave him money for the first time and enabled him, after each pro fight, to fly one more of his seven siblings up from the Caribbean to New York City and attempt to re-create something that exploded in his childhood in St. Thomas, back when his absentee father cleared out for good and headed to America, when his mother left to take a cooking job for the governor in Puerto Rico, when his brothers and sisters were scattered like shrapnel, landing in the homes of their mother's relatives and friends.

Emile landed hardest: on his knees, on the bricks at Aunt Blanche's house, holding cinder blocks overhead as long as he could, knowing that when his arms dropped, her switch would rake his back. That was his punishment for dawdling in his daily task of hauling water in a steel drum up the hill to her house. He loathed living there so much that he begged to enter Mandal, St. Thomas's home for wayward and orphaned boys, and finally was accepted. Somehow, as the oldest child in the family, he felt responsible to gather all its splintered pieces one day and glue them back together.

He's twenty-three now, living with Mama and all her brood in the five-bedroom house he's just bought in Queens Village. A champ but still a child, leaping into the referee's arms to hug him the first time he takes the title from Paret and then, when the astonished ref fumbles him onto the canvas, doing a backward somersault. Running up $100 candy bills in the gift shop at the Concord Hotel, where he trains in the Catskills, doling out gum and grins to everyone, falling asleep with a wad of Bazooka in his mouth that Albert has to scoop out.

So sweet — maybe too sweet, the men in the city's boxing gyms have begun to whisper. They've started adding things up: that high-pitched singsong voice . . . those Sunday mornings singing tenor at St. James Missionary Church . . . those pants as tight as tape on his broomstick legs . . . those young Latino males who seem to appear wherever he does . . . that teenager he always lets use his car and calls his "son." But what's this all add up to? It can't be *that*, not in 1962 or even 2002: a prizefighter, a champion, a limp wrist with a knockout punch? It's the ultimate contradiction, the perfect smoke, so dense that Emile himself can't see through it. "It was irreconcilable . . . to be homosexual and a world champion," says Sugar. "As long as he was beating the s —— out of people, it gave lie to the slander. You couldn't confirm it, you couldn't deny it, you just had to put it . . . *over there*."

"Besides," says Bob Jackson, a New York City trainer who was just getting started at the time, "we're like the police, the blue wall. There's a code. We might talk among ourselves about it, but nobody would talk in public about something like that." Nobody . . . except a desperate man.

Paret has taken a beating in three straight fights, including that dubious decision over Griffith; the most recent one, when he went up in weight to fight middleweight Gene Fullmer, was so frightful that even the cheap-seat sadists left the arena with a hollow in the pit of their guts. But Benny's still dangerous because he can catch a wrecking ball with his chin and remain vertical, then take five or six more for good measure, then — *what?* — blink away the fog and flatten you . . . the way he did just moments ago to Emile, in the sixth round of this third fight. Clancy got in Emile's face after the round and shouted, "Emile, look, when you go inside I want you to keep punching until Paret holds you or the referee breaks you! But you keep punching *until* he does that!"

Midway through the twelfth, Emile stuns Benny with a short right. Benny reels into a corner, eats another hammer, then another. His head and shoulders slump. The only way to nail his jaw now is with uppercuts, and so that's what Emile begins to hurl — or rather, that's what hurls out of Emile, an eruption of fury so mechanically precise that it seems to come from an engine house in hell rather than from the realm of human kinetics. At last Benny tilts, but the turnbuckle keeps him from collapsing, from saving himself, and now begins the terrible ticktock of his cranium, left-right-left-right-left-right, combinations bursting from Emile faster than eye and brain can process.

The ref! Where's the ref? *Who's* the ref? Ruby Goldstein, a victim of his own expertise, a respected pro who knows this sport so well that he *knows* Emile's not a big finisher, *knows* Paret's a chronic possum, *knows* the Hispanics in the house will riot if he stops this fight just as their possum's about to pounce. Goldstein is caught flat-footed as eighteen punches land in six seconds — twenty-nine consecutive unanswered punches in all — bouncing brain against skull again and again. Eyes puffed shut, blood oozing from his nose and his cheek, Benny slithers down the ropes, at last, as Goldstein grabs Emile and his corner men run to wrap him too.

Silence falls over the ring. "I think we just saw a gay murder," a colleague murmurs to Pete Hamill. But even now, in the face of death, Emile remains an innocent. "I'm very proud to be the welterweight champion again," he tells the TV audience, "and I hope Paret is feeling very good."

Paret leaves in a coma, on a stretcher. It's not Emile's fault, of course. It's not the fighter's job to stop throwing punches. But now he's done it. Now that Benny lies near death, the media feel compelled to reveal the insult that would've been swept under the rug, the word that lit the fuse that may have exploded Paret's life. When the *New York Times* boxing writer Howard Tuckner attempts to explain to his tender readership that *maricón* is gutter Spanish for homosexual, an editor changes the word so that it appears as "anti-man." "A butterfly is an anti-man!" Tuckner later rages to Hamill. "A *rock* is an anti-man!"

For hours, just after the fight, Emile tries to gain entry to Paret's hospital room, finally gives up and races down the street, trying to run right out of his own skin. He ends up on Forty-second Street, where passersby who've heard the news shower him with insults.

Paret dies ten days later. There's smoke hanging over his death, a half-dozen contributing causes: the ref's hesitation . . . the havoc in Paret's head wrought by Fullmer's fists three months earlier . . . the lack of a careful medical exam before this fight . . . the hunger of Paret's manager, Manuel Alfaro, to squeeze one more payday — some boxing insiders allege — from a shot fighter who told his wife the day before the bout that he didn't feel right and didn't want to fight. "Fullmer ate the meal, but Emile picked up the check," says trainer Bob Jackson. But all that is far too much ambiguity for the cerebral cortex of homo sapiens, much less for fifteen inches of newspaper ink. So Emile goes down in boxing history as the man who killed Paret for calling him a faggot.

What happens to a child when he kills a man?

Nightmares. Decades of them. Dreams of Benny walking down the street, calling out greetings, extending his hand . . . but when Emile takes it, it's as cold and clammy as last week's trout, awaking Emile in a bath of his own sweat. Dreams of one empty seat at a fight. "May I sit there?" asks Emile. A voice says yes, but as he takes the seat it dawns on Emile that it's Benny's voice, and now he must sit beside the dead man and watch two men wallop each other's heads for an entire night.

Emile grows afraid of sleep. Afraid of silence. Afraid of *alone*. Here comes the hate mail from Latinos convinced that Emile ended Paret's life on purpose. Here come the questions about Paret's death from every interviewer from now till kingdom come. Here comes the public outcry to banish boxing, and the seven-man commission appointed by New York governor Nelson Rockefeller to investigate the tragedy and the sport. There go the fights on TV.

Sixteen weeks later, at lunch on the day of his next fight, against Ralph Dupas, Emile buries his head in his hands. When he backs Dupas into *that* corner, Paret's coffin, he jumps back as if shocked and lets the contender escape. Emile wins by guile in fifteen rounds. "After Paret," he'll admit years later, "I never wanted to hurt a guy again. I was so scared to hit someone. I was always holding back."

He wants to quit, but where else can he get what boxing gives him? How else can he play *father*, put siblings and nephews and nieces through college, pay poor people's rents, buy friends cars, outfit kids' baseball teams, buy meals for the homeless? Kids trail him everywhere. He becomes the Pied Piper of Chelsea, the Manhattan neighborhood near Clancy's gym, even takes home a pair of white twins from their quarreling parents while the couple iron out their differences. He doesn't just give to people. He gives his *last*.

He turns on the glitz. Brand-new Lincolns, sprinkled with glitter. Seven dozen suits, from baby blue to chartreuse, and double-breasted red sweaters festooned with white buttons, mother of pearl. Hmmm. But, hey, he's from the Caribbean; those tropical guys all love bright colors. Big black leather bag strapped over his shoulder, tiny white poodle cradled in his arm. But, hey, it's the '60s: is he being gay . . . or feeling groovy? "I'm *nobody's* faggot," he says to the few who screw up the courage to ask. But what does that mean?

Women keep flocking to him, and Emile seems happy to accommodate them all. A singer at the Concord Hotel named Ce'Vara gives him a picture of herself and signs it: 1. *God.* 2. *Earth.* 3. *Emile.* Not a bad ranking for any boxer. They're firecrackers, these ladies with whom he'll merengue or mambo or mashed potato the night away. He cuts a single for Columbia Records entitled "A Little Bit More."

> She brings out the tiger in me
> She makes me feel like a man
> And she tries so hard to please me
> Anytime that she can

You know the old saying. Where there's smoke . . . well, does there *have* to be fire? No, there doesn't. That's what Emile's co-manager Howie Albert concludes. Otherwise why would he have blown even more smoke right up the writers' nostrils — the myth that Emile's job, in Albert's millinery, is *hat designer*? Why had he brought a dozen bonnets to Emile's press conference before the Gaspar Ortega fight in '61 and beamed as the flashbulbs popped and Emile placed the fuzziest one of all on Ortega's head for the cameras? Rest easy, America. *This Milliner Is No Sissy.* Honest, that's the caption beneath the photograph the Associated Press sent across the land. And Emile, God bless him, rose to the occasion, actually began to design a few chapeaus and pick up the lingo. "The Jackie Kennedy pillbox will remain in vogue," he told the *Los Angeles Times*. "But hats will come in a greater variety of shapes and materials than ever this year. We're featuring maribu, ostrich, novelty braids, feathers, and velours. With the bouffant coiffure still in vogue look for higher pillboxes." *Howwwwieeeee* . . .

But now Howie can't win. He needs the feathers and velours even more, to warm and fuzzy up a man marked as a murderer. "I have a date with a killer, Emile Griffith," declares Brian Curvis just before their '64 match in London. Curvis's terrified wife, Barbara, says she's not coming to the fight, no way. But the killer's lost all killer instinct. Clancy has to smack him between rounds to get his blood up. His boxer's a craftsman now, fond of clinching, targeting belly and spleen rather than jaw and temple, staying *away* from cuts when he opens them, staying busy enough with his hands to keep opponents crouched behind theirs . . . but never again *exploding*. He decisions Mr. Curvis in fifteen rounds. He presents Mrs. Curvis with a hat.

It all keeps growing smokier, one complication wreathed around the next. The event that exposes the question about Emile's sexuality — Paret's death — provides him with the perfect cover: how can a fighter whose fists killed a man *not* be a man? Oh, but, at what cost. Because now *two* things can come whistling out of the dark to ambush Emile.

Safest thing to do? Keep everyone smiling. When he gets knocked out in the first round by Hurricane Carter in '63, the press surrounds him in the locker room, everyone lost for words. Who knows where such a deadly silence might turn? "Merry Christmas!" he suddenly shouts, cracking up everyone. He'll never be without a pet phrase, a red herring to yelp, the rest of his life.

Safest thing to do? Keep running. More and more at night, he slips away alone, ends up in the gay bars near the Port Authority on Eighth Avenue or down in Greenwich Village, throwing down seven-and-sevens. He doesn't disguise himself or change his name. Hell, sometimes he doesn't even change after fighting in a Garden main event, showing up at bars wearing his boxing trunks and shoes, no shirt . . . and a mink coat. He's a child, not a plotter, not a calculating man. It's illegal in New York for two men to be on a dance floor without a woman present, so when the lights flash on, that's a warning to break the clinch, push your partner away because the cops are raiding the joint again. The men in Trix and The Anvil marvel: *A boxer . . . here? A world champ?* But they protect him, just as the boxing world does.

Kathy Hogan, owner of several of Emile's haunts, learns to smell a bender coming. She empties Emile's pockets, sometimes fifteen or twenty grand, takes the jewelry and the poodle and the mink so he doesn't lose them all. Four or five days later, when the wad of hundreds that she let him keep is gone, he returns, groaning, "Mommy's gonna kill me! I think I got robbed," and she puts him in a cab with his cash and baubles and pooch and tells the cabbie not to dare stop anywhere — but Mommy's.

But he never lets his nightlife affect his training. He's still ready at the crack of dawn to run his five miles through the Catskills. Still brilliant enough as a boxer to win the world welterweight championship back from Luis Rodriguez, to jump in weight and take the world middleweight title from Dick Tiger, to retain it twice against Joey Archer, to lose it to Nino Benvenuti in fifteen rounds and then win it back. Even with hell's engine house padlocked.

It's 1967. Mike Wallace concludes his groundbreaking *60 Minutes* segment entitled "The Homosexuals" with these words: "The dilemma of the homosexual: told by the medical profession he is sick; by the law that he's a criminal; shunned by employers, rejected by heterosexual society. Incapable of a fulfilling relationship with a woman, or for that matter, with a man. At the center of his life, he remains anonymous. A displaced person. An outsider."

Emile flies to St. Thomas a few years later. He enters a bar named Bamboshay. He sees a twenty-four-year-old knockout on the dance floor, a former member of a world-touring dance troupe named Prince Rupert and the Slave Girls. She's wearing blue hot pants. Emile's wearing brown hot pants. But, hey, it's 1971. Might just be disco fever. Emile and Mercedes "Sadie" Donastorg begin to do the bump at 11:00 P.M. They don't stop until 4:00 A.M. Dropping her off at her mother's house, he says, "Sadie, marry me."

She says, "What? Are you crazy? You don't even know me."

He says, "That's what I want, that's what I want, I want to marry you."

Cooler heads prevail. He returns to America.

They get married two months later. Smokin' Joe Frazier makes a smokin' best man. So maybe all the whispers *are* wrong. Now Howie Albert has a retort for writers who nudge him and ask The Question: "Go ask his wife."

They move into an apartment and he adopts her daughter, Christine. Emile goes and goes, to training camp, to fights in Buenos Aires, Los Angeles, Paris. Sadie and Christine stare out that apartment window at Weehawken, New Jersey. Less than two years into the marriage, they're gone.

"Emile said I was a distraction because he had to keep his mind on what he was doing," says Sadie, "but we remain friends."

What else could anyone be with Emile? He doesn't just cry, "My pleasure!" when he's asked by strangers for autographs. He writes "(Smile)" beneath his name and thanks *them*. Benvenuti, after they fight a third time, flies Emile to Italy so his newborn son will have the world's sunniest godfather, then keeps flying him back, just to feel the sunshine again.

Color, nationality, status, sex, age . . . none of it matters to Emile. It's a beautiful thing, and a blurry thing too: nobody can tell anymore who's a friend, who's a lover, who's a "son," who's a sponge. It maddens his family, never knowing who'll be at Emile's elbow when he materializes at 5:00 A.M., whom he'll leave in their house when he vanishes again. He'll just sit there, smiling blankly at everything his brother Franklin hisses at him until finally he hisses *that* word, and then Emile nearly loses his mind. Off he goes again, looking for family someplace else.

He finds it in 1979. Finds it two years after Clancy calls him to his home and tells him it's over, at age thirty-nine, after 111 pro fights and more main events — 26 — than anyone else in the combined history of the old and new Madison Square Gardens. Finds it at the Secaucus youth detention facility in New Jersey, where Emile, having burned up most of his ring earnings, works supervising wayward boys. Every day Luis Rodrigo, a sixteen-year-old whose father died fifteen years earlier in a four-story fall at a construction site, runs to the front door to hug him. When Luis finishes his punishment for breaking and entering, he asks Emile to be his father. Of course, says Emile. He takes to calling the boy Emile, the way his own father, Emile Sr. — long ago and far away and never often enough — called him. Luis moves into Emile's apartment. When administrators find out about their relationship, Emile loses his job.

That's how he ends up training boxers in New York City by day and tending bar at Jack Miller's Pub in Jersey City by night. Of course, somebody has to yell *Stop!* every time Emile pours a drink for a customer, then Emile has to test that drink to make sure he didn't stop too soon, then Emile has to take a gulp from every bottle on the wall to make sure inventory's up to snuff. They all fall in love with him, the Irish and Scottish regulars, but none more than the man's man who owns the place: big, silver-haired Jack Miller. He takes Emile's five world title belts from a paper bag under Emile's bed and displays them on the bar's wall. He makes sure Emile has money and a warm place to sleep. He becomes Emile's "poppy," as Clancy and Albert were before him. His wife, Alice, becomes Emile's "mommy," as Clancy's wife, Nancy, and bar owner Kathy Hogan once were.

On good nights, Jack and Emile turn out the lights in the pub, strip off their shirts, put on wigs, dial up Kate Smith on the jukebox, and lead the boys — two-deep around the bar holding up cigarette lighters — in singing "God Bless America." On the best nights, Emile leaps onto the bar and keeps stripping, down to his briefs, blond wig, and granny glasses, while whooping wives stuff fivers in his wriggling waistband and he yelps, "Oooh-la-la Sasson!"

At last, one day over drinks, Jack looks his buddy in the eye and asks, "Emile, are you a homosexual?"

"What do you think?" asks Emile.

"I don't think so," says Jack.

"That's all that matters," says Emile.

At the wake, after Jack dies, Emile pulls him out of his coffin to hug him and sob on his chest.

It's 1992. A 265-pound NFL offensive lineman named Roy Simmons discloses that he's gay, seventeen years after running back Dave Kopay did. But both men, of course, have waited until they're safely retired. "It will take someone *extremely* talented and famous to come out while he's still playing in one of the major sports," says Charles Kaiser, author of *The Gay Metropolis*. "It'll happen. But until there's someone who's both good enough and has the fortitude to take all the abuse, we won't have our Jackie Robinson."

It's a summer evening. Emile gets off an airplane at JFK. He should be exhausted. He should go straight to his mother's house in Queens Village, where he's moved back into the finished basement along with Luis. He has just flown back from Australia, where the boxer he trains, junior welterweight Juan LaPorte, has lost to Kostya Tszyu. Emile takes a cab to Manhattan.

He ends up in Hombre, a gay bar on West Forty-first Street hard by the Port Authority. He can relax more in gay bars than in straight ones, he tells people, because the people there are far less likely to challenge him to a fight. But suddenly he feels so woozy that he wonders if someone put something in his drink. He steps outside. Here comes the smoke.

A gang of men jumps him, beats him with pipes, robs him, and leaves him for dead on the street. Later he staggers onto the wrong train, but finally, after hours have passed, he stumbles home. That's what Emile tells LaPorte, who comes to the Griffith home at the request of Emile's frightened mother and takes him to the hospital.

The men catch him stepping into a cab, slam the door on his body over and over again until he drops. That's what Keith Stechman, a friend, says Emile told him.

Two guys start a fight in the bar. He follows them outside to break it up and two more join them, all turning on him, trying to take his money and beating him with baseball bats. That's what Butch Miller, Jack Miller's son, says Emile told the Miller family.

They kick him with heavy boots, kick every part of his body as if he were a dog. That's what Luis Rodrigo, the first to find him when he staggers home, says Emile told him.

He nearly dies in the hospital. His battered kidneys fail, he goes on dialysis, then his spine gets infected. The severity and site of the beating suggests a gay bashing, a hate crime, but no one will ever know. By the time Emile comes home, two months later, he remembers almost nothing of it. It vanishes in smoke.

He wakes up each dawn, in his sixty-seventh year, lights a cigarette, and inhales three or four times, just enough to create a few puffs of smoke. It rises from the single mattress on the floor on which he sleeps; wafts through the tiny efficiency apartment that he, Luis, and a friend of Luis's share; floats over cardboard boxes and suitcases and shoes and buckets and barbells crammed everywhere. Curls around the heads and fists of boxing trophy figurines poking through old black plastic bags just inside the front door.

Emile rubs out the cigarette before it's half done. Luis, forty-two, fixes him breakfast and hands him the medication for gout and dementia that Ring 8 — an organization that looks out for indigent fighters — pays $300 for each month. He lays out Emile's clothes in matching colors and puts Emile's bracelet on him, each gesture's tender patience rewarded with a tender *thank you*, their relationship sealed when adoption papers were signed not long ago.

Then Luis leaves for Manhattan, where he works in a mailroom elbow to elbow with Benny Paret Jr. Yes, Emile's son and Benny's son, bent over the same bins of manila envelopes every day together, both hired by *Ring of Fire* director Klores to work in his public relations firm.

Emile dozes when Luis leaves for work. There's nothing to do in Hempstead, Long Island, he grumbles, but he didn't want to live alone, and that's where Luis wanted to move — away from the temptations of the city and Luis's old cocaine habit — after Emile's mother died in 1997 and the family sold the house in Queens Village a few years later.

In the afternoon, after he watches his favorite show, *Judge Judy,* Emile grows lonely. He takes a walk through downtown Hempstead, stops at the bodega and the bar to bid hello to the regulars, sits in the park and makes goo-goo sounds and tickling gestures toward the toddlers until they smile. He's fine near the apartment; he won't get lost. But a few times a year he boards the N-6 bus to Queens, switches to the F train to Forty-second Street and returns to his old haunts, and worries the hell out of Luis.

Twice a week Stechman picks him up and takes him to the Starrett City Boxing Club on the edge of Brooklyn. The champ goes around the room giving out bubble gum and advice, handshakes and grins. "Don't start!" he yelps, out of the blue, to young boxers and old trainers. "I'll call Judge Judy!"

He's beloved at the city's gyms and all its boxing gatherings. Larry Holmes hugs him. Gerry Cooney kisses him. Most of them have shared moments with him like the one Ron Ross will never forget, the night Ross grabbed the microphone at a surprise fortieth wedding anniversary celebration that his daughters threw for him and began singing "It Had to Be You" to his wife — when he heard another voice, a tenor. He turned and saw Emile, who'd come to know the Ross family during the three years that Ron worked on Emile's biography, standing and singing along as tears streamed down his cheeks.

It's way too late now. Hate's missed the boat. Funny how that works, how it doesn't matter anymore to the boxing fraternity whether Emile is or isn't. They've gotten to know *him.* "All I see when I look at him," says trainer Randy Stevens, "is love."

Now, of course, if it's somebody else you're talking about, some other boxer who might be gay . . . "Promoters wouldn't touch him," says former light heavyweight champ Jose Torres. "It wouldn't bother me, but most fighters would hate him. And then, if someone loses to him? *You lost to this gay guy? Get out of town!*"

"A gay boxer would be ostracized," says Showtime boxing analyst Steve Farhood. "It would take amazing courage."

"Better kick everybody's ass first, then tell 'em you're gay," says trainer Jimmy O'Pharrow.

Five times world champion. That's sufficient ass kicked. And still not enough, not nearly enough, for Emile to have been a Jackie Robinson, nor even to look back a quarter-century after retiring and tell us what it was like for him, so the sports world can learn and begin to move forward. But it's not even fair to compare. Because Jackie and everyone else could see the barrier he was facing — it was right there on his skin — while Emile couldn't even go near his wall, the wall that hides the scariest thing. No, not homosexuality, not exactly, but something that's all tangled up with it. It's the thing, when two men fight, that's more frightening than the punishment meted out by the one who dominates: *the weakness of the one who submits.* That's every boxer's, every athlete's, deepest fear. That's what must be kept locked in the closet. That's why Pete Williams, who was "outed" by a magazine, could be the Pentagon's TV spokesman in the first Gulf War, the face of America's war machine . . . but a gay man can't be a boxer. That's why it's still 1962, when it comes to sports and male sexuality, while the rest of the country moves ahead.

Today is Thursday. Emile says, "I'm *not* gay! It's craziness. I go to gay bars to see my friends. What's the difference? I have my drink and talk to people, same as any bar. Then I finish and go outside. I don't do anything wrong."

Today is Friday. Emile says, "I will dance with anybody. I've chased men and women. I like men and women both. But I don't like that word: *homosexual, gay,* or *faggot.* I don't know what I am. I love men and women the same, but if you ask me which is better . . . I like women."

Tomorrow is Saturday. He may say something else. That's just how smoke is. Especially since the beating.

"The beating?" he says. His eyes flash. "What beating?"

The one in the early '90s, when those men beat you up.

"Me? Beat up?" says Emile Griffith. "I beat *them.*"

PAMELA COLLOFF

She's Here. She's Queer.
She's Fired.

FROM TEXAS MONTHLY

IN BLOOMBURG THERE ISN'T A STOP SIGN, or even a blinking yellow light, at the center of town — just a bend in a winding two-lane
road that meanders through the woods toward the Arkansas state
line. Every now and then a logging truck piled high with pulp-
wood rumbles by on its way to the paper mill, scattering twigs and
pine needles onto the blacktop below. Otherwise the town is quiet.
There is no Dairy Queen, or any diversions to speak of; the closest
movie theater is thirty miles away, in Texarkana. Even Bloomburg's
1A high school is too small and too poor to have its own football team. But every November, when teenagers scrawl "Go Wildcats!" in white shoe polish on the back windows of their pickups,
the boys' and girls' varsity basketball teams try to make the town
proud.

Bloomburg never had much to brag about until six years ago,
when the school district hired a young coach out of Arkansas
named Merry Stephens. She was the first female coach in Bloomburg history, and also one of its toughest. When just seven girls
tried out for the Lady Wildcats during her first year in Bloomburg,
Stephens had them practice by playing against the boys. If they
were used to making fifty lay-ups at practice, she told them to do
twice as many. It wasn't long before the Lady Wildcats started winning. Stephens led the team to the state playoffs three times, and in
2004, when the team had grown to twenty-five players, the Lady
Wildcats made it all the way to the final four. "Half the town went
with them," said one parent of the six-hour drive to Georgetown,

just north of Austin. "We'd never had a team do so well." The Lady
Wildcats didn't win the championship, but they were welcomed
back as heroes. When the team's bus pulled into town, people
stood on their porches and cheered, and the volunteer fire department led an impromptu parade.

But even after the local Wal-Mart named Stephens Teacher of
the Year and the district had chosen her as its Coach of the Year
no fewer than three times, many residents felt uneasy about her.
Stephens, it was rumored, was a lesbian. And in an area where min-
isters preach against homosexuality from the pulpit and tracts de-
nouncing the theory of evolution sit next to cash registers in convenience stores, Stephens's sexual orientation was not an issue that
most residents of Bloomburg, or its school board, could overlook.
In December, just nine months after the Lady Wildcats had gone to
the finals, Stephens was abruptly put on leave. The woman she
lived with, a teacher's aide and school bus driver named Sheila
Dunlap, was dismissed. The board's actions made this otherwise
placid town of 374 people erupt in controversy and became the
central issue of the school board election in May. "It's divided this
town," said history teacher Thresha Jones. "You've got people who
feel that Merry and Sheila were done wrong. And then you've got
people who think that what the school board did was the only right
thing to do."

Anyone who has looked through the classifieds for a job is familiar
with the fine print at the bottom of most help-wanted ads: "We do
not discriminate on the basis of race, color, religion, sex, or national origin." Employers can add the words "sexual orientation" to
the list, but Texas law does not require them to do so. In fact, Texas
offers no legal protections in the workplace from discrimination
based on sexual orientation. Sixteen states have amended their em-
ployment laws to offer such safeguards, and seven others have man-
dated these protections just for their state employees; the Texas
Legislature has not. Indeed, at the Capitol this spring, the mood
was hardly magnanimous when it came to homosexuality. Both the
House and the Senate approved a proposed constitutional amendment, which voters will decide on in November, to ban same-sex
marriage. (State law already prohibits it, but legislators want to go
further by adding a provision to the constitution.) And while is-

sues like school finance and balancing the budget languished, the House made it a priority to pass an amendment to the Child Protective Services reform bill that both required foster parents to disclose their sexual orientation and barred gays and lesbians from becoming foster parents. (The Senate version of the bill removed this requirement.) Of the four House bills that would have outlawed employer discrimination against gays and lesbians, all died in committee.

In Bloomburg, Stephens did not become the target of employer discrimination until several years into her tenure there, after she had been made the school's athletic director. But the whispering started not long after she began coaching the Lady Wildcats, in the late summer of 1999. Stephens was pretty and vivacious, and at thirty-four, she was old enough to have a husband and kids. So why wasn't she married, people wondered? "They would ask me, 'Is your boyfriend coming to the next ball game?' or, 'When are you planning on settling down?'" Stephens said one afternoon this spring as we talked in the two-story log house outside town that she shares with Dunlap. "I'd have to change the subject or talk about the last boyfriend I'd had. If I told the truth, I knew my career would be over." Still, as months and then more than a year passed without any sign of a boyfriend, the tomboyish Stephens remained the subject of gossip and innuendo. When she began spending a lot of time with Dunlap, it only fueled speculation. Who had sent her that bouquet of flowers at school? And what about her and Dunlap? Hadn't they been sitting awfully close to each other at the last basketball game? "The talk of the town was 'Are they or aren't they?'" said Anna Doll, the owner of a local beauty salon, Style'n. "It's been a five-year-long gossip session."

Secrets are hard to keep in a town whose residents are nearly all related by blood or marriage. At Style'n, and over morning coffee at the Shell Mart, the talk was that Stephens and Dunlap were an item. Dunlap was an unlikely person to have the town talking; a reserved mother of two who was born and raised in Bloomburg, she had never lived anywhere but her hometown. She had married her high school sweetheart during her junior year, when she was seventeen; at the time, she was a forward for the Lady Wildcats. But she had been unhappy in her marriage for many years, and at the end of 1999 she filed for divorce, separating from her husband of twenty-four years. A year later, Stephens moved in. "We had become friends at school, and then we started spending a lot of time together outside of school," said Dunlap, who was in charge of keeping the scoreboard at the Lady Wildcats games. "It just got to where we didn't want to be apart." For a while, she and Stephens denied that they were romantically involved; the recently divorced Dunlap needed someone to share expenses with, they told people who were nosy enough to ask, and Stephens, who had been commuting from her home an hour's drive away, needed a place to live. "People *knew*, but they didn't know for sure," Dunlap said. "Besides, it wasn't nobody's business but ours. We went to school, we did our jobs, and we came home."

But at least two members of the school board, Jimmy Lightfoot and Ronnie Peacock, made it their business. Lightfoot, who is Dunlap's uncle, was not happy about the fact that Stephens had moved in with his niece. "Jimmy Lightfoot and I would walk laps around the track at school when I moved back here from Texarkana," said Suzanne Bishop, a well-liked grandmother who challenged Lightfoot for his seat on the school board this spring. "He said, 'Merry Stephens has to go.' He told me several times that he didn't think Merry Stephens should be teaching kids because she had broken up a family." (Dunlap denies that was the case.) Peacock was equally blunt. In a deposition taken this February, former Bloomburg school board president Derous Byers recalled that Peacock had told him several times that the board should terminate Stephens's contract because she was a lesbian. "I've told him that you cannot fire anyone based on their lifestyles," Byers testified. "He made the comment that we're bonded or insured for a million dollars apiece and that we ought to fire her and see what happens."

Lightfoot and Peacock would find an ally in Jerry Hendrick, the school's guidance counselor. When Bloomburg's superintendent retired in 2003, they supported Hendrick's getting the job. Although he was not certified to be a superintendent, he quickly set a new tone, demoting Stephens from athletic director to coach and cutting her salary by several thousand dollars.

Stephens had not received a single reprimand during her four years in Bloomburg, but once Hendrick was promoted, she was called into his office or the principal's on an almost daily basis. "They singled me out," said Stephens. "I think they thought I would leave if they made my job miserable enough." The harassment was also obvious to many of her colleagues. "The administration was determined to get rid of her," said teacher Thresha Jones. "They would create things to write her up on so they could put it in her file." Jones remembers when Stephens missed a day of school so she could attend her grandmother's funeral; although the protocol was to inform the school secretary of a planned absence, which Stephens had done, she later received a stern written warning for failing to tell Hendrick himself. "If she ran to the store for five minutes, she was written up, but none of us ever were," said Jones. "She was held to a different standard." Some parents were troubled by what they saw as well. "She was put under the microscope at school, at basketball practice, at every game," said Style'n's Anna Doll, whose son graduated in May. "They made her life a living hell."

By the end of the 2003–2004 school year, the pressure had become too much. Although Stephens was at the height of her career — the Lady Wildcats had gone to the finals only a couple months earlier — she was sleeping little, and for the first time in her life, she had begun to have panic attacks. Burned out, she decided to apply for a classroom position in hope of diffusing the situation. "I thought if I stopped coaching and got out of the limelight that the harassment would stop," she said. "That was very hard for me, but I was desperate." Stephens was given seven classes to teach starting last August, including an upper-level science course — an unusually heavy workload that often required her to put in eighteen-hour days to finish her lesson plans and grade homework. Dunlap became persona non grata as well. "Hendrick sent word through his secretary that my office was to be moved into a broom closet," said Dunlap. "It had no heat or air and no room for a desk. Rain came in through the ceiling. I think Hendrick thought that I would quit right then and there, but I took it as a challenge. I decided I was going to do my job so well that they couldn't fire me even if they wanted to."

But on December 8, Dunlap was suddenly let go. "I asked Hendrick, 'You're firing me for what reason?' and he couldn't name one," Dunlap said. Like most of the school's support staff —

from the custodian to the cafeteria workers — Dunlap was an "at will" employee and had no recourse; under Texas law, she could be fired without cause. After fifteen years of being entrusted to drive the district's children to school, Dunlap was given less than an hour to pack up her things. Five days later, Lightfoot made a motion to fire Stephens as well. The school board voted 4–3 to begin proceedings to terminate her contract, alleging insubordination; Stephens was told to hand over her keys and grade book and was put on administrative leave. But when Michael Shirk, an attorney with the Texas State Teachers Association, began to take depositions in preparation for a hearing on Stephens's proposed termination, it became apparent that the district had no case; unlike at-will employees, Texas teachers cannot be fired without cause. "What doomed these administrators from the start was their hubris and obvious bigotry," noted Shirk. (Hendrick, principal Billy Don Frost, Lightfoot, Peacock, and other board members did not respond to interview requests for this story.) The district settled with Stephens and paid out the last year and a half of her contract after she agreed not to pursue any further legal action.

For Stephens, what stings the most is the belief held by some in Bloomburg that her sexual orientation made her unfit to teach. Helping to bolster this view was the fact that a former player of Stephens's, who had since left for college, announced last year that she was a lesbian. In a move that Stephens believes sealed her fate with the administration, the girl's parents met with the school board early last December and laid the blame for their daughter's sexual orientation on her former coach. "I know that some people in Bloomburg think that being gay is contagious," said Stephens. "And they think that whatever the school district had to do to buy out my contract was money well spent. But why on earth would I want any student of mine to be gay and have to go through the hell that Sheila and I have?"

In the end, the school board's actions left many in Bloomburg uneasy. One of them was Tim Reed, the pastor at First Baptist Church. "Some folks here are proud of what happened," he said as we talked in his office this May, two days before the school board election. "But there's nothing to be proud of about what happened here." Reed is not exactly liberal when it comes to social issues; for starters, he preaches that homosexuality is a sin. "But unless we're going to remove every abomination from the school district, I don't see why we should focus on one at the exclusion of all others," he said. "Maybe we should have a crusade against gossipers too. Let's cut their tongues out and run them out of town! There might be three of us left."

In April, Reed had delivered a sermon that caused something of a sensation in Bloomburg. If Merry Stephens and Sheila Dunlap ever walked through the doors of First Baptist Church, he had instructed, members were to stand up, offer the women a seat, and make them feel welcome. "It's easy to condemn people when you haven't walked in their shoes," he reminded the faithful. He went on to preach from John 8:7, in which Jesus cautions a mob that is preparing to stone an adulterous woman to death: "He who is without sin among you, let him throw a stone at her first." Reed gave his flock a meaningful stare from the pulpit and asked, "Who among *you* can cast the first stone?" His message resonated in Bloomburg, where some had begun to wonder aloud why certain school board members, who had been all too willing to sit in judgment on Stephens and Dunlap, did not cast a more critical eye on their own human failings. Others were upset that the school board had voted to remove Derous Byers as its president shortly after he gave his deposition in Stephens's case. And still others pointed to the fact that the district had urgent business to attend to; the district's accountability rating had dropped from "exemplary" to "acceptable."

The school board election on May 14 became a referendum of sorts. Lightfoot was up for reelection, and one of his challengers was Suzanne Bishop, who had criticized his handling of the firings. Perhaps sensing that it might be a tight race, Lightfoot ran a half-page ad in the newspaper, next to a letter written by his pastor at New Hope Baptist Church. The pastor didn't mention Stephens and Dunlap by name, but he might as well have. "If we don't stand for God's standards, He will remove His blessing from the school and the city," it read. "If Believers hide from the sin and pretend not to see it, God will send His judgment . . . If you live in the Bloomburg School District you need to vote and have your voice heard!!!"

At seven o'clock in the evening on election day, when all the votes had been cast, locals gathered in the parking lot of Bloomburg High School to await the results. Lightfoot nervously circled the parking lot in his car. Peacock, whose term will be up next year, watched the proceedings from his front yard, across the street. Stephens and Dunlap had decided to get out of town for the weekend; both unemployed, they had driven to a county fair outside Beaumont to operate a concession stand. It was a way to pay the bills, since moving is not an option; although Dunlap's daughter is grown, her son, who lives in town with his father, is still in high school. And for all the second-guessing that had swept through Bloomburg about the way in which the school board had stripped Stephens and Dunlap of their careers, there has never been talk of giving either of them her job back.

"There are more people here than at a ball game!" one woman exclaimed as she surveyed the forty or so people in the school parking lot.

"We should have brought our folding chairs," said another.

At half past seven, Jerry Hendrick strode outside and announced that Suzanne Bishop had won handily, with 135 votes. Coming in a close second was a more conservative challenger, Brian Cloninger, who would get the other empty seat on the board. A cheer went up from the crowd as each name was called out. Of the five candidates, Lightfoot came in a distant last.

BEN PAYNTER

So You Wanna Be a Cowboy?

FROM THE PITCH

Just because this is gay rodeo doesn't mean Shorty likes to see men acting like women. While finishing a cigarette a few moments ago, he heard two men catcalling effeminately to each other.

"Shit," he said quietly. "Those are the ones who give us names."

Later, realizing the insult to gay culture's time-honored tradition of campy behavior, he backpedals. "How can I put this without stepping on anyone's toes?" he wonders. "Uh, well, I'm not into the more feminine-acting type. For me, it seems like a show, an act in some way."

For Shorty, being an authentic cowboy is about more than whether the boots and the belt match the hat. It's about strutting your low-hanging brass.

That's why he's running for Mr. Missouri Gay Rodeo Association. He wants to make sure the next state representative for this little-known clique of homosexual cowboys will know how to handle a rope.

He's out to prove something as he approaches a cattle chute, one of six metal-barred hoosegows beneath an American flag–draped grandstand at the Wyandotte County Fairgrounds. It's a cut-rate venue with concrete-hard clay that, until a week ago, was littered with shrapnel from a demolition derby. Beyond the bleachers are trailers, campsites, and booths stocked with sexually evocative wares: leather collars, chaps, and T-shirts with slogans like IF YOU CAN ROPE ME, YOU CAN RIDE ME! A full bar has been pouring to sunburned men and women since midmorning.

Shorty, whose real name is Nelson Mueller, stands a wiry six feet six inches tall. He sports a horseshoe mustache and a golden belt buckle that reads BODACIOUS.

Clad in a protective vest, he lowers himself into a chute that holds a spotted steer with a set of horns that look like sharpened handlebars. He surveys the animal's weaponry, estimating each prong at ten inches, maybe longer.

"Of course, I'm not a size man."

He's a chute dogger — a term for steer wrestlers. When the gates open, he'll try to drag the steer into the arena, then pile-drive it to the ground. Putting the moves on something this big doesn't always go as planned. At a rodeo in Oklahoma earlier this year, he was trampled and suffered a deep bruise on his right biceps. In Denver, the animal reared up and kicked him. Yesterday, he drew a "butt boy," a steer that ducked its head but kept its ass in the air until Shorty finally kicked it. That took about eight seconds — forever in this sport in which the object is to get 'em laid as fast as you can.

Now it's a Sunday in early September, the last day of competition at the Show Me State Rodeo. And because final scores are tabulated by combining both days' times, he'll need to finish fast — in three seconds or less — to stay in contention for the first-place silver belt buckle.

When Shorty joined the Missouri Gay Rodeo Association in July 2003, it was obvious that the organization had some holes to fill. This year he was appointed group historian and assumed scrapbooking duty. Then he decided to do something relatively unprecedented: actually compete in rodeo events.

The organizers of the gay rodeo circuit standardized their rules back in 1982 so that gay cowboys could compete on almost the same level as their straight counterparts. There are traditional roping events in which contestants stand still or ride horses to lasso moving steers, or two-rider teams rope steers by their heads and haunches. There are traditional speed events, such as barrel racing, flag racing, and pole bending. And there are traditional roughstock events: steer, bronc, and bull riding, all pure machismo.

But gay rodeo also involves camp events, which is where things get queer. There's steer decorating, a partner event in which one cowboy ties a ribbon to a steer's tail while another removes a rope from its horns. There's the wild drag race, a threesome event requiring a man and a woman to drag a steer into the arena and someone dressed in drag to mount it and ride across a dirt finish line. And there's goat dressing, in which partners chase down a tethered goat to pull a pair of jockey-style underwear onto it.

Last January, before his first rodeo, in Phoenix, Shorty enrolled in a one-day rodeo school hoping to learn two powerhouse events: chute dogging and steer riding. After he witnessed a woman break her arm getting thrown, he thought about his limited health insurance and chickened out of riding steers.

Pinning rough stock remained an interest, though.

He struck out on the circuit after Phoenix, hitting competitions in Tulsa and Oklahoma City, Oklahoma; Albuquerque, New Mexico; Wichita, Kansas; Denver; and Chicago.

Now, at the Wyandotte County Fairgrounds, he watches four opponents get bucked off or disqualified immediately. The steers are bolting fast and pissed, sometimes dragging would-be desperados with them. That's the kind of rough ride Shorty likes. "I like to get down there, grab and go. I like to get in and get the hell out."

In the chute, he maneuvers the steer into a broad headlock, reaching a gloved hand around its skull, gripping its chin, and inserting his fingers into its mouth. He places his other hand on the horn in front of him, like it's a steering wheel.

At the buzzer, his gate swings open and man and animal rush out dragging each other like chained inmates in a jailbreak. Shorty leans down on the steer's outside horn and twists its head skyward. The motions come fast but time moves slowly. The ride lasts one . . . two . . . three long seconds before he body-slams the animal to the turf.

Shorty's story is similar to those of many MGRA members reared in the small towns surrounding Kansas City.

He dreamed of growing up to be a John Wayne type; he just never figured he'd want to ride into the sunset with another cowboy.

Born in Sweet Springs, Missouri, he was one of five brothers who all turned out to be truckers. The other boys dressed in relaxed jeans and listened to hard rock, but Shorty embraced his hick heritage, fancying tight jeans and flannel. As a kid, his emotions rebelled. He found other men attractive.

"You didn't know who was or who wasn't. Actually everybody

wasn't," he says of gay people in his hometown, about halfway between Kansas City and Columbia on Interstate 70. So he stayed in the closet. "I mean way back beneath the dirty clothes."

As a boy, he distracted himself with horses, learning to ride at the nearby rodeo grounds. He knew breeds like most gearheads know what's under their hoods. He worked long hours on local farms, feeding cows, castrating hogs, and breaking ponies, until he found a chore he liked well enough to start calling it a career — driving cross-state for a feed company. He fathered a child when he was eighteen but didn't marry the mother — throughout his twenties, Shorty's real love was a horse named Babe. When she died, it nearly broke his heart. At thirty-three, he married another woman, but that lasted less than a year.

By the time Shorty was forty, he realized he was lonely as hell. He'd bought himself his sixth horse, a new foal, but that didn't satisfy him, so he set out for the gay clubs in Columbia and Kansas City, moseying awkwardly among the dolled-up boys under disco lights.

Three years ago, he discovered Sidekicks, a Western-themed gay bar near Fortieth Street and Main, and decided to trade country living for midtown's more progressive pace. He took a part-time gig DJing at the bar and eventually secured a day job driving trucks for an Olathe glass company. Sidekicks is the Missouri Gay Rodeo Association's local watering hole, which is how Shorty eventually heard about the group.

As a spectator at his first gay rodeo in 2003, he immediately noticed the paradox: when cowboys who like cowboys move to the city to express themselves, most have to leave their horses behind.

And there's no place in the city to practice roping or riding, so when the rodeo comes to town, most first-time contestants gravitate toward the camp events.

"You don't have to have a horse, and you don't have to learn how to rope," explains Rocky Kuhn, a forty-eight-year-old circuit veteran who lives on a farm near Bethany. He's ridden gay rodeo for the past twelve years, first in Washington, D.C., and then, for the past decade, in Missouri. Kuhn competes in everything except broncs and bulls, usually placing in all eleven of his events. His favorites are flag racing, chute dogging, and pole bending.

This season, he also finished first in wild drag, but he doesn't tout this as a major accomplishment. "I do very well in wild drag, but I really don't like it that much," he says. "A lot of it is luck, as opposed to skill. It's in what animal you get."

In gay rodeo, he says, rough-stock events have a particularly low turnout. Overall, just eight bull riders and nine bronc riders competed nationally this season, compared with the more than two hundred who entered wild drag.

This isn't the archetypal posse of wranglers Shorty envisioned. Too much giddy, too little giddyup.

In late November, the battle to determine Missouri's best all-around gay cowboy will be settled in the usual way: with an elaborate beauty pageant.

In truth, the MGRA functions more like a drinking club than a group bent on refuting stereotypes.

Ad hoc homo rodeos had been in full swing in Reno, Nevada, and Denver for more than a decade before 1985, when delegates from separate rodeo groups in Texas, Arizona, Colorado, and California formalized as the International Gay Rodeo Association. In 1986, the Missouri Gay Rodeo Association joined the umbrella organization, which now holds more than twenty rodeos across the United States and Canada. Originally, in the '70s, the events were designed to increase awareness and raise money for charities such as the Muscular Dystrophy Association. Mainstream philanthropy didn't stop gay rodeo from encountering occasional bigotry, though. For the first rodeo, ranchers withheld their livestock; in the late '80s, one small town reneged on the arena lease. By the early '80s, auxiliary festivities such as drag shows, sing-a-thons, and the crowning of rodeo royalty became draws that rivaled the livestock events, and charitable proceeds were split between mainstream and gay causes.

The MGRA hosted its first rodeo in Kansas City in 1993; the group now has roughly 150 members, with separate chapters in Joplin and Springfield, says Mandy Barbarell, a drag queen who is the group's trustee. (Last year, St. Louis formed its own organization, the Gateway Gay Rodeo Association.)

The Kansas City chapter has just eighty members, barely enough to fill a corner in the city's larger gay clubs. And the group seems to have more groupies than rustlers. The association's only real form of self-promotion consists of a few bar crawls that function as re-cruiting drives.

"We try not to be too pushy. You show up in a martini bar with a bunch of dudes in Western shirts and Western hats, and people tend to ask questions," says president Chuck Kirkwood, who grew up on a farm in Oklahoma and volunteers as an event timer. "It's a way to catch some of the lifestyle we grew up with and share similar interests."

That's why the association's annually anointed ambassadors — Mr. Missouri Gay Rodeo (a man), Ms. Missouri Gay Rodeo (a woman), Miss Missouri Gay Rodeo (a drag queen), and MsTer Missouri Gay Rodeo (a drag king) — need never rope or ride. Though they're judged in four categories — horsemanship, an interview, a Western-wear pageant, and a talent show in which the contestant must perform a country song — the MGRA allows would-be caballeros to forgo mounting a horse and simply sketch their riding principles on a chalkboard.

Missouri's is one of the few gay rodeo associations that allows cowboys to be theoretical. Mr. MGRA 2003, Steven Hammontree, has no real horsemanship experience but recently signed with Wild Oats Records in Nashville. He's just released an album called *Breakin' Loose.* The so-called Cowboy Steve has been performing at clubs such as Missy B's, Sidekicks, and the now-defunct Cabaret for a decade. He says winning the title didn't get him the record deal, but carting merchandise to MGRA events has been a handy way to cross-promote. "It definitely helps me with my career," he says.

Being a real cowboy isn't a requirement, says the current Mr. MGRA, Jack Truman, who also lives on a farm outside of Kansas City. "It's just something they encourage on a national level," he says. "It's just nice to know they [contestants] know some aspect of rodeo and are not just . . . looking *purty.*"

In fact, times may be changing. The current Mr. IGRA, Ken Pool from Colorado, was a favored rope, speed, and rough-stock competitor with no performance experience.

Meanwhile, Shorty isn't exactly the sweetheart of the stage. Sure, he's stumbled up for karaoke once in a while, but he says singing makes him more nervous than tackling a steer.

"Everyone is watching you onstage," he says. "This competition is strictly by memory. It's a whole different aspect of performing."

He's bought background tracks for songs by Alan Jackson, George Strait, Vince Gill, and Tracy Byrd, but as of mid-October, he hasn't done much practicing. Not wanting to bother his roommate, he sings in his Jeep during morning commutes.

Shorty's competition for the Missouri title will be Kevin Lynn Beagley, a Northland hotel manager with shoulder-length blond hair who joined the organization last December and decided to make an immediate run for the title. He's a thirty-five-year-old aspiring singer-songwriter whose stage name is Kevin Lynn.

Lynn has no plans to go butch. He says he can saddle up if necessary, but he explains that he was always more interested in local 4-H bake-offs. "I also know my limitations," he adds. "I myself love to watch."

Shorty knows he's not supposed to trash-talk the competition.

In fact, rule number 8 in the IGRA Royalty's Abbreviated Guide to Dealing with the Media and the Public mandates: "When in doubt . . . be *perky* . . . Imagine you always have the ability to sprinkle happy dust on all those around you. Avoid discussing any IGRA (this includes your association and your chapter) dirty laundry where *anyone* can hear you."

Still, he can't help being a little catty. "His reasons are totally different than mine," Shorty says of Lynn. "I don't like him running for the position because he just wants that title."

According to Shorty, the unofficial slogan of gay rodeo is "We bring all the cowboys to town that you haven't slept with."

This is the kind of scene Shorty usually tries to avoid: on September 1, the day before the rodeo at the Wyandotte County Fairgrounds, last year's MGRA royalty and this year's candidates saddled barstools for a kickoff party at Sidekicks. Dudes were packed tightly together in a backroom that reeked of cigarette smoke and citrus cologne. Some leaned against a wooden fence surrounding a dance floor, thrusting their buckles at one another beneath an electric sunset.

This was the chance for candidates to court their blocs — bargoers who support the organization but don't seem to follow rodeo. A representative sampling included Tom, a closeted thirty-four-year-old from Warrensburg who is ignorant of the year's candidates; Bill, a thirty-three-year-old "fan of cowboys" who didn't belong to MGRA but might join sometime; and another guy in his late twenties who said loudly that he hoped Shorty didn't win because he never showed up to events like this. (Shorty admits that he sang at just one MGRA revue this year.)

But Shorty was expected to be here on this night to further his campaign. The shindig was a typical drag show. Men dressed like women and strutted like divas, lip-synching with the enthusiasm of high school talent-show contestants. Locals in the lineup included Miss MGRA 2005 Onyx Diamanté and Trixie, who lifted her skirt to reveal some unidentified plumbing.

Dressed in a red shirt, tamping a Marlboro into an ashtray, Kevin Lynn, a veteran performer at local revues, perched at a table beside a metal briefcase filled with musical selections — Cher, Janis Joplin, and Martina McBride. He wore a baby-blue contestant sash festooned with buttons supporting his candidacy.

Shorty hadn't arrived by the time Lynn took the stage and pointed two fingers in the air as though firing a make-believe six-shooter, or by the time he pulled a fresh black Stetson from a nearby box for his second number.

Though he was expected to sing, Shorty never showed. He claimed he got a flat tire trucking out of Omaha. After that, he decided he'd rather get sleep for the weekend's competition than stump at some bar.

It's a talent he's hesitant to admit, but Shorty can pull underwear onto a goat faster than just about anyone you've ever seen.

He discovered this gift accidentally. After Shorty dropped out of steer-riding school in Phoenix, his friend Destiny B. Childs (a purple-rouged drag queen from Washington, D.C., who is the current Miss International Gay Rodeo Association) needed a partner for wild drag and goat dressing and asked him to join her. Shorty swallowed his pride and obliged. When they took fifth place in the event that weekend, Shorty developed more than a passing interest. The event rewards natural sprinters, and he was lean and quick. It seemed the perfect low-skill alternative to sitting in the stands.

"It's basically something to do," he says. "I go, 'This is fun and easy and kinda crazy.'"

He was also good, earning enough points in chute dogging and goat dressing to finish second out of roughly forty rookies competing in a regional series with stops in Phoenix, Albuquerque, and Denver.

He's a competitor in whatever he does, and now, as the crowd gathers at the Wyandotte County Fairgrounds to cheer for the afternoon's camp events, it's his goat-dressing skills that will endear him.

At the sound of the buzzer, Shorty and his partner, Teeny Copafeelya, a short, middle-aged lesbian from Omaha, sprint from a dirt line in the center of the arena toward a goat tied to a rope that's anchored to a cinder block. He has ditched his hat, unholstered his cell phone, and traded his boots for a pair of softball cleats to pick up time.

The goat bucks at the end of its rope as Shorty and Teeny close in rapidly. Teeny, her arms thrust through the leg holes of a pair of blue underwear, gets there first and steps on the rope.

The duo met earlier this year in Wichita and found that they worked well together. Teeny had competed for seven years and burned through different partners before Shorty proved himself a smooth underwear handler.

Dressing goats is a sport of skill and chance. Sometimes the "lil bitch" is a runner. Sometimes her milk bag will leak all over you. Other times she can shake the undies off after you leave, getting you disqualified.

"Even something as simple and stupid as goat dressing, you still have to have strategy to get the best time," Shorty says. His basic game plan is pretty simple: "Wedgie the hell out of them."

He grabs the animal by its haunches and lifts its rear end into the air. When Teeny clamps her hands down on its haunches, Shorty releases his grip and slides the drawers straight off her arms and onto the animal and then pulls up hard. Then they turn and sprint back across the starting line. Shorty pumps his fist, whooping for the crowd.

He retreats to his shirtless boyfriend, Will McDonald, a computer programmer from St. Louis, while his offensive lineman–sized opponents take turns goosing the shell-shocked goats. He and McDonald have spent most of the morning hawking beer from a stand in the shadow of the bleachers. They were introduced at a rodeo in Chicago last weekend, and McDonald has since joined the MGRA to volunteer.

"We just kind of met," Shorty admits later. He says he's already thinking long-term. "Believe it or not, I'm not doing the hookup thing, but we met at a rodeo."

The loudspeaker announces that his time was just more than ten seconds, good enough for first place in today's heat and good enough to keep him in contention for the first-place silver buckle.

Earlier, Shorty confided that it might be sort of embarrassing to win first place overall in goat dressing. But now, as the drag queens cheer, he seems to have forgotten that.

"But the buckle? Who gets the buckle?" he chants hopefully to himself.

Last night in the fairground auditorium, which is reminiscent of an elementary school cafeteria, Shorty donned a low-cut, hot-pink dress and strutted for the other IGRA members as part of a charity auction. The garment went for $65. It was his first time in drag. He says he was told to get used to it. If he wins Mr. MGRA, he'll be playing dress-up for charity more often.

Now, after today's chute dogging and goat dressing, he will have to confront his stage fright by singing in a post-awards show in the same auditorium.

Folding chairs are parked at long golden plastic–covered tables topped by gold and silver stars. A small stage is set with the life-sized glittery silhouettes of a pair of cowboys near a banner announcing tonight's theme: WHEN THE DUST SETTLES LEGENDS ARE BORN. (Actually, the theme is supposed to be AFTER THE ROPING AND RIDING IT'S TIME TO RODEO, but because of a miscommunication, the set has been designed with the same theme as last year.)

The day's bull-riding event was a slaughter — none of the six riders managed to stay up for the six seconds necessary to score. Half the competitors were viciously tossed or trampled and required medical attention from on-site paramedics. Wild drag was more of a fashion show than a competition. One guy wore a hot-pink wig and a racing jumpsuit with boob and butt implants. Another wore an orange wig, a pink top, and a skirt revealing his bikini briefs.

Still, the awards ceremony lasted about two hours, with ribbons offered to even fifth-place finishers in the thirteen categories of men's and women's events.

About thirty people linger after the ceremony to hear the singers.

Cowboy Steve keeps their attention. Shorty stands in the shadows next to Lynn.

Before stepping out to sing, Shorty faces Lynn and admits that he has a problem he's never had to deal with. His throat is raw from a day spent yelling and eating dust and smoking countless cigarettes. This is something Great American Cowboys shouldn't have to think about: how too much hollerin' might affect one's dulcet tones.

"Try a little bit of lemon in water," Lynn tells him gently.

There isn't any water handy, so he reaches crudely into a condiment cup on a nearby bar, grabs a lemon rind, and tosses it directly into his mouth.

He performs Alan Jackson's "Little Bitty," leaning away from the audience, speaking the lyrics more than singing them, in a deep, commanding rasp. Shorty forgets a verse and stumbles to find his place, but Jackson's voice is faintly audible in the backing track, and he manages to pick up the lyrics again for the chorus.

> Well, it's all right to be little bitty
> Little hometown or a big old city
> Might as well share, might as well smile
> Life goes on for a little bitty while

Shorty's finishing *Yee-ha!* is the only part of the act that sounds authentic.

On November 10, Shorty will have a chance to compete against the country's best cowboys at the IGRA National Finals in Dallas.

In a goat-dressing showdown.

The top twenty competitors in each event make the finals. Nationally, Shorty placed forty-seventh out of ninety-nine in chute dogging. But in goat dressing, which attracted 164 participants over the course of the season, Shorty and Teeny came up big, finishing twenty-fifth and thirty-second, respectively, to earn an invitation to the finals as alternates. Rocky Kuhn will be there in Dallas too. He finished among the top three in calf roping, breakaway roping, team roping, and flag racing and placed well enough to represent Missouri in the rest of his eleven events.

All of them will probably face camera crews from Hero Unit Productions, a company that's been at tour stops in Oklahoma

City, Minneapolis, Denver, Atlanta, Los Angeles, and San Francisco filming a seven-part documentary series for broadcast on the gay cable station OUTtv this fall. In Atlanta, the crew's presence caused a minor disruption when at least eight competitors dropped out because they were afraid of going public, Shorty says. He reckons the publicity will be a good thing. He even two-stepped with a male producer while the cameras rolled in Denver.

His feelings about actually winning the goat-dressing title are mixed.

"To be a world champion in goat dressing would actually be quite embarrassing because it means I can dress a goat faster than anyone else can," he says. He thinks for a moment. "It's not really embarrassing — it's just, how should I put this? It's just kind of a letdown. Aw, I can't find the right word for it . . . I mean, I would rather be there in chute dogging, but at the same time, I placed well enough my rookie year to get to finals. If you have the chance to win the belt buckle for chute dogging or goat dressing, what would you rather have?"

Nonetheless, when he enters the arena in Dallas, he'll be representing Missouri and looking to win. He'd be an unlikely hero in an obscure event. But isn't that how frontier legends begin?

JEFF PEARLMAN

Mom's the Word

FROM NEWSDAY

WITHIN THE FOUR WALLS of the major league clubhouse, the concept of homosexuality fits about as comfortably as a pair of mittens on a porcupine. For the most part, men who love men and women who love women are not gays or lesbians, but "queers" and "dykes." Trip over a mitt and you're a "faggot." As for ideas of civil unions and gay marriage — forget about it.

"Baseball is very set in its ways," Cincinnati Reds outfielder Jacob Cruz said. "Always has been."

Within these confines, there is a man who seems to hover above it all. He is a twenty-five-year-old right-handed relief pitcher with the Reds, a quiet Long Island kid with blazing brown eyes and a blazing ninety-five-mile-per-hour fastball. He is as open as he needs to be, not afraid to tell the truth about his family but aware that its implications might not sit perfectly with the forty or so other young men who surrounded him recently in the Reds' spring training clubhouse.

"I'm a blue-state guy in a red-state sport," Joe Valentine said. "But that won't stop me from being proud of who I am."

Who is Joe Valentine?

He is a 1997 graduate of Deer Park High School.

He is a former All-American at Jefferson Davis Community College in Alabama.

He is a happily married North Babylon resident who wants to start a family.

He is a potential future closer for the Reds.

One more thing. Consider the following dialogue, which took place on a lazy spring training morning between a pitcher fighting to make the club and a baseball writer wrapping up another run-of-the-mill Grapefruit League interview.

Joe, can I give your parents a call?

"Sure."

Okay, what are their names?

"Deb and Doreen."

That's right: Joe Valentine is the son of two gay women.

He tells you this without an iota of emphasis, almost as if he were explaining the mechanics of a slider or giving directions to the nearest 7-Eleven. There is no additional explanation, no awkward pause for effect. Nothing.

"It's no different than having a mother and father," he said. "These are the two women who raised me, and they are wonderful people. It's just not a big deal to me. Why should it be?"

In an enlightened world, it shouldn't. But major league baseball is to enlightenment what Pauly Shore is to career longevity. It took until 1959 for every team to have at least one black player. There never has been a female umpire. And in the history of the league, no active player has ever come out of the closet to express his homosexuality.

"I've got nothing against those people," Washington Nationals relief pitcher T. J. Tucker said recently. "But I don't get why anyone would want to be like that."

Moments after Tucker's comment, a Nationals front-office employee approached a reporter and asked him not to bring the subject of homosexuality into the clubhouse. "Makes the players uncomfortable," the employee said.

Years ago, then-Giants second baseman Jeff Kent was changing out of his uniform when he glanced at the nearby reporters and cracked, "There are no queers here, are there?" The comment barely raised an eyebrow.

Valentine is aware of the stigma. That is why his family asked that this story not be published until Valentine secured a spot on the major league roster.

"We've almost never been treated badly," said Deb Valentine, Joe's birth mother. "But we live in the real world, and you don't 100 percent know how people will react."

Here's the startling thing: thus far in Joe Valentine's life, few have reacted.

Born in Las Vegas on Christmas Eve 1979, Joe is the biological son of Deb Valentine and a man she prefers not to discuss, a man Joe does not know. Deb declined to discuss the circumstances of the pregnancy, but when she delivered Joe at Sunrise Hospital, the person by her side was Doreen Price, her life partner since they first met in a bowling alley in 1975.

At the time, homosexuality was an unacceptable lifestyle in approximately 99 percent of America. Las Vegas was the 1 percent.

"Vegas was Vegas," Deb said. "Open-minded. Accepting. Embracing. Doreen was my coach in the hospital, and nobody there raised an eyebrow. Vegas was ten times more liberal than New York is even today. Being gay just wasn't a big deal."

The couple operated a hair salon in Las Vegas, and in 1982 moved to North Babylon, where they opened Hair Studio 231, which lasted four years. When Joe was just sixteen months old, Doreen was throwing him a baseball. At two, he fielded his first grounder with his nose.

"Blood all over," Doreen said. "But we wiped it off, and he was back looking for the baseball."

At age five, Joe signed up for Little League, and by eight he was one of the best athletes around. His gift was a strong right arm. His Little League coach for two seasons? Doreen, who had played competitive softball.

"Joe could always throw," she said. "I mean, he had a real powerful arm. And he kept working and working to get better. I think we knew he was a special kind of baseball player."

Remarkably — and against all hardball logic — Valentine rarely pitched. He was a catcher whose greatest joy came from nailing a hapless runner trying to swipe second. Young Joe loved everything about squatting behind the plate. The power of calling a game. The dirt crumbling between his fingers. The pop-pop-pop of rawhide meeting leather. The collisions at home.

"I wanted to be in the middle of the action," he said. "Not making random appearances here and there."

By the time he arrived at Deer Park as a sophomore in 1994 (Joe attended St. Anthony's in Huntington as a freshman), Valentine was one of the better young ballplayers on Long Island.

"He was exceptional," Deer Park coach Carmine Argenziano said. "Even when we had pitchers who had poor moves and couldn't hold anyone on, no one would run on Joe. He was a weapon back there."

In fact, Argenziano once said, "He used to throw it back to our pitchers harder than they threw it to him. It was scary."

Meanwhile, Deb and Doreen attended every Deer Park game. People in the stands assumed Deb was Joe's "mom" and Doreen his "aunt," and none of the three would argue.

"If it eases what people need to believe," Doreen said, "so be it."

Joe swears he never has been embarrassed by his family. It is all he has ever known. But the unpredictability of facial expressions that greet "These are my mothers" is, well, awkward.

Making things easier, the two women never held hands, kissed, or hugged at the games. Partially to avoid controversy, but also because it's not who they are.

"We went to watch baseball," Doreen said. "We're not trying to make statements."

By the end of his senior year, most of his teammates and their parents knew Joe was the product of a gay relationship. Heck, the kids used to hang out at Joe's house.

"One day I heard a teacher talking about Joe, and that he had two mothers," Argenziano said. "I was shocked, truly shocked. But you know what? I also didn't care. Those two women did a helluva job raising one fine man. A helluva job."

College recruiters began showing up during Valentine's senior season in 1997. Not big-time schools like Arizona State and Miami, but local colleges willing to overlook his so-so hitting ability.

After batting .370 as a senior and making his second All-County team, Valentine played for the Bayside Yankees, a summer-league team that has produced more than twenty major league players. During Valentine's first summer with Bayside, coach Marc Cuseta often was frustrated by his catcher's refusal to take the mound.

"You know how high school kids are," Cuseta said. "They wanna be the star, bat third, and be in the lineup every day. Joe was no different."

But when it finally became clear to Valentine that his future as a catcher was limited because of his hitting, he relented. In the summer of 1998, Bayside turned him into its closer, and after several weeks of just throwing midnineties fastballs and hoping they sailed over the plate, Valentine picked up the slider that's now his major league "out" pitch.

Valentine accepted a scholarship to Dowling College but grew frustrated with the program and left during his first semester. Eventually, Cuseta called an old pal, Keith Griffin, the baseball coach at Jefferson Davis Community College in Brewton, Alabama, and told him about an under-the-radar pitcher with an infinite upside.

Joe Valentine was moving to the heart of the Bible Belt.

With his gay parents.

They expected the worst. When Deb and Doreen followed Joe south and settled into an apartment in nearby Pensacola, Florida, they envisioned one hostile face after another. This was Alabama, after all, onetime home of church bombings and tree lynchings. Perhaps if they played it cool, nobody would notice. But inevitably, someone would get the picture, that Joe's "aunt" (wink-wink) wasn't his aunt.

It didn't take long.

"I remember people finding out and thinking it was something to joke about," Valentine said. "They'd say, 'Oh, so you must be gay, huh?'"

"What?" Valentine would reply.

"Well, you must be gay," one person said. "But how come you don't act all foo-fooey? You're not elegant. You're just a regular guy."

"What the hell is 'foo-fooey'?" Valentine says now. "People can be so incredibly narrow-minded. But I'm not someone who starts fights over this stuff. I'm a patient guy."

Deb and Doreen attended every Jefferson Davis game that season, becoming unofficial team mothers as their son compiled an 8–1 record and was named to the NJCAA All-Region XXII team. They'd invite Joe's teammates out for lunch and dinner. Sometimes even cook. Gay? Straight? Most of the players were just happy to be looked after.

"If you're a good boy, I don't care if you're from Mars," Griffin said. "And Joe was as good a boy as I've ever had around. He's hardworking, he's very competitive, and he's got a big heart. I'll tell you, very few seemed to care that his parents were gay. They were wonderful people. And Joe — he's a man's man."

Valentine's decision to attend Jefferson Davis was a good one. In June 1999, he was selected by the Chicago White Sox in the twenty-sixth round of the amateur draft.

Throughout his six-year, four-organization professional baseball career, Joe Valentine rarely has volunteered information about his parents. Again, it's not that he's embarrassed. But why risk starting trouble?

Every so often, however, when he's comfortable, Valentine lets his guard down.

Three years ago, while playing for the Double-A Birmingham Barons, Valentine roomed with Gary Majewski, a right-handed pitcher from Houston. One night they were watching TV, shooting the breeze. "I don't remember how we got on the subject," said Majewski, now with the Nationals. "He just sort of told me. I was like, 'Um, okay.' Joe is a cool dude."

And Valentine can play. After bouncing from the White Sox to the Tigers to the White Sox to the A's to the Reds, he made his big league debut with Cincinnati in 2003 (a forgettable two innings and 18.00 ERA). He pitched in twenty-four games last season, going 2–3 with four saves and a 5.22 ERA. He initially struggled in spring training this year but made the Reds out of camp. Against the Mets on Thursday, Valentine pitched the eighth inning of a 6–1 Reds victory, allowing two hits and one unearned run and striking out two.

Deb and Doreen, who are retired and live in North Port, Florida, plan on seeing Joe pitch as often as possible. And when they show up in the family area after games, surrounded by the brigade of wives and husbands and kids, their son will, as always, proudly greet them with a hug. They are his loved ones. His moms.

"I don't see myself as an activist for gay rights, although I will speak up if I need to," Valentine said. "I think people need to judge others for who they are. Not by any prejudiced ideas or thoughts. I'm a baseball player who was raised by two wonderful, loving mothers. How can anyone criticize that?"

LINDA ROBERTSON

XXL

FROM THE MIAMI HERALD

STOCKAR MCDOUGLE, son of a chef, is the largest Miami Dolphin at six-four, 348 pounds. He wears size 16 cleats, size 46 pants, a size 62 suit jacket, and a size 15 ring. He is a mountain of a man, but a mountain who can run the 40-yard dash in 5.2 seconds and bench-press 450 pounds.

McDougle's teammate, Wade Smith, majored in eating as a college senior, adding 25 pounds to impress NFL scouts. He has packed on almost 100 pounds in seven years to remake himself as a football player. He longs for the day when his wife can see him slim down from 315 to 220 because that is "the real me."

University of Miami tackle Eric Winston insists he won't bulk up as Smith did. He hopes his reputation as a master of the "pancake block" and his 312 pounds will be enough to make it in the NFL.

Teenager Kevin Perez, 275 pounds and growing, dreams of being a pro. So he drinks three high-calorie "Gainer" shakes per day to supplement frozen pizzas for breakfast and mounds of Cuban food for dinner. The Miami Killian High player hired a personal trainer. The focus on body expansion paid off; he signed a scholarship to Georgia.

Like Perez, Pace High's Javon Hill — six-four, 330 pounds — makes his classmates look Lilliputian. He was taller than his teachers in elementary school and banned from age-group leagues for fear of crushing opponents.

Add up these five offensive linemen and you get three-quarters of a ton of massive muscle. They are part of a trend that shows no signs of tapering. It's the boom of the bulge in football. Players have grown bigger at every position at every level, especially in the past ten years along the line of scrimmage.

The 2005 opening day rosters of the NFL included an unprecedented 332 players who weighed three hundred pounds or more. Thirty years ago, there were none.

"When I played, a three-hundred-pounder was a freak," said UM associate head coach Art Kehoe, forty-eight, and a former Hurricanes offensive lineman. "Today, if you don't weigh three hundred pounds you are a freak."

Former Dolphin Bob Heinz was considered the team's behemoth when he played defensive tackle at 265 pounds from 1969 to 1977. "I'm lucky I played in a different era," Heinz said. "It would be scary to play now."

A National Bigness

Like American houses, Hummers, and hamburgers, football players are a reflection of the bigness of our society. The average male weighs twenty-five pounds more than he did forty years ago, and two-thirds of Americans are overweight — one-third obese.

But the increase in size of football players has outpaced that of the general population. Linemen are about sixty-four pounds heavier than they were forty years ago. While big might be better for the spectacle of the game, as Sumo-like players wrestle in the trenches, it is likely to have harmful repercussions on athletes' health. They are incredible, vulnerable hulks.

San Francisco Forty-Niner Thomas Herrion collapsed and died after a preseason game. An autopsy revealed that the six-four, 335-pound offensive lineman's right coronary artery was nearly blocked. Chris Stewart, a six-one, 290-pound seventeen-year-old, died of heat stroke last summer while practicing in Oklahoma City. Complications from heat stroke caused the death of 335-pound Minnesota Vikings offensive tackle Korey Stringer in 2001. Two retired linemen died young in recent years: former Saint Frank Warren died of a heart attack in 2002, and former Packer and Eagle Reggie White died last December as a result of a respiratory ailment associated with sleep apnea.

Increased Risk

The extra weight they carried as players put them at increased risk for the problems that killed them.

"My concern about the humongous players of today is what's going to happen when they retire," said Dolphin Hall of Famer Larry Little, who weighed 265 as a player and gained 20 pounds upon retirement. "We're going to have a lot of four-hundred-pound people walking around — or being buried."

A University of North Carolina endocrinologist's study categorizing 56 percent of NFL players as fat was criticized by the league for not taking into account their lean muscle, but inside NFL locker rooms, shirtless linemen can't hide the fact that many of them could use girdles or bras. They are built like oak trees, with thick trunks and limbs, but have all-too-human bellies hanging over their waistbands.

"Some guys carry a gut, and you have to if you want to hold your ground against a three-hundred-twenty-pound defensive lineman," Smith said. "When I go back home, my friends say, 'Man, you got big.' And I say, 'That's what it takes to play in the NFL.'"

Football's XXL athletes are prime candidates for chronic pain. Almost inescapable is damage to the musculoskeletal frame, under strain to support three-hundred-plus pounds of flesh through countless explosive thrusts, twists, and collisions.

"All my players are coming back to me in their forties and fifties for ankle, knee, and hip replacements, and with spinal problems and arthritis," said Dr. Pierce Scranton, who was team physician for the Seattle Seahawks for seventeen years. "They were fed like Kobe beef cows to get huge, and now they are paying one hell of a price."

Sleep apnea, a brief cessation of breathing, afflicts 34 percent of NFL linemen compared to 4 percent of the general population, according to a 2003 study printed in the *New England Journal of Medicine.*

The NFL's largest players are 50 percent more likely to suffer from cardiovascular disease than the average person, Dr. Sherry Baron found in a National Institute of Occupational Safety and Health study. The risk to linemen was six times higher than that to smaller NFL players.

The body mass index (BMI) of NFL retirees has increased steadily in the past twenty-five years, with a sharp turn upward in the 1990s, according to Dr. Kevin Guskiewicz, research director of the University of North Carolina's Center for the Study of Retired Athletes. BMI is equal to weight (in kilograms) divided by height (in meters) squared. Anything over 30 is classified as obese. The average BMI of players from the 1990s is 32, and plenty are in the 40s.

He also compared the BMIs of the 2003 Carolina Panthers defensive line (37–38) with those of the "Steel Curtain" Pittsburgh linemen of the 1970s (28–30).

"The game has changed, and not gradually," Guskiewicz said. "Unless we have six-eight and six-nine players, the BMI will continue to go up."

NFL retirees age faster than normal, Guskiewicz found. Among other ailments, they reported high rates of hypertension and diabetes, which are usually linked to being overweight.

"The ex-players tend to convert lean mass into adipose [fat], and the heart is really being taxed," Guskiewicz said. Most players pledge to shed weight upon retirement. But their good intentions are usually foiled by hefty eating habits and the lingering effects of injuries. It hurts too much to exercise. Heinz ballooned during retirement, and only after having knee and hip replacements was he able to take up golf and bike riding and lose weight.

Fiercer Collisions

Bigger players mean more violent collisions. Dr. Tim Gay, a University of Nebraska physicist, figures a 50 percent increase in the mass of linemen since the NFL was founded in 1920 plus a 10 percent increase in speed equals a doubling of the kinetic energy along the line of scrimmage.

"I think we're going to see more injuries because improvements in equipment have leveled off," he said.

The NFL Players Association (NFLPA) counted 4,200 injuries last season.

"The injury rate is steady at 100 percent; everybody gets injured," said Michael Duberstein, who retired recently after twenty-four years as the NFLPA's research director. "What remains to be seen is how the increase in size will affect the type and severity of injuries."

Scranton predicts that every player will wind up with arthritis and nearly all will need synthetic joints. The movements of a 300-pound lineman will typically place 450 pounds of force on the hip and 700 pounds on the ankle.

"Keep in mind that the joint cartilage of a five-three, one-hundred-twenty-pound woman is exactly the same structurally and biologically as that of a three-hundred-twenty-pound man," Scranton said. "Subject it repetitively to thousands of pounds of force and you will wear it out."

Former Dolphins O-lineman Ron Heller has had both knees and a shoulder replaced in the past eighteen months. He is forty-three. After eight years of pain, anti-inflammatory injections, and reliance on a motorized scooter to get around, he can go fishing and hiking on his Montana ranch near the Beartooth Mountains. In twelve NFL seasons, he went from being the heaviest lineman (285) in Tampa to the lightest lineman (305) in Miami. He's down to 255.

"I had fifteen surgeries as a player," said Heller, a sales manager for a cattle supplement maker. "My wife would beg me not to play hurt. In between my last five games as a Dolphin I didn't practice and used crutches because my knees swelled so bad. Being big exacerbated everything."

"Fans Are Awed"

"The size thing — fans are awed by it and coaches are fixated on it. People will say proudly, 'My son is already up to two-eighty,' and I'll see the kid and think, *Boy, he is fat.* I believe it's time to examine whether the three-hundred-pound benchmark is counterproductive."

Players sound fatalistic when they talk about how they have sacrificed their bodies for the game. The reward is an NFL salary — $1.4 million on average.

"We are gladiators. It worries you, but it's the life we've chosen, and this is how we feed our families," said Vernon Carey, who has dropped 30 pounds to 340 since being drafted out of the University of Miami by the Dolphins. His body fat is still high at 26 percent.

McDougle said he was saddened by Herrion's death but never pictured himself in Herrion's shoes.

"You see the news but you don't see it, otherwise you couldn't do this for a living," he said. 'If I'm smart and want to live to old age, I will lose weight when I retire. I know I feel better at three-forty than I did at three-sixty. It's murder toting too much of yourself around."

Mankind has gotten larger since he traded spear for drive-through window, but it's not just evolution of the species that accounts for the growth spurt in football. It's evolution of the game. Blocking rules have been liberalized to protect quarterbacks so they can throw more passes. Offensive linemen can extend their arms and use their hands to tie up defenders. Less attention is paid to footwork and the choreography of pull blocking and trapping, and more is placed on upper-body leverage — like Greco-Roman wrestling — and straight-ahead bull rushing.

Ex-linemen lament the loss of finesse and agility for the gain in power and bulk. "I see a lot of belly bumping," Little said. "They want a big guy to plug the middle and a bigger guy to bulldoze him out of there."

Said Heinz: "When I started, you couldn't hold at all. Now there is holding on every play."

Use of Steroids

In the 1970s and 1980s, it was not uncommon for linemen to use steroids, say players and coaches. Heller recalled guys coming back from the offseason twenty pounds heavier and "strong as an ox."

Once the NFL banned steroids and started testing for them in 1987, reliance on the drugs declined. Players had to find other ways to get bigger and stronger. Weight lifting had been nearly nonexistent; Little said he did push-ups until the Dolphins put a Universal machine in a storage room. But succeeding generations learned they could pile on pounds and muscle in the weight room and at the training table.

"Prior to testing, a great deal of linemen used steroids and freely admitted it," Scranton said. "I saw guys who retired and shrunk fifty pounds, and they'd tell me, 'I'm off the juice, Doc.' Since 1987, the science of conditioning and nutrition has taken over. Players know how to induce their bodies to get bigger."

Teams built high-tech weight rooms and hired strength and conditioning coaches and dietitians. Players were given detailed plans for sculpting their bodies to the ideal parameters.

"Years ago, a three-hundred-forty-pounder was a fat slob, plain and simple," said former Dolphins, Cowboys, and UM coach Jimmy Johnson. "Now he does not have much excess flab. These guys are working year-round to be fit, not just two weeks before training camp."

Johnson coached what was the biggest, fiercest offensive line in history when the Cowboys won Super Bowls in 1992 and 1993. The strategy was simple: overpower the defense and hand the ball to Emmitt Smith. Other teams copied the Dallas blueprint. While some, notably the Denver Broncos, have reverted to more complex blocking schemes, most still seek to build an impenetrable wall. At the 2005 NFL combine, fifty-eight of the sixty-one linemen weighed 300-plus. The other three weighed 299 or 298.

But bigness alone won't suffice, players and coaches say.

"Most guys are more athletic than they appear and healthier than an average person who is thirty pounds lighter," Wade Smith said. "If you are giant but slow you won't survive in the NFL."

Kehoe wants his linemen to have no more than 20 percent body fat; otherwise they tend to be lumbering, breathless, and injury-prone.

When Little was coach at Bethune-Cookman, he cut players he deemed "sloppy."

"I've seen huge guys who can't bust a grape," he said. "I also had a three-hundred-fifty-pound kid who could do a three-sixty dunk. You can't always go by the number on the scale."

Yet numbers are dictating which players get noticed. As the game has grown, so have the stakes and the stars. Big kids are identified early, almost as in the old Soviet and current Chinese systems of selecting promising athletes according to body type. Coaches look for youngsters with long arms and large parents. They are groomed throughout their teens.

Perez, the Killian High blue-chip tackle, attended the University of Miami camp, Down and Dirty camp, and Nike combine.

"Looking at the college rosters and going to the camps forces you to gain weight," Perez said. "I realized a two-hundred-fifty-pounder wouldn't get recruited by a top Division I school. Bottom line, they're making an investment in you."

Perez has gained ninety pounds since his freshman year.

UM's Winston doesn't plan to add more weight for February's NFL combine.

"Not Worth It"

"I don't want to do that to my body," he said. "It's not worth it when you're done playing by age thirty."

Where does it end? Aaron Gibson, a six-seven guard who needed a custom-enlarged helmet from Riddell, was the NFL's first four-hundred-pound man. The Bears released him earlier this year.

"I don't see it reaching a plateau," Johnson said. "Not as long as they keep getting bigger *and* faster *and* stronger. Not as long as you've got quarterbacks throwing sixty-two times in a game."

Hill, the senior coveted by Duke, was teased as a kid. He was a supersized oddity. But today he is Superman.

"When I hear the 'Ooh' of the crowd after a big pop, that gives me a jolt of energy. When I hear my mom ringing her cowbell in the stands, that feels good."

He recalled going to games when his older sister was a cheerleader.

"I thought the players were monsters," he said with a chuckle. "Now I guess I'm the monster."

MICHAEL SOKOLOVE

Clang!

FROM THE NEW YORK TIMES MAGAZINE

BEHOLD THE SLAM-DUNK, the pulse-quickening, throw-it-down, in-your-face signature move of the National Basketball Association. The dunk is a declaration of power and dominance, of machismo. In a team game, an ensemble of five players a side, it is an expression of self. In a sport devoted to selling sneakers, the dunk is a marketing tour de force, the money shot at the end of every worthy basketball sequence. (When you see the shoes in the thirty-second spot, what is the wearer of those shoes always doing?) Next weekend in Denver, the cultural moment that is the NBA All-Star Game will take place, an event set annually amid a weekend of concerts, lavish parties, and showy displays of fashion. On such a big stage (and with defensive standards momentarily relaxed), the game itself is sure to be a veritable dunkathon, a string of self-satisfied throw-downs by the league's biggest stars. If I had my way, at the conclusion of the game the dunk would be taken out of commission. Banned as a first step toward rescuing a game that has strayed far from its roots, fundamentals, and essential appeal.

The addiction to the dunk is emblematic of the direction in which basketball — like all major pro sports, really — has been heading: less nuance, more explosive force. Greater emphasis on individual heroics and personal acclaim, less on such quaint values as teamwork and sacrifice. Basketball's muscled-up, minimally skilled dunker is the equivalent of baseball's steroid-fueled home run slugger or the guided-missile NFL linebacker, his helmet aimed at anything that moves. It is all part of a video-game aesthetic being transplanted into our real games: the athlete as action hero, an essentially antisocial lone wolf set apart from teammates, dedicated to his own personal glory and not bound by much of anything, even the laws of gravity. (Last month the sports media giant ESPN entered into an $850 million partnership with Electronic Arts, the video-game company that turns real-life athletes into digitized figures, further blurring the distinction between flesh-and-blood athletes and the superhumans we have come to expect in the sports arena.)

In November, an ugly incident, a brawl between NBA players and fans in Detroit, led some commentators to conclude that pro basketball is populated by thugs. (My online search of the keywords "NBA" and "thug" a month later produced more than four hundred hits.) But the fight was an aberration; NBA players are, in my experience, as gentlemanly as (or more so than) athletes in other pro sports. The NBA doesn't have a thug problem; it has a basketball problem. Its players are the best athletes in all of pro sports — oversize, swift, and agile — but weirdly they are also the first to have devolved to a point where they can no longer play their own game.

Unbelievable as it may seem, you can make millions in today's NBA without having even one semi-reliable way to put the ball in the basket — no jump shot, no hook shot, no little twelve-foot bank shot. In fact, the entire area between dunking range and the three-point line, what used to be prime real estate for scoring, is now a virtual dead zone. (The three-point shot is the other one of the NBA's twin addictions, but more on that later.) Richard Hamilton of the Detroit Pistons, last year's NBA champion, has been just about knighted for his ability to consistently sink the "midrange" jumper, which used to be an entry-level requirement into the NBA — if you couldn't do that, you had to find another line of work. But not anymore. This generation of players is so young, so green, so unschooled (four years of college is now exceedingly rare), so raised on a diet of ESPN highlights, that many have nothing but so-called NBA bodies.

Last year, the New Jersey Nets scored fifty-six points in a playoff game. Fifty-six! "We just missed shots," said a Nets player. No kidding. Wilt Chamberlain once averaged more than fifty points a game, all by himself. Two decades ago, teams averaged about one hundred and ten points a game; this year, the figure is about ninety-six points per game (which is actually three points better than last season). Presented with players bent on executing high-light-reel dunks — but who otherwise do not pass well, shoot well, or move effectively to open spots on the floor — many NBA coaches have slowed the pace to a plodding, unwatchable crawl. And the more important the game, the more slowly it is played. "It's an incongruity," Rod Thorn, the president of the Nets, told me. "We have better athletes than ever, but they play at a slower pace. The reason is they're not as sound fundamentally, so the coaches feel that the faster they play, the more mistakes they'll make."

The dunk, by the way, has been banned once before, for reasons other than the one I am proposing. In 1965, a seven-foot-one basketball player of uncommon grace and coordination graduated from Power Memorial Academy in New York City and enrolled at UCLA, then the dominant force in college basketball. In his first season, Kareem Abdul-Jabbar (then known as Lew Alcindor) led UCLA to a national championship. Faced with the probability that no other team would have any chance at a title for the duration of Abdul-Jabbar's stay, the NCAA outlawed "basket stuffing," aka the dunk. No one said straight out that the new rule was meant to handicap the young giant, but it immediately became known as the Alcindor rule. UCLA still thrived, winning national championships in both of Abdul-Jabbar's remaining two seasons. "After the so-called Alcindor rule was passed . . . some skeptics said he wouldn't be as great," John Wooden, the legendary UCLA coach, observed years later. "They ignored his tremendous desire and determination. He worked twice as hard on banking shots off the glass, his little hook across the lane, and his turnaround jumper."

In other words, Abdul-Jabbar, already skilled, became even more so. His "sky hook" — released five to ten feet from the basket, with his right arm fully extended and the ball cradled in one hand — remains the most devastatingly effective, and most beautiful, shot in the history of the game. A close second, in terms of grace, might be the "finger roll" of Julius Erving, in which high-flying Dr. J glided above defenders and let the ball roll toward the hoop with his palm facing up, as if he were a waiter extending a serving tray. It is no coincidence that Erving played his college basketball within the years (1967 to 1976) that the Alcindor rule was in effect: the finger roll is the kind of move you invent when the option of just powering it to the basket and stuffing it is not available.

Earl Monroe, a stylish guard who played for the New York Knicks in the 1970s, employed "tempo changes only Thelonious Monk would understand," the music and social critic Nelson George has written. Many others over the years have seen basketball as jazz, an apt comparison when the game is played well — as an amalgam of creativity, individuality, collaboration, improvisation, and structure. Much of what makes basketball interesting is the give and take, the constant tension, between individual expression and team concepts. On the best teams, players take their turns as soloists, but not at the expense of others in the quintet.

The most obvious aspect of basketball, especially at the NBA level, is the extraordinary athleticism of the players. What is less apparent is that the outcome of games, more so than in any other major sport, is determined by a series of social interactions. Basketball coaches have long taught that the ball must be "shared" — passed from player to player until it ends up in the hands of the one with the best possible shot. Players are urged constantly to "talk" on defense — communicate about the alignment and movements of offensive players — and to "give help," meaning that a defender is not just responsible for the man he is guarding but also for sliding over to help a teammate who has been beaten by his own man. With just five players on the court at a time and rosters that consist of just twelve men, NBA teams are intimate groups, extended families almost, and the ones that succeed cover for individual weaknesses and stress their strengths. They play as if they are aware of, and care for, one another.

One reason that fans of a certain age remember and still cherish the great Knicks teams of the early '70s is because they seemed to be such a functional, appealing social unit. The guards Walt "Clyde" Frazier, Dick Barnett, and Earl Monroe were sort of urban hipsters. Bill Bradley, the dead-eye shooter and future United States senator, was an Ivy League wonk nicknamed "Dollar Bill" by his teammates for the presumed cost of the bargain-basement suits he wore. Willis Reed and Dave DeBusschere did the dirty work under the basket and were so blue-collar in their approach to the game that it wasn't hard to imagine them carrying lunch buckets to some MTA rail yard. They meshed seamlessly on the court, elevating the concept of sharing the ball (Coach Red Holzman's mantra was "hit the open man") to something like an art form. The same could be said of the Los Angeles Lakers of Magic Johnson and Abdul-Jabbar in the '80s, the so-called Showtime teams. The multitalented Johnson, in particular, was understood to have sacrificed his own scoring in order to involve teammates in a free-flowing, high-scoring offense.

Few teams play like that anymore because basketball culture in America is broken in ways that go beyond the addiction to dunking or the decline in fundamentals like shooting. It has always been possible to identify extraordinary basketball talent at very young ages. The game's phenoms present early, like female gymnasts or violin prodigies (and unlike athletes in, say, football or baseball, where seemingly talented twelve-year-olds often just fizzle out). What has changed in basketball is that a whole constellation has been created for the phenoms; they are separated out and sent off to dwell in a world of their own. An industry of tout sheets and recruiting services identifies them as early as fifth or sixth grade, and they begin traveling a nationwide circuit of tournaments with their high-powered youth teams. In the summer, the best high school players attend showcases sponsored by the big sneaker companies. (The latest of the prodigies earned cover notice on *Sports Illustrated* in January. "Meet Demetrius Walker," the headline said. "He's 14 Years Old. You're Going to Hear From Him.")

Quite understandably, these young stars, rather than being prone to sharing the ball, are apt to believe they own it. "I'm amazed when guys make it out of that system with any sense of perspective at all," said Jeff Van Gundy, the former Knicks coach now coaching the Houston Rockets. "It's not natural to be that catered to at such a young age. We've got kids being named the 'best eleven-year-old basketball player in America.' How the hell do you recover from that?"

As Van Gundy knows too well, many do not recover. The NBA's upper tier, its elite performers (the American ones, as opposed to the increasing number of foreign-born players), now typically come out of a system in which they have been pointed toward the "next level" since grammar school. They have never played in the present tense. Their high school coach and teammates may well have been secondary to their peer group of nationally recognized megastars. If they stopped off in college before turning pro, it was probably for just a year or two. It is not often easy to coach such a player because he is likely to see himself as a finished product, in no need of instruction, polishing, or discipline. (My favorite college coach, John Chaney of Temple University, recently benched a couple of players because they showed up for the team bus without the winter hats he requires in cold weather. Unsurprisingly, Chaney rarely lands any of the nation's most coveted recruits.)

Stephon Marbury, the twenty-seven-year-old, $14-million-a-year point guard of the New York Knicks and one of the most celebrated schoolboy players ever, is in many ways the embodiment of modern basketball culture. Even among other very good players in his Coney Island neighborhood (including his three older brothers, who all went on to play college ball), he stood out as gifted. As a ninth-grader, he was an instant starter at Abraham Lincoln High, the perennial New York City powerhouse. A basketball luminary since grammar school, he had been so eagerly awaited that after just one high school game, Newsday proclaimed that the "era of Stephon Marbury" had begun.

One night earlier this season at the press table at Madison Square Garden, I was seated next to Jeff Lenchiner, the editor of *InsideHoops.com*, an online magazine for basketball aficionados. During a lull in the game, he turned his laptop computer toward me and directed me to watch an electronic file of Stephon Marbury highlights, an array of breathtaking moves: crossover dribbles that left defenders looking as if they were stuck in cement; spinning, twisting drives to the basket; soaring dunks. The last clip showed the six-foot-two Marbury rising up for a jump shot over a taller defender. At his peak, just as the ball left his hand, his sneakers looked to be about three feet above the floor. "Look at him!" Lenchiner shouted. "It's like he's in a video game. He's got thrusters!"

Marbury played one year of college basketball at Georgia Tech before jumping to the NBA. A dazzling ball handler, utterly fearless about driving to the hoop against bigger defenders, he has compiled high scoring averages and high assist totals (an assist is a pass that leads directly to a basket) in the pros while at the same time often leaving the strong impression that he does not play well with others. But then again, the concept of being part of a team is one that seems to elude a great many NBA players. Prodigies as kids, they see themselves as virtuosos, leading men with "supporting casts" (a favorite phrase of Michael Jordan's) rather than players with teammates.

On his first pro team, the Minnesota Timberwolves, Marbury chafed at sharing the spotlight with another young talent, Kevin Garnett, and forced a trade. Marbury has yet to play on a team that advanced past one round of the playoffs, even as, in the last three of his four NBA stops (in nine seasons), he has been his team's unquestioned marquee performer. Marbury this year publicly proclaimed himself the best point guard in the NBA. The Knicks promptly lost fourteen of their next sixteen games, and the coach, Lenny Wilkins, resigned along the way.

Few of the NBA's younger stars want to share top billing. Tracy McGrady left the Toronto Raptors rather than stay with another superstar, Vince Carter (who also happened to be his cousin). Allen Iverson of the Philadelphia Seventy-Sixers is much admired for his grit and competitive spirit, but it is not unusual for him to fire up thirty or more shots in a game in which no teammate takes as many as fifteen. Kobe Bryant and Shaquille O'Neal famously could not get along in Los Angeles, and with Shaq's trade, Kobe has been left on a vastly inferior Lakers team, a trade-off he seemed willing to make.

Marbury was among a dozen NBA players who went to Athens last August to represent the United States at the Summer Olympics. Since NBA players began competing at the Olympics in 1992, the Americans had never lost a game, let alone failed to win the gold medal. But in Athens, the U.S. truly dominated only one game — against the scrappy but overmatched Angolans. The NBA players, who collectively earn more than $100 million a year, suffered relatively close losses to Lithuania and Argentina. They squeaked by Greece, which did have the home-court advantage. Stunningly, the U.S. Olympians were blown off the court by the commonwealth of Puerto Rico.

In the midst of this tournament, as it was going downhill, Isiah Thomas, the president of the Knicks, called Marbury from New York. Marbury's game had been muted; he wasn't taking many shots or being very aggressive. His defense was so lax that the

Puerto Rican point guard, Carlos Arroyo, scored twenty-four points on him (as compared with Marbury's two). "I was just honest with him," Thomas said, recalling the conversation. "I told him he was playing like" something that can't be reprinted here. Thomas advised Marbury: "Remember who you are." In other words, be the man, be the wizard of Coney Island. But only one person at a time, of course, can be that kind of player.

After his talk with Thomas, Marbury responded with a record-breaking barrage of three-pointers in a close victory over Spain, nearly single-handedly preserving the U.S. medal hopes. But the next night he failed to make any three-pointers, and the Americans lost the game to Argentina, and with it any hope for a gold medal. (They settled for a bronze.)

The Olympic basketball tournament amounted to an indictment of U.S. basketball. If you had just watched the games in Athens and knew nothing of basketball history, it would have been reasonable to conclude that the sport had been invented and popularized in, say, Argentina or Italy — and was just starting to catch on in the United States. Other teams passed better, shot more accurately, played better defense. (Foul shooting is generally regarded as a matter of discipline and repetition. With enough practice, most players can become proficient. It's worth noting that in Athens, the gold medal–winning U.S. women's team made 76 percent of its foul shots while the men connected on a woeful 67 percent.)

The American men, in defeat, chose to focus on how much better the rest of the world's players have become and how unfamiliar the U.S. players were with one another and the somewhat different style and rules of international basketball. The larger point, they would not face: after a month together and with the noted basketball teacher Larry Brown of the Detroit Pistons as their coach, they still played as strangers. Seasoned jazz musicians can pick up together in a lounge and play the standards and sound pretty damn good — they would know all the changes in "Stompin' at the Savoy" — but the American basketballers had no common basketball language. Five old heads on lunch hour at a gym in North Philly or Harlem could have meshed better.

This season, some good things are starting to happen in the NBA, possibly because the Olympic debacle was such an eye-opener. Scoring has started to edge up for the first time in years, and some coaches have begun to trust their teams to play a fast-breaking style. After years of exporting the game, the NBA is importing not just players but also a style of play from abroad. The high-scoring Phoenix Suns have been the surprise team of the NBA season so far. Their coach, Mike D'Antoni, holds dual Italian and U.S. citizenship and has spent most of his career playing and coaching in Europe. The Suns' point guard, the master orchestrator of their run-and-gun offense, is Steve Nash, a Canadian. (The Suns signed him as a free agent to replace their point guard of last season, Stephon Marbury.)

The San Antonio Spurs do not play at the frenzied pace of the Suns, but they are one of the NBA's best teams and, within the coaching fraternity, probably the most admired. On offense, they are a five-man whirl of movement. A player who passes the ball cuts to the basket. The player receiving a pass either shoots, makes a move toward the hoop, or quickly passes to someone else. They execute the old-school "give and go" play — a player passes to a teammate, cuts, then gets it right back. "The Spurs are the gold standard," Van Gundy said.

As the Spurs took the floor for a November game in San Antonio against the Knicks, I looked in my program and noted the backgrounds of the players in their starting lineup. Rasho Nesterovic is from Slovenia; Tony Parker, from France; Manu Ginobili, star of the gold medal–winning Olympic team, from Argentina; and Tim Duncan, the Spurs' power forward and best player, from St. Croix in the U.S. Virgin Islands. Among the Spurs starters, only Bruce Bowen was born on U.S. soil, and he spent four years after college toiling for minor league teams in the United States and on the European pro circuit. A key reserve, Beno Udrih, is another Slovenian.

For Marbury, playing the Spurs must have felt like being back in Athens. Their style is sometimes called Euro-ball, but it is really nothing new: constant motion on offense, hit the open man. It's the game that used to be played in the United States but was forsaken for a more static style.

The Knicks got off to an early lead, spurred by one of Marbury's highlight-reel moments: he stole a pass, raced the ball toward his offensive end, and shoveled a no-look, behind-the-back, left-handed pass to Nazr Mohammed, who finished the sequence with a dunk. Eventually, though, the Spurs' teamwork and Duncan's strong inside presence took over. What kept me fascinated, even after the game was no longer competitive, was that the two teams played according to entirely different geometries. The Spurs made a series of angled passes that usually culminated with the final one advancing the ball closer to the basket. The Knicks' offense consisted of Marbury using his speed off the dribble to dart inside the lane, and then, when the Spurs' defense collapsed on him, he passed the ball back out, farther from the basket — often to beyond the three-point line where teammates were standing still, awaiting a pass.

"They do that even on a fast break, not just the Knicks but most of the rest of the teams," Walt Frazier explained to me. A Knicks broadcaster now, Frazier diagrammed this on a tablecloth as he spoke. He was quite agitated. "One guy's got the ball in the middle, and these two guys on the wing here, they should be cutting to the basket, right? But, no, here they go way out here, to three-point land, and they get the ball and shoot it. You're six feet from the hoop; why pass it back out twenty-five feet? And then people wonder why teams can't score eighty points."

I am guessing that the league's commissioner, David Stern, the best and the brightest of all sports executives, will not take my suggestion and decommission the dunk shot. It's too much of a crowd-pleaser — just two points, but so much money in the bank. But I do hope that college and high school basketball will again ban dunking, so that players on the way up have some chance of acquiring something other than a repertory of slam dunks.

The three-point shot is another matter altogether. No reason it should not just disappear. "The dagger!" announcers sometimes call it, as if it were the shock-and-awe of the hardwood, a weapon that brings opposing players to their knees. The three-pointer is a corruption of the sport, a perversion of a century of basketball wisdom that held that the whole point of the game was to advance the ball closer to the basket. If its intent was to increase scoring, the three-point shot definitely has not done that, and if it was to make the game more wide open and exciting, it hasn't accomplished that either. The unintended consequence of the three-pointer has been to make the game more static as players "spot up" outside the arc, waiting for the pass that will lead to the dagger.

*

"Michael Jeffrey Jordan is almost certainly more popular than Jesus," *Playboy* declared in 1992. "What's more, he has better endorsement deals."

Money, of course, is at the root of many, probably most, of the NBA's ills. Because Jordan established that one man can become a brand unto himself, that he can personally elevate a company — no one was more responsible for making Nike into a worldwide cultural force — the NBA is now the only pro league in which a player can become an endorsement king without playing for a winning team. If he's a spectacular enough dunker, it can happen, even if he plays in some NBA outpost.

Jordan created this world, but it's important to remember that he did not grow up in it. Until he was deep into high school, few outside of his hometown had heard of him. When he needed coaching, he was still listening — which is part of what made him worth watching. The same cannot be said of many of his heirs in the sneaker-shilling game.

The power of the shoe deal (and the hoped-for shoe deal) in basketball cannot be overstated. It induces kids to skip college and go right to the NBA because endorsement money from Nike and other companies can dwarf the salaries they make from playing ball. The shoe deal is specifically what is making the NBA younger — which, in turn, is what is degrading the quality of play.

Sebastian Telfair of Coney Island was a phenom from an early age, pointed toward bigger things and therefore on the radar of the sneaker companies — just like his cousin, Stephon Marbury. He went to an Adidas-sponsored camp. The teams he played for as a kid, right up through high school, were outfitted in Adidas. Last spring, he took the shoe money, a reported $15 million — from Adidas, of course — and skipped right from Lincoln High to the NBA. "I've been Adidas all my life," he said at the press conference to announce his NBA ascension. I saw him play the other night. He looked small and lost.

A snapshot from today's NBA: the locker room of the New York Knicks, where in each dressing cubicle a necktie hangs on a hook, pre-knotted. Isiah Thomas, the team president, has ordered players to wear suits and ties to the arenas, a grown-up enough thing. But during games, a team functionary goes around knotting the ties so that when a player gets dressed afterward, all he has to do is slip the tie over his head and tighten it rather than actually having to make the knot himself.

One other snapshot: the Knicks bench, with twelve players, one head coach, and six assistant coaches. The Dallas Mavericks have employed as many as ten assistants, nearly one per player. I checked into how many assistants Red Holzman had with the old Knicks. The answer: none. He coached by himself. It was explained to me by people around the league that in the modern NBA, a half-dozen or more assistant coaches are needed to help fill in the gaps for young players. In essence, they teach remedial basketball for millionaires.

What the NBA needs, most of all, is to get older. Last summer, eight first-round draft choices were high school kids; four were college seniors. There are some true prodigies out there, young men ready to go straight from seventh-period English to the NBA. But not that many. The most notable recent one is LeBron James of the Cleveland Cavaliers, who somehow survived intense high school fame to emerge as a mature, team-oriented professional basketball player.

For most, though, the NBA is a bad place to learn, no matter how many coaches are available as tutors. The league is increasingly stocked with athletes who might have ripened in college — if they had not been picked so young. They end up stunted. The players are paid, but the fans, and the game, are being cheated.

KATY VINE

Brooklyn Heights

FROM TEXAS MONTHLY

DURING THE SATURDAY GAME of the March 2004 Adidas All-American West Coast Evaluation Camp in Los Angeles, one of those perennial shoe company–sponsored all-star gatherings for high school basketball players, a few of the game's top women's college coaches must have wondered if they were suffering from some sort of collective amnesia. How else to explain having never heard of Brooklyn Pope, the five-foot-eleven-inch girl wearing the thick, wire-rimmed glasses who was running circles around some of the best players in the country? Every other rising senior on the court that day had been on their recruiting radar for years. Many of them had already committed to one of the big dogs: Juanita Ward to Mississippi, Charde Houston to UConn, Kirsten Thompson to Arizona State. But as the game dragged on, the unheralded and unsigned Brooklyn Pope was making her high-profile opponents look stone-tired.

In the second half, she took a pass on a wide-open fast break and appeared to be heading for a routine lay-up. Instead, she picked up her dribble and took two giant steps inside the key. Rising up to the backboard with the ball held high in her right hand, she hammered it into the basket. Then, as if to make sure everyone was watching, she hung on the rim for a few seconds on the way down. Never mind that the ball clanked off the back of the rim and ricocheted toward half-court: some unknown player under six feet tall had just tried to dunk in a *girls' high school basketball game.* And so the one hundred or so coaches in the stands hopped to their feet and did what you'd expect any leader of a big-time program to do:

they pointed to the school logos on their shirts and shouted toward Brooklyn as if to say, "Pick me! Pick me!"

But why hadn't they seen this girl before? Where had she been hiding?

Brooklyn Pope was only in the eighth grade.

If Brooklyn is reading this story, her coaches would rather that she stop right here. No need to let her get a big head, they'd say, from all the praise about to be lavished upon her. But it's hard to imagine that anything could surprise the fifteen-year-old small forward at this point. By last February, when Brooklyn was leading Fort Worth's Dunbar Lady Wildcats to their first-ever Texas high school basketball 4A final four in Austin — as a freshman — she was already the talk of the Stop Six neighborhood. Wherever she went, neighbors bragged about how she was already six feet two and still growing. About how she was averaging 16.8 points, 8.5 rebounds, and 3 blocked shots a game. How before the season even began she'd already won Most Outstanding Player at the Adidas Elite 100 Superstar Camp in September and *Slam* magazine had gushed that she'd "outhustled, outsmarted, and pretty much outplayed everybody on the court" in July's Adidas Top Ten Girls All-American Basketball Camp in Atlanta. Even the man who ran the West Coast camp, Ray Mayes, testified: "I think Brooklyn will be the best player to come out of Texas, period. And one of the top five to play the game. I haven't seen a kid with that much broad skill and ability in a long time. LeBron James, maybe, is the last time I saw somebody play with that skill at that age." That seemingly impossible comparison didn't sit well with some of the talkers, though, who said that with Brooklyn's size and dribbling skill, she should really be compared to Magic Johnson.

Hype like this is probably inevitable when you're the first female superstar at Dunbar, an institution best known as the home of the winningest high school boys' coach in the country, seventy-seven-year-old Robert Hughes, and therefore the home of one of the most rabid basketball communities in the country. And it's been like this for Brooklyn since the seventh grade, when she opened the mailbox to find her first recruiting letter, from Princeton. Since then she's accumulated so much fan mail from scouts — at UCLA, Duke, UConn, Stanford, Baylor, Texas Tech, Tennessee,

UT-Austin, and every other upper-echelon college program — that her mailman told her he wants a raise. No matter that she won't be able to step onto the court at anyone's university for another three years. Brooklyn is a can't-miss recruit, the coaches say, the kind of impact athlete who can relieve the pressure of a few losing seasons or even save their jobs just by signing her name. So they stare at their keyboards searching for new and inventive ways to praise her. Like the letter from Notre Dame that arrived a week after a camp Brooklyn attended in July: "We had the opportunity to see you at the Adidas Top Ten camp in Atlanta and all I can say is 'Wow.' That move in the all-star game? I don't even know what to say." Brooklyn Pope, in other words, already knows that she's been tagged the Next Big Thing.

She also knows she isn't supposed to believe any of it. From the time she was nine years old, her coaches have been preaching humility and teamwork and respect. They tell her that the recruiters and the scouts and the player-ranking websites are a dangerous hype machine that will forget her just as quickly as it has built her up. They tell her that being able to dunk won't be enough to make her a special player. Last year, after all, Candace Parker, a high school senior from Illinois, won the slam-dunk contest at the McDonald's All American High School Basketball Game — against a field full of boys. To get to the next level, she's told, she'll have to learn to play vanilla. Don't let your head get full of helium, the coaches say. Can't let yourself think you're all that. But when you're a fifteen-year-old freshman being told repeatedly that you *are* all that — and told just as often not to believe a word of it — how do you know whom to listen to?

This was the predicament Brooklyn found herself in a few days before the 2005 high school final four. The Dunbar boys' team had already lost in the regional quarterfinals, leaving her with the community's undivided attention. During the Lady Wildcats' recent run in the playoffs, as they'd notched wins against Denison (75–58), Stephenville (74–33), Lubbock Estacado (46–43), and Denton (62–45), Brooklyn had become an undisputed force. In the final two regional playoff games in San Angelo, she had played Magic-like all-around basketball, pouring in twenty-nine points, grabbing sixteen rebounds, and tallying up nine blocks. But to the chagrin of her coaches, the ones who tell her she needs to stick to the fundamentals, she had also attempted another dunk. It was a miss. And so heading to the semifinals in Austin, the girl with the unstoppable talent, whose game was about to be on the biggest stage of her short career, was caught between playing to a crowd wondering what she would pull off next and listening to the coaches who begged her to play vanilla.

Away from the court, Brooklyn looks like the friendly, noncompetitive twin of the intimidating jock pictured in the newspapers. She'll don a letter jacket and a T-shirt, but her large gold hoop earrings give her casual attire a dash of confident femininity. Unlike many high school freshmen females over six feet, she rarely slouches, which makes her seem Amazonian. She has the air of someone who enjoys her size and her personality. I asked her why she likes to try to dunk. "It puts the momentum back into my teammates," she told me. "The crowd loses it, and if we have the crowd, we have the game. They determine the game. Their excitement brings it. If I dunk in a real close game and the whole crowd loses their minds on our side — so that even the other side has to clap? It makes the other team mad at us, like they messed up." Then she thinks about it for another moment, as if she's trying to construct a sentence that won't sound obnoxiously overconfident. "My doing this as a freshman just blows the lid off the expectations of the game," she said. "There's a different reaction when [WNBA star] Lisa Leslie dunks than when I dunk. Because of my age, I get more hype. Leslie just kinda puts it in there, whereas when I put it in, I'm like, 'Whoa! I can feel it.' I make it so we all can feel it."

The Stop Six neighborhood, so named for its position on the old Dallas–Fort Worth train line, is a little like a basketball incubator. There is a hoop on almost every block. Most guys at Dunbar High School wear basketball jerseys whether they're on a team or not. At the Martin Luther King Community Center gym, which sits just a few blocks south of Brooklyn's house and a few blocks north of Dunbar's gym, there is always a game of pickup being played. The girls who grow up playing here don't always learn the fundamentals of the traditional girls' game, sometimes referred to as "thump-thump" basketball, where the ball gets tossed around for a long while before somebody takes a shot. Playing against their older brothers and male classmates, they learn to play fast and tough, picking up aggressive moves that sometimes earn them fouls in girls' games.

It's a more modern style of play that has been developing elsewhere and is slowly changing the women's game. Gordon Loucks, who covers high school basketball for *Texas Girls Basketball Report* and has watched between three hundred and four hundred teams a season for the past eighteen years, said he witnessed a change starting around 1997, when the WNBA held its first game. "There's definitely influences coming down from the WNBA," Loucks says. "We're in the drive to be more appealing and entertaining. There's less fundamentals, more athleticism. That's the sad part to watch, because you're losing what a lot of us hold pretty dear. But there's not a lot you can do about it." Of course, some say the change is good for the girls: a more intense game translates into ticket sales, a greater fan base, and careers in professional leagues.

The evolving style has certainly benefited girls' basketball at Dunbar. When thirty-one-year-old coach Andrea Robinson took over the Lady Wildcats three years ago, the team hadn't made the playoffs in a decade. All the attention was on the boys' team, which had won twenty-seven consecutive district titles under Coach Hughes. But Robinson's teams found success — Dunbar made the playoffs in her first year — and their crowds have grown. Now the Stop Six girls grow up dreaming of playing on the Dunbar varsity squad the same way the Stop Six boys do. This year, playing a fast-paced style with Brooklyn, sophomore LaShandra "LaLa" Hill, junior Victoria Davis, and junior Jerin Smith setting the tone, the Lady Wildcats were 29–4.

But going into the semifinals, none of the Lady Wildcats had had much experience in high-pressure games. Meanwhile, their opponents, Dallas Lincoln, were last year's state champions and hadn't lost a game in Texas in three years. Lincoln had five seniors on the team, and forwards Simone Cooks and Dominic Seals would be going on to play Division I college basketball next year. The celebratory "Na Na Hey Hey Kiss Him Good-bye" song was probably already cued up on the Lincoln bus. Even Dunbar's fans believed their team would probably lose in Austin and then go home happy to have had a winning season. One observer willing to give Brooklyn and her teammates a chance was Coach Hughes, who's been to the state semifinals thirteen times. He told the naysayers,

"Sometimes a team is so young they don't know enough to get nervous."

And from the opening tip of their Friday night contest, his comment seemed prescient. Before a raucous crowd of 4,575, Dunbar jumped out to an early lead. Brooklyn, in her number 32 jersey (same as Magic's), wore her hair tied up in a softball-size poof of a ponytail near the top of her head and contacts to replace her lucky Coke-bottle glasses. She had her game face on from the outset: her eyebrows diving toward her nose and her nostrils flared, she yelled at her team on the court, trying to keep up the intensity. During the second quarter, with the game still tight, Brooklyn had a chance to dunk on a fast break, but she took the lay-up instead.

Deep into the second half, however, Dunbar's aggressive defense had worn down its opponent, forcing twenty-two turnovers. With two minutes and sixteen seconds left on the clock and her team up by nineteen points, Brooklyn picked up a loose ball at midcourt and hit her stride on another open break. For a moment, you could hear the little squeals of anticipation coming from the spectators. Brooklyn went up for the dunk and came up just short, but as the ball slipped off her fingers, she managed to tap it forward over the rim, where it bounced off the backboard and through the net. On the way down, she grabbed the rim with her hand, and the crowd was hushed as the *thunngggg* hung in the air.

Seated next to me at the Frank Erwin Center was Rick Sherley, the executive director of the Texas Association of Basketball Coaches. The whole game he had remained tight-lipped about Brooklyn. "I've heard of her" was all he'd said. But now he turned to me and laughed. I asked if he had ever seen a girl attempt a dunk during a high school game, and he shook his head.

"How long were you a coach?" I asked.

"Thirty-two years," he said. Then he leaned over. "She's got another three years to get better?" he quipped.

Outside the locker room after the game, a reporter from the *Fort Worth Star-Telegram* asked Brooklyn why she'd tried to dunk. Why hadn't she gone for the lay-up, as her coach had instructed? "I wanted to give the next team we play a stomachache," she said.

Brooklyn's dad likes to tell the story of how his daughter first got "discovered." A hoops fanatic, Tony Pope Sr. is six feet four and would have played for Coach Hughes back when he went to Dunbar, but doctor's orders after a bout with rheumatic fever kept him off the team. Instead, he passed his love of the sport on to his two sons, Tony Jr. and Tim, and to his only daughter, Brooklyn. He became so impressed with her early talent that when she was only nine years old, he brought her to a local Amateur Athletic Union club, Team Ichiban, a rigorous March-to-September all-star group directed by Gene Watts. Over the years, Watts has earned a name for himself for developing talent. (Most recently, he trained UT star and 2004 ESPN.com National Freshman of the Year Tiffany Jackson.) Taking Brooklyn to Team Ichiban would be a reality check. If Watts said Brooklyn was good, she was *good*.

She was already five feet eight when she walked into Watts's gym. The coach put her out in a scrimmage with a team of thirteen-year-olds and passed her the ball.

"Let's see what you've got," he said.

Brooklyn took her defender down the court, weaving in and out and then spinning under the basket before banging a shot off the glass. As the ball dropped through the hoop, Watts blew his whistle and called a time-out. Then he brought all the girls to center court and asked them to estimate the new player's age.

"Thirteen," they guessed.

"She's only nine years old," he told them.

But while Brooklyn was good enough to play with girls four years her senior, there was a catch. "Her attitude was horrible," Watts remembered. If things didn't go her way, he said, she threw a tantrum. "I kicked her out of practice about every day for the first two months just to get her to understand no one is above the program." The other players told her about the dangers of "helium" and "hype" and how she'd better be ready to meet someone who would be better than her. Whether it was the lessons or just maturity, Brooklyn gradually came around, playing two and a half hours a day with either Team Ichiban or her school's team. She started memorizing the maxims about staying humble, hoping the stale-sounding phrases would sink in.

Brooklyn's mom, Janice, admits that while Tony was teaching their daughter to dribble, she was wishing that Brooklyn would show more interest in gymnastics (which Brooklyn vetoed) or classical piano (which she flat-out didn't have time for). But even in second grade, when Brooklyn was wearing matching socks and hair bows to go with her dresses, she'd be out on the playground at lunchtime, barefoot, throwing a ball into a trash can. When her grade school teacher asked the students to write about what they loved most, Brooklyn wrote in large, perfectly formed round letters, "I like basketball 24–7. 24–7 means 24 hours a day, 7 days a week."

And she was a die-hard gym rat years before other girls in her class. The MLK Center's late-night supervisor Wayne "Spanky" Lewis, himself an old player from Hughes's 1965 state championship team, knew what he was looking at when he first saw Brooklyn coming in to play pickup games with the guys. Usually girls would be there to attract a guy's attention. Brooklyn, on the other hand, consistently played to win, and the boys ratcheted up their game to avoid defeat by a girl. Lewis, who predicted she'd be famous someday, started calling her "Brooke Shields." That was six years before she surpassed him in height.

When Brooklyn finally arrived at Dunbar, Coach Robinson knew her job wouldn't be as simple as handing the new kid the ball. Dealing with a gifted player is tricky. "You want to structure her, but you don't want to take away her talent," said Robinson. And the game has to stay fun. "[At the San Angelo playoffs], she attempted to dunk it, and she came to me afterward and said, 'Coach, I don't know what happened. I was just going at it really hard and it just happened.'" Robinson laughed. "So you accidentally *dunk?*"

Robinson and other coaches say they are often taken aback by Brooklyn's knowledge of the sport. When she isn't playing, she and her dad watch old VHS tapes from the public library, memorizing big games and talking shop. At home, her older brothers grill her about televised games. Which player is doing what? Why? What should he be doing instead? She studies basketball history and the players whose posters neatly adorn one of her bedroom walls. At her house one night, she curled up on the couch and started talking about her favorite players in her low, silky voice. She didn't just know which players were great; she knew *why* they were great: "Of course I like Michael Jordan — he's the typical choice as a favorite — but I also like Bill Russell because he was the champion. I like LeBron James because he passed expectations. I like Magic Johnson because he did the unexpected thing: he played guard at six-foot-nine back in the days when you had a five-foot-eleven, six-foot guard. [Magic's] a big old dude that could play center."

She also understands that some of those players knew the art of trash-talking. One night we went out to Wing Stop with her next-door neighbor E'Tasha Keeton, who plays ninth-grade volleyball at Dunbar. Brooklyn is a giant compared with the petite E'Tasha, a sweet-faced girl who is pleased to have finally reached one hundred pounds this year. E'Tasha often flashed a smile while we talked, while Brooklyn struck a cool pose, playing the straight man.

"Brooke, you know, she's fun," E'Tasha told me, teasing her friend. "She brags a lot, though." Then she took my tape recorder and began to pretend to interview the superstar: "With all this stuff about Brooklyn Pope, do you get a big head?"

Brooklyn slipped on her sunglasses and leaned back, perhaps imagining herself at a postgame news conference. "No," she said. "I stay down to earth. I keep it real for myself and others."

"What would you say about your playing? Overall, how is your game?"

"Real talented. I have a lot of faith in my game."

They continued like this, Brooklyn teetering on the verge of remaining humble until E'Tasha began a brief exchange about who was better than whom at what, like the time they played each other in eighth-grade basketball. Then E'Tasha offered a challenge. "Look at that little bitty box over there in the corner. Who's going to get through that thing quicker, me or you?"

"Me," said Brooklyn, "because I'd bust it up while you're trying to crawl through."

"Uh-*uhhhh!*" said E'Tasha.

"I win!" Brooklyn said with her arms in the air.

"I will win. You will lose," said E'Tasha. "You would lose in volley-ball too."

"I would spike it," countered Brooklyn.

"No, you would not. Your height doesn't matter!"

At this, Brooklyn simply put her hand up in front of her.

"Don't wave your hand at me!"

"I'm just tryin' to get some *air*," said Brooklyn.

A sea of bright-blue T-shirts marked the sections that held the Dunbar Lady Wildcats fans at the Erwin Center, in Austin, for the 4A championship game on March 5 against Angleton. One of the

Dunbar fans told me she hadn't missed more than five boys' basket-ball home games since 1974, and several of the men were wearing T-shirts that read "Stop Six." Among the crowd was Hughes, who had been down to Austin with the boys from Dunbar thirteen times over the years and was a month from announcing his retirement. "Usually, when you go down to the Erwin Center," he said, "the only seat worth a dime is the seat next to your team. Any other seat is unsatisfying. But this is not me looking at a team I don't know."

I took a seat in an area adjacent to the tightly packed Dun-bar crowd, where the two men next to me were leaning back in their chairs, talking about Brooklyn. "So this girl from Dunbar can dunk?" one asked.

"So they say," said the other.

"I read in the paper she wanted to scare the other team."

"I guess if you can do it."

Dunbar jumped out to an early lead, shooting an astounding 63 percent from the field in the first half. But it couldn't pull away. Each trip down the court, concerned that her team was losing pa-tience, Coach Robinson would yell at her players — "Calm down! Calm down!" Before heading into the locker room, Angleton had cut Dunbar's eleven-point first-quarter lead to seven.

And in the second half Angleton was matching Dunbar basket for basket. When Brooklyn started playing aggressive defense, she quickly picked up her second and third fouls, and while she sat on the bench, Angleton continued closing in, pulling to 41–40 by the beginning of the fourth quarter. The Dunbar fans were now stand-ing and hoarse, shouting with exasperation, "Come *on*, ladies!" "Defense!"

When she finally got back in the game, Brooklyn immediately helped swing the momentum. She pulled in a long, downcourt pass near the sideline, and, after barely maintaining her balance to stay inbounds, she drove in for a lay-up. After trading a few more baskets, Dunbar pulled ahead 53–49. Then, with fifty-seven sec-onds on the clock, Dunbar guard Victoria Davis stood at the free-throw line. She hit the first shot, and the crowd cheered. When she missed the second, Brooklyn stepped in once again to make the big play. Moving in off the key, she grabbed the offensive rebound and made a quick put-back for two points. Angleton would make one more free throw, but when the buzzer sounded, Dunbar had won, 56–50.

The team ran to center court, crashing into a heap on the floor and then rolling over one another like puppies. As the sea of blue T-shirts finished a round of high-fives in the stands, Brooklyn posed for photographs with her teammates, then she held her index finger high in the air and led the team in a cheer: "D! H! S! D! H! S!"

"This is the first championship for the Lady Wildcats . . ." said the announcer over the loudspeaker. Then he read an announcement passed to him from Coach Hughes: "Stop Six will rock the night."

Try to remember when you were a freshman in high school. You didn't have a driver's license yet. Maybe you had braces. Chances are, especially if you were a girl, you tried to find a spot in the world where you wouldn't be horribly embarrassed just to exist. So when the announcement was made that the fifteen-year-old freshman with so much hype had been named the tournament MVP, was it anything but beautiful when she slowly strutted off the court wearing her flashy sunglasses, proudly reveling in the spotlight? A few days later, Coach Hughes would tell her that if he ever saw her showboating with her shades like that again, he'd make her run laps. But that would come later. On that night in March, as she posed for the cameras with her arms folded across her chest, Brooklyn Pope had earned every bit of her delightful brashness.

Okay, Brooke, you can quit reading now.

The Magician

FROM THE ATLANTIC MONTHLY

AT MIDNIGHT on a bitterly cold January 15 the lobby of the Executive West Hotel near the Louisville, Kentucky, airport was crowded with men and a few women, all waiting anxiously for the guest of honor.

A man in a yellow windbreaker came through the front door and walked toward the registration desk. A murmur rose from the crowd. Everyone stared at him, a small brown man with slitlike eyes, a wispy Fu Manchu mustache, and no front teeth. He wore a soiled T-shirt and wrinkled, baggy jeans. He moved hunched over, his eyes lowered.

People clustered around him. Men flipped open their cell phones and called their friends to say, "He's here!" They introduced him to their girlfriends. The man looked embarrassed. Another man thrust his cell phone at him and said, "Please say hello to my son; he's been waiting up all night." The small man mumbled a few words in broken English. Then the hotel clerk asked him his name. He said, "Reyes." Someone called out, "Just put down 'the Magician.'"

Efren Reyes, fifty, was born in poverty, the fifth of nine children, in a dusty little town in the Philippines without electricity or running water. When he was five, his parents sent him to live with his uncle, who owned a pool hall in Manila. Efren cleaned up the pool hall and watched. He was fascinated by the way the players made the balls move around the table and fall into pockets — and by the way money changed hands after a game. At night he slept on a pool table and dreamed of combinations. He had mastered the game in his head before he finally picked up a pool cue, at the age of eight. He stood on a pile of Coke crates to shoot, two hours in the morning and two hours at night. At nine he played his first money game, and at twelve he won $100; he sent $90 home to his family. Soon he was the best pool shooter in Manila. His friends would wait for him in the pool hall after school, hand him his cue when he walked in the door, and back him in gambling games. He was the best pool shooter in the Philippines when he quit school, at fifteen. By the time he was in his twenties, no one in the Philippines would play him any longer, so he toured Asia. He wrote down in a notebook the names of the best pool shooters in the world, and proceeded to beat them one by one. He became a legend. People who had seen him play recounted the impossible shots he had made. They called him a genius, the greatest pool shooter who had ever lived. Even people who had never seen him play, including many in the United States, soon heard the legend of Efren Reyes, "the Magician."

In 1985 a small brown man, a stranger, entered Red's pool hall and nightclub, in Houston, Texas. He said he was Cezar Morales, and he offered to play all comers. Over the next twenty-one days he played the best pool shooters in the Southwest, and won $81,000. The players he beat argued among themselves about who was the better pool shooter, Cezar Morales or the legendary Efren Reyes. Shortly before he returned to the Philippines, they learned that Morales and Reyes were one and the same.

Over the next eighteen years Reyes won every major pool tournament and title in the world: the U.S. Open, the Challenge of Champions, the World Pool League Championship. He was named Player of the Year in 1995, and World Champion in 1999. He won the biggest prize in all of pool — $160,000 — in Japan, $100,000 in Hong Kong, and around $50,000 in a number of other tournaments. The Philippines Jaycees named him an "outstanding Filipino," and the government awarded him the Philippines Legion of Honor. He endorsed McDonald's, and Puyat sporting goods, and San Miguel beer. One of the first things visitors see when they enter the Manila airport is the image of Efren Reyes. His closest friend was Fernando Poe Jr., who campaigned for the presidency of the Philippines before his recent death.

Reyes and about six hundred other pool shooters, mostly men, had come to the Executive West in Louisville to compete in the Derby City Classic pool tournament, three events over nine days, for prize money totaling more than $180,000. They warmed up on seven practice tables off the Boozeseller Lounge, and played their games on twenty-eight tournament tables in a huge conference room down a long hallway. The first event consisted of nine-ball bank games, in which the object ball must hit at least one cushion before being pocketed; the second of one-pocket games, in which each player picks a corner pocket and must deposit all his balls in that pocket: and the third of nine-ball games, in which the balls must be shot in order, 1 to 9, with the last being the money ball. The winners and high finishers in each event were eligible for the overall best-in-tourney prize of $20,000.

The Derby City Classic is not like most other tournaments — or even matches seen on ESPN, with the referees in black tuxedos, and a ring of polite, hushed fans. The DCC is a gambler's event; the players are less interested in the tournament matches that end at midnight than in the gambling games that run from midnight until 7:00 A.M., or the craps games and Texas Hold 'Em poker that run twenty-four hours a day in the hotel rooms.

The DCC is nine days of hustling pool, cards, and dice for men with such nicknames as Shannon the Cannon, the Scorpion, Scott the Shot, Kid Delicious, Spanish Mike, Goose, the Hurricane, Kid Confidence, the Killer Pixie, and Piggy Banks, and a few women — called, say, the Black Widow or Ming.

I found Spanish Mike, Reyes's trusted adviser, having breakfast in the hotel restaurant. He is a big-bellied man of seventy, from Philadelphia by way of Puerto Rico. "Efren is a poor loser," he told me. "When he plays for money, his eyes get like a snake's. That's his strength, the money. And his knowledge. Sometimes I don't see a shot, but I see his eyes going fast and I know he sees one. Efren is a genius."

Tournament action was in full sway on all twenty-eight tables in the conference room. Spectators drifted from table to table, watching the action, or sat on folding chairs against the walls. On a raised platform at one side of the room Scott the Shot, the tourney emcee, spoke into his microphone: "All starting times are approximate. If the schedules on the wall read ten A.M., the match could start at five P.M. 'Approximate' means within twenty-four hours."

Scott the Shot — Scott Smith — is fifty-seven, with a spiky gray crew cut; he wore a shiny gray suit and a tie showing Bugs Bunny playing pool.

Ming, in black silk pants, flounced around coquettishly at table 13. The Black Widow, Jeanette Lee, was practicing with her husband, George Breedlove, on table 25. She wore a tight black sweater with a rhinestone black widow spider on it. Earl "the Pearl" Strickland played on table 4. A long, lean North Carolinian who was considered the best nine-ball player of the 1990s, he had hit a dry spell that made him touchy and suspicious. He has a reputation for arguing with referees and fans, who, he claims, "laugh at me." At table 10 was Johnny Archer, the Scorpion, a hunched, sinister-looking man with a black pirate's goatee who was voted Player of the Decade for the 1990s. Ralf Souquet, a trim, bald little man who resembles Tweety Bird, was playing on table 9. A thirty-five-year-old from Germany, he was the 1996 World Pool Association world nine-ball champion. Reyes played a twenty-one-year-old from Ohio on table 8. This was the young Ohioan's first tournament — "and I drew the number-one player in the world," he said, trying not to hyperventilate. It didn't help that Reyes had drawn a small crowd, which applauded his masterly shots and laughed at his self-deprecation. Reyes smiled when he missed a shot, scratched his scalp, slumped down in his chair between shots, and hung his head as if he were the most pitiful pool shooter in the world. But his disconsolation was not an act; his Filipino friends say he's a simple, humble guy who's astonished by his fame.

Scott Smith said into his mike, "What does a professional pool player have in common with a medium-size pizza? . . . Neither can feed a family of four." His audience laughed, but it's true: the best players in the world earn about $100,000 a year from tournaments. That's why they like to play gambling games.

Every great pool player has three talents to varying degrees: the ability to make shots; the ability to control the cue ball to set up the next shot, which is called playing position; and the intelligence to read the balls spread out on a table so as to determine the order of successive shots.

Souquet plays a maddeningly slow and methodical game, which tends to disrupt the rhythm of his opponent. Archer plays a cautious and precise game, preferring to rely on position to avoid difficult shots. Strickland is an explosive shot maker who can be unbeatable when he is in "high gear," according to Scott the Shot. Reyes plays a fast, flamboyant game, marked by his ability to control the cue ball and make seemingly impossible shots, to read the layout of a table at a glance (he claims to be able to see as far as eight shots ahead), and — his genius — to see possibilities that lesser mortals can't imagine.

"Efren has more imagination and creativity than the rest of us," Archer says. "We're more basic. He takes one glance and sees it all. He knows things we don't. A few times he's taken a shot I couldn't even envision until after he made it, and I saw it was an easier shot than I'd thought."

"Three times a match he'll take shots I don't see," Souquet says. "He's in a different league than the rest of us. He's the greatest player who ever lived. But he's beatable. I'm probably his worst opponent, because I throw off his rhythm. I usually play by the book. He does wild stuff I wouldn't do, shots I would never take. I like to play Efren, because he is the greatest player. I consider him a friend. But I wouldn't play him in a gambling game. No one in the world will, unless he gives them a spot." In pool parlance a "spot" is the advantage a good player will give a lesser player to entice him into a game. In a game of one-pocket Reyes might offer a spot of nine to six, meaning he would have to make nine balls in a rack to win, and his opponent would have to make only six.

"He's the best I've ever seen," Strickland says. "The luckiest too. The fans love him and disrespect me." In 1996 in Hong Kong, Strickland and Reyes played a match for $100,000, winner take all. The first player to win 120 games of nine-ball would get the money. They played several hours a day for three days. By the end of the third day Strickland was ahead, 117 games to 116. Then Reyes ran out the last four games to win the match.

A year before that match, in Reno, Nevada, Reyes beat Strickland in a nine-ball game with what has become known as "the Shot."

"It was the greatest shot ever made in pool," Archer told me. "Efren's cue ball was behind the nine, so he couldn't hit the object ball, the five. It was a no-escape shot. But Efren hit the cue ball off two rails before it cut in the five *and* gave him perfect position for the six."

In Kentucky, Reyes won his match with the Ohioan easily and moved quickly down the hallway before anyone could intercept him. He is embarrassed by his fans' adulation. When he got to the indoor swimming pool, he sat down at a table and began to talk in the heavy Tagalog accent he calls Pampanga. He articulated each word carefully.

"I now like be famous," he said. "But not morning when fans call me sleeping." He smiled his elfin, mischievous smile, his eyes closing.

Reyes has two kinds of fans: pool aficionados who worship his genius, and Filipinos who worship him. When he plays in Asia and the Middle East, he stays in fancy hotels, many of them staffed by Filipino waitresses, maids, janitors. They see him as one of their own, a man who has pulled himself up from poverty to become world-famous. After his matches they bring him his favorite Filipino dishes of fried fish and chicken and rice. He takes staffers out with him to karaoke bars, where he sings and buys them drinks.

With his fame came money beyond his wildest dreams. "As kid I have no dreams," he told me. "Pool just sport. I never thought make money with pool. Now, I like my kids finish school and family be good." (When he's not on the road he lives with his wife, Susan, and three children in a country town in the Philippines called Angeles City.) "I support all my family, my wife's family. Forty-four, but more kids coming." He smiled his guileless smile. "I give just to family. I don't want anything to me."

Reyes's life today in Angeles City is not much different from the life he saw around him as a child. He putters around his house and front porch in flip-flops, shorts, and a T-shirt. Chickens peck in his front yard or waddle onto his porch and through the house. The house is a meeting place for all the neighborhood children, his relatives, and his cronies. They drink beer all day, play mahjong, have hot soup–eating contests, and hold cockfights. Reyes rarely plays pool at home. But he does play chess, a recent passion. He learned chess the same way he learned pool — in his head first.

Reyes says the only player he fears today in nine-ball is Strickland. "But many young players are good now," he told me. "Archer. Ralf. Mika [Immonen], from Finland. It a young man's game. My game only fifty percent of when I younger." In pool, as in most sports, a player's best years are behind him by the time he reaches forty. After that the eyes begin to go — and then, with aches and pains, the stroke. Finally, Spanish Mike told me at breakfast, wiggling his fingers, "the nerves go."

Scott Smith worked his way along the crowded hallway outside the conference room. Before he entered, a man burst through the door and shouted, "Efren's got a game!" The crowd surged toward the door and poured into the conference room, where spectators were leaving the games they had been watching to hurry toward table 25, in the far corner. The tournament players watched the crowd rush away from them as if in a fire drill. People stood four and five rows deep around Reyes's table, with those in the back standing on chairs, boxes, anything they could find.

Reyes was shooting one-pocket for $500 a game against Ricky Byrd, a pool-hall owner from Alabama. Reyes had given him a spot of nine to three. The crowd watched in rapt silence as Reyes won the first game. Byrd dug into his pocket, pulled out a wad of $100 bills fastened with a rubber band, peeled off five, and handed them to Reyes.

A man was practicing by himself on table 26. He looked over at Reyes and the crowd and said softly, "I feel like a fool, but I'm too scared to move."

When Reyes lost the second game, he gave Byrd $500. Byrd handed the money to a big, light-skinned black man with a stubble of beard, who stood against one wall. The man was wearing a Phillies baseball cap turned backward, a T-shirt, and gray sweatpants. Sitting beside him was Spanish Mike, watching the action through tinted glasses. Some men in the crowd were talking on their cell phones, giving their friends a play-by-play of the action.

Reyes won the sixth and seventh games, to go ahead by one. Then Byrd won the next four games. Reyes was sitting on a chair against the wall. He didn't get up for the next game. One of the fans said into his cell phone, "Efren's in a trap." Finally Reyes shook his head no. He quit. A small man stepped out of the crowd and said to Byrd, "Play Efren nine-four."

Byrd shook his head. The crowd muttered, and some called out, "Play him nine-four!" But Byrd refused to reduce his advantage.

Finally Byrd turned and pointed at the burly man in the Phillies cap. "Let Efren play Cliff," he said. "I'll put up five dimes [$5,000] on Cliff if Efren plays him eight-seven."

All eyes turned toward Reyes, sitting on his chair. He stood and said, "I play."

The crowd erupted, people yelling into their cell phones, "Efren's playing Cliff for five dimes!" Men started shouting: "I'll take five nickels [$500] of that action." "I'll take a dime." Dozens of men waved fistfuls of bills at the small man from the crowd. He collected the bills — maybe $20,000 in side bets — and wrote names on a piece of paper. Meanwhile, Spanish Mike produced a wad of bills. He counted out $5,000 and handed it to the small man. Byrd did the same. The game was set: $5,000, winner take all. Reyes would have to pocket eight balls a rack to win, and Cliff only seven. The first man to win eight games would win the $5,000.

The first game began with an audience of more than four hundred fans, all sitting on one side of the room. The series lasted six hours, full of unbelievable tension and skill. The spectators were witness to the game of a lifetime, between two men who, though rated the top two one-pocket players in the world, had rarely played each other.

Cliff Joyner, in his early forties, is from North Carolina. Despite his bulk, Joyner plays a game every bit as nuanced and delicate as Reyes's. He studied the balls and then tapped the cue ball so that it came to rest behind another ball, leaving Reyes without a shot. This is called a "safety." Joyner's strategy was to play a series of safeties against Reyes, hoping he'd become frustrated and take a wild shot that would leave an open table Joyner could easily run.

But Reyes didn't take the bait. He played Joyner safety after safety. He waited. He studied every one of Joyner's safeties to see if he could find a shot in it that neither Joyner nor any other pool player in the world could even conceive of. In this way the two men nibbled away at each other: safety after safety, then a shot, a pocketed ball, more safeties; each man winning a game, losing a game; the games going on and on for agonizing minutes, the crowd silent, holding its collective breath, until finally the two men were tied at six games each.

Reyes won the thirteenth game to go ahead, 7–6. Joyner began the fourteenth game by pocketing four balls in a row. Then he played Reyes a weak safety by mistake, and Reyes pocketed seven balls in a row before finding himself without a shot. He played Joyner safe. Joyner returned the favor and played Reyes an impossible safety that was rewarded by applause from the fans.

Reyes studied the balls. His cue ball was against the rail, next to a corner pocket. The object ball was against the rail a few inches from the other side of the same pocket. To win Reyes would have to pocket the object ball in the far corner pocket on his side of the table. That seemed impossible. So he aimed his cue at the cue ball to play a safety. He hit the ball too hard, however, and both the object ball and the cue ball went spinning around the table, hitting one cushion after another in what was such a terrible mistake that groans rose in unison from the audience. The paths of the two balls crossed in the middle of the table; the cue ball headed for another rail, while the object ball moved on a forty-five-degree angle. The audience suddenly realized where it was heading. The four hundred fans jumped screaming from their seats as the object ball rolled slowly toward Reyes's pocket and dropped in.

Pandemonium filled the room, people shouting, applauding, yelling into their cell phones. Reyes gave a little punch in the air with his fist and then sat and hung his head. He had just won $5,000 on a shot that no one else could ever have seen, one rivaling the shot he once made against Strickland. That's why he is called "the Magician."

KURT STREETER

Making the Time Count

FROM THE LOS ANGELES TIMES*

THE TIMEKEEPER CARRIED HIS BELL. Once he had used it to control boxing matches. Now he used it to honor the dead.

Slowly and wordlessly, he walked, with shuffling half steps, the four blocks from his dark Hollywood apartment to the restaurant.

He stood in front of a group of people: retired boxers, referees, and fight fans. Many were stooped and shaky. For years, every Tuesday, when his body was not betraying him, the timekeeper had been meeting them here.

He placed his bell on a table. Then he spoke of three boxers who had just fallen for the last time.

Jerry Moore. Great puncher, he would remember telling the group. *Great manager. Friend to us all.*

Tears welled in their eyes.

Coley Wallace. Once beat Marciano. This was in the amateurs, 1948. I was there.

Heads bowed.

Max Schmeling. Lived ninety-nine years. Deserves our utmost respect. He beat Joe Louis, who was the greatest of them all.

With a small hammer, he tapped the bell ten times, a steady rhythm . . . *bing, bing, bing, bing* . . . to pay tribute.

They surrounded the timekeeper, telling him how important he was.

*

* Italics designate statements recalled by subjects in the story. Statements heard by the writer are enclosed in quotation marks.

Arnie Koslow is a lonely man. He is eighty and lives by himself in a bare-walled studio apartment filled with dust, cardboard boxes, a framed photo of his parents — and his bell.

He does not have much left.

He never had a wife and never had children.

He has aching feet, unreliable kidneys, a bad heart, and a thin body that seems to grow slighter by the week.

Among his greatest possessions has always been time; he loves and respects its steady march. Now, though, even time is slipping through his fingers. Arnie Koslow knows this because of the condition he is in. "A senior and weak," he says, frankly. "I could die any day. I'm not afraid of it."

A boxing enthusiast since his childhood in Brooklyn, he became a highly regarded timekeeper. He had been an awful boxer and never made much of a mark as a manager's assistant. But he found his niche as a timekeeper — a job that offers little recognition, although boxing could not go on without it.

He worked more than 1,500 fights, almost all in Los Angeles. He kept time for youth bouts, sideshow bouts, and big-time professional fights. Boxing: the stage, the drama, the ugliness, and the beautiful precision of it all. Keeping time: watching seconds turn into minutes, minutes into moments, moments into memory.

In his life, they became intertwined.

"I've always been one to reminisce about days gone by," he says, his voice still tinged by Brooklyn. "As I get older, the things I remember, it's like they are becoming clearer and clearer in my mind. Like a movie. Oh, I miss so much of it. Miss it bad. But I've had a great life. Had my friends. Survived the war. There were two women I loved . . .

"And boxing, the greatest sport in the world. I was lucky to be a part of it."

"It Just Grabbed Me"

He was nine, and it was an amateur fight: the New York Golden Gloves, the first bout he ever saw. He cannot recall who fought, but he can still smell the roasted hot dogs and hear the crowd yell. Two boxers stepped into the ring. They were lean. One was in dark trunks, the other in white. "It just grabbed me," he says. "From that moment. Love."

Two years later, he saw his first professional fight. "Dexter Park, Long Island, June 7, 1937," he says. "I remember it specifically. That was the night Jean Harlow died. Ah, Harlow, what a dame . . . The opening bout was a four-rounder. Then there was a six-rounder.

"You know what? I used to know the first one hundred bouts I ever saw. But now I can't remember all one hundred. It's age, and it makes me mad. But that night, the big shot coming up was Petey Scalzo. Then the main event: Freddie 'Red' Cochran. Did I tell you? He just died. I rung my bell for him. I rung that one at home. I was all by myself. In the apartment. Sometimes I can't make it to the restaurant, so I ring it right there. These guys are heroes, larger than life. When they die they deserve to be honored by somebody."

Arnie Koslow's family was poor, so he worked odd jobs to cobble together enough nickels and dimes to pay for the subway and the seventy-five cents for admission to the local fights. His weeks were filled with boxing. Mondays at Dexter Park. Tuesdays at the Broadway Arena. Fridays at the old Madison Square Garden. Saturday nights at the Ridgewood Grove.

On Sunday afternoons, he rode the train from his neighborhood of mostly Polish immigrants into Manhattan to watch a live radio show that featured boxing greats. In the waiting room, he met a string of champions. One day, a large man in a gray suit sat next to him. It was Joe Louis, the heavyweight title holder.

"I look at him and I say, 'Mr. Louis, can I have your autograph?' Did I ever tell you? His hand covered the whole pencil, and his writing, it was so small? Anyways I says to him, 'Thank you, Mr. Louis.'

"And he says to me, 'You're welcome.' You are welcome? Joe Louis spoke to me? One of the thrills of my life."

Power in His Hand

Not long afterward, Arnie Koslow began to box. In his first match, he took a beating. After a few more fights and a few more beatings, he quit.

He joined the Army. Soon he was on the shores of Normandy,

ten days after D-day, part of a company heading through France, then into Germany. Grenades. Bullets. Snipers. Death. Moments that still come to him in nightmares. But he had boxing.

"Did I ever tell you," he asks, "about Phillips?"

Indeed he has, but he tells the story again anyway.

It was cold, sometime in February 1945. He was in a British hospital, suffering trench foot. Good God, there were doctors talking about amputation. But he knew he was still himself when he found out about a championship bout in Manchester — Al Phillips, one of the best fighters in Europe, would fight Nel Tarleton — and he, Arnie Koslow, tried to break out of the hospital to see it.

He took another man's uniform and hobbled through the door. A military policeman caught him before he got off the grounds, and he missed the bout. But inside of himself he knew he was okay and that he would survive, even if they told him to go back to the battle. He knew this because, in spite of everything, he was still holding tight to the thing that made him whole: boxing.

When the war ended, he returned to New York. He fell for a girl, Sylvia, eighteen, brown-haired and sweet. They kissed on their first date. But he hated New York's weather. He wanted a new start, to be part of a new boxing scene. Like thousands of others after World War II, he came to Los Angeles. In early 1951, he climbed into an old Dodge and drove all the way. Sylvia came out west for a while. But then she moved home and stayed.

He met another woman, Louise. Fell for her too. But they argued too much, and soon it was over.

Maybe it was just bad luck; he's not sure. Both times, things ended so badly that he looks down at the ground in sorrow, even today. He knew his chances at having a family were gone.

At first he worked as a sound technician at a recording studio and lived in low-rent apartments on the outskirts of Hollywood. Then it occurred to him: "I got used to it, not having a family, being alone."

It's not hard to guess what made it easier: boxing. During the 1950s and '60s, Los Angeles was a boxing hotbed. He saw "the great Davey Moore, Jerry Quarry, Sonny Liston, Joe Frazier." If there was a fight, especially a big-time fight, he was there, at the Olympic Auditorium or maybe the old Hollywood Legion, happy as he could be, because the boxing was as good as any in New York.

Then, one evening in the early '70s, he went to a bout in East L.A. The timekeeper was a no-show. Somebody asked him to step in.

They gave him a stopwatch and told him to sit at ringside. They said to make sure that each round lasted exactly three minutes and that each break between the rounds lasted exactly one minute.

He had power, control of the bell. When he rang it, the fighting started and stopped.

It wasn't long before he was a timekeeper at boxing matches all over Los Angeles, dressed in his black-and-white-striped uniform, a stopwatch on a cord around his neck, always arriving early so he could test the bell and the acoustics long before the crowd came.

"I was just drawn to the whole process," he says. "I just felt important, like what I did mattered. I never wanted to give that up."

"One Light Touch . . ."

Timekeepers toil in obscurity, with hardly a nod from boxers, managers, promoters, referees, or fans.

Unless they make a mistake and, say, allow a round to go extra seconds, and there is a knockout.

Arnie Koslow made few mistakes. He loved the precision that came with keeping the time. He tracked each round, each break, and when a fighter hit the canvas, he began the official count — "one, two, three, four . . ." — shouting so loudly he could be heard above the crowd, slapping a hand hard on the canvas with each beat, until the referee took over.

Then there was the bell.

For many fights, he brought his own. It was a humble bell. Black. Eighteen inches in diameter, affixed to a small wooden panel. It had a particularly high pitch that he liked. Although he bought it mail order for just $80, he still holds his bell with the same loving gentleness with which a concert violinist would caress a Stradivarius.

"I see it as a musical instrument," he says. He is cradling the bell in his apartment, looking at it with admiration. "Even the technique. It's all in the wrist. It's physics. You bing it low, the sound will resonate — up."

The only bell better than his, he says, was the one at the Olympic Auditorium. It was big, brown, and, he thinks, once a brake drum in an old Ford truck. No bell sounded as good as that one. "The best. Absolutely.

"Did I ever tell you about that bell?"

He imagines it is in front of him. He lifts his right hand, as if clutching a hammer. "One light touch . . ." His hand moves, as if he were hitting it. "The sound. Oh, the sound . . ."

His voice rises as he remembers all the bells he rang at his favorite fights. Julio Cesar Chavez. Oscar De La Hoya. George Foreman.

Then he begins to remember the ugly fights, and his voice falls to a whisper. Two of them: among the worst days of his life.

September 19, 1980. Arnie Koslow rang the bell for Johnny Owen when he fought Lupe Pintor at the Olympic Auditorium for the world bantamweight title. A right to the head in the twelfth round sent Owen crumpling to the canvas. He went into a coma. Three weeks later, he died.

September 1, 1983. Arnie Koslow rang the bell for Francisco "Kiko" Bejines in his bantamweight title fight against Alberto Davila at the Olympic Auditorium. In the final round, Bejines was hit with a jab that dropped him like a bag of crushed bricks. His head slammed back, he sprawled against the ropes, and his eyes stared into nothingness. It was a stare from the beach at Normandy. Bejines, too, went into a coma. Three days later, he died.

Arnie Koslow would have given back all of his time in boxing, every bit of it, he says, if those two fighters could have lived.

Every boxer tempts fate. Some become champions. Others achieve greatness but go unrecognized. Some have little talent and endure beatings. Some die.

And his own fate?

By the mid-1990s, as he turned seventy, his health began to fail. He fought a terrible battle with colon cancer, and boxing began to phase him out. Suddenly, from the state officials who decide, he stopped getting work. He doesn't know why. He refuses to blame his age. He worked a kickboxing bout in the Los Angeles suburbs. "Reduced to karate," Koslow scoffs.

Then it was over.

What had made him happiest, what had made him feel useful and alive, was taken away completely.

"It eats at me," he says. "I miss it, but this is a fact I have to live with. Boxing is full of risk, and it is highly subjective. But not the timekeeper's part. Those seconds passing? That's a fact. We work with the facts. Every second, time is ticking. Time is not gonna wait for you. Funny thing is, it's the same in life.

"The moment you are born the clock starts. That's a fact."

Sparring with Ghosts

Now it's 2005. March 15. Tuesday. Lunch.

He sits inside the restaurant, the Old Spaghetti Factory.

He doesn't have his bell. He brings it only when someone has died.

Thirty men and five women have assembled in a yellow-walled room, elderly boxers, trainers, referees, officials, and fans. They call themselves the Golden State Boxers Assn. They have been meeting for lunch on Tuesdays for three decades.

The boxers talk while they eat. They tell crude jokes. They conjure up their toughest foes and bravest victories. They try to put together enough money — $10 here, $20 there — to help other old fighters: men who are sick or poor, maybe homeless, unable to pay their bills, maybe even about to run out of time forever.

They sit in the middle of the room: Joey Barnum, a top-ranked lightweight in the 1940s; Art Aragon, who enchanted Los Angeles with his flair in the 1950s; Danny Valdez, a title contender in the 1960s; and Bobby Chacon, twice a world champion, one of the toughest fighters of the 1970s and '80s.

Some are vital still. They stand and throw punches into the air, suddenly young again. But others limp and shake, slur their words, and have trouble keeping track of the past.

"It's sort of sad," Arnie Koslow says, under his breath. He looks at Chacon, a smiling, boisterous man, but so shell-shocked he must constantly write notes to himself, reminders so he does not forget where he was, where he should be, or who should be around him. On a portable DVD player, they watch one of Chacon's greatest moments, a fifteen-round title fight. "Knew I had 'em here!" Chacon shouts in a mumble, raising his hands.

The men clap and shout. They pat him on the back.

"Bobby, you were the best!"

"Bobby, Bobby . . . Oh, man!"

Arnie Koslow grimaces. Is Chacon shell-shocked because of the boxing? He tries to answer his own question. "I don't know. I've seen high school football players in bad shape too. I believe boxing, if the rules are applied properly, is a very safe contact sport. Some say it's that dementia, caused by boxing. That Alzheimer's."

One of the old boxers interrupts. "It ain't the all-timers," he says. "Just people getting old is all."

Arnie Koslow laughs. "Getting old. Don't I know it." He shakes his head. "Getting old. Jeez."

"Kid, I Saw Louis Fight"

Tuesday again. May 9. Lunch.

"Hey, Arnie, who was the best fighter ever?"

"Louis."

"Better than Sugar Ray Robinson?"

"He was great. [But] I liked Louis."

"Better than Ali?" asks another man, in his fifties. Then the man adds: "I don't know about that."

"I do. Kid, I saw Louis fight. At his peak, he could take apart any man. I saw Ray Robinson fight too. This must have been in the late thirties. In Manhattan. I think it was Harlem, and it was the Golden Gloves. He had it all. But Louis, he was my idol. Did I ever tell you about the time I met him at Sam Taub's radio show . . . ?"

Nearby, someone stands and makes a plea. "We gotta help out the Bossman," the man says, referring to Eddie "Bossman" Jones, a light heavyweight who sparred with Ali. The Bossman, he reports, is down on his luck in South Los Angeles.

Arnie Koslow shakes his head. "He could hit. Whew, the Bossman could really hit. It's a shame." He would give money, if he had any.

An hour later, he walks stiffly down the front steps of the restaurant.

"These people here are family," he says. "It keeps me going. God, it keeps me going."

The March of Time

This summer, Arnie Koslow nearly died. Kidney stones and two heart attacks, he says. In July, after more than a month in a veterans hospital, he came back home: weak, bone-thin, thirty pounds gone from his frame.

He began missing Tuesdays at the Old Spaghetti Factory. He couldn't walk that far. Rarely did anyone come to pick him up.

Rarely did he have visitors at all.

Now, on most Tuesdays at lunchtime, he sits alone in his room, waiting for Meals-on-Wheels, a tired man with crinkly skin, his wavy hair mostly gray. He turns up his TV so loud people can hear it on the sidewalk. He reads the sports pages. He looks at the framed picture of his parents.

Sometimes he screams, mad as hell at what his body has become.

He jots down stream-of-consciousness memories in a black journal with a wire binder: he writes about New York and Normandy, rainstorms and retirement, boxing and his bell.

He writes about time.

"Time on my hands. If memory serves me right, 'Time on my hands' [was] the opening line of a beautiful love song in the 1930s. Strange for me to think of that, because I haven't actually been in love for such a long time . . .

"So what does that leave me with? Let's see. What is time? Time waits for no one . . . [and time] reminds me of a wonderful job I had for years in the sport of boxing.

"I was the boxing timekeeper."

TIM ZIMMERMANN

Raising the Dead

FROM OUTSIDE

TEN MINUTES INTO HIS DIVE, Dave Shaw started to look for the bottom. Utter blackness pressed in on him from all sides, and he directed his high-intensity light downward, hoping for a flash of rock or mud. Shaw, a fifty-year-old Aussie, was in an alien world, more than 800 feet below the surface pool that marks the entrance to Bushman's Hole, a remote sinkhole in the Northern Cape province of South Africa and the third-deepest freshwater cave known to man.

Shaw's stocky five-foot-ten body was encased in a black crushed-neoprene drysuit. On his back he carried a closed-circuit re-breather set, which, unlike traditional open-circuit scuba gear, was recycling the gas Shaw breathed, scrubbing out the carbon dioxide he exhaled and adding back oxygen. He carried six cylinders of gas, splayed alongside him like mutant appendages. On the surface, Shaw would barely have been able to move. But in the water, descending the shot line guiding him from the cave's entrance to the bottom, he was weightless and graceful, a black creature with just a flash of skin showing behind his mask, gliding downward without emitting a single bubble to disrupt the ethereal silence.

Only two divers had ever been to this depth in Bushman's before. One of them, a South African named Nuno Gomes, had claimed a world record in 1996 when he hit bottom, on open-circuit gear, at 927 feet. Gomes had turned immediately for the surface. But Shaw, a Cathay Pacific Airways pilot based in Hong Kong and a man who had become one of the most audacious explorers in cave diving, didn't strive for depth alone. He planned to bottom out Bushman's Hole at a depth that no rebreather had ever been taken, connect a light reel of cave line to the shot line, and then swim off to perform the sublime act of having a look around. At that moment late last October, cocooned in more than a billion gallons of water, Dave Shaw was a very happy man.

Shaw touched down on the cave's sloping bottom well up from where Gomes had landed, clipped off the cave reel, and started swimming. There was no time to waste. Every minute he spent on the bottom — his VR3 dive computer said he was now approaching 886 feet — would add more than an hour of decompression time on the way up. Still, Shaw felt remarkably relaxed, sweeping his light left and right, reveling in the fact that he was the first human ever to lay line at this depth. Suddenly, he stopped. About fifty feet to his left, perfectly illuminated in the gin-clear water, was a human body. It was on its back, the arms reaching toward the surface. Shaw knew immediately who it was: Deon Dreyer, a twenty-year-old South African who had blacked out deep in Bushman's ten years earlier and disappeared. Divers had been keeping an eye out for him ever since.

Shaw turned immediately, unspooling cave line as he went. Up close, he could see that Deon's tanks and dive harness, snugged around a black-and-tan wetsuit, appeared to be intact. Deon's head and hands, exposed to the water, were skeletonized, but his mask was eerily in place on the skull. Thinking he should try to bring Deon back to the surface, Shaw wrapped his arms around the corpse and tried to lift. It didn't move. Shaw knelt down and heaved again. Nothing. Deon's air tanks and the battery pack for his light appeared to be firmly embedded in the mud underneath him, and Shaw was starting to pant from exertion.

This isn't wise, he chastised himself. *I'm at 270 meters and working too hard.* He was also already a minute over his planned bottom time. Shaw quickly tied the cave reel to Deon's tanks, so the body could be found again, and returned to the shot line to start his ascent.

Approaching 400 feet, almost an hour into the dive, Shaw met up with his close friend Don Shirley, a forty-eight-year-old British expat who runs a technical-diving school in Badplaas, South Africa. After Shirley checked that Shaw was okay and retrieved some spare gas cylinders hanging on the shot line below, Shaw showed him an underwater slate on which he had written 270M, FOUND BODY. Shirley's eyebrows shot up inside his mask, and he reached out to shake his friend's hand.

Shirley left Shaw, who had another eight hours and forty minutes of decompression to complete. As Shirley ascended, it occurred to him that Shaw would not be able to resist coming back to try to recover Deon. Shirley would have been content to leave the body where it was, but Shaw was a man who dived to expand the limits of the possible. He had just hit a record depth on a rebreather, and now he had the opportunity to return a dead boy to his parents and, in the process, do something equally stunning: make the deepest body recovery in the history of diving.

"Dave felt very connected with Deon," Shirley says. "He had found him, so it was like a personal thing that he should bring him back."

When Shaw finally surfaced in the late-afternoon African sun, he removed his mask and said, "I want to try to take him out."

Deep-water divers have always been the daredevils of the diving community, pushing far into the dark labyrinths of water-filled holes and extreme ocean depths. It's a small global fraternity — there are no more than a dozen members — and in the history of recreational diving, only six people other than Shaw have ever pulled off successful dives below 820 feet. (More people have walked on the moon, Don Shirley likes to point out.) At least three ran into serious trouble in the process (including Nuno Gomes, who got stuck in the mud on the bottom of Bushman's Hole for two minutes before escaping). And two have since died: American Sheck Exley, who drowned while diving the world's deepest sinkhole, Mexico's 1,080-foot-deep Zacatón, in April 1994; and Britain's John Bennett, who disappeared while diving a wreck off the coast of South Korea in March 2004.

"Today extreme divers are far exceeding any reasonable physiology capabilities," says American Tom Mount, a pioneer in technical diving and the owner of the Miami Shores, Florida–headquartered International Association of Nitrox and Technical Divers (IANTD). "Equipment can go to those depths, but your body might not be able to."

Aside from the dangers of getting trapped or lost, breathing deep-dive gas mixes — usually a combination of helium, nitrogen, and oxygen known as trimix — at extreme underwater pressure can kill you in any number of ways. For example, at depth, oxygen can become toxic, and nitrogen acts like a narcotic — the deeper you go, the stupider you get. Divers compare narcosis to drinking martinis on an empty stomach, and, depending on the gas mix you're using, at 800-plus feet you can feel like you've downed at least four or five of them all at once. Helium is no better; it can send you into nervous, twitching fits. Then, if you don't breathe slowly and deeply, carbon dioxide can build up in your lungs and you'll black out. And if you ascend too quickly, all the nitrogen and helium that has been forced into your tissues under pressure can fizz into tiny bubbles, causing a condition known as the bends, which can result in severe pain, paralysis, and death. To try to avoid getting the bends, extreme divers spend hours on ascent, sitting at targeted depths for carefully calculated periods of decompression to allow the gases to flush safely from their bodies. As divers say, if you do the depth, you do the time.

For any diver who can stomach the risks, Bushman's Hole is world-class. It's located on the privately owned Mount Carmel game farm, eleven thousand acres of rolling, ocher-earthed veldt sparsely thatched with silky bushman grass and dotted with sun-baked termite mounds. Not until you top a small rise a few miles from the farm dwellings do you notice a break in the clean sweep of the land, where the earth starts to fall in on itself as if a giant hammer had come smashing down. The resulting crater is hundreds of feet from rim to rim and walled on one side by a sheer cliff. If you hike down the steep, stony path on the opposite side, you come to a small, swimming pool–size basin of water, covered in a green carpet of duckweed. This is the entrance to Bushman's Hole.

No one had any idea how deep Bushman's was until Nuno Gomes arrived. On his first visit, in 1981, the Johannesburg-based Gomes dived to almost 250 feet, dropping down through a narrow chimney that opens up into an enormous chamber below 150 feet. In 1988, he set an African depth record of just over 400 feet, and Bushman's reputation as a deep diver's cave started to spread. In 1993, Sheck Exley showed up. Supported by a team that included Gomes, Exley became the first diver to hit bottom, touching down at 863 feet on the hole's sloping floor.

During the Exley expedition, Gomes performed a sonar scan of the hole. It revealed Bushman's to be the largest freshwater cave ever discovered, with a main chamber that was approximately 770 feet by 250 feet across and more than 870 feet deep. (Gomes later found a maximum depth of at least 927 feet.)

Diving Bushman's is exhilarating. The narrow entrance is claustrophobic, but once you reach the vast main chamber, it's like spacewalking. For a young cave diver like Deon Dreyer, it must have been irresistible. Deon grew up in the modest town of Vereeniging, about thirty-five miles south of Johannesburg, and loved adventure in all its forms. He shot his first buck at the age of ten. By seventeen he was racing a souped-up car around local tracks, tinkering with his motorcycle, and designing obscenely loud car stereos. Another of his passions was diving. "He couldn't sit still, never, ever, ever," says his younger brother, Werner, now twenty-seven.

Deon had logged about two hundred dives when he was invited to join some South Africa Cave Diving Association divers at Bushman's Hole over the 1994 Christmas break. They planned a descent to 492 feet and asked Deon to dive support. He was thrilled. Two weeks before the expedition, Deon's grandfather passed away. Sitting around a barbecue with his family one night, Deon spoke with boyish hubris. "He said if he had a choice of how to go out in life, he'd like to go out diving," recalls his father, Theo, fifty-one, the owner of a business that sells and services two-way radios.

Deon's mother, Marie, a petite fifty-year-old, begged Deon not to go. In 1993, Bushman's Hole had already taken the life of a diver named Eben Leyden, who blacked out at 200 feet. (A dive buddy rushed him to the surface, but Leyden didn't survive.) And then, on December 17, 1994, the hole claimed Deon Dreyer.

For Marie and Theo, the nightmare started with a policeman's knock at the door. They rushed to Mount Carmel, where slowly the story came out. The team had been doing a practice dive. On the way back up, at 196 feet, Deon appeared to be fine, exchanging hand signals with his buddy. The group continued ascending. At 164 feet they suddenly noticed a light below them. A quick, confused diver count came up one short. Team leader Dietloff Giliomee wasn't sure what was happening. Then another diver, in the eerie glow of his submersible light, dragged his finger across his throat. Giliomee desperately started swimming down but stopped when he realized the light below him was already more than 100 feet deeper and fading fast. "I decided it was a suicide chase," he wrote in the accident report.

No one knows for sure what killed Deon. The best guess is deep-water blackout from carbon dioxide buildup. Two weeks after the accident, Theo paid to bring in a small, remotely operated sub used by the De Beers mining company. It found Deon's dive helmet on the vast floor of Bushman's, but there was no sign of his body. Resigning themselves to the idea that Deon would stay in the hole for eternity, Theo and Marie placed a commemorative plaque on a rock wall above the entry pool. "He had the most majestic grave in the country," Theo says. "And I said, 'Well, this will be his final resting place.'"

But on October 30, 2004, Dave Shaw called Theo and said, "I will go and fetch your son." Theo immediately responded, "Yes, absolutely yes." More than anything, he realized, he wanted to see his boy again.

If recovering Deon from the bottom of Bushman's Hole was a feat of extraordinary ambition and danger, combining extreme depth with demanding work, Shaw and Shirley were just the guys to pull it off. On his first dive, in 1999, with his then-seventeen-year-old son, Steven, in the Philippines, Shaw had found a sport whose challenges he couldn't resist. He quickly pushed past the standard reef tours and went wreck diving. Soon enough he discovered the caves, and he was hooked.

As an airline pilot, Shaw could dive all over the world — in Asia, the United States, Mexico, and South Africa. He was born in the small town of Katanning, in Western Australia, and from the age of three, when he built his first toy aircraft out of cardboard, Shaw knew he wanted to fly. By the time he was eighteen, in 1973, he was working as a crop duster. That same year he met the Melbourne-raised Ann Broughton at a youth camp in Perth. He took her up in an airplane on their first date, and twenty months later they were married. In 1981, Shaw became a missionary pilot, moving with Ann to Papua New Guinea, where Steven was born. A daughter, Lisa, followed in 1983, and the Shaws relocated briefly to Tanzania before moving to New South Wales, Australia, where eventually Shaw began flying corporate jets. In 1989, he settled in with Cathay Pacific, moving his family to Hong Kong.

Shaw loved to poke around deep underwater, so he was commit-

ted to the closed-circuit rebreather for its remarkable efficiency
and the warm, moist gas recycling produces. The oxygen supply
is automatically monitored and adjusted by a digital controller
strapped to a forearm, and pretty much the only oxygen consumed
is that which the diver metabolizes. In contrast, divers using traditional open-circuit scuba (the majority of divers today) inhale
ice-cold mixes and exhale huge volumes of gas into the water.
(Rebreather divers like to call them "bubble blowers.") As a result,
extreme open-circuit divers often need a dozen or more gas cylinders, constantly court hypothermia, and, without automatic control of their oxygen levels, end up breathing — and absorbing —
more helium and nitrogen, running up a greater decompression
tab. When Nuno Gomes went to the bottom of Bushman's Hole on
open circuit in 1996, he didn't hang around at all, used more than
54,000 liters of gas, and had to spend almost twelve hours in the water. When Shaw went to the bottom on his rebreather, he tooled
around exploring, used only 5,800 liters of gas, and got back to the
surface in nine hours and forty minutes.

The chief drawbacks to rebreathers are that they are expensive
(upwards of $5,000), require the diver to constantly monitor the
digital controller settings (open-circuit divers just have to breathe),
and, until Shaw came along, had not been proved at great depths.
But Shaw was convinced that rebreathers were the future of diving.
In 2003, he purchased a rare Mk15.5 rebreather, developed by the
U.S. Navy for deep submarine evacuation, and modified it with a
Hammerhead controller that he filled with paraffin oil, as a sort of
internal shock absorber that would help the components withstand
intense pressures. Then he set about diving his custom rig to suc-
cessively greater depths.

Don Shirley, an understated man with steel-frame glasses and a
scraggly beard, was a kindred spirit. He grew up in Surrey, England,
and spent twenty-two years as an electronics specialist in the British
Army, which took him through the Falklands War and to the Per-
sian Gulf. He dived every spare minute he had, specializing in deep
wrecks off the coast of Britain. In 1997, he retired from the army
and moved to South Africa, looking to start a new life as a technical-diving trainer in an exotic English-speaking land. He and a
partner set up the South African franchise of IANTD, alongside a
deep, flooded asbestos mine in the beautiful grassy hills a couple

hundred miles east of Johannesburg. He dubbed the spot Komati Springs, spent hundreds of hours a year in the water, teaching technical and cave diving, and developed the mine, with its deep shafts, into a premier dive site. In 2003, he married Andre Truter, a feisty thirty-eight-year-old Afrikaner with short brown hair and a sly smile. Together they live in a thatch-roofed bungalow, surrounded by a pack of rambunctious dogs with names like Sheck and Argon.

In the fall of 2002, a bearded man with an Australian twang appeared at Shirley's dive center. "Hi, I'm Dave Shaw," the man said. "Do you mind if I go dive your hole?" Shirley sized up the bluff Aussie and liked what he saw. Soon Shaw was flying in regularly to dive, and Shirley went with him whenever he had time. In October 2003, at Komati Springs, Shaw set a rebreather cave record of 597 feet, with Shirley diving backup. Two days later, Shirley, with Shaw just behind him, became the first diver to reach the very end of the mine's deepest shaft, at 610 feet. Shaw and Shirley had logged more than a hundred hours underwater together in the nearly two and a half years they'd known each other. "It was stunning being in the water with Dave, very relaxed," Shirley says.

Shirley introduced Shaw to the enticing depths of Bushman's in June 2004. Shaw turned up with his modified Mk15.5 and dived it to 725 feet, another world record for a closed-circuit rebreather in a cave. His DUI drysuit and Thinsulate underwear kept him warm. He peed happily into the water via a valve in his drysuit that had a catheter running to a condom (informally known as "the Urinator"), and topped up, intermittently pulling his regulator out of his mouth, on candy bars and water lowered in a string bag at shallow decompression stops. He fell in love with the place.

In November 2004, back home in his apartment in Hong Kong, Shaw was in almost daily e-mail and phone contact with Shirley. The Big Dive, as they started to call it, was set for early January, and one of the most elusive questions was the condition of Deon's body. The forensics experts they consulted weren't sure but guessed the corpse would be mostly bone. Shaw decided he'd better try to get it into a body bag for the trip to the surface or risk having it fall apart. Together with Ann, he designed a silk bag with drawstrings, long enough to fit over Deon's fins.

Ann, a forty-nine-year-old deputy head principal at Hong Kong's

German Swiss International School, was nervous about the dangers her husband faced. "I want someone to ring me as soon as you are on your way up," she insisted. Shaw agreed but gave Ann the impression the dive would be taking place a day later than scheduled. That way, he could just call her when he was back on the surface and say, "Don't worry. It's all over and I'm fine." If he wasn't fine, he gently told Ann, he would arrange to have someone call Michael Vickers, their minister at Hong Kong's Anglican Resurrection Church.

On the evening of Saturday, January 1, Ann made the forty-five-minute drive to Hong Kong's Chep Lap Kok airport with 250 pounds of dive gear in her car. Shaw had been flying that day, and she met him at the Cathay Pacific offices and drove him to the departure area for his flight to South Africa. They sat together in a coffee bar. "You're not crying, are you?" he asked. "No," Ann replied bravely. Shaw got up to leave for his flight. He didn't say, "I love you." He didn't need to. She knew.

Shaw arrived in Johannesburg six days before the dive. His first stop was Komati Springs, where he practiced getting a body into the bag underwater, with Shirley playing the part of Deon's corpse. At 66 feet, it went smoothly, taking Shaw only a couple of minutes. A day later, he and Shirley drove to Mount Carmel, where seven South African rebreather divers, handpicked by Shirley, and a police team from Cape Town and Pretoria (since there was a dead body involved) were assembling. The dive would go off on the coming Saturday, January 8, and Shirley's dive plan was like an underwater symphony. Shaw was looking at a dive that would last roughly twelve hours, and would hit the water around 6:00 A.M. All the other divers would key off Shaw's dive time and head for specific target depths either to help look after Shaw or pass Deon's body to the surface. The first diver Shaw would meet on the way back up was Shirley, at 725 feet. He would hand the body bag over, and, if things went well, Deon would be out of the water about eighty minutes after Shaw's dive had started.

Shirley had done everything in his power to minimize the risks. He planned to have thirty-five backup cylinders of gas in the water — enough so that he, Shaw, and even some support divers could survive total rebreather failure. He arranged for a rope-and-sling system to be set up that could haul a diver on a stretcher up the cliffs of the hole to a recompression chamber that the police trucked in. To cope with any medical emergencies, Shirley had recruited a doctor — Jack Meintjies, a specialist in diving physiology at the University of Stellenbosch, outside Cape Town — to be on hand. When Meintjies realized that up to nine divers would be in the water, and learned the depths they would be going to, he almost backed out. "There were too many potential bodies. You are dealing with multiple divers going deep, and that's serious," Meintjies says.

Shaw, for one, was quietly confident. At Mount Carmel, he stressed repeatedly that the effort was an "attempted" body recovery. "The dive is huge," he told a collection of reporters and cameramen gathered a day before the dive. "No one has ever attempted anything even vaguely approximating a body recovery from these sorts of depths." He also talked about his motivation with the team. "I think what you are doing for the Dreyers is great," said Peter "Big B" Herbst, a forty-two-year-old dive instructor and the owner of Reef Divers, a dive shop and tour operator in Pretoria. Shaw looked at him, winked, and said, "Face it, B, we're doing this for the adventure of it."

Shaw did have one wrinkle to sort out. He had partnered up with South African documentary filmmaker Gordon Hiles to chronicle the recovery of Deon. Hiles had designed an underwater camera housing for a lightweight, low-light Sony HC20 Handy-cam and attached it to a Petzl climbing helmet. Shaw was not used to wearing a helmet. He liked to carry a high-intensity light on the back of his hand, and if he needed both hands underwater, Shaw would normally sling the light and cable around his neck so it wouldn't snag on anything. The helmet cam would make it hard to do that. Shaw tried the device in the swimming pool at Mount Carmel and decided he was comfortable with the design and weight. He told Hiles that, instead of slinging his light around his neck, he would occasionally set it out to the side.

Three days before the dive, Shaw carried the camera on an acclimatization dive to 500 feet. It came out in perfect running order. "A very impressive bit of gear," Shaw said to Hiles. "I'm sure you'll be impressed with my video footage as well." Everyone laughed.

The divers gathered for one last briefing on Friday. It was a warm, beautiful evening, and Shaw had some final points to make.

"The most important person on this dive is you. If you have a problem, deal with your problem and forget about me," he told the team. "It's better to have one person dead than two." He had a separate, private conversation with Shirley, who had upgraded his rebreather for the dive with an oil-filled Hammerhead controller so he could get all the way to the bottom of Bushman's if he had to. Shirley had asked his friend, "If you have problems, do you want me to come down?"

Shaw considered the question and answered, "Yes, but only come down if I signal."

Shirley and Shaw had one last message for the gathered team. "If Dave doesn't make it, if I don't make it, we stay there," said Shirley. "That's the end of the story. We don't want to be recovered."

At 4:00 A.M. on Saturday, January 8, Shaw and Shirley rose in the dark to prepare for the dive. It had been a rough night for Shirley. The previous evening, as he was changing the battery on his new Hammerhead controller, a wire snapped. Without the unit, he wouldn't be able to make the dive. Shirley was devastated. Shaw felt deeply for his friend but was prepared to proceed without him. He put Shirley and Peter Herbst in touch with Juergensen Marine, the Hammerhead manufacturer. At 9:00 P.M. — the cutoff time he had set for himself — Shaw went to bed. With the help of Juergensen, a soldering iron, and some tinfoil, Herbst managed to jury-rig a fix. The Hammerhead powered up, and Shirley was a go again.

In the gray predawn light, Shaw and Shirley began the ten-minute drive to the hole, listening to iPods to relax. Shaw had bought two in Hong Kong, loaded them with mixes he called Deep Cave 1 and Deep Cave 2, and given one to Shirley as a gift. (Shirley's favorite tune for the ride to the crater was Led Zeppelin's "Whole Lotta Love.") At the water, they started squeezing into their drysuits. Knowing how long he might be underwater, Shirley added an adult diaper to his ensemble. The rest of the team — the support divers, the police divers, the paramedics — assembled as well, and the rocky, uneven ground around the surface pool became crowded, dive equipment spilling over every flat surface. Verna van Schaik, thirty-five, a South African who had set the outright women's depth record of 725 feet at Bushman's in October, settled in with a large sheaf of dive tables. Shirley had asked her to run the dive as surface marshal, and van Schaik, who has magenta hair and a dolphin tattoo on her right ankle, was hoping she was going to have an easy day.

At 6:13 A.M., video camera whirring quietly on his head, Shaw shook Shirley's hand, said, "I'll see you in twenty minutes," and ducked into the dark waters of Bushman's Hole. A few minutes later, Theo and Marie Dreyer made their way to the water's edge. They had come late so that Shaw wouldn't feel any additional pressure to bring Deon back.

Shaw dropped quickly, letting the shot line squeak through his fingers. He hit the bottom in just over eleven minutes, more than a minute and a half faster than he had planned, and immediately started swimming along the cave line. As soon as the corpse loomed ahead, he pulled out the body bag. Then he knelt alongside Deon and went to work. He almost certainly could feel the narcosis kicking in. The helium and reduced nitrogen of his trimix would have limited the effect, but it was probably still as if he had downed four or five martinis. He had been on the bottom of Bushman's Hole, at 886 feet, for just over a minute.

Thirteen minutes after Shaw submerged, Shirley got the go signal from van Schaik and dropped toward his rendezvous point with Shaw, at 725 feet. Approaching 500 feet, he looked down. The water was so clear he could see Shaw's light almost 400 feet below him. It was about where he expected it would be, in the region of the shot line. There was only one problem: the light wasn't moving. Shirley knew instantly that something had gone very wrong. By this time, more than twenty minutes into his dive, Shaw should have been ascending. Shirley should have seen bubbles burbling up as Shaw vented the expanding gases in his rebreather and drysuit. But there was no movement. No bubbles. Nothing but a lonely, still light.

There is no room for emotion or panic in the bowels of a dark hole. Shirley stayed calm, his actions becoming almost automatic. Shaw hadn't signaled for help, but Shirley would be going to the bottom. A motionless diver at 886 feet is almost certainly a dead diver, but it was Dave Shaw down there. Shirley had to see if there was anything he could do, or at least clip Shaw to the shot line so his body could be recovered. *Okay, here we go then,* he said to himself.

At about 800 feet, deeper than he had ever been, Shirley heard the slight, sharp crack of enormous pressure crushing something, and then there was a thud. He looked down: the Hammerhead controller on his left forearm was a wreck. Without it, Shirley would have to constantly monitor the oxygen levels in his rebreather and inject oxygen into his breathing loop manually. It was a full-time occupation, an emergency routine at a life-threatening depth. Shirley was certain that if he went down to Shaw he would join him for eternity. He got his rebreather back under control and started back up the shot line, flipping through the alternate decompression profiles he was carrying with him on slates. He was facing at least another ten hours in the water. After a few minutes, Shaw's light was swallowed by the darkness below him.

Back on the surface, van Schaik and the crowd around the hole had no idea what was going on far beneath them. Twenty-nine minutes after Shaw had gone under (and about six minutes after Shirley had seen that his light was not moving), support divers Dusan Stojakovic, forty-eight, and Mark Andrews, thirty-nine, started their dive to rendezvous with Shaw at 492 feet. As they closed on their target depth, they realized there were no lights coming up, and no sign of Shirley or Shaw. Their plan called for them to wait two to four minutes. They stayed for six. Then it was time to go. "There's no heroics in this diving," Stojakovic says bluntly. "You dive your plan."

Before Andrews and Stojakovic started up, they peered once more into the void. This time they could see a light, but they couldn't tell who it was. Andrews took out an underwater slate and wrote, DID NOT MEET D + D, @ 150 [METERS] FOR 6 MIN. 1 LIGHT BELOW? NOT SURE D'S LIGHT OFF. On the way up, they passed Peter Herbst, and then Lo Vingerling, sixty, another support diver, who were on their way down. They showed each the slate and continued ascending. They needed to get the slate to the surface.

Herbst is a bearish Afrikaner with unruly graying hair and a love of a good joke. He's also a first-rate diver who never shies from a tough job. The single light meant there was trouble, and without hesitation Herbst descended past his target of 275 feet. Whoever was underneath him might need help, and Shirley was one of his best friends. Just a little deeper, just a little deeper, he kept telling himself. As the diver got closer he found himself praying, *Please, please, God, let it be Don.*

Just past 400 feet, Herbst pulled even. It was Shirley. *Sorry, Dave,* Herbst silently apologized. He flashed Shirley the okay sign and got one back. Then Shirley asked Herbst for a slate. He scribbled on it for a second and returned it. It read, DAVE NOT COMING BACK. Now it really hit Herbst. No Deon. No Dave. Reflexively, he peered deep into the hole. He saw nothing, just blackness. He checked Shirley again, and Shirley indicated that he should head up. Lo Vingerling was the next diver to reach Shirley. He signaled that he would drop down to do a last sweep for Shaw. Shirley stopped him, then drew his hand across his throat.

On the surface, the Dreyers waited nervously. It had been more than an hour since Shaw submerged, and the police divers were due to return with their son's body any minute. Theo wrapped his arms around Marie, and they peered into the dark pool. A nervous hush settled over the group. It was broken by the rattling of stones inside a plastic Energade bottle. The bottle was attached to a line dropping twenty feet into the hole, so that the divers could send slates up as they sat decompressing.

It was the slate from Andrews and Stojakovic, and was passed to van Schaik. Somehow, instead of "1 light below," van Schaik understood the slate to read "no lights below." She assumed it was saying that both Shaw and Shirley were gone. Within minutes, the police divers surfaced, empty-handed. In an instant, the entire, noble enterprise fell apart. Divers were dying. There was thirty seconds of stunned silence around the hole, then van Schaik calmly announced, "Okay, we are on our emergency plan."

Within twenty minutes, another slate arrived. It was from Shirley, and it had been raced to the surface by the next diver to reach him, Stephen Sander, thirty-nine, a former police-special-forces diver. DAVE NOT COMING BACK, it stated bluntly, repeating the slate Shirley had given to Herbst. On the flip side it detailed Shirley's new decompression profile. Van Schaik felt some relief — one of her two dead divers was alive — but glancing at the figures on the slate, she could see that Shirley had gone very deep and would run the risk of getting bent as he came up.

For the Dreyers it had been a tragic half-hour. A day that had started out promising the recovery of their son's body was now going to end with Shaw and Deon both at the bottom of Bushman's Hole. The Dreyers backed away from the water, helpless to do anything, and made their way to the farmhouse. Marie was in agony, crying and thinking about Shaw's wife and family. She wandered into Shaw's room and saw his shoes, wallet, cell phone, and clothes, all neatly laid out. *It's like he's coming back soon to use it all again,* Marie thought. But she knew he wasn't.

Derek Hughes, an underwater cameraman who was working with Gordon Hiles, also left. Before the dive, Shaw had asked him to call Michael Vickers, the Shaws' minister, if there was trouble. Hughes climbed to the top of the crater to get cell-phone reception and placed the call. Vickers asked him if he was sure Shaw wasn't coming back. Hughes waited another two hours before making the trip up the crater to call Vickers again. He was sure.

It was 7:00 P.M. Saturday evening in Hong Kong, and Ann Shaw was in her living room. Her twenty-one-year-old daughter, Lisa, was with her, on break from the Royal Melbourne Institute of Technology. The doorbell rang, and Ann opened the door to see Vickers, accompanied by two friends from church. Ann thought the dive wasn't taking place until the next day, but as soon as she saw the somber group, she knew. Vickers explained that Dave was five hours late. He suggested there was still a chance he could reappear. "Oh, no, he won't," Ann replied. "Not if he's been down there so long."

Ann, who has a deep faith in God, tried to believe that there was some higher purpose in what was happening. More than anything, though, she was struck by how completely her life had changed in the brief time it took Vickers to relay the news. The last time she'd had that feeling was thirty years earlier, at nineteen, as she walked down the aisle to be married, with Dave Shaw, himself just twenty, waiting for her at the altar.

Back at the hole, van Schaik didn't have time to think much about Shaw. With five other divers in the water and only two reserve divers on the surface, she had to focus on Don Shirley. She sent Gerhard Du Preez, thirty-one, into the hole to find him, with instructions to check everyone on his way down. Du Preez found Shirley just below the ceiling of the main chamber, checked that he was okay, then turned immediately for the surface to report back.

Alone again, Shirley continued his retreat. As he approached the chamber ceiling at about 164 feet, he started feeling faint. Instinct told him to get off his rebreather and onto his open-circuit bailout before he lost consciousness. He stuffed the regulator into his mouth, and as soon as he did, the cave started to spin around him. Shirley didn't know it yet, but a small bubble of helium had formed in his left inner ear, causing extreme vertigo. He was in a washing machine, and off the shot line. In the dark, all he could see with his light as he spun was black, followed by the flash of the cave roof, then black. He saw a flash of white go by, and then again. It was the shot line, and without thinking he thrust out his hand to grab it. That grab kept him alive. If he had missed, he would have drifted off, lost in the blackness. Up or down, it wouldn't really have mattered. Depth or the bends would have finished him, and van Schaik and her divers would have returned to an empty line.

The washing machine finally slowed just long enough for Shirley to read the backlit screen of his primary VR3. It showed he had come up to 114 feet. It also warned him that he needed to be down at 151 feet. Hand over hand, Shirley descended. As he reached his new depth, nausea hit him and he started to vomit. Shirley would feel the heave coming, pull the regulator from his mouth, throw up, and then replace the regulator. Fighting the vertigo and nausea, he managed to grab some spare gas cylinders from the cluster clipped onto the shot line nearby. The thought that he might die never occurred to him. I will survive, I will survive, he kept telling himself.

After about twenty minutes, Truwin Laas, thirty-one, van Schaik's second reserve diver, appeared. Shirley scratched on his slate, I'M HAVING A BAD TIME. I'VE GOT VERTIGO AND I'M VOMITING. Laas made sure Shirley was breathing the right gas mix for the depth, decided he was stable, and left quickly to update van Schaik. Shirley, alone again, started cycling repeatedly through a subroutine of survival, asking himself, Where should I be now? How long should I be here? And where do I have to go? Each breath was a conscious act that got harder as he tired. Suck, hold, exhale. Suck, hold, exhale. I will survive. I will survive.

Now the marathon began. Van Schaik started cycling divers down to stay with Shirley. Du Preez, Laas, Sander, and Vingerling dived repeatedly that day, racking up three or four dives apiece despite the risk of getting the bends themselves. (Herbst, who was out of action for hours with a suspected minor bend, went down once more; Andrews and Stojakovic had been too deep to dive again.) The divers clipped Shirley to the shot line in case he convulsed or passed out, unclipping him only to move him from one decompression stop to another. Every movement brought a new round of vomiting. "It was heartbreaking to hear," Vingerling says, mimicking the spastic violence of Shirley's dry heaves.

Before the dive, Shirley had told the team that if anything went wrong, his wife, Andre, was to be given the bad news straight and fast. Andre, who had stayed behind at Komati Springs to run the dive center, had been getting regular updates. After one call, a slate was taken to Shirley. MESSAGE FROM ANDRE, I LOVE YOU, it read, and then, YOU'D BETTER HANG IN THERE OR ELSE.

After more than ten hours in the water, Shirley finally reached a depth of twenty feet. He was exhausted and approaching hypothermia, but he stayed there decompressing for almost two hours. The next circle of hell was at just ten feet and had to be endured, according to the tables, for a full two hours and twenty minutes. As soon as Shirley settled in, a sharp pain flared in his left leg, a sign that more bends could be on the way. It was time to take his chances on the surface. LOWER LEFT LEG HURT. COULD BE LACK OF USE? he wrote on a slate. Soon after, Sander appeared. I'M HERE TO TAKE YOU HOME, he wrote.

Shirley was carried out. He had been in Bushman's Hole almost twelve and a half hours. "Don't cut the drysuit," he managed to growl when he saw Du Preez coming at him with a pair of shears. Shirley was winched up the cliff face, and within twenty-two minutes he was in the recompression chamber.

Over the next few days, as word spread of Shaw's death, the Dreyers and most of the dive team went home. Andre Shirley arrived on Sunday, after driving all night from Badplaas, to take her husband for additional recompression treatments in Pretoria. But Herbst stayed at the hole, and he was in a grim mood. It had been left to him to retrieve all the lines and gas cylinders that still hung in Bushman's depths, work he had started on Monday. By Wednesday, he was ready to go after the deepest cylinders, and he had called in his Afrikaner diving buddy Petrus Roux to help, with the police assisting at shallower depths. Standing at the water's edge, the police team held an impromptu memorial service for Shaw. Police diving superintendent Ernst Strydom and Roux read from the Bible. Herbst hadn't planned to say anything, but emotion gripped him, and a few words came.

"I'm going to miss you, mate," he said, as if Shaw could hear. "It's a good place. Rest here, stay here." The group sang "Amazing Grace" as black clouds threatened rain. And then Herbst and Roux dived into the hole.

They dropped to 300 feet and attached lifting buoys to the shot line to raise the cylinders still at 500 feet to a more manageable depth. When they returned to the surface, they were approached by police diver Gert Nel, who had been helping to clear lines in the chimney. "Did you see them?" Nel asked quietly. "See what?" Herbst asked. "The bodies," Nel said. "We saw Deon and Dave stuck in the cave at 20 meters."

Herbst rested up and returned to the water. As soon as he cleared the narrow neck of the chimney, his cave light locked on to Shaw, floating eerily upright, his arms spread wide and the back of his head and shoulders jammed against the ceiling. Shaw's light was hanging below. Looped around it was the cave line he had attached to Deon in October, and cradled almost perfectly in the line, its legs hanging down as if on a swing, was the headless body of Deon Dreyer. Herbst realized that Shaw's light must've gotten tangled in the cave line. When Herbst and Roux had lifted the shot line with the buoys, it had pulled the cave line — and with it Deon and Shaw — off the bottom. As Shaw ascended, the gases in his body, as well as those in his suit, rebreather, and buoyancy wing, had started to expand. Up he had gone, dragging Deon with him.

Herbst brought Deon out first. The police team laid a white body bag along the water's edge and lifted Deon into it. There was a surprising firmness under the wetsuit, and Strydom was shocked to get a whiff of rotting flesh. One of Deon's flippered feet fell off. A policeman tossed it into the bag alongside the body, and the zipper was closed. Shaw had died doing it, but Deon's body had finally been taken back from Bushman's Hole.

Shaw was recovered next. It was a distressing job. His body was grotesquely swollen from the change of depth and pressure, and it was locked by rigor mortis in the free-fall position. Herbst, standing in the surface pool, had to cut Shaw out of his equipment. "That was quite bad," he says, choking up.

Herbst cut the helmet cam free too. Gordon Hiles, who had been filming the morning's work, was relieved to see that the camera's housing was still intact. Herbst was exhausted, with a pounding headache. He needed to call Don Shirley and Ann Shaw. But more than anything, he wanted to see what was on that video.

It's not an easy thing to watch a person die, especially if that person is a friend. Less than an hour after the helmet cam was removed from Shaw's head, as Hiles made a copy of the video for the police at the top of the crater, Herbst watched the film of Shaw's last dive. Later, he and Shirley (who calls it "a snuff tape") examined it frame by frame, backward and forward, multiple times, to try and understand every nuance of Shaw's death.

The picture is dark, and sometimes hard to see. But along with the sounds of Shaw's breathing, picked up with perfect clarity by the camera in the stillness of the cave, the video tells the tale of Shaw's final moments. When Shaw reaches the body of Deon Dreyer, he is twelve minutes and twenty-two seconds into the dive, and he's been on the bottom for just over a minute. He pulls the body bag out and starts to try and work it over Deon's legs. As he does, a cloud of silt obscures the picture. When it clears, Deon's body, its head having fallen off, is floating in front of Shaw.

This was totally unexpected. Deon, as it turned out, was not completely skeletal, and he was no longer stuck in the silt. Instead of decomposing, his corpse had mummified into a soaplike composition that gave it mass and neutral buoyancy. And for some reason — no one has an explanation — the body had become unstuck from the mud as soon as Shaw started working on it. "The fact that the body was now loose, and not pinned to the ground, was not one of the scenarios that we had thought about," Shirley sighs. "The body was not meant to be floating." It's a lot easier to slip a bag over an immobile body than a body floating and rolling in front of you at 886 feet.

Shaw starts fumbling and, for the first time, lets out an audible grunt of effort.

Herbst, listening intently through headphones, heard the steadily increasing distress in Shaw's breathing and knew there was trouble coming. "Breathe slower, man, breathe slower," he urged out loud. Watching the video with a clear head, it is hard not to wonder why Shaw didn't just turn around right then and abandon the dive. In October, he had turned for the surface as soon as his breathing rate increased. Now he was panting, and Deon, who was attached to the cave line, was floating free. The body could have been pulled up. "All the options involved putting the bag on," Shirley explains. "He's sticking with his plan. Which is what you've got to do." Still, when Shirley first saw the video, he couldn't stop himself from pleading, "Leave it, leave it, leave the body now. It's loose and can come up."

Shaw, however, is responding only to the pounding of his narcosis and his determination to finish the job. He keeps working to control the body, letting go of his cave light so he can use both hands. Deon is rolling and turning in front of him, resisting Shaw's efforts to get him into the bag. Shaw has been at it for two minutes, and the cave line is seemingly everywhere. It snags on his cave light, and Shaw pauses to clear it.

At this, Shirley and Herbst bridled. A cave diver should never let gear float loose. "It's a recipe for disaster," says Shirley, who will always regret not being present when Shaw told Hiles he would put the light to the side at times. "Do not do that," he would have warned him.

Now Shaw is acting confused. He is working at the torso, instead of the feet. His movements have lost purpose. After more than two and a half minutes of work — and three minutes and forty-nine seconds on the bottom — Shaw pulls his shears out, fumbling to open them. The plan was for him to cut the dive tanks away as he rolled the bag over Deon. Shaw's breathing rate continues to increase. Suddenly he loses his footing on the sloping bottom. He scrambles back to the body in a cloud of silt. The grunts of effort, hateful little bursts of sound, are painfully frequent.

Shirley and Herbst guess that Shaw's narcosis was then closer to six or seven martinis. "You focus on the one thing. You don't focus on the dive anymore," Herbst says. "The one thing becomes everything. And I think with Dave it became the body, the body, the body."

Still, Shaw keeps checking the time on his dive computer. After five and a half minutes on the bottom, he's aware enough to know he has to leave, but he doesn't get far. The video shows the bottom moving beneath him. Then Shaw's forward progress stops. His errant cave light has apparently snagged the cave line tied to Deon's tanks. Shaw knows he has caught something and turns awkwardly. His breathing starts to sound desperate. He pulls at the cat's cradle of cave line, as if trying to sort it out. Every breath is now a sharp grunt. Shaw struggles to move forward again but is anchored by the weight of Deon's body. The shears are still in his hand, but he never cuts anything. The pace of his breathing keeps accelerating, and there is a tragic, gasping quality to it, so painful to listen to that Herbst and Shirley will no longer watch the video with sound.

Twenty-one minutes into the dive, the sounds finally start to fade. Dave Shaw, with carbon dioxide suffusing his lungs, is starting to pass out. He is dying. It's heartbreaking to watch. A minute later there is no movement.

Don Shirley survived that day, but he didn't walk away unscathed. He emerged from the recompression chamber at Bushman's, which was pressurized to a depth of 98 feet to shrink the helium bubble in his head, after seven hours, disoriented and barely able to stand. He was so weak that Herbst dragged a mattress over from the police camp so Shirley could sleep right there. Over the next two weeks, he endured ten more chamber sessions, for a total of twenty-seven hours of treatment. It was more than a month before he could think clearly or walk down a crowded street without his perception and balance running haywire. "When I first saw him, I got a hell of a shock," Andre Shirley says. "He could not walk without support, and his thinking patterns had been affected. He would sound sane, but two minutes later he would forget what he'd said."

Shirley has improved with time, but the helium bend left him with permanent damage that has impaired his balance. In May he went diving again for the first time, with Peter Herbst hovering protectively alongside. He closed his eyes, turned somersaults, and with relief discovered that the Big Dive had not taken one of the things he loves most. "A cave is a place where I live," Shirley says.

A week after Shaw died, Gordon Hiles brought the video to a guest house in Pretoria, where Shirley was staying while undergoing recompression treatment at the Eugene Marais Hospital, and Shirley finally watched it. "It was difficult to see, but I really wanted to know firsthand what went on," he says. Later that day, Shirley took the video to the hospital, where he met with Herbst and Dr. Frans Cronje, medical director of Divers Alert Network Southern Africa, who was overseeing Shirley's treatment and assisting with the official accident investigation. They watched the video on a large screen and spent hours poring over every detail.

Shirley was so focused on what he was watching that he started mimicking Shaw's breathing. Then, determined to "see for myself what happened," Shirley volunteered for an unusual experiment. As Cronje carefully observed, Shirley sat with a CO_2 monitor in his mouth and headphones on his ears, watching the video one more time. Every time Shaw breathed, Shirley breathed. Eventually Shirley was huffing through thirty-six shallow, extremely rapid breaths a minute.

"There was extreme hyperventilation," Cronje says. "On a rebreather at that depth, it would have been very ineffective." Shirley's breathing became so distorted that by the time Shaw faded to just six breaths per minute and then lost consciousness, Shirley was also on the verge of blacking out. His hands were weak and he could barely move. Cronje concluded that Shaw had passed out from carbon dioxide buildup and eventually drowned.

It took Shirley a full half-hour to bring his breathing back under control.

"I actually died with Dave," he says.

Nuno Gomes is the last person alive today who knows what it's like to dive to the bottom of Bushman's Hole, and he understands why Shaw had trouble reacting to a body that was suddenly floating instead of anchored. "You don't think of a new plan while you are down there. It doesn't work. Your mind is clouded. You cannot do it," Gomes says. But he also wonders whether Shaw should have done more buildup dives to increase his tolerance for narcosis — much the way a climber will try to acclimatize to altitude — and his ability to recognize when it reaches dangerous levels. "When he started putting the body in the bag and it didn't work, he should have immediately turned around and left," Gomes says.

Gomes is an open-circuit diver, and his priority is setting records. (In June, he reclaimed the world depth record, reaching 1,044 feet in the Red Sea.) "I didn't think it was worth the risk of a diver losing his life to recover the remains of Deon Dreyer," he says flatly. Even so, Gomes honors Shaw as a fallen comrade. "It was a noble dive, a heroic dive. He did what he believed in, and I've got to say he had a lot of courage," Gomes says. "At the end of the day, he achieved what he wanted to achieve, even though he paid for it with his life."

None of the divers who were with Shaw in Bushman's Hole think the dive was reckless. As support diver Mark Andrews puts it, "If you asked me about the chances before the dive, I'd have said there is a ninety-nine percent chance of success, and a one percent chance he'll have to leave the body. And zero percent that Dave wasn't coming back."

Verna van Schaik, who is used to people telling her she is pushing too deep, is sorry Shaw died but not sorry for him. "Dave was going to go back," she says. "The fact that Deon was there just made it more interesting and more exciting. Dave knew the risks. They were his risks, and he took them."

Every diver there that day will keep diving, and instead of second-guessing Shaw, they say they are proud of him. "Dave took rebreather diving where it has never been before. People never knew about [rebreathers] until he died showing what can be done," Peter Herbst says. "Two hundred meters [656 feet] was a damned deep dive on a rebreather. This guy went half as deep again. He made the envelope bigger."

Ten days after Bushman's Hole gave the bodies back, Theo and Marie Dreyer went to see their son. When the morgue attendant asked them to step in, Marie wasn't sure what to expect. When she saw a fully fleshed-out body, her tears stopped, and she felt happy. There was no head, but lying in front of her was her boy. Theo marveled that Deon's legs still held their athletic shape. Marie couldn't believe he was still in his Jockey underwear. "We saw him," she explains, her eyes shining. Overwhelmed, she stepped forward and took her dead son in her arms.

Ann Shaw had hoped her husband would rest forever in Bushman's Hole. When Herbst called to tell her that his body had been recovered, she was completely unnerved. After some anguish, she decided Shaw's ashes should be scattered in South Africa, the place he had come to love so much. Ann continues to live and work in Hong Kong. Every once in a while, when she has a problem with the computer, or needs help in the kitchen, she finds herself thinking, *Why did you do this to me? Because now I have to do everything.* But it's not anger she feels, just loss. "He needed to dive, and I accepted that," she says. "I wasn't about to change him or to tie him down."

Lisa Shaw, in a eulogy for her father, wrote, "I know having faced death before that my father was unafraid and was completely at peace with the prospect. I know and he knew that the Lord would be right there ready to take him on to new adventures. I am also at peace because he died doing something he loved; very few of us will ever get that privilege." Steven Shaw, who is twenty-three and is studying for a master's degree at the Melbourne College of Divinity, finds some solace that his father died helping others. "But now I'm feeling more just sad that Dad's gone," he says.

Shirley misses Shaw too and has a picture of himself with Shaw, peering out of a recompression chamber, on his computer's screen saver. "Dave died exploring and trying to achieve something he wanted to do," Shirley says. "That to me is better than dying in a car crash." Still, every day Shirley thinks, *Ah, I've got to tell Dave that —* only to remember that he can't.

Shaw is not far, though. On a beautiful evening in May, Don and Andre Shirley took a bottle of wine and a small wooden box to the summit of a mountain a short drive from their home. Below them, the rich, pungent grasslands of Mpumalanga swept all the way to the distant horizon, and the Komati River glinted in the golden light. Next to a wild fig tree, the couple raised their glasses in a quiet toast. As the sun dipped low, they opened the box and threw Shaw's ashes into the air. The ashes hung for an instant, a cloud of a man. Then the African earth took them, and Dave Shaw was gone.

A (Fishing) Hole in One

FROM THE LOS ANGELES TIMES MAGAZINE

A GUY IN A CAMOUFLAGE JACKET is pacing in the almost empty parking lot behind a municipal golf course east of Los Angeles. His eyes, still adjusting to the fading light, dart from a group of workers loitering outside their trucks to a chain-link fence bordering the course.

"Hold on," he says, then whips out his cell phone and speed-dials.

"Hi, Mom."

He asks her if he's got the right location. Is this where she sees the gate as she walks her dogs?

She says that it is.

John tucks a plastic box under his arm and walks quickly up a one-lane dirt road toward the undulating fairways. He tries to keep his eyes down and his goateed chin pinned to his chest, but more than once he gives in to the urge to glance back at the men standing under the lights. John decides that they're not watching him. "It doesn't look like I'm doing anything wrong," he says.

A few hundred yards down the road he finds the gate, just where Mom said it would be. It's open. John slogs through the thick grass in the direction of the only light — an anemic fluorescent coil above the distant entrance to a concrete restroom. The sounds of ducks quacking and the buzzing of the nearby 10 Freeway ride on cool air with a distinctive odor: two parts freshly cut grass, one part pesticide.

John stops at the edge of an amoeba-shaped pond. He pulls a tiny flashlight from his breast pocket, pops it in his mouth and then plucks a mock Roboworm from the plastic box. Within seconds it's skewered on a barbless hook that dangles from a fishing rod. John scans the course from right to left and back again — all's clear — and with a snap of his wrist the rubber bait soars over the water. A tiny ripple appears in the glow of an almost full moon, confirming touchdown.

John, a thirty-four-year-old with the thick physique of a rugby player, lives nearby and works odd jobs when he isn't poaching. He belongs to a semi-secret, completely unorganized underground of sport fishermen who sneak onto golf courses across the country to make sport of unsuspecting bass, catfish, and whatever else swims among the sunken golf balls. In southern California, these guerrilla anglers, who divulge their misdemeanors on the condition of anonymity, can pick from hundreds of private and public courses with at least one body of water guarding a green or lining a fairway. Some of the most committed covertly plant desired species in the ponds, creating an urban version of the neighborhood fishing hole.

Bass fishermen are particularly attracted to these off-limits, or "low fishing pressure" in angler-speak, waters because they tend to obsess about the size of their catches. You've seen these guys on the Outdoor Life Network. They schlep boats equipped with electronic fish finders to huge lakes stocked with hatchery fish, including Castaic and Pyramid in southern California, in hopes of hauling in something the weight of a chain saw. But the behemoths are few and far between. "If you find a pond with big bass in it, it's usually one that has NO TRESPASSING signs around it and requires a nighttime mission," says Chuck Bauer, a noted big-bass specialist and veteran golf course poacher from Dallas. "The more protected the pond is, the bigger the fish are."

Bass, like deer, get wilier with age, Bauer says. "There are always a few of them big old bucks with huge horns. The same thing with bass. A fourteen-pound bass is going to be much smarter than a ten-pound bass. Three-pound bass? They're dumb."

If left unmolested, bass can grow a pound a year on a diet of ducklings and fish, including smaller bass. What makes golf course bass so appealing to poachers is that they gain size without getting wise to the tactics that anglers use against their scaly counterparts in sanctioned waters. They bulk up and stay dumb.

Catfish are no smarter. Ask Rick, a color-correction technician in the film industry, who often fishes off the Santa Monica Pier during his lunch hour. He says he caught a five-pounder on a spinnerbait down in Sylmar, at a little executive course called El Cariso. "You wouldn't think there would be any fish, but I caught a big catfish," he says.

He snagged the lunker during the day by stashing a rod in a golf bag with his driver and irons. It's tricky to combine fishing with a round of golf, Rick concedes, but the glacial pace of the sport presents time, usually while waiting for a chance to hit from the tee, to sneak off to the water's edge. "I break out a little miniature steel pole, with two eyes on it and a casting reel," Rick says.

The odds of being detected are low. Consider that an 18-hole golf course covers from 100 to 400 acres, with many holes roughly 375 yards long from tee to green. There are rarely more than three foursomes in sight of each other per hole. Changes in elevation, trees, mounds, bunkers, even high grass can obscure poachers. Marshals patrol the courses, but their job is to prod slowpokes. There was a time, Rick says, he was asked by one course never to return.

John also is an avid golfer. Though he prefers poaching at night, when it's easier to conceal a rod, he understands why Rick casts in daylight. "You've got some time, you're waiting on another foursome, and you see a fish. You might want to make a couple of casts," he says. "I'm not saying it's something the golf course will approve of."

The Roboworm plops into the water again, and again. The largemouths that John hopes to hook on this cold night just aren't biting. In an attempt to get his fishing head on, John clams up. Yet another cast — *kerplunk!* — and he's all business now.

It's around dusk, and before leaving his apartment for the night mission, John sifts through a small tackle box of homemade bait, looking for the ideal worm with which to lure a bass. "I do a lot of my own hand pouring," he says. "Me and a good buddy of mine have made replicas of popular worms. We buy the plastic, scents, and colors and mold them ourselves. You can save quite a bit of money."

John, it turns out, is a former warden for the California Department of Fish and Game, and he's seriously into fish. They're everywhere in the living room of his apartment, mounted on the walls, swimming in a gurgling aquarium, and pictured in weathered piscatorial manuals and old scrapbooks lining the bookshelves.

Tonight, because of the cool temperature and low light, he selects one of his six-inch cinnamon Roboworm knockoffs, which he'll Texas rig — a method of securing a hook to bait so it'll slip through weeds — on a four-pound test line. He chooses this "presentation" also because of the sound it will produce: a clicking, not unlike like that of a crayfish bumping against rocks. Furthermore, its unexposed hook will enable the worm to slide easily through rocks, trees, and crevices and into the places where the bass will be hanging out.

Presentation is everything to a bass master. Water and weather conditions dictate lure selection, and a poorly chosen bait (the wrong type, color, size, or movement) or incorrect setup almost guarantees an angler will walk away empty-handed. In fact, the weather dictates if it's worth fishing at all. Low barometric pressure, according to Chuck Bauer, puts bass in a sort of stasis. Cold weather does the same. "It takes a lot of education and knowledge to become proficient, to know that every day you're going to catch a fish." Fishing for less savvy and passive types of fish isn't nearly as challenging, or fun, Bauer says.

Catfish are a lazy man's fish and, bass masters say, trout aren't much better. Just like golf, bass fishing is jampacked with tips, techniques, and "top secret" information guaranteed to help anglers hook the predatory fish again and again. When even the color of one's clothing can affect bass behavior (a bright white shirt on a sunny day alerts older, wiser and, hence, bigger bass to the presence of an angler), you know there's a lot to learn.

But shirt color doesn't mean a thing when you sneak onto a golf course to fish at night. The "youthful fun," as Bauer puts it, of fishing on a golf course is just one reason anglers risk a trespassing or poaching citation. The maximum fine for poaching at a public course, says the Department of Fish and Game, is $1,000 and/or one year in county jail — a misdemeanor. However, the punishment doled out is usually a slap on the wrist, which is what John once received when he got busted fishing a nearby golf course lake after dark.

They may break the law, but most poachers scrupulously follow catch-and-release etiquette. Perhaps it's because they're sensitive. Or they like the idea of hooking the same fish another day. Or maybe the thought of eating a bass that lives in reclaimed water grosses them out. "If I'm that hungry I can go to McDonald's and order a Filet-o-Fish sandwich," John says.

Here's another theory: the poachers don't deplete the supply because they planted the fish there in the first place. Though he won't admit to stocking bass, John refers to the fish he's trying to catch as "pets," and says he's eager to see how they're doing. With his tackle box and fishing rod in hand, John kicks his screen door closed and heads toward the car that will take him to the golf course. The puny trunk of the Japanese two-door can't accommodate John's one-piece rod, so he sticks it out the window, where it will stay for the mile-long trip.

John's frustrated. Cold air means slow bass and slow bass mean slow fishing, and John's just reeling way too fast. He's been casting for nearly an hour and the only thing he has to show for it are some weeds dangling off the Roboworm. The green slime is annoying him almost as much as the turtles wreaking havoc on the bass nests. "I despise them," he grumbles.

In an attempt to draw out some bass and elude the weeds, John's relocated twice around the perimeter of the lake. But even with the weeds in the distance, and the moon directly in his face assisting his sight, he's got nothing to show for his efforts. Worse, his line is now in a snarl, what he refers to as a "bird's nest." The temperature has dropped into the upper forties, but John refuses to quit. "When I come here I want to at least get one. Just to prove to myself that I can get 'em," he says as he starts to untangle the line.

The rod jolts. John jerks it to set the hook. "What are the odds of that?" he says, chuckling. As soon as he stops paying attention, he lands one. Since the bird's nest has completely jammed his reel, John has to pull the fish toward shore, and for the first time tonight he seems confident in what he's doing. He flicks on the flashlight while pulling pliers out of his pocket, all the while tending to the aggravated bass.

Suddenly the fish jumps into the faint moonlight.

John sticks the light in his mouth and shines it in the direction of the spastic fish, calmly pulling it closer and closer. The fish tires and surrenders. John grabs the line and hoists the bass out of the water.

"Florida-strain largemouth, sixteen inches, small, couple of pounds," he says clinically, sticking his thumb into its mouth and clamping down on its lower lip to paralyze it. He shines the light up and down its body, revealing surprisingly subtle, beautiful fins and a fist-sized mouth with tiny recessed teeth, before using the pliers to take out the hook.

The largemouth is now hanging vertically, mouth up, frozen in midair. John knows every inch of it, but he can't say for sure if he's caught this one before. There are no easily identifiable characteristics such as a lost eye or a broken hook stuck in its mouth.

After a few minutes of airtime, John cradles the head in his left hand and underbelly in his right. He lowers the fish into the water, swishing it back and forth a couple of times. While the flashlight casts a dim light onto the murky water, the shocked fish pauses for a second to gather itself. Then, with a sudden kick of its tail fin, it darts away.

A tiny smile creeps across John's face as he heads to the parking lot. Back in the apartment, John's roommate has left the TV on, a rerun of *That '70s Show.* John dumps his rod and tackle box into the hall closet next to a vinyl golf bag. From his cage in the kitchen, a sun conure named Herman is chirping away to the sitcom's amplified laugh track.

John's beat. As he kicks back to soak up some four-camera comedy, his arm rests on a skinned bobcat draped over the couch. John takes off the fishing license that's been hanging around his neck and tosses it on the coffee table. "I wear it whenever I'm fishing," he had said when he put it on. "I don't care whether I need it or not."

Contributors' Notes

Notable Sports Writing of 2005

Contributors' Notes

James Brown is the author of several novels, including *Lucky Town* and *Final Performance*. He has received the Nelson Algren Award for Short Fiction, a National Endowment for the Arts Fellowship in Fiction Writing, and a Chesterfield Film Writing Fellowship from Universal/Amblin Entertainment. His writing has been featured in the *Los Angeles Times Magazine*, *Denver Quarterly*, and the *New England Review*. He lives with his family in Lake Arrowhead, California.

Pamela Colloff, a native New Yorker, is a senior editor at *Texas Monthly* magazine. In 2001, she was nominated for a National Magazine Award for Public Interest. She lives in Austin, Texas.

Jeff Duncan has been a staff writer at the *New Orleans Times-Picayune* since 1999. He covered LSU athletics and the New Orleans Saints beat during his first six years before switching to the city desk to cover Hurricane Katrina and the storm's aftermath in August 2005. He has worked as a newspaper reporter throughout the South, including stops at the *Louisville Courier-Journal*, *USA Today*, *Florida Today*, the (Monroe, Louisiana) *News-Star*, and the *St. Petersburg Times*.

Steve Friedman is writer-at-large for the Rodale Sports Group, and his work has appeared in *Esquire*, where he was a contributing editor, and *GQ*, where he was senior editor, as well as in *Outside*, *Ski*, the *Washington Post*, the *New York Times*, and other publications. He is the author of *The Gentleman's Guide to Life* and, with former NBA player Jayson Williams, *Loose Balls*. A St. Louis native and graduate of Stanford University, he lives in Manhattan. This is his fifth appearance in *The Best American Sports Writing*.

GREG GARBER has worked as a reporter at ESPN for fifteen years, focusing on the NFL. He contributes regularly to the NFL Countdown and has won several Emmy awards. He has worked as a reporter at ESPN.com since 2001 and is also the author of more than twenty books. From 1986 to 2001, he was a sportswriter for the *Hartford Courant*, where his beats included the NFL and professional tennis. Garber is married, has two children, and lives in Connecticut.

DAVID GRANN has been a staff writer at *The New Yorker* since July 2003. His stories have also appeared in the *New York Times Magazine*, the *Atlantic Monthly*, the *Washington Post*, the *Wall Street Journal*, and *The New Republic*, where he is a contributing editor. Before joining *The New Yorker*, Grann was a senior editor at *The New Republic*. Grann holds master's degrees in international relations from the Fletcher School of Law and Diplomacy and in creative writing from Boston University.

PAT JORDAN is the author of thirteen books, among them the memoirs *A Nice Tuesday* and *A False Spring* and the novels *aka Sheila Doyle* and *aka Sheila Weinstein*. His short story "The Hustle" will appear in Otto Penzler's anthology *Murder at the Racetrack*. He can be reached at Patjordanstories.com.

DAN KOEPPEL is a contributing editor to *National Geographic Adventure*, and his work has appeared *in Men's Journal*, *Popular Science*, *Wired*, and the *New York Times Magazine*. His memoir *To See Every Bird on Earth* was published in 2005. He was elected to the Mountain Bike Hall of Fame in 2003.

JONATHAN MILES is a contributing editor for *Men's Journal*. His work has appeared in the *New York Times*, *Sports Afield*, *Salon*, and many other publications.

J. R. MOEHRINGER is a reporter for the western bureau of the *Los Angeles Times*. His story "Resurrecting the Champ" appeared in *The Best American Sports Writing of the Century*. He is the author of the critically acclaimed memoir *The Tender Bar*.

STEVE ONEY is a senior writer for *Los Angeles* magazine. His articles have also appeared in *Esquire*, *Playboy*, and *Premiere*. His 2003 book on the Leo Frank murder case, *And the Dead Shall Rise*, won the American Bar Association's Silver Gavel Award for best book on America's legal system, the Jewish Book Council's National Jewish Book Award for best work of Jewish history, and the Southern Book Critics Circle prize for best nonfiction book about the South. *And the Dead Shall Rise* was also a finalist for the J. Anthony Lukas Prize, awarded jointly by Harvard and Columbia.

BEN PAYNTER has been a staff writer at *The Pitch*, a weekly newspaper in Kansas City, since 2003. He is a graduate of the University of Missouri at Columbia and has contributed to *Details* and NationalGeographic.com.

JEFF PEARLMAN covered major league baseball for six years as a senior writer at *Sports Illustrated*, where he received national attention for his article on controversial relief pitcher John Rocker. He is the author of *The Bad Guys Won*. Now a features writer for *Newsday*, Pearlman lives in New York with his wife, Catherine, and daughter, Casey.

NEAL POLLACK is the author of *Alternadad, Chicago Noir,* and *The Neal Pollack Anthology of American Literature.*

S. L. PRICE is a senior writer at *Sports Illustrated* and author of *Pitching Around Fidel.* A graduate of the University of North Carolina, this is his third appearance in *The Best American Sports Writing.*

LINDA ROBERTSON is a columnist and feature writer at the *Miami Herald.* Born in Midland, Michigan, she was once Miami's fastest high school miler, later graduated from the University of North Carolina, and now lives in Coral Gables with her husband, Andres Viglucci, and children, Nicolas, Natalie, and Sofia. She is a former president of the Association for Women in Sports Media. She has appeared in *The Best American Sports Writing* six times.

CHARLIE SCHROEDER is a writer, radio producer, actor, and golf instructor. He has written for the *Los Angeles Times Magazine, Golf, Fore,* and *Modern Humorist* and has appeared on television in the series *Ed* and *Sex in the City.* He is working with Dr. David Wright on a series of golf psychology books. He lives in Los Angeles with his wife, Wendy, and teaches golf at the Tregnan Golf Academy.

No other writer has appeared in *The Best American Sports Writing* more frequently than *Sports Illustrated* senior writer GARY SMITH, here making his eleventh appearance. An anthology of his work, *Beyond the Game,* was published in 2000.

MICHAEL SOKOLOVE is a contributing writer for the *New York Times Magazine* and the author of *The Ticket Out: Darryl Strawberry and the Boys of Crenshaw* and *Hustle: The Myth, Life, and Lies of Pete Rose.* He lives in Bethesda, Maryland, with his wife and three children.

PAUL SOLOTAROFF is a contributing editor for *Rolling Stone* and *Men's Journal.* He is writing a memoir called *The Body Shop* about his adventures in the steroid labyrinth of bodybuilding. He lives in New York City with his son.

KURT STREETER is a general assignment reporter who writes about everyday people living uncommon lives. He also has covered the Los Angeles Police Department and transportation. He came to the *Los Angeles Times* six years ago from the *Baltimore Sun*, where he covered Baltimore's inner city. He has been a documentary and radio producer and had a short stint in the minor leagues of professional tennis. A 1989 graduate of the University of California at Berkeley, where he captained the tennis team, he lives in Los Angeles with his wife, Vanashree.

KATY VINE is a senior editor at *Texas Monthly*. This is her second consecutive appearance in *The Best American Sports Writing*.

Sports Illustrated senior writer L. JON WERTHEIM covers tennis for the magazine and is a regular contributor to SI.com. He is the author of *Venus Envy* and *Transition Game* and is working on a book about pool champion Kid Delicious, to be published by Houghton Mifflin in 2007.

TIM ZIMMERMANN is a correspondent at *Outside* and an avid sailor and diver. He is the author of *The Race: The First Nonstop, Round-the-World, No-Holds-Barred Sailing Competition.* "Raising the Dead" was a finalist for the National Magazine Award for Feature Writing. His work has also appeared in *Sports Illustrated, Men's Journal,* and numerous sailing magazines. Prior to writing about the adventure world, he was diplomatic correspondent at *U.S. News & World Report.* He lives in Washington, D.C., with his wife and two young children.

Notable Sports Writing of 2005

Selected by Glenn Stout

THE B·E·S·T AMERICAN SERIES®

Introducing our newest addition to the BEST AMERICAN *series*

THE BEST AMERICAN COMICS 2006. Harvey Pekar, guest editor, Anne Elizabeth Moore, series editor. This newcomer to the best-selling series — the first Best American annual dedicated to the finest in graphic storytelling and literary comics — includes stories culled from graphic novels, pamphlet comics, newspapers, magazines, mini-comics, and the Web. Edited by the subject of the Oscar-nominated film *American Splendor*, Harvey Pekar, the collection features pieces by Robert Crumb, Chris Ware, Kim Deitch, Jaime Hernandez, Alison Bechdel, Joe Sacco, Lilli Carré, and Lynda Barry, among others.

ISBN-10: 0-618-71874-5 / ISBN-13: 978-0-618-71874-0 $22.00 POB

Alongside our perennial favorites

THE BEST AMERICAN SHORT STORIES® 2006. Ann Patchett, guest editor, Katrina Kenison, series editor. This year's most beloved short fiction anthology is edited by Ann Patchett, author of *Bel Canto*, a 2002 PEN/Faulkner Award winner and a National Book Critics Circle Award finalist. The collection features stories by Tobias Wolff, Donna Tartt, Thomas McGuane, Mary Gaitskill, Nathan Englander, and others. "Story for story, readers can't beat the *Best American Short Stories* series" (*Chicago Tribune*).

ISBN-10: 0-618-54351-1 / ISBN-13: 978-0-618-54351-9 $28.00 CL
ISBN-10: 0-618-54352-X / ISBN-13: 978-0-618-54352-6 $14.00 PA

THE BEST AMERICAN NONREQUIRED READING 2006. Edited by Dave Eggers, introduction by Matt Groening. This "enticing . . . funny, and wrenching" (*Cleveland Plain Dealer*) collection highlights a bold mix of fiction, nonfiction, screenplays, alternative comics, and more from publications large, small, and online. With an introduction by Matt Groening, creator of *The Simpsons* and *Futurama*, this volume features writing from *The Onion, The Daily Show, This American Life*, Judy Budnitz, Joe Sacco, and others.

ISBN-10: 0-618-57050-0 / ISBN-13: 978-0-618-57050-8 $28.00 CL
ISBN-10: 0-618-57051-9 / ISBN-13: 978-0-618-57051-5 $14.00 PA

THE BEST AMERICAN ESSAYS® 2006. Lauren Slater, guest editor, Robert Atwan, series editor. Since 1986, *The Best American Essays* has annually gathered outstanding nonfiction writing, establishing itself as the premier anthology of its kind. Edited by the best-selling author of *Prozac Diary*, Lauren Slater, this year's "delightful collection" (*Miami Herald*) highlights provocative, lively writing by Adam Gopnik, Scott Turow, Marjorie Williams, Poe Ballantine, and others.

ISBN-10: 0-618-70531-7 / ISBN-13: 978-0-618-70531-3 $28.00 CL
ISBN-10: 0-618-70529-5 / ISBN-13: 978-0-618-70529-0 $14.00 PA

THE BEST AMERICAN MYSTERY STORIES™ 2006. Scott Turow, guest editor, Otto Penzler, series editor. This perennially popular anthology is sure to appeal to mystery fans of every variety. The 2006 volume, edited by Scott Turow, author of the critically acclaimed *Ordinary Heroes* and *Presumed Innocent*, features both mystery veterans and new talents, offering stories by Elmore Leonard, Ed McBain, James Lee Burke, Joyce Carol Oates, Walter Mosley, and others.

ISBN-10: 0-618-51746-4 / ISBN-13: 978-0-618-51746-6 $28.00 CL
ISBN-10: 0-618-51747-2 / ISBN-13: 978-0-618-51747-3 $14.00 PA

THE B·E·S·T AMERICAN SERIES®

THE BEST AMERICAN SPORTS WRITING™ 2006. Michael Lewis, guest editor, Glenn Stout, series editor. "An ongoing centerpiece for all sports collections" (*Booklist*), this series stands in high regard for its extraordinary sports writing and top-notch editors. This year's guest editor, Michael Lewis, the acclaimed author of the bestseller *Moneyball*, brings together pieces by Gary Smith, Pat Jordan, Paul Solotaroff, Linda Robertson, L. Jon Wertheim, and others.

> ISBN-10: 0-618-47021-2 / ISBN-13: 978-0-618-47021-1 $28.00 CL
> ISBN-10: 0-618-47022-0 / ISBN-13: 978-0-618-47022-8 $14.00 PA

THE BEST AMERICAN TRAVEL WRITING 2006. Tim Cahill, guest editor, Jason Wilson, series editor. Tim Cahill is the founding editor of *Outside* magazine and a frequent contributor to *National Geographic Adventure*. This year's collection captures the traveler's wandering spirit and ever-present quest for adventure. Giving new life to armchair journeys are Alain de Botton, Pico Iyer, David Sedaris, Gary Shteyngart, George Saunders, and others.

> ISBN-10: 0-618-58212-6 / ISBN-13: 978-0-618-58212-9 $28.00 CL
> ISBN-10: 0-618-58215-0 / ISBN-13: 978-0-618-58215-0 $14.00 PA

THE BEST AMERICAN SCIENCE AND NATURE WRITING 2006. Brian Greene, guest editor, Tim Folger, series editor. Brian Greene, the best-selling author of *The Elegant Universe* and the first physicist to edit this prestigious series, offers a fresh take on the year's best science and nature writing. Featuring such authors as John Horgan, Daniel C. Dennett, and Dennis Overbye, among others, this collection "surprises us into caring about subjects we had not thought to examine" (*Cleveland Plain Dealer*).

> ISBN-10: 0-618-72221-1 / ISBN-13: 978-0-618-72221-1 $28.00 CL
> ISBN-10: 0-618-72222-X / ISBN-13: 978-0-618-72222-8 $14.00 PA

THE BEST AMERICAN SPIRITUAL WRITING 2006. Edited by Philip Zaleski, introduction by Peter J. Gomes. Featuring an introduction by Peter J. Gomes, a best-selling author, respected minister, and the Plummer Professor of Christian Morals at Harvard University, this year's edition of this "excellent annual" (*America*) gathers pieces from diverse faiths and denominations and includes writing by Michael Chabon, Malcolm Gladwell, Mary Gordon, John Updike, and others.

> ISBN-10: 0-618-58644-X / ISBN-13: 978-0-618-58644-8 $28.00 CL
> ISBN-10: 0-618-58645-8 / ISBN-13: 978-0-618-58645-5 $14.00 PA

THE BEST AMERICAN GOLD GIFT BOX 2006. Boxed in rich gold metallic, this set includes *The Best American Short Stories 2006*, *The Best American Mystery Stories 2006*, and *The Best American Sports Writing 2006*.

> ISBN-10: 0-618-80126-X / ISBN-13: 978-0-618-80126-8 $40.00 PA

THE BEST AMERICAN SILVER GIFT BOX 2006. Packaged in a lavish silver metallic box, this set features *The Best American Short Stories 2006*, *The Best American Travel Writing 2006*, and *The Best American Spiritual Writing 2006*.

> ISBN-10: 0-618-80127-8 / ISBN-13: 978-0-618-80127-5 $40.00 PA

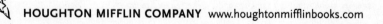 **HOUGHTON MIFFLIN COMPANY** www.houghtonmifflinbooks.com